TEXAS INSTRUMENTS

BAII PLUS Rebate Terms and Conditions

This offer is valid only for BAII PLUS purchases between July 1, 1997 and March 31, 1999. All claims must be postmarked by April 30, 1999. Allow 8 to 10 weeks for processing. All purchases must be made in the U.S. or Canada. Rebates will be sent only to addresses in the U.S. and Canada and paid in U.S. dollars. Not redeemable at any store. Send this completed form along with the cash register receipt (original or copy) and the UPC bar code to the address indicated. This original mail-in certificate must accompany your request and may not be duplicated or reproduced. Offer valid only as stated on this form. Offer void where prohibited, taxed, licensed, or restricted. Limit one rebate per household or address. Texas Instruments reserves the right to discontinue this program at any time and without notice.

Yes! I Want $5 Back On My Purchase of the BAII PLUS.

Foundations of Finance
The Logic and Practice of Financial Management
Second Edition

Arthur J. Keown
Virginia Polytechnic Institute and State University
R. B. Pamplin Professor of Finance

J. William Petty
Baylor University
Carouth Professor of Entrepreneurship

David F. Scott, Jr.
University of Central Florida
Holder, Phillips-Schenck Chair in American Private Enterprise
and Professor of Finance

John D. Martin
University of Texas at Austin
Margaret and Eugene McDermott Professor of Banking and Finance

Prentice Hall
Upper Saddle River, New Jersey 07458

Acquisitions Editor: Paul Donnelly
Assistant Editor: Gladys Soto
Editorial Assistant: Mary Beth Sanok
Editor-in-Chief: James Boyd
Marketing Manager: Patrick Lynch
Production Editor: Cynthia Regan
Managing Editor: Dee Josephson
Manufacturing Buyer: Kenneth J. Clinton
Manufacturing Supervisor: Arnold Vila
Senior Designer: Ann France
Interior Design: York Production Services
Cover Design: Maureen Eide
Illustrator (Interior): York Production Services
Composition: York Graphic Services
Cover Art/Photo: © Rob Day / SIS

Copyright © 1998, 1994 by Prentice-Hall, Inc.
A Simon & Schuster Company
Upper Saddle River, New Jersey 07458

Library of Congress Cataloging–in–Publication Data
Foundations of finance: the logic and practice of financial management/
    Arthur J. Keown … [et al.].—2nd ed.
      p. cm
    Includes index.
    ISBN 0-13-748153-5 (alk. paper)
    1. Corporations—Finance.   I. Keown, Arthur J.
    HG4026.F67 1998
    658.15—dc21   97-27019
                                                                       CIP

Prentice-Hall International (UK) Limited, London
Prentice-Hall of Australia Pty. Limited, Sydney
Prentice-Hall Canada, Inc., Toronto
Prentice-Hall Hispanoamericana, S.A., Mexico
Prentice-Hall of India Private Limited, New Delhi
Prentice-Hall of Japan, Inc., Tokyo
Simon & Schuster Asia Pte. Ltd., Singapore
Editora Prentice-Hall do Brasil, Ltda., Rio de Janeiro

Printed in the United States of America

10 9 8 7 6 5 4 3

To my parents, from whom I learned the most.

—Arthur J. Keown

In memory and appreciation of my parents, John and Kate Petty, for their enduring love and constant encouragement.

—J. William Petty

To my wife, Peggy.

—David F. Scott, Jr.

In loving memory of my mother, who was ever encouraging, and to my father, whose life I seek to emulate.

—John D. Martin

CONTENTS

Chapter 6
Valuation and Characteristics of Bonds 171

Chapter 7
Valuation and Characteristics of Stock 196

Chapter 8
The Meaning and Measurement of Risk and Return 221

Chapter 13

Dividend Policy and Internal Financing 402

Chapter 14

Introduction to Working-Capital Management 435

Chapter 15

Liquid Asset Management 457

Chapter 16

International Business Finance

Chapter 17

Changes and Challenges in Finance

PREFACE

In finance, our goal is to create wealth. This is done by providing customers with the best product and service possible, and it is the market response that determines whether we reach our goal. We are very proud of the market reaction to the first edition of *Foundations of Finance;* the market's response to it was overwhelming. With its success comes an even greater responsibility to deliver the finest possible textbook and supplementary package possible in the Second Edition. To do this we have taken a two-pronged approach of refinement, based upon users' comments, and of remaining the innovative leaders in the field, focusing on value-added innovations.

From students and instructors alike, the reaction to the First Edition was that it was "intuitive"—allowing the reader "to see the forest from the trees"—and it was "lively and easy to read." In the second edition of *Foundations of Finance*, we have tried to build on these strengths, introducing the latest concepts and developments in finance in a practical and intuitive manner.

Pedagogy That Works

This book provides the student with a conceptual understanding of the financial decision making process, rather than just an introduction to the tools and techniques of finance. For the student, it is all too easy to lose sight of the logic that drives finance and focus instead on memorizing formulas and procedures. As a result, students have a difficult time understanding the interrelationships between the topics covered. Moreover, later in life when the problems encountered do not match the textbook presentation, students may find themselves unprepared to abstract from what they learned. To overcome this problem, the opening chapter presents ten underlying principles or axioms of finance, which serve as a springboard for the chapters and topics that follow. In essence, the student is presented with a cohesive, interrelated perspective from which future problems can be approached.

With a focus on the big picture, we provide an introduction to financial decision making rooted in current financial theory and in the current state of world economic conditions. This focus is perhaps most apparent in the attention given to the capital markets and their influence on corporate financial decisions. What results is an introductory treatment of a discipline rather than the treatment of a series of isolated problems that face the financial manager. The goal of this text is not merely to teach the tools of a discipline or trade but also to enable students to abstract what is learned to new and yet unforeseen problems—in short, to educate the student in finance.

Innovations and Distinctive Features of the Second Edition

New: Introduction of an Integrated Learning System The text has been reorganized around the learning objectives that appear at the beginning of each chapter to provide the instructor and student with an easy-to-use integrated learning system. Numbered icons identifying each objective appear next to the related material throughout the text and in the summary allowing easy location of material related to each objective.

New: Opening Vignettes   Each chapter begins with a new current, real-world story about a financial decision faced by a company related to the chapter material that follows. These vignettes have been carefully prepared to stimulate student interest in the topic to come and can be used as a lecture tool to stimulate class discussion.

New: Key Terms Identified in the Margins   Key terms are highlighted in the margin with definitional material italicized in the text and can also be found in the glossary in the back of the book, making it easier for the student to check their understanding of key terms. At the end of each chapter key terms are listed along with page numbers as a study checklist for students.

New: Comprehensive End-of-Chapter Problems   A new comprehensive problem has been added at the end of almost every chapter covering all the major topics included in that chapter. This comprehensive problem can be used as a lecture or review tool by the professor. For the student, the comprehensive end-of-chapter problems provide an opportunity to apply all the concepts presented within the chapter in a realistic setting, thereby strengthening their understanding of the material.

Ten Axioms of Finance   The fundamental principles that drive the practice of corporate finance are presented in the form of ten axioms. These axioms first appear in Chapter 1 and thereafter appear in in-text inserts called "Back to the Foundations." These inserts serve to refocus the students' attention upon the underlying principles behind what is being done. In effect, they serve to keep the student from being so wrapped up in specific calculations that the interrelationships and overall scheme are lost.

Pause and Reflect   In-text inserts titled Pause and Reflect appear throughout the text, serving to direct the student's attention to the "big picture." The use of these Pause and Reflect inserts coupled with the use of the ten axioms keeps the student from losing sight of the interrelationships and motivating factors behind what is being done.

Financial Management in Practice   Strong emphasis is also placed upon practice, where practice is used to demonstrate both the relevance of the topics discussed and the implementation of theory. Moreover, to add life to the discussion, "Financial Management in Practice" boxed inserts are provided throughout the text.

Financial Calculators   The use of financial calculators has been integrated throughout this text, especially with respect to the presentation of the time value of money, where appropriate calculator solutions appear in the margin.

Content Updating   In response to both the continued development of financial thought and reviewer comments, changes have been made in the text. Some of these changes include:

Chapter 1   In response to comments from reviewers and adopters, we have simplified the tax section of Chapter 1, focusing on those aspects of the tax code that affect financial decisions directly. In addition, again in response to comments from reviewers and adopters, a tenth axiom, "All Risk Is Not Equal—Some Risk Can Be Diversified Away and Some Cannot," has been introduced. This axiom provides an intuitive presentation of the logic behind the concepts of systematic and unsystematic risk.

Chapter 2   Several changes are spread throughout this chapter in response to suggestions from reviewers. The relationship of Federal Reserve monetary policy to the cost of capital is related through the *opportunity cost of funds* concept. The relationship between risk and return (Axiom 1) is clarified with the incorporation of sharper and more complete graphics. Interest rate levels and inflation rates over the 1981–1995 period are studied within the context of explaining interest rate determinants. The significant difference between real and nominal interest rates is put into context of a financial analyst's viewpoint on the subject.

Chapter 3 The use of a firm familiar and of interest to the students—the McDonald's Corporation—has been introduced to demonstrate the use of financial ratios.

Chapter 4 Much of this chapter was rewritten and simplified to make it accessible to the non-accounting student. For example, the mathematical presentation from the first edition has been replaced by a more intuitive discussion including simple examples to illustrate the concepts involved.

Chapter 5 The mathematics of continuous compounding have been dropped from this chapter in an attempt to eliminate unnecessary and confusing mathematics. In addition, annuities due have been introduced, reflecting their importance and the importance of understanding the time value of money calculations.

Chapter 7 This chapter has been revised to reflect the use of the Internet by companies to communicate with the firm's investors. In addition, this chapter now includes a tutorial on how to read stock quotes in the *Wall Street Journal.*

Chapter 8 New real-world examples have been introduced that illustrate how diversification across different types of assets affects a portfolio's risk and average returns.

Chapter 9 Based on the comments from adopters and reviewers the presentation of the discounted payback period has been dropped.

Chapter 10 In response to comments from reviewers and adopters, we have simplified the approach to risk adjustment in capital budgeting by eliminating the presentation of the certainty-equivalent approach.

Chapter 11 The entire chapter has been re-written with the objective of simplifying the materials presented and the methods used in their presentation. We have eliminated the discussion of multiple "break points" in the marginal cost of capital schedule. Although the discussion of break points is valid, it adds unnecessary complexity to the discussion of the cost of capital concept.

The problem set has been edited and expanded to reflect the revision to the chapter content. Overall this chapter, which is traditionally a very difficult one for introductory students, has been simplified and refocused on the core concept of the weighted average cost of capital.

Chapter 12 At the suggestion of reviewers this chapter was streamlined in several places, while retaining the proper emphasis on the relationship between financial leverage use and capital structure design. Real-world discussions revolve around the Coca-Cola Company, Chevron Corporation, and Phillips Petroleum.

Chapter 15 The chapter includes actual company examples and discussions that include General Motors, the Walt Disney Company, and IBM. The yield structure on marketable securities is studied over a 16-year period to emphasize fundamental rate and risk differentials. This chapter has also been shortened at the request of reviewers.

Chapter 17 The discussion of executive compensation has been updated to reflect current developments.

Supplements

Instructor's Manual with Solutions The Instructor's Manual, which was prepared by the authors, contains the following four elements for each chapter: a chapter orientation, which offers the instructor a simple statement of the author's intent for the chapter as well as providing a useful point of departure for in-class lecture; a chapter outline for easy reference to key issues; answers to all end-of-chapter questions in the text; and a second set of alternative problems with answers.

Test Item File   The Test Item File, prepared by the authors, provides more than 1400 multiple-choice, true/false, and short-answer questions with complete and detailed answers. We have carefully examined all the test questions as to their appropriateness and updated them where needed.

The Test Item File is designed for use with the Prentice Hall Custom Test, a computerized package that allows users to custom design, save, and generate classroom tests. This Windows-based test program permits professors to edit and add or delete questions from the test item file, and to export files to various word processing programs, including WordPerfect and Microsoft Word.

The New York Times "Themes of the Times"   *The New York Times* and Prentice Hall are sponsoring "Themes of the Times," a program designed to enhance student access to current information of relevance in the classroom. Through this program, the core subject matter provided in the text is supplemented by a collection of articles from one of the world's most distinguished newspapers, *The New York Times*. These articles demonstrate the vital, ongoing connections between what is learned in the classroom and what is happening in the world around us. To enjoy the wealth of information of *The New York Times* daily, a reduced subscription rate is available. For information, call toll-free: 1-800-631-1222.

PHLIP **PHLIP (Prentice Hall's Learning through the Internet Partnership) at http://www.prenhall.com/phlip**   Developed by Dan Cooper at Marist College, PHLIP provides academic support for faculty adopting this text. From the PHLIP Web site you can download supplements and lecture aids such as instructor's manuals, lecture notes, PowerPoint presentations, problem and case solutions, and chapter outlines. We have chosen to deliver information electronically so you can be assured that you are getting the very latest in support materials.

PHLIP also helps you bring current events into the classroom. Through services such as PHLIPping Through The News, you and your students can access the most current articles of relevance to economics. Tony Pizelo of Spokane Community College and Metropolitan Investment Securities reviews the most current articles and prepares topic summaries, discussion questions, group activities, and research ideas for those articles. Updated every two weeks, these stories are keyed to specific chapters in the text providing the instructor with an infinite and invaluable teaching tool. Call your Prentice Hall sales representative to get the necessary username and password to access these digital supplements or contact Prentice Hall Sales directly at **college_sales@prenhall.com** and we'll have your local representative contact you right away.

PowerPoint Presentation Graphics   Prepared by Terry Maness, the Dean of Baylor University's College of Business, these PowerPoint graphics provide individual lecture outlines to accompany *Foundations of Finance*. These lectures are class tested and can be used as is or easily modified to reflect your specific presentation needs.

Spreadsheet Problem Disk   (Available for download at **http://www.prenhall. com/phlip** [click on Finance and then Student Supplements]) In addition to the solutions being provided in the Instructor's Manual, we have also developed spreadsheet solutions to almost all of the end-of-chapter problems. The solutions have been prepared in Excel, but they can be converted into Lotus. The user can change the assumptions in the problem and thereby generate new solutions.

Color Transparencies   Approximately 150 four-color acetates of the major figures in the text are available. In addition, a complete set of transparency masters will be available to download from the Prentice Hall web site.

Study Guide   Also written by the authors, the Study Guide contains several innovative features to help the student of *Foundations of Finance*. Each chapter begins with an overview of the key points of the chapter, which can serve both as a preview and quick survey of the chapter content and as a review. There are problems (with detailed solutions) and self-tests that can be used to aid in the preparation of outside assignments and to study for examinations. The problems are keyed to the end-of-chapter problems in the text in order to provide direct and meaningful student aid. Multiple-choice and true/false questions are also included to provide a self-test over the descriptive chapter material.

The Study Guide also offers a tutorial on capital budgeting that can help the student work through this important topic on an individual basis at his or her own pace. A helpful teacher's note on understanding the rationale and logic of the internal rate of return is also included in this Study Guide. Students frequently learn the procedure for computing a project's internal rate of return but fail to grasp the meaning or the reason for its computation. This brief note helps the student better understand this important concept and tool of finance.

A complete article from *Financial Practice and Education* appears at the end of the Study Guide, which demonstrates the use of a variety of financial calculators. Students have found the article extremely helpful in getting started at using a financial calculator. Finally, in addition to the tables giving compound sum and present value interest factors, the Study Guide now includes tables that show how to compute the interest factors using a financial calculator.

Student Lecture Notes (Available for download at **http://www.prenhall.com/ phlip** [click on Finance and then Student Supplements]) The Student Lecture Notes provides the student with a printed copy of all the PowerPoint presentation graphics in a workbook format.

FinCoach Version C (ISBN 0-13-552275-7) FinCoach, a Windows-based software designed to teach the student, within a matter of hours, how to solve practically any mathematical problem in corporate finance, is also available to the students. It provides a step-by-step problem-solving guide with over 5 million practice problems and self-tests in valuation of single cash flows, valuation of multiple cash flows, valuation of infinitely many cash flows, bond valuation, stock valuation, cost of capital, portfolio diversification, CAPM, project and firm valuation, NPV, IRR, and Profitability Index. It allows the student to save problems, review them, print them, and more. FinCoach Version C is available through any college bookstore.

As a final, but important, comment to the teacher, we know how frustrating errors in a textbook or instructor's manual can be. Thus, we have worked diligently to provide you with as error-free a book as possible. Not only did we check and recheck the answers ourselves, but Prentice Hall hired faculty members at other universities to check the accuracy of the problem solutions. We, therefore, make the following offer to users of *Foundations of Finance.*

Any professor or student identifying an error of substance (e.g., an incorrect number in an example or problem) in *Foundations of Finance*, in either the text or the instructor's manual, that has not been previously reported to the authors will receive a $10 reward. If a series of related errors occurs resulting from an original error, the reward will be limited to a maximum of $20 for the group of errors. Please report any errors to Art Keown at the following address:

Art Keown
Department of Finance
Virginia Tech
Blacksburg, VA 24061-0221

Acknowledgments

We gratefully acknowledge the assistance, support, and encouragement of those individuals who have contributed to *Foundations of Finance*. Specifically, we wish to recognize the very helpful insights provided by many of our colleagues. For their careful comments and helpful reviews of the text, we are indebted to:

Ibrahim J. Affaneh
Indiana University of Pennsylvania

Sung C. Bae
Bowling Green State University

Laurey Berk
University of Wisconsin, Green Bay

Ronald W. Best
University of South Alabama

Laurence E. Blose
University of North Carolina Charlotte

Robert Boldin
Indiana University of Pennsylvania

Michael Bond
Cleveland State University

Waldo L. Born
Eastern Illinois University

Paul Bursik
St. Norbert College

Anthony K. Byrd
University of Central Florida

P. R. Chandy
University of North Texas

Santosh Choudhury
Norfolk State University

K. C. Chen
California State University, Fresno

Jeffrey S. Christensen
Youngstown State University

M. C. Chung
*California State University
  Sacramento*

Steven M. Dawson
University of Hawaii

Yashwant S. Dhatt
University of Southern Colorado

John W. Ellis
Colorado State University

Suzanne Erickson
Seattle University

Slim Feriani
George Washington University

Greg Filbeck
Miami University

Ken Halsey
Wayne State College

James D. Harriss
*University of North Carolina
  Wilmington*

Dr. Linda C Hittle
San Diego State University

Gerry Jensen
Northern Illinois University

Steve Johnson
University of Texas at El Paso

Ravi Kamath
Cleveland State University

James D. Keys
Florida International University

Reinhold P. Lamb
University of North Carolina Charlotte

Larry Lang
University of Wisconsin

George B. F. Lanigan
*University of North Carolina
  Greensboro*

William R. Lasher
Nichols College

David E. Letourneau
Winthrop University

Ilene Levin
University of Minnesota—Duluth

Michael McMillan
*Northern Virginia Community
  College*

Judy E. Maese
New Mexico State University

Abbas Mamoozadeh
Slippery Rock University

James E. McNulty
Florida Atlantic University

Grant McQueen
Brigham Young University

Emil Meurer
University of New Orleans

Stuart Michelson
Eastern Illinois University

Eric J. Moon
San Francisco State University

Scott Moore
John Carroll University

Rick H. Mull
Fort Lewis College

M. P. Narayanan
University of Michigan

William E. O'Connell Jr.
College of William & Mary

Jeffrey H. Peterson
St. Bonaventure University

Mario Picconi
University of San Diego

Stuart Rosenstein
Clemson University

Ivan C. Roten
Arizona State University

Marjorie A. Rubash
Bradley University

Joseph Stanford
Bridgewater State College

David Suk
Rider University

Elizabeth Sun
San Jose State University

R. Bruce Swensen
Adelphi University

Philip R. Swensen
Utah State University

Lee Tenpao
Niagara University

Paul A. Vanderheiden
*University of Wisconsin,
Eau Claire*

Nikhil P. Varaiya
San Diego State University

K. G. Viswanathan
Hofstra University

Al Webster
Bradley University

Patricia Webster
Bradley University

Herbert Weinraub
Michigan State University

Herbert Weinraub
University of Toledo

Sandra Williams
Moorhead State University

Tony R. Wingler
*University of North Carolina
Greensboro*

Wold Zemedkun
Norfolk State University

Marc Zenner
Indiana University

We also wish to thank a wonderful group of people at Prentice Hall. To Paul Donnelly we owe an immeasurable debt of gratitude. He has continued to push us to make sure that we deliver the finest possible textbook and supplementary package possible. His efforts go well beyond what one might expect from the best of editors. We also offer our personal expression of appreciation to Gladys Soto for her editorial deftness; to MaryBeth Sanok for her superb coordinating skills. To Cynthia Regan, our Production Editor, we express a very special thank you. Her skills in coordinating this revision through a very complex production process and keeping it all on schedule while maintaining extremely high quality earns her a "beyond-the-call-of-duty" applause from all of us! Our appreciation to the people at Prentice Hall would be extremely incomplete without the mention of the highly professional Prentice Hall field sales people and their managers. In our opinion they are the best in the business and we are delighted with their dedicated performance each year. We continue to salute Victoria McWilliams of Arizona State West for her help on the initial edition. Her comments and insights added greatly to the value of the book. We thank Glenn Furney at Texas Instruments for his help in bringing to life the use of calculators in the teaching of financial management.

As a final word, we express our sincere thanks to those using *Foundations of Finance* in the classroom. We thank you for making us a part of your team. Always feel free to give any of us a call when you have questions or needs.

A.J.K.
J.W.P.
D.F.S.
J.D.M.

An Introduction to the Foundations of Financial Management— The Ties That Bind

LEARNING OBJECTIVES

After reading this chapter you should be able to

1. Identify the goal of the firm.

2. Compare the various legal forms of business organization and explain why the corporate form of business is the most logical choice for a firm that is large or growing.

3. Describe the corporate tax features that affect business decisions.

4. Explain the 10 axioms that form the foundations of financial management.

5. State the general topics to be covered in the remainder of this text.

Goal of the Firm • Legal Forms of Business Organization • Federal Income Taxation • Ten Axioms That Form the Foundations of Financial Management • Overview of the Text

In 1995 AT&T Corporation's Chief Executive Officer Robert E. Allen made headlines when he received, in addition to a salary of $1.15 million, a $1.5 million bonus and a tenfold increase in stock options—all during a year in which AT&T barely broke even due to $5.4 billion in restructuring charges and announced plans to eliminate 40,000 jobs. In addition, in 1995 the heads of about 30 major companies received compensation 212 times higher than the pay of the average American employee—this figure is up fivefold from 1965, when the multiple was 44.

In this chapter we will examine this problem, although we aren't as concerned with how much a firm's CEO earns as with whether the compensation package helps align the interests of the shareholders with those of the management. We will see that this alignment between managers and shareholders is necessary for the goal of the firm that we develop to be realized. We will also see that aligning the interests of the shareholders and the managers serves as one of the basic axioms of finance developed in this chapter. Moreover, the tax laws have been recently changed to encourage corporations to incorporate pay for performance into the management contracts, thereby aligning the interests of shareholders and managers.

Financial management is concerned with the maintenance and creation of wealth. Consequently, this course focuses on decision making with an eye to creating wealth. In introducing decision-making techniques we will emphasize the logic behind those techniques, thereby ensuring that you don't lose sight of the concepts when dealing with the calculations. To the first-time student of finance this may sound a bit overwhelming, but as we will see, the techniques and tools introduced in this text are all motivated by 10 underlying principles, or axioms, that will guide us through the decision-making process.

To lay a foundation for what will follow, we will begin by introducing the goal of the firm—maximization of shareholder wealth—which we will use as a guide in developing rules for decision making. Several alternative business forms, focusing on the corporate form and the tax environment in which the corporation exists, will then be introduced. In discussing the tax environment, we will concentrate only on that portion of the tax code that affects business decisions. Our attention will then turn to the 10 axioms that form the foundation of financial management. Although these axioms may seem quite simple or even trivial, they will provide the driving force behind all that follows. They will also provide the threads that tie the concepts and techniques introduced in the chapters together, all driven to create wealth.

GOAL OF THE FIRM

In this text we designate the goal of the firm to be *maximization of shareholder wealth*, by which we mean maximization of the price of the existing common stock. Not only will this goal directly benefit the shareholders of the company, but it will also provide benefits to society. This will come about as scarce resources are directed to their most productive use by businesses competing to create wealth. With this goal in place, our job as a financial manager becomes to create wealth for the shareholders. To better understand this goal, we will first discuss profit maximization as a possible goal for the firm. Then we will compare it to maximization of shareholder wealth to see why, in financial management, the latter is the more appropriate goal for the firm.

Profit Maximization

In microeconomics courses, profit maximization is frequently given as the goal of the firm. Profit maximization stresses the efficient use of capital resources, but it is not specific with respect to the time frame over which profits are to be measured. Do we maximize profits over the current year, or do we maximize profits over some longer period? A financial manager could easily increase current profits by eliminating research and development expenditures and cutting down on routine maintenance. In the short run, this might result in increased profits, but this clearly is not in the best long-run interests of the firm. If we are to base financial decisions on a goal, that goal must be precise, not allow for misinterpretation, and deal with all the complexities of the real world.

In microeconomics, profit maximization functions largely as a theoretical goal, with economists using it to prove how firms behave rationally to increase profit. Unfortunately, it ignores many real-world complexities that financial managers must address in their decisions. In the more applied discipline of financial management, firms must deal every day with two major factors not considered by the goal of profit maximization: uncertainty and timing.

Microeconomics courses ignore uncertainty and risk to present theory more easily. Projects and investment alternatives are compared by examining their expected values or weighted average profits. Whether one project is riskier than another does not enter into these calculations; economists do discuss risk, but only tangentially.[1] In reality, projects differ a great deal with respect to risk characteristics, and to disregard these differences in the practice of financial management can result in incorrect decisions. As we will discover later in this chapter, there is a very definite relationship between risk and expected return—that is, investors demand a higher expected return for taking on added risk—and to ignore this relationship would lead to improper decision making.

Another problem with the goal of profit maximization is that it ignores the timing of the project's returns. If this goal is only concerned with this year's profits, we know it inappropriately ignores profit in future years. If we interpret it to maximize the average of future profits, it is also incorrect. Inasmuch as investment opportunities are available for money in hand, we are not indifferent to the timing of the returns. Given equivalent cash flows from profits, we want those cash flows sooner rather than later. Thus, the real-world factors of uncertainty and timing force us to look beyond a simple goal of profit maximization as a decision criterion. We will turn now to an examination of a more robust goal for the firm: maximization of shareholder wealth.

Maximization of Shareholder Wealth

In formulating the goal of maximization of shareholder wealth we are doing nothing more than modifying the goal of profit maximization to deal with the complexities of the operating environment. We have chosen maximization of shareholder wealth— that is, maximization of the market value of the existing shareholders' common stock—because the effects of all financial decisions are thereby included. Investors react to poor investment or dividend decisions by causing the total value of the firm's stock to fall, and they react to good decisions by pushing up the price of the stock. In effect, under this goal, good decisions are those that create wealth for the shareholder.

Obviously, there are some serious practical problems in direct use of this goal and in using changes in the firm's stock to evaluate financial decisions. Many things affect stock prices; to attempt to identify a reaction to a particular financial decision would simply be impossible. Fortunately, that is not necessary. To employ this goal, we need not consider every stock price change to be a market interpretation of the worth of our decisions. Other factors, such as changes in the economy, also affect stock prices. What we will focus on is the effect that our decision *should* have on the stock price if everything else were held constant. The market price of the firm's stock reflects the value of the firm as seen by its owners and takes into account the complexities and complications of the real-world risk. As we follow this goal throughout our discussions, we must keep in mind one more question: Who exactly are the shareholders? The answer: Shareholders are the legal owners of the firm.

| LEGAL FORMS OF BUSINESS ORGANIZATION | OBJECTIVE 2 |

In the chapters ahead we will focus on financial decisions for corporations. Although the corporation is not the only legal form of business available, it is the most logical choice for a firm that is large or growing. It is also the dominant business form in

---

[1]See, for example, Robert S. Pindyck and Daniel Rubenfield, *Microeconomics*, 2d ed. (New York: Macmillan, 1992), pp. 244–46.

terms of sales in this country. In this section we will explain why this is so. This will in turn allow us to simplify the remainder of the text, as we will assume that the proper tax code to follow is the corporate tax code, rather than examine different tax codes for different legal forms of businesses. Keep in mind that our primary purpose is to develop an understanding of the logic of financial decision making. Taxes will become important only when they affect our decisions, and our discussion of the choice of the legal form of the business is directed at understanding why we will limit our discussion of taxes to the corporate form.

Legal forms of business organization are diverse and numerous. However, there are three categories: the sole proprietorship, the partnership, and the corporation. To understand the basic differences between each form, we need to define each one and understand its advantages and disadvantages. As the firm grows, we will see the advantages of the corporation begin to dominate. As a result, most large firms take on the corporate form.

Sole Proprietorship

sole proprietorship

The **sole proprietorship** is *a business owned by an individual.* The owner maintains title to the assets and is responsible, generally without limitation, for the liabilities incurred. The proprietor is entitled to the profits from the business but must also absorb any losses. This form of business is initiated by the mere act of beginning the business operations. Typically, no legal requirement must be met in starting the operation, particularly if the proprietor is conducting the business in his or her own name. If a special name is used, an assumed-name certificate should be filed, requiring a small registration fee. Termination occurs on the owner's death or by the owner's choice. Briefly stated, the sole proprietorship is for all practical purposes the absence of any formal *legal* business structure.

Partnership

partnership

The primary difference between a **partnership** and a sole proprietorship is that the partnership has more than one owner. A partnership is *an association of two or more persons coming together as co-owners for the purpose of operating a business for profit.* Partnerships fall into two types: (1) general partnerships and (2) limited partnerships.

General Partnership

general partnership

In a **general partnership** *each partner is fully responsible for the liabilities incurred by the partnership.* Also, any partner's ill conduct even having the appearance of relating to the firm's business renders the remaining partners liable as well. The relationship among partners is dictated entirely by the partnership agreement, which may be an oral commitment or a formal document.

Limited Partnership

limited partnership

In addition to the general partnership, in which all partners are jointly liable without limitation, many states provide for a **limited partnership.** The state statutes permit *one or more of the partners to have limited liability, restricted to the amount of capital invested in the partnership.* Several conditions must be met to qualify as a limited partner. First, at least one general partner must remain in the association for whom the privilege of limited liability does not apply. Second, the names of the limited partners may not appear in the name of the firm. Third, the limited partners may not participate in the management of the business. If one of these restrictions is violated, all partners forfeit their right to limited liability. In essence, the intent of the statutes creating the limited partnership is to provide limited liability for a person whose interest in the partnership is purely as an investor. That individual may not assume a management function within the organization.

Corporation

The **corporation** has been a significant factor in the economic development of the United States. As early as 1819 Chief Justice John Marshall set forth the legal definition of a corporation as "an artificial being, invisible, intangible, and existing only in the contemplation of law."[2] This entity *legally functions separate and apart from its owners*. As such, the corporation can individually sue and be sued, and purchase, sell, or own property; and its personnel are subject to criminal punishment for crimes. However, despite this legal separation, the corporation is composed of owners who dictate its direction and policies. The owners elect a board of directors, whose members in turn select individuals to serve as corporate officers, including president, vice-president, secretary, and treasurer. Ownership is reflected in common stock certificates, designating the number of shares owned by its holder. The number of shares owned relative to the total number of shares outstanding determines the stockholder's proportionate ownership in the business. Because the shares are transferable, ownership in a corporation may be changed by a shareholder simply remitting the shares to a new shareholder. The investor's liability is confined to the amount of the investment in the company, thereby preventing creditors from confiscating stockholders' personal assets in settlement of unresolved claims. Finally, the life of a corporation is not dependent on the status of the investors. The death or withdrawal of an investor does not affect the continuity of the corporation. The management continues to run the corporation when stock is sold or when it is passed on through inheritance.

Comparison of Organizational Forms

Owners of new businesses have some important decisions to make in choosing an organizational form. Whereas each business form seems to have some advantages over the others, we will see that as the firm grows and needs access to the capital markets to raise funds, the advantages of the corporation begin to dominate.

Why Large and Growing Firms Choose the Corporate Form: Ease in Raising Capital

Because of the limited liability, the ease of transferring ownership through the sale of common shares, and the flexibility in dividing the shares, the corporation is the ideal business entity in terms of attracting new capital. In contrast, the unlimited liabilities of the sole proprietorship and the general partnership are deterrents to raising equity capital. Between the extremes, the limited partnership does provide limited liability for limited partners, which has a tendency to attract wealthy investors. However, the impracticality of having a large number of partners and the restricted marketability of an interest in a partnership prevent this form of organization from competing effectively with the corporation. Therefore, when developing our decision models we will assume we are dealing with the corporate form. The taxes incorporated in these models will deal only with the corporate tax codes. Because our goal is to develop an understanding of the management, measurement, and creation of wealth, and not to become tax experts, we will only focus on those characteristics of the corporate tax code that will affect our financial decisions.

---

[2]*The Trustees of Dartmouth College* v. *Woodard*, 4 Wheaton 636 (1819).

Before presenting the 10 axioms of finance that will provide the conceptual underpinnings for what will follow, we will examine those tax features that will affect our decisions. We will describe the environment and set up the ground rules under which financial decisions are made. As the nation's politics change, so does the tax system. The purpose of looking at the current tax structure is not to become tax experts, but rather to gain an understanding of taxes and how they affect business decisions. There is a good chance that corporate tax rates may change significantly before you enter the workforce. However, although rates may change, taxes will continue to remain a cash outflow and therefore something to avoid. Thus, we will pay close attention to which expenses are and are not deductible for tax purposes, and in doing so focus on how taxes affect business decisions.

Objectives of Income Taxation

Originally, the sole objective of the federal government in taxing income was to generate financing for government expenditures. Although this purpose continues to be important, social and economic objectives have been added. For instance, a company may receive possible reductions in taxes if (1) it undertakes certain technological research, (2) it pays wages to certain economically disadvantaged groups, or (3) it locates in certain economically depressed areas. Other socially oriented stipulations in the tax laws include exemptions for dependents, old age, and blindness and a reduction in taxes on retirement income. In addition, the government uses tax legislation to stabilize the economy. In recessionary periods taxes may be reduced, giving the public more discretionary income in the hope that this income will be spent to increase the demand for products and thereby generate new jobs.

In short, three objectives may be given for the taxation of revenues: (1) the provision of revenues for government expenditures, (2) the achievement of socially desirable goals, and (3) economic stabilization.

Types of Taxpayers

To understand the tax system, we must first ask, "Who is the taxpayer?" For the most part, there are three basic types of taxable entities: individuals, corporations, and fiduciaries. Individuals include company employees, self-employed persons owning their own businesses, and members of a partnership. Income is reported by these individuals in their personal tax returns.[3] The corporation, as a separate legal entity, reports its income and pays any taxes related to these profits. The owners (stockholders) of the corporation need not report these earnings in their personal tax returns, except when all or a part of the profits are distributed in the form of dividends. Finally, fiduciaries, such as estates and trusts, file a tax return and pay taxes on the income generated by the estate or trust which isn't distributed to (and included in the taxable income of) a beneficiary.

Although taxation of individual and fiduciary income is an important source of income to the government, neither is especially relevant to the financial manager. Since most firms of any size are corporations, we will restrict our discussion to the corporation. A caveat is necessary, however. Tax legislation can be quite complex, with numerous exceptions to most general rules. The laws can also change quickly, and certain details discussed here may no longer apply in the near future. It sometimes is true that "a little knowledge is a dangerous thing."

---

[3]Partnerships report only the income from the partnership. The income is then reported again by each partner, who pays any taxes owed.

Table 1–1
J and S Corporation Taxable Income

Sales		$50,000,000
Cost of goods sold		23,000,000
Gross profit		$27,000,000
Operating expenses		
Administrative expenses	$4,000,000	
Depreciation expenses	1,500,000	
Marketing expenses	4,500,000	
Total operating expenses		10,000,000
Operating income (earnings before interest and taxes)		$17,000,000
Other income		0
Interest expense		1,000,000
Taxable income		$16,000,000

Dividends paid to common stockholders ($1,000,000) are not tax-deductible expenses.

Computing Taxable Income

The **taxable income** for a corporation is based on *the gross income from all sources, except for allowable exclusions, less any tax-deductible expenses.* **Gross income** equals *the firm's dollar sales from its products or services less the cost of producing or acquiring them.* Tax-deductible expenses include any operating expenses, such as marketing expenses and administrative expenses. Also, *interest expense* paid on the firm's outstanding debt is a tax-deductible expense. However, dividends paid to the firm's stockholders, are *not* deductible expenses, but rather distributions of income. Other taxable income includes interest income and dividend income.

    To demonstrate how to compute a corporation's taxable income, consider the J and S Corporation, a manufacturer of home accessories. The firm, originally established by Kelly Stites, had sales of $50 million for the year. The cost of producing the accessories totaled $23 million. Operating expenses were $10 million. The corporation has $12.5 million in debt outstanding, with an 8 percent interest rate, which resulted in $1 million interest expense ($12,500,000 × .08 = $1,000,000). Management paid $1 million in dividends to the firm's common stockholders. No other income, such as interest or dividend income, was received. The taxable income for the J and S Corporation would be $16 million, as shown in Table 1–1.

    Once we know the J and S Corporation's taxable income, we can next determine the amount of taxes the firm will owe.

Computing the Taxes Owed

The taxes to be paid by the corporation on its taxable income are based on the corporate tax rate structure. The specific rates effective for the corporation, as of 1997, are given in Table 1–2 on page 8. Under the Revenue Reconciliation Act of 1993 a new top marginal corporate tax rate of 35 percent was added for taxable income in excess of $10 million. Also, a surtax of 3 percent was imposed on taxable income between $15 million and $18,333,333. This, in combination with the previously existing 5 percent surtax on taxable income between $100,000 and $335,000, recaptures the benefits of the lower marginal rates and as a result both the average and marginal tax rates on taxable income above $18,333,333 become 35 percent.

Table 1–2
Corporate Tax Rates

15%	$	0–$50,000
25%	$	50,001–$75,000
34%		$75,001–$10,000,000
35%		over $10,000,000

Additional surtax:
- 5% on income between $100,000 and $335,000.
- 3% on income between $15,000,000 and $18,333,333.

For example, the tax liability for the J and S Corporation, which had $16 million in taxable earnings, would be $5,530,000, calculated as follows:

EARNINGS	×	MARGINAL TAX RATE	=	TAXES
$ 50,000	×	15%	=	$ 7,500
25,000	×	25%	=	6,250
9,925,000	×	34%	=	3,374,500
6,000,000	×	35%	=	2,100,000
				$5,488,250

Additional surtaxes
- Add 5% surtax on income between
  $100,000 and $335,000
  (5% × [$335,000 − $100,000])   11,750
- Add 3% surtax on income between
  $15,000,000 and $18,333,333
  (3% × [$16,000,000 − $15,000,000])   30,000

Total tax liability	$5,530,000

marginal tax rate   The tax rates shown in Table 1–2 are defined as the **marginal tax rates,** or *rates applicable to the next dollar of income.* For instance, if a firm has earnings of $60,000 and is contemplating an investment that would yield $10,000 in additional profits, the tax rate to be used in calculating the taxes on this added income is 25 percent; that is, the marginal tax rate is 25 percent. However, if the corporation already expects $20 million without the new investment, the extra $10,000 in earnings would be taxed at 35 percent, the marginal tax rate. In the example, where the J and S Corporation has taxable income of $16 million, its marginal tax rate is 38 percent (this is because $16 million falls into the 35% tax bracket *with* a 3% surtax); that is, any additional income from new investments will be taxed at a rate of 38 percent. However, after taxable income exceeds $18,333,333, the marginal tax rate declines to 35 percent, when the 3 percent surtax no longer applies.

For financial decision making, it's the *marginal tax rate* rather than the average tax rate that we will be concerned with. As will become increasingly clear throughout the text, we always want to consider the tax consequences of any financial decision. The appropriate rate to be used in the analysis is the marginal tax rate, because it is this rate that will be applicable for any changes in earnings as a result of the decision being made. Thus, when making financial decisions involving taxes, always use the marginal tax rate in your calculations.[4]

The tax rate structure used in computing the J and S Corporation's taxes assumes that the income occurs in the United States. Given the globalization of the economy, it may well be that some of the income originates in a foreign country. If so, the tax rates, and the method of taxing the firm, frequently vary. As financial manager, you would minimize the firm's taxes by reporting as much income as possible in the low-tax-rate countries and as little as possible in the high-tax-rate countries. Of course, other factors, such as political risk, may discourage your efforts to minimize taxes across national borders.

Other Tax Considerations

In addition to the fundamental computation of taxes, several other aspects of the existing tax legislation have relevance for the financial manager. These are (1) the dividend income exclusion for corporations, (2) the effects of depreciation on the firm's taxes, and (3) the recognition of capital gains and losses. Let's look at each of these tax provisions in turn.

Dividend Exclusion

A corporation may normally exclude 70 percent of any dividends received from another corporation. For instance, if corporation A owns common stock in corporation B and receives dividends of $1,000 in a given year, only $300 will be subject to tax, and the remaining $700 (70 percent of $1,000) will be tax exempt. If the corporation receiving the dividend income is in a 34 percent tax bracket, only $102 in taxes (34 percent of $300) will result.[5]

Depreciation

Depreciation is *the means by which an asset's value is expensed over its useful life for federal tax purposes.* Essentially, there are three methods for computing depreciation expenses: (1) straight-line depreciation, (2) the double-declining balance method, and (3) the modified accelerated cost recovery system. Any one of the three methods results in the same depreciation expense over the life of the asset; however, the last two approaches allow the firm to take the depreciation earlier as opposed to later, which in turn defers taxes until later. Assuming a time value of money, there is an advantage to using the accelerated techniques. (Chapter 5 fully explains the time value of money.) Also, management may use straight-line depreciation for reporting income to the shareholders while still using an accelerated method for calculating taxable income.

depreciation

---

[4]On taxable income between $335,000 and $10 million, both the marginal and average tax rates equal 34 percent, owing to the imposition of the 5 percent surtax that applies to taxable income between $100,000 and $335,000. After the company's taxable income exceeds $18,333,333, both the marginal and average tax rates equal 35 percent, because the 3 percent surtax on income between $15 million and $18,333,333 eliminates the benefits of having the first $10 million of income taxed at 34 rather than 35 percent.

[5]If corporation A owns at least 20 percent of corporation B, but less than 80 percent, 80 percent of any dividends received may be excluded from taxable income. If 80 percent or more is owned, all the dividends received may be excluded.

Capital Gains and Losses

capital gain (or loss)

An important tax consideration prior to 1987 was the preferential tax treatment for **capital gains (or losses);** that is, *gains (or losses) from the sale of assets not bought or sold in the ordinary course of business.* The Tax Reform Act of 1986 repealed any special treatment of capital gains and while the Revenue Reconciliation Act of 1993 reinstituted preferential treatment in certain unique circumstances, in general, capital gains are taxed at the same rates as ordinary income. However, if a corporation has capital losses that exceed capital gains in any year, these net capital losses may not be deducted from ordinary income. The net losses may, however, be carried back and applied against net capital gains in each of the three years before the current year. If the loss is not completely used in the three prior years, any remaining loss may be carried forward and applied against any net gains in each of the next five years. For example, if a corporation has an $80,000 net capital loss in 1996, it may apply this loss against any net gains in 1993, 1994, and 1995. If any loss remains, it may be carried forward and applied against any gains through 2001.

Other Tax Concerns

net operating loss carryback and carryforward

As mentioned earlier, taxes are used not only to raise money, but also to promote socially desirable goals and to maintain economic stability. One way in which both of these goals are met is through the creation and retention of jobs. As a result, to keep struggling firms afloat, there is a tax provision that allows a corporation with an operating loss (which is simply a loss from operating a business) to apply this loss against income in other years. This is commonly referred to as a **net operating loss carryback and carryforward.** *This tax feature allows firms that lose money to recapture taxes they had previously paid, carrying losses back up to three years or forward up to fifteen years to offset profits,* which hopefully allows them to deal with the problems that resulted in the loss. The bottom line here is that the government wants to keep as many people employed as possible and to keep the markets as competitive as possible, and to do this they have set up a tax code that helps those in trouble stay afloat.

Corporate Taxes: An Example

To illustrate certain portions of the tax laws for a corporation, assume that the Griggs Corporation had sales during the past year of $5 million; its cost of goods sold was $3 million; and it incurred operating expenses of $1 million. In addition, it received $185,000 in interest income and $100,000 in dividend income from another corporation. In turn, it paid $40,000 in interest and $75,000 in dividends. Also, it sold old machinery, which had originally cost $350,000, for $200,000. The equipment, purchased five years ago, was being depreciated (straight-line) over a 10-year life and had a book value of $175,000. Finally, the company sold a piece of land for $100,000 that had cost $50,000 six years ago. Given this information, the firm's taxable income is $1,250,000, as computed in the top part of Table 1–3.

Based on the tax rates from Table 1–2, Grigg's tax liability is $425,000, as shown at the bottom of Table 1–3. Note that the $75,000 Griggs paid in dividends is not tax deductible. Also, since the firm's taxable income exceeds $335,000, and the 5 percent surtax no longer applies, the marginal tax rate and the average tax rate both equal 34 percent; that is, we could have computed Grigg's tax liability as 34 percent of $1,250,000, or $425,000.

Table 1-3
Griggs Corporation Tax Computations

Sales			$5,000,000
Cost of goods sold			(3,000,000)
Gross profit			$2,000,000
Operating expenses			(1,000,000)
Operating income			$1,000,000
Other taxable income and expenses:			
Interest income		$185,000	
Dividend income	$100,000		
Less 70% exclusion	70,000	30,000	
Interest expense		(40,000)	175,000
Gain on sale of equipment:			
Selling price		$200,000	
Book value		175,000	25,000
Gain on land sale:			
Selling price		$100,000	
Cost		(50,000)	$ 50,000
Total taxable income			$1,250,000

Tax computation:

15%	×	$50,000	=	$ 7,500
25%	×	25,000	=	6,250
34%	×	1,175,000	=	399,500
		$1,250,000		

Add 5% surtax for income between $100,000 and $335,000	$ 11,750
Tax liability	$425,000

TEN AXIOMS THAT FORM THE FOUNDATIONS OF FINANCIAL MANAGEMENT

OBJECTIVE 4

To the first-time student of finance, the subject matter may seem like a collection of unrelated decision rules. This could not be further from the truth. In fact, our decision rules, and the logic that underlies them, spring from 10 simple axioms that do not require knowledge of finance to understand. *However, while it is not necessary to understand finance in order to understand these axioms, it is necessary to understand these axioms in order to understand finance.* Keep in mind that although these axioms may at first appear simple or even trivial, they will provide the driving force behind all that follows. These axioms will weave together concepts and techniques presented in this text, thereby allowing us to focus on the logic underlying the practice of financial management.

Axiom 1:
The Risk-Return Trade-off—We Won't Take on Additional Risk Unless We Expect to Be Compensated with Additional Return

At some point we have all saved some money. Why have we done this? The answer is simple: to expand our future consumption opportunities. We are able to invest those savings and earn a return on our dollars because some people would rather forgo future consumption opportunities to consume more now. Assuming there are a lot of different people that would like to use our savings, how do we decide where to put our money?

First, investors demand a minimum return for delaying consumption that must be greater than the anticipated rate of inflation. If they didn't receive enough to compensate for anticipated inflation, investors would purchase whatever goods they desired ahead of time or invest in assets that were subject to inflation and earn the rate of inflation on those assets. There isn't much incentive to postpone consumption if your savings are going to decline in terms of purchasing power.

Investment alternatives have different amounts of risk and expected returns. Investors sometimes choose to put their money in risky investments because these investments offer higher expected returns. The more risk an investment has, the higher will be its expected return. This relationship between risk and expected return is shown in Figure 1–1.

Notice that we keep referring to *expected* return rather than *actual* return. We may have expectations of what the returns from investing will be, but we can't peer into the future and see what those returns are actually going to be. If investors could see into the future, no one would have invested money in the dressmaker Leslie Fay, whose stock dropped 43 percent on April 5, 1993, when it announced it was filing for bankruptcy. Until after the fact, you are never sure what the return on an investment will be. That is why General Motors bonds pay more interest than U.S. Treasury bonds of the same maturity. The additional interest convinces some investors to take on the added risk of purchasing a General Motors bond.

This risk-return relationship will be a key concept as we value stocks, bonds, and proposed new projects throughout this text. We will also spend some time determining how to measure risk. Interestingly, much of the work for which the 1990 Nobel Prize for Economics was awarded centered on the graph in Figure 1–1 and how to measure risk. Both the graph and the risk-return relationship it depicts will reappear often in this text.

Axiom 2:

The Time Value of Money—A Dollar Received Today Is Worth More Than a Dollar Received in the Future

A fundamental concept in finance is that money has a time value associated with it: A dollar received today is worth more than a dollar received a year from now. Because we can earn interest on money received today, it is better to receive money earlier rather

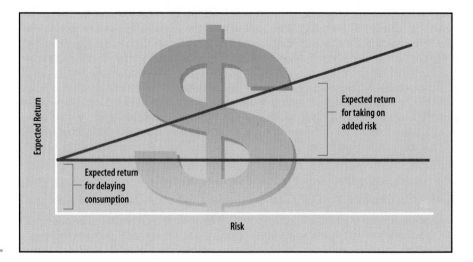

Figure 1–1
The Risk-Return Relationship

than later. In your economics courses, this concept of the time value of money is referred to as the opportunity cost of passing up the earning potential of a dollar today.

In this text we focus on the creation and measurement of wealth. To measure wealth or value we will use the concept of the time value of money to bring the future benefits and costs of a project back to the present. Then, if the benefits outweigh the costs, the project creates wealth and should be accepted; if the costs outweigh the benefits, the project does not create wealth and should be rejected. Without recognizing the existence of the time value of money, it is impossible to evaluate projects with future benefits and costs in a meaningful way.

To bring future benefits and costs of a project back to the present, we must assume a specific opportunity cost of money, or interest rate. Exactly what interest rate to use is determined by **Axiom 1: The Risk-Return Trade-off,** which states investors demand higher returns for taking on more risky projects. Thus, when we determine the present value of future benefits and costs, we take into account that investors demand a higher return for taking on added risk.

Axiom 3:
Cash—Not Profits—Is King

In measuring wealth or value we will use cash flows, not accounting profits, as our measurement tool. Cash flows are received by the firm and can be reinvested. Accounting profits, on the other hand, are shown when they are earned rather than when the money is actually in hand. A firm's cash flows and accounting profits may not occur together. For example, capital expenses, such as the purchase of new equipment or a building, are depreciated over several years, with the annual depreciation subtracted from profits. However, the cash flow associated with this expense generally occurs immediately. Therefore, cash outflows involving paying money out and cash inflows that can be reinvested correctly reflect the timing of the benefits and costs.

At this point, the first three axioms we have presented can be used to determine the value of any asset, be it a business, a new project, or a financial asset like a share of stock or a bond. In future chapters we will provide the techniques for determining the value of an asset based on these axioms.

Axiom 4:
Incremental Cash Flows—It's Only What Changes That Counts

In making business decisions, we are concerned with the results of those decisions: What happens if we say yes versus what happens if we say no? **Axiom 3** states that we should use cash flows to measure the benefits that accrue from taking on a new project. We are now fine-tuning our evaluation process so that we only consider **incremental** cash flows. The incremental cash flow is the difference between the cash flows if the project is taken on versus what they will be if the project is not taken on.

Not all cash flows are incremental. For example, when Leaf Inc., a manufacturer of sports cards, introduced Donruss Triple Play Baseball Cards in 1992, the product competed directly with the company's Leaf and Donruss baseball cards. There is no doubt that some of the sales dollars that ended up with Donruss Triple Play Cards would have been spent on Donruss or Leaf Cards if Triple Play Cards had not been available. Although the Leaf corporation meant to target the low-cost end of the baseball cards market held by Topps, there was no question that Triple Play sales bit into—actually cannibalized—sales from the company's existing product lines. The *difference* between revenues generated by introducing the new cards versus maintaining the original series is the incremental cash flows. This difference reflects the true impact of the decision.

What is important is that we *think* incrementally. Our guiding rule in deciding whether a cash flow is incremental is to look at the company with and without the new product. In fact, we will take this incremental concept beyond cash flows and look at all consequences from all decisions on an incremental basis.

Axiom 5:
The Curse of Competitive Markets—Why It's Hard to Find Exceptionally Profitable Projects

Our job as financial managers is to create wealth. Therefore, we will look closely at the mechanics of valuation and decision making. We will focus on estimating cash flows, determining what the investment earns, and valuing assets and new projects. But it will be easy to get caught up in the mechanics of valuation and lose sight of the process of creating wealth. Why is it so hard to find projects and investments that are exceptionally profitable? Where do profitable projects come from? The answers to these questions tell us a lot about how competitive markets operate and where to look for profitable projects.

In reality, it is much easier evaluating profitable projects than finding them. If an industry is generating large profits, new entrants are usually attracted. The additional competition and added capacity can result in profits being driven down to the required rate of return. Conversely, if an industry is returning profits below the required rate of return, then some participants in the market drop out, reducing capacity and competition. In turn, prices are driven back up. This is precisely what happened in the VCR video rental market in the mid-1980s. This market developed suddenly with the opportunity for extremely large profits. Because there were no barriers to entry, the market quickly was flooded with new entries. By 1987 the competition and price cutting produced losses for many firms in the industry, forcing them to flee the market. As the competition lessened with firms moving out of the video rental industry, profits again rose to the point where the required rate of return could be earned on invested capital.

In competitive markets, extremely large profits simply cannot exist for very long. Given that somewhat bleak scenario, how can we find good projects—that is, projects that return more than the required rate of return? Although competition makes them difficult to find, we have to invest in markets that are not perfectly competitive. The two most common ways of making markets less competitive are to differentiate the product in some key way or to achieve a cost advantage over competitors.

Product differentiation insulates a product from competition, thereby allowing prices to stay sufficiently high to support large profits. If products are differentiated, consumer choice is no longer made by price alone. For example, in the pharmaceutical industry, patents create competitive barriers. Schering's Claritin, used in the treatment of allergies, and Hoffman–La Roche's Valium, a tranquilizer, are protected from direct competition by patents.

Service and quality are also used to differentiate products. For example, Caterpillar Tractor has long prided itself on the quality of its construction and earthmoving machinery. As a result, it has been able to maintain its market share. Similarly, much of Toyota's and Honda's brand loyalty is based on quality. Service can also create product differentiation, as shown by McDonald's fast service, cleanliness, and consistency of product that brings customers back.

Whether product differentiation occurs because of advertising, patents, service, or quality, the more the product is differentiated from competing products, the less competition it will face and the greater the possibility of large profits.

Economies of scale and the ability to produce at a cost below competition can effectively deter new entrants to the market and thereby reduce competition. The retail hardware industry is one such case. In the hardware industry there are fixed costs that are independent of the store's size. For example, inventory costs, advertising expenses, and managerial salaries are essentially the same regardless of annual sales.

Therefore, the more sales that can be built up, the lower the per-sale dollar cost of inventory, advertising, and management. Restocking from warehouses also becomes more efficient as delivery trucks can be used to full potential.

Regardless of how the cost advantage is created—by economies of scale, proprietary technology, or monopolistic control of raw materials—the cost advantage deters new market entrants while allowing production at below industry cost. This cost advantage has the potential of creating large profits.

The key to locating profitable investment projects is to first understand how and where they exist in competitive markets. Then the corporate philosophy must be aimed at creating or taking advantage of some imperfection in these markets, either through product differentiation or creation of a cost advantage, rather than looking to new markets or industries that appear to provide large profits. Any perfectly competitive industry that looks too good to be true won't be for long.

Axiom 6:
Efficient Capital Markets—The Markets Are Quick and the Prices Are Right

Our goal as financial managers is the maximization of shareholder wealth. Decisions that maximize shareholder wealth lead to an increase in the market price of the existing common stock. To understand this relationship, as well as how securities such as bonds and stocks are valued or priced in the financial markets, it is necessary to have an understanding of the concept of **efficient markets.** *These are markets in which the values of all assets and securities at any instant in time fully reflect all available information.*

efficient markets

Whether a market is efficient has to do with the speed with which information is impounded into security prices. An efficient market is characterized by a large number of profit-driven individuals who act independently. In addition, new information regarding securities arrives in the market in a random manner. Given this setting, investors adjust to new information immediately and buy and sell the security until they feel the market price correctly reflects the new information. Under the efficient market hypothesis, information is reflected in security prices with such speed that there are no opportunities for investors to profit from publicly available information. Investors competing for profits ensure that security prices appropriately reflect the expected earnings and risks involved and thus the true value of the firm.

What are the implications of efficient markets for us? First, the price is right. Stock prices reflect all publicly available information regarding the value of the company. This means we can implement our goal of maximization of shareholder wealth by focusing on the effect each decision *should* have on the stock price if everything else is held constant. Second, earnings manipulations through accounting changes will not result in price changes. Stock splits and other changes in accounting methods that do not affect cash flows are not reflected in prices. Market prices reflect expected cash flows available to shareholders. Thus, our preoccupation with cash flows to measure the timing of the benefits is justified.

As we will see, it is indeed reassuring that prices reflect value. It allows us to look at prices and see value reflected in them. While it may make investing a bit less exciting, it makes corporate finance much less uncertain.

Axiom 7:
The Agency Problem—Managers Won't Work for the Owners Unless It's in Their Best Interest

Although the goal of the firm is the maximization of shareholder wealth, in reality the agency problem may interfere with the implementation of this goal. The **agency problem** *results from the separation of management and the ownership of the firm.* For

agency problem

example, a large firm may be run by professional managers who have little or no ownership in the firm. Because of this separation of the decision makers and owners, managers may make decisions that are not in line with the goal of maximization of shareholder wealth. They may approach work less energetically and attempt to benefit themselves in terms of salary and perquisites at the expense of shareholders.

The costs associated with the agency problem are difficult to measure, but occasionally we see the problem's effect in the marketplace. For example, if the market feels management of a firm is damaging shareholder wealth, we might see a positive reaction in stock price to the removal of that management. In 1989, on the day following the death of John Dorrance, Jr., chairman of Campbell's Soup, Campbell's stock price rose about 15 percent. Some investors felt that Campbell's relatively small growth in earnings might be improved with the departure of Dorrance. There was also speculation that Dorrance was the major obstacle to a possible positive reorganization.

If the management of the firm works for the owners, who are actually the shareholders, why doesn't the management get fired if they don't act in the shareholders' best interest? *In theory*, the shareholders pick the corporate board of directors and the board of directors in turn picks the management. Unfortunately, *in reality* the system frequently works the other way around. Management selects the board of director nominees and then distributes the ballots. In effect, shareholders are offered a slate of nominees selected by the management. The end result is management effectively selects the directors, who then may have more allegiance to managers than to shareholders. This in turn sets up the potential for agency problems with the board of directors not monitoring managers on behalf of the shareholders as they should.

We will spend considerable time monitoring managers and trying to align their interests with shareholders. Managers can be monitored by auditing financial statements and managers' compensation packages. The interests of managers and shareholders can be aligned by establishing management stock options, bonuses, and perquisites that are directly tied to how closely their decisions coincide with the interest of shareholders. The agency problem will persist unless an incentive structure is set up that aligns the interests of managers and shareholders. In other words, what is good for shareholders must also be good for managers. If that is not the case, managers will make decisions in their best interest rather than maximizing shareholder wealth.

Axiom 8:
Taxes Bias Business Decisions

Hardly any decision is made by the financial manager without considering the impact of taxes. When we introduced **Axiom 4,** we said that only incremental cash flows should be considered in the evaluation process. More specifically, the cash flows we will consider will be *after-tax incremental cash flows to the firm as a whole.*

When we evaluate new projects, we will see income taxes play a significant role. When the company is analyzing the possible acquisition of a plant or equipment, the returns from the investment should be measured on an after-tax basis. Otherwise, the company will not truly be evaluating the true incremental cash flows generated by the project.

The government also realizes taxes can bias business decisions and uses taxes to encourage spending in certain ways. If the government wants to encourage spending on research and development projects, it might offer an *investment tax credit* for such investments. This would have the effect of reducing taxes on research and development projects, which would in turn increase the after-tax cash flows from those projects. The increased cash flow would turn some otherwise unprofitable research and development projects into profitable projects. In effect, the government can use taxes as a tool to direct business investment to research and development projects, to the inner cities, and to projects that create jobs.

Taxes also play a role in determining a firm's financial structure, or mix of debt and stock. Although this subject has been the focus of intense controversy for over three decades, one aspect remains constant: The tax laws give debt financing a definite cost advantage over stock. As we noted when we examined how taxes are computed, *interest payments are a tax-deductible expense, whereas dividend payments to stockholders may not be used as deductions in computing a corporation's taxable profits.* Interest payments lower profits, which are not a cash flow item, and this in turn lowers taxes due, which are a cash flow item. In effect, paying interest as opposed to dividends reduces taxes.

Axiom 9:
All Risk Is Not Equal—Some Risk Can Be Diversified Away, and Some Cannot

Much of finance centers around **Axiom 1, The Risk-Return Trade-off.** But before we can fully use **Axiom 1** we must decide how to measure risk. As we will see, risk is difficult to measure. **Axiom 9** introduces you to the process of diversification and demonstrates how it can reduce risk. We will also provide you with an understanding of how diversification makes it difficult to measure a project's or an asset's risk.

You are probably already familiar with the concept of diversification. There is an old saying, "don't put all your eggs in one basket." Diversification allows good and bad events or observations to cancel each other out, thereby reducing total variability without affecting expected return.

To see how diversification complicates the measurement of risk, let us look at the difficulty Louisiana Gas has in determining the level of risk associated with a new natural gas well-drilling project. Each year Louisiana Gas might drill several hundred wells, with each well having only a 1 in 10 chance of success. If the well produces, the profits are quite large, but if it comes up dry, the investment is lost. Thus, with a 90 percent chance of losing everything, we would view the project as being extremely risky. However, if Louisiana Gas each year drills 2,000 wells, all with a 10 percent, independent chance of success, then they would typically have 200 successful wells. Moreover, a bad year may result in only 190 successful wells, while a good year may result in 210 successful wells. If we look at all the wells together, the extreme good and the bad results tend to cancel each other out and the well-drilling projects taken together do not appear to have much risk or variability of possible outcome.

The amount of risk in a gas well project depends upon our perspective. Looking at the well standing alone, it looks like a lot; however, if we consider the risk that each well contributes to the overall firm risk, it is quite small. This occurs because much of the risk associated with each individual well is diversified away within the firm. From the point of view of a diversified shareholder, much of the risk that a project contributes to the firm is further diversified away as the shareholder adds the Louisiana Gas stock to other stocks in his or her portfolio. The risk of an investment varies depending upon the perspective of the individual considering the risk.

Perhaps the easiest way to understand the concept of diversification is to look at it graphically. Consider what happens when we combine two projects, as depicted in Figure 1–2 on page 18. In this case, the cash flows from these projects move in opposite directions, and when they are combined, the variability of their combination is totally eliminated. Notice that the return has not changed—both the individual projects' and their combination's return averages 10 percent. In this case the extreme good and bad observations cancel each other out. The degree to which the total risk is reduced is a function of how the two sets of cash flows or returns move together.

As we will see for most projects and assets, some risk can be eliminated through diversification, while some risk cannot. This will become an important distinction later in our studies. *For now, we should realize that the process of diversification can reduce risk, and as a result, measuring a project's or an asset's risk is very*

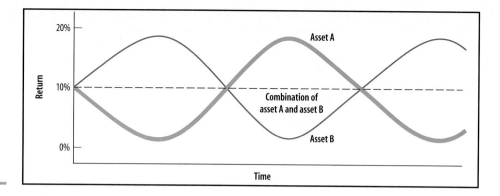

Figure 1–2
Reducing Risk through Diversification

difficult. A project's risk changes depending on whether you measure (1) the project's risk when it is standing alone, (2) the amount of risk a project contributes to a firm, or (3) the amount of risk that this project contributes to the stockholder's portfolio.

Axiom 10:
Ethical Behavior Is Doing the Right Thing, and Ethical Dilemmas Are Everywhere in Finance

Ethics, or rather a lack of ethics in finance, is a recurring theme in the news. During the late 1980s and early 1990s the fall of Ivan Boesky and Drexel, Burnham, Lambert, and the near collapse of Salomon Brothers seemed to make continuous headlines. Meanwhile, the movie *Wall Street* was a hit at the box office and the book *Liar's Poker*, by Michael Lewis, chronicling unethical behavior in the bond markets, became a best-seller. As the lessons of Salomon Brothers and Drexel, Burnham, Lambert illustrate, ethical errors are not forgiven in the business world. Not only is acting in an ethical manner morally correct, it is congruent with our goal of maximization of shareholder wealth.

Ethical behavior means "doing the right thing." A difficulty arises, however, in attempting to define "doing the right thing." The problem is that each of us has his or her own set of values, which forms the basis for our personal judgments about what is the right thing to do. However, every society adopts a set of rules or laws that prescribe what it believes to be "doing the right thing." In a sense, we can think of laws as a set of rules that reflect the values of the society as a whole, as they have evolved. For purposes of this text, we recognize that individuals have a right to disagree about what constitutes "doing the right thing," and we will seldom venture beyond the basic notion that ethical conduct involves abiding by society's rules. However, we will point out some of the ethical dilemmas that have arisen in recent years with regard to the practice of financial management. These dilemmas generally arise when some individual behavior is found to be at odds with the wishes of a large portion of the population, even though that behavior is not prohibited by law. Ethical dilemmas can therefore provide a catalyst for debate and discussion, which may eventually lead to a revision in the body of the law. So as we embark on our study of finance and encounter ethical dilemmas, we encourage you to consider the issues and form your own opinion. At this point you might want to look at the Ethics in Financial Management box on page 19. It illustrates that many times ethical questions are not easily answered, but they must be dealt with on a day-to-day basis.

Many students ask, "Is ethics really relevant?" This is a good question and deserves an answer. First, although business errors can be forgiven, ethical errors tend to end careers and terminate future opportunities. Why? Because *unethical behavior*

Is It Wrong to Tell a Lie?

In a February 1996 article in the *Journal of Business Ethics*, 400 people were asked to play the role of a fictional executive named Todd Fogler, who is faced with an ethical decision. The authors found that 47 percent of the top executives, 41 percent of the controllers, and 76 percent of the graduate-level business students they studied were willing to commit fraud by understating write-offs that cut into their companies' profits. When you hear about a study like this, the initial reaction of many students is that such ethical dilemmas are only the concerns of the top executives. They aren't—they are everywhere, and they are faced by everyone.

A teacher might not be able to change ethical standards in a college classroom, but he or she can teach students how to analyze questions so that they can bring to bear whatever ethical standards they have when they make decisions.

If you haven't already done so, there is no better time than now to develop a rule or set of rules against which you can measure the "rightness" or "wrongness" of your decisions and actions. It may be nothing more provocative than "Do unto others as you would have them do unto you." Or it may be a question or set of questions that you consistently ask: How would I feel about explaining to my parents or children what I did? How would I feel if the action I took were described, in detail, on the front page of my local newspaper? Have I avoided even the appearance of a conflict of interest in my decision? Would my action infringe on the liberty or constitutional rights of others?

Let's begin our look at ethical dilemmas in finance by asking this question: Is it wrong to tell a lie?

One of the roles of the financial manager is to transmit financial information to people outside the company. Occasionally, the facts that the financial manager must transmit and explain aren't particularly flattering to the firm. This presents the dilemma of whether it is unethical to tell a lie.

For example, at the annual stockholders' meeting a senior financial manager is reviewing her company's financial performance for the previous year. The news is not good. Sales dropped 30 percent, and profits were down 50 percent. A stockholder asks the manager, "What caused this drastic decline and has it been corrected?" The manager knows that the primary cause of the decline was a series of poor top-management decisions made over the past several years, but she also knows that's not what her colleagues want her to say. Furthermore, she personally believes the decline is far from over, but she recognizes that's not what the stockholders want to hear.

Should this financial manager lie? Is lying always wrong, or is it acceptable under certain circumstances? What, if any, would those circumstances be? What do you think?

Adapted by permission from Stephen P. Robbins, *Management*, 3d ed., p. 11. Copyright 1991 by Prentice Hall, Inc.

---

eliminates trust, and without trust businesses cannot interact. Second, *the most damaging event a business can experience is a loss of the public's confidence in its ethical standards.* In finance we have seen several recent examples of such events. It was the ethical scandals involving insider trading at Drexel, Burnham, Lambert that brought down that firm. In 1991 the ethical scandals involving attempts by Salomon Brothers to corner the Treasury bill market led to the removal of its top executives and nearly put the company out of business.

Beyond the question of ethics is the question of social responsibility. In general, corporate social responsibility means that a corporation has responsibilities to society beyond the maximization of shareholder wealth. It asserts that a corporation answers to a broader constituency than shareholders alone. As with most debates that center on ethical and moral questions, there is no definitive answer. One opinion is that because financial managers are employees of the corporation, and the corporation is owned by the shareholders, the financial managers should run the corporation in such a way that shareholder wealth is maximized and then allow the shareholders to decide if they would like to fulfill a sense of social responsibility by passing on any of the profits to deserving causes. This is the view presented by Milton Friedman in the Ethics in Financial Management box, "Milton Friedman on the Social Responsibility of Corporations." Very few corporations consistently act in this way. For example, Bristol-Myers Squibb Co. has an ambitious program to give away heart medication to those who cannot pay for it. This program came in the wake of an American Heart Association report showing that many of the nation's working poor face severe health risks because they cannot afford heart drugs. Clearly, Bristol-Myers Squibb felt it had a social responsibility to provide this medicine to the poor at no cost.

How do you feel about this decision?

A Final Note on the Axioms

Hopefully, these axioms are as much statements of common sense as they are theoretical statements. These axioms provide the logic behind what is to follow. We will build on them and attempt to draw out their implications for decision making. As we continue, try to keep in mind that while the topics being treated may change from chapter to chapter, the logic driving our treatment of them is constant and rooted in these 10 axioms.

OBJECTIVE 5   **OVERVIEW OF THE TEXT**

In this text we will focus on the maintenance and creation of wealth. Although this will involve attention to decision-making techniques, we will emphasize the logic behind those techniques to ensure that you do not lose sight of the concepts driving finance and the creation of wealth. The text begins by discussing the goal of the firm, a goal that is to be used in financial decision making. It also presents the legal and tax environment in which these decisions are to be made. Since this environment sets the ground rules, it is necessary to understand it before decision rules can be formulated. The 10 guiding axioms that provide the underpinnings for what is to follow are then presented. In Chapter 2, the financial markets and interest rates are examined, looking at both the determinants of interest rates and their effect on business decisions. Chapters 3 and 4 introduce the basic financial tools the financial manager uses to maintain control over the firm and its operations. These tools enable the financial manager to locate potential problem areas and plan for the future.

In Chapter 5 our focus turns to how the firm and its assets are valued. It begins with an examination of the mathematics of finance and the concept of the time value of money. An understanding of this topic allows us to compare benefits and costs that occur in different time periods. Valuation of fixed-income securities is then examined in Chapter 6. Valuation models that attempt to explain how different financial decisions affect the firm's stock price are examined in Chapter 7. We move on in Chapter 8 to develop an understanding of the meaning and measurement of risk and return.

Using the valuation principles just developed, our discussion in Chapter 9 turns to the capital-budgeting decision, which involves the financial evaluation of investment proposals in fixed assets. We then examine, in Chapter 10, the measurement of cash flows and introduce methods to incorporate risk in the analysis. In Chapter 11, we will examine the financing of a firm's chosen projects, looking at what costs are associated with alternative ways of raising new funds.

Chapter 12 examines the firm's capital structure along with the impact of leverage on returns to the enterprise. It is followed in Chapter 13 with a discussion of the determination of the dividend-retained earnings decision. Chapters 14 and 15 deal with working-capital management and the management of current assets. We will dis-

Milton Friedman on the
Social Responsibility of Corporations

There is a difference between acting in a socially responsible way and acting ethically. Milton Friedman does a good job of stating the argument that the corporations do not have "social responsibility." This view is far from universally held. The purpose of the following is to make you think about this issue.

In a free-enterprise, private-property system, a corporate executive is an employee of the owners of the business. He has direct responsibility to his employers. That responsibility is to conduct the business in accordance with their desires, which generally will be to make as much money as possible while conforming to the basic rules of the society, both those embodied in law and those embodied in ethical custom.

Of course, the corporate executive is also a person in his own right. As a person, he may have many other responsibilities that he recognizes or assumes voluntarily—to his family, his conscience, his feelings of charity, his church, his clubs, his city, his country. He may feel impelled by these responsibilities to devote part of his income to causes he regards as worthy, to refuse to work for particular corporations, even to leave his job, for example, to join his coun-

try's armed forces. If we wish, we may refer to some of these responsibilities as "social responsibilities." But in these respects he is acting as a principal, not an agent; he is spending his own money or time or energy, not the money of his employers or the time or energy he has contracted to devote to their purposes. If these are "social responsibilities," they are the social responsibilities of individuals, not of business.

What does it mean to say that the corporate executive has a "social responsibility" in his capacity as a businessman? If this statement is not pure rhetoric, it must mean that he is to act in some way that is not in the interest of his employers. For example, that he is to refrain from increasing the price of the product in order to contribute to the social objective of preventing inflation, even though a price increase would be in the best interests of the corporation. Or that he is to make expenditures on reducing pollution beyond the amount that is in the best interests of the corporation or that is required by law in order to contribute to the social objective of improving the environment. Or that, at the expense of corporate profits, he is to hire "hard-core" unemployed instead of better-qualified available

workmen to contribute to the social objective of reducing poverty.

In each of these cases, the corporate executive would be spending someone else's money for a general social interest. Insofar as his actions with his "social responsibility" reduce returns to stockholders, he is spending their money. Insofar as his actions raise the price to customers, he is spending the customers' money. Insofar as his actions lower the wages of some employees, he is spending their money.

The stockholders or the customers or the employees could separately spend their own money on the particular actions if they wished to do so. The executive is exercising a distinct "social responsibility," rather than serving as an agent of the stockholders or the customers or the employees, only if he spends the money in a different way than they would have spent it.

But if he does this, he is in effect imposing taxes, on the one hand, and deciding how the tax proceeds shall be spent, on the other.

Source: Milton Friedman, "The Social Responsibility of Business Is to Increase Its Profits," *New York Times Magazine* (September 13, 1970), 33, 122–26. Copyright 1970 by The New York Times Company. Reprinted by permission.

cuss methods for determining the appropriate investment in cash, marketable securities, inventory, and accounts receivable, as well as the risks associated with these investments and the control of these risks.

Chapter 16 provides an introduction to international financial management, focusing on how financial decisions are affected by the international environment. The final chapter in the text, Chapter 17, deals with future changes in finance and the dynamic nature of the discipline. It focuses on areas of change in finance: the development of the futures and options markets, recent innovations in corporate restructuring and raising capital, attempts to deal with the agency problem, and recent challenges to the concept of market efficiency and how assets are valued.

SUMMARY

OBJECTIVE 1

This chapter outlines the framework for the maintenance and creation of wealth. In introducing decision-making techniques aimed at creating wealth, we emphasize the logic behind those techniques. This chapter begins with an examination of the goal of the firm.

The commonly accepted goal of profit maximization is contrasted with the more complete goal of maximization of shareholder wealth. Because it deals well with uncertainty and time in a real-world environment, the goal of maximization of shareholder wealth is found to be the proper goal for the firm.

OBJECTIVE 2

The legal forms of business are examined. The sole proprietorship is a business operation owned and managed by an individual. Initiating this form of business is simple and generally does not involve any substantial organizational costs. The proprietor has complete control of the firm but must be willing to assume full responsibility for its outcomes.

The general partnership, which is simply a coming together of two or more individuals, is similar to the sole proprietorship. The limited partnership is another form of partnership sanctioned by states to permit all but one of the partners to have limited liability if this is agreeable to all partners.

The corporation increases the flow of capital from public investors to the business community. Although larger organizational costs and regulations are imposed on this legal entity, the corporation is more conducive to raising large amounts of capital. Limited liability, continuity of life, and ease of transfer in ownership, which increase the marketability of the investment, have contributed greatly in attracting large numbers of investors to the corporate environment. The formal control of the corporation is vested in the parties who own the greatest number of shares. However, day-to-day operations are managed by the corporate officers, who theoretically serve on behalf of the common stockholders.

OBJECTIVE 3

The tax environment is presented. In introducing taxes we focus on taxes that affect our business decisions. Three taxable entities exist: the individual, including partnerships; the corporation; and the fiduciary. Only information on the corporate tax environment is given here.

For the most part, taxable income for the corporation is equal to the firm's operating income plus capital gains less any interest expense. The corporation is allowed an income exclusion of 70 percent of the dividends received from another corporation.

Tax consequences have a direct bearing on the decisions of the financial manager. The relationships are grounded in the taxability of investment income and the difference in tax treatment for interest expense and dividend payments. Also, shareholders' tax status may influence their preference between gains from stock sale and dividends, which in turn may influence corporate dividend policy.

OBJECTIVE 4

An examination of the 10 axioms on which finance is built is presented. The techniques and tools introduced in this text are all motivated by these 10 principles or axioms. They are:

Axiom 1: The Risk-Return Trade-off—We Won't Take on Additional Risk Unless We Expect to Be Compensated with Additional Return

Axiom 2: The Time Value of Money—A Dollar Received Today Is Worth More Than a Dollar Received in the Future

Axiom 3: Cash—Not Profits—Is King

Axiom 4: Incremental Cash Flows—It's Only What Changes That Counts

Axiom 5: The Curse of Competitive Markets—Why It's Hard to Find Exceptionally Profitable Projects

Axiom 6: Efficient Capital Markets—The Markets Are Quick and the Prices Are Right

Axiom 7: The Agency Problem—Managers Won't Work for the Owners Unless It's in Their Best Interest

Axiom 8: Taxes Bias Business Decisions

Axiom 9: All Risk Is Not Equal—Some Risk Can Be Diversified Away, and Some Cannot

Axiom 10: Ethical Behavior Is Doing the Right Thing, and Ethical Dilemmas Are Everywhere in Finance

This chapter closes with an overview of the text.

OBJECTIVE 5

KEY TERMS

Agency Problem, 15

Capital Gain (or Loss), 10

Corporation, 5

Depreciation, 9

Efficient Markets, 15

General Partnership, 4

Gross Income, 7

Limited Partnership, 4

Marginal Tax Rate, 8

Net Operating Loss Carryback and Carryforward, 10

Partnership, 4

Sole Proprietorship, 4

Taxable Income, 7

STUDY QUESTIONS

1-1. What are some of the problems involved in the use of profit maximization as the goal of the firm? How does the goal of maximization of shareholder wealth deal with those problems?

1-2. Compare and contrast the goals of profit maximization and maximization of shareholder wealth.

1-3. Firms often involve themselves in projects that do not result directly in profits; for example, IBM and Mobil Oil frequently support public television broadcasts. Do these projects contradict the goal of maximization of shareholder wealth? Why or why not?

1-4. What is the relationship between financial decision making and risk and return? Would all financial managers view risk-return trade-offs similarly?

1-5. Define (a) sole proprietorship, (b) partnership, and (c) corporation.

1-6. Identify the primary characteristics of each form of legal organization.

1-7. Using the following criteria, specify the legal form of business that is favored: (a) organizational requirements and costs, (b) liability of the owners, (c) continuity of business, (d) transferability of ownership, (e) management control and regulations, (f) ability to raise capital, and (g) income taxes.

1-8. Does a partnership pay taxes on its income? Explain.

1-9. When a corporation receives a dividend from another corporation, how is it taxed?

1-10. What is the purpose of the net operating loss carryback and carryforward?

SELF-TEST PROBLEM

ST-1. (*Corporate Income Tax*)   The Dana Flatt Corporation had sales of $2 million this past year. Its cost of goods sold was $1.2 million, and its operating expenses were $400,000. Interest expenses on outstanding debts were $100,000, and the company paid $40,000 in preferred stock dividends. The corporation received $10,000 in preferred stock dividends and interest income of $12,000. The firm sold stock that had been owned for two years for $40,000; the original cost of the stock was $30,000. Determine the corporation's taxable income and its tax liability.

STUDY PROBLEMS

1-1. (*Corporate Income Tax*)   The William B. Waugh Corporation is a regional Toyota dealer. The firm sells new and used trucks and is actively involved in the parts business. During the most recent year the company generated sales of $3 million. The combined cost of goods sold and the operating expenses were $2.1 million. Also, $400,000 in interest expense was paid during the year. The firm received $6,000 during the year in dividend income from 1,000 shares of common stock that had been purchased three years previously. However, the stock was sold toward the end of the year for $100 per share; its initial cost was $80 per share. The company also sold land that had been recently purchased and had been held for only four months. The selling price was $50,000; the cost was $45,000. Calculate the corporation's tax liability.

1-2. (*Corporate Income Tax*)   Sales for L. B. Menielle, Inc., during the past year amounted to $5 million. The firm provides parts and supplies for oil field service companies. Gross profits for the year were $3 million. Operating expenses totaled $1 million. The interest and dividend income from securities owned were $20,000 and $25,000, respectively. The firm's interest expense was $100,000. The firm sold securities on two occasions during the year, receiving a gain of $40,000 on the first sale but losing $50,000 on the second. The stock sold first had been owned for four years; the stock sold second had been purchased three months prior to the sale. Compute the corporation's tax liability.

1-3. (*Corporate Income Tax*)   Sandersen, Inc., sells minicomputers. During the past year the company's sales were $3 million. The cost of its merchandise sold came to $2 million, and cash operating expenses were $400,000; depreciation expense was $100,000, and the firm paid $150,000 in interest on bank loans. Also, the corporation received $50,000 in dividend income but paid $25,000 in the form of dividends to its own common stockholders. Calculate the corporation's tax liability.

1-4. (*Corporate Income Tax*)   A. Don Drennan, Inc., had sales of $6 million during the past year. The company's cost of goods sold was 70 percent of sales; operating expenses, including depreciation, amounted to $800,000. The firm sold a capital asset (stock) for $75,000, which had been purchased five months earlier at a cost of $80,000. Determine the company's tax liability.

1-5. (*Corporate Income Tax*)   The Robbins Corporation is an oil wholesaler. The company's sales last year were $1 million, with the cost of goods sold equal to $600,000. The firm paid interest of $200,000, and its cash operating expenses were $100,000. Also, the firm received $40,000 in dividend income while paying only $10,000 in dividends to its preferred stockholders. Depreciation expense was $150,000. Compute the firm's tax liability. Based on your answer, does management need to take any additional action?

1-6. (*Corporate Income Tax*)   The Fair Corporation had sales of $5 million this past year. The cost of goods sold was $4.3 million, and operating expenses were $100,000. Dividend income totaled $5,000. The firm sold land for $150,000 that had cost $100,000 five months ago. The firm received $150 per share from the sale of 1,000 shares of stock. The stock was purchased for $100 per share three years ago. Determine the firm's tax liability.

1-7. (*Corporate Income Tax*)   Sales for J. P. Hulett, Inc., during the past year amounted to $4 million. The firm supplies statistical information to engineering companies. Gross profits totaled $1 million, and operating and depreciation expenses were $500,000 and $350,000, respectively. Dividend income for the year was $12,000. Compute the corporation's tax liability.

1-8. (*Corporate Income Tax*)   Anderson & Dennis, Inc., sells computer software. The company's past year's sales were $5 million. The cost of its merchandise sold came to $3 million. Operating expenses were $175,000, plus depreciation expenses totaling $125,000. The firm paid $200,000 interest on loans. The firm sold stock during the year, receiving a $40,000 gain on a stock owned six years but losing $60,000 on stock held four months. Calculate the company's tax liability.

1-9. (*Corporate Income Tax*)   G. R. Edwin, Inc., had sales of $6 million during the past year. The cost of goods sold amounted to $3 million. Operating expenses totaled $2.6 million, and interest expense was $30,000. Determine the firm's tax liability.

1-10. (*Corporate Income Tax*)   The Analtoly Corporation is an electronics dealer and distributor. Sales for the last year were $4.5 million, and cost of goods sold and operating expenses totaled $3.2 million. Analtoly also paid $150,000 in interest expense, and depreciation expense totaled $50,000. In addition, the company sold securities for $120,000 that it had purchased four years earlier at a price of $40,000. Compute the tax liability for Analtoly.

1-11. (*Corporate Income Tax*)   Utsumi Inc. supplies wholesale industrial chemicals. Last year the company had sales of $6.5 million. Cost of goods sold and operating expenses amounted to 70 percent of sales, and depreciation and interest expenses were $75,000 and $160,000, respectively. Furthermore, the corporation sold 40,000 shares of Sumitono Industries for $10 a share. These shares were purchased a year ago for $8 each. In addition, Utsumi received $60,000 in dividend income. Compute the corporation's tax liability.

COMPREHENSIVE PROBLEM

The final stage in the interview process for an Assistant Financial Analyst at Caledonia Products involves a test of your understanding of basic financial concepts and of the corporate tax code. You are given the following memorandum and asked to respond to the questions. Whether or not you are offered a position at Caledonia will depend on the accuracy of your response.

To: Applicants for the position of Financial Analyst
From: Mr. V. Morrison, CEO, Caledonia Products
Re: A test of your understanding of basic financial concepts and of the Corporate Tax Code

Please respond to the following questions:

a. What are the differences between the goals of profit maximization and maximization of shareholder wealth? Which goal do you think is more appropriate?

b. What does the risk-return trade-off mean?

c. Why are we interested in cash flows rather than accounting profits in determining the value of an asset?

d. What is an efficient market and what are the implications of efficient markets for us?

e. What is the cause of the agency problem and how do we try to solve it?

f. What do ethics and ethical behavior have to do with finance?

g. Define (1) sole proprietorship, (2) partnership, and (3) corporation.

h. The Carrickfergus Corporation had sales of $4 million this past year. Its cost of goods sold was $2.4 million, and its operating expenses were $600,000. Interest expenses on outstanding debts were $300,000, and the company paid $60,000 in preferred stock dividends. The corporation received $30,000 in preferred stock dividends and interest income of $22,000. The firm sold stock that had been owned for two years for $100,000; the original cost of the stock was $60,000. Determine the corporation's taxable income and its tax liability.

SELF–TEST SOLUTION

SS–1.

Sales		$2,000,000
Cost of goods sold		1,200,000
Gross profit		800,000
Tax-deductible expenses:		
Operating expenses	$400,000	
Interest expenses	100,000	500,000
		$ 300,000
Other income:		
Interest income		12,000
Preferred dividend income	$ 10,000	
Less 70% exclusion	$ 7,000	3,000
Taxable ordinary income		$ 315,000
Gain on sale:		
Selling price	$ 40,000	
Cost	30,000	10,000
Taxable income		$ 325,000
Tax liability		
.15 × $50,000 =	$ 7,500	
.25 × 25,000 =	6,250	
.34 × 250,000 =	85,000	
5% surtax	11,250	
	$110,000	

The Financial Markets and Interest Rates

The Mix of Corporate Securities Sold in the Capital Market • Why Financial Markets Exist • Financing of Business: The Movement of Funds through the Economy • Components of the U.S. Financial Market System • The Investment Banker • Private Placements • Flotation Costs • Regulation • More Recent Regulatory Developments • Rates of Return in the Financial Markets • Interest Rate Determinants in a Nutshell • The Term Structure of Interest Rates

F rom February 4, 1994, through January 31, 1996, the Federal Reserve System (Fed), the nation's central bank, voted to change the "target" federal funds rate on 10 different occasions. Seven of these interest rate changes were in the upward direction. The federal funds rate is a short-term market rate of interest, influenced by the Fed, that serves as a sensitive indicator of the direction of future changes in interest rates. In early 1994, the central bank feared that inflationary pressures were building up in the U.S. economy and decided to take action, via raising nominal short-term interest rates, to stem those pressures by slowing down aggregate economic growth. The Fed remained committed to a course of higher interest rates throughout 1994 and the first half of 1995; then on July 6, 1995, these monetary policy makers reversed course and began a series of interest rate decreases. These policy actions and the resultant changes are shown in the table on the following page.

From a financial management viewpoint the seven overt actions by the Fed to raise rates caused the *opportunity cost of funds* to rise. This means the firm's cost of capital funds rose, which in turn made it more difficult for real

Changes in the Target Federal Funds Rate
February 1994–January 1996

Date	Old Target Rate %	New Target Rate %
1994		
February 4	3.00	3.25
March 22	3.25	3.50
April 18	3.50	3.75
May 17	3.75	4.25
August 16	4.25	4.75
November 19	4.75	5.50
1995		
February 1	5.50	6.00
July 6	6.00	5.75
December 19	5.75	5.50
1996		
January 31	5.50	5.25

capital projects to be financed and be included in the firm's capital budget. The three decisions to lower the target federal funds rate had the exact opposite effect; that is, the firm's cost of capital funds decreased. In this latter case, the firm can take on more capital projects.

Also note that the commercial bank prime lending rate typically changes in the same direction and at about the same time that an upward shift in the federal funds rate occurs. Thus, the transmission of the central bank's policy move to the explicit cost of funds that the firm faces in the financial markets happens quickly.

As you read this chapter you will learn about (a) the importance of financial markets to a developed economy, (b) how funds are raised in the financial markets, and (c) the fundamentals of interest rate determination. This will help you, as a financial executive, understand the likely effects of federal policy actions on your firm's ability to do business.

WHAT'S AHEAD

At times internally generated funds will not be sufficient to finance all of the firm's proposed expenditures. In these situations, the corporation may find it necessary to attract large amounts of financial capital externally.[1] This chapter focuses on the market environment in which long-term capital is raised. It also introduces and covers the logic behind the determination of interest rates and required rates of return in the capital markets. We will explore interest rate levels and risk differentials over recent time periods and will study several theories that attempt to explain the shape of the *term structure of interest rates*. Ensuing chapters will discuss the distinguishing features of the instruments by which long-term funds are raised. Long-term funds are raised in the capital market. By the term *capital market*, we mean all institutions and procedures that facilitate transactions in long-term financial instruments (like common stocks and bonds).

Business firms in the nonfinancial corporate sector of the U.S. economy rely heavily on the nation's financial market system to raise cash. Table 2–1 displays the relative internal and external sources of funds for such corporations over the 1981–1993 period. Notice that the percentage of external funds raised in any given year can vary substantially from that of other years. In 1982, for example, the nonfinancial business sector raised only 25.4 percent of its funds by external means (in the financial markets). This was substantially less than the 39.4 percent raised externally only one year earlier, during 1981. In more recent years the same type of significant adjustment made by financial managers is evident. For example, during 1988 nonfinancial firms raised 36.3 percent of new funds in the external markets. By the end of 1991 this proportion dropped drastically to 9.7 percent.

Such adjustments illustrate an important point: The financial executive is perpetually on his or her toes regarding market conditions. Changes in market conditions influence the precise way corporate funds will be raised.

The financial market system must be both organized and resilient. Periods of economic recession, for instance, test the financial markets and those firms that continually use the markets. Economic contractions are especially challenging to financial decision makers because all recessions are *unique*. This forces financing policies to become unique.

During the 1981–1982 recession, which lasted 16 months, interest rates remained high during the worst phases of the downturn. This occurred because policy makers at the Federal Reserve System decided to wring a high rate of inflation out of the econ-

---

[1]By *externally generated*, we mean that the funds are obtained by means *other* than through retentions or depreciation. Funds from these latter two sources are commonly called *internally generated* funds.

Table 2-1
Nonfinancial Corporate Business Sources of Funds

Year	Total Sources ($ Billions)	Percent Internal Funds	Percent External Funds
1993	557.4	82.9	17.1
1992	560.5	78.2	21.8
1991	471.7	90.3	9.7
1990	535.5	76.9	23.1
1989	567.9	70.4	29.6
1988	634.2	63.7	36.3
1987	564.7	66.6	33.4
1986	538.8	62.5	37.5
1985	493.8	71.3	28.7
1984	511.4	65.8	34.2
1983	444.6	65.7	34.3
1982	331.7	74.6	25.4
1981	394.4	60.6	39.4

Source: *Economic Report of the President*, February 1995, p. 384.

omy by means of a tight monetary policy. Simultaneously, stock prices were depressed. These business conditions induced firms to forgo raising funds via external means. During 1982 we notice that 74.6 percent of corporate funds were generated internally (see Table 2–1).

The same general pattern followed after the 1990–1991 recession ended in the first quarter of 1991. During 1991 businesses paid down their short-term borrowings and relied on internally generated sources for 90.3 percent of their net financing needs. As economic policy shapes the environment of the financial markets, managers must understand the meaning of the economic ups and downs and remain *flexible* in their decision-making processes.

The sums involved in tapping the capital markets can be vast. To be able to distribute and absorb security offerings of enormous size, an economy must have a well-developed financial market system. To use that system effectively, the financial officer must have a basic understanding of its structure. Accordingly, this chapter explores the rudiments of raising funds in the capital market.

PAUSE AND REFLECT

In Chapter 12 we will learn how to assess leverage use—both operating and financial leverage. In addition, we will examine the corporate financing decision in Chapter 12. Portions of those discussions will identify financial managers' confirmed preferences for raising funds through new debt contracts. The next section presents some near-term history of that financing behavior.

THE MIX OF CORPORATE SECURITIES SOLD IN THE CAPITAL MARKET

When corporations decide to raise cash in the capital market, what type of financing vehicle is most favored? Many individual investors think that common stock is the answer to this question. This is understandable, given the coverage of the level of common stock prices by the popular news media. All the major television networks, for instance, quote the closing price of the Dow Jones Industrial Average on their nightly news broadcasts. Common stock, though, is not the financing method relied on most heavily by corporations. The answer to this question is *corporate bonds. The corporate debt markets clearly dominate the corporate equity markets when new funds are being raised.* This is a long-term relationship—it occurs year after year. Table 2–2 bears this out.

In Table 2–2 we see the total volume (in millions of dollars) of domestic corporate securities sold for cash over the 1981–1995 period. The percentage breakdown among common stock, preferred stock, and bonds is also displayed. We will learn from our discussions of the cost of capital and planning the firm's financing mix that the U.S. tax system inherently favors debt as a means of raising capital. Quite simply, interest expense is deductible from other income when computing the firm's federal tax liability, whereas the dividends paid on both preferred and common stock are not.

Financial executives responsible for raising corporate cash know this. When they have a choice between marketing new bonds and marketing new preferred stock, the outcome is usually in favor of bonds. The after-tax cost of capital on the debt is less than that incurred on the preferred stock. Likewise, if the firm has unused debt capacity and the general level of equity prices is depressed, financial executives favor the issuance of debt securities over the issuance of new common stock. It is always good to keep some benchmark figures in your head. The average (unweighted) mix

Table 2–2
Corporate Securities Offered for Cash (Domestic Offerings), 1981–1995

Year	Total Volume ($ Millions)	Percent Common Stock	Percent Preferred Stock	Percent Bonds and Notes
1995	477,579	12.1	2.3	85.6
1994	425,620	11.2	2.9	85.9
1993	588,583	14.0	3.3	82.7
1992	456,515	12.5	4.7	82.8
1991	352,245	13.7	4.9	81.4
1990	212,712	9.1	1.9	89.0
1989	213,617	12.2	2.9	84.9
1988	244,670	14.7	2.7	82.6
1987	262,725	16.4	3.9	79.7
1986	248,722	23.7	4.9	71.4
1985	133,460	27.5	5.3	67.2
1984	95,287	23.3	4.5	72.2
1983	103,355	43.9	7.7	48.4
1982	73,397	32.3	6.7	61.0
1981	64,500	39.5	2.6	57.9

Source: *Economic Report of the President*, January 1989, p. 415, and *Federal Reserve Bulletin*, Table 1.46, various issues.

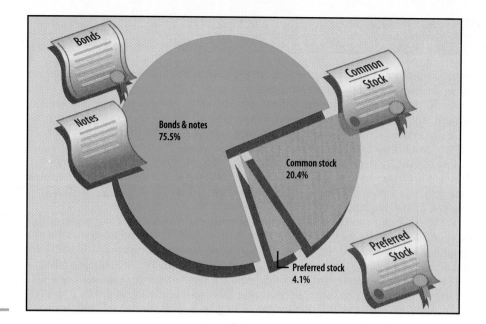

Figure 2–1
Corporate External Financing Patterns, 1981–1995

of corporate securities sold for cash over the 1981–1995 period follows. This *excludes* private debt placements or the bonds and notes categories would be a bit higher. Figure 2–1 illustrates this financing pattern.

Common stock	20.4%
Preferred stock	4.1
Bonds and notes	75.5
Total	100.0%

When you borrow money from a commercial bank to finance a purchase of stereo equipment or take out a mortgage to pay for a new home, you have used this country's financial market system. The average individual (and you are not that because of your study of financial management) tends to take the reality of the financial markets for granted. But they were not always there, and they have evolved amid much controversy over a long period.

Recent years have produced heated debates over alterations in our financial system; this just illustrates the dynamic nature of these markets. Much of that debate followed the collapse of the equity markets on Monday, October 19, 1987, when the Dow Jones Industrial Average fell by an unprecedented 508 points. Like banks, the equity markets are another piece of our complex financial market system. One reason underdeveloped countries are underdeveloped is that they lack a financial market system that has the confidence of those who must use it. Without such a system, real assets (like your home) do not get produced at an adequate rate and the populace suffers. We learn next why financial markets exist.

In this chapter we cover material that introduces the financial manager to the processes involved in raising funds in the nation's capital markets and also cover the logic that lies behind the determination of interest rates and required rates of return in those capital markets.

We will see that the United States has a highly developed, complex, and competitive system of financial markets that allows for the quick transfer of savings from those economic units with a surplus of savings to those economic units with a savings deficit. Such a system of highly developed financial markets allows great ideas (like the personal computer) to be financed and increases the overall wealth of the economy. Consider your wealth, for example, compared to that of the average family in Russia. Russia lacks a complex system of financial markets to facilitate transactions in financial claims (securities). As a result, real capital formation there has suffered.

Thus, we return now to **Axiom 6: Efficient Capital Markets—The Markets Are Quick and the Prices Are Right.** Financial managers like our system of capital markets because they trust them. This trust stems from the fact that the markets are "efficient." Managers trust prices in the securities markets because those prices quickly and accurately reflect all available information about the value of the underlying securities. This means that expected risks and expected cash flows matter more to market participants than do simpler things like accounting changes and the sequence of past price changes in a specific security. With security prices and returns (like interest rates) competitively determined, more financial managers (rather than fewer) participate in the markets and help ensure the basic concept of efficiency.

WHY FINANCIAL MARKETS EXIST

Financial markets are *institutions and procedures that facilitate transactions in all types of financial claims.* The purchase of your home, the common stock you may own, and your life insurance policy all took place in some type of financial market. Why do financial markets exist? What would the economy lose if our complex system of financial markets were not developed? We will address these questions here.

financial markets

Some *economic units*, such as households, firms, or governments, spend more during a given period than they earn. Other economic units spend *less* on current consumption than they earn. For example, business firms in the aggregate usually spend more during a specific period than they earn. Households in the aggregate spend less on current consumption than they earn. As a result, some mechanism is needed to facilitate the transfer of savings from those economic units with a surplus to those with a deficit. That is precisely the function of financial markets. Financial markets exist in order to allocate the supply or savings in the economy to the demanders of those savings. The central characteristic of a financial market is that it acts as the vehicle through which the forces of demand and supply for a specific type of financial claim (such as a corporate bond) are brought together.

Now, why would the economy suffer without a developed financial market system? The answer is that the wealth of the economy would be less without the financial markets. The rate of capital formation would not be as high if financial markets did not exist. This means that the net additions during a specific period to the stocks of (1) dwellings, (2) productive plant and equipment, (3) inventory, and (4) consumer durables would occur at lower rates. Figure 2–2 on page 34 helps clarify the rationale behind this assertion. The abbreviated balance sheets in the figure refer to firms or any other type of economic units that operate in the private as

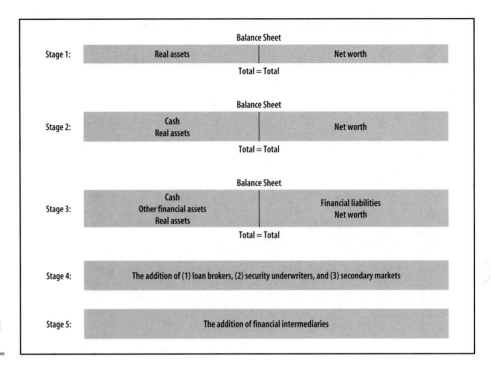

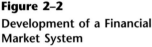

Figure 2–2
Development of a Financial
Market System

opposed to governmental sectors of the economy. This means that such units cannot issue money to finance their own activities.

At stage 1 in Figure 2–2 only real assets exist in the hypothetical economy. **Real assets** are *tangible assets like houses, equipment, and inventories.* They are distinguished from **financial assets,** which represent *claims for future payment on other economic units.* Common and preferred stocks, bonds, bills, and notes all are types of financial assets. If only real assets exist, then savings for a given economic unit, such as a firm, must be accumulated in the form of real assets. If the firm has a great idea for a new product, that new product can be developed, produced, and distributed only out of company savings (retained earnings). Furthermore, all investment in the new product must occur simultaneously as the savings are generated. If you have the idea, and we have the savings, there is no mechanism to transfer our savings to you. This is not a good situation.

At stage 2, paper money (cash) comes into existence in the economy. Here, at least, you can *store* your own savings in the form of money. Thus, you can finance your great idea by drawing down your cash balances. This is an improvement over stage 1, but there is still no effective mechanism to transfer our savings to you. You see, we will not just hand you our dollar bills. We will want a receipt.

The concept of a receipt that represents the transfer of savings from one economic unit to another is a monumental advancement. The economic unit with excess savings can lend the savings to an economic unit that needs them. To the lending unit these receipts are identified as "other financial assets" in stage 3 of Figure 2–2. To the borrowing unit, the issuance of financial claims (receipts) shows up as "financial liabilities" on the stage 3 balance sheet. The economic unit with surplus savings will earn a rate of return on those funds. The borrowing unit will pay that rate of return, but it has been able to finance its great idea.

In stage 4 the financial market system moves further toward full development. Loan brokers come into existence. These brokers help locate pockets of excess savings and channel such savings to economic units needing the funds. Some economic units will actually purchase the financial claims of borrowing units and sell them at a higher price to other investors; this process is called *underwriting*. Underwriting will be discussed in more detail later in this chapter. In addition, **secondary markets** develop. Secondary markets simply represent *trading in already existing financial claims*. If you buy your brother's General Motors common stock, you have made a secondary market transaction. Secondary markets reduce the risk of investing in financial claims. Should you need cash, you can liquidate your claims in the secondary market. This induces savers to invest in securities.

The progression toward a developed and complex system of financial markets ends with stage 5. Here, financial intermediaries come into existence. You can think of financial intermediaries as the major financial institutions with which you are used to dealing. These include commercial banks, savings and loan associations, credit unions, life insurance companies, and mutual funds. Financial intermediaries share a common characteristic. They offer *their own financial claims*, called **indirect securities,** to economic units with excess savings. The proceeds from selling their indirect securities are then used to purchase the *financial claims of other economic units*. These latter claims can be called **direct securities.** Thus, a mutual fund might sell mutual fund shares (their indirect security) and purchase the common stocks (direct securities) of some major corporations. A life insurance company sells life insurance policies and purchases huge quantities of corporate bonds. Financial intermediaries thereby involve many small savers in the process of capital formation. This means there are more "good things" for everybody to buy.

A developed financial market system provides for a greater level of wealth in the economy. In the absence of financial markets, savings are not transferred to the economic units most in need of those funds. It is difficult, after all, for a household to build its own automobile. The financial market system makes it *easier* for the economy to build automobiles and all the other goods that economic units like to accumulate.

PAUSE AND REFLECT

The movement of financial capital (funds) throughout the economy just means the movement of savings to the ultimate user of those savings. Some sectors of the economy save more than other sectors. As a result, these savings are moved to a productive use—say to manufacture that Corvette you want to buy.

The price of using someone else's savings is expressed in terms of interest rates. The financial market system helps to move funds to the most-productive end use. Those economic units with the most promising projects should be willing to bid the highest (in terms of rates) to obtain the savings. The concepts of financing and moving savings from one economic unit to another are now explored.

FINANCING OF BUSINESS: THE MOVEMENT OF FUNDS THROUGH THE ECONOMY

OBJECTIVE 4

The Financing Process

We now understand the crucial role that financial markets play in a capitalist economy. At this point we will take a brief look at how funds flow across some selected sectors of the U.S. economy. In addition, we will focus a little more closely on the process of financial intermediation that was introduced in the preceding section. Some actual data are used to sharpen our knowledge of the financing process. We will see that financial institutions play a major role in bridging the gap between savers and borrowers in the economy. Nonfinancial corporations, we already know, are significant borrowers of financial capital.

Table 2–3 shows how funds were supplied and raised by the major sectors of our economy in 1993. Households were the largest net suppliers of funds to the financial markets. This is the case, by the way, year in and year out. In 1993, households made available $155.0 billion in funds to other sectors. That was the excess of their funds supplied over their funds raised in the markets. In the jargon of economics, the household sector is a *savings-surplus* sector.

By contrast, the nonfinancial business sector is a *savings-deficit* sector. In 1993, nonfinancial corporations raised $11.0 billion *more* in the financial markets than they supplied to the markets. This too is a consistent long-term relationship. The nonfinancial business sector is typically a savings-deficit sector.

Next, it can also be seen that the U.S. government sector was a savings-deficit sector for 1993. In 1993 the federal government raised $285.0 billion in excess of the funds it supplied to the financial markets. This highlights a serious problem for the entire economy and for the financial manager. Persistent federal deficits have increased the role of the federal government in the market for borrowed funds. The last time the federal government posted a budget surplus was 1969; the last time prior to that was 1960. The federal government has thus become a "quasi-permanent" savings-deficit sector. Most financial economists agree that this tendency puts upward pressure on interest rates in the financial marketplace and thereby raises the general (overall) cost of capital to corporations. This phenomenon has become known as *crowding-out:* The private borrower is pushed out of the financial markets in favor of the government borrower.

Table 2–3 further highlights how important *foreign* financial investment is to the activity of the U.S. economy. As the federal government has become more of a "confirmed" savings-deficit sector, the need for funds has been increasingly supplied by foreign interests. Thus, in 1993, the foreign sector *supplied* a net $82.8 billion to the domestic capital markets. As recently as 1982, the foreign sector *raised*—rather than supplied—$30.8 billion in the U.S. financial markets! This illustrates the dynamic nature of financial management.

Table 2–3 demonstrates that the financial market system must exist to facilitate the orderly and efficient flow of savings from the surplus sectors to the deficit sectors of the economy. The result during long periods is that the nonfinancial business sector is *typically* dependent on the household sector to finance its investment needs. The governmental sectors—especially the federal government—are quite reliant on foreign financing.

Table 2–3

Sector View of Flow of Funds in U.S. Financial Markets for 1993 (Billions of Dollars)

	[1]	[2]	[2] − [1]
SECTOR	FUNDS RAISED	FUNDS SUPPLIED	NET FUNDS SUPPLIED
Households[a]	$325.4	$480.4	$155.0
Nonfinancial corporate business	94.0	83.0	−11.0
U.S. government	286.0	1.0	−285.0
State and local governments	60.1	15.9	−44.2
Foreign	187.2	270.0	82.8

[a]Includes personal trusts and nonprofit organizations.
Source: Flow of Funds Accounts, Second Quarter 1994, Flow of Funds Section (Washington, DC: Board of Governors of the Federal Reserve System, September 20, 1994).

As we noted in the preceding section, the financial market system includes a complex network of intermediaries that assist in the transfer of savings among economic units. Two intermediaries will be highlighted here: life insurance companies and pension funds. They are especially important participants in the capital market of the country.

Because of the nature of their business, life insurance firms can invest heavily in long-term financial instruments. This investment tendency arises for two key reasons: (1) life insurance policies usually include a *savings element* in them, and (2) their liabilities liquidate at a very predictable rate. Thus, life insurance companies invest in the "long end" of the securities markets. This means that they favor (1) mortgages and (2) corporate bonds as investment vehicles rather than shorter-term-to-maturity financial instruments like Treasury bills. To a lesser extent, they acquire corporate stocks for their portfolios.

Over recent years, about 47 percent of the financial assets of life insurance firms are represented by corporate stocks and bonds. We see that life insurance companies are an important financial intermediary. By issuing life insurance policies (indirect securities), they can acquire direct securities (corporate stocks and bonds) for their investment portfolios. Their preference, by far, is for bonds over stocks.

Let us now direct our attention to another financial intermediary, private pension funds. In comparison with life insurance companies, three factors are emphasized. First, since 1960, private pension funds have grown at a *much faster rate* than have the insurance companies. Second, a *greater proportion* of the financial asset mix of the pension funds is devoted to *corporate stocks* and bonds. Third, the pension funds *invest more heavily* in corporate stocks than they do in corporate bonds. Over recent years, about 62 percent of the financial assets of private pension funds have been tied up in corporate stocks and bonds. These financial institutions also are significant *sources* of business financing in this country. The pension funds play the same *intermediary* role as does the life insurance subsector of the economy.

Movement of Savings

Figure 2–3 on page 38 provides a useful way to summarize our discussion of (1) why financial markets exist and (2) the movement of funds through the economy. It also serves as an introduction to the role of the investment banker—a subject discussed in detail later in this chapter.

We see that savings are ultimately transferred to the business firm in need of cash in three ways.

1. **The direct transfer of funds.** Here the firm seeking cash sells its securities directly to savers (investors) who are willing to purchase them in hopes of earning a reasonable rate of return. New business formation is a good example of this process at work. The new business may go directly to a saver or group of savers called venture capitalists. The venture capitalists will lend funds to the firm or take an equity position in the firm if they feel the product or service the new firm hopes to market will be successful.

2. **Indirect transfer using the investment banker.** In a common arrangement under this system, the managing investment-banking house will form a syndicate of several investment bankers. The syndicate will buy the entire issue of securities from the firm that is in need of financial capital. The syndicate will then sell the securities at a higher price than it paid for them to the investing public (the savers). Merrill Lynch Capital Markets and The First Boston Corporation are examples of investment-banking firms. They tend to be called "houses" by those who work in the financial community. Notice that under this second method of transferring savings, the securities being issued just pass through the investment-banking firm. They are not transformed into a different type of security.

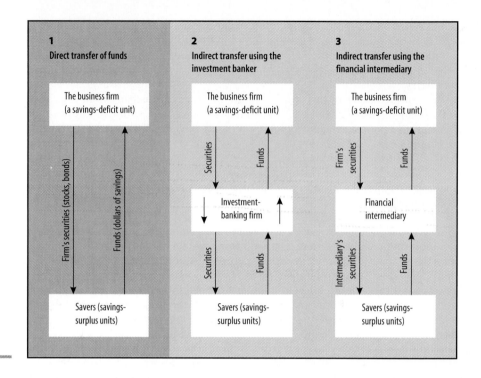

Figure 2–3
Three Ways to Transfer Financial Capital in the Economy

3. **Indirect transfer using the financial intermediary.** This is the type of system life insurance companies and pension funds operate within. The financial intermediary collects the savings of individuals and issues its own (indirect) securities in exchange for these savings. The intermediary then uses the funds collected from the individual savers to acquire the business firm's (direct) securities, such as stocks and bonds.

We all benefit from the three transfer mechanisms displayed in Figure 2–3. Capital formation and economic wealth are greater than they would be in the absence of this financial market system.

PAUSE AND REFLECT

Because the United States enjoys such a developed system of financial markets, the terms used to discuss operations in those markets are numerous—some would say limitless. The financial executive, and those who work close to the financial executive, need to master a basic understanding of the commonly used terms and financing situations. There is just no getting around this requirement. But if you can learn the terminology of baseball, basketball, or football, you can do the same relative to the financial markets. It may, in fact, pay off in a much wealthier fashion for you.

OBJECTIVE 5

COMPONENTS OF THE U.S. FINANCIAL MARKET SYSTEM

Numerous approaches exist for classifying the securities markets. At times, the array can be confusing. An examination of four sets of dichotomous terms can help provide a basic understanding of the structure of the U.S. financial markets.

Public Offerings and Private Placements

When a corporation decides to raise external capital, those funds can be obtained by making a public offering or a private placement. In a **public offering** *both individual and institutional investors have the opportunity to purchase the securities*. The securities are usually made available to the public at large by a managing investment-banking firm and its underwriting (risk-taking) syndicate. The firm does not meet the ultimate purchasers of the securities in the public offering. The public market is an impersonal market.

In a **private placement,** also called a **direct placement,** the securities are offered and sold to a *limited number of investors*. The firm will usually hammer out, on a face-to-face basis with the prospective buyers, the details of the offering. In this setting the investment-banking firm may act as a finder by bringing together potential lenders and borrowers. The private placement market is a more personal market than its public counterpart.

public offering

private placement
direct placement

Primary Markets and Secondary Markets

Primary markets are *those in which securities are offered for the first time to potential investors*. A new issue of common stock by AT&T is a primary market transaction. This type of transaction increases the total stock of financial assets outstanding in the economy.

primary markets

As mentioned in our discussion of the development of the financial market system, *secondary markets* represent transactions in currently outstanding securities. If the first buyer of the AT&T stock subsequently sells it, he or she does so in the secondary market. All transactions after the initial purchase take place in the secondary market. The sales do *not* affect the total stock of financial assets that exist in the economy. Both the money market and the capital market, described next, have primary and secondary sides.

Money Market and Capital Market

Money Market

The key distinguishing feature between the money and capital markets is the maturity period of the securities traded in them. The **money market** refers to *all institutions and procedures that provide for transactions in short-term debt instruments* generally issued by borrowers with very high credit ratings. By financial convention, *short-term* means maturity periods of one year or less. Notice that equity instruments, either common or preferred, are not traded in the money market. The major instruments issued and traded are U.S. Treasury bills, various federal agency securities, bankers' acceptances, negotiable certificates of deposit, and commercial paper. Keep in mind that the money market is an intangible market. You do not walk into a building on Wall Street that has the words "Money Market" etched in stone over its arches. Rather, the money market is primarily a telephone market.

money market

Capital Market

The **capital market** refers to *all institutions and procedures that provide for transactions in long-term financial instruments. Long-term* here means having maturity periods that extend beyond one year. In the broad sense this encompasses term loans and financial leases, corporate equities, and bonds. The funds that comprise the firm's capital structure are raised in the capital market. Important elements of the capital market are the organized security exchanges and the over-the-counter markets.

capital market

Organized Security Exchanges and Over-the-Counter Markets

organized security exchanges

over-the-counter markets

Organized security exchanges are *tangible entities;* they physically occupy space (such as a building or part of a building), and *financial instruments are traded on their premises.* The **over-the-counter markets** include *all security markets except the organized exchanges.* The money market, then, is an over-the-counter market. Because both markets are important to financial officers concerned with raising *long-term capital*, some additional discussion is warranted.

Organized Security Exchanges

For practical purposes there are seven major security exchanges in the United States.[2] These are the (1) New York Stock Exchange, (2) American Stock Exchange, (3) Midwest Stock Exchange, (4) Pacific Stock Exchange, (5) Philadelphia Stock Exchange, (6) Boston Stock Exchange, and (7) Cincinnati Stock Exchange. The New York Stock Exchange (NYSE) and the American Stock Exchange (AMEX) are called *national* exchanges, whereas the others are loosely described as *regionals.* All of these seven active exchanges are registered with the Securities and Exchange Commission (SEC). Firms whose securities are traded on the registered exchanges must comply with reporting requirements of both the specific exchange and the SEC.

An indication of the importance of the NYSE to our financial market system is reflected in something known as "consolidated tape volume." The Consolidated Tape prints all of the transactions on stocks that are listed on the NYSE and are traded on other organized markets. These markets include the exchanges mentioned earlier plus over-the-counter markets. In 1995, the NYSE accounted for 82.1 percent of consolidated volume.[3]

The business of an exchange, including securities transactions, is conducted by its *members.* Members are said to occupy "seats." There are 1,366 seats on the NYSE, a number that has remained constant since 1953. Major brokerage firms own seats on the exchanges. An officer of the firm is designated to be the member of the exchange, and this membership permits the brokerage house to use the facilities of the exchange to effect trades. During 1994 the prices of seats that were exchanged for cash ranged from a low of $760,000 to a high of $830,000.[4] The record price, by the way, was $1.15 million paid on September 21, 1987—just prior to the October 19 market debacle.

Stock Exchange Benefits   Both corporations and investors enjoy several benefits provided by the existence of organized security exchanges. These include

1. **Providing a continuous market.** This may be the most important function of an organized security exchange. A continuous market provides a series of continuous security prices. Price changes from trade to trade tend to be smaller than they would be in the absence of organized markets. The reasons are that there is a relatively large sales volume in each security, trading orders are executed quickly, and the range between the price asked for a security and the offered price tends to be narrow. The result is that price volatility is reduced.

---

[2]Others include (1) The Honolulu Stock Exchange, which is unregistered; (2) the Board of Trade of the City of Chicago, which does not now trade stocks; and (3) the Chicago Board Options Exchange, Inc., which deals in options rather than stocks. The cities of Colorado Springs, Salt Lake City, and Spokane also have small exchanges. From time to time you may hear of the New York Futures Exchange (NYFE). This subsidiary of the NYSE was incorporated on April 5, 1979. Trading on the NYFE is in futures contracts and options contracts.

[3]New York Stock Exchange, *Fact Book* (New York, 1995), p. 8.

[4]New York Stock Exchange, *Fact Book* (New York, 1995), p. 105.

2. **Establishing and publicizing fair security prices.** An organized exchange permits security prices to be set by competitive forces. They are not set by negotiations off the floor of the exchange, where one party might have a bargaining advantage. The bidding process flows from the supply and demand underlying each security. This means the specific price of a security is determined in the manner of an auction. In addition, the security prices determined at each exchange are widely publicized.

3. **Helping business raise new capital.** Because a continuous secondary market exists where prices are competitively determined, it is easier for firms to float new security offerings successfully. This continuous pricing mechanism also facilitates the determination of the offering price of a new issue. This means that comparative values are easily observed.

Listing Requirements To receive the benefits provided by an organized exchange, the firm must seek to have its securities listed on the exchange. An application for listing must be filed and a fee paid. The requirements for listing vary from exchange to exchange; those of the NYSE are the most stringent. The general criteria for listing fall into these categories: (1) profitability, (2) size, (3) market value, and (4) public ownership. To give you the flavor of an actual set of listing requirements, those set forth by the NYSE are displayed in Table 2–4.[5]

Over-the-Counter Markets

Many publicly held firms do not meet the listing requirements of major stock exchanges. Others may want to avoid the reporting requirements and fees required to maintain listing. As an alternative their securities may trade in the over-the-counter markets. On the basis of sheer numbers (not dollar volume), more stocks are traded over-the-counter than on organized exchanges. As far as secondary trading in corporate bonds is concerned, the over-the-counter markets are where the action is. In a typical year, more than 90 percent of corporate bond business takes place over-the-counter.

Most over-the-counter transactions are done through a loose network of security traders who are known as broker-dealers and brokers. Brokers do not purchase se-

---

Table 2–4
NYSE Listing Requirements

Profitability
Earnings before taxes (EBT) for the most recent year must be at least $2.5 million. For the two years preceding that, EBT must be at least $2.0 million.

Size
Net tangible assets must be at least $18.0 million.

Market Value[a]
The market value of publicly held stock must be at least $18.0 million.

Public Ownership
There must be at least 1.1 million publicly held common shares. There must be at least 2,000 holders of 100 shares or more.

---

[a]The market value is tied to the level of common stock prices prevailing in the marketplace at the time of the listing application. From time to time the $18.0 million requirement noted above may be lessened. Under current regulations of the NYSE, the requirement can never be less than $9.0 million.

---

[5]New York Stock Exchange, *Fact Book* (New York, 1995), p. 33.

curities for their own account, whereas dealers do. Broker-dealers stand ready to buy and sell specific securities at selected prices. They are said to "make a market" in those securities. Their profit is the spread or difference between the price they will pay for a security (bid price) and the price at which they will sell the security (asked price).

Price Quotes

The availability of prices is not as continuous in the over-the-counter market as it is on an organized exchange. Since February 8, 1971, however, when a computerized network called NASDAQ came into existence, the availability of prices in this market has improved substantially. NASDAQ stands for National Association of Security Dealers Automated Quotation System. It is a telecommunications system that provides a national information link among the brokers and dealers operating in the over-the-counter markets. Subscribing traders have a terminal that allows them to obtain representative bids and ask prices for thousands of securities traded over-the-counter. NASDAQ is a quotation system, not a transactions system. The final trade is still consummated by direct negotiation between traders.

NASDAQ price quotes for many stocks are published daily in the *Wall Street Journal*. This same financial newspaper also publishes prices on hundreds of other stocks traded over-the-counter. Local papers supply prices on stocks of regional interest. Finally, the National Quotation Bureau publishes daily "pink sheets," which contain prices on about 8,000 securities; these sheets are available in the offices of most security dealers.

PAUSE AND REFLECT

We touched briefly on the investment-banking industry and the investment banker earlier in this chapter when we described various methods for transferring financial capital (see Figure 2–3 on page 38). The investment banker is to be distinguished from the commercial banker in that the former's organization is not a permanent depository for funds. Later it will be shown, however, that a trend is under way in this country to let commercial banks perform more functions and services that since 1933 have belonged almost exclusively to the investment-banking industry. For the moment, it is important for you to learn about the role of the investment banker in the funding of commercial activity.

OBJECTIVE 6   ## THE INVESTMENT BANKER

Most corporations do not raise long-term capital frequently. The activities of working-capital management go on daily, but attracting long-term capital is, by comparison, episodic. The sums involved can be huge, so these situations are considered of great importance to financial managers. Because most managers are unfamiliar with the subtleties of raising long-term funds, they enlist the help of an expert. That expert is an investment banker.

Definition

investment banker

The **investment banker** is *a financial specialist involved as an intermediary in the merchandising of securities.* He or she acts as a "middle person" by facilitating the flow of savings from those economic units that want to invest to those units that want to raise funds. We use the term investment banker to refer both to a given individual and to the organization for which such a person works, variously known as an investment-banking firm or an investment-banking house. Although these firms are called investment bankers, they perform no depository or lending functions. The activities of commercial banking and investment banking as we know them today were separated by the Banking Act of 1933 (also known as the Glass-Steagall Act of 1933). Just what does this middleman role involve? That is most easily understood in terms of the basic functions of investment banking.

Functions

The investment banker performs three basic functions: (1) underwriting, (2) distributing, and (3) advising.

Underwriting

The term **underwriting** is borrowed from the field of insurance. It means *assuming a risk*. The investment banker assumes the risk of selling a security issue at a satisfactory price. A satisfactory price is one that will generate a profit for the investment-banking house.

underwriting

    The procedure goes like this. The managing investment banker and its syndicate will buy the security issue from the corporation in need of funds. The **syndicate** is *a group of other investment bankers who are invited to help buy and resell the issue*. The managing house is the investment-banking firm that originated the business because its corporate client decided to raise external funds. On a specific day, the firm that is raising capital is presented with a check in exchange for the securities being issued. At this point the investment-banking syndicate owns the securities. The corporation has its cash and can proceed to use it. The firm is now immune from the possibility that the security markets might turn sour. If the price of the newly issued security falls below that paid to the firm by the syndicate, the syndicate will suffer a loss. The syndicate, of course, hopes that the opposite situation will result. Its objective is to sell the new issue to the investing public at a price per security greater than its cost.

syndicate

Distributing

Once the syndicate owns the new securities, it must get them into the hands of the ultimate investors. This is the distribution or selling function of investment banking. The investment banker may have branch offices across the United States, or it may have an informal arrangement with several security dealers who regularly buy a portion of each new offering for final sale. It is not unusual to have 300 to 400 dealers involved in the selling effort. The syndicate can properly be viewed as the security wholesaler, and the dealer organization can be viewed as the security retailer.

Advising

The investment banker is an expert in the issuance and marketing of securities. A sound investment-banking house will be aware of prevailing market conditions and can relate those conditions to the particular type of security that should be sold at a given time. Business conditions may be pointing to a future increase in interest rates. The investment banker might advise the firm to issue its bonds in a timely fashion to avoid the higher yields that are forthcoming. The banker can analyze the firm's capital structure and make recommendations as to what general source of capital should be issued. In many instances the firm will invite its investment banker to sit on the board of directors. This permits the banker to observe corporate activity and make recommendations on a regular basis.

Distribution Methods

Several methods are available to the corporation for placing new security offerings in the hands of final investors. The investment banker's role is different in each of these. Sometimes, in fact, it is possible to bypass the investment banker. These methods are described in this section. Private placements, because of their importance, are treated separately later in the chapter.

Negotiated Purchase

In a negotiated underwriting, the firm that needs funds makes contact with an investment banker, and deliberations concerning the new issue begin. If all goes well, a *method* is negotiated for determining the price the investment banker and the syndicate will pay for the securities. For example, the agreement might state that the syndicate will pay $2 less than the closing price of the firm's common stock on the day before the offering date of a new stock issue. The negotiated purchase is the most prevalent method of securities distribution in the private sector. It is generally thought to be the most profitable technique as far as investment bankers are concerned.

Competitive Bid Purchase

The method by which the underwriting group is determined distinguishes the competitive bid purchase from the negotiated purchase. In a competitive underwriting, several underwriting groups bid for the right to purchase the new issue from the corporation that is raising funds. The firm does not directly select the investment banker. The investment banker that underwrites and distributes the issue is chosen by an auction process. The syndicate willing to pay the greatest dollar amount per new security will win the competitive bid.

Most competitive bid purchases are confined to three situations, compelled by legal regulations: (1) railroad issues, (2) public utility issues, and (3) state and municipal bond issues. The argument in favor of competitive bids is that any undue influence of the investment banker over the firm is mitigated and the price received by the firm for each security should be higher. Thus, we would intuitively suspect that the cost of capital in a competitive bid situation would be less than in a negotiated purchase situation. Evidence on this question, however, is mixed. One problem with the competitive bid purchase as far as the fund-raising firm is concerned is that the benefits gained from the advisory function of the investment banker are lost. It may be necessary to use an investment banker for advisory purposes and then by law exclude the banker from the competitive bid process.

Commission or Best-Efforts Basis

Here, the investment banker acts as an agent rather than as a principal in the distribution process. The securities are *not* underwritten. The investment banker attempts to sell the issue in return for a fixed commission on each security actually sold. Unsold securities are returned to the corporation. This arrangement is typically used for more speculative issues. The issuing firm may be smaller or less established than the investment banker would like. Because the underwriting risk is not passed on to the investment banker, this distribution method is less costly to the issuer than a negotiated or competitive bid purchase. On the other hand, the investment banker only has to give it his or her "best effort." A successful sale is not guaranteed.

Privileged Subscription

Occasionally, the firm may feel that a distinct market already exists for its new securities. When a *new issue is marketed to a definite and select group of investors*, it is called a **privileged subscription.** Three target markets are typically involved: (1) current stockholders, (2) employees, or (3) customers. Of these, distributions directed at current stockholders are the most prevalent. Such offerings are called *rights offerings.* In a privileged subscription the investment banker may act only as a selling agent. It is also possible that the issuing firm and the investment banker might sign a *standby agreement,* which would obligate the investment banker to underwrite the securities that are not accepted by the privileged investors.

Direct Sale

In a **direct sale** *the issuing firm sells the securities directly to the investing public without involving an investment banker.* Even among established corporate giants this procedure is relatively rare. A variation of the direct sale, though, was used more frequently in the 1970s than in previous decades. This involves the private placement of a new issue by the fund-raising corporation *without* the use of an investment banker as an intermediary. Texaco, Mobil Oil, and International Harvester (now Navistar) are examples of large firms that have followed this procedure.[6]

Industry Leaders

All industries have their leaders, and investment banking is no exception. We have discussed investment bankers in general at some length in this chapter. Table 2–5 gives us some idea who the major players are within the investment-banking industry. It lists the top 10 houses in 1995 based on the dollar volume of security issues that were managed. The number of issues the house participated in as lead manager is also identified, along with its share of the market.

Table 2–5
Leading U.S. Investment Bankers, 1995
(Domestic Debt and Equity Issues)

	FIRM	UNDERWRITING VOLUME (BILLIONS OF DOLLARS)	PERCENT OF MARKET
1.	Merrill Lynch	$122.3	17.9%
2.	Lehman Brothers	70.3	9.9
3.	Goldman Sachs	68.5	9.7
3.	Morgan Stanley	68.5	9.7
5.	Salomon Brothers	68.1	9.6
6.	CS First Boston	64.6	9.1
7.	J.P. Morgan	40.2	5.7
8.	Bear, Sterns	25.4	3.6
9.	Donaldson, Lufkin & Jenrette	22.2	3.1
10.	Smith Barney	20.7	2.9

Source: Securities Data Co., as reported in the *Wall Street Journal,* January 2, 1996, p. R-38.

---

[6]See Wyndham Robertson, "Future Stock at Morgan Stanley," *Fortune* 97 (February 27, 1978), pp. 88, 90.

PRIVATE PLACEMENTS

Private placements are an alternative to the sale of securities to the public or to a restricted group of investors through a privileged subscription. Any type of security can be privately placed (directly placed). This market, however, is clearly dominated by debt issues. Thus, we restrict this discussion to debt securities. From year to year the volume of private placements will vary greatly. Table 2–6 shows, though, that the private placement market is always a significant portion of the U.S. capital market.

The major investors in private placements are large financial institutions. Based on the volume of securities purchased, the three most important investor groups are (1) life insurance companies, (2) state and local retirement funds, and (3) private pension funds.

In arranging a private placement the firm may (1) avoid the use of an investment banker and work directly with the investing institutions or (2) engage the services of an investment banker. If the firm does not use an investment banker, of course, it does not have to pay a fee. Conversely, investment bankers can provide valuable advice in the private placement process. They are usually in contact with several major institutional investors; thus, they will know if a firm is in a position to invest in its proposed offering, and they can help the firm evaluate the terms of the new issue.

Private placements have advantages and disadvantages compared with public offerings. The financial manager must carefully evaluate both sides of the question. The advantages associated with private placements are these:

1. **Speed.** The firm usually obtains funds more quickly through a private placement than a public offering. The major reason is that registration of the issue with the SEC is not required.
2. **Reduced flotation costs.** These savings result because the lengthy registration statement for the SEC does not have to be prepared, and the investment-banking underwriting and distribution costs do not have to be absorbed.
3. **Financing flexibility.** In a private placement the firm deals on a face-to-face basis with a small number of investors. This means that the terms of the issue can

Table 2–6

Publicly and Privately Placed Corporate Debt Placed Domestically
(Gross Proceeds of All New U.S. Corporate Debt Issues)

Year	Total Volume ($ Millions)	Percent Publicly Placed	Percent Privately Placed
1994	$441,287	82.8%	17.2%
1993	608,255	80.1	19.9
1992	443,911	85.2	14.8
1991	361,860	79.3	20.7
1990	276,259	68.5	31.5
1989	298,813	60.7	39.3
1988	329,919	61.3	38.7
1987	301,447	69.5	30.5
1986	313,502	74.2	25.8
1985	165,754	72.1	27.9
1984	109,903	66.9	33.1
1983	68,370	69.1	30.9
1982	53,636	81.7	18.3
1981	45,092	84.5	15.5

Source: Federal Reserve Bulletin, various issues including June 1996, p. A31.

be tailored to meet the specific needs of the company. For example, all of the funds need not be taken by the firm at once. In exchange for a commitment fee the firm can "draw down" against the established amount of credit with the investors. This provides some insurance against capital market uncertainties, and the firm does not have to borrow the funds if the need does not arise. There is also the possibility of renegotiation. The terms of the debt issue can be altered. The term to maturity, the interest rate, or any restrictive covenants can be discussed among the affected parties.

The following disadvantages of private placements must be evaluated:

1. **Interest costs.** It is generally conceded that interest costs on private placements exceed those of public issues. Whether this disadvantage is enough to offset the reduced flotation costs associated with a private placement is a determination the financial manager must make. There is some evidence that on smaller issues, say $500,000 as opposed to $30 million, the private placement alternative would be preferable.
2. **Restrictive covenants.** Dividend policy, working-capital levels, and the raising of additional debt capital may all be affected by provisions in the private-placement debt contract. That is not to say that such restrictions are always absent in public debt contracts. Rather, the financial officer must be alert to the tendency for these covenants to be especially burdensome in private contracts.
3. **The possibility of future SEC registration.** If the lender (investor) should decide to sell the issue to a public buyer before maturity, the issue must be registered with the SEC. Some lenders, then, require that the issuing firm agree to a future registration at their option.

FLOTATION COSTS

OBJECTIVE 8

flotation costs

The firm raising long-term capital incurs two types of **flotation costs:** (1) *the underwriter's spread* and (2) *issuing costs.* Of these two costs, the underwriter's spread is the larger. The *underwriter's spread* is simply the difference between the gross and net proceeds from a given security issue expressed as a percent of the gross proceeds. The *issue costs* include (1) printing and engraving, (2) legal fees, (3) accounting fees, (4) trustee fees, and (5) several other miscellaneous components. The two most significant issue costs are printing and engraving and legal fees.

Data published by the SEC have consistently revealed two relationships about flotation costs. First, the costs associated with issuing common stock are notably greater than the costs associated with preferred stock offerings. In turn, preferred stock costs exceed those of bonds. Second, flotation costs (expressed as a percent of gross proceeds) decrease as the size of the security issue increases.

In the first instance, the stated relationship reflects the fact that issue costs are sensitive to the risks involved in successfully distributing a security issue. Common stock is riskier to own than corporate bonds. Underwriting risk is, therefore, greater with common stock than with bonds. Thus, flotation costs just mirror these risk relationships. In the second case, a portion of the issue costs is fixed. Legal fees and accounting costs are good examples. So, as the size of the security issue rises, the fixed component is spread over a larger gross proceeds base. As a consequence, average flotation costs vary inversely with the size of the issue.

PAUSE AND REFLECT

Since late 1986, there has been a renewal of public interest in the regulation of the country's financial markets. The key event was a massive insider trading scandal that made the name Ivan F. Boesky one of almost universal recognition—but, unfortunately, in a negative sense. This was followed by the October 19, 1987, crash of the equity markets. More recently, in early 1990, the investing community (both institutional and individual) became increasingly concerned over a weakening in the so-called junk bond market. The upshot of all of this enhanced awareness is a new appreciation of the crucial role that regulation plays in the financial system. The basics are presented below.

REGULATION

Following the severe economic downturn of 1929–1932, Congressional action was taken to provide for federal regulation of the securities markets. State statutes (blue sky laws) also govern the securities markets where applicable, but the federal regulations are clearly more pressing and important. The major federal regulations are reviewed here.

Primary Market Regulations

The new issues market is governed by the Securities Act of 1933. The intent of the act is important. It aims to provide potential investors with accurate, truthful disclosure about the firm and the new securities being offered to the public. This does *not* prevent firms from issuing highly speculative securities. The SEC says nothing whatsoever about the possible investment worth of a given offering. It is up to the investor to separate the junk from the jewels. The SEC does have the legal power and responsibility to enforce the 1933 act.

Full public disclosure is achieved by the requirement that the issuing firm file a registration statement with the SEC containing requisite information. The statement details particulars about the firm and the new security being issued. During a minimum 20-day waiting period, the SEC examines the submitted document. In numerous instances the 20-day wait has been extended by several weeks. The SEC can ask for additional information that was omitted in order to clarify the original document. The SEC can also order that the offering be stopped.

During the registration process a preliminary prospectus (the red herring) may be distributed to potential investors. When the registration is approved, the final prospectus must be made available to the prospective investors. The prospectus is actually a condensed version of the full registration statement. If, at a later date, the information in the registration statement and the prospectus is found to be lacking, purchasers of the new issue who incurred a loss can sue for damages. Officers of the issuing firm and others who took part in the registration and marketing of the issue may suffer both civil and criminal penalties.

Generally, the SEC defines public issues as those that are sold to more than 25 investors. Some public issues need not be registered. These include

1. Relatively small issues where the firm sells less than $1.5 million of new securities per year.
2. Issues that are sold entirely intrastate.
3. Issues that are basically short-term instruments. This translates into maturity periods of 270 days or less.
4. Issues that are already regulated or controlled by some other federal agency. Examples here are the Federal Power Commission (public utilities) and the Interstate Commerce Commission (railroads).

The most recognizable inside trader of them all, Mr. Ivan F. Boesky, was scheduled to be set free on April 6, 1990, after a three-year prison sentence. The piece below discusses his opportunities to manage money for others.

How do you feel about an individual who violated the 1934 act being allowed in law to operate as a professional money manager? Once free, Boesky will even be able to resume the life of a money manager—assuming, of course, that people will trust him. Although the November 14, 1986, agreement with the Securities & Exchange Commission barred him for life from the securities business, a loophole in the 1940 statute governing investment advisers allows Boesky to invest for up to 14 people, as long as he doesn't advertise his services. As Boesky lawyer Harvey L. Pitt observes: "If I had 14 people, each with a billion dollars, I could manage $14 billion." An obvious point—but startling nonetheless.

Source: "How Life on the Outside Looks for an Inside Trader," *Business Week*, January 15, 1990, pp. 27–28.

Secondary Market Regulations

Secondary market trading is regulated by the Securities Exchange Act of 1934. This act created the SEC to enforce federal securities laws. The Federal Trade Commission enforced the 1933 act for one year. The major aspects of the 1934 act can be best presented in outline form:

1. Major security exchanges must register with the SEC. This regulates the exchanges and places reporting requirements on the firms whose securities are listed on them.
2. Insider trading is regulated. Insiders can be officers, directors, employees, relatives, major investors, or anyone having information about the operation of the firm that is not public knowledge. If an investor purchases the security of the firm in which the investor is an insider, he or she must hold it for at least six months before disposing of it. Otherwise, profits made from trading the stock within a period of less than six months must be returned to the firm. Furthermore, insiders must file with the SEC a monthly statement of holdings and transactions in the stock of their corporation.[7]
3. Manipulative trading of securities by investors to affect stock prices is prohibited.
4. The SEC is given control over proxy procedures.
5. The Board of Governors of the Federal Reserve System is given responsibility for setting margin requirements. This affects the flow of credit into the securities markets. Buying securities on margin simply means using credit to acquire a portion of the subject financial instruments.

---

[7]On November 14, 1986, the SEC announced that Ivan F. Boesky had admitted to illegal inside trading after an intensive investigation. Boesky at the time was a very well-known Wall Street investor, speculator, and arbitrageur. Boesky was an owner or part owner in several companies, including an arbitrage fund named Ivan F. Boesky & Co. L. P. Boesky agreed to pay the U.S. government $50 million, which represented a return of illegal profits, another $50 million in civil penalties; to withdraw permanently from the securities industry; and to plead guilty to criminal charges. The far-reaching investigation continued into 1987 and implicated several other prominent investment figures.

MORE RECENT REGULATORY DEVELOPMENTS

Securities Acts Amendments of 1975

The Securities Acts Amendments of 1975 touched on three important issues. First, Congress mandated the creation of a national market system (NMS). Only broad goals for this national exchange were identified by Congress. Implementation details were left to the SEC and, to a much lesser extent, the securities industry in general. Congress was really expressing its desire for (1) widespread application of auction market trading principles, (2) a high degree of competition across markets, and (3) the use of modern electronic communication systems to link the fragmented markets in the country into a true NMS. The NMS is still a goal toward which the SEC and the securities industry are moving. Agreement as to its final form and an implementation date have not occurred.

A second major alteration in the habits of the securities industry also took place in 1975. This was the elimination of fixed commissions (fixed brokerage rates) on public transactions in securities. This was closely tied to the desire for an NMS in that fixed brokerage fees provided no incentive for competition among brokers. A third consideration of the 1975 amendments focused on such financial institutions as commercial banks and insurance firms. These financial institutions were prohibited from acquiring membership on stock exchanges in order to reduce or save commissions on their own trades.

Shelf Registration

shelf registration
shelf offering

On March 16, 1982, the SEC began a new procedure for registering new issues of securities. Formally it is called SEC Rule 415; informally the process is known as a **shelf registration,** or a **shelf offering.** The essence of the process is rather simple. Rather than go through the lengthy, full registration process each time the firm plans an offering of securities, it can get a blanket order approved by the SEC. *A master registration statement that covers the financing plans of the firm over the coming two years is filed with the SEC.* On approval, the firm can market some or all of the securities over this two-year period. The securities are sold in a piecemeal fashion, or "off the shelf." Prior to each specific offering, a short statement about the issue is filed with the SEC.

Corporations raising funds approve of this new procedure. The tedious, full registration process is avoided with each offering pulled off the shelf. This should result in a saving of fees paid to investment bankers. Moreover, an issue can more quickly be brought to the market. Also, if market conditions change, an issue can easily be redesigned to fit the specific conditions of the moment.

As is always the case, there is another side to the story. Recall that the reason for the registration process in the first place is to give investors useful information about the firm and the securities being offered. Under the shelf registration procedure some of the information about the issuing firm becomes old as the two-year horizon unfolds. Some investment bankers feel they do not have the proper amount of time to study the firm when a shelf offering takes place. This is one of those areas of finance where more observations are needed before any final conclusions can be made. Those observations will only come with the passage of time.

RATES OF RETURN IN THE FINANCIAL MARKETS

Earlier in this chapter in discussing "the financing process" we noted that net users of funds (savings-deficit economic units) must compete with one another for the funds supplied by net savers (savings-surplus economic units). Consequently, to obtain financing for projects that will benefit the firm's stockholders, that firm must offer the supplier (savings-surplus unit) a rate of return *competitive* with the next best investment alternative available to that saver (investor). This *rate of return on the next best investment alternative to the saver* is known as the supplier's **opportunity cost of funds.** The opportunity cost concept is crucial in financial management and will be referred to often.

opportunity cost of funds

Next we will review the levels and variability in rates of return that have occurred over the lengthy period of 1926–1995. This review focuses on returns from a wide array of financial instruments. In both Chapters 8 and 11 we will discuss at length the concept of an *overall* cost of capital. Part of that overall cost of capital is attributed to interest rate levels at given points in time. So we will follow this initial broad look at interest rate levels with a discussion of the more recent period of 1981–1995.

PAUSE AND REFLECT

Opportunity cost is one of the most important concepts in financial management. It matters not that your firm's debt has a cost of 12 percent; the more important issue in making financial decisions is what it would cost the firm to issue the debt today. Put another way, would you loan a firm money at 13 percent if you could earn 15 percent on a similar investment? Not if you have any "smarts."

Rates of Return over Long Periods

History can tell us a great deal about the returns that investors earn in the financial markets. A primary source for a historical perspective comes from Ibbotson and Sinquefield's *Stocks, Bonds, Bills, and Inflation*, which examines the realized rates of return for a wide variety of securities spanning the period from 1926 through 1995.[8] As part of their study, Ibbotson and Sinquefield calculated the average annual rates of return investors earned over the preceding 69 years, along with the average inflation rate for the same period. They also calculated the standard deviations of the returns for each type of security. The concept of standard deviation comes from our statistical colleagues, who use this measurement to indicate quantitatively how much dispersion or variability there is around the mean, or average, value of the item being measured—in this case, the rates of return in the financial markets.

Ibbotson and Sinquefield's results are summarized in Figure 2–4 on page 52. These returns represent the average inflation rate and the average observed rates of return for different types of securities. The average inflation rate was 3.2 percent for the period covered by the study. We will refer to this rate as the "inflation-risk premium."

---

[8]Roger G. Ibbotson and Rex A. Sinquefield, *Stocks, Bonds, Bills, and Inflation: Historical Returns* (Chicago: Dow Jones–Irwin, 1996).

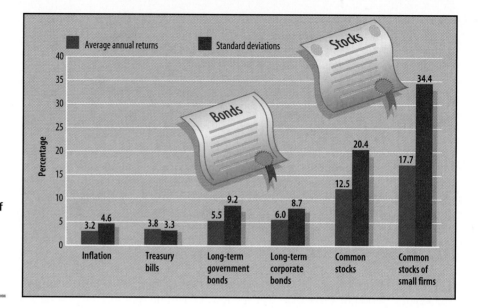

Figure 2–4

Average Annual Returns and Standard Deviations of Returns, 1926–1995

Source: Roger G. Ibbotson and Rex A. Sinquefield, *Stocks, Bonds, Bills, and Inflation: Historical Returns* (Chicago: Dow Jones–Irwin, 1996), p. 33. © Ibbotson Associates.

The investor who earns only the rate of inflation has earned no "real return." That is, the *real return* is the return earned above the rate of increase in the general price level for goods and services in the economy, which is the inflation rate. In addition to the danger of not earning above the inflation rate, investors are concerned about the risk of the borrower defaulting or failing to repay the loan when due. Thus, we would expect a default-risk premium for long-term corporate bonds over long-term government bonds. The premium for 1926–1995, as shown in Figure 2–4, was 0.5 percent, or what is called 50 basis points (6.0 percent on long-term corporate bonds minus 5.5 percent on long-term government bonds). We would also expect an even greater risk premium for common stocks vis-à-vis long-term corporate bonds, since the variability in average returns is greater for common stocks. The Ibbotson and Sinquefield study verifies such a risk premium, with common stocks (all firms) earning 6.5 percent more than the rate earned on long-term corporate bonds (12.5 percent for common stocks minus 6.0 percent for long-term corporate bonds).

Remember that these returns are "averages" across many securities and over an extended period of time. However, these averages reflect the conventional wisdom regarding risk premiums: The greater the risk, the greater will be the expected returns. Such a relationship is shown in Figure 2–5, where the average returns are plotted against their standard deviations; note that higher average returns have historically been associated with higher dispersion in these returns.

OBJECTIVE 10

Interest Rate Levels over Recent Periods

The *nominal* interest rates on some key fixed-income securities are displayed within both Table 2–7 and Figure 2–6 (see page 54) for the most recent 1981–1995 time frame. The rate of inflation at the consumer level is also presented in those two exhibits. This allows us to observe quite easily several concepts that were mentioned in the section above. Specifically, we can observe (1) the inflation-risk premium, (2) the default-risk premium across the several instruments, and (3) the approximate real return for each instrument. Looking at the mean (average) values for each security and the inflation rate at the bottom of Table 2–7 will facilitate the discussion.

Notice that the average inflation rate over this more recent period is higher than reported in the longer period covered by the Ibbotson and Sinquefield analysis. Over

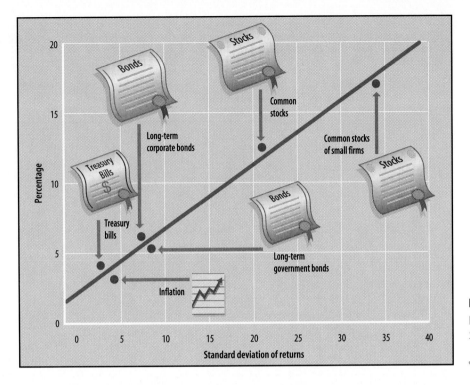

Figure 2–5
Rates of Return and Standard Deviations, 1926–1995

the period 1981–1995 the consumer price index (December to December change) increased by an average of 3.93 percent each year. According to the logic of the financial markets, investors will *require* a nominal rate of interest that exceeds the inflation rate or else their realized *real* return will be negative. Earning a negative return over long periods of time (like 15 years) is not very smart.

Table 2–7 indicates that investor rationality prevailed. For example, the average inflation-risk premium demanded on U.S. Treasury bills with a three-month maturity was 3.15 percent (or 315 basis points). That is, an average 7.08 percent yield on Treasury bills over the period *minus* the average inflation rate of 3.93 percent over the same period produces a premium of 3.15 percent.

The default-risk premium is also evident in Table 2–7 and Figure 2–6. If we array the securities in these two exhibits from low risk to high risk, the following tabulation results:

Security	Yield
3-month Treasury bills	7.08
30-year Treasury bonds	9.31
Aaa corporate bonds	10.03

Again, the basic rationale of the financial markets prevailed. The default-risk premium on high-rated (Aaa) corporate bonds relative to long-term Treasury bonds of 30-year maturity was 0.72 percent.

The array above can also be used to identify another factor that affects interest rate levels. It is referred to as the "maturity premium." This maturity premium arises even if securities possess equal (or approximately equal) odds of default. This is the case with Treasury bills and Treasury bonds, for instance, since the full faith and credit of the U.S. government stands behind these financial contracts. They are considered risk free (i.e., possessing no chance of default).

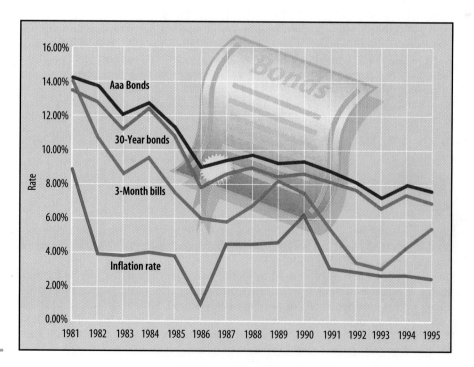

Table 2–7
Interest Rate Levels and Inflation Rates
1981–1995

Year	3-Month Treasury Bills %	30-Year Treasury Bonds %	Aaa Rated Corporate Bonds %	Inflation Rate %
1981	14.08	13.44	14.17	8.9
1982	10.69	12.76	13.79	3.9
1983	8.63	11.18	12.04	3.8
1984	9.52	12.39	12.71	4.0
1985	7.49	10.79	11.37	3.8
1986	5.98	7.80	9.02	1.1
1987	5.82	8.58	9.38	4.4
1988	6.68	8.96	9.71	4.4
1989	8.12	8.45	9.26	4.6
1990	7.51	8.61	9.32	6.1
1991	5.42	8.14	8.77	3.1
1992	3.45	7.67	8.14	2.9
1993	3.02	6.59	7.22	2.7
1994	4.29	7.37	7.97	2.7
1995	5.51	6.88	7.59	2.5
Mean	7.08	9.31	10.03	3.93

Source: *Federal Reserve Bulletin*, various issues, and *Federal Reserve Statistical Releases* H.15 (519), G.13 (415), various issues.

Figure 2–6
Interest Rate Levels and
Inflation Rates, 1981–1995

Notice that Treasury bonds with a 30-year maturity commanded a 2.23 percent yield differential over the shorter, three-month-to-maturity Treasury bonds. This provides an estimate of the maturity premium demanded by investors over this specific 1981–1995 period. More precisely, the **maturity premium** can be defined as:

The additional return required by investors in longer-term securities (bonds in this case) to compensate them for the greater risk of price fluctuations on those securities caused by interest rate changes.

When you study the basic mathematics of financial decisions in Chapter 5 and the characteristics of fixed-income securities in Chapter 6, you will learn how to quantify this maturity premium that is imbedded in nominal interest rates.

One other type of risk premium that helps determine interest rate levels needs to be identified and defined. It is known as the "liquidity premium." The **liquidity premium** is defined as:

The additional return required by investors in securities that cannot be quickly converted into cash at a reasonably predictable price.

The secondary markets for small-bank stocks, especially community banks, provide a good example of the liquidity premium. A bank holding company that trades on the New York Stock Exchange, like Barnett Bank, will be more liquid to investors than, say, the common stock of Citizens National Bank of Leesburg, Florida. Such a liquidity premium will be reflected across the spectrum of financial assets, from bonds to stocks.

maturity premium

liquidity premium

BACK TO THE FOUNDATIONS

Our first axiom, **Axiom 1: The Risk-Return Trade-off—We Won't Take on Additional Risk Unless We Expect to Be Compensated with Additional Return,** established the fundamental risk-return trade-offs that govern the financial markets. We are now trying to provide you with an understanding of the kinds of risks that are rewarded in the risk-return trade-off presented in **Axiom 1.**

INTEREST RATE DETERMINANTS IN A NUTSHELL

OBJECTIVE 11

Our review of rates of return and interest rate levels in the financial markets permits us to synthesize our introduction to the different types of risks that impact interest rates. We can, thereby, generate a simple equation with the **nominal** (i.e., observed) **rate of interest** being the output variable from the equation. The nominal interest rate, also called the "quoted" rate, *is the interest rate paid on debt securities without an adjustment for any loss in purchasing power.* It is the rate that you would read about in the *Wall Street Journal* for a specific fixed-income security. That equation follows:

nominal rate of interest

$$k = k^* + IRP + DRP + MP + LP \qquad (2\text{-}1)$$

where: k = the nominal or observed rate of interest on a specific fixed-income security.

k^* = the real risk-free rate of interest; it is the required rate of interest on a fixed-income security that has no risk and in an economic environment of zero inflation. This can be reasonably thought of as the rate of interest demanded by investors in U.S. Treasury securities during periods of no inflation.

IRP = the inflation-risk premium.

DRP = the default-risk premium.

MP = the maturity premium.

LP = the liquidity premium.

Sometimes in analyzing interest rate relationships over time it is of use to focus on what is called the "nominal risk-free rate of interest." Again, by nominal we mean "observed." So let us designate the nominal risk-free interest rate as k_{rf}. Drawing, then, on our discussions and notation from above we can write this expression for k_{rf}:

$$k_{rf} = k^* + IRP \tag{2-2}$$

This equation just says that the nominal risk-free rate of interest is equal to the real risk-free interest rate plus the inflation-risk premium. It also provides a quick and *approximate* way of estimating the risk-free rate of interest, k^*, by solving directly for this rate. This basic relationship in equation (2–2) contains important information for the financial decision maker. It has also for years been the subject of fascinating and lengthy discussions among financial economists. We will look more at the substance of the real rate of interest in the next section. In this following section we will improve on equation (2–2) by making it more *precise*.

The Effects of Inflation on Rates of Return and the Fisher Effect

real rate of interest

When a rate of interest is quoted, it is generally the nominal, or observed rate. The **real rate of interest,** on the other hand, represents *the rate of increase in actual purchasing power, after adjusting for inflation.* For example, if you have $100 today and lend it to someone for a year at a nominal rate of interest of 11.3 percent, you will get back $111.30 in one year. But if during the year prices of goods and services rise by 5 percent, it will take $105 at year end to purchase the same goods and services that $100 purchased the beginning of the year. What was your increase in purchasing power over the year? The quick and dirty answer is found by subtracting the inflation rate from the nominal rate, 11.3% − 5% = 6.3%, but this is not exactly correct. To be more precise, let the nominal rate of interest be represented by k_{rf}, the anticipated rate of inflation by IRP, and the real rate of interest by k^*. Using these notations, we can express the relationship among the nominal interest rate, the rate of inflation, and the real rate of interest as follows:

$$\Rightarrow \quad 1 + k_{rf} = (1 + k^*)(1 + IRP) \tag{2-3}$$

or

$$k_{rf} = k^* + IRP + (k^* \cdot IRP)$$

Consequently, the nominal rate of interest (k_{rf}) is equal to the sum of the real rate of interest (k^*), the inflation rate (IRP), and the product of the real rate and the inflation rate. This relationship among nominal rates, real rates, and the rate of inflation has come to be called the *Fisher effect*.[9] It means that the observed nominal rate of interest includes both the real rate and an *inflation premium* as noted in the previous section.

Substituting into equation (2–3) using a nominal rate of 11.3 percent and an inflation rate of 5 percent, we can calculate the real rate of interest, k^*, as follows:

$$k_{rf} = k^* + IRP + (k^* \cdot IRP)$$
$$.113 = k^* + .05 + .05k^*$$
$$k^* = .06 = 6\%$$

Thus, at the new higher prices, your purchasing power will have increased by only 6 percent, although you have $11.30 more than you had at the start of the year. To

---

[9]This relationship was analyzed many years ago by Irving Fisher. For those who want to explore "Fisher's theory of interest" in more detail, a fine overview is contained in Peter N. Ireland, "Long-Term Interest Rates and Inflation: A Fisherian Approach," *Federal Reserve Bank of Richmond, Economic Quarterly* 82 (Winter 1996), pp. 22–26.

see why, let's assume that at the outset of the year one unit of the market basket of goods and services costs $1, so you could purchase 100 units with your $100. At the end of the year you have $11.30 more, but each unit now costs 1.05 (remember the 5 percent rate of inflation). How many units can you buy at the end of the year? The answer is $111.30 ÷ $1.05 = 106, which represents a 6 percent increase in real purchasing power.[10]

Inflation and Real Rates of Return: The Financial Analyst's Approach

While the algebraic methodology presented in the section above is strictly correct, few practicing analysts or executives use it. Rather, they will employ some version of the following relationship, an approximation method, to estimate the real rate of interest over a selected past time frame.

$$\text{(nominal interest rate)} - \text{(inflation rate)} = \text{real interest rate}$$

The concept is straightforward, but implementation requires that several judgments be made. For example, which interest rate series and maturity period should be used? Suppose we settle for using some U.S. Treasury security as a surrogate for a nominal risk-free interest rate. Then, should we use the yield on 3-month U.S. Treasury bills or, perhaps, that on 30-year Treasury bonds? Guess what? There is no absolute answer to the question.

So, we can have a real risk-free short-term interest rate, as well as a real risk-free long-term interest rate, and several variations in between. In essence, it just depends on what the analyst wants to accomplish. We could also calculate the real rate of interest on some rating class of corporate bonds (like Aaa-rated bonds) and have a risky real rate of interest as opposed to a real risk-free interest rate.

Further, the choice of a proper inflation index is equally challenging. Again, we have several choices. We could use the consumer price index, the producer price index for finished goods, or some price index out of the national income accounts, like the gross domestic product chain price index. Again, there is no precise scientific answer as to which specific price index to use. Logic and consistency do narrow the boundaries of the ultimate choice.

Let's tackle a very basic (simple) example. Suppose that an analyst wants to estimate the approximate real interest rate on (1) 3-month Treasury bills, (2) 30-year Treasury bonds, and (3) Aaa-rated corporate bonds over the 1981–1995 time frame. Further, the annual rate of change in the consumer price index (measured from December to December) is considered a logical measure of past inflation experience. Guess what? Most of our work is already done for us in Table 2–7. Some of the data from Table 2–7 are displayed below.

SECURITY	MEAN NOMINAL YIELD %	MEAN INFLATION RATE %	INFERRED REAL RATE %
Treasury bills	7.08	3.93	3.15
Treasury bonds	9.31	3.93	5.38
Corporate bonds	10.03	3.93	6.10

Notice that the mean yield over the 15 years from 1981 to 1995 on all three classes of securities has been used as a reasonable proxy for the ex-post return. Likewise,

---

[10]In Chapter 5 we will study more about the time value of money.

the mean inflation rate over the same time period has been used as an estimate of the inflation-risk premium (IRP from our earlier notation). The last column provides the approximation for the real interest rate on each class of securities.

Thus, over the 15-year examination period the real rate of interest on 3-month Treasury bills was 3.15 percent versus 5.38 percent on 30-year Treasury bonds, versus 6.10 percent on Aaa-rated corporate bonds. These three estimates (approximations) of the real interest rate provide a rough guide to the increase in real purchasing power associated with an investment position in each security. Remember that the real rate on the corporate bonds is expected to be greater than that on long-term government bonds because of the default-risk premium (DRP) placed on the corporate securities. We move in the next section to a discussion of the maturity premium (MP).

OBJECTIVE 12 | **THE TERM STRUCTURE OF INTEREST RATES**

term structure of interest rates
yield to maturity

The relationship between a debt security's rate of return and the length of time until the debt matures is known as the **term structure of interest rates** or the **yield to maturity.** For the relationship to be meaningful to us, all the factors other than maturity, meaning factors such as the chance of the bond defaulting, must be held constant. Thus, *the term structure reflects observed rates or yields on similar securities, except for the length of time until maturity, at a particular moment in time.*

Figure 2–7 shows an example of the term structure of interest rates. The curve is upward sloping, indicating that longer terms to maturity command higher returns, or yields. In this hypothetical term structure, the rate of interest on a 5-year note or bond is 11.5 percent, whereas the comparable rate on a 20-year bond is 13 percent.

Observing Historical Term Structures of Interest Rates

As we might expect, the term structure of interest rates changes over time, depending on the environment. The particular term structure observed today may be quite different from the term structure a month ago and different still from the term structure one month from now. A perfect example of the changing term structure, or yield curve, was witnessed during the early days of the Persian Gulf crisis in August 1990. Figure 2–8 shows the yield curves one day prior to the Iraqi invasion of Kuwait and then again just three weeks later. The change is noticeable, particularly for long-term

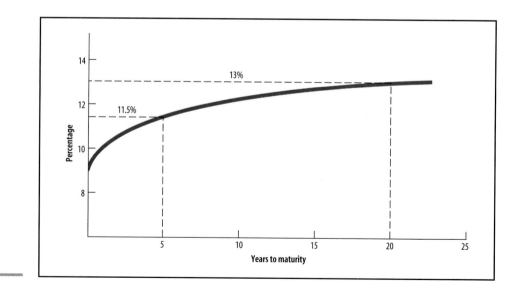

Figure 2–7
The Term Structure of
Interest Rates

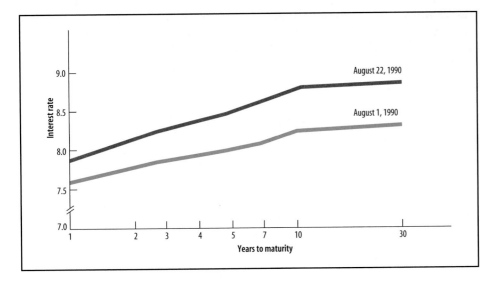

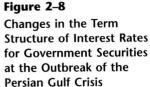

Figure 2–8
Changes in the Term
Structure of Interest Rates
for Government Securities
at the Outbreak of the
Persian Gulf Crisis

interest rates. Investors quickly developed new fears about the prospect of increased inflation to be caused by the crisis and consequently increased their required rates of return.

Although the upward-sloping term-structure curves in Figures 2–7 and 2–8 are the ones most commonly observed, yield curves can assume several shapes. Sometimes the term structure is downward sloping; at other times it rises and then falls (hump-backed); and at still other times it may be relatively flat. Figure 2–9 shows some yield curves at different points in time.

Trying to Explain the Shape of the Term Structure

A number of theories may explain the shape of the term structure of interest rates at any point. Three possible explanations are prominent: (1) the unbiased expectations theory, (2) the liquidity preference theory, and (3) the market segmentation theory.[11] Let's look at each in turn.

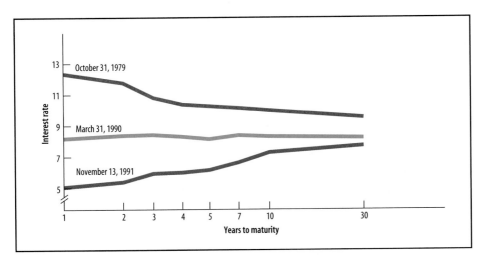

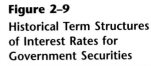

Figure 2–9
Historical Term Structures
of Interest Rates for
Government Securities

---

[11] See Richard Roll, *The Behavior of Interest Rates: An Application of the Efficient Market Model to U.S. Treasury Bills* (New York: Basic Books, 1970).

The Unbiased Expectations Theory

unbiased expectations theory

The **unbiased expectations theory** says that *the term structure is determined by an investor's expectations about future interest rates.* [12] To see how this works, consider the following investment problem faced by Mary Maxell. Mary has $10,000 that she wants to invest for two years, at which time she plans to use her savings to make a down payment on a new home. Wanting not to take any risk of losing her savings, she decides to invest in U.S. government securities. She has two choices. First, she can purchase a government security that matures in two years, which offers her an interest rate of 9 percent per year. If she does this, she will have $11,881 in two years, calculated as follows: [13]

Principal amount	$10,000
Plus: Year 1 interest (.09 × $10,000)	900
Principal plus interest at the end of year 1	$10,900
Plus: Year 2 interest (.09 × $10,900)	981
Principal plus interest at the end of year 2	$11,881

Alternatively, Mary could buy a government security maturing in one year that pays an 8 percent rate of interest. She would then need to purchase another one-year security at the end of the first year. Which alternative Mary will prefer obviously depends in part on the rate of interest she expects to receive on the government security she will purchase a year from now. We cannot tell Mary what the interest rate will be in a year; however, we can at least calculate the rate that will give her the same two-year total savings she would get from her first choice, or $11,881. The interest rate can be calculated as follows:

Savings needed in two years	$11,881
Savings at the end of year 1	
$10,000(1 + .08)	$10,800
Interest needed in year 2	$1,081

For Mary to receive $1,081 in the second year, she would have to earn about 10 percent on her second-year investment, computed as follows:

$$\frac{\text{interest received in year 2}}{\text{investment made at beginning of year 2}} = \frac{\$1,081}{\$10,800} = 10\%$$

So the term structure of interest rates for our example consists of the one-year interest rate of 8 percent and the two-year rate of 9 percent. This exercise also gives us information about the *expected* one-year rate for investments made one year hence.

---

[12]Irving Fisher thought of this idea in 1896. The theory was later refined by J. R. Hicks in *Value and Capital* (London: Oxford University Press, 1946) and F. A. Lutz and V. C. Lutz in *The Theory of Investment in the Firm* (Princeton, NJ: Princeton University Press, 1951).

[13]We could also calculate the principal plus interest for Mary's investment using the following compound interest equation: $\$10,000(1 + .09)^2 = \$11,881$. We will study the mathematics of compound interest in Chapter 5.

In a sense, the term structure contains implications about investor expectations of future interest rates; thus, this explains the unbiased expectations theory of the term structure of interest rates.

Although we can see a relationship between current interest rates with different maturities and the investor's expectations about future interest rates, is this the whole story? Are there influences other than the investor's expectations about future interest rates? Probably, so let's continue to think about Mary's dilemma.

Liquidity Preference Theory

In presenting Mary's choices, we have suggested that she would be indifferent to a choice between the two-year government security offering a 9 percent return and two consecutive one-year investments offering 8 and 10 percent, respectively. However, that would be so only if she is unconcerned about the risk associated with not knowing the rate of interest on the second security as of today. If Mary is risk averse (that is, she dislikes risk), she might not be satisfied with expectations of a 10 percent return on the second one-year government security. She might require some additional expected return to be truly indifferent. Mary might in fact decide that she will expose herself to the uncertainty of future interest rates only if she can reasonably *expect* to earn an additional .5 percent in interest, or 10.5 percent, on the second one-year investment. This *risk premium* (additional required interest rate) to compensate for the risk of changing future interest rates is nothing more than the maturity premium **(MP)** introduced earlier, and this concept underlies the liquidity preference theory of the term structure.[14] In the **liquidity preference theory,** *investors require maturity premiums to compensate them for buying securities that expose them to the risks of fluctuating interest rates.*

liquidity preference theory

Market Segmentation Theory

The **market segmentation theory** is the third popular theory of the term structure of interest rates. This concept is built on the notion that legal restrictions and personal preferences limit choices for investors to certain ranges of maturities. For example, commercial banks prefer short- to medium-term maturities as a result of the short-term nature of their deposit liabilities. They prefer not to invest in long-term securities. Life insurance companies, on the other hand, have long-term liabilities, so they prefer longer maturities in investments. At the extreme, the market segmentation theory implies that *the rate of interest for a particular maturity is determined solely by demand and supply for a given maturity and that it is independent of the demand and supply for securities having different maturities.* A more moderate version of the theory allows investors strong maturity preferences, but it also allows them to modify their feelings and preferences if significant yield inducements occur.

market segmentation theory

SUMMARY

This chapter centers on the market environment in which corporations raise long-term funds, including the structure of the U.S. financial markets, the institution of investment banking, and the various methods for distributing securities. It also discusses the role of interest rates in allocating savings to ultimate investment.

---

[14]This theory was first presented by John R. Hicks in *Value and Capital* (London: Oxford University Press, 1946), pp. 141–145, with the risk premium referred to as the liquidity premium. For our purposes we will use the term *maturity premium (MP)* to describe this risk premium, thereby keeping our terminology consistent within this chapter.

Mix of corporate securities sold

When corporations go to the capital market for cash, the most favored financing method is debt. The corporate debt markets clearly dominate the equity markets when new funds are raised. The U.S. tax system inherently favors debt capital as a fund-raising method. In an average year over the 1981–1995 period, bonds and notes made up 75.5 percent of external cash that was raised.

Primarily because of the transactions costs involved, corporations prefer to finance new investments out of internally generated funds before external sources of funds are tapped. Table 2–1 on page 30 showed that from 76.9 to 90.3 percent of business sources of funds over the 1990–1993 period were generated via internal sources.

Why financial markets exist

The function of financial markets is to allocate savings efficiently in the economy to the ultimate demander (user) of the savings. In a financial market the forces of supply and demand for a specific financial instrument are brought together. The wealth of an economy would not be as great as it is without a fully developed financial market system.

Financing of business

Every year households are a net supplier of funds to the financial markets. The non-financial business sector is always a net borrower of funds. Both life insurance companies and private pension funds are important buyers of corporate securities. Savings are ultimately transferred to the business firm seeking cash by means of (1) the direct transfer, (2) the indirect transfer using the investment banker, or (3) the indirect transfer using the financial intermediary.

Components of the U.S. financial market system

Corporations can raise funds through public offerings or private placements. The public market is impersonal in that the security issuer does not meet the ultimate investors in the financial instruments. In a private placement, the securities are sold directly to a limited number of institutional investors.

The primary market is the market for new issues. The secondary market represents transactions in currently outstanding securities. Both the money and capital markets have primary and secondary sides. The money market refers to transactions in short-term debt instruments. The capital market, on the other hand, refers to transactions in long-term financial instruments. Trading in the money and capital markets can occur in either the organized security exchanges or the over-the-counter market. The money market is exclusively an over-the-counter market.

Investment banker

The investment banker is a financial specialist involved as an intermediary in the merchandising of securities. He or she performs the functions of (1) underwriting, (2) distributing, and (3) advising. Major methods for the public distribution of securities include (1) the negotiated purchase, (2) the competitive bid purchase, (3) the commission or best-efforts basis, (4) privileged subscriptions, and (5) direct sales. The direct sale bypasses the use of an investment banker. The negotiated purchase is the most profitable distribution method to the investment banker. It also provides the greatest amount of investment-banking services to the corporate client.

Private placements

OBJECTIVE 7

Privately placed debt provides an important market outlet for corporate bonds. Major investors in this market are (1) life insurance firms, (2) state and local retirement funds, and (3) private pension funds. Several advantages and disadvantages are associated with private placements. The financial officer must weigh these attributes and decide if a private placement is preferable to a public offering.

Flotation costs

OBJECTIVE 8

Flotation costs consist of the underwriter's spread and issuing costs. The flotation costs of common stock exceed those of preferred stock, which, in turn, exceed those of debt. Moreover, flotation costs as a percent of gross proceeds are inversely related to the size of the security issue.

Regulation

The new issues market is regulated at the federal level by the Securities Act of 1933. It provides for the registration of new issues with the SEC. Secondary market trading is regulated by the Securities Exchange Act of 1934. The Securities Acts Amendments of 1975 placed on the SEC the responsibility for devising a national market system. This concept is still being studied. The shelf registration procedure (SEC Rule 415) was initiated in March 1982. Under this regulation and with the proper filing of documents, firms that are selling new issues do not have to go through the old, lengthy registration process each time the firm plans an offering of securities.

The logic of rates of return and interest rate determination

OBJECTIVE 9
OBJECTIVE 10
OBJECTIVE 11
OBJECTIVE 12

The financial markets give managers an informed indication of investors' opportunity costs. The more efficient the market, the more informed the indication. This information is a useful input about the rates of return that investors require on financial claims. In turn, this will become useful to financial managers as they estimate the overall cost of capital used as a screening rate in the capital budgeting process.

Rates of return on various securities are based on the underlying supply of loanable funds (savings) and demand for those loanable funds. In addition to a risk-free return, investors will want to be compensated for the potential loss of purchasing power resulting from inflation. Moreover, investors require a greater return the greater the default-risk, maturity premium, and liquidity premium are on the securities being analyzed.

KEY TERMS

Capital Market, 39

Direct Placement, 39

Direct Sale, 45

Direct Securities, 35

Financial Assets, 34

Financial Markets, 33

Flotation Costs, 47

Indirect Securities, 35

Investment Banker, 42

Liquidity Preference Theory, 61

Liquidity Premium, 55

Market Segmentation Theory, 61

Maturity Premium, 55

Money Market, 39

Nominal Rate of Interest, 55

Opportunity Cost of Funds, 51

Organized Security Exchanges, 40

Over-the-Counter Markets, 40

Primary Markets, 39

Private Placement, 39

STUDY QUESTIONS

2-1. What are financial markets? What function do they perform? How would an economy be worse off without them?

2-2. Define in a technical sense what we mean by *financial intermediary*. Give an example of your definition.

2-3. Distinguish between the money and capital markets.

2-4. What major benefits do corporations and investors enjoy because of the existence of organized security exchanges?

2-5. What are the general categories examined by an organized exchange in determining whether an applicant firm's securities can be listed on it? (Specific numbers are not needed here, but rather areas of investigation.)

2-6. Why do you think most secondary-market trading in bonds takes place over-the-counter?

2-7. What is an investment banker, and what major functions does he or she perform?

2-8. What is the major difference between a negotiated purchase and a competitive bid purchase?

2-9. Why is an investment-banking syndicate formed?

2-10. Why might a large corporation want to raise long-term capital through a private placement rather than a public offering?

2-11. As a recent business school graduate, you work directly for the corporate treasurer. Your corporation is going to issue a new security and is concerned with the probable flotation costs. What tendencies about flotation costs can you relate to the treasurer?

2-12. When corporations raise funds, what type of financing vehicle (instrument or instruments) is most favored?

2-13. What is the major (most significant) savings-surplus sector in the U.S. economy?

2-14. Identify three distinct ways that savings are ultimately transferred to business firms in need of cash.

2-15. Explain the term *opportunity cost* with respect to cost of funds to the firm.

2-16. Compare and explain the historical rates of return for different types of securities.

2-17. Explain the impact of inflation on rates of return.

2-18. Define the term structure of interest rates.

2-19. Explain the popular theories for the rationale of the term structure of interest rates.

STUDY PROBLEMS

2-1. (*Real Interest Rates: Financial Analyst's Method*)   The chief financial officer of your firm has asked you for an approximate answer to this question: What was the increase in real purchasing power associated with both 3-month Treasury bills and

30-year Treasury bonds over the 1991–1995 period? Hints: (a) Consult Table 2–7 in the text, and (2) simple averages on the key variables will provide a defensible response to your boss. Also, the chief financial officer wants a short explanation should the 3-month real rate turn out to be *less* than the 30-year real rate.

2-2. (*Inflation and Interest Rates*)   What would you expect the nominal rate of interest to be if the real rate is 4 percent and the expected inflation rate is 7 percent?

2-3. (*Inflation and Interest Rates*)   Assume the expected inflation rate to be 4 percent. If the current real rate of interest is 6 percent, what ought the nominal rate of interest be?

2-4. (*Inflation and Interest Rates*)   Assume the expected inflation rate to be 5 percent. If the current real rate of interest is 7 percent, what would you expect the nominal rate of interest to be?

2-5. (*Term Structure of Interest Rates*)   You want to invest your savings of $20,000 in government securities for the next two years. Currently, you can invest either in a security that pays interest of 8 percent per year for the next two years or in a security that matures in one year but pays only 6 percent interest. If you make the latter choice, you would then reinvest your savings at the end of the first year for another year.

   a. Why might you choose to make the investment in the one-year security that pays an interest rate of only 6 percent, as opposed to investing in the two-year security paying 8 percent? Provide numerical support for your answer. Which theory of term structure have you supported in your answer?

   b. Assume your required rate of return on the second-year investment is 11 percent; otherwise, you will choose to go with the two-year security. What rationale could you offer for your preference?

COMPREHENSIVE PROBLEM

You have been asked to provide a reasonable estimate of the nominal interest rate for a new issue of Aaa-rated bonds to be offered by Big Truck Producers, Inc. The final format that the chief financial officer of Big Truck has requested is that of equation (2–1) in the text. Your assignment also requires that you consult the data in Table 2–7.

   Some agreed-upon procedures related to generating estimates for key variables in equation (2–1) follow.

a. The financial market environment over the 1993–1995 period is considered representative of the prospective tone of the market near the time of offering the new bonds to the investing public. This means that 3-year averages will be used as benchmarks for some of the variable estimates. All estimates will be rounded off to hundredths of a percent; thus, 6.288 becomes 6.29 percent.

b. The real risk-free rate of interest is the difference between the calculated average yield on 3-month Treasury bills and the inflation rate.

c. The default-risk premium is estimated by the difference between the average yield on Aaa-rated bonds and 30-year Treasury bonds.

d. The maturity premium is estimated by the difference between the average yield on 30-year Treasury bonds and 3-month Treasury bills.

e. Big Truck's bonds will be traded on the New York Exchange for Bonds so the liquidity premium will be slight. It will be greater than zero, however, because the secondary market for the firm's bonds is more uncertain than that of some other truck producers. It is estimated at 3 basis points. A basis point is one hundredth of 1 percent.

   Now place your output into the format of equation (2–1) so that the nominal interest rate can be estimated and the size of each variable can also be inspected for reasonableness and discussion with the chief financial officer.

Chapter

3

LEARNING OBJECTIVES

After reading this chapter you should be able to

1. Construct and analyze a firm's basic financial statements, including the balance sheet, income statement, and cash flow statement.
2. Interpret the meaning of a firm's cash flow statement.
3. Calculate a comprehensive set of financial ratios and use them to evaluate the financial health of a company.
4. Apply the Du Pont analysis in evaluating the firm's performance.
5. Explain the limitations of ratio analysis.

Evaluating a Firm's Financial Performance and Measuring Cash Flow

Basic Financial Statements • Financial Ratio Analysis • The Du Pont Analysis: An Integrative Approach to Ratio Analysis • Limitation of Ratio Analysis

E valuating the performance of a firm using its financial statements can be a tricky business. The difficulty is generally not due to deliberate attempts by corporate managers and their accountants to mislead you. The problem relates to the substantial flexibility inherent in the set of rules and principles that accountants follow in preparing a firm's financial statements (generally accepted accounting principles, or GAAP). For example, consider the words of wisdom offered by Warren Buffet in the 1990 annual report of Berkshire Hathaway, Inc.

> The term "earnings" has a precise ring to it. And when an earnings figure is accompanied by an unqualified auditor's certificate, a naive reader might think it comparable in certitude to pi, calculated to dozens of decimal places. In reality, however, earnings can be as pliable as putty when a charlatan heads the company reporting them. Eventually truth will surface, but in the meantime a lot of money can change hands. Indeed, some important American fortunes have been created by the monetization of accounting mirages. . . .

> So where does this leave the analyst who attempts to evaluate the financial performance of a firm using its financial statements? The answer is that one must indeed "look through" the numbers in the statements and seek to understand the subtle differences in accounting practice and the effect that they can have on reported earnings. Analyzing financial performance using accounting statements is not simply a mechanical process. It requires the analyst not only to "crunch the numbers" but to understand where the numbers came from.

With this caveat from one of the most successful investors ever, we begin our study of how to interpret and use a firm's financial statements.

WHAT'S AHEAD

Chapter 3 reviews the firm's basic financial statements and discusses the use of financial ratios to analyze them. The basic financial statements include the income statement, balance sheet, and cash flow statement. We first review the basic format of the firm's financial statements with particular attention given to the cash flow statement. This statement is important in financial analysis because it focuses on cash rather than income or profits. Our discussion of financial ratios incorporates four categories of ratios: firm liquidity, operating profitability, financing decisions, and return on equity. We conclude our discussion of financial statements analysis with an overview of an integrative approach to ratio analysis known as Du Pont analysis.

In Chapter 2, we looked at the workings of the financial markets. We found that these markets provide the means for bringing together investors (savers) with the users of capital (businesses that provide products and services to the consumer). There we looked at the world as the economist sees it, with an eye for understanding the marketplace where managers go to acquire capital. It is these financial markets that determine the value of a firm, and given our goal of maximizing shareholder value, no issue is more fundamental to our study. However, we now want to alter our perspective. In this chapter, we will see the world of finance more as the accountant sees it.

Although some might argue that the accountant has less to say to us than the economist, it is an undeniable fact that a significant part of the data used in financial management is provided by the accountant. We also know that this information is used mostly in planning, evaluating, and controlling a firm's financial performance and in measuring its cash flows. These issues are significant for several reasons. Remembering **Axiom 3,** we know that **Cash—Not Profits—Is King.** Although profit is thought to be important by many in finance, we will argue that the investor should assign a greater significance to the firm's cash flows.

Axiom 7 gives us our second reason for wanting to understand a company's financial position. This axiom tells us there may be a problem resulting from the conflict of interest that can develop between a firm's manager and its common stockholders (owners). Although the management is an agent of the owners, experience suggests that managers do not always act in the best interest of the owners.[1] The incentives for the managers are at times different from those of the owners. Thus, the firm's common stockholders, as well as other providers of capital (such as bankers), have a need for information that can be used to monitor the managers' actions. Be-

---

[1]See "Corporate Governance's Sorry History," *Wall Street Journal*, April 18, 1996, p. C1, and "Another Victory for Myopia," *The Economist*, December 2, 1995, pp. 19–22, for a discussion of this potential conflict of interest between managers and stockholders.

cause the owners of large companies do not have access to internal information about the firm's operations, they must rely on public information from any and all sources. One of the main sources of such information comes from the company's financial statements provided by the firm's accountants. Although this information is by no means perfect, it is an important source used by outsiders to assess a company's activities.

BACK TO THE FOUNDATIONS

Two axioms are especially important in this chapter: **Axiom 3** tells us that **Cash—Not Profits—Is King.** At times, cash is more important than profits. Thus, in this chapter, considerable time will be devoted to learning how to measure cash flows. **Axiom 7** warns us there may be a conflict between management and owners, especially in large firms where managers and owners have different incentives. That is, **Managers Won't Work for the Owners Unless It's in Their Best Interest** to do so. In this chapter, we will learn how to use data from the firm's public financial statements to monitor management's actions.

In addition to the investors, the managers themselves have a need for financial information to evaluate their decisions. If they are to have any hope of evaluating their own decisions and the decisions of others within their organization, they need to understand the financial consequences of their decisions. Only with this information can a financial decision maker plan and control activities within the firm effectively.[2]

PAUSE AND REFLECT

Financial statement analysis has probably been introduced in your basic accounting courses. However, the evaluation of financial performance is so important to the financial manager that a review is appropriate here.

OBJECTIVE 1

BASIC FINANCIAL STATEMENTS

As we set the stage for gaining a better understanding of financial management, it is imperative to know the "coin of the realm" used to describe a company's financial position. To a large extent, this "coin" is the firm's financial or accounting statements.

We can think of financial statements as consisting of certain pieces of important information about the firm's operations that are reported in the form of (1) an income statement, (2) a balance sheet, and (3) a cash flow statement. We will look at each of these statements in turn.

PAUSE AND REFLECT

The double-entry system of accounting used in this country dates back to about 3600 B.C., with the first published work describing the system by Luca Pacioli of Venice in A.D. 1494. Although the details of the double-entry system can be overwhelming to the novice, the mathematical content of these financial statements is straightforward and may be expressed as follows:

1. *Balance sheet or statement of financial position*
   liabilities + owner's equity = assets

---

[2]Chapter 4 develops the use of financial planning and control techniques based on the firm's pro forma or projected financial statements.

2. *Income statement or statement of results from operations*
   revenues + gains − expenses − losses = income
3. *Cash flow statement*
   cash inflow − cash outflow = change in cash

The Income Statement

An **income statement** *measures the financial results of a firm's operations for a specific period, such as a year.* It is helpful to think of the income statement as comprising four types of activities:

income statement

1. The cost of selling the product or service;
2. The cost of producing or acquiring the goods or services sold;
3. The expenses incurred in marketing and distributing the product or service to the customer, along with administrative operating expenses; and
4. The financing costs of doing business, for example, interest paid to creditors and dividend payments to the preferred stockholders.

These "income-statement activities" are represented graphically in Figure 3–1. In this figure, we observe that the top part of the income statement, beginning with sales

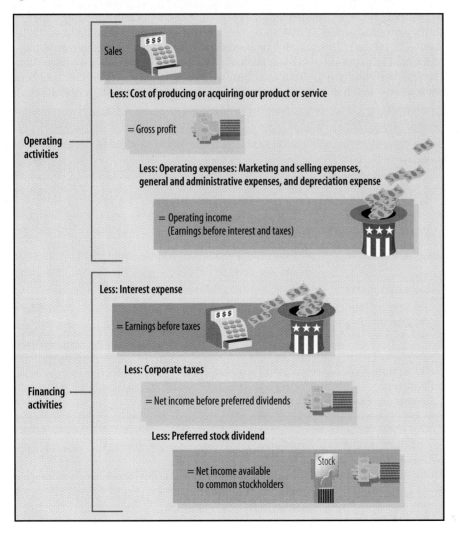

Figure 3–1
The Income Statement: An Overview

and continuing down through the **operating income** or **earnings before interest
and taxes,** is affected solely by the first three activities, or what is considered the
firm's operating activities. No financing costs are included to this point.

financing costs
earnings before taxes
tax expenses
net income available to common stockholders (net income)

Below the line reporting operating income, we see the results of the firm's financing decisions, along with the taxes that are due on the company's income. Here
the company's **financing costs** are shown, first in the form of *interest expenses* and
then *preferred dividends*. The tax rates imposed on the company's **earnings before
taxes** determine the amount of the *tax liability*, or the **tax expenses.**[3] The final
number, **net income available to common stockholders** (frequently just called **net
income**), is the *income that may be distributed to the company's owners or reinvested* in the company, provided of course there is cash available to do so. As we shall
see later, however, the fact that a firm has a positive net income does not necessarily mean it has any cash—possibly a surprising result to us, but one we shall come
to understand.

An example of an income statement is provided in Table 3–1 for the McDonald's
Corporation. As shown in the table, McDonald's had sales of $8,362 million for the 12-
month period ending December 31, 1994, and the cost of goods sold was $4,452 mil-
lion. (The numbers for McDonald's are expressed in millions, so McDonald's sales were
actually about $8.4 billion, with cost of goods sold of almost $4.5 billion.) The result
is a gross profit of $3,910 million ($3.9 billion). The firm then had $1,696 million in op-
erating expenses, which included selling or marketing expenses, general and administrative expenses, and depreciation expenses. After deducting operating expenses, the
firm's operating profits (earnings before interest and taxes) amounted to $2,214 mil-
lion ($2.2 billion). This amount represents the before-tax profits generated as if the
McDonald's Corporation were an all-equity company. To this point, we have calculated
the profits resulting only from operating activities, as opposed to financing decisions
such as how much debt or equity is used to finance the company's operations.[4]

Table 3–1
The McDonald's Corporation Income Statement for 1994 ($ Millions)

Sales		$8,362
Cost of goods sold		4,452
Gross profit		$3,910
Operating expenses:		
Marketing expenses and general and		
administrative expenses	$1,218	
Depreciation	478	
Total operating expenses		$1,696
Operating income		$2,214
Interest expense		373
Earnings before taxes		$1,841
Income taxes		662
Net income available to common stockholders		$1,179

Net income available to common stockholders	$1,179
Dividends	539
Change in retained earnings	$640

[3]Notice that interest is a tax-deductible expense, while preferred dividends are paid after taxes have
been calculated.

[4]The McDonald's Corporation financial statements presented in this chapter have been simplified considerably with some loss of accuracy in details but in so doing avoids unnecessary complexity.

We next deduct McDonald's interest expense (the amount paid for using debt financing) of $373 million to arrive at the company's earnings before tax of $1,841 million ($1.84 billion). Finally, we deduct the income taxes of $662 million to leave the net income available to common stockholders of $1,179 ($1.18 billion). At the bottom of the income statement, we also see the amount of common dividends paid by the firm to its owners in the amount of $539 million, leaving $640 million, which increases retained earnings in the firm's 1994 balance sheet.

The Balance Sheet

Whereas the income statement reports the results from operating the business for a period of time, such as a year, the **balance sheet** provides a *snapshot of the firm's financial position at a specific point in time*, presenting its asset holdings, liabilities, and owner-supplied capital. Assets represent the resources owned by the firm, whereas the liabilities and owners' equity indicate how those resources are financed.

balance sheet

The difference between the timing of an income statement and a balance sheet may be represented graphically as follows.

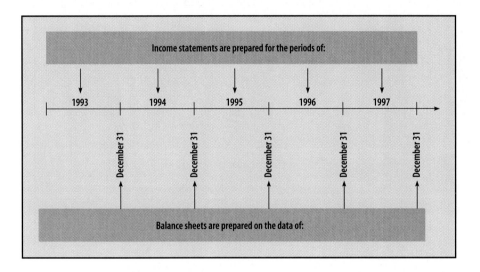

Here we see five periods of operations, 1993 through 1997. There would be an income statement for the period of January 1 through December 31 for each of the five years' operations and a balance sheet reporting the company's financial position as of December 31 of each year. Thus, the balance sheet on December 31, 1997, is a statement of the company's financial position at that particular date, which is the result of all financial transactions since the company began its operations.

Figure 3–2 on page 72 gives us the basic ingredients of a balance sheet. In the figure, the assets fall into three categories:

1. **Current assets**—consisting primarily of *cash, marketable securities, accounts receivable, inventories, and prepaid expenses*;
2. **Fixed or long-term assets**—comprising *equipment, buildings, and land*; and
3. **Other assets**—all assets not otherwise included in the firm's current assets or fixed assets, such as *patents, long-term investments in securities, and goodwill.*

current assets

fixed or long-term assets

other assets

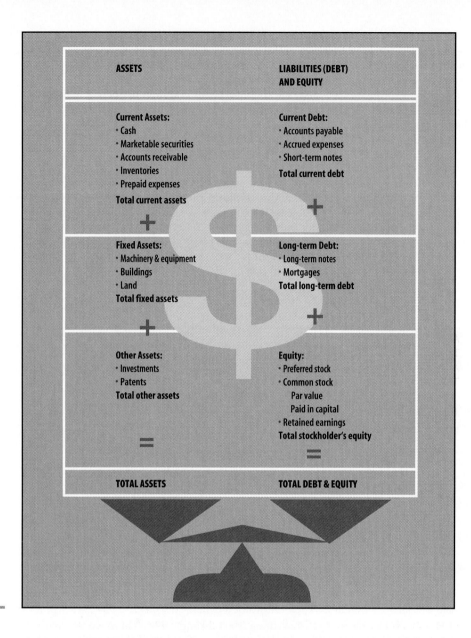

Figure 3–2
The Balance Sheet: An Overview

In reporting the dollar amounts of these various assets, the conventional practice is to report the value of the assets and liabilities on a historical cost basis. Thus, the balance sheet is not intended to represent the current market value of the company, but rather reports the historical transactions recorded at their cost. Determining a fair value of the business is a different matter.

The remaining part of the balance sheet (the right-hand side of Figure 3–2), headed "Liabilities and Equity," indicates how the firm has financed its investments in assets. The principal sources of financing are debt (liabilities) and equity. The **debt** consists of *such sources as credit extended from suppliers* (accounts payable) or a *loan from a bank* (including notes payable and mortgages). The **equity** includes the *stockholders' investment in the firm* (par value plus paid in capital) and the *cumulative profits retained in the business up to the date of the balance sheet,* or **retained earnings.**

Table 3–2
The McDonald's Corporation Balance Sheets for December 31, 1993 and 1994 ($ Millions)

ASSETS	1993	1994	CHANGE
Cash	$186	$180	$ (6)
Accounts receivables	315	379	64
Inventories	44	51	7
Prepaid expenses	119	131	12
Total current assets	$664	$741	$ 77
Gross fixed assets	$13,459	$15,185	$1,726
Accumulated depreciation	3,378	3,856	478
Net fixed assets	$10,081	$11,329	$1,248
Investments	537	659	122
Other assets	755	864	109
Total assets	$12,037	$13,593	$1,556
LIABILITIES AND EQUITY			
LIABILITIES			
Short-term notes payable	$ 223	$ 1,415	$1,192
Accounts payable	396	509	113
Taxes payable	56	25	(31)
Accrued expenses	429	502	73
Total current liabilities	$ 1,104	$ 2,451	$1,347
Long-term notes payable	4,659	4,199	(460)
Total liabilities	$ 5,763	$ 6,650	$ 887
EQUITY			
Common stock (par value and paid in capital)	$ 349	$ 378	$ 29
Retained earnings	5,925	6,565	640
Total equity	$ 6,274	$ 6,943	$ 669
Total liabilities and equity	$12,037	$13,593	$1,556

Balance sheets for the McDonald's Corporation are presented in Table 3–2 for both December 31, 1993, and December 31, 1994, along with the changes in each amount between years. By referring to the two balance sheets, we can see the financial position of the firm both at the beginning and end of 1994. Furthermore, by examining the two balance sheets, along with the income statement for 1994, we will have a more complete picture of the firm's operations. We are then able to see what McDonald's looked like at the beginning of 1994 (balance sheet on December 31, 1993), what happened during the year (income statement for 1994), and the final outcome at the end of the year (balance sheet on December 31, 1994). Our perspective of 1994 is shown graphically in Figure 3–3 on page 74.

The balance sheet data for the McDonald's Corporation show that the firm ended the prior year (1993) with about $12 billion ($12,037 million) in assets, compared to $13.6 billion ($13,593 million) a year later at the end of 1994. Most of this growth was in long-term assets, namely, an increase of $1.7 billion ($1,726 million) in gross plant and equipment, also called fixed assets. In the bottom half of the balance sheet, we should notice the growth in debt and equity primarily occurred in the short-term notes payable (an increase of $1,192 million), along with an increase in retained earnings of $640 million. These increases in debt (liabilities) and equity were offset in part by a decrease of $460 million in long-term notes payable.

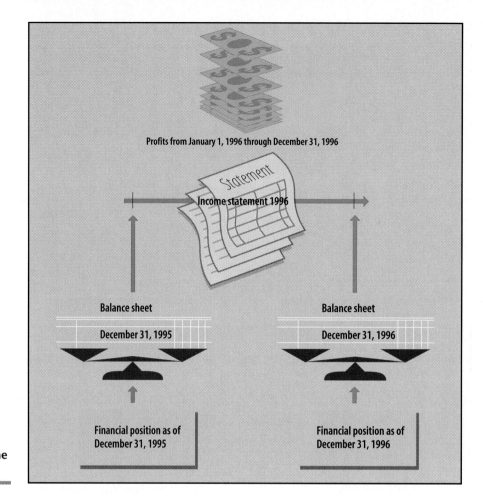

Figure 3–3
Visual Perspective of the Relationship between the McDonald's Corporation Balance Sheets and Income Statement

The Cash Flow Statement

PAUSE AND REFLECT

In this section, we will learn how to construct a firm's cash flow statement. We could limit our study to interpreting the statement and not get into the computations. However, experience suggests that our understanding of cash flows is limited if we do not know what drives the numbers. Also, without the computations, we will not be able to grasp the relationship between a firm's profits and its cash flows—an item of considerable importance.

cash flow statement

The final statement for consideration is the **cash flow statement,** which shows *the actual cash flows generated by the firm for the year.* The primary categories for this statement are presented in Figure 3–4. Here we see that the cash flows generated are divided into three main areas: (1) cash flows from operations, (2) investments made by the firm, and (3) financing transactions, such as issuing stock and borrowing or repaying debt.

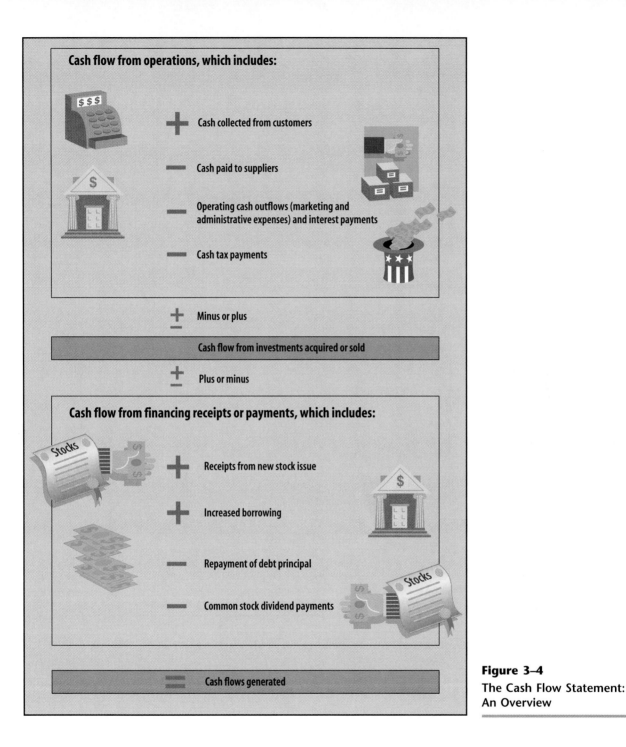

Cash flow from operations, which includes:

+ Cash collected from customers

− Cash paid to suppliers

− Operating cash outflows (marketing and administrative expenses) and interest payments

− Cash tax payments

± Minus or plus

Cash flow from investments acquired or sold

± Plus or minus

Cash flow from financing receipts or payments, which includes:

+ Receipts from new stock issue

+ Increased borrowing

− Repayment of debt principal

− Common stock dividend payments

= Cash flows generated

Figure 3–4
The Cash Flow Statement: An Overview

Table 3–3 on page 76 shows a cash flow statement for the McDonald's Corporation. The data needed to construct a cash flow statement come from two sources: (1) balance sheets for the beginning of 1994 (actually December 31, 1993) and the end of 1994, and (2) the income statement for 1994. Let's look at the computations required in determining the cash flow for McDonald's. To do so, we will need to make frequent use of the company's income statement (Table 3–1) and the balance sheets (Table 3–2).

Table 3–3

The McDonald's Corporation Cash Flow Statement for 1994
($ Millions)

Cash inflows received from customers		
Net sales	$ 8,362	
Less increase in accounts receivable	(64)	
Cash inflows from customers		$ 8,298
Cash paid to suppliers		
Cost of goods sold	$(4,452)	
Plus increase in inventory	(7)	
Less increase in accounts payable	113	
Cash paid to suppliers		$(4,346)
Other operating cash outflows		
Marketing expenses and general and administration expenses	$(1,218)	
Interest expense	(373)	
Plus increase in prepaid expenses	(12)	
Less increase in accrued expenses	73	
Other operating cash outflows		$(1,530)
Cash tax payments		
Provision for taxes	$ (662)	
Plus decrease in taxes payable	(31)	
Cash tax payments		$ (693)
Cash flows from operations		$ 1,729
Cash flow—investment activities		
Increase in gross plant and equipment	$(1,726)	
Increase in investments	(122)	
Increase in other assets	(109)	
Total investments		$(1,957)
Cash flow—financing activities		
Increase in short-term notes	$ 1,192	
Decrease in long-term notes	(460)	
Issue common stock	29	
Common stock dividends	(539)	
Total financial receipts		$ 222
Net change in cash		$ (6)

Cash Flows from Operations

cash flows from operations

As already noted, a firm's **cash flows from operations** consist of (1) *collections from customers*, (2) *payments to suppliers for the purchase of materials*, (3) *other operating cash outflows*, such as marketing and administrative expenses and interest payments, and (4) *cash tax payments.*

1. **Collections from customers.** Our beginning point is to determine how much the firm has collected from its customers. We know how much they sold (sales revenue), but we want to know what was actually collected in cash. To find this number, we simply take the firm's sales and subtract the change in accounts receivable. For example, if a firm were to have $200,000 in sales during a year, but its accounts receivable increased from $50,000 to $70,000, or by $20,000, that means that $20,000 of the sales were not collected. Thus, the firm's collections were only $180,000 ($200,000 − $20,000). For the McDonald's Corporation, sales were $8,362

million (about $8.4 billion), but accounts receivable increased $64 million from $315 million to $379 million. (See the change in accounts receivables in Table 3–2). Thus, actual collections were $8,298 million ($8.3 billion), calculated as $8.362 million less $64 million. So we see that the firm's sales and its cash collections from customers are essentially the same.

2. **Payments to suppliers.** When a firm purchases products from suppliers, the firm's inventories are increased. When the product is sold, the inventory decreases, and cost of goods sold in the income statement increases. Thus, total purchases of products from suppliers are reflected in the cost of goods sold plus any increase in inventories. Then the firm will either pay for the products or rely on additional credit from the supplier, which is shown in accounts payable in the balance sheet. The actual payment to suppliers may therefore be calculated as follows:

$$\begin{pmatrix} \text{payment} \\ \text{to suppliers} \end{pmatrix} = \begin{pmatrix} \text{cost of} \\ \text{goods sold} \end{pmatrix} + \begin{pmatrix} \text{change in} \\ \text{inventories} \end{pmatrix} - \begin{pmatrix} \text{change in} \\ \text{accounts} \\ \text{payable} \end{pmatrix} \qquad \textbf{(3–1)}$$

For McDonald's, the cost of goods sold for 1994 was $4,452 million ($4.45 billion); inventories increased from $44 million to $51 million, or by $7 million, and accounts payable increased $113 million, from $396 million to $509 million. Thus, payments to suppliers were $4.346 million, computed as follows:

$$\begin{pmatrix} \text{payment} \\ \text{to suppliers} \end{pmatrix} = \begin{pmatrix} \text{cost of} \\ \text{goods sold} \end{pmatrix} + \begin{pmatrix} \text{change in} \\ \text{inventories} \end{pmatrix} - \begin{pmatrix} \text{change in} \\ \text{accounts} \\ \text{payable} \end{pmatrix}$$
$$= \$4,452 + \$7 - \$113 \text{ million}$$
$$= \$4,346 \text{ million}$$

3. **Other operating cash outflows and interest payments.** We next calculate the actual cash outflows listed as operating expenses and interest expense in the income statement. We only include those operating expenses that are cash outflows and not such items as depreciation expense or other noncash items. In addition, we adjust as follows for the changes in prepaid expenses and accrued expenses:
   a. We add any changes in prepaid expenses; even though they have not been expensed on an accrual basis, they have been paid.
   b. We deduct the changes in accrued expenses and interest payable; although these items have been expensed, they have not yet been paid.
   We see in Table 3–3 that the other operating cash outflows for McDonald's came to $1,530 million, the combination of marketing expenses, general and administrative expenses (without any depreciation expense), interest expense, plus the $12 million increase in prepaid expenses, and less the $73 million increase in accrued expenses.[5]

4. **Cash tax payments.** The tax expense shown in a firm's income statement is oftentimes not the actual amount paid at that time. The provision for taxes in the income statement is the amount attributable to the income reported, but the company may be permitted to defer part of the payment. Thus, the cash payment would equal the provision for taxes reported in the income statement less (plus) any increase (decrease) in accrued or deferred taxes in the balance sheet. For the McDonald's Corporation, the cash tax payment is $693 million—the $662 in the pro-

---

[5]In the income statement, we made a point to compute operating income before deducting interest expenses; that is, operating income or earnings before interest and taxes represents the profits from operations without regard to financing costs, such as interest. Now when calculating cash flows from operations, we deduct interest payments. Why the inconsistency? The answer is that our cash flow statement follows the conventional format used by accountants.

vision for taxes in the income statement plus the $31 million decrease in taxes payable as reflected from a comparison of the two balance sheets in Table 3–2.

The final cash flows from operations are shown to be $1,729 million, the net change from the above cash flows ($8,298 − $4,346 − $1,530 − $693 million).

Cash Flows—Investment Activities

cash flows from investment activities

Now that we have calculated the cash flows that were generated from the day-to-day operations at McDonald's, we next want to determine *the amount of cash used for investments by the firm*—the **cash flows from investment activities.** As shown in Table 3–3, $1,957 million ($1.96 billion) was expended for investments during 1994, including $1,726 million ($1.73 billion) for fixed assets (an increase from $13,459 million to $15,185 million); plus the $122 million increase in investments ($659 − $537 million) and the $109 million increase in other assets ($864 − $755 million).

Cash Flows—Financing Activities

cash flows from financing activities

The last area is **cash flows from financing activities,** including any *cash inflows or outflows to or from the firm's investors, both lenders of debt and owners.* For the McDonald's Corporation, the firm received a net positive cash flow from financing activities in the amount of $222 million. The company borrowed an additional $1,192 million ($1.2 billion) in short-term debt, decreased the firm's long-term debt (a cash outflow) by $460 million, issued $29 million in common stock, and paid $539 million in common stock dividends.

We may now summarize the cash flows for the McDonald's Corporation as follows:

Cash flows from operations		
Collections from customers	$8,298	
Payments to suppliers	(4,346)	
Other operating cash flows	(1,530)	
Cash tax payments	(693)	
Total cash flows from operations		$1,729
Cash flows—investment activities		(1,957)
Cash flows—financing activities		222
Total cash flows		($6)

Thus, the total cash flows generated by the McDonald's Corporation from all its activities come to a negative $6 million in 1994. (We should also note that the firm's change in cash balances is shown in the 1993 and 1994 balance sheets decreased by that exact amount as well.)

Measuring Cash Flows from Operations: An Alternative Approach

direct method

The format used in Table 3–3 to measure cash flow from operations is called the **direct method.** It *begins with the cash flow collected from the firm's customers and then subtracts the different cash outflows occurring in regular operations of the business,* such as the money paid to suppliers and for employee wages, just to mention two examples. We could also measure cash flow from operations by the **indirect method.** This approach, which gives us the same answer as the direct method,

indirect method

is shown for the McDonald's Corporation in Table 3–4. In this table, we see that the indirect method *begins with net income and then adds back all expenses related to the firm's operations that did not result in a cash outflow for the period.* So, in a sense, the two methods for arriving at cash flow from operations differ only in terms of whether we start at the top (direct method) or the bottom (indirect method) of the income statement. Both methods simply convert the firm's statement of net income to its cash flow equivalent.

The McDonald's Corporation: What Have We Learned?

Based on our review of the McDonald's Corporation's financial statements, we can now draw some conclusions. To this point, we have learned that:

- The firm has used its cash flows from operations and from new financing to expand the asset base of the company.
- The main sources of new financing for the firm came from borrowing short term.
- McDonald's has little in the way of current assets, especially accounts receivable and inventory. Most of the firm's investments are in fixed assets.
- The primary use of the firm's cash flows during 1994 went to investing in fixed assets and reducing long-term debt.

To better understand the small investment in accounts receivable and inventories and the large amounts in fixed assets, we have to think about the nature of McDonald's business. For a restaurant business, inventories will be small—you don't want to keep a lot of lettuce on hand. Also, many of the restaurants are owned by franchisees and not the McDonald's Corporation itself; thus, McDonald's has no inventory whatsoever related to these units. Regarding accounts receivable, the business is largely a cash operation, with the receivables being primarily money owed the firm by the franchises. On the other hand, the McDonald's Corporation owns the real estate for all the stores, whether company-owned or a franchise, which explains the large amount of fixed assets. So by looking at the financial statements for the McDonald's Corporation, we have gained a better understanding of the business.

Table 3–4
The Indirect Method for Measuring Cash Flows from Operations
The McDonald's Corporation for Year Ending December 31, 1994
($ Millions)

Net income available to common stockholders (from the income statement)		$1,179
Add (deduct) to reconcile net income to net cash flow		
Depreciation expense		478
Less		
Increase in accounts receivable	$(64)	
Increase in inventories	(7)	
Increase in prepaid expenses	(12)	(83)
Plus		
Increase in accounts payable	113	
Increase in accrued expenses	73	
Increase (less decrease) in taxes payable	(31)	155
Cash flows from operations		$1,729

Profits and Cash Flows

As a final thought about measuring cash flows, there is a popular belief that income plus depreciation is a reasonable measure of a company's cash flows. For instance, taking net income available to common stockholders for McDonald's of $1,179 million and adding back depreciation of $478 million gives us $1,657 million. Given conventional thought, someone might be tempted to use this amount as an estimate of the firm's cash flows. However, from the cash flow statement, we can see that the cash flows actually decreased $6 million. Thus, we can conclude that calculating a firm's cash flow is more complicated than merely adding depreciation expense back to net income. The changes in asset balances resulting from growth are just as important in determining the firm's cash flows as is profits, maybe even more important sometimes. Hence, management, particularly of a growth company, is well advised not to limit its attention to profits, but also focus on cash flows, because they are not the same thing.

Interpreting the Cash Flow Statement

As already noted, there are three basic categories of activities related to a firm's cash flows, these being

- Cash flows from operations
- Cash flows related to the investment or sale of assets (investment activities)
- Cash flows related to financing the firm (financing activities)

To help us understand the basic nature of a firm's cash flows, consider the following cash flow patterns with respect to the above three categories:

	CASH FLOW RELATED TO		
CASH FLOW PATTERN	OPERATIONS	INVESTMENTS	FINANCING
1	+	−	+
2	+	+	−
3	+	−	−
4	−	+	+

For example, a firm with cash flow pattern 1, as is the case of McDonald's, has positive cash flows from operations, negative investment cash flows, and positive cash flows from financing. How would we describe this company? It is a firm that is using its cash flows from operations and new financing to expand the firm's operations. On the other hand, a company with cash flow pattern 2 is one that is using its positive cash flows from operations and selling off assets to pay down debt and pay owners. Cash flow pattern 3 depicts a firm that is using cash flows from operations to expand the business and to pay down debt and pay owners. Finally, cash flow pattern 4 describes a company that is encountering cash flow problems from operations, which are being covered by selling assets and by borrowing more and/or acquiring more equity financing. There are obviously other possible cash flow patterns—four to be exact—but the above cash flow patterns are sufficient to see the process to be used in interpreting the cash flow statement.[6]

---

[6]For a more complete discussion of these cash flow patterns, see Benton E. Gup, William D. Samson, Michael T. Dugan, Myung J. Kim, and Thawatfchai Jittrapanun, "An Analysis of the Statement of Cash Flow Patterns," *Financial Practice and Education*, Fall 1993, pp. 72–79.

To this point, we have examined financial statements in absolute dollar terms for the purpose of coming to understand a firm's financial position. We chose to use the financial statements for the McDonald's Corporation to illustrate the format and content of the statements. We next want to restate the *accounting data in relative terms*, or what we call **financial ratios.** Financial ratios help us identify some of the financial strengths and weaknesses of a company. The ratios give us two ways of making meaningful comparisons of a firm's financial data: (1) we can examine the ratios across time (say for the last five years) to identify any trends; and (2) we can compare the firm's ratios with those of other firms.

financial ratios

In making a comparison of our firm with other companies, we could select a peer group of companies, or we could use industry norms published by firms such as Dun & Bradstreet, Robert Morris Associates, Standard & Poor's, and Prentice Hall. Dun & Bradstreet, for instance, annually publishes a set of 14 key ratios for each of 125 lines of business. Robert Morris Associates, the association of bank loan and credit officers, publishes a set of 16 key ratios for more than 350 lines of business. In both cases, the ratios are classified by industry and by firm size to provide the basis for more meaningful comparisons.

PAUSE AND REFLECT

Mathematically, a financial ratio is nothing more than a ratio whose numerator and denominator are comprised of financial data. Sound simple? Well, in concept it is. The objective in using a ratio when analyzing financial information is simply to standardize the information being analyzed so that comparisons can be made between ratios of different firms or possibly the same firm at different points in time. So try to keep this in mind as you read through the discussion of financial ratios. All we are doing is trying to standardize financial data so that we can make comparisons with industry norms or other standards.

In learning about ratios, we could simply study the different types or categories of ratios, or we could use ratios to answer some important questions about a firm's operations. We prefer the latter approach and choose the following four questions as a map in using financial ratios:

1. How liquid is the firm?
2. Is management generating adequate *operating* profits on the firm's assets?
3. How is the firm financing its assets?
4. Are the owners (stockholders) receiving an adequate return on *their* investment?

Let's look at each of these questions in turn. In doing so, we will use the balance sheet (Table 3–2) and the income statement (Table 3–3) for the McDonald's Corporation to demonstrate how these questions can be answered.

Question 1: How liquid is the firm?

The **liquidity** of a business is defined as its *ability to meet maturing debt obligations.* That is, does or will the firm have the resources to pay the creditors when the debt comes due?

liquidity

There are two ways to approach the liquidity question. First, we can look at the firm's assets that are relatively liquid in nature and compare them to the amount of the debt coming due in the near term.[7] Second, we can look at how quickly the firm's liquid assets are being converted into cash.

Measuring Liquidity: Approach 1

The first approach compares (a) cash and the assets that should be converted into cash within the year with (b) the debt (liabilities) that is coming due and payable within the year. The assets here are the *current assets*, and the debt is the *current liabilities* in the balance sheet. Thus, we could use the following measure, called the **current ratio,** to estimate a company's relative liquidity:

current ratio

$$\text{current ratio} = \frac{\text{current assets}}{\text{current liabilities}} \qquad (3\text{--}2)$$

Furthermore, remembering that the three primary current assets include (1) cash, (2) accounts receivable, and (3) inventories, we could make our measure of liquidity more restrictive by *excluding inventories*, the least liquid of the current assets, in the numerator. This revised ratio is called the **acid-test** (or **quick**) **ratio,** and is calculated as follows:

acid-test (quick) ratio

$$\text{acid-test ratio} = \frac{\text{current assets} - \text{inventories}}{\text{current liabilities}} \qquad (3\text{--}3)$$

To demonstrate how to compute the current ratio and acid-test ratio, we will use the 1994 balance sheet for the McDonald's Corporation (refer to Table 3–2). To have a standard for comparison, we could use industry norms published by Dun & Bradstreet or any of the other sources mentioned above. However, we had difficulty at finding industry norms that we thought represented comparable companies—not an unusual problem in practice. Thus, we chose instead to calculate the average ratios for a group of similar firms or what could be called a *peer group*. The results for these first two ratios are as follows:

	McDonald's Corporation	Peer-Group Average
current ratio $= \dfrac{\text{current assets}}{\text{current liabilities}}$		
$= \dfrac{\$741M}{\$2,451M} = 0.30$		0.90
acid-test ratio $= \dfrac{\text{current assets} - \text{inventories}}{\text{current liabilities}}$		
$= \dfrac{\$741M - \$51M}{\$2,451M} = 0.28$		0.62

So, in terms of the current ratio and acid-test ratio, McDonald's is significantly less liquid than the average peer-group firm. McDonald's only has $0.30 in current assets for every $1 in current liabilities (debt), compared to $0.90 for comparable firms, and only $0.28 in current assets less inventories per $1 of current debt, compared to $0.62 for the peer group. Given the conventional wisdom that firms should maintain about $2 in current assets for every $1 in current debt—an idea that fails to recognize the unique needs of various companies—McDonald's, and even the industry itself, is less liquid than most other companies.

---

[7]This approach has long been used in the finance community; however, it really measures solvency, not liquidity. A firm is solvent when its assets exceed its liabilities, which is in essence what we will be measuring by this approach. For an in-depth discussion of this issue, see Chapter 2 of Terry S. Maness and John T. Zietlow, *Short-Term Financial Management* (New York: Dryden Press, 1997).

Measuring Liquidity: Approach 2

The second view of liquidity examines the firm's ability to convert accounts receivable and inventory into cash on a timely basis. The conversion of accounts receivable into cash may be measured by computing *how long it takes to collect the firm's receivables*; that is, how many days of sales are outstanding in the form of accounts receivable? We can answer this question by computing the **average collection period:** average collection period

$$\text{average collection period} = \frac{\text{accounts receivable}}{\text{daily credit sales}} \qquad \textbf{(3–4)}$$

If we assume all the McDonald's Corporation's 1994 sales ($8,362 million in Table 3–1) to be credit sales, as opposed to some cash sales, then the firm's average collection period is 16.5 days, compared to a peer-group norm of 6 days:

McDonald's Corporation	Peer-Group Average
$\dfrac{\text{average collection}}{\text{period}} = \dfrac{\text{accounts receivable}}{\text{daily credit sales}}$	
$= \dfrac{\$379M}{\$8,362M \div 365} = 16.5 \text{ days}$	6 days

Thus, McDonald's does not collect its receivables as quickly as the average firm in the comparison group—16.5 days compared to only 6 days for the industry. The short collection period for the industry is undoubtedly the result of being in the restaurant industry, which has more cash sales than most industries. By our using total sales, as opposed to credit sales, in our calculation, we have understated the actual collection period, both for McDonald's and for the industry. Nevertheless, the fact remains that McDonald's does extend longer credit terms than do its competitors.

We could have reached the same conclusion by measuring *how many times accounts receivable are "rolled over" during a year*, or the **accounts receivable turnover ratio.** For instance, the McDonald's Corporation turns its receivables over 22.1 times a year.[8] accounts receivable turnover ratio

McDonald's Corporation	Peer-Group Average
$\dfrac{\text{accounts}}{\text{receivable}} = \dfrac{\text{credit sales}}{\text{accounts receivable}}$ turnover	$\textbf{(3–5)}$
$= \dfrac{\$8,362M}{\$379M} = 22.1 \text{ times/year}$	60.81 times/year

Whether we use the average collection period or the accounts receivable turnover ratio, the conclusion is the same. The McDonald's Corporation is slower at collecting its receivables than competing firms.[9]

We now want to know the same thing for inventories that we just determined for accounts receivable: *How many times are we turning over inventories during the year?* In this manner, we gain some insight into the liquidity of inventories. The **inventory turnover ratio** is calculated as follows: inventory turnover ratio

---

[8]We could also measure the accounts receivable turnover by dividing 365 days by the average collection period: 365/16.5 = 22.1.

[9]Although it will not be discussed here, one tool for further assessing the liquidity of a firm's receivables is an aging of accounts receivable schedule. Such a schedule identifies the number and dollar value of accounts outstanding for various periods. For example, accounts that are less than 10 days old, 11 to 20 days, and so forth might be examined. Still another way to construct the schedule would involve analyzing the length of time to eventual collection of accounts over a past period. For example, how many accounts were outstanding less than 10 days when collected, between 10 and 20 days, and so forth.

$$\text{inventory turnover} = \frac{\text{cost of goods sold}}{\text{inventory}} \qquad \textbf{(3–6)}$$

Note that sales in this ratio is replaced by cost of goods sold. Since the inventory (the denominator) is measured at cost, we want to use a cost-based measure of sales in the numerator. Otherwise, our answer would vary from one firm to the next solely due to differences in how each firm marks up its sales over costs.[10]

Given that the McDonald's Corporation's cost of goods sold was $4,452 million (Table 3–1) and its inventory was $51 million (Table 3–2) the firm's 1994 inventory turnover, along with the peer-group average, is as follows:

McDonald's Corporation	**Peer-Group Average**
$\dfrac{\text{inventory}}{\text{turnover}} = \dfrac{\text{cost of goods sold}}{\text{inventory}}$	
$= \dfrac{\$4,452\text{M}}{\$51\text{M}} = 87.3 \text{ times/year}$	56.3 times/year

Given the above results, we can conclude that McDonald's is clearly excellent in its management of inventory, turning its inventory over 87.3 times per year compared to 56.3 times for the peer group. In other words, McDonald's sells its inventory in 4.2 days on average (365 days ÷ 87.3 times), while the average firm takes 6.5 days (365 days ÷ 56.3 times).

Thus, when it comes to McDonald's liquidity, we see that the firm has low current and acid-test ratios, but that the firm collects its receivables in about 17 days and turns its inventory over 87 times per year, indicating that these assets are relatively liquid.

Question 2: Is management generating adequate operating profits on the firm's assets?

We now begin a different line of thinking that will carry us through all the remaining questions. At this point, we want to know if the profits are sufficient relative to the assets being invested. The question is similar to a question one might ask about the interest being earned on a savings account at the bank. When you invest $1,000 in a savings account and receive $40 in interest during the year, you are earning a 4 percent return on your investment ($40 ÷ $1,000 = .04 = 4%). With respect to the McDonald's Corporation, we want to know something similar: the rate of return management is earning on the firm's assets.

In answering this question, we have several choices as to how we measure profits: gross profits, operating profits, or net income. Gross profits would not be an acceptable choice because it does not include some important information, such as the cost of marketing and distributing the firm's product. Thus, we should choose between operating profits and net income. For our purposes, we prefer to use operating profits, because this measure of firm profits is calculated before the costs of the company's financing policies have been deducted. Because financing is explicitly considered in our next question, we want to isolate only the operating aspects of the company's profits at this point. In this way, we are able to compare the profitability of firms with different debt-to-equity mixes. Therefore, to examine the *level of operating profits relative to the assets*, we would use the **operating income return on investment** (OIROI):

operating income return on investment

$$\frac{\text{operating income}}{\text{return on investment}} = \frac{\text{operating income}}{\text{total assets}} \qquad \textbf{(3–7)}$$

---

[10]Whereas our logic may be correct to use cost of goods sold in the numerator, practicality may dictate that we use sales instead. Some suppliers of peer-group norm data use sales in the numerator. Thus, for consistency in our comparisons, we too may need to use sales.

The operating income return on investment for the McDonald's Corporation for 1994 (based on the financial data in Table 3–1 and Table 3–2), and the corresponding peer-group norm, are shown below:

McDonald's Corporation	**Peer-Group Average**

$$\begin{array}{c} \text{operating income} \\ \text{return on investment} \end{array} = \frac{\text{operating income}}{\text{total assets}}$$

$$= \frac{\$2,214M}{\$13,593M} = .163 = 16.3\% \qquad\qquad 13.2\%$$

Hence, we see that the McDonald's Corporation is earning an above-average return on investment relative to the average firm in the peer group. Management is generating more income on $1 of assets than similar firms.[11]

If we were the managers of the McDonald's Corporation, we should not be satisfied with merely knowing that we are earning more than a competitive return on the firm's assets. We should also want to know *why we are above average*. To understand this issue, we may separate the operating income return on investment, OIROI, into two important pieces: the operating profit margin and the total asset turnover. The firm's OIROI is a multiple of these two ratios and may be shown algebraically as follows:

$$\text{OIROI} = \left(\begin{array}{c}\text{operating}\\\text{profit margin}\end{array}\right) \times \left(\begin{array}{c}\text{total asset}\\\text{turnover}\end{array}\right) \qquad \textbf{(3–8a)}$$

or more completely,

$$\text{OIROI} = \frac{\text{operating income}}{\text{sales}} \times \frac{\text{sales}}{\text{total assets}} \qquad \textbf{(3–8b)}$$

The first component of the OIROI, the **operating profit margin,** is an extremely important variable in understanding a *company's operating profitability*. It is important that we know exactly what drives this ratio. In coming to understand the ratio, think about the makeup of the ratio, which may be expressed as follows:

operating profit margin

$$\frac{\text{operating income}}{\text{sales}} =$$

$$\frac{\text{total sales} - \text{cost of goods sold} - \begin{array}{c}\text{general and}\\\text{administrative}\\\text{expenses}\end{array} - \begin{array}{c}\text{marketing}\\\text{expenses}\end{array}}{\text{sales}}$$

Because total sales equals the number of units sold times the sales price per unit, and the cost of goods sold equals the number of units sold times the cost of goods sold per unit, we may conclude that the driving forces of the operating profit margin are the following:

1. The number of units of product sold;[12]
2. The average selling price for each product unit;
3. The cost of manufacturing or acquiring the firm's product;

---

[11]The **return on assets** (ROA) is often used as an indicator of a firm's profitability and is measured as follows: return on assets = net income ÷ total assets.

return on assets

We choose not to use this ratio because *net income* is influenced both by operating decisions and how the firm is financed. We want to restrict our attention only to operating activities; financing is considered later in questions 3 and 4. Nevertheless, sometimes the peer-group norm for operating income return on investment is not available. Instead, return on assets is provided. If so, we have no option but to use the return on assets for measuring the firm's profitability.

[12]The number of units affects the operating profit margin only if some of the firm's costs and expenses are fixed. If a company's expenses are all variable in nature, then the ratio would not change as the number of units sold increases or decreases, because the numerator and the denominator would change at the same rate.

Intel Announces Lower Than Expected Profits

The following excerpts were taken from an article appearing in the *Wall Street Journal* regarding Intel's announcement that the firm's profits would not be as good as expected. The reason: lower profit margins as a result of carrying too much inventory. Don Clark, the author of the article, suggests that the firm's stock will be negatively affected.

Intel, based in Santa Clara, California, said profits were hurt because it bought too many memory chips for use in motherboards, the circuit boards

that contain most electronic components in PCs. Andrew Grove, Intel's chief executive officer, said the company took unusually large write downs that totaled about $70 million.

Intel said the write downs helped push down its gross profit margin (gross profit ÷ sales) to 48 percent from 52 percent in the preceding quarter. Looking ahead, the company projected that margins will stay in the "high 40s" in the first quarter [1996].

Those comments are expected to be another blow to investors, who have hammered high-tech stocks in general recently and have been particularly tough on Intel. Intel's stock is down more than 40% since July [1995], and investors were especially nervous about the fourth-quarter report.

Source: Excerpts taken from Don Clark, "Intel Confirms Investors Worries," *Wall Street Journal*, January 17, 1996, p. A3, A5.

---

4. The ability to control general and administrative expenses; and
5. The ability to control expenses in marketing and distributing the firm's product.

These influences are also apparent simply by looking at the income statement and thinking about what is involved in determining the firm's operating profits or income.[13]

total asset turnover

As shown in Equation 3–8b, the **total asset turnover** is the second component of the operating income return on investment. *The total asset turnover measures the dollar sales per one dollar of assets.* The ratio is calculated as follows:

$$\frac{\text{Total asset}}{\text{turnover}} = \frac{\text{sales}}{\text{total assets}} \qquad (3\text{--}9)$$

This ratio indicates how efficiently a firm is using its assets in generating sales. For instance, if Company A can generate $3 in sales with $1 in assets, compared to $2 in sales per asset dollar for Company B, we may say that Company A is using its assets more efficiently in generating sales, which is a major determinant in the firm's operating income return on investment.

Let's again return to the McDonald's Corporation to apply the above concepts. Continuing to rely on the firm's financial statements in Table 3–1 and Table 3–2, we can compute the operating profit margin and total asset turnover for McDonald's as follows:

net profit margin

---

[13]We could have used the **net profit margin,** rather than the operating profit margin, which is measured as follows: net profit margin = net income ÷ sales.

The net profit margin *measures the amount of net income per one dollar of sales.* However, because net income includes both operating expenses and interest expense, this ratio is influenced both by operating activities and financing activities. We prefer to defer the effect of financing decisions until questions 3 and 4, which follow shortly.

	McDonald's Corporation	**Peer-Group Average**

$$\text{operating profit margin} = \frac{\text{operating income}}{\text{sales}}$$

$$= \frac{\$2,214\text{M}}{\$8,362\text{M}} = .265 = 26.5\% \qquad\qquad 8\%$$

	McDonald's Corporation	**Peer-Group Average**

$$\text{total asset turnover} = \frac{\text{sales}}{\text{total assets}}$$

$$= \frac{\$8,362\text{M}}{\$13,593\text{M}} = 0.62 \qquad\qquad 1.64$$

Recalling that:

$$\text{OIROI} = \left(\begin{array}{c}\text{operating} \\ \text{profit margin}\end{array}\right) \times \left(\begin{array}{c}\text{total asset} \\ \text{turnover}\end{array}\right)$$

we see that for the McDonald's Corporation,

$$\text{OIROI}_{\text{McD}} = 26.5\% \times 0.62 = .163 = 16.3\%$$

and for the peer group, this same ratio is

$$\text{OIROI}_{\text{pg}} = 8\% \times 1.64 = .132 = 13.2\%$$

Clearly, the McDonald's Corporation is more than competitive when it comes to keeping costs and expenses in line relative to sales, as is reflected by the operating profit margin. In other words, management is extremely effective in managing the five driving forces of the operating profit margin listed above. In terms of its high operating profit margin, McDonald's has no equal. However, when we look at the total asset turnover, we can see that the firm is not using its assets efficiently. The McDonald's Corporation generates only about $.62 in sales per dollar of assets, whereas the competition produces $1.64 in sales from every dollar in assets.

We should not stop here with our analysis of McDonald's asset utilization; we should dig deeper. We have concluded that the assets are not being used efficiently, but now we should try to determine which assets are the problem. Are we overinvested in all assets or more so in accounts receivable or inventory or fixed assets? To answer this question, we merely examine the turnover ratios for the primary assets held by the firm—accounts receivables, inventories, and fixed assets. We have already calculated these ratios for accounts receivable and inventories, which are repeated as follows:

	McDonald's Corporation	**Peer-Group Average**

Accounts receivable turnover:

$$\frac{\text{credit sales}}{\text{accounts receivable}} = \frac{\$8,362\text{M}}{\$379\text{M}} = 22.1 \qquad\qquad 60.8$$

Inventory turnover:

$$\frac{\text{cost of goods sold}}{\text{inventory}} = \frac{\$4,452\text{M}}{\$51\text{M}} = 87.3 \qquad\qquad 56.3$$

We next calculate a firm's fixed assets turnover ratio as follows:

$$\text{fixed assets turnover} = \frac{\text{sales}}{\text{fixed assets}} \qquad\qquad \text{(3–10)}$$

For the McDonald's Corporation:

	Peer-Group Average

$$\frac{\text{sales}}{\text{net fixed assets}} = \frac{\$8,362\text{M}}{\$11,329\text{M}} = 0.74 \qquad\qquad 2.0$$

McDonald's Corporations' situation is now clearer. The company has excessive accounts receivables, which we had known from our earlier discussions, and also there is too large an investment in fixed assets for the sales being produced. It would appear that these two asset categories are not being managed well, and the consequence is a lower overall or total asset turnover ratio. Moreover, given the far greater amount invested in fixed assets ($11.3 billion) than accounts receivable ($379 million)—see the balance sheet in Table 3–2—the heart of the problem is with the firm's large amount of fixed assets relative to the firm's sales.

Question 3: How is the firm financing its assets?

We now turn for the moment to the matter of how the firm is financed. (We shall return to the firm's profitability shortly.) The basic issue is the use of debt versus equity: Do we finance the assets more by debt or equity? In answering this question, we will use two ratios. (Many more could be used.) First, we simply ask *what percentage of the firm's assets are financed by debt*, including *both* short-term and long-term debt, realizing the remaining percentage must be financed by equity. We would compute the **debt ratio** as follows:[14]

debt ratio

$$\text{debt ratio} = \frac{\text{total debt}}{\text{total assets}} \qquad \textbf{(3–11)}$$

For the McDonald's Corporation, debt as a percentage of total assets is 49 percent (taken from McDonald's balance sheet in Table 3–2) compared to a peer-group norm of 66 percent. The computation is as follows:

McDonald's Corporation	**Peer-Group Average**
$\text{debt ratio} = \dfrac{\text{total debt}}{\text{total assets}}$	
$= \dfrac{\$6,650\text{M}}{\$13,593\text{M}} = .49 = 49\%$	66%

Thus, the McDonald's Corporation uses significantly less debt than the average firm in the peer group.

Our second perspective regarding the firm's financing decisions comes by looking at the income statement. When we borrow money, there is a minimum requirement that the firm pay the interest on the debt. Thus, it is informative to compare the amount of operating income that is available to service the interest with the amount of interest that is to be paid. Stated as a ratio, we compute *the number of times we are earning our interest*. Thus, a **times interest earned** ratio is commonly used when examining the firm's debt position and is computed in the following manner:

times interest earned

$$\text{times interest earned} = \frac{\text{operating income}}{\text{interest}} \qquad \textbf{(3–12)}$$

Based on the income statement for the McDonald's Corporation (Table 3–1), the firm's times interest earned is 5.94, computed as follows:

McDonald's Corporation	**Peer-Group Average**
$\text{times interest earned} = \dfrac{\text{operating income}}{\text{interest}}$	
$= \dfrac{\$2,214\text{M}}{\$373\text{M}} = 5.94$	4.0

[14]We will often see the relationship stated in terms of debt to equity, or the debt-equity ratio, rather than debt to total assets. We come to the same conclusion with either ratio.

Thus, the McDonald's Corporation is able to service its interest expense without any great difficulty. In fact, the firm's operating income could fall to as little as one-sixth (1/5.94) its current level and still have the income to pay the required interest. We should remember, however, that interest is not paid with income but with cash and that the firm may be required to repay some of the debt principal as well as the interest. Thus, the times interest earned is only a crude measure of the firm's capacity to service its debt. Nevertheless, it does give us a general indication of a company's debt capacity.

Question 4: Are the owners (stockholders) receiving an adequate return on their investment?

Our one remaining question looks at the *accounting return on the common stock-holders' investment* or **return on common equity;** that is, we want to know if the earnings available to the firm's owners or common equity investors is attractive when compared to the returns of owners of companies in the peer-group.

return on common equity

We measure the return to the owners as follows:

$$\text{return on common equity} = \frac{\text{net income}}{\text{common equity (including par, paid in capital and retained earnings)}} \qquad (3\text{--}13)$$

The return on common equity for the McDonald's Corporation and the peer group are 17 percent and 20 percent, respectively:

McDonald's Corporation	**Peer-Group Average**

$$\frac{\text{return}}{\text{on common equity}} = \frac{\text{net income}}{\text{common equity}}$$

$$\frac{\$1,179}{\$6,943} = .17 = 17\% \qquad\qquad 20\%$$

It would appear that the owners of the McDonald's Corporation are not receiving a return on their investment equivalent to what owners involved with competing businesses receive. However, we should also ask, "Why not?" To answer, we need to draw on what we have already learned, namely that:

1. The McDonald's Corporation is more profitable in its operations than its competitors. (Remember, the operating income return on investment, OIROI, was 16.3 percent for McDonald's compared to 13.2 percent for the competition.) Thus, this fact would suggest that McDonald's should have a higher, not a lower, return on common equity.

2. McDonald's uses considerably less debt (more equity) financing than does the average firm in the peer group. As we will see shortly, the more debt a firm uses, the higher its return on equity will be, provided that the firm is earning a return on investment greater than its cost of debt. Thus, the competition, on average, provides a higher return for its shareholders by using more debt, not by being better at generating profits on the firm's assets. That's the good news. The bad news for the competitors' shareholders is the more debt a firm uses, the greater the company's financial risk, which translates to more risk for the shareholders as well.

To help us understand the foregoing conclusion about the reason for McDonald's lower return on common equity and its implications, consider the following example.

THE EFFECT OF USING DEBT ON NET INCOME: AN EXAMPLE

Firms A and B are identical in size, both having $1,000 in total assets and both having an operating income return on investment of 14 percent. However, they are different in one respect: Firm A uses no debt, but Firm B finances 60 percent of its investments with debt at an interest cost of 10 percent. For the sake of simplicity, we will assume there are no income taxes. The financial statements for the two companies would be as follows:

	FIRM A	FIRM B
Total assets	$1,000	$1,000
Debt (10% interest rate)	$ 0	$ 600
Equity	1,000	400
Total	$1,000	$1,000
Operating income (OIROI = 14%)	$ 140	$ 140
Interest expense (10%)	0	60
Net profit	$ 140	$ 80

Computing the return on common equity for both companies, we see that Firm B has a much more attractive return to its owners, 20 percent compared to Firm A's 14 percent:

$$\text{return on equity} = \frac{\text{net income}}{\text{common equity}}$$

$$\text{Firm A: } = \frac{\$140}{\$1,000} = .14 = 14\% \quad \text{Firm B: } \frac{\$80}{\$400} = .20 = 20\%$$

Why the difference? The answer is straightforward. Firm B is earning 14 percent on its investments, but is only having to pay 10 percent for its borrowed money. The difference between the return on the firm's investments and the interest rate, 14 percent less the 10 percent, goes to the owners, thus boosting Firm B's return on equity above that of Firm A. We are seeing the results of *favorable* financial leverage at work, where we borrow at 10 percent and invest at 14 percent. The result is an increase in the return on equity.

If debt enhances the owners' returns, why would we not use lots of it all the time? We may continue our example to find the answer. Assume now that the economy falls into a deep recession, business declines sharply, and Firms A and B only earn a 6 percent operating income return on investment. Let's recompute the return on common equity now.

	FIRM A	FIRM B
Operating income (OIROI = 6%)	$60	$60
Interest expense	0	60
Net profit	$60	$ 0

$$\text{Firm A: } \frac{\$60}{\$1,000} = .06 = 6\% \qquad \text{Firm B: } \frac{\$0}{\$400} = .00 = 0\%$$

Now the use of leverage has a negative influence on the return on equity, with Firm B earning less than Firm A for its owners. This results from the fact that now Firm B earns less than the interest rate of 10 percent; consequently, the equity investors have to make up the difference. Thus, financial leverage is a two-edged sword; when times are good, financial leverage can make them very, very good, but when times are bad, financial leverage makes them very, very bad. Thus, financial leverage can potentially enhance the returns of the equity investors, but it also increases the uncertainty or risk for the owners. ■

Let's review what we have learned about the use of financial ratios in evaluating a company's financial position. We have presented all the ratios for the McDonald's Corporation in Table 3–5. The ratios are grouped by the issue being addressed: liquidity, operating profitability, financing, and profits for the owners. As before, we use some ratios for more than one purpose, namely the turnover ratios for accounts receivable and inventories. These ratios have implications both for the firm's liquidity and its prof-

Table 3–5
McDonald's Corporation Financial Ratio Analysis

FINANCIAL RATIOS	McDONALD'S CORPORATION	PEER-GROUP AVERAGE
1. FIRM LIQUIDITY		
current ratio $= \dfrac{\text{current assets}}{\text{current liabilities}}$	$\dfrac{\$741M}{\$2,451M} = 0.30$	0.90
acid-test ratio $= \dfrac{\text{current assets} - \text{inventories}}{\text{current liabilities}}$	$\dfrac{\$741M - \$51M}{\$2,451M} = 0.28$	0.62
average collection period $= \dfrac{\text{accounts receivable}}{\text{daily credit sales}}$	$\dfrac{\$379M}{\$8,362M \div 365} = 16.5$	6 days
accounts receivable turnover $= \dfrac{\text{credit sales}}{\text{accounts receivable}}$	$\dfrac{\$8,362M}{\$379M} = 22.1$	60.8
inventory turnover $= \dfrac{\text{cost of goods sold}}{\text{inventory}}$	$\dfrac{\$4,452M}{\$51M} = 87.3$	56.3
2. OPERATING PROFITABILITY		
operating income return on investment $= \dfrac{\text{operating income}}{\text{total assets}}$	$\dfrac{\$2,214M}{\$13,593M} = 16.3\%$	13.2%
operating profit margin $= \dfrac{\text{operating income}}{\text{sales}}$	$\dfrac{\$2,214M}{\$8,362M} = 26.5\%$	8.0%
total asset turnover $= \dfrac{\text{sales}}{\text{total assets}}$	$\dfrac{\$8,362M}{\$13,593M} = 0.62$	1.64
accounts receivable turnover $= \dfrac{\text{credit sales}}{\text{accounts receivable}}$	$\dfrac{\$8,362M}{\$379M} = 22.1$	60.8
inventory turnover $= \dfrac{\text{cost of goods sold}}{\text{inventory}}$	$\dfrac{\$4,452M}{\$51M} = 87.3$	56.3
fixed assets turnover $= \dfrac{\text{sales}}{\text{net fixed assets}}$	$\dfrac{\$8,362M}{\$11,329M} = 0.74$	2.0
3. FINANCING DECISIONS		
debt ratio $= \dfrac{\text{total debt}}{\text{total assets}}$	$\dfrac{\$6,650M}{\$13,593M} = 49\%$	66.0%
times interest earned $= \dfrac{\text{operating income}}{\text{interest}}$	$\dfrac{\$2,214M}{\$373M} = 5.94$	4.0
4. RETURN ON EQUITY		
return on equity $= \dfrac{\text{net income}}{\text{common equity}}$	$\dfrac{\$1,179M}{\$6,943M} = 17.0\%$	20.0%

itability; thus, they are listed in both areas. Also, we have included both average collection period and accounts receivable turnover; typically, we would only use one in our analysis, because they are just different ways of expressing the same thing.

OBJECTIVE 4

THE DU PONT ANALYSIS: AN INTEGRATIVE APPROACH TO RATIO ANALYSIS

In the previous section, we used ratio analysis to answer four questions thought to be important in understanding a company's financial position. The last three of the four questions dealt with a company's earnings capabilities and the common stockholders' return on the equity capital. In our analysis, we measured the return on equity as follows:

$$\text{return on equity} = \frac{\text{net income}}{\text{common equity}} \tag{3-14}$$

Du Pont analysis

Another approach can be used to evaluate a firm's return on equity. The **Du Pont analysis**, is *a method used to analyze a firm's profitability and return on equity.* Figure 3–5 shows graphically the Du Pont technique, modified somewhat from the original format developed by the management at the Du Pont Corporation. Beginning at the top of the figure, we see that the return on equity is calculated as follows:

$$\text{return on equity} = \left(\frac{\text{return}}{\text{on assets}}\right) \div \left(1 - \frac{\text{total debt}}{\text{total assets}}\right) \tag{3-15}$$

where the return on assets, or ROA, equals:

$$\text{return on assets} = \frac{\text{net income}}{\text{total assets}} \tag{3-16}$$

Thus, we see that the return on equity is a function of (1) the firm's overall profitability (net income relative to the amount invested in assets), and (2) the amount of debt used to finance the assets. We also know that the return on assets may be represented as follows:

$$\text{return on assets} = \left(\frac{\text{net profit}}{\text{margin}}\right) \times \left(\frac{\text{total asset}}{\text{turnover}}\right) \tag{3-17}$$
$$= \left(\frac{\text{net income}}{\text{sales}}\right) \times \left(\frac{\text{sales}}{\text{total assets}}\right)$$

Combining equations (3–15) and (3–17) gives us the basic Du Pont equation that shows the firm's return on equity as follows:

$$\text{return on equity} = \left(\frac{\text{net profit}}{\text{margin}}\right) \times \left(\frac{\text{total asset}}{\text{turnover}}\right) \div \left(1 - \frac{\text{total debt}}{\text{total assets}}\right) \tag{3-18}$$
$$= \left(\frac{\text{net income}}{\text{sales}}\right) \times \left(\frac{\text{sales}}{\text{total assets}}\right) \div \left(1 - \frac{\text{total debt}}{\text{total assets}}\right)$$

Using the Du Pont equation and the diagram in Figure 3–5 allows management to see more clearly what drives the return on equity and the interrelationships among the net profit margin, the asset turnover, and the debt ratio. Management is provided with a road map to follow in determining their effectiveness in managing the firm's resources to maximize the return earned on the owners' investment. In addition, the manager or owner can determine why that particular return was earned.

Let's return to the McDonald's Corporation to demonstrate the use of the Du Pont analysis. Taking the information from the McDonald's Corporation's income statement (Table 3–1) and balance sheet as of December 31, 1994 (Table 3–2), we can calculate the company's return on equity as follows:

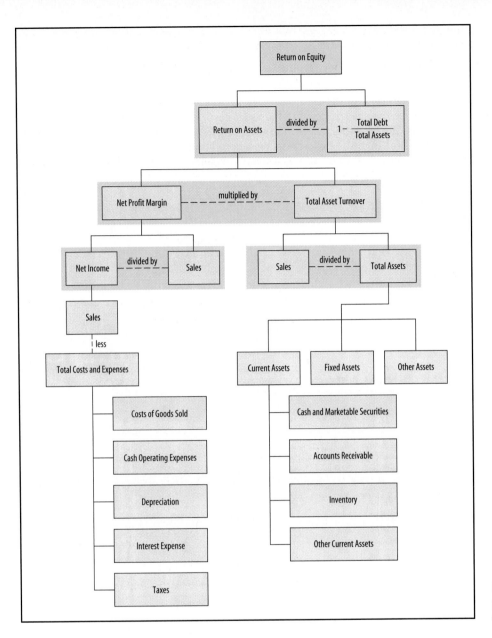

Figure 3–5
Du Pont Analysis

$$\text{return on equity} = \left(\frac{\text{net income}}{\text{sales}}\right) \times \left(\frac{\text{sales}}{\text{total assets}}\right) \div \left(1 - \frac{\text{total debt}}{\text{total assets}}\right)$$

$$= \left(\frac{\$1{,}179}{\$8{,}362}\right) \times \left(\frac{\$\ 8{,}362}{\$13{,}593}\right) \div \left(\frac{1 - \$6{,}650}{\$13{,}593}\right)$$

$$= \frac{14.1\% \times 0.615\%}{(1 - 0.489)}$$

$$= 16.98\%$$

We can also visualize the relationships graphically for the McDonald's Corporation, as shown in Figure 3–6 on page 94.

If the McDonald's Corporation's management wants to improve the company's return on equity, they should carefully examine Figure 3–6 for possible avenues. As we study the figure, we quickly see that improvement in the return on equity can come in one or more of four ways:

1. Increase sales without a disproportionate increase in costs and expenses.
2. Reduce the firm's cost of goods sold or operating expenses shown in the left-hand side of Figure 3–6.
3. Increase the sales relative to the asset base, either by increasing sales or by reducing the amounts invested in company assets. From our earlier examination of the McDonald's Corporation, we learned that the firm had excessive accounts receivables and fixed assets. Thus, management needs to reduce these assets

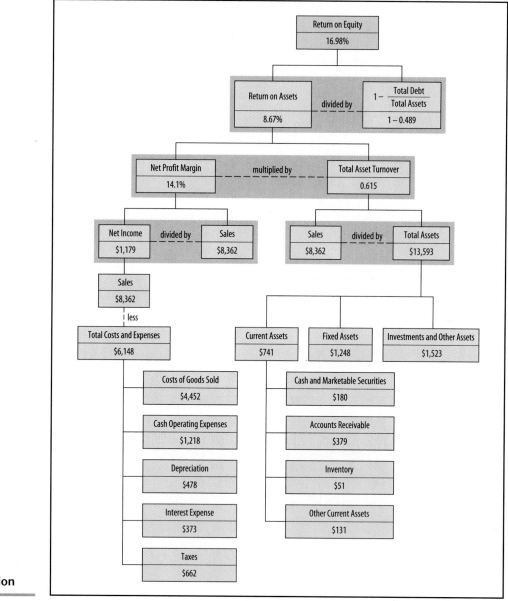

Figure 3–6

Du Pont Analysis: McDonald's Corporation

to the point possible, which would in turn result in an increase in the return on assets and then the return on equity.

4. Increase the use of debt relative to equity, but only to the extent that it does not unduly jeopardize the firm's financial position.

The choice between using the four-question approach as described earlier or the Du Pont analysis is largely a matter of personal preference. Both approaches are intended to let us see the variables that determine a firm's profitability. There are, however, limitations to either technique because of the inherent limitations in using financial ratios—a topic addressed in the next section.

Limitations of Ratio Analysis

OBJECTIVE 5

We have shown how financial ratios may be used to understand a company's financial position, but anyone who works with these ratios ought to be aware of the limitations involved in their use. The following list includes some of the more important pitfalls that may be encountered in computing and interpreting financial ratios:

1. It is sometimes difficult to identify the industry category to which a firm belongs when the firm engages in multiple lines of business. Thus, we frequently must select our own set of peer firms and construct tailor-made norms. Such was the case with our analysis of the McDonald's Corporation.

2. Published industry averages are only approximations and provide the user with general guidelines rather than scientifically determined averages of the ratios of all or even a representative sample of the firms within an industry.

3. Accounting practices differ widely among firms and can lead to differences in computed ratios. For example, the use of last-in, first-out (LIFO) in inventory valuation can, in a period of rising prices, lower the firm's inventory account and increase its inventory turnover ratio as compared with that of a firm that uses first-in, first-out (FIFO). In addition, firms may choose different methods of depreciating their fixed assets.

4. Financial ratios can be too high or too low. For example, a current ratio that exceeds the industry norm may signal the presence of excess liquidity, which results in a lowering of overall profits in relation to the firm's investment in assets. On the other hand, a current ratio that falls below the norm indicates the possibility that the firm has inadequate liquidity and may at some future date be unable to pay its bills on time.

5. An industry average may not provide a desirable target ratio or norm. At best an industry average provides a guide to the financial position of the average firm in the industry. It does not mean it is the ideal or best value for the ratio. Thus, we may choose to compare our firm's ratios with a self-determined peer group or even a single competitor.[15]

6. Many firms experience seasonality in their operations. Thus, balance sheet entries and their corresponding ratios will vary with the time of year when the statements are prepared. To avoid this problem, an average account balance should be used (for several months or quarters during the year) rather than the

---

[15]See Donald F. Cunningham and John T. Rose, "Industry Norms in Financial Statement Analysis: A Comparison of RMA and D&B Benchmark Data," *The Credit and Financial Management Review*, 1995, pp. 42–48, for a comparison of the industry financial ratios provided by Robert Morris and Associates with those of Dun & Bradstreet. They find significant differences within the same industry classifications. This finding points out the need to carefully consider the choice of an industry norm. In fact, your analysis may require that you construct your own norm from, say, a list of the four or five firms in a particular industry that might provide the most appropriate standard of comparison for the firm being analyzed.

year-end total. For example, an average of month-end inventory balances might be used to compute a firm's inventory turnover ratio when the firm is subject to a significant seasonality in its sales (and correspondingly in its investment in inventories).

In spite of their limitations, financial ratios provide us with a very useful tool for assessing a firm's financial conditions. We should, however, be aware of these potential weaknesses when performing a ratio analysis. In many cases the real value derived from analyzing financial ratios is that they tell us what questions to ask.

SUMMARY

OBJECTIVE 1

Construct and analyze a firm's basic financial statements, including the balance sheet, income statement, and cash flow statement

Three basic financial statements are commonly used to describe the financial condition and performance of the firm: the balance sheet, the income statement, and the cash flow statement. The balance sheet provides a picture of the firm's assets, liabilities, and owners' equity on a particular date, whereas the income statement reflects the net revenues from the firm's operations over a given period. The cash flow statement combines information from both the balance sheet and income statement to describe sources and uses of cash for a given period in the firm's history.

OBJECTIVE 2

Interpret the meaning of a firm's cash flow statement

There are three basic categories of activities related to a firm's cash flows, these being:

- Cash flows from operations
- Cash flows related to the investment or sale of assets (investment activities)
- Cash flows related to financing the firm (financing activities)

The first category, cash flows from operations, converts the income statement from an accrual basis to a cash basis. Also, by identifying the positive or negative signs of these three areas of cash flows, we gain an understanding of where cash is coming from and how it is being used.

OBJECTIVE 3

Calculate a comprehensive set of financial ratios and use them to evaluate the financial health of a company

Financial ratios are the principal tool of financial analysis. Sometimes referred to simply as benchmarks, ratios standardize financial information so that comparisons can be made between firms of varying sizes.

Two groups find financial ratios useful. The first is comprised of managers who use them to measure and track company performance over time. The focus of their analysis is frequently related to various measures of profitability used to evaluate the performance of the firm from the perspective of the owners. The second group of users of financial ratios includes analysts external to the firm who, for one reason or another, have an interest in the firm's economic well-being. An example of this group would be a loan officer of a commercial bank who wishes to determine the credit worthiness of a loan applicant. Here the focus of the analysis is on the firm's previous use of financial leverage and its ability to pay the interest and principal associated with the loan request.

Financial ratios may be used to answer at least four questions: (1) How liquid is the company? (2) Is management effective at generating operating profits on the firm's assets? (3) How is the firm financed? (4) Are the returns earned by the common stockholders adequate?

Two methods may be used in analyzing financial ratios. The first involves trend analysis for the firm over time; the second involves making ratio comparisons with a selected peer group of similar firms. In our example, a peer group was chosen for analyzing the financial position of the McDonald's Corporation.

Apply the Du Pont analysis in evaluating the firm's performance

OBJECTIVE 4

Another approach frequently used to evaluate a firm's profitability and the return on equity is the Du Pont analysis. The basic format of the Du Pont analysis dissects the return on equity into three drivers, represented as follows:

$$\frac{\text{return}}{\text{on equity}} = \left(\frac{\text{net income}}{\text{sales}}\right) \times \left(\frac{\text{sales}}{\text{total assets}}\right) \div \left(1 - \frac{\text{total debt}}{\text{total assets}}\right)$$

Explain the limitations of ratio analysis

OBJECTIVE 5

The following limitations may be encountered in computing and interpreting financial ratios:

1. It is sometimes difficult to identify an appropriate industry category.
2. Published industry averages are only approximations rather than scientifically determined averages.
3. Accounting practices differ widely among firms and can lead to differences in computed ratios.
4. Some financial ratios can be too high or too low, which makes the results more difficult to interpret.
5. An industry average may not provide a desirable target ratio or norm.
6. Many firms experience seasonality in their operations. Thus, ratios will vary with the time of year when the statements are prepared.

In spite of their limitations, financial ratios provide us with a very useful tool for assessing a firm's financial condition.

KEY TERMS

Accounts Receivable Turnover Ratio, 83

Acid-Test (Quick) Ratio, 82

Average Collection Period, 83

Balance Sheet, 71

Cash Flow Statement, 74

Cash Flows from Financing Activities, 78

Cash Flows from Investment
    Activities, 78

Cash Flows from Operations, 76

Current Assets, 71

Current Ratio, 82

Debt, 72

Debt Ratio, 88

Direct Method, 78

Du Pont Analysis, 92

Earnings before Taxes, 70

Equity, 72

Financial Ratios, 81

Financing Costs, 70

Fixed or Long-term Assets, 71

Income Statement, 69

Indirect Method, 78

Inventory Turnover Ratio, 83

Liquidity, 81

Net Income Available to Common
    Stockholders (Net Income), 70

STUDY QUESTIONS

3-1. The basic financial statements of an organization consist of the balance sheet, income statement, and cash flow statement. Describe the nature of each and explain how their functions differ.

3-2. Describe the eight cash flow patterns that can exist in a cash flow statement (the direct method).

3-3. Why is it that the preferred stockholders' equity section of the balance sheet would change only when new shares are sold or repurchased, whereas the common equity section would change from year to year regardless of whether new shares are bought or sold?

3-4. Discuss the reasons why net income for a particular period does not necessarily reflect a firm's cash flow during that period.

3-5. Describe the "four-question approach" to using financial ratios.

3-6. Discuss briefly the two perspectives that can be taken in performing ratio analyses.

3-7. Where can we obtain industry norms? What are the limitations of industry average ratios? Discuss briefly.

SELF-TEST PROBLEMS

ST-1. (*Ratio Analysis and Short-term Liquidity*) Ray's Tool and Supply Company of Austin, Texas, has been expanding its level of operation for the past two years. The firm's sales have grown rapidly as a result of the expansion in the Austin economy. However, Ray's is a privately held company, and the only source of available funds it has is a line of credit with the firm's bank. The company needs to expand its inventories to meet the needs of its growing customer base but also wishes to maintain a current ratio of at least 3. If Ray's current assets are $6 million, and its current ratio is now 4, how much can it expand its inventories (financing the expansion with its line of credit) before the target current ratio is violated?

ST-2. (*Ratio Analysis*)   The statements for M & G Industries are presented below:

M & G Industries Balance Sheet
For December 31, 1996 and 1997

	1996	1997
Cash	$ 9,000	$ 500
Accounts receivable	12,500	16,000
Inventories	29,000	45,500
Total current assets	$ 50,500	$ 62,000
Land	20,000	26,000
Buildings and equipment	70,000	100,000
Less: allowance for depreciation	(28,000)	(38,000)
Total fixed assets	$ 62,000	$ 88,000
Total assets	$112,500	$150,000
Accounts payable	$ 10,500	$ 22,000
Short-term bank notes	17,000	47,000
Total current liabilities	$ 27,500	$ 69,000
Long-term debt	28,750	22,950
Common stock	31,500	31,500
Retained earnings	24,750	26,550
Total debt and equity	$112,500	$150,000

M & G Industries Income Statement
For the Years Ended December 31, 1996 and 1997

	1996	1997
Sales (all credit)	$125,000	$160,000
Cost of goods sold	75,000	96,000
Gross profit	$ 50,000	$ 64,000
Operating expenses		
Fixed cash operating expenses	$ 21,000	$ 21,000
Variable operating expenses	12,500	16,000
Depreciation	4,500	10,000
Total operating expenses	$ 38,000	$ 47,000
Earnings before interest and taxes	$ 12,000	$ 17,000
Interest expense	3,000	6,100
Earnings before taxes	$ 9,000	$ 10,900
Taxes	4,500	5,450
Net income	$ 4,500	$ 5,450

a. Based on the preceding statements, complete the following table:

M & G Industries Ratio Analysis			
	INDUSTRY AVERAGES	**ACTUAL 1996**	**ACTUAL 1997**
Current ratio	1.80		
Acid-test ratio	.70		
Average collection period	37.00		
Inventory turnover	2.50		
Debt ratio	58%		
Times interest earned	3.80		
Gross profit margin	38%		
Operating profit margin	10%		
Total asset turnover	1.14		
Fixed asset turnover	1.40		
Operating income return on investment	11.4%		
Return on total assets	4.0%		
Return on common equity	9.5%		

b. Evaluate the firm's financial position using the "four-question approach" described in the chapter.

ST-3. (*Cash Flow Statement*)

    a. Using the indirect method, prepare a cash flow statement for M & G Industries for 1997, using information given in Self-Test Problem ST-2.

    b. How does this statement supplement your ratio analysis from Self-Test Problem ST-2? Explain.

STUDY PROBLEMS

3-1. (*Ratio Analysis*) The Mitchem Marble Company has a target current ratio of 2.0 but has experienced some difficulties financing its expanding sales in the past few months. At present the firm has a current ratio of 2.5 with current assets of $2.5 million. If Mitchem expands its receivables and inventories using its short-term line of credit, how much additional short-term funding can it borrow before its current ratio standard is reached?

3-2. (*Ratio Analysis*)   The balance sheet and income statement for the J. P. Robard Mfg. Company are as follows:

BALANCE SHEET ($000)	
Cash	$ 500
Accounts receivable	2,000
Inventories	1,000
Current assets	3,500
Net fixed assets	4,500
Total assets	$8,000
Accounts payable	$1,100
Accrued expenses	600
Short-term notes payable	300
Current liabilities	$2,000
Long-term debt	2,000
Owners' equity	4,000
Total liabilities and owners' equity	$8,000

INCOME STATEMENT ($000)	
Net sales (all credit)	$8,000
Cost of goods sold	(3,300)
Gross profit	4,700
Operating expenses	
(includes $500 depreciation)	(3,000)
Operating income	1,700
Interest expense	(367)
Earnings before taxes	$1,333
Income taxes (40%)	(533)
Net income	$ 800

Calculate the following ratios:

Current ratio

Times interest earned

Inventory turnover

Total asset turnover

Operating profit margin

Operating income return on investment

Debt ratio

Average collection period

Fixed asset turnover

Gross profit margin

Return on equity

3-3. (*Analyzing Operating Income Return on Investment*)   The R. M. Smithers Corporation earned an operating profit margin of 10 percent based on sales of $10 million and total assets of $5 million last year.

    a. What was Smithers' total asset turnover ratio?

    b. During the coming year the company president has set a goal of attaining a total asset turnover of 3.5. How much must firm sales rise, other things being the same, for the goal to be achieved? (State your answer in both dollars and percentage increase in sales.)

    c. What was Smithers' operating income return on investment last year? Assuming the firm's operating profit margin remains the same, what will the operating income return on investment be next year if the total asset turnover goal is achieved?

3-4. (*Using Financial Ratios*)   The Brenmar Sales Company had a gross profit margin (gross profits ÷ sales) of 30 percent and sales of $9 million last year. Seventy-five percent of the firm's sales are on credit and the remainder are cash sales. Brenmar's current assets equal $1.5 million, its current liabilities equal $300,000, and it has $100,000 in cash plus marketable securities.

    a. If Brenmar's accounts receivable are $562,500, what is its average collection period?

    b. If Brenmar reduces its average collection period to 20 days, what will be its new level of accounts receivable?

    c. Brenmar's inventory turnover ratio is 9 times. What is the level of Brenmar's inventories?

3-5. (*Ratio Analysis*)   Using Pamplin Inc.'s financial statements shown on the following pages:

    a. Compute the following ratios for both 1996 and 1997.

	INDUSTRY NORM 1997
Current ratio	5.00
Acid-test (quick) ratio	3.00
Inventory turnover	2.20
Average collection period	90.00
Debt ratio	0.33
Times interest earned	7.00
Total asset turnover	0.75
Fixed asset turnover	1.00
Operating profit margin	20%
Return on common equity	9%

    b. How liquid is the firm?

    c. Is management generating adequate operating profit on the firm's assets?

    d. How is the firm financing its assets?

    e. Are the common stockholders receiving a good return on their investment?

Pamplin Inc. Balance Sheet
At 12/31/96 and 12/31/97

ASSETS

	1996	1997
Cash	$ 200	$ 150
Accounts receivable	450	425
Inventory	550	625
Current assets	$1,200	$1,200
Plant and equipment	$2,200	$2,600
Less: accumulated depreciation	(1,000)	(1,200)
Net plant and equipment	$1,200	$1,400
Total assets	$2,400	$2,600

[handwritten: — Cash Flow From Invest. 2600 - 2200]

LIABILITIES AND OWNERS' EQUITY

	1996	1997
Accounts payable	$ 200	$ 150
Notes payable—current (9%)	0	150
Current liabilities	$ 200	$ 300
Bonds (8 1/3% interest)	$ 600	$ 600
Owners' equity		
Common stock	$ 300	$ 300
Paid-in capital	600	600
Retained earnings	700	800
Total owners' equity	$1,600	$1,700
Total liabilities and owners' equity	$2,400	$2,600

Pamplin Inc. Income Statement
For Years Ending 12/31/96 and 12/31/97

	1996		1997	
Sales (all credit)		$1,200		$1,450
Cost of goods sold		700		850
Gross profit		$ 500		$ 600
Operating expenses	30		40	
Depreciation	220	250	200	240
Operating income		$ 250		$ 360
Interest expense		50		64
Net income before taxes		$ 200		$ 296
Taxes (40%)		80		118
Net income		$ 120		$ 178

3-6. (*Cash Flow Statement*)   Prepare a cash flow statement for Pamplin Inc. for the year ended December 31, 1997 (problem 3-5). Use both the direct method and the indirect method in calculating cash flow from operations. Interpret your results.

3-7. (*Cash Flow Statement*)   (a) Prepare a cash flow statement for the Waterhouse Co. for the year 1997. Use both the direct method and the indirect method in calculating cash flow from operations. (b) What were the firm's primary sources and uses of cash?

	1996	1997
Cash	$ 75,000	$ 82,500
Receivables	102,000	90,000
Inventory	168,000	165,000
Prepaid expenses	12,000	13,500
Total current assets	$357,000	$351,000
Gross fixed assets	325,500	468,000
Accumulated depreciation	(94,500)	(129,000)
Patents	61,500	52,500
Total assets	$649,500	$742,500
Accounts payable	$124,500	$112,500
Taxes payable	97,500	105,000
Total current liabilities	$222,000	$217,500
Mortgage payable	150,000	0
Preferred stock	0	225,000
Additional paid-in capital— preferred	0	6,000
Common stock	225,000	225,000
Retained earnings	52,500	69,000
Total liabilities and equity	$649,500	$742,500

Additional Information

1. The only entry in the accumulated depreciation account is the depreciation expense for the period.
2. The only entries in the retained earning account are for dividends paid in the amount of $18,000 and for the net income for the year.
3. Expenses include a $9,000 amortization of patents.
4. The income statement for 1997 is as follows:

Sales (all credit)	$187,500
Cost of goods sold	111,000
Gross profit	76,500
Operating expenses	32,000
Provision for taxes	10,000
Net income	$ 34,500

(Cost of goods sold included depreciation expense of $34,500)

3-8. (*Review of Financial Statements*)   Prepare a balance sheet and income statement at December 31, 1997 for the Sharpe Mfg. Co. from the scrambled list of items below.

Accounts receivable	$120,000
Machinery and equipment	700,000
Accumulated depreciation	236,000
Notes payable	100,000
Net sales	800,000
Inventory	110,000
Accounts payable	90,000
Long-term debt	160,000
Cost of goods sold	500,000
Operating expenses	280,000
Common stock	320,000
Cash	96,000
Retained earnings—prior year	?
Retained earnings—current year	?

3-9. (*Financial Ratios—Investment Analysis*)   The annual sales for Salco, Inc., were $4.5 million last year. The firm's end-of-year balance sheet appeared as follows:

Current assets	$ 500,000	Liabilities	$1,000,000
Net fixed assets	1,500,000	Owners' equity	1,000,000
	$2,000,000		$2,000,000

The firm's income statement for the year was as follows:

Sales	$4,500,000
Less: cost of goods sold	(3,500,000)
Gross profit	$1,000,000
Less: operating expenses	(500,000)
Operating income	$500,000
Less: interest expense	(100,000)
Earnings before taxes	$400,000
Less: taxes (50%)	(200,000)
Net income	$200,000

a. Calculate Salco's total asset turnover, operating profit margin, and operating income return on investment.

b. Salco plans to renovate one of its plants, which will require an added investment in plant and equipment of $1 million. The firm will maintain its present debt ratio of .5 when financing the new investment and expects sales to remain constant, while the operating profit margin will rise to 13 percent. What will be the new operating income return on investment for Salco after the plant renovation?

c. Given that the plant renovation in part b occurs and Salco's interest expense rises by $50,000 per year, what will be the return earned on the common stockholders' investment? Compare this rate of return with that earned before the renovation.

3-10. (*Cash Flow Statement*) The consolidated balance sheets of the TMU Processing Company are presented below for May 31, 1996 and May 31, 1997 (millions of dollars). TMU earned $14 million after taxes during the year ended May 31, 1997, and paid common dividends of $10 million.

	MAY 31 1996	MAY 31 1997
Cash	$ 10	$ 8
Accounts receivable	12	22
Inventories	8	14
Current assets	$ 30	$ 44
Gross fixed assets	$100	$110
Less: accumulated depreciation	(40)	(50)
Net fixed assets	$ 60	$ 60
Total assets	$ 90	$104
Accounts payable	$ 12	$ 9
Notes payable	7	7
Long-term debt	11	24
Common stock	20	20
Retained earnings	40	44
Total liabilities	$ 90	$104

a. Prepare a statement of cash flow for 1997 for TMU Processing Company. (Hint: You will only be able to use the indirect method.)

b. Interpret your findings.

3-11. (*Financial Analysis and Cash Flow Problem*) The T. P. Jarmon Company manufactures and sells a line of exclusive sportswear. The firm's sales were $600,000 for the year just ended, and its total assets exceeded $400,000. The company was started by Mr. Jarmon just 10 years ago and has been profitable every year since its inception. The chief financial officer for the firm, Brent Vehlim, has decided to seek a line of credit from the firm's bank totaling $80,000. In the past the company has relied on its suppliers to finance a large part of its needs for inventory. However, in recent months tight money conditions have led the firm's suppliers to offer sizable cash discounts to speed up payments for purchases. Mr. Vehlim wants to use the line of credit to supplant a large portion of the firm's payables during the summer months, which are the firm's peak seasonal sales period.

The firm's two most recent balance sheets were presented to the bank in support of its loan request. In addition, the firm's income statement for the year just ended was provided to support the loan request. These statements are found in the following tables:

T. P. Jarmon Company, Balance Sheet
For 12/31/96 and 12/31/97

ASSETS

	1996	1997
Cash	$ 15,000	$ 14,000
Marketable securities	6,000	6,200
Accounts receivable	42,000	33,000
Inventory	51,000	84,000
Prepaid rent	1,200	1,100
Total current assets	$115,200	$138,300
Net plant and equipment	286,000	270,000
Total assets	$401,200	$408,300

LIABILITIES AND EQUITY

	1996	1997
Accounts payable	$ 48,000	$ 57,000
Notes payable	15,000	13,000
Accruals	6,000	5,000
Total current liabilities	$ 69,000	$ 75,000
Long-term debt	$160,000	$150,000
Common stockholders' equity	$172,200	$183,300
Total liabilities and equity	$401,200	$408,300

T. P. Jarmon Company, Income Statement
For the Year Ended 12/31/97

Sales (all credit)		$600,000
Less: cost of goods sold		460,000
Gross profits		$140,000
Less: operating and interest expenses		
General and administrative	$30,000	
Interest	10,000	
Depreciation	30,000	
Total		70,000
Earnings before taxes		$70,000
Less: taxes		27,100
Net income available to common stockholders		$42,900
Less: cash dividends		31,800
Change in retained earnings		$11,100

Jan Fama, associate credit analyst for the Merchants National Bank of Midland, Michigan, was assigned the task of analyzing Jarmon's loan request.

a. Calculate the financial ratios for 1997 corresponding to the industry norms provided as follows:

	Ratio Norm
Current ratio	1.8
Acid-test ratio	0.9
Debt ratio	0.5
Times interest earned	10.0
Average collection period	20.0
Inventory turnover (based on cost of goods sold)	7.0
Return on common equity	12.0%
Gross profit margin	25.0%
Operating income return on investment	16.8%
Operating profit margin	14.0%
Total asset turnover	1.20
Fixed asset turnover	1.80

b. Which of the ratios reported above in the industry norms do you feel should be most crucial in determining whether the bank should extend the line of credit?

c. Prepare a cash flow statement for Jarmon covering the year ended December 31, 1997. Interpret your findings.

d. Use the information provided by the financial ratios and the cash flow statement to decide if you would support making the loan.

e. Use the Du Pont analysis to evaluate the firm's financial position.

3-12. (*Preparing the Cash Flow Statement*) Comparative balance sheets for December 31, 1996 and December 31, 1997, for the Abrams Mfg. Company are found below:

	1996	1997
Cash	$ 89,000	$100,000
Accounts receivable	64,000	70,000
Inventory	112,000	100,000
Prepaid expenses	10,000	10,000
Total current assets	275,000	280,000
Plant and equipment	238,000	311,000
Accumulated depreciation	(40,000)	(66,000)
Total assets	$473,000	$525,000
Accounts payable	$ 85,000	$ 90,000
Accrued liabilities	68,000	63,000
Total current debt	153,000	153,000
Mortgage payable	70,000	0
Preferred stock		100,000
Additional paid-in capital		
Preferred stock		20,000
Common stock	205,000	205,000
Retained earnings	45,000	47,000
Total debt and equity	$473,000	$525,000

Abrams 1997 income statement is found below:

Sales (all credit)	$184,000
Cost of goods sold	60,000
Gross profit	$124,000
Selling, general, and administrative expenses	44,000
Depreciation expense	26,000
Operating income	$54,000
Interest expense	4,000
Earnings before taxes	$50,000
Taxes	26,000
Preferred stock dividends	10,000
Net income	$24,000

Additional Information

1. The only entry in the accumulated depreciation account is for 1997 depreciation.
2. The firm paid $22,000 in dividends during 1997.

Prepare a 1997 statement of cash flow for Abrams using the indirect method only.

3-13. (*Analyzing the Cash Flow Statement*)   Identify any financial weaknesses revealed in the cash flow statement for the Westlake Manufacturing Co.

Westlake Manufacturing Co. Statement of Cash Flow for Current Year		
Cash flow from operating activities		
Net income	$ 540,000	
Add (deduct) to reconcile net income to cash flow		
Decrease in accounts receivable	40,000	
Increase in inventories	(240,000)	
Increase in prepaid expenses	(10,000)	
Depreciation expense	60,000	
Decrease in accrued wages	(50,000)	
Net cash flow from operations		$ 340,000
Cash flow from investing activities		
Sale (purchase) of plant and equipment		2,400,000
Cash flow from financing activities		
Issuance of bonds	$1,000,000	
Repayment of short-term debt	(3,000,000)	
Payment of long-term debt	(500,000)	
Payment of dividends	(1,000,000)	
Net cash from financing activities		(3,500,000)
Net increase (decrease) in cash for the period		($ 760,000)

COMPREHENSIVE PROBLEM

PepsiCo's income statement for 1995 and the balance sheets for December 31, 1994, and December 31, 1995, are provided below. PepsiCo is considered to be in the beverages industry (Standard Industrial Code 2080).

a. Go to your library and find industry norms for the beverages industry.

b. Are there any ratios that are not provided for the industry that prevent you from using the "four-question approach" as described in this chapter? How would you adapt your approach to compensate for any missing industry norms?

c. Compute the financial ratios for PepsiCo for 1995, and using your industry norms, evaluate the firm in the following areas:

   (1) liquidity

   (2) operating profitability

   (3) financing policies

   (4) return on the shareholders' investment

d. Prepare a cash flow statement for PepsiCo. Interpret your findings.

PepsiCo, Inc.
Income Statement For Year Ending 1995

Net sales		$30,421
Costs and expenses, net		
Costs of sales	$14,886	
Selling, general, and administrative expenses[a]	11,712	
Amortization of intangible assets[b]	316	
— Impairment of long-lived assets[c]	520	$27,434
Operating profit		$ 2,987
Interest expense		(682)
Interest income		127
Income before income taxes		$ 2,432
Provision for income taxes		826
Net income		$ 1,606

[a]Selling expenses and general and administrative expenses include $1,740 in depreciation and amortization (non-cash expenses).

[b]Amortization of intangible assets is a non-cash expense for the purposes of writing off the intangible assets over time—much like depreciation of fixed assets.

[c]Impairment of long-lived assets (plant and equipment or fixed assets) is a non-cash expense, also similar to depreciation.

PepsiCo, Inc.
Balance Sheet
December 31, 1994 and 1995

	1995	1994
ASSETS		
Current assets		
Cash and cash equivalents	$ 382	$ 331
Short-term investments, at cost	1,116	1,157
Accounts and notes receivable, less allowance		
$150 in 1995 and $151 in 1994	2,407	2,051
Inventories	1,051	970
Prepaid expenses	590	563
Total current assets	$ 5,546	$ 5,072
Investments in unconsolidated affiliates	1,635	1,295
Property, plant, and equipment, net	9,870	9,883
Intangible assets, net	7,584 +316	7,842
Other assets	797	700
Total assets	$25,432	$24,792
LIABILITIES AND SHAREHOLDERS EQUITY		
Current liabilities		
Accounts payable	$ 1,556	$ 1,452
Accrued compensation and benefits	815	753
Short-term borrowings	706	678
Accrued marketing	469	546
Income taxes payable	387	672
Other current liabilities	1,297	1,169
Total current liabilities	$ 5,230	$ 5,270
Long-term debt	8,509	8,841
Other liabilities	2,495	1,852
Deferred income taxes	1,885	1,973
Shareholders' equity		
Capital stock, par value 1 2/3 cents per share:		
authorized 1,800 shares, issued 863 shares	$ 14	$ 14
Capital in excess of par value	1,060	935
Retained earnings	8,730	7,739
Currency translation adjustment and other	(808)	(471)
	$ 8,996	$ 8,217
Less: treasury stock, at cost: 75 shares and		
73 shares in 1995 and 1994, respectively	(1,683)	(1,361)
Total shareholders' equity	$ 7,313	$ 6,856
Total liabilities and shareholders' equity	$25,432	$24,792

Handwritten margin notes:

13   9870
−520   or   + 520
−1740   +1740

12130 − 9883 =
(2247)

SS–1

Note that Ray's current ratio before the inventory expansion is as follows:

$$\text{current ratio} = \$6{,}000{,}000/\text{current liabilities} = 4$$

Thus, the firm's level of current liabilities is $1.5 million. If the expansion in inventories is financed entirely with borrowed funds, then the change in inventories is equal to the change in current liabilities, and the firm's current ratio after the expansion can be defined as follows:

$$\text{current ratio} = \frac{\$6{,}000{,}000 + \text{change in inventory}}{\$1{,}500{,}000 + \text{change in inventory}} = 3$$

Note that we set the new current ratio equal to the firm's target of 3. Solving for the change in inventory in the above equation, we determine that the firm can expand its inventories by $750,000 and finance the expansion with current liabilities and still maintain its target current ratio.

SS–2

a.

M & G Industries Ratio Analysis			
	INDUSTRY AVERAGES	**ACTUAL 1996**	**ACTUAL 1997**
Current ratio	1.80	1.84	0.90
Acid-test ratio	0.70	0.78	0.24
Average collection period (based on a 365-day year and end-of-year figures)	37.00	36.50	36.50
Inventory turnover	2.50	2.59	2.11
Debt ratio	58%	50%	61.3%
Times interest earned	3.80	4.00	2.79
Gross profit margin	38%	40%	40%
Operating profit margin	10%	9.6%	10.6
Total asset turnover	1.14	1.11	1.07
Fixed asset turnover	1.40	2.02	1.82
Operating income return on investment	11.4%	10.67%	11.3%
Return on common equity	9.5%	8.0%	9.4%

b. M & G's liquidity is poor, as suggested by the low current ratio and acid-test ratio; also, inventories are turning slowly. In 1997, management is doing a satisfactory job at generating profits on the firm's operating assets, as indicated by the operating income return on investment. Note that the operating income return on investment in 1997 is average, owing to a slightly above average operating profit margin combined with a slightly below average asset turnover. The problem with the asset turnover ratio comes from a slow inventory turnover.

M & G has increased its use of debt to the point of using slightly more debt than the average company in the industry. As a result, the firm's coverage of interest has decreased to a point well below the industry norm.

As of 1997, M & G's return on equity is average because the operating income return on investment and the debt ratio are average.

SS–3

a.

M & G Industries Cash Flow Statement For the Year Ended December 31, 1994	
Cash flows from operating *activities*	
Net income (from the income statement)	$ 5,450
Add (deduct) to reconcile net income to net cash flow	
Increase in accounts payable	11,500
Increase in inventories	(16,500)
Depreciation expense	10,000
Increase in accounts receivable	(3,500)
Net cash inflow from operating activities	$ 6,950
Cash flows from investing *activities*	
Purchase of land	($ 6,000)
Purchase of plant and equipment	(30,000)
Net cash outflow from investing activities	(36,000)
Cash flows from financing *activities*	
Cash inflows	
Increase in bank notes	$30,000
Cash outflows	
Decrease in long-term debt	(5,800)
Common stock dividend	(3,650)
Net cash inflow from financing activities	20,550
Net increase (decrease) in cash during period	($ 8,500)
Cash balance at the beginning of the period	$ 9,000
Cash balance at the end of the period	$ 500

b. The cash flow statement is an important supplement to ratio analysis. This statement directs analysts' attention to where M & G Industries obtained financing during the period and how those funds were spent. For example, a very large portion of M & G's funds came from an increase in bank notes and an increase in accounts payable. In addition, the largest uses of funds were additions to buildings and equipment and increases in inventories. Thus, M & G did little in the most recent operating period to alleviate the financial problems we noted earlier in our ratio analysis. In fact, M & G aggravated matters by purchasing fixed assets using short-term sources of financing. It would appear that another short-term loan at this time is *not* warranted.

Financial Forecasting, Planning, and Budgeting

LEARNING OBJECTIVES

After reading this chapter you should be able to

1. Use the percent of sales method to forecast the financing requirements of a firm.

2. Calculate a firm's sustainable rate of growth.

3. Describe the limitations of the percent of sales forecast method.

4. Prepare a cash budget and use it to evaluate the amount and timing of a firm's financing needs.

Financial Forecasting • Financial Planning and Budgeting • Computerized Financial Planning

F orecasting is an integral part of the planning process, yet there are countless examples where our ability to predict the future is simply awful. Declining birthrates during the seventies was widely attributed to the women's liberation movement. Believing that the lower birthrates were permanent, school administrators began closing elementary schools. Then in the eighties birthrates and consequently school enrollments increased again as a result of the fact that childless couples had simply deferred having children until later in life. Still another example of poor forecasting relates to projections of oil prices that were prevalent during the mid-eighties. Oil prices were roughly $30 a barrel and many firms were developing new reserves that would cost well over this amount to produce. Why? Oil prices were projected to continue to rise and many thought the price might eventually reach $50 a barrel by the end of the decade. Then in January 1986 the collapse of the oil producers' cartel in combination with the benefits of energy conservation efforts produced a dramatic drop in oil prices to below $10 a barrel. Although these cases are dramatic they are by no means unique.

If forecasting the future is so difficult, and plans are built on forecasts, why do firms engage in planning efforts? Obviously, they do, but why? The answer, oddly enough, does not lie in the accuracy of the firm's projections, for planning offers its greatest value when the future is the most uncertain. The reason is that planning is the process of thinking about what the future might bring and devising strategies for dealing with the likely outcomes. Planning is thinking in advance, and thinking in advance provides an opportunity to devise contingency plans that can be quickly and easily initiated should the need arise. This increased speed of response to uncertain events means that the firm can reduce the costs of responding to adverse circumstances and quickly respond to take advantage of unexpected opportunities.

WHAT'S AHEAD

Chapter 4 has two primary objectives: First, it develops an appreciation for the role of forecasting in the firm's financial planning process. Basically, forecasts of future sales revenues and their associated expenses give the firm the information needed to project its future needs for financing. Also, this chapter provides an overview of the firm's budgetary system, including the cash budget, the pro forma (planned) income statement, and pro forma balance sheet. Pro forma financial statements give us a useful tool for analyzing the effects of the firm's forecasts and planned activities on its financial performance, as well as its needs for financing. In addition, pro forma statements can be used as a benchmark or standard to compare against actual operating results. Used in this way, pro forma statements are an instrument for controlling or monitoring the firm's progress throughout the planning period.

BACK TO THE FOUNDATIONS

Financial decisions are made today in light of our expectations of an uncertain future. Financial forecasting involves making estimates of the future financing requirements of the firm. **Axiom 3: Cash—Not Profits—Is King** speaks directly to this problem. Remember that effective financial management requires that consideration be given to cash flow and when it is received or dispersed.

FINANCIAL FORECASTING

OBJECTIVE 1

Forecasting in financial management is used to estimate a firm's future financial needs. The basic steps involved in predicting those financing needs are the following: *Step 1:* Project the firm's sales revenues and expenses over the planning period. *Step 2:* Estimate the levels of investment in current and fixed assets that are necessary to support the projected sales. *Step 3:* Determine the firm's financing needs throughout the planning period.

Sales Forecast

The key ingredient in the firm's planning process is the sales forecast. This projection is generally derived using information from a number of sources. At a minimum, the sales forecast for the coming year would reflect (1) any past trend in sales that is expected to carry through into the new year, and (2) the influence of any events that might materially affect that trend.[1] An example of the latter would be

---

[1]A complete discussion of forecast methodologies is outside the scope of this book. The interested reader will find the following references helpful: F. Gerard Adams, *The Business Forecasting Revolution* (Oxford: Oxford University Press, 1986); C. W. J. Granger, *Forecasting in Business and Economics*, 2d ed. (Boston: Academic Press, 1989); and Paul Newbold and Theodore Bos, *Introductory Business Forecasting* (Cincinnati: Southwestern, 1990).

the initiation of a major advertising campaign or a change in the firm's pricing policy.

Forecasting Financial Variables

Traditional financial forecasting takes the sales forecast as a given and makes projections of its impact on the firm's various expenses, assets, and liabilities. The most commonly used method for making these projections is the percent of sales method.

Percent of Sales Method of Financial Forecasting

percent of sales method

The **percent of sales method** involves *estimating the level of an expense, asset, or liability for a future period as a percent of the sales forecast.* The percentage used can come from the most recent financial statement item as a percent of current sales, from an average computed over several years, from the judgment of the analyst, or from some combination of these sources.

Figure 4–1 presents a complete example that uses the percent of sales method of financial forecasting. In this example each item in the firm's balance sheet that varies with sales is converted to a percentage of 1997 sales of $10 million. The forecast of the new balance for each item is then calculated by multiplying this percentage times the $12 million in projected sales for the 1998 planning period. The method of forecasting future financing is not as precise or detailed as the method using a cash budget, which is presented later; however, it offers a relatively low-cost and easy-to-use first approximation of the firm's financing needs for a future period.

Note that in the example in Figure 4–1, both current and fixed assets are assumed to vary with the level of firm sales. This means that the firm does not have

Assets	Present (1997)	Percent of Sales (1995 Sales = $10M)	Projected (Based on 1998 Sales = $12M)
Current assets	$2.0M	$\frac{\$2M}{\$10M} = 20\%$	$.2 \times \$12M = \$2.4$ M
Net fixed assets	$4.0M	$\frac{\$4M}{\$10M} = 40\%$	$.4 \times \$12M = \underline{\$4.8M}$
Total	$6.0M		$7.2M
Liabilities and Owners' Equity			
Accounts payable	$1.0M	$\frac{\$1M}{\$10M} = 10\%$	$.10 \times \$12M = \$1.2M$
Accrued expenses	1.0M	$\frac{\$1M}{\$10M} = 10\%$	$.10 \times \$12M = \$1.2M$
Notes payable	.5M	NA[a]	no change	.5M
Long-term debt	$2.0M	NA[a]	no change	2.0M
Total liabilities	$4.5M			$4.9M
Common stock	$.1M	NA[a]	no change	$.1M
Paid-in capital	.2M	NA[a]	no change	.2M
Retained earnings	1.2M		$1.2M [.05 \times \$12M \times (1 - .5)] =$	1.5M[b]
Common equity	$1.5M			$1.8M
Total	$6.0M		Total financing provided	$6.7M
			Discretionary financing needed	.5M[c]
			Total	$7.2M

[a] Not applicable. These accounts balances are assumed not to vary with sales.
[b] Projected retained earnings equals the beginning level ($1.2M) plus projected net income less any dividends paid. In this case net income is projected to equal 5 percent of sales, and dividends are projected to equal half of net income: $.05 \times \$12M \times (1 - .5) = \$300,000$.
[c] Discretionary financing needed equals projected total assets ($7.2M) less projected total liabilities ($4.9M) less projected common equity ($1.8), or $7.2M - 4.9M - 1.8M = \$500,000$.

Figure 4–1

Using the Percent of Sales Method to Forecast Future Financing Requirements

Now You See It . . .

Cash flow is at least as important a measure of corporate health as reported earnings. But put a dozen investors in a room and you'll get almost as many different definitions.

After grappling with the problem for more than six years, the Financial Accounting Standards Board has come up with the beginnings of a more precise definition. It would require all companies to use the same format to explain how cash and cash equivalents change from one reporting period to the next. The proposal still leaves companies with room for flexibility but will make investors' lives much easier. Why? Companies will have to show sources and uses of cash in three areas: operations, investing, and financing.

Let's take a specific case: Lowe's Cos., the North Carolina-based retailer of building materials. The company said in its annual report that cash flow amounted to $2.31 per share in 1985 as compared with $2.20 the year before. An investor looking at these numbers might have assumed Lowe's had plenty of cash left over for dividends and other purposes.

Not necessarily so. Although Lowe's used a generally accepted definition of cash flow, it was not a strict definition. It failed to subtract the cash absorbed by higher inventories and receivables. Lowe's ended the year with hardly more cash than it started the year, and its long-term debt almost doubled from 1984 to 1985—despite the positive cash flow.

Does it really matter how you measure cash flow? Very much. While Lowe's is healthy—the increased inventory and receivables simply reflect growth in revenues— there are situations where a company can go broke while reporting positive cash flow. How can this be? Simple.

Suppose inventories and receivables rise faster than sales, reflecting slow pay by customers on unsold goods. Under the simpler method of reporting cash flow (which would not include working-capital components), such a company could report a positive cash flow even while it was fast running out of cash.

When the smoke clears, investors will still need to do lots of homework. It's never enough to know just what the numbers are. You still have to figure out what the numbers mean. Again, Lowe's is an example. Even if it were forced to report a negative cash flow, it would still be a very healthy business; it would cease being one only if inventories and receivables increased faster than sales and the company's credit were deteriorating.

When it comes to some things, the more you try simplifying them, the more complicated they become.

_____

Source: Excerpted by permission of Forbes (February 9, 1987): 70. © Forbes Inc. 1987

---

sufficient productive capacity to absorb a projected increase in sales. Thus, if sales were to rise by $1, fixed assets would rise by $.40, or 40 percent of the projected increase in sales. If the fixed assets the firm currently owns were sufficient to support the projected level of new sales, then fixed assets should not be allowed to vary with sales. If this were the case, then fixed assets would not be converted to a percent of sales and would be projected to remain unchanged for the period being forecast.

Also, we note that accounts payable and accrued expenses are the only liabilities allowed to vary with sales. Both these liability accounts might reasonably be expected to rise and fall with the level of firm sales; hence the use of the percent of sales forecast. Because these two categories of current liabilities normally vary directly with the level of sales, they are often referred to as sources of **spontaneous financing,** which include *the trade credit and other accounts payable that arise "spontaneously in the firms day-to-day operations"*. Chapter 14, which discusses working-capital management, has more to say about these forms of financing. Notes payable, long-term debt, common stock, and paid-in capital are not assumed to vary directly with the level of firm sales. These sources of financing are termed **discretionary financing,** *which require an explicit decision on the part of the firm's management every*

spontaneous financing

discretionary financing

time funds are raised. An example is a bank note which requires that negotiations be undertaken and an agreement signed setting forth the terms and conditions for the financing. Finally, we note that the level of retained earnings does vary with estimated sales. The predicted change in the level of retained earnings equals the estimated after-tax profits (projected net income) equal to 5 percent of sales or $600,000 less the common stock dividends of $300,000.

Thus, using the example from Figure 4–1, we estimate that firm sales will increase from $10 million to $12 million, which will cause the firm's need for total assets to rise to $7.2 million. These assets will then be financed by $4.9 million in existing liabilities plus spontaneous liabilities; $1.8 million in owner funds, including $300,000 in retained earnings from next year's sales; and finally, $500,000 in discretionary financing, which can be raised by issuing notes payable, selling bonds, offering an issue of stock, or some combination of these sources.

In summary, we can estimate the firm's discretionary financing needs (DFN), using the percent of sales method of financial forecasting, by following a four-step procedure:

Step 1: Convert each asset and liability account that varies directly with firm sales to a percent of the current year's sales.

EXAMPLE: CURRENT ASSETS AS A PERCENT OF SALES

$$\frac{\text{current assets}}{\text{sales}} = \frac{\$2M}{\$10M} = .2 \text{ or } 20\%$$

Step 2: Project the level of each asset and liability account in the balance sheet using its percent of sales multiplied by projected sales or by leaving the account balance unchanged where the account does not vary with the level of sales.

EXAMPLE: PREDICTING CURRENT ASSETS

$$\text{projected current assets} =$$
$$\text{projected sales} \times \frac{\text{current assets}}{\text{sales}} = \$12M \times .2 = \$2.4M$$

Step 3: Project the addition to retained earnings available to help finance the firm's operations. This equals projected net income for the period less planned common stock dividends.

EXAMPLE: PREDICTING ADDITIONAL RETAINED EARNINGS

$$\text{projected addition to retained earnings} =$$
$$\text{projected sales} \times \frac{\text{net income}}{\text{sales}} \times \left(1 - \frac{\text{cash dividends}}{\text{net income}}\right)$$
$$= \$12M \times .05 \times (1 - .5) = \$300,000$$

Step 4: Project the firm's DFN as the projected level of total assets less projected liabilities and owners' equity.

EXAMPLE: PREDICTING DISCRETIONARY FINANCING NEEDS

$$\text{discretionary financing needed} =$$
$$\text{projected total assets} - \text{projected total liabilities} - \text{projected owner's equity}$$
$$= \$7.2M - \$4.9M - \$1.8M = \$500,000$$

Are you beginning to wonder exactly where finance comes into financial forecasting? To this point, financial forecasting looks for all the world like financial statement forecasting. The reason is that we have adopted the accountant's model of the firm, the balance sheet, as the underlying structure of the financial forecast. The key to financial forecasting is the identification of the firm's anticipated future financing requirements. These requirements can be identified as the "plug" figure, or simply the number that balances a pro forma balance sheet.

Analyzing the Effects of Profitability and Dividend Policy on DFN

Projecting discretionary financing needed we can quickly and easily evaluate the sensitivity of our projected financing requirements to changes in key variables. For example, using the information from the preceding example, we evaluate the effect of net profit margins (NPMs) equal to 1 percent, 5 percent, and 10 percent in combination with dividend payout ratios of 30 percent, 50 percent, and 70 percent as follows:

Discretionary Financing Needed for Various Net Profit Margins and Dividend Payout Ratios

NET PROFIT MARGIN	DIVIDEND PAYOUT RATIOS (DIVIDENDS ÷ NET INCOME)		
	30%	50%	70%
1%	$716,000	$740,000	$764,000
5%	380,000	500,000	620,000
10%	(40,000)	200,000	440,000

If these values for the net profit margin represent reasonable estimates of the possible ranges of values the firm might experience, and if the firm is considering dividend payouts ranging from 30 percent to 70 percent, then we estimate that the firm's financing requirements will range from ($40,000), which represents a surplus of $40,000, to a situation where it would need to acquire $764,000. Lower net profit margins mean higher funds requirements. Also, higher dividend payout percentages, other things remaining constant, lead to a need for more discretionary financing. This is a direct result of the fact that a high-dividend-paying firm retains less of its earnings.

Analyzing the Effects of Sales Growth on a Firm's Discretionary Financing Needs

In Figure 4–1 we analyzed the discretionary financing needs for a firm whose sales were expected to grow from $10 million to $12 million during the coming year. Recall that the 20 percent expected increase in sales led to an increase in the firm's needs for financing in the amount of $500,000. We referred to this added financing requirement as the firm's discretionary financing needs (DFN), since all these funds must be raised from sources such as bank borrowing or a new equity issue which require that management exercise its discretion in selecting the source. In this section we want to investigate how a firm's DFN varies with different rates of anticipated growth in sales.

Table 4–1 on page 120 contains an expansion of the financial forecast found in Figure 4–1. Specifically, we use the same assumptions and prediction methods that underlie Figure 4–1 but apply them to sales growth rates of −5 percent to 20 percent. DFN for these sales growth rates ranges from ($625,000) to $500,000. When DFN is

Table 4–1
Discretionary Financing Needs and the Rate of Growth in Firm Sales

			GROWTH RATE IN FIRM SALES			
			−10%	0%	10%	20%
			PRO FORMA INCOME STATEMENTS			
CURRENT SALES (1997)	$10,000,000	SALES	9,000,000	10,000,000	11,000,000	12,000,000
NET INCOME ÷ SALES	5%	NET INCOME	450,000	500,000	550,000	600,000
DIVIDENDS ÷ EARNINGS	50%	DIVIDENDS	225,000	250,000	275,000	300,000
ASSETS		**FORECAST MODEL**	**PRO FORMA BALANCE SHEETS**			
Current assets	2,000,000	20% of sales	1,800,000	2,000,000	2,200,000	2,400,000
Net fixed assets	4,000,000	40% of sales	3,600,000	4,000,000	4,400,000	4,800,000
Total assets	6,000,000		5,400,000	6,000,000	6,600,000	7,200,000
LIABILITIES AND OWNERS' EQUITY						
Accounts payable	1,000,000	10% of sales	900,000	1,000,000	1,100,000	1,200,000
Accrued expenses	1,000,000	10% of sales	900,000	1,000,000	1,100,000	1,200,000
Notes payable	500,000	Constant	500,000	500,000	500,000	500,000
Current liabilities	2,500,000		2,300,000	2,500,000	2,700,000	2,900,000
Long-term debt	2,000,000	Constant	2,000,000	2,000,000	2,000,000	2,000,000
Total liabilities	4,500,000		4,300,000	4,500,000	4,700,000	4,900,000
Common stock	100,000	Constant	100,000	100,000	100,000	100,000
Paid-in capital	200,000	Constant	200,000	200,000	200,000	200,000
Retained earnings	1,200,000	Plus new retained earnings	1,425,000	1,450,000	1,475,000	1,500,000
Common equity	1,500,000		1,725,000	1,750,000	1,775,000	1,800,000
Total financing requirements = total assets			5,400,000	6,000,000	6,600,000	7,200,000
Total financing available			6,025,000	6,250,000	6,475,000	6,700,000
Discretionary financing needed (DFN) = Total Assets − Total Financing Available			(625,000)	(250,000)	125,000	500,000

negative, this means that the firm has more money than it needs to finance the assets used to generate the projected sales. Alternatively, when DFN is positive, this means that the firm must raise additional funds in this amount either by borrowing or issuing stock. We can calculate DFN using the following relationship:

$$DFN = \begin{bmatrix} \text{predicted} \\ \text{change in} \\ \text{total assets} \end{bmatrix} - \begin{bmatrix} \text{predicted} \\ \text{change in} \\ \text{spontaneous liabilities} \end{bmatrix} - \begin{bmatrix} \text{predicted} \\ \text{change in} \\ \text{retained earnings} \end{bmatrix} \quad (4\text{–}1)$$

Notice that in defining DFN we only consider changes in spontaneous liabilities, which you will recall are those liabilities that arise more or less automatically in the course of doing business (examples include accrued expenses and accounts payable). In Table 4–1 the only liabilities that are allowed to change with sales are spontaneous liabilities so that we can calculate the change in spontaneous liabilities simply by comparing total liabilities at the current sales level with total liabilities for the predicted sales level.

Equation (4–1) can be used to estimate the DFN numbers found in Table 4–1. For example, where sales are expected to grow at a rate of 10 percent (i.e., g equals 10 percent), DFN can be calculated as follows:

$$\text{DFN}(g = 10\%) = (\$6,600,000 - 6,000,000) - (\$4,700,000 - 4,500,000) - (\$1,475,000 - 1,200,000) = \$125,000$$

Sometimes analysts prefer to calculate a firm's **external financing needs (EFN)**, which include *all the firm's needs for financing beyond the funds provided internally through the retention of earnings.* Thus,

external financing needs

$$\text{EFN} = \begin{bmatrix} \text{predicted} \\ \text{change in} \\ \text{total assets} \end{bmatrix} - \begin{bmatrix} \text{predicted} \\ \text{change in} \\ \text{retained earnings} \end{bmatrix} \qquad \textbf{(4–2)}$$

For an anticipated growth in sales of 10 percent, EFN equals $325,000. The difference between EFN and DFN equals the $200,000 in added spontaneous financing that the firm anticipates receiving when its sales rise from $10 million to $11 million. We prefer to use the DFN concept, as it focuses the analyst's attention on the amount of funds that the firm must actively seek to meet the firm's financing requirements.

Figure 4–2 contains a graphical representation of the relationship between growth rates for sales and DFN. The straight line in the graph depicts the level of DFN for each of the different rates of growth in firm sales. For example, if sales grow by 20 percent, then the firm projects DFN of $500,000, which must be raised externally by borrowing or a new equity offering. Note that where firm sales grow at 6.667 percent, the firm's DFN will be exactly zero. For firms that have limited sources of external financing or choose to grow through internal finance plus spontaneous financing, it is important that they be able to estimate the sales growth rate that they can "afford," which in this case is 6.667 percent.

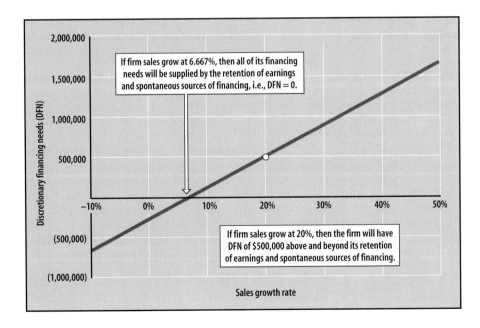

Figure 4–2

Sales Growth and the Discretionary Financing Needs of the Firm

The Sustainable Rate of Growth

The **sustainable rate of growth** (g^*) represents *the rate at which a firm's sales can grow if it wants to maintain its present financial ratios and* does not *want to resort to the sale of new equity shares.*[2] A simple formula can be derived for g^* where we assume that a firm's assets and liabilities all grow at the same rate as its sales, that is,

$$\text{sustainable rate of growth } (g^*) = \text{ROE} (1 - b) \qquad \textbf{(4–3)}$$

ROE is the firm's return on equity, which was defined in Chapter 3 as follows:

$$\text{ROE} = \frac{\text{net income}}{\text{common equity}}$$

and b is the firm's dividend payout ratio, that is, $\frac{\text{dividends}}{\text{net income}}$. The term $(1 - b)$ is sometimes referred to as the **plowback ratio** since it indicates *the fraction of earnings that are reinvested or plowed back into the firm.* Equation (4–3) is deceptively simple. Recall that ROE can also be written as follows:

$$\text{ROE} = \left(\frac{\text{net income}}{\text{sales}}\right) \times \left(\frac{\text{sales}}{\text{assets}}\right) \times \left(\frac{\text{common equity}}{\text{assets}}\right)$$

Consequently, a firm's sustainable rate of growth is determined by its ROE (i.e., its anticipated net profit margin, asset turnover, and capital structure), as well as its dividend policy.

EXAMPLE: CALCULATING THE SUSTAINABLE RATE OF GROWTH

Consider the three firms found below:

Firm	Net Profit Margin	Asset Turnover	Leverage	Plowback Ratio	g^*
A	15%	2	0.3	50%	4.5%
B	15%	2	0.3	100%	9.0%
C	15%	2	0.5	100%	15.0%

Comparing Firms A and B we see that the only difference is that Firm A pays out half its earnings in common dividends (i.e., plows back half its earnings) whereas Firm B retains or plows back all of its earnings. The net result is that Firm B with its added source of internal equity financing can grow at twice the rate of Firm A (9 percent compared to only 4.5 percent). Similarly, comparing Firms B and C we note that they differ only in that Firm B finances only 30 percent of its assets with equity whereas Firm C finances 50 percent of its assets with equity. The result is that Firm C's sustainable rate of growth is 15 percent compared to only 9 percent for Firm B.

Before leaving our discussion of the sustainable rate of growth concept, it is important that we stress the underlying assumptions behind equation (4–2). For this equation to accurately depict a firm's sustainable rate of growth, the following assumptions must hold: First, the firm's assets must vary as a constant percent of sales

[2]For an extensive discussion of this concept see Robert C. Higgins, "Sustainable Growth with Inflation," *Financial Management* (Autumn 1981): 36–40.

(i.e., even fixed assets expand and contract directly with the level of firm sales). Second, the firm's liabilities must all vary directly with firm sales. This means that the firm's management will expand its borrowing (both spontaneous and discretionary) in direct proportion with sales to maintain its present ratio of debt to assets. Finally, the firm pays out a constant proportion of its earnings in common stock dividends regardless of the level of firm sales. Since all three of these assumptions are only rough approximations to the way that firms actually behave, equation (4–3) provides a crude approximation of the firm's actual sustainable rate of growth. However, an estimate of g^* using equation (4–3) can be a very useful first step in the firm's financial planning process.

Limitations of the Percent of Sales Forecast Method

OBJECTIVE 2

The percent of sales method of financial forecasting provides reasonable estimates of a firm's financing requirements only where asset requirements and financing sources can be accurately forecast as a constant percent of sales. For example, predicting inventories using the percent of sales method involves the following predictive equation, where the subscript t to the period that is being forecast.

$$\text{inventories}_t = \left[\frac{\text{inventories}}{\text{sales}}\right] \cdot \text{sales}_t$$

Figure 4–3a on page 124 depicts this predictive relationship. Note that the percent-of-sales predictive model is simply a straight line that passes through the origin (that is, has a zero intercept). There are some fairly common instances in which this type of relationship fails to describe the relationship between an asset category and sales. Two such examples involve assets for which there are scale economies and assets that must be purchased in discrete quantities ("lumpy assets").

Economies of scale are sometimes realized from investing in certain types of assets. For example, a new computer system may support a firm's operations over a wide range of firm sales. This means that these assets do not increase in direct proportion to sales. Figure 4–3b on page 124 reflects one instance in which the firm realizes economies of scale from its investment in inventory. Note that inventories as a percent of sales decline from 120 percent where sales are $100, to 30 percent where sales equal $1,000. This reflects the fact that there is a fixed component of inventories (in this case $100) that the firm must have on hand regardless of the level of sales, plus a variable component (20 percent of sales). In this instance the predictive equation for inventories is as follows:

$$\text{inventories}_t = a + b \text{ sales}_t$$

In this example, a is equal to 100 and b equals .20.[3]

Figure 4–3c on page 125 is an example of *lumpy assets*, that is, assets that must be purchased in large, nondivisible components. For example, if the firm spends $500 on plant and equipment, it can produce up to $100 in sales per year. If it spends another $500 (for a total of $1,000), then it can support sales of $200 per year, and so forth. Note that when a block of assets is purchased, it creates excess capacity until sales grow to the point where the capacity is fully used. The result is a step function like the one depicted in Figure 4–3c. Thus, if the firm does not expect sales to exceed the current capacity of its plant and equipment, there would be no projected need for added plant and equipment capacity.

---

[3]Economies of scale are evidenced here by the nonzero intercept value. However, scale economies can also result in nonlinear relationships between sales and a particular asset category. Later, when we discuss cash management, we will find that one popular cash management model predicts a nonlinear relationship between the optimal cash balance and the level of cash transactions.

ETHICS IN FINANCIAL MANAGEMENT

To Bribe or Not to Bribe

In many parts of the world, bribes and payoffs to public officials are considered the norm in business transactions. This raises a perplexing ethical question. If paying bribes is not considered unethical in a foreign country, should you consider it unethical to make these payments?

This situation provides an example of an ethical issue that gave rise to legislation. The Foreign Corrupt Practices Act of 1977 (as amended in the Omnibus Trade and Competi-

tiveness Act of 1988) established criminal penalties for making payments to foreign officials, political parties, or candidates in order to obtain or retain business. Ethical problems are frequently areas just outside the boundaries of current legislation and often lead to the passage of new legislation.

Consider the following question: If you were involved in negotiating an important business deal in a foreign country, and the success or fail-

ure of the deal hinged on whether you paid a local government official to help you consummate the deal, would you authorize the payment? Assume that the form of the payment is such that you do not expect to be caught and punished; for example, your company agrees to purchase supplies from a family member of the government official at a price slightly above the competitive price.

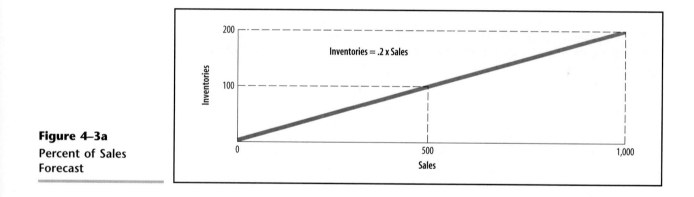

Figure 4–3a
Percent of Sales
Forecast

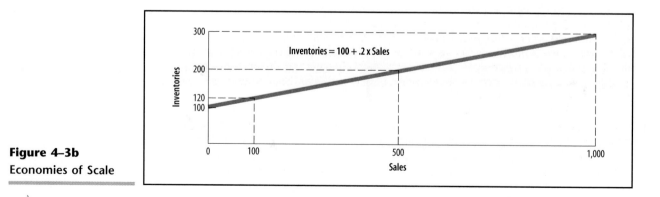

Figure 4–3b
Economies of Scale

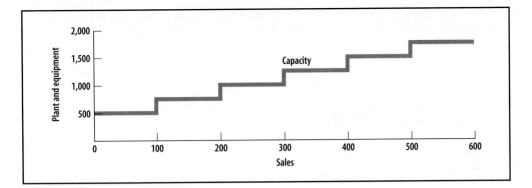

Figure 4–3c
Economies of Scale and Lumpy Investments

FINANCIAL PLANNING AND BUDGETING

As we noted earlier, the principal virtue of the percent of sales method of financial forecasting is its simplicity. To obtain a more precise estimate of the amount and timing of the firm's future financing needs, we require a cash budget. The percent of sales method of financial forecasting provides a very useful, low-cost forerunner to the development of the more detailed cash budget, which the firm will ultimately use to estimate its financing needs.

BACK TO THE FOUNDATIONS

Budgets have many important uses; however, their use as a tool of managerial control is critically important and often overlooked in the study of financial management. **Axiom 7: The Agency Problems—Managers Won't Work for Owners Unless It's in Their Best Interest** speaks to the root source of the problem, and budgets provide one tool for attempting to deal with it. Specifically, budgets provide management with a tool for evaluating performance and consequently maintaining a degree of control over employee actions.

Budget Functions

A **budget** is simply *a forecast of future events.* For example, students preparing for final exams make use of time budgets, which help them allocate their limited preparation time among their courses. Students also must budget their financial resources among competing uses, such as books, tuition, food, rent, clothes, and extracurricular activities.

budget

Budgets perform three basic functions for a firm. First, they indicate the amount and timing of the firm's needs for future financing. Second, they provide the basis for taking corrective action in the event budgeted figures do not match actual or realized figures. Third, budgets provide the basis for performance evaluation. Plans are carried out by people, and budgets provide benchmarks that management can use to evaluate the performance of those responsible for carrying out those plans and, in turn, to control their actions. Thus, budgets are valuable aids in both the planning and controlling aspects of the firm's financial management.

OBJECTIVE 4

The Cash Budget

cash budget

The **cash budget** represents a *detailed plan of future cash flows* and is composed of four elements: cash receipts, cash disbursements, net change in cash for the period, and new financing needed.

EXAMPLE: CONSTRUCTING A CASH BUDGET

To demonstrate the construction and use of the cash budget, consider Salco Furniture Company, Inc., a regional distributor of household furniture. Management is in the process of preparing a monthly cash budget for the upcoming six months (January through June 1998). Salco's sales are highly seasonal, peaking in the months of March through May. Roughly 30 percent of Salco's sales are collected one month after the sale, 50 percent two months after the sale, and the remainder during the third month following the sale.

Salco attempts to pace its purchases with its forecast of future sales. Purchases generally equal 75 percent of sales and are made two months in advance of anticipated sales. Payments are made in the month following purchases. For example, June sales are estimated at $100,000, thus April purchases are .75 × $100,000 = $75,000. Correspondingly, payments for purchases in May equal $75,000. Wages, salaries, rent, and other cash expenses are recorded in Table 4–2 on pages 128–129, which gives Salco's cash budget for the six-month period ended in June 1998. Additional expenditures are recorded in the cash budget related to the purchase of equipment in the amount of $14,000 during February and the repayment of a $12,000 loan in May. In June Salco will pay $7,500 interest on its $150,000 in long-term debt for the period of January–June 1998. Interest on the $12,000 short-term note repaid in May for the period January through May equals $600 and is paid in May.

Salco currently has a cash balance of $20,000 and wants to maintain a minimum balance of $10,000. Additional borrowing necessary to maintain that minimum balance is estimated in the final section of Table 4–2. Borrowing takes place at the beginning of the month in which the funds are needed. Interest on borrowed funds equals 12 percent per annum, or 1 percent per month, and is paid in the month following the one in which funds are borrowed. Thus, interest on funds borrowed in January will be paid in February equal to 1 percent of the loan amount outstanding during January.

The financing-needed line in Salco's cash budget determines that the firm's cumulative short-term borrowing will be $36,350 in February, $65,874 in March, $86,633 in April, and $97,599 in May. In June the firm will be able to reduce its borrowing to $79,875. Note that the cash budget indicates not only the amount of financing needed during the period but also when the funds will be needed.

Fixed versus Flexible Budgets

The cash budget given in Table 4–2 for Salco, Inc., is an example of a fixed budget. Cash flow estimates are made for a single set of monthly sales estimates. Thus, the estimates of expenses and new financing needed are meaningful only for the level of sales for which they were computed. To avoid this limitation, several budgets corresponding to different sets of sales estimates can be prepared. Such a flexible budgeting fulfills two basic needs: First, it gives information regarding the firm's possible financing needs, and second, it provides management with a control mechanism. That is, management can compare actual performance against budgeted figures. In this way management can evaluate the performance of subordinates who are responsible for the various cost and revenue items contained in the budget.

This second function deserves some additional comment. Costs vary with the actual level of sales experienced by the firm. Thus, if the budget is to be used as a standard for performance evaluation or control, it must be constructed to match realized sales and production figures. This can involve much more than simply adjusting cost figures up or down in proportion to the deviation of actual from planned sales; that is, costs may not vary in strict proportion to sales, just as inventory levels may not vary as a constant percent of sales. Thus, preparation of a flexible budget involves reestimating all the cash expenses that would be incurred at each of several possible sales levels. This process might utilize a variation of the percent of sales method discussed earlier.

Budget Period

There are no strict rules for determining the length of the budget period. However, as a general rule, it should be long enough to show the effect of management policies yet short enough so that estimates can be made with reasonable accuracy. Applying this rule of thumb to the Salco example in Table 4–2, it appears that the six-month budget period is too short. The reason is that we cannot tell whether the planned operations of the firm will be successful over the coming fiscal year. That is, for most of the first six-month period, the firm is operating with a cash flow deficit. If this does not reverse in the latter six months of the year, then a reevaluation of the firm's plans and policies is clearly in order.

Longer-range budgets are also prepared in the form of the capital-expenditure budget. These budgets detail the firm's plans for acquiring plant and equipment over a 5-year, 10-year, or even longer period. Furthermore, firms often develop comprehensive long-range plans extending up to 10 years into the future. These plans are generally not as detailed as the annual cash budget, but they do consider such major components as sales, capital expenditures, new-product development, capital funds acquisition, and employment needs.

ETHICS IN FINANCIAL MANAGEMENT

Put yourself in the shoes of Ben Tolbert, who is the CFO of Bonajet Enterprises. Ben's CEO is scheduled to meet with a group of outside analysts tomorrow to discuss the firm's financial forecast for the last quarter of the year. Ben's analysis suggests that there is a very real prospect that the coming quarter's results could be very disappointing. How would you handle Ben's dilemma?

As Ben looks over a draft of the report he must submit to the company CEO, he becomes increasingly concerned. Although the forecast is below initial expectations, this is not what worries Ben. The problem is that some of the basic assumptions underlying his prediction might not come true. If this is the case, then the company's performance for the last quarter of the year will be dramatically below its annual forecast. The result would be a potentially severe reaction in the investment community causing a downward adjustment of unknown proportions in the firm's stock price.

Bonajet's CEO is a no-nonsense guy who really doesn't like to see his CFO hedge his predictions, so Ben is under pressure to decide whether to ignore the downside prospects or make them known to his CEO. Complicating matters is the fact that the worst-case scenario would probably give rise to a reorganization of Bonajet that would lead to substantial layoffs of its workforce. Here is Ben's dilemma: What should he tell the CEO in their meeting tomorrow morning?

Table 4–2

Salco Furniture Co., Inc., Cash Budget for the Six Months Ended June 30, 1998

WORKSHEET	OCT.	NOV.	DEC.	JAN.
Sales	$55,000	$62,000	$50,000	$60,000
Collections:				
First month (30%)				15,000
Second month (50%)				31,000
Third month (20%)				11,000
Total				$57,000
Purchases (75% of sales in two months)			$56,250	66,000
Payments (one-month lag)				$56,250
Cash budget				
Cash receipts				
Collections (see worksheet)				$57,000
Cash disbursements:				
Payments (see worksheet)				$56,250
Wages and salaries				3,000
Rent				4,000
Other expenses				1,000
Interest expense on existing debt ($12,000 note and $150,000 in long-term debt)				
Taxes				
Purchase of equipment				
Loan repayment ($12,000 note due in May)				
Total disbursements:				$64,250
Net monthly change				$(7,250)
Plus: Beginning cash balance				20,000
Less: Interest on short-term borrowing				—
Equals: Ending cash balance before short-term no borrowing				$12,750
Financing needed[a]				—
Ending cash balance				$12,750
Cumulative borrowing				—

[a]The amount of financing that is required to raise the firm's ending cash balance up to its $10,000 desired cash balance.
[b]Negative financing needed simply means the firm has excess cash that can be used to retire a part of its short-term borrowing from prior months.

COMPUTERIZED FINANCIAL PLANNING

Personal computers and spreadsheet software have reduced the tedium of the planning and budgeting process immensely. The number and variety of financial spreadsheet programs has expanded dramatically since the introduction of the original VisiCalc program. These include Lotus 1-2-3 and Excel, among others. In addition, there

FEB.	MAR.	APR.	MAY	JUNE	JULY	AUG.
$75,000	$88,000	$100,000	$110,000	$100,000	$80,000	$75,000
18,000	22,500	26,400	30,000	33,000		
25,000	30,000	37,500	44,000	50,000		
12,400	10,000	12,000	15,000	17,600		
55,400	62,500	75,900	89,000	100,600		
75,000	82,500	75,000	60,000	56,250		
66,000	75,000	82,500	75,000	60,000		
55,400	62,500	75,900	89,000	100,600		
66,000	75,000	82,500	75,000	60,000		
10,000	7,000	8,000	6,000	4,000		
4,000	4,000	4,000	4,000	4,000		
500	1,200	1,500	1,500	1,200		
			600			
				7,500		
	4,460			5,200		
14,000						
			12,000			
94,500	91,660	96,000	99,100	81,900		
(39,100)	(29,160)	(20,100)	(10,100)	18,700		
12,750	10,000	10,000	10,000	10,000		
—	(364)	(659)	(866)	(976)		
(26,350)	(19,524)	(10,759)	(966)	27,724		
36,350	29,524	20,759	10,966	(17,724)[b]		
10,000	10,000	10,000	10,000	10,000		
36,350	65,874	86,633	97,599	79,875		

is a growing set of products referred to as "expert systems," which attempt to mimic the decisions of experts. To date, these efforts have produced a limited number of financial applications software related to such things as the capital-budgeting decision, but they offer an opportunity to expand the capabilities of the financial manager of the future.

OBJECTIVE 1

This chapter develops the role of forecasting within the context of the firm's financial-planning activities. Forecasts of the firm's sales revenues and related expenses provide the basis for projecting future financing needs. The most popular method for forecasting financial variables is the percent of sales method.

OBJECTIVE 2

The percent of sales method presumes that the asset or liability being forecast is a constant percent of sales for all future levels of sales. There are instances where this assumption is not reasonable and consequently the percent of sales method does not provide reasonable predictions. One such instance arises where there are economies of scale in the use of the asset being forecast. For example, the firm may need at least $10 million in inventories to open its doors and operate even for sales as low as $100 million per year. If sales double to $200 million, inventories may only increase to $15 million. Thus, inventories do not increase with sales in a constant proportion. A second situation where the percent of sales method fails to work properly is where asset purchases are lumpy. That is, if plant capacity must be purchased in $50 million increments, then plant and equipment will not remain a constant percent of sales.

How serious are these possible problems and should we use the percent of sales method? Even in the face of these problems, the percent of sales method predicts reasonably well where predicted sales levels do not differ drastically from the level used to calculate the percent of sales. For example, if the current sales level used in calculating percent of sales for inventories is $40 million, then we can feel more comfortable forecasting the level of inventories corresponding to a new sales level of $42 million than where sales are predicted to rise to $60 million.

OBJECTIVE 3

A firm's sustainable rate of growth is the maximum rate at which its sales can grow if it is to maintain its present financial ratios and not have to resort to issuing new equity. We calculate the sustainable rate of growth as follows:

$$\text{sustainable rate of growth } (g^*) = \text{ROE } (1 - b)$$

where ROE is the return earned on common equity and b is the dividend payout ratio (that is, the ratio of dividends to earnings). Consequently, a firm's sustainable rate of growth increases with ROE and decreases with the fraction of its earnings paid out in dividends.

OBJECTIVE 4

The cash budget is the primary tool of financial forecasting and planning. It contains a detailed plan of future cash flow estimates and is comprised of four elements or segments: cash receipts, cash disbursements, net change in cash for the period, and new financing needed. Once prepared, the cash budget also serves as a tool for monitoring and controlling the firm's operations. By comparing actual cash receipts and disbursements to those in the cash budget, the financial manager can gain an appreciation for how well the firm is performing. In addition, deviations from the plan serve as an early warning system to signal the onset of financial difficulties ahead.

KEY TERMS

STUDY QUESTIONS

4-1. Discuss the shortcomings of the percent of sales method of financial forecasting.

4-2. Explain how a fixed cash budget differs from a variable or flexible cash budget.

4-3. What two basic needs does a flexible (variable) cash budget serve?

4-4. What would be the probable effect on a firm's cash position of the following events?

  a. Rapidly rising sales

  b. A delay in the payment of payables

  c. A more liberal credit policy on sales (to the firm's customers)

  d. Holding larger inventories

4-5. How long should the budget period be? Why would a firm not set a rule that all budgets be for a 12-month period?

4-6. A cash budget is usually thought of as a means of planning for future financing needs. Why would a cash budget also be important for a firm that has excess cash on hand?

4-7. Explain why a cash budget would be of particular importance to a firm that experiences seasonal fluctuations in its sales.

SELF-TEST PROBLEMS

ST-1. (*Financial Forecasting*) Use the percent of sales method to prepare a pro forma income statement for Calico Sales Co., Inc. Projected sales for next year equal $4 million. Cost of goods sold equals 70 percent of sales, administrative expense equals $500,000, and depreciation expense is $300,000. Interest expense equals $50,000 and income is taxed at a rate of 40 percent. The firm plans to spend $200,000 during the period to renovate its office facility and will retire $150,000 in notes payable. Finally, selling expense equals 5 percent of sales.

ST-2. (*Cash Budget*) Stauffer, Inc., has estimated sales and purchase requirements for the last half of the coming year. Past experience indicates that it will collect 20 percent of its sales in the month of the sale, 50 percent of the remainder one month after the sale, and the balance in the second month following the sale. Stauffer prefers to pay for half its purchases in the month of the purchase and the other half the following month. Labor expense for each month is expected to equal 5 percent of that month's sales, with cash payment being made in the month in which the expense is incurred. Depreciation expense is $5,000 per month; miscellaneous cash expenses are $4,000 per month and are paid in the month incurred. General and administrative expenses of $50,000 are recognized and paid monthly. A $60,000 truck is to be purchased in August and is to be depreciated on a straight-line basis over 10 years with no expected salvage value. The company also plans to pay a $9,000 cash dividend to stockholders in July. The company feels that a minimum cash balance of $30,000 should be maintained. Any borrowing will cost 12 percent annually, with interest paid in the month following the month in which the funds are borrowed. Borrowing takes place at the beginning of the month in which the need for funds arises. For example, if during the month of July the firm should need to borrow $24,000 to maintain its $30,000 desired minimum balance, then $24,000 will be taken out on July 1 with interest owed for the entire month of July. Interest for the month of July would then be paid on August 1. Sales and purchase estimates are shown on page 132. Prepare a cash budget for the months of July and August (cash on hand June 30 was $30,000, while sales for May and June were $100,000 and purchases were $60,000 for each of these months).

Month	Sales	Purchases
July	$120,000	$50,000
August	150,000	40,000
September	110,000	30,000

STUDY PROBLEMS

4-1. (*Financial Forecasting*) Zapatera Enterprises is evaluating its financing requirements for the coming year. The firm has only been in business for one year, but its chief financial officer predicts that the firm's operating expenses, current assets, net fixed assets, and current liabilities will remain at their current proportion of sales.

Last year Zapatera had $12 million in sales with net income of $1.2 million. The firm anticipates that next year's sales will reach $15 million with net income rising to $2 million. Given its present high rate of growth, the firm retains all its earnings to help defray the cost of new investments.

The firm's balance sheet for the year just ended is found below:

Zapatera Enterprises, Inc.

BALANCE SHEET

	12/31/97	% OF SALES
Current assets	$3,000,000	25%
Net fixed assets	6,000,000	50%
Total	$9,000,000	

LIABILITIES AND OWNERS' EQUITY

Accounts payable	$3,000,000	25%
Long-term debt	2,000,000	NA[6]
Total liabilities	$5,000,000	
Common stock	1,000,000	NA
Paid-in capital	1,800,000	NA
Retained earnings	1,200,000	
Common equity	4,000,000	
Total	$9,000,000	

[6]Not applicable. This figure does not vary directly with sales and is assumed to remain constant for purposes of making next year's forecast of financing requirements.

Estimate Zapatera's total financing requirements (i.e., total assets) for 1998 and its net funding requirements (discretionary financing needed).

Month	Sales	Month	Sales
January	$15,000	March	$30,000
February	20,000	April (projected)	40,000

4-2. (*Pro Forma Accounts Receivable Balance Calculation*) On March 31, 1997, the Sylvia Gift Shop had outstanding accounts receivable of $20,000. Sylvia's sales are roughly evenly split between credit and cash sales, with the credit sales collected half in the month after the sale and the remainder two months after the sale. Historical and projected sales for the gift shop are given below:

 a. Under these circumstances, what should the balance in accounts receivable be at the end of April?

 b. How much cash did Sylvia realize during April from sales and collections?

4-3. (*Financial Forecasting*) Sambonoza Enterprises projects its sales next year to be $4 million and expects to earn 5 percent of that amount after taxes. The firm is currently in the process of projecting its financing needs and has made the following assumptions (projections):

1. Current assets will equal 20 percent of sales, while fixed assets will remain at their current level of $1 million.

2. Common equity is currently $0.8 million, and the firm pays out half its after-tax earnings in dividends.

3. The firm has short-term payables and trade credit that normally equal 10 percent of sales, and has no long-term debt outstanding.

What are Sambonoza's financing needs for the coming year?

4-4. (*Financial Forecasting—Percent of Sales*) Tulley Appliances, Inc., projects next year's sales to be $20 million. Current sales are at $15 million based on current assets of $5 million and fixed assets of $5 million. The firm's net profit margin is 5 percent after taxes. Tulley forecasts that current assets will rise in direct proportion to the increase in sales, but fixed assets will increase by only $100,000. Currently, Tulley has $1.5 million in accounts payable (which vary directly with sales), $2 million in long-term debt (due in 10 years), and common equity (including $4 million in retained earnings) totaling $6.5 million. Tulley plans to pay $500,000 in common stock dividends next year.

 a. What are Tulley's total financing needs (i.e., total assets) for the coming year?

 b. Given the firm's projections and dividend payment plans, what are its discretionary financing needs?

 c. Based on your projections, and assuming that the $100,000 expansion in fixed assets will occur, what is the largest increase in sales the firm can support without having to resort to the use of discretionary sources of financing?

4-5. (*Pro Forma Balance Sheet Construction*) Use the following industry-average ratios to construct a pro forma balance sheet for Carlos Menza, Inc.

Total asset turnover	2 times
Average collection period (assume a 365-day year)	9 days
Fixed asset turnover	5 times
Inventory turnover (based on cost of goods sold)	3 times
Current ratio	2 times
Sales (all on credit)	$4.0 million
Cost of goods sold	75% of sales
Debt ratio	50%

		Current liabilities	
Cash		Long-term debt	
Accounts receivable	_____	Common stock plus	_____
Net fixed assets	$_____	Retained earnings	$_____

4-6. (*Cash Budget*) The Sharpe Corporation's projected sales for the first eight months of 1998 are as follows:

January	$ 90,000	May	$300,000
February	120,000	June	270,000
March	135,000	July	225,000
April	240,000	August	150,000

Of Sharpe's sales, 10 percent is for cash, another 60 percent is collected in the month following sales, and 30 percent is collected in the second month following sales. November and December sales for 1997 were $220,000 and $175,000, respectively.

Sharpe purchases its raw materials two months in advance of its sales equal to 60 percent of their final sales price. The supplier is paid one month after it makes delivery. For example, purchases for April sales are made in February and payment is made in March.

In addition, Sharpe pays $10,000 per month for rent and $20,000 each month for other expenditures. Tax prepayments of $22,500 are made each quarter, beginning in March. The company's cash balance at December 31, 1997, was $22,000; a minimum balance of $15,000 must be maintained at all times. Assume that any short-term financing needed to maintain the cash balance would be paid off in the month following the month of financing if sufficient funds are available. Interest on short-term loans (12 percent) is paid monthly. Borrowing to meet estimated monthly cash needs takes place at the beginning of the month. Thus, if in the month of April the firm expects to have a need for an additional $60,500, these funds would be borrowed at the beginning of April with interest of $605 (.12 × 1/12 × $60,500) owed for April and paid at the beginning of May.

  a. Prepare a cash budget for Sharpe covering the first seven months of 1998.

  b. Sharpe has $200,000 in notes payable due in July that must be repaid or renegotiated for an extension. Will the firm have ample cash to repay the notes?

4-7. (*Percent of Sales Forecasting*) Which of the following accounts would most likely vary directly with the level of firm sales? Discuss each briefly.

	Yes	No		Yes	No
Cash	___	___	Notes payable	___	___
Marketable securities	___	___	Plant and equipment	___	___
Accounts payable	___	___	Inventories	___	___

4-8. (*Financial Forecasting—Percent of Sales*) The balance sheet of the Thompson Trucking Company (TTC) follows:

Thompson Trucking Company Balance Sheet, December 31, 1997 ($ millions)

Current assets	$10	Accounts payable	$5
Net fixed assets	15	Notes payable	0
Total	$25	Bonds payable	10
		Common equity	10
		Total	$25

TTC had sales for the year ended 12/31/97 of $50 million. The firm follows a policy of paying all net earnings out to its common stockholders in cash dividends. Thus, TTC generates no funds from its earnings that can be used to expand its operations. (Assume that depreciation expense is just equal to the cost of replacing worn-out assets.)

a. If TTC anticipates sales of $80 million during the coming year, develop a pro forma balance sheet for the firm for 12/31/98. Assume that current assets vary as a percent of sales, net fixed assets remain unchanged, accounts payable vary as a percent of sales, and use notes payable as a balancing entry.

b. How much "new" financing will TTC need next year?

c. What limitations does the percent of sales forecast method suffer from? Discuss briefly.

4-9. (*Financial Forecasting—Discretionary Financing Needs*) The most recent balance sheet for the Armadillo Dog Co. is shown in the following table. The company is about to embark on an advertising campaign, which is expected to raise sales from the current level of $5 million to $7 million by the end of next year. The firm is currently operating at full capacity and will have to increase its investment in both current and fixed assets to support the projected level of new sales. In fact, the firm estimates that both categories of assets will rise in the direct proportion to the projected increase in sales.

Armadillo Dog Biscuit Co., Inc. ($ millions)

	PRESENT LEVEL	PERCENT OF SALES	PROJECTED LEVEL
Current assets	$2.0		
Net fixed assets	3.0		
Total	$5.0		
Accounts payable	$0.5		
Accrued expenses	0.5		
Notes payable	—		
Current liabilities	$1.0		
Long-term debt	$2.0		
Common stock	0.5		
Retained earnings	1.5		
Common equity	$2.0		
Total	$5.0		

The firm's net profits were 6 percent of the current year's sales but are expected to rise to 7 percent of next year's sales. To help support its anticipated growth in asset needs next year, the firm has suspended plans to pay cash dividends to its stockholders. In past years a $1.50 per share dividend has been paid annually.

Armadillo's payables and accrued expenses are expected to vary directly with sales. In addition, notes payable will be used to supply the funds that are needed to finance next year's operations and that are not forthcoming from other sources.

a. Fill in the table and project the firm's needs for discretionary financing. Use notes payable as the balancing entry for future discretionary financing needs.

b. Compare Armadillo's current ratio and debt ratio (total liabilities/total assets) before the growth in sales and after. What was the effect of the expanded sales on these two dimensions of Armadillo's financial condition?

c. What difference, if any, would have resulted if Armadillo's sales had risen to $6 million in one year and $7 million only after two years? Discuss only; no calculations required.

4-10. (*Forecasting Discretionary Financing Needs*) Fishing Charter, Inc., estimates that it invests 30 cents in assets for each dollar of new sales. However, 5 cents in profits are produced by each dollar of additional sales, of which 1 cent can be reinvested in the firm. If sales rise from their current level of $5 million by $500,000 next year, and the ratio of spontaneous liabilities to sales is .15, what will be the firm's need for discretionary financing? (*Hint:* In this situation you do not know what the firm's existing level of assets is, nor do you know how those assets have been financed. Thus you must estimate the change in financing needs and match this change with the expected changes in spontaneous liabilities, retained earnings, and other sources of discretionary financing.)

4-11. (*Preparation of a Cash Budget*) Harrison Printing has projected its sales for the first eight months of 1998 as follows:

January	$100,000	April	$300,000	July	$200,000
February	120,000	May	275,000	August	180,000
March	150,000	June	200,000		

Harrison collects 20 percent of its sales in the month of the sale, 50 percent in the month following the sale, and the remaining 30 percent two months following the sale. During November and December of 1997 Harrison's sales were $220,000 and $175,000, respectively.

Harrison purchases raw materials two months in advance of its sales equal to 65 percent of its final sales. The supplier is paid one month after delivery. Thus, purchases for April sales are made in February and payment is made in March.

In addition, Harrison pays $10,000 per month for rent and $20,000 each month for other expenditures. Tax prepayments of $22,500 are made each quarter beginning in March. The company's cash balance as of December 31, 1997, was $22,000; a minimum balance of $20,000 must be maintained at all times to satisfy the firm's bank line of credit agreement. Harrison has arranged with its bank for short-term credit at an interest rate of 12 percent per annum (1 percent per month) to be paid monthly. Borrowing to meet estimated monthly cash needs takes place at the end of the month, and interest is not paid until the end of the following month. Consequently, if the firm were to need to borrow $50,000 during the month of April, then it would pay $500 (= .01 × $50,000) in interest during May. Finally, Harrison follows a policy of repaying its outstanding short-term debt in any month in which its cash balance exceeds the minimum desired balance of $20,000.

a. Harrison needs to know what its cash requirements will be for the next six months so that it can renegotiate the terms of its short-term credit agreement with its bank, if necessary. To evaluate this problem, the firm plans to evaluate the impact of a ±20 percent variation in its monthly sales efforts. Prepare a six-month cash budget for Harrison and use it to evaluate the firm's cash needs.

b. Harrison has a $20,000 note due in June. Will the firm have sufficient cash to repay the loan?

4-12. (*Sustainable Rate of Growth*) ADP, Inc., is a manufacturer of specialty circuit boards in the personal computer industry. The firm has experienced phenomenal sales growth over its short five-year life. Selected financial statement data are found in the following table:

	19n5	19n4	19n3	19n2	19n1
Sales	$3,000	$2,200	$1,800	$1,400	$1,200
Net income	150	110	90	70	60
Assets	2,700	1,980	1,620	1,260	1,080
Dividends	60	44	36	28	24
Common equity	812	722	656	602	560
Liabilities	1,888	1,258	964	658	520
Liabilities and equity	2,700	1,980	1,620	1,260	1,080

a. Calculate ADP's sustainable rate of growth for each of the five years of its existence.

b. Compare the actual rates of growth in sales to the firm's sustainable rates calculated in part a. How has ADP been financing its growing asset needs?

4-13. (*Sustainable Rate of Growth*) The Carrera Game Company has experienced a 100 percent increase in sales over the last five years. The company president, Jack Carrera, has become increasingly alarmed by the firm's rising debt level even in the face of continued profitability.

	19n7	19n6	19n5	19n4	19n3
Sales	$60,000	$56,000	$48,000	$36,000	$30,000
Net income	3,000	2,800	2,400	1,800	1,500
Assets	54,000	50,400	43,200	32,400	27,000
Dividends	1,200	1,120	960	720	600
Common equity	21,000	19,200	17,520	16,080	15,000
Liabilities	33,000	31,200	25,680	16,320	12,000
Liabilities and equity	54,000	50,400	43,200	32,400	27,000

a. Calculate the debt-to-assets ratio, return on common equity, actual rate of growth in firm sales, and retention ratio for each of the five years of data provided above.

b. Calculate the sustainable rates of growth for Carrera for each of the last five years. Why has the firm's borrowing increased so dramatically?

4-14. (*Forecasting Inventories*) Findlay Instruments produces a complete line of medical instruments used by plastic surgeons and has experienced rapid growth over the last five years. In an effort to make more accurate predictions of its financing requirements, Findlay is currently attempting to construct a financial-planning model based on the percent of sales forecasting method. However, the firm's chief financial analyst (Sarah Macias) is concerned that the projections for inventories will be seriously in error. She recognizes that the firm has begun to accrue substantial economies of scale in its inventory investment and has documented this fact in the following data and calculations:

YEAR	SALES (000)	INVENTORY (000)	% OF SALES
19n1	$15,000	1,150	7.67%
19n2	18,000	1,180	6.56%
19n3	17,500	1,175	6.71%
19n4	20,000	1,200	6.00%
19n5	25,000	1,250	5.00%
		Average	6.39%

a. Plot Findlay's sales and inventories for the last five years. What is the relationship between these two variables?

b. Estimate firm inventories for 19n6 where firm sales are projected to reach $30 million. Use the average percent of sales for the last five years, the most recent percent of sales, and your evaluation of the true relationship between the sales and inventories from part a to make three predictions.

COMPREHENSIVE PROBLEM

Phillips Petroleum is an integrated oil and gas company with headquarters in Bartlesville, Oklahoma, where it was founded in 1917. The company engages in petroleum exploration and production worldwide. In addition, it engages in natural gas gathering and processing, as well as petroleum refining and marketing primarily in the United States. The company has three operating groups—Exploration and Production, Gas and Gas Liquids, and Downstream Operations, which encompasses Petroleum Products and Chemicals.

In the mid-eighties Phillips engaged in a major restructuring following two failed takeover attempts, one led by T. Boone Pickins and the other by Carl Ichan.[*] The restructuring resulted in a $4.5 billion plan to exchange a package of cash and debt securities for roughly half the company's shares and to sell $2 billion worth of assets. Phillip's long-term debt increased from $3.4 billion in late 1984 to a peak of $8.6 billion in April 1985.

During 1992 Phillips was able to strengthen its financial structure dramatically. Its subsidiary Phillips Gas Company completed an offering of $345 million of Series A 9.32% Cumulative Preferred Stock. As a result of these actions and prior year's debt reductions, the company lowered its long-term debt-to-capital ratio over the last five years from 75 percent to 55 percent. In addition, the firm refinanced over a billion dollars of its debt at reduced rates. A company spokesman said that "Our debt-to-capital ratio is still on the high side, and we'll keep working to bring it down. But the cost of debt is manageable, and we're beyond the point where debt overshadows everything else we do."[†]

Summary Financial Information for Phillips Petroleum Corporation: 1986–1992 (in millions of dollars except for per share figures)

	1986	1987	1988	1989	1990	1991	1992
Sales	$10,018.00	$10,917.00	$11,490.00	$12,492.00	$13,975.00	$13,259.00	$12,140.00
Net income	228.00	35.00	650.00	219.00	541.00	98.00	270.00
EPS	0.89	0.06	2.72	0.90	2.18	0.38	1.04
Current assets	2,802.00	2,855.00	3,062.00	2,876.00	3,322.00	2,459.00	2,349.00
Total assets	12,403.00	12,111.00	11,968.00	11,256.00	12,130.00	11,473.00	11,468.00
Current liabilities	2,234.00	2,402.00	2,468.00	2,706.00	2,910.00	2,503.00	2,517.00
Long-term debt	5,758.00	5,419.00	4,761.00	3,939.00	3,839.00	3,876.00	3,718.00
Total liabilities	10,409.00	10,289.00	9,855.00	9,124.00	9,411.00	8,716.00	8,411.00
Preferred stock	270.00	205.00	0.00	0.00	0.00	0.00	359.00
Common equity	1,724.00	1,617.00	2,113.00	2,132.00	2,719.00	2,757.00	2,698.00
Dividends per share	2.02	1.73	1.34	0.00	1.03	1.12	1.12

Source: Phillips Annual Reports for the years 1986–1992.

Highlights of Phillips' financial condition spanning the years 1986–1992 are found above. These data reflect the modern history of the company as a result of its financial restructuring following the downsizing and reorganization of Phillips' operations begun in the mid-eighties.

---

[*]This discussion is based on a story in the *New York Times*, January 7, 1986.
[†]From *SEC Online*, 1992.

Phillips' management is currently developing its financial plans for the next five years and wants to develop a forecast of its financing requirements. As a first approximation they have asked you to develop a model that can be used to make "ballpark" estimates of the firm's financing needs under the proviso that existing relationships found in the firm's financial statements remain the same over the period. Of particular interest is whether Phillips will be able to further reduce its reliance on debt financing. You may assume that Phillips' projected sales (in millions) for 1993 through 1997 are as follows: $13,000; $13,500; $14,000; $14,500; and $15,500.

a. Project net income for 1993–1997 using the percent of sales method based on an average of this ratio for 1986–1992.

b. Project total assets and current liabilities for the period 1993–1997 using the percent of sales method and your sales projections from part a.

c. Assuming that common equity increases only as a result of the retention of earnings and holding long-term debt and preferred stock equal to their 1992 balances, project Phillips' discretionary financing needs for 1993–1997. (*Hint:* Assume that total assets and current liabilities vary as a percent of sales as per your answers to part b above. In addition, assume that Phillips plans to continue to pay its dividends of $1.12 per share in each of the next five years.)

SELF–TEST SOLUTIONS

SS–1.

Calico Sales Co., Inc., Pro Forma Income Statement		
Sales		$4,000,000
Cost of goods sold (70%)		(2,800,000)
Gross profit		1,200,000
Operating expense		
Selling expense (5%)	$200,000	
Administrative expense	500,000	
Depreciation expense	300,000	(1,000,000)
Net operating income		200,000
Interest		(50,000)
Earnings before taxes		150,000
Taxes (40%)		(60,000)
Net income		$90,000

Although the office renovation expenditure and debt retirement are surely cash outflows, they do not enter the income statement directly. These expenditures affect expenses for the period's income statement only through their effect on depreciation and interest expense. A cash budget would indicate the full cash impact of the renovation and debt retirement expenditures.

	May	June	July	August
Sales	$100,000	$100,000	120,000	$150,000
Purchases	60,000	60,000	50,000	40,000
Cash receipts:				
Collections from month of sale (20%)	20,000	20,000	24,000	30,000
1 month later (50% of uncollected amount)		40,000	40,000	48,000
2 months later (balance)			40,000	40,000
Total receipts			$104,000	$118,000
Cash disbursements:				
Payments for purchases—				
From 1 month earlier			$30,000	$25,000
From current month			$25,000	20,000
Total			$55,000	$45,000
Miscellaneous cash expenses			4,000	4,000
Labor expense (5% of sales)			6,000	7,500
General and administrative expense				
($50,000 per month)			50,000	50,000
Truck purchase			0	60,000
Cash dividends			9,000	—
Total disbursements			$(124,000)	$(166,500)
Net change in cash			(20,000)	(48,500)
Plus: beginning cash balance			30,000	30,000
Less: interest on short-term borrowing				
(1% prior month's borrowing)				(200)
Equals: ending cash balance—without borrowing			10,000	(18,700)
Financing needed to reach target cash balance			20,000	48,700
Cumulative borrowing			$20,000	$68,700

The Time Value of Money

Compound Interest • Present Value • Annuities • Annuities Due • Amortized Loans • Compound Interest with Nonannual Periods • Present Value of an Uneven Stream • Perpetuities

LEARNING OBJECTIVES

After reading this chapter you should be able to

1. Explain the mechanics of compounding, that is, how money grows over time when it is invested.

2. Discuss the relationship between compounding and bringing money back to the present.

3. Define an ordinary annuity and calculate its compound or future value.

4. Differentiate between an ordinary annuity and an annuity due, and determine the future and present value of an annuity due.

5. Determine the future or present value of a sum when there are nonannual compounding periods.

6. Determine the present value of a perpetuity.

I n business, there is probably no other single concept with more power or applications than that of the time value of money. It has been the topic Homer (Sidney Homer that is), who, in his landmark book, *A History of Interest Rates,* noted that if $1,000 were invested for 400 years at 8 percent interest, it would grow to $23 quadrillion—that would work out to approximately $5 million per person on earth. He was not giving a plan to make the world rich, but effectively pointing out the power of the time value of money.

The time value of money is certainly not a new concept. Benjamin Franklin had a good understanding of how it worked when he left £1,000 each to Boston and Philadelphia. With the gift, he left instructions that the cities were to lend the money, charging the going interest rate, to worthy apprentices. Then, after the money had been invested in this way for 100 years, they were to use a portion of the investment to build something of benefit to the city and hold some back for the future. Two hundred years later, Franklin's Boston gift resulted in the construction of the Franklin Union, has helped countless medical students with loans, and still has over $3 million left in the account. Philadelphia, likewise, has reaped a significant reward from his gift. Bear in mind that all this has come from a gift of £2,000 with some serious help from the time value of money.

The power of the time value of money can also be illustrated through a story Andrew Tobias tells in his book *Money Angles.* There he tells of a peasant who wins a chess tournament put on by the king. The king then asks the peasant what he would like as the prize. The peasant answers that he would like for his village one piece of grain to be placed on the first square of his chessboard, two pieces of grain on the second square, four pieces on the third, eight on the fourth, and so forth. The king, thinking he was getting off easy, pledged on his word of honor that it would be done. Unfortunately for the king, by the time all 64 squares on the chessboard were filled, there were 18.5 million trillion grains of wheat on the board—the kernels were compounding at a rate of 100 percent over the 64 squares of the chessboard. Needless to say, no one in the village ever went hungry, in fact, that is so much wheat that if the kernels were one-quarter inch long (quite frankly, I have no idea how long a kernel of wheat is, but Andrew Tobias's guess is one-quarter inch), if laid end to end they could stretch to the sun and back 391,320 times.

Understanding the techniques of compounding and moving money through time are critical to almost every business decision. It will help you to understand such varied things as how stocks and bonds are valued, how to determine the value of a new project, how much you should save for children's education, and how much your mortgage payments will be.

In the next five chapters, we will focus on determining the value of the firm and the desirability of investment proposals. A key concept that underlies this material is the *time value of money;* that is, a dollar today is worth more than a dollar received a year from now. Intuitively this idea is easy to understand. We are all familiar with the concept of interest. This concept illustrates what economists call an *opportunity cost* of passing up the earning potential of a dollar today. This opportunity cost is the time value of money.

In evaluating and comparing investment proposals, we need to examine how dollar values might accrue from accepting these proposals. To do this, all dollar values must first be comparable; since a dollar received today is worth more than a dollar received in the future, we must move all dollar flows back to the present or out to a common future date. An understanding of the time value of money is essential, therefore, to an understanding of financial management, whether basic or advanced.

BACK TO THE FOUNDATIONS

In this chapter we develop the tools to incorporate **Axiom 2: The Time Value of Money—A Dollar Received Today Is Worth More Than a Dollar Received in the Future** into our calculations. In coming chapters we will use this concept to measure value by bringing the benefits and costs from a project back to the present.

OBJECTIVE 1

COMPOUND INTEREST

Most of us encounter the concept of compound interest at an early age. Anyone who has ever had a savings account or purchased a government savings bond has received compound interest. **Compound interest** occurs when *interest paid on the investment during the first period is added to the principal and then, during the second period, interest is earned on this new sum.*

compound interest

For example, suppose we place $100 in a savings account that pays 6 percent interest, compounded annually. How will our savings grow? At the end of the first year we have earned 6 percent, or $6 on our initial deposit of $100, giving us a total of $106 in our savings account. The mathematical formula illustrating this phenomenon is

$$FV_1 = PV(1 + i) \tag{5-1}$$

where FV_1 = the future value of the investment at the end of one year
i = the annual interest (or discount) rate
PV = the present value, or original amount invested at the beginning of the first year

In our example

$$FV_1 = PV(1 + i)$$
$$= \$100(1 + .06)$$
$$= \$100(1.06)$$
$$= \$106$$

Carrying these calculations one period further, we find that we now earn the 6 percent interest on a principal of \$106, which means we earn \$6.36 in interest during the second year. Why do we earn more interest during the second year than we did during the first? Simply because we now earn interest on the sum of the original principal, or present value, and the interest we earned in the first year. In effect we are now earning interest on interest; this is the concept of compound interest. Examining the mathematical formula illustrating the earning of interest in the second year, we find

$$FV_2 = FV_1(1 + i) \qquad (5\text{--}2)$$

which, for our example, gives

$$FV_2 = \$106(1.06)$$
$$= \$112.36$$

Looking back at equation (5–1), we can see that FV_1, or \$106, is actually equal to $PV(1 + i)$, or \$100(1 + .06). If we substitute these values into equation (5–2), we get

$$FV_2 = PV(1 + i)(1 + i)$$
$$= PV(1 + i)^2 \qquad (5\text{--}3)$$

Carrying this forward into the third year, we find that we enter the year with \$112.36 and we earn 6 percent, or \$6.74 in interest, giving us a total of \$119.10 in our savings account. Expressing this mathematically:

$$FV_3 = FV_2(1 + i) \qquad (5\text{--}4)$$
$$= \$112.36(1.06)$$
$$= \$119.10$$

If we substitute the value in equation (5–3) for FV_2 into equation (5–4), we find

$$FV_3 = PV(1 + i)(1 + i)(1 + i)$$
$$= PV(1 + i)^3 \qquad (5\text{--}5)$$

By now a pattern is beginning to be evident. We can generalize this formula to illustrate the value of our investment if it is compounded annually at a rate of i for n years to be

$$FV_n = PV(1 + i)^n \qquad (5\text{--}6)$$

where
FV_n = the future value of the investment at the end of n years
n = the number of years during which the compounding occurs
i = the annual interest (or discount) rate
PV = the present value or original amount invested at the beginning of the first year

Table 5–1 on page 144 illustrates how this investment of \$100 would continue to grow for the first 10 years at a compound interest rate of 6 percent. Notice how the amount of interest earned annually increases each year. Again, the reason is that each year interest is received on the sum of the original investment plus any interest earned in the past.

Table 5–1
Illustration of Compound Interest Calculations

Year	Beginning Value	Interest Earned	Ending Value
1	$100.00	$ 6.00	$106.00
2	106.00	6.36	112.36
3	112.36	6.74	119.10
4	119.10	7.15	126.25
5	126.25	7.57	133.82
6	133.82	8.03	141.85
7	141.85	8.51	150.36
8	150.36	9.02	159.38
9	159.38	9.57	168.95
10	168.95	10.13	179.08

When we examine the relationship between the number of years an initial investment is compounded for and its future value graphically, as shown in Figure 5–1, we see that we can increase the future value of an investment by either increasing the number of years for which we let it compound or by compounding it at a higher interest rate. We can also see this from equation (5–6), since an increase in either i or n while PV is held constant will result in an increase in FV_n.

PAUSE AND REFLECT

Keep in mind that future cash flows are assumed to occur at the end of the time period during which they accrue. For example, if a cash flow of $100 occurs in time period 5, it is assumed to occur at the end of time period 5, which is also the beginning of time period 6. In addition, cash flows that occur in time $t = 0$ occur right now; that is, they are already in present dollars.

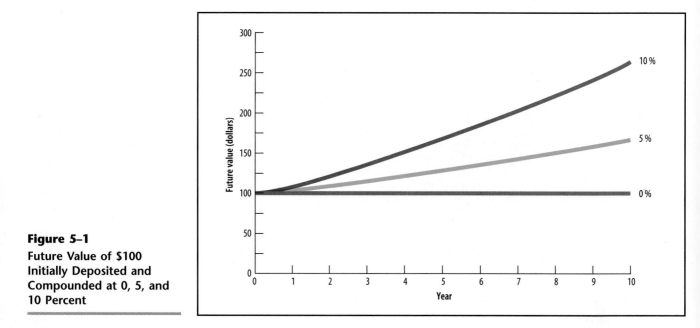

Figure 5–1

Future Value of $100 Initially Deposited and Compounded at 0, 5, and 10 Percent

If we place $1,000 in a savings account paying 5 percent interest compounded annually, how much will our account accrue to in 10 years? Substituting $PV = \$1000$, $i = 5$ percent, and $n = 10$ years into equation (5–6), we get

$$FV_n = PV(1 + i)^n \qquad\qquad \textbf{(5–6)}$$
$$= \$1,000(1 + .05)^{10}$$
$$= \$1,000(1.62889)$$
$$= \$1,628.89$$

Thus, at the end of 10 years we will have $1,628.89 in our savings account.

As the determination of future value can be quite time-consuming when an investment is held for a number of years, the **future-value interest factor** for i and n (**$FVIF_{i,n}$**) defined as $(1 + i)^n$, has been compiled in the back of the book for various values of i and n. An abbreviated compound interest or future-value interest factor table appears in Table 5–2, with a more comprehensive version of this table appearing in Appendix B at the back of this book. Alternatively, the $FVIF_{i,n}$ values could easily be determined using a calculator. Note that the compounding factors given in these tables represent the value of $1 compounded at rate i at the *end* of the nth year. Thus, to calculate the future value of an initial investment we need only to determine the $FVIF_{i,n}$ using a calculator or the tables at the end of the text and multiply this times the initial investment. In effect, we can rewrite equation (5–6) as follows:

future-value interest factor

$$FV_n = PV(FVIF_{i,n}) \qquad\qquad \textbf{(5–6a)}$$

If we invest $500 in a bank where it will earn 8 percent compounded annually, how much will it be worth at the end of seven years? Looking at Table 5–2 in the row $n = 7$ and column $i = 8$ percent, we find that $FVIF_{8\%,7yr}$ has a value of 1.714. Substituting this into equation (5–6a), we find

$$FV_n = PV(FVIF_{8\%,7yr})$$
$$= \$500(1.714)$$
$$= \$857$$

Table 5–2
$FVIF_{i,n}$ or the Compound Sum of $1

N	1%	2%	3%	4%	5%	6%	7%	8%	9%	10%
1	1.010	1.020	1.030	1.040	1.050	1.060	1.070	1.080	1.090	1.100
2	1.020	1.040	1.061	1.082	1.102	1.124	1.145	1.166	1.188	1.210
3	1.030	1.061	1.093	1.125	1.158	1.191	1.225	1.260	1.295	1.331
4	1.041	1.082	1.126	1.170	1.216	1.262	1.311	1.360	1.412	1.464
5	1.051	1.104	1.159	1.217	1.276	1.338	1.403	1.469	1.539	1.611
6	1.062	1.126	1.194	1.265	1.340	1.419	1.501	1.587	1.677	1.772
7	1.072	1.149	1.230	1.316	1.407	1.504	1.606	1.714	1.828	1.949
8	1.083	1.172	1.267	1.369	1.477	1.594	1.718	1.851	1.993	2.144
9	1.094	1.195	1.305	1.423	1.551	1.689	1.838	1.999	2.172	2.358
10	1.105	1.219	1.344	1.480	1.629	1.791	1.967	2.159	2.367	2.594
11	1.116	1.243	1.384	1.539	1.710	1.898	2.105	2.332	2.580	2.853
12	1.127	1.268	1.426	1.601	1.796	2.012	2.252	2.518	2.813	3.138
13	1.138	1.294	1.469	1.665	1.886	2.133	2.410	2.720	3.066	3.452
14	1.149	1.319	1.513	1.732	1.980	2.261	2.579	2.937	3.342	3.797
15	1.161	1.346	1.558	1.801	2.079	2.397	2.759	3.172	3.642	4.177

Thus, we will have $857 at the end of seven years.

In the future we will find several uses for equation (5–6); not only will we find the future value of an investment, but we can also solve for PV, i, or n. In any case, we will be given three of the four variables and will have to solve for the fourth.

EXAMPLE

How many years will it take for an initial investment of $300 to grow to $774 if it is invested at 9 percent compounded annually? In this problem we know the initial investment, $PV = \$300$; the future value, $FV_n = \$774$; the compound growth rate, $i = 9$ percent; and we are solving for the number of years it must compound for, $n = ?$ Substituting the known values in equation (5–6), we find

$$FV_n = PV(1 + i)^n$$
$$\$774 = \$300(1 + .09)^n$$
$$2.58 = (1 + .09)^n$$

Thus, we are looking for a value of 2.58 in the $FVIF_{i,n}$ tables, and we know it must be in the 9 percent column. Looking down the 9 percent column for the value closest to 2.58, we find that it occurs in the $n = 11$ row. Thus, it will take 11 years for an initial investment of $300 to grow to $774 if it is invested at 9 percent compounded annually. ■

EXAMPLE

At what rate must $100 be compounded annually for it to grow to $179.10 in 10 years? In this case we know the initial investment, $PV = \$100$; the future value of this investment at the end of n years, $FV_n = \$179.10$; and the number of years that the initial investment will compound for, $n = 10$ years. Substituting into equation (5–6), we get

$$FV_n = PV(1 + i)^n \qquad \textbf{(5–6)}$$
$$\$179.10 = \$100(1 + i)^{10}$$
$$1.791 = (1 + i)^{10}$$

We know we are looking in the $n = 10$ row of the $FVIF_{i,n}$ table for a value of 1.791, and we find this in the $i = 6$ percent column. Thus, if we want our initial investment of $100 to accrue to $179.10 in 10 years, we must invest it at 6 percent. ■

Moving Money through Time with the Aid of a Financial Calculator

Time value of money calculations can be made simple with the aid of a *financial calculator*. In solving time value of money problems with a financial calculator, you will be given three of four variables and will have to solve for the fourth. Before presenting any solutions using a financial calculator, we will introduce the calculator's five most common keys. (In most time value of money problems, only four of these keys are relevant.) These keys are:

Menu Key	Description
N	Stores (or calculates) the total number of payments or compounding periods.
I/Y	Stores (or calculates) the interest or discount rate.
PV	Stores (or calculates) the present value of a cash flow or series of cash flows.
FV	Stores (or calculates) the future value, that is, the dollar amount of a final cash flow or the compound value of a single flow or series of cash flows.
PMT	Stores (or calculates) the dollar amount of each annuity payment deposited or received at the end of each year.

When you use a financial calculator, remember that outflows generally have to be entered as negative numbers. In general, each problem will have two cash flows: one an outflow with a negative value, and one an inflow with a positive value. The idea is that you deposit money in the bank at some point in time (an outflow), and at some other point in time you take money out of the bank (an inflow). Also, every calculator operates a bit differently with respect to entering variables. Needless to say, it is a good idea to familiarize yourself with exactly how your calculator functions.

As stated above, in any problem you will be given three of four variables. These four variables will always include N and I/Y; in addition, two out of the final three variables—PV, FV, and PMT—will also be included. To solve a time value of money problem using a financial calculator, all you need to do is enter the appropriate numbers for three of the four variables and then press the key of the final variable to calculate its value. It is also a good idea to enter zero for any of the five variables not included in the problem in order to clear that variable.

Now let's solve the previous example using a financial calculator. We were trying to find at what rate must $100 be compounded annually for it to grow to $179.10 in 10 years. The solution using a financial calculator would be as follows:

Step 1: Input Values of Known Variables

Data Input	Function Key	Description
10	N	Stores N = 10 years
−100	PV	Stores PV = −$100
179.10	FV	Stores FV = $179.10
0	PMT	Clears PMT to = 0

Step 2: Calculate the value of the unknown variable

Function Key	Answer	Description
CPT		
I/Y	6.00%	Calculates I/Y = 6.00%

Any of the problems in this chapter can easily be solved using a financial calculator; and the solutions to many examples using a Texas Instruments BAII Plus financial calculator are provided in the margins. If you are using the TI BAII Plus, make sure that you have selected both the "END MODE" and "one payment per year" (*P/Y* = 1). This sets the payment conditions to a maximum of one payment per period occurring at the end of the period. One final point, you will notice that solutions using the present-value tables versus solutions using a calculator may vary slightly—a result of rounding errors in the tables.

For further explanation of the TI BAII Plus, see Appendix A at the end of the book.

PAUSE AND REFLECT

The concepts of compound interest and present value will follow us through the remainder of this book. Not only will they allow us to determine the future value of any investment, but they will allow us to bring the benefits and costs from new investment proposals back to the present and thereby determine the value of the investment in today's dollars.

OBJECTIVE 2 | **PRESENT VALUE**

Up until this point we have been moving money forward in time; that is, we know how much we have to begin with and are trying to determine how much that sum will grow in a certain number of years when compounded at a specific rate. We are now going to look at the reverse question: What is the value in today's dollars of a sum of money to be received in the future? The answer to this question will help us determine the desirability of investment projects in Chapters 9 and 10. In this case we are moving future money back to the present. We will be determining the **present value** of a lump sum, which in simple terms is the *current value of a future payment*. What we will be doing is, in fact, nothing other than inverse compounding. The differences in these techniques come about merely from the investor's point of view. In compounding we talked about the compound interest rate and the initial investment; in determining the present value we will talk about the discount rate and present value. Determination of the discount rate is the subject of Chapter 11 and can be defined as the rate of return available on an investment of equal risk to what is being discounted. Other than that, the technique and the terminology remain the same, and the mathematics are simply reversed. In equation (5–6) we were attempting to determine the future value of an initial investment. We now want to determine the initial investment or present value. By dividing both sides of equation (5–6) by $(1 + i)^n$, we get

present value

$$PV = FV_n \left[\frac{1}{(1 + i)^n} \right] \tag{5–7}$$

where FV_n = the future value of the investment at the
end of n years
n = the number of years until the payment
will be received
i = the annual discount (or interest) rate
PV = the present value of the future sum of money

Because the mathematical procedure for determining the present value is exactly the inverse of determining the future value, we also find that the relationships among n, i, and PV are just the opposite of those we observed in future value. The present

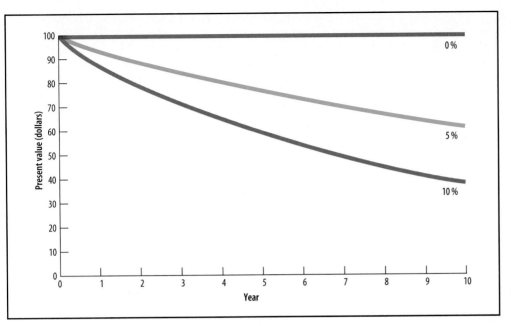

Figure 5–2

Present Value of $100 to Be Received at a Future Date and Discounted Back to the Present at 0, 5, and 10 Percent

value of a future sum of money is inversely related to both the number of years until the payment will be received and the discount rate. Graphically, this relationship can be seen in Figure 5–2.

PAUSE AND REFLECT

Although the present value equation [equation (5–7)] will be used extensively in evaluating new investment proposals, it should be stressed that the present value equation is actually the same as the future value or compounding equation [equation (5–6)], where it is solved for PV.

EXAMPLE

What is the present value of $500 to be received 10 years from today if our discount rate is 6 percent? Substituting $FV_{10} = \$500$, $n = 10$, and $i = 6$ percent into equation (5–7), we find

$$PV = \$500\left[\frac{1}{(1 + .06)^{10}}\right]$$

$$= \$500\left(\frac{1}{1.791}\right)$$

$$= \$500(.558)$$

$$= \$279$$

Thus, the present value of the $500 to be received in 10 years is $279.

To aid in the computation of present values, the **present-value interest factor** for i and n (**$PVIF_{i,n}$**), defined as $[1/(1 + i)^n]$, has been compiled for various combinations of i and n and appears in Appendix C at the back of this book. An abbreviated version of Appendix C appears in Table 5–3 on page 150. A close examination shows that the values in Table 5–3 are merely the inverse of those found in Table 5–2 and Appendix B. This, of course, is as it should be, as the values in Appendix B are $(1 + i)^n$ and those in Appendix C are $[1/(1 + i)^n]$. Now, to determine the present value

CALCULATOR SOLUTION

DATA INPUT	FUNCTION KEY
10	N
6	I/Y
500	FV
0	PMT

FUNCTION KEY	ANSWER
CPT	
PV	–279.20

present-value interest factor

Table 5–3

$PVIF_{i,n}$ or the Present Value of $1

N	1%	2%	3%	4%	5%	6%	7%	8%	9%	10%
1	.990	.980	.971	.962	.952	.943	.935	.926	.917	.909
2	.980	.961	.943	.925	.907	.890	.873	.857	.842	.826
3	.971	.942	.915	.889	.864	.840	.816	.794	.772	.751
4	.961	.924	.888	.855	.823	.792	.763	.735	.708	.683
5	.951	.906	.863	.822	.784	.747	.713	.681	.650	.621
6	.942	.888	.837	.790	.746	.705	.666	.630	.596	.564
7	.933	.871	.813	.760	.711	.655	.623	.583	.547	.513
8	.923	.853	.789	.731	.677	.627	.582	.540	.502	.467
9	.914	.837	.766	.703	.645	.592	.544	.500	.460	.424
10	.905	.820	.744	.676	.614	.558	.508	.463	.422	.386
11	.896	.804	.722	.650	.585	.527	.475	.429	.388	.350
12	.887	.789	.701	.625	.557	.497	.444	.397	.356	.319
13	.879	.773	.681	.601	.530	.469	.415	.368	.326	.290
14	.870	.758	.661	.577	.505	.442	.388	.340	.299	.263
15	.861	.743	.642	.555	.481	.417	.362	.315	.275	.239

of a sum of money to be received at some future date, we need only determine the value of the appropriate $PVIF_{i,n}$, either by using a calculator or consulting the tables, and multiply it by the future value. In effect we can use our new notation and rewrite equation (5–7) as follows:

$$PV = FV_n(PVIF_{i,n}) \qquad \text{(5–7a)}$$

EXAMPLE

What is the present value of $1,500 to be received at the end of 10 years if our discount rate is 8 percent? By looking at the $n = 10$ row and $i = 8$ percent column of Table 5–3, we find the $PVIF_{8\%, 10yr}$ is .463. Substituting this value into equation (5–7a), we find

$$PV = \$1,500(.463)$$
$$= \$694.50$$

Thus, the present value of this $1,500 payment is $694.50. ∎

Again, we only have one present-value–future-value equation; that is, equations (5–6) and (5–7) are identical. We have introduced them as separate equations to simplify our calculations; in one case we are determining the value in future dollars and in the other case the value in today's dollars. In either case the reason is the same: to compare values on alternative investments and to recognize that the value of a dollar received today is not the same as that of a dollar received at some future date. We must measure the dollar values in dollars of the same time period. Because all present values are comparable (they are all measured in dollars of the same time period), we can add and subtract the present value of inflows and outflows to determine the net present value of an investment.

EXAMPLE

What is the present value of an investment that yields $500 to be received in 5 years and $1,000 to be received in 10 years if the discount rate is 4 percent? Substituting the values of $n = 5$, $i = 4$ percent, and $FV_5 = \$500$; and $n = 10$, $i = 4$ percent, and $FV_{10} = \$1000$ into equation (5–7) and adding these values together, we find

$$PV = \$500\left[\frac{1}{(1 + .04)^5}\right] + \$1,000\left[\frac{1}{(1 + .04)^{10}}\right]$$

$$= \$500(PVIF_{4\%, \, 5 \text{ yr}}) + \$1,000(PVIF_{4\%, 10 \text{ yr}})$$

$$= \$500(.822) + \$1,000(.676)$$

$$= \$411 + \$676$$

$$= \$1,087$$

Again, present values are comparable because they are measured in the same time period's dollars. ■

OBJECTIVE 3

ANNUITIES

An **annuity** is a *series of equal dollar payments for a specified number of years.* When we talk about annuities we will be referring to **ordinary annuities** unless otherwise noted. With an ordinary annuity *the payments occur at the end of each period.* Because annuities occur frequently in finance—for example, as bond interest payments—we will treat them specially. Although compounding and determining the present value of an annuity can be dealt with using the methods we have just described, these processes can be time-consuming, especially for larger annuities. Thus, we have modified the formulas to deal directly with annuities.

annuity
ordinary annuities

Compound Annuities

A **compound annuity** involves *depositing or investing an equal sum of money at the end of each year for a certain number of years and allowing it to grow.* Perhaps we are saving money for education, a new car, or a vacation home. In any case we want to know how much our savings will have grown by some point in the future.

compound annuity

Actually, we can find the answer by using equation (5–6), our compounding equation, and compounding each of the individual deposits to its future value. For example, if to provide for a college education we are going to deposit $500 at the end of each year for the next five years in a bank where it will earn 6 percent interest, how much will we have at the end of five years? Compounding each of these values using equation (5–6), we find that we will have $2,818.50 at the end of five years.

$$FV_5 = \$500(1 + .06)^4 + \$500(1 + .06)^3 + \$500(1 + .06)^2$$
$$+ \$500(1 + .06) + \$500$$

$$= \$500(1.262) + \$500(1.191) + \$500(1.124)$$
$$+ \$500(1.060) + \$500$$

$$= \$631.00 + \$595.50 + \$562.00 + \$530.00 + \$500.00$$
$$= \$2,818.50$$

From examining the mathematics involved and the graph of the movement of money through time in Table 5–4 (see page 152), we can see that this procedure can be generalized to

$$FV_n = PMT\left[\sum_{t=0}^{n-1}(1 + i)^t\right] \qquad \textbf{(5–8)}$$

where FV_n = the future value of the annuity at the end of the nth year

YEAR		0	1	2	3	4	5
DOLLAR DEPOSITS AT END OF YEAR			500	500	500	500	500

$500.00
530.00
562.00
595.50
631.00

Future value of the annuity | $2,818.50

PMT = the annuity payment deposited or received at the end of each year

i = the annual interest (or discount) rate

n = the number of years for which the annuity will last

To aid in compounding annuities, the **future-value interest factor for an annuity** for i and n (**$FVIFA_{i,n}$**), defined as $\left[\sum_{t=0}^{n-1}(1+i)^t\right]$, is provided in Appendix D for various combinations of n and i; an abbreviated version is shown in Table 5–5.[1]

Using this new notation, we can rewrite equation (5–8) as follows:

$$FV_n = PMT(FVIFA_{i,n}) \tag{5–8a}$$

Reexamining the previous example, in which we determined the value after five years of $500 deposited in the bank at 6 percent at the end of each of the next five years, we would look in the $i = 6$ percent column and $n = 5$ row and find the value of the $FVIFA_{6\%,\,5yr}$ to be 5.637. Substituting this value into equation (5–8a), we get

$$FV_5 = \$500(5.637)$$
$$= \$2,818.50$$

This is the same answer we obtained earlier using equation (5–6).

Rather than ask how much we will accumulate if we deposit an equal sum in a savings account each year, a more common question is how much we must deposit each year to accumulate a certain amount of savings. This problem frequently occurs with respect to saving for large expenditures and pension funding obligations.

For example, we may know that we need $10,000 for education in eight years; how much must we deposit in the bank at the end of each year at 6 percent interest to have the college money ready? In this case we know the values of n, i, and FV_n in equation (5–8); what we do not know is the value of PMT. Substituting these example values in equation (5–8), we find

$$\$10,000 = PMT\left[\sum_{t=0}^{8-1}(1+.06)^t\right]$$

$$\$10,000 = PMT(FVIFA_{6\%,\,8\,yr})$$

$$\$10,000 = PMT(9.897)$$

CALCULATOR SOLUTION

DATA INPUT	FUNCTION KEY
5	N
6	I/Y
0	PV
500	PMT

FUNCTION KEY	ANSWER
CPT	
FV	–2,818.55

CALCULATOR SOLUTION

DATA INPUT	FUNCTION KEY
8	N
6	I/Y
10,000	FV
0	PV

FUNCTION KEY	ANSWER
CPT	
PMT	–1,010.36

---

[1]Another useful analytical relationship for FV_n is $FV_n = PMT[(1+i)^n - 1]/i$.

Table 5–5
$FVIFA_{i,n}$, or the Sum of an Annuity of $1 for n Years

N	1%	2%	3%	4%	5%	6%	7%	8%	9%	10%
1	1.000	1.000	1.000	1.000	1.000	1.000	1.000	1.000	1.000	1.000
2	2.010	2.020	2.030	2.040	2.050	2.060	2.070	2.080	2.090	2.100
3	3.030	3.060	3.091	3.122	3.152	3.184	3.215	3.246	3.278	3.310
4	4.060	4.122	4.184	4.246	4.310	4.375	4.440	4.506	4.573	4.641
5	5.101	5.204	5.309	5.416	5.526	5.637	5.751	5.867	5.985	6.105
6	6.152	6.308	6.468	6.633	6.802	6.975	7.153	7.336	7.523	7.716
7	7.214	7.434	7.662	7.898	8.142	8.394	8.654	8.923	9.200	9.487
8	8.286	8.583	8.892	9.214	9.549	9.897	10.260	10.637	11.028	11.436
9	9.368	9.755	10.159	10.583	11.027	11.491	11.978	12.488	13.021	13.579
10	10.462	10.950	11.464	12.006	12.578	13.181	13.816	14.487	15.193	15.937
11	11.567	12.169	12.808	13.486	14.207	14.972	15.784	16.645	17.560	18.531
12	12.682	13.412	14.192	15.026	15.917	16.870	17.888	18.977	20.141	21.384
13	13.809	14.680	15.618	16.627	17.713	18.882	20.141	21.495	22.953	24.523
14	14.947	15.974	17.086	18.292	19.598	21.015	22.550	24.215	26.019	27.975
15	16.097	17.293	18.599	20.023	21.578	23.276	25.129	27.152	29.361	31.772

$$\frac{\$10,000}{9.897} = PMT$$

$$\$1,010.41 = PMT$$

Thus, we must deposit $1,010.41 in the bank at the end of each year for eight years at 6 percent interest to accumulate $10,000 at the end of eight years.

EXAMPLE

How much must we deposit in an 8 percent savings account at the end of each year to accumulate $5,000 at the end of 10 years? Substituting the values $FV_{10} = \$5,000$, $n = 10$, and $i = 8$ percent into equation (5–8), we find

$$\$5,000 = PMT\left[\sum_{t=0}^{10-1}(1+.08)^t\right] = PMT(FVIFA_{8\%,\ 10\ yr})$$

$$\$5,000 = PMT(14.487)$$

$$\frac{\$5,000}{14.487} = PMT$$

$$\$345.14 = PMT$$

Thus, we must deposit $345.14 per year for 10 years at 8 percent to accumulate $5,000.

CALCULATOR SOLUTION

DATA INPUT	FUNCTION KEY
10	N
8	I/Y
5,000	FV
0	PV

FUNCTION KEY	ANSWER
CPT	
PMT	–345.15

PAUSE AND REFLECT

A timeline often makes it easier to understand time value of money problems. By visually plotting the flow of money you can better determine which formula to use. Arrows placed above the line are inflows, whereas arrows below the line represent outflows. One thing is certain: Timelines reduce errors.

Present Value of an Annuity

Pension funds, insurance obligations, and interest received from bonds all involve annuities. To compare them, we need to know the present value of each. While we can find this by using the present-value table in Appendix C, this can be time-consuming, particularly when the annuity lasts for several years. For example, if we wish to know what $500 received at the end of the next five years is worth to us given the appropriate discount rate of 6 percent, we can simply substitute the appropriate values into equation (5–7), such that

$$PV = \$500\left[\frac{1}{(1+.06)}\right] + \$500\left[\frac{1}{(1+.06)^2}\right] + \$500\left[\frac{1}{(1+.06)^3}\right]$$

$$+ \$500\left[\frac{1}{(1+.06)^4}\right] + \$500\left[\frac{1}{(1+.06)^5}\right]$$

$$= \$500(.943) + \$500(.890) + \$500(.840) + \$500(.792) + \$500(.747)$$

$$= \$2,106$$

Thus, the present value of this annuity is $2,106.00. From examining the mathematics involved and the graph of the movement of these funds through time in Table 5–6, we see that this procedure can be generalized to

$$PV = PMT\left[\sum_{t=1}^{n} \frac{1}{(1+i)^t}\right] \tag{5–9}$$

where PMT = the annuity payment deposited or received at the end of each year

i = the annual discount (or interest) rate

PV = the present value of the future annuity

n = the number of years for which the annuity will last

To simplify the process of determining the present value of an annuity, the **present-value interest factor for an annuity** for i and n ($PVIFA_{i,n}$), defined as $\left[\sum_{t=1}^{n} \frac{1}{(1+i)^t}\right]$ has been compiled for various combinations of i and n in Appendix E with an abbreviated version provided in Table 5–7.[2]

present-value-interest factor for an annuity

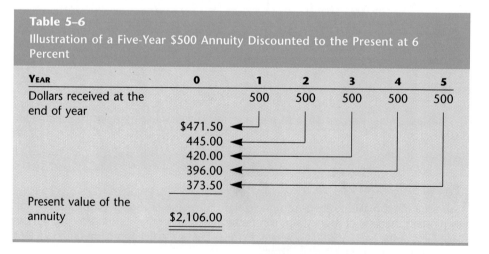

Table 5–6
Illustration of a Five-Year $500 Annuity Discounted to the Present at 6 Percent

YEAR	0	1	2	3	4	5
Dollars received at the end of year		500	500	500	500	500
	$471.50					
	445.00					
	420.00					
	396.00					
	373.50					
Present value of the annuity	$2,106.00					

---

[1]Another useful analytical relationship for PV is $PV = PMT[1 - 1/(1+i)^n]/i$.

Table 5-7

PVIFA$_{i,n}$, or the Present Value of an Annuity of $1

N	1%	2%	3%	4%	5%	6%	7%	8%	9%	10%
1	0.990	0.980	0.971	0.962	0.952	0.943	0.935	0.926	0.917	0.909
2	1.970	1.942	1.913	1.886	1.859	1.833	1.808	1.783	1.759	1.736
3	2.941	2.884	2.829	2.775	2.723	2.673	2.624	2.577	2.531	2.487
4	3.902	3.808	3.717	3.630	3.546	3.465	3.387	3.312	3.240	3.170
5	4.853	4.713	4.580	4.452	4.329	4.212	4.100	3.993	3.890	3.791
6	5.795	5.601	5.417	5.242	5.076	4.917	4.767	4.623	4.486	4.355
7	6.728	6.472	6.230	6.002	5.786	5.582	5.389	5.206	5.033	4.868
8	7.652	7.326	7.020	6.733	6.463	6.210	5.971	5.747	5.535	5.335
9	8.566	8.162	7.786	7.435	7.108	6.802	6.515	6.247	5.995	5.759
10	9.471	8.983	8.530	8.111	7.722	7.360	7.024	6.710	6.418	6.145
11	10.368	9.787	9.253	8.760	8.306	7.887	7.499	7.139	6.805	6.495
12	11.255	10.575	9.954	9.385	8.863	8.384	7.943	7.536	7.161	6.814
13	12.134	11.348	10.635	9.986	9.394	8.853	8.358	7.904	7.487	7.103
14	13.004	12.106	11.296	10.563	9.899	9.295	8.746	8.244	7.786	7.367
15	13.865	12.849	11.938	11.118	10.380	9.712	9.108	8.560	8.061	7.606

Using this new notation we can rewrite equation (5–9) as follows:

$$PV = PMT(PVIFA_{i,n}) \qquad \textbf{(5–9a)}$$

Solving the previous example to find the present value of $500 received at the end of each of the next five years discounted back to the present at 6 percent, we look in the $i = 6$ percent column and $n = 5$ row and find the PVIFA$_{6\%, 5yr}$ to be 4.212. Substituting the appropriate values into equation (5–9a), we find

$$PV = \$500(4.212)$$
$$= \$2,106$$

This, of course, is the same answer we calculated when we individually discounted each cash flow to the present. The reason is that we really only have *one* table; the Table 5–7 value for an *n*-year annuity for any discount rate i is merely the sum of the first *n* values in Table 5–3. We can see this by comparing the value in the present-value-of-an-annuity table (Table 5–8) for $i = 8$ percent and $n = 6$ years, which is 4.623, with the sum of the values in the $i = 8$ percent column and $n = 1, \ldots, 6$ rows of the present-value table (Table 5–3), which is equal to 4.623, as shown in Table 5–8.

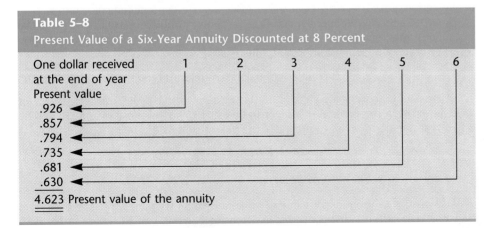

Table 5-8
Present Value of a Six-Year Annuity Discounted at 8 Percent

One dollar received at the end of year   1   2   3   4   5   6

Present value
.926
.857
.794
.735
.681
.630
4.623 Present value of the annuity

CALCULATOR SOLUTION

DATA INPUT	FUNCTION KEY
10	N
5	I/Y
1,000	PMT
0	FV

FUNCTION KEY	ANSWER
CPT	
PV	−7,721.73

What is the present value of a 10-year $1,000 annuity discounted back to the present at 5 percent? Substituting $n = 10$ years, $i = 5$ percent, and $PMT = \$1,000$ into equation (5–9), we find

$$PV = \$1,000\left[\sum_{t=1}^{10} \frac{1}{(1 + .05)^t}\right] = \$1,000(PVIFA_{5\%, \, 10 \, yr})$$

Determining the value for the $PVIFA_{5\%, \, 10 \, yr}$ from Table 5–7, row $n = 10$, column $i = 5$ percent, and substituting it in, we get

$$\begin{aligned} PV &= \$1,000(7.722) \\ &= \$7,722 \end{aligned}$$

Thus, the present value of this annuity is $7,722. ◼

As with our other compounding and present-value tables, given any three of the four unknowns in equation (5–9), we can solve for the fourth. In the case of the present-value-of-an-annuity table we may be interested in solving for *PMT*, if we know i, n, and *PV*. The financial interpretation of this action would be: How much can be withdrawn, perhaps as a pension or to make loan payments, from an account that earns i percent compounded annually for each of the next n years if we wish to have nothing left at the end of n years? For example, if we have $5,000 in an account earning 8 percent interest, how large an annuity can we draw out each year if we want nothing left at the end of five years? In this case the present value, *PV*, of the annuity is $5,000, $n = 5$ years, $i = 8$ percent, and *PMT* is unknown. Substituting this into equation (5–9), we find

CALCULATOR SOLUTION

DATA INPUT	FUNCTION KEY
5	N
8	I/Y
5,000	PV
0	FV

FUNCTION KEY	ANSWER
CPT	
PMT	−1,252.28

$$\begin{aligned} \$5,000 &= PMT(3.993) \\ \$1,252.19 &= PMT \end{aligned}$$

Thus, this account will fall to zero at the end of five years if we withdraw $1,252.19 at the end of each year.

OBJECTIVE 4 — **ANNUITIES DUE**

annuity due

Because **annuities due** are really just *ordinary annuities where all the annuity payments have been shifted forward by one year,* compounding them and determining their present value is actually quite simple. Remember, with an annuity due, each annuity payment occurs at the beginning of each period rather than at the end of the period. Let's first look at how this affects our compounding calculations.

Since an annuity due merely shifts the payments from the end of the year to the beginning of the year, we now compound the cash flows for one additional year. Therefore, the compound sum of an annuity due is simply

$$FV_n(\text{annuity due}) = PMT(FVIFA_{i,n})(1 + i) \tag{5–10}$$

For example, earlier we calculated the value of a five-year ordinary annuity of $500, invested in the bank at 6 percent to be $2,818.50. If we now assume this to be a five-year annuity due, its future value increases from $2,818.50 to $2,987.61.

$$\begin{aligned} FV_5 &= \$500(FVIFA_{5\%, \, 5 \, yr})(1 + .06) \\ &= \$500(5.637)(1.06) \\ &= \$2,987.61 \end{aligned}$$

Likewise, with the present value of an annuity due, we simply receive each cash flow one year earlier—that is, we receive it at the beginning of each year rather than at the end of each year. Thus, since each cash flow is received one year earlier, it is discounted back for one less period. To determine the present value of an annuity due, we merely need to find the present value of an ordinary annuity and multiply that by $(1 + i)$, which in effect cancels out one year's discounting.

$$PV(\text{annuity due}) = PMT(PVIFA_{i,n})(1 + i) \qquad \textbf{(5–11)}$$

Reexamining the earlier example where we calculated the present value of a five-year ordinary annuity of $500 given an appropriate discount rate of 6 percent, we now find that if it is an annuity due rather than an ordinary annuity, the present value increases from $2,106 to $2,232.36,

$$
\begin{aligned}
PV &= \$500(PVIFA_{6\%,\ 5\ yrs})(1 + .06) \\
&= \$500(4.212)(1.06) \\
&= \$2,232.36
\end{aligned}
$$

The result of all this is that both the future and present values of an annuity due are larger than those of an ordinary annuity because in each case all payments are received earlier. Thus, when *compounding* an annuity due, it compounds for one additional year, while when *discounting* an annuity due, the cash flows are discounted for one less year. While annuities due are used with some frequency in accounting, their usage is quite limited in finance. Therefore, in the remainder of this text, whenever the term *annuity* is used, you should assume that we are referring to an ordinary annuity.

AMORTIZED LOANS

This procedure of solving for PMT, the annuity payment value when i, n, and PV are known, is also used to determine what payments are associated with paying off a loan in equal installments over time. *Loans that are paid off this way, in equal periodic payments,* are called **amortized loans.** For example, suppose a firm wants to purchase a piece of machinery. To do this, it borrows $6,000 to be repaid in four equal payments at the end of each of the next four years, and the interest rate that is paid to the lender is 15 percent on the outstanding portion of the loan. To determine what the annual payments associated with the repayment of this debt will be, we simply use equation (5–9) and solve for the value of PMT, the annual annuity. Again we know three of the four values in that equation, PV, i, and n. PV, the present value of the future annuity, is $6,000; i, the annual interest rate, is 15 percent; and n, the number of years for which the annuity will last, is four years. PMT, the annuity payment received (by the lender and paid by the firm) at the end of each year, is unknown. Substituting these values into equation (5–9), we find

amortized loan

$$\$6,000 = PMT\left[\sum_{t=1}^{4} \frac{1}{(1 + .15)^t}\right]$$

$$\$6,000 = PMT(PVIFA_{15\%,\ 4\ yr})$$

$$\$6,000 = PMT(2.855)$$

$$\$2,101.58 = PMT$$

To repay the principal and interest on the outstanding loan in four years the annual payments would be $2,101.58. The breakdown of interest and principal payments is given in the *loan amortization schedule* in Table 5–9 on page 158, with very minor rounding error. As you can see, the interest payment declines each year as the loan outstanding declines.

CALCULATOR SOLUTION

DATA INPUT	FUNCTION KEY
4	N
15	I/Y
6,000	PV
0	FV

FUNCTION KEY	ANSWER
CPT PMT	–2,101.59

Table 5–9

Loan Amortization Schedule Involving a $6,000 Loan at 15 Percent to Be Repaid in Four Years

Year	Annuity	Interest Portion of the Annuity[a]	Repayment of the Principal Portion of the Annuity[b]	Outstanding Loan Balance after the Annuity Payment
1	$2,101.58	$900.00	$1,201.58	$4,798.42
2	2,101.58	719.76	1,381.82	3,416.60
3	2,101.58	512.49	1,589.09	1,827.51
4	2,101.58	274.07	1,827.51	

[a]The interest portion of the annuity is calculated by multiplying the outstanding loan balance at the beginning of the year by the interest rate of 15 percent. Thus, for year 1 it was $6,000 × .15 = $900.00, for year 2 it was $4,798.42 × .15 = $719.76, and so on.
[b]Repayment of the principal portion of the annuity was calculated by subtracting the interest portion of the annuity (column 2) from the annuity (column 1).

OBJECTIVE 5

COMPOUND INTEREST WITH NONANNUAL PERIODS

Until now we have assumed that the compounding or discounting period is always annual; however, it need not be, as evidenced by savings and loan associations and commercial banks that compound on a quarterly, daily, and in some cases continuous basis. Fortunately, this adjustment of the compounding period follows the same format as that used for annual compounding. If we invest our money for five years at 8 percent interest compounded semiannually, we are really investing our money for 10 six-month periods during which we receive 4 percent interest each period. If it is compounded quarterly, we receive 2 percent interest per period for 20 three-month periods. This process can easily be generalized, giving us the following formula for finding the future value of an investment for which interest is compounded in nonannual periods:

$$FV_n = PV\left(1 + \frac{i}{m}\right)^{mn} \tag{5–12}$$

where FV_n = the future value of the investment at the end of n years

n = the number of years during which the compounding occurs

i = annual interest (or discount) rate

PV = the present value or original amount invested at the beginning of the first year

m = the number of times compounding occurs during the year

We can see the value of intrayear compounding by examining Table 5–10. Since interest is earned on interest more frequently as the length of the compounding period declines, there is an inverse relationship between the length of the compounding period and the effective annual interest rate.

Table 5–10
The Value of $100 Compounded at Various Intervals

	For 1 Year at i Percent			
$i =$	**2%**	**5%**	**10%**	**15%**
Compounded annually	$102.00	$105.00	$110.00	$115.00
Compounded semiannually	102.01	105.06	110.25	115.56
Compounded quarterly	102.02	105.09	110.38	115.87
Compounded monthly	102.02	105.12	110.47	116.08
Compounded weekly (52)	102.02	105.12	110.51	116.16
Compounded daily (365)	102.02	105.13	110.52	116.18

	For 10 Years at i Percent			
$i =$	**2%**	**5%**	**10%**	**15%**
Compounded annually	$121.90	$162.89	$259.37	$404.56
Compounded semiannually	122.02	163.86	265.33	424.79
Compounded quarterly	122.08	164.36	268.51	436.04
Compounded monthly	122.12	164.70	270.70	444.02
Compounded weekly (52)	122.14	164.83	271.57	447.20
Compounded daily (365)	122.14	164.87	271.79	448.03

EXAMPLE

If we place $100 in a savings account that yields 12 percent compounded quarterly, what will our investment grow to at the end of five years? Substituting $n = 5$, $m = 4$, $i = 12$ percent, and $PV = \$100$ into equation (5–12), we find

$$FV_5 = \$100\left(1 + \frac{.12}{4}\right)^{4 \cdot 5}$$

$$= \$100(1 + .03)^{20}$$

$$= \$100(1.806)$$

$$= \$180.60$$

Thus, we will have $180.60 at the end of five years. Notice that the calculator solution is slightly different because of rounding errors in the tables, and that it also takes on a negative value.

CALCULATOR SOLUTION

DATA INPUT	FUNCTION KEY
20	N
3	I/Y
100	PV
0	PMT

FUNCTION KEY	ANSWER
CPT	
FV	−180.61

PRESENT VALUE OF AN UNEVEN STREAM

While some projects will involve a single cash flow and some annuities, many projects will involve uneven cash flows over several years. Chapter 9, which examines investments in fixed assets, presents this situation repeatedly. There we will be comparing not only the present value of cash flows between projects but also the cash inflows and outflows within a particular project, trying to determine that project's present value. However, this will not be difficult because the present value of any cash flow is measured in today's dollars and thus can be compared, through addition for inflows and subtraction for outflows, to the present value of any other cash flow also measured in today's dollars. For example, if we wished to find the present value of the following cash flows:

Year	Cash Flow	Year	Cash Flow
1	$500	6	500
2	200	7	500
3	−400	8	500
4	500	9	500
5	500	10	500

given a 6 percent discount rate, we would merely discount the flows back to the present and total them by adding in the positive flows and subtracting the negative ones. However, this problem is complicated by the annuity of $500 that runs from years 4 through 10. To accommodate this, we can first discount the annuity back to the beginning of period 4 (or end of period 3) by multiplying it by the value of $PVIFA_{6\%,\ 7\ yr}$ and get its present value at that point in time. We then multiply this value times the $PVIF_{6\%,\ 3\ yr}$ in order to bring this single cash flow (which is the present value of the seven-year annuity) back to the present. In effect we discount twice, first back to the end of period 3, then back to the present. This is shown graphically in Table 5–11 and numerically in Table 5–12. Thus, the present value of this uneven stream of cash flows is $2,657.94.

EXAMPLE

What is the present value of an investment involving $200 received at the end of years 1 through 5, a $300 cash outflow at the end of year 6, and $500 received at the end of years 7 through 10, given a 5 percent discount rate? Here we have two annuities, one that can be discounted directly back to the present by multiplying it by the value of the $PVIFA_{5\%,\ 5\ yr}$ and one that must be discounted twice to bring it back to the present. This second annuity, which is a four-year annuity, must first be discounted back to the beginning of period 7 (or end of period 6) by multiplying it by the value of the $PVIFA_{5\%,\ 4\ yr}$. Then the present value of this annuity at the end of period 6 (which can be viewed as a single cash flow) must be discounted back to the present by multiplying it by the value of the $PVIF_{5\%,\ 6\ yr}$.

To arrive at the total present value of this investment, we subtract the present value of the $300 cash outflow at the end of year 6 from the sum of the present value

Table 5–11

Illustration of an Example of Present Value of an Uneven Stream Involving One Annuity Discounted to the Present at 6 Percent

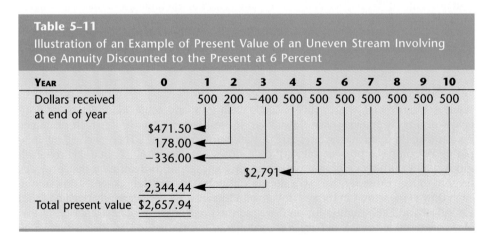

Year	0	1	2	3	4	5	6	7	8	9	10
Dollars received at end of year		500	200	−400	500	500	500	500	500	500	500
	$471.50										
	178.00										
	−336.00										
							$2,791				
	2,344.44										
Total present value	$2,657.94										

Table 5–12

Determination of the Present Value of an Example with Uneven Stream Involving One Annuity Discounted to the Present at 6 Percent

1. Present value of $500 received at the end of one year = $500(.943) =	$471.50
2. Present value of $200 received at the end of two years = $200(.890) =	178.00
3. Present value of a $400 outflow at the end of three years = −400(.840) =	−336.00
4. (a) Value at the end of year 3 and a $500 annuity, years 4 through 10 = $500(5.582) = $2,791.00	
(b) Present value of $2,791.00 received at the end of year 3 = $2,791(.840) =	2,344.44
5. Total present value =	$2,657.94

of the two annuities. Table 5–13 shows this graphically; Table 5–14 on page 162 gives the calculations. Thus, the present value of this series of cash flows is $1,964.66. ▮

PERPETUITIES

A **perpetuity** is *an annuity that continues forever*; that is, every year from its establishment this investment pays the same dollar amount. An example of a perpetuity is preferred stock that pays a constant dollar dividend infinitely. Determining the present value of a perpetuity is delightfully simple; we merely need to divide the constant flow by the discount rate. For example, the present value of a $100 perpetuity discounted back to the present at 5 percent is $100/.05 = $2,000. Thus, the equation representing the present value of a perpetuity is

perpetuity

$$PV = \frac{PP}{i} \qquad\qquad (5\text{–}13)$$

where PV = the present value of the perpetuity

PP = the constant dollar amount provided by the perpetuity

i = the annual interest (or discount) rate

Table 5–13

Illustration of an Example of the Present Value of an Uneven Stream Involving Two Annuities Discounted to the Present at 5 Percent

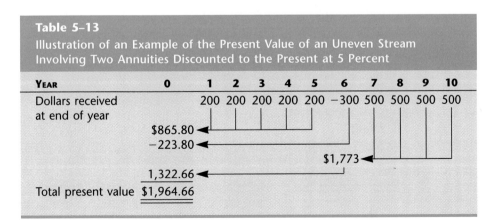

YEAR	0	1	2	3	4	5	6	7	8	9	10
Dollars received at end of year		200	200	200	200	200	−300	500	500	500	500

$865.80

−223.80

$1,773

1,322.66

Total present value $1,964.66

Bringing Australs Back to the Present

From **Axiom 1: The Risk-Return Tradeoff—We Won't Take on Additional Risk Unless We Expect to Be Compensated with Additional Return,** we found that investors demand a return for delaying consumption as well as an additional return for taking on added risk. The discount rate that we use to move money through time should reflect this return for delaying consumption; and as the Fisher effect showed in Chapter 2, this discount rate should reflect anticipated inflation. In the United States anticipated inflation is quite low, although it does tend to fluctuate over time. Elsewhere in the world, however, the inflation rate is difficult to predict because it can be dramatically high and undergo huge fluctuations.

Let's look at Argentina, keeping in mind that similar examples abound in Central and South America and Eastern Europe. At the beginning of 1992, Argentina introduced the fifth currency in 22 years, the new peso. The austral, the currency that was replaced, was introduced in June 1985 and was initially equal in value of $1.25 U.S. currency. Five and a half years later it took 100,000 australs to equal one dollar. Inflation had reached the point where the stack of money needed to buy a candy bar was bigger and weighed more than the candy bar itself, and many workers received their weeks' wages in grocery bags. Needless to say, if we were to move australs through time, we would have to use an extremely high interest or discount rate. Unfortunately, in countries suffering from hyperinflation, inflation rates tend to fluctuate dramatically, and this makes estimating the expected inflation rate even more difficult. For example, in 1989 the inflation rate in Argentina was 4,924 percent, in 1990 it dropped to 1,344 percent in 1991 it was only 84 percent, in 1992, only 18 percent and in 1995 it had fallen to 3.9 percent. However, as inflation in Argentina dropped, inflation in Brazil heated up, going from 426 percent in 1991, to 1,094 percent in 1995. Finally, at the extreme, in 1993 in Serbia the inflation rate reached 360,000,000,000,000,000 percent.

EXAMPLE

What is the present value of a $500 perpetuity discounted back to the present at 8 percent? Substituting $PP = \$500$ and $i = .08$ into equation (5–11), we find

$$PV = \frac{\$500}{.08} = \$6,250$$

Thus, the present value of this perpetuity is $6,250.

Table 5–14

Determination of the Present Value of an Example with Uneven Stream Involving Two Annuities Discounted to the Present at 5 Percent

1. Present value of first annuity, years 1 through 5 = $200(4.329)	$865.80
2. Present value of $300 cash outflow = −$300(.746) =	−223.80
3. (a) Value at end of year 6 of second annuity, years 7 through 10 = $500(3.546) = $1,773.00	
(b) Present value of $1,773.00 received at the end of year 6 = $1,773.00(.746) =	1,322.66
4. Total present value =	$1,964.66

To make decisions, financial managers must compare the costs and benefits of alternatives that do not occur during the same time period. Whether to make profitable investments or to take advantage of favorable interest rates, financial decision making requires an understanding of the time value of money. Managers who use the time value of money in all of their financial calculations assure themselves of more logical decisions. The time value process first makes all dollar values comparable; because money has a time value, it moves all dollar flows either back to the present or out to a common future date. All time value formulas presented in this chapter actually stem from the single compounding formula $FV_n = PV(1 + i)^n$. The formulas are used to deal simply with common financial situations, for example, discounting single flows, compounding annuities, and discounting annuities. Table 5–15 provides a summary of these calculations.

Table 5–15
Summary of Time Value of Money Equations[*]

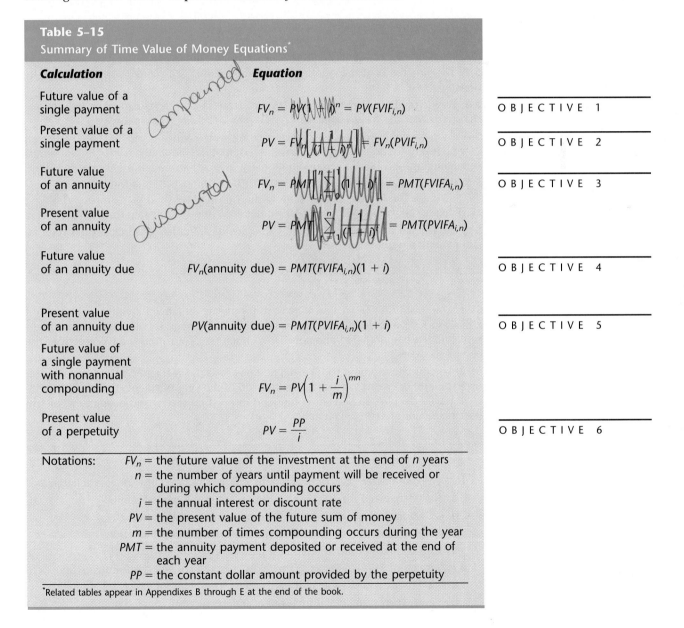

Calculation	Equation	
Future value of a single payment	$FV_n = PV(1 + i)^n = PV(FVIF_{i,n})$	OBJECTIVE 1
Present value of a single payment	$PV = FV\left[\dfrac{1}{(1+i)^n}\right] = FV_n(PVIF_{i,n})$	OBJECTIVE 2
Future value of an annuity	$FV_n = PMT\left[\sum_{t=0}^{n-1}(1+i)^t\right] = PMT(FVIFA_{i,n})$	OBJECTIVE 3
Present value of an annuity	$PV = PMT\left[\sum_{t=1}^{n}\dfrac{1}{(1+i)^t}\right] = PMT(PVIFA_{i,n})$	
Future value of an annuity due	$FV_n(\text{annuity due}) = PMT(FVIFA_{i,n})(1 + i)$	OBJECTIVE 4
Present value of an annuity due	$PV(\text{annuity due}) = PMT(PVIFA_{i,n})(1 + i)$	OBJECTIVE 5
Future value of a single payment with nonannual compounding	$FV_n = PV\left(1 + \dfrac{i}{m}\right)^{mn}$	
Present value of a perpetuity	$PV = \dfrac{PP}{i}$	OBJECTIVE 6

Notations: FV_n = the future value of the investment at the end of n years
     n = the number of years until payment will be received or during which compounding occurs
     i = the annual interest or discount rate
     PV = the present value of the future sum of money
     m = the number of times compounding occurs during the year
     PMT = the annuity payment deposited or received at the end of each year
     PP = the constant dollar amount provided by the perpetuity

[*]Related tables appear in Appendixes B through E at the end of the book.

KEY TERMS

Amortized Loan, 157

Annuity, 151

Annuity Due, 156

Compound Annuity, 151

Compound Interest, 142

Future-value Interest Factor ($FVIF_{i,n}$), 145

Future-value Interest Factor for an Annuity ($FVIFA_{i,n}$), 152

Ordinary Annuity, 151

Perpetuity, 161

Present Value, 148

Present-value Interest Factor ($PVIF_{i,n}$), 149

Present-value Interest Factor for an Annuity ($PVIFA_{i,n}$), 154

STUDY QUESTIONS

5-1. What is the time value of money? Why is it so important?

5-2. The processes of discounting and compounding are related. Explain this relationship.

5-3. How would an increase in the interest rate (i) or a decrease in the holding period (n) affect the future value (FV_n) of a sum of money? Explain why.

5-4. Suppose you were considering depositing your savings in one of three banks, all of which pay 5 percent interest; bank A compounds annually, bank B compounds semiannually, and bank C compounds daily. Which bank would you choose? Why?

5-5. What is the relationship between the $PVIF_{i,n}$ (Table 5–3) and the $PVIFA_{i,n}$ (Table 5–7)? What is the $PVIFA_{10\%, \, 10 \, yr}$? Add up the values of the $PVIF_{10\%, \, n}$, for $n = 1, \, \ldots,$ 10. What is this value? Why do these values have the relationship they do?

5-6. What is an annuity? Give some examples of annuities. Distinguish between an annuity and a perpetuity.

SELF-TEST PROBLEMS

ST-1. You place $25,000 in a savings account paying an annual compound interest of 8 percent for three years and then move it into a savings account that pays 10 percent interest compounded annually. How much will your money have grown at the end of six years?

ST-2. You purchase a boat for $35,000 and pay $5,000 down and agree to pay the rest over the next 10 years in 10 equal annual end-of-the-year payments that include principal payments plus 13 percent compound interest on the unpaid balance. What will be the amount of each payment?

STUDY PROBLEMS

5-1. (*Compound Interest*) To what amount will the following investments accumulate?
  a. $5,000 invested for 10 years at 10 percent compounded annually
  b. $8,000 invested for 7 years at 8 percent compounded annually
  c. $775 invested for 12 years at 12 percent compounded annually
  d. $21,000 invested for 5 years at 5 percent compounded annually

5-2. (*Compound Value Solving for n*) How many years will the following take?
  a. $500 to grow to $1,039.50 if invested at 5 percent compounded annually
  b. $35 to grow to $53.87 if invested at 9 percent compounded annually

c. $100 to grow to $298.60 if invested at 20 percent compounded annually

d. $53 to grow to $78.76 if invested at 2 percent compounded annually

5-3. (*Compound Value Solving for i*) At what annual rate would the following have to be invested?

a. $500 to grow to $1,948.00 in 12 years

b. $300 to grow to $422.10 in 7 years

c. $50 to grow to $280.20 in 20 years

d. $200 to grow to $497.60 in 5 years

5-4. (*Present Value*) What is the present value of the following future amounts?

a. $800 to be received 10 years from now discounted back to the present at 10 percent

b. $300 to be received 5 years from now discounted back to the present at 5 percent

c. $1,000 to be received 8 years from now discounted back to the present at 3 percent

d. $1,000 to be received 8 years from now discounted back to the present at 20 percent

5-5. (*Compound Annuity*) What is the accumulated sum of each of the following streams of payments?

a. $500 a year for 10 years compounded annually at 5 percent

b. $100 a year for 5 years compounded annually at 10 percent

c. $35 a year for 7 years compounded annually at 7 percent

d. $25 a year for 3 years compounded annually at 2 percent

5-6. (*Present Value of an Annuity*) What is the present value of the following annuities?

a. $2,500 a year for 10 years discounted back to the present at 7 percent

b. $70 a year for 3 years discounted back to the present at 3 percent

c. $280 a year for 7 years discounted back to the present at 6 percent

d. $500 a year for 10 years discounted back to the present at 10 percent

5-7. (*Compound Value*) Stanford Simmons, who recently sold his Porsche, placed $10,000 in a savings account paying annual compound interest of 6 percent.

a. Calculate the amount of money that will have accrued if he leaves the money in the bank for 1, 5, and 15 years.

b. If he moves his money into an account that pays 8 percent or one that pays 10 percent, rework part (a) using these new interest rates.

c. What conclusions can you draw about the relationship between interest rates, time, and future sums from the calculations you have done above?

5-8. (*Compound Interest with Nonannual Periods*) Calculate the amount of money that will be in each of the following accounts at the end of the given deposit period.

ACCOUNT	AMOUNT DEPOSITED	ANNUAL INTEREST RATE	COMPOUNDING PERIOD (COMPOUNDED EVERY __ MONTHS)	DEPOSIT PERIOD (YEARS)
Theodore Logan III	$ 1,000	10%	12	10
Vernell Coles	95,000	12	1	1
Thomas Elliott	8,000	12	2	2
Wayne Robinson	120,000	8	3	2
Eugene Chung	30,000	10	6	4
Kelly Cravens	15,000	12	4	3

5-9. (*Compound Interest with Nonannual Periods*)

    a. Calculate the future sum of $5,000 given that it will be held in the bank five years at an annual interest rate of 6 percent.

    b. Recalculate part (a) using a compounding period that is (1) semiannual and (2) bimonthly.

    c. Recalculate parts (a) and (b) for a 12 percent annual interest rate.

    d. Recalculate part (a) using a time horizon of 12 years (annual interest rate is still 6 percent).

    e. With respect to the effect of changes in the stated interest rate and holding periods on future sums in parts (c) and (d), what conclusions do you draw when you compare these figures with the answers found in parts (a) and (b)?

5-10. (*Solving for i with Annuities*) Nicki Johnson, a sophomore mechanical engineering student, receives a call from an insurance agent, who believes that Nicki is an older woman ready to retire from teaching. He talks to her about several annuities that she could buy that would guarantee her an annual fixed income. The annuities are as follows:

Annuity	Initial Payment into Annuity (at $t = 0$)	Amount of Money Received per Year	Duration of Annuity (Years)
A	$50,000	$8,500	12
B	$60,000	$7,000	25
C	$70,000	$8,000	20

If Nicki could earn 11 percent on her money by placing it in a savings account, should she place it instead in any of the annuities? Which ones, if any? Why?

5-11. (*Future Value*) Sales of a new finance book were 15,000 copies this year and were expected to increase by 20 percent per year. What are expected sales during each of the next three years? Graph this sales trend and explain.

5-12. (*Future Value*) Reggie Jackson, formerly of the New York Yankees, hit 41 home runs in 1980. If his home-run output grew at a rate of 10 percent per year, what would it have been over the following five years?

5-13. (*Loan Amortization*) Mr. Bill S. Preston, Esq., purchased a new house for $80,000. He paid $20,000 down and agreed to pay the rest over the next 25 years in 25 equal annual end-of-year payments that include principal payments plus 9 percent compound interest on the unpaid balance. What will these equal payments be?

5-14. (*Solving for* PMT *of an Annuity*) To pay for your child's education you wish to have accumulated $15,000 at the end of 15 years. To do this you plan on depositing an equal amount into the bank at the end of each year. If the bank is willing to pay 6 percent compounded annually, how much must you deposit each year to obtain your goal?

5-15. (*Solving for i in Compound Interest*) If you were offered $1,079.50 ten years from now in return for an investment of $500 currently, what annual rate of interest would you earn if you took the offer?

5-16. (*Future Value of an Annuity*) In 10 years you are planning on retiring and buying a house in Oviedo, Florida. The house you are looking at currently costs $100,000 and is expected to increase in value each year at a rate of 5 percent. Assuming you can earn 10 percent annually on your investments, how much must you invest at the end of each of the next 10 years to be able to buy your dream home when you retire?

5-17. (*Compound Value*) The Aggarwal Corporation needs to save $10 million to retire a $10 million mortgage that matures on December 31, 2006. To retire this mortgage, the company plans to put a fixed amount into an account at the end of each year for 10 years, with the first payment occurring on December 31, 1997. The Aggarwal Corporation expects to earn 9 percent annually on the money in this account. What equal annual contribution must it make to this account to accumulate the $10 million by December 31, 2006?

5-18. (*Compound Interest with Nonannual Periods*) After examining the various personal loan rates available to you, you find that you can borrow funds from a finance company at 12 percent compounded monthly or from a bank at 13 percent compounded annually. Which alternative is more attractive?

5-19. (*Present Value of an Uneven Stream of Payments*) You are given three investment alternatives to analyze. The cash flows from these three investments are as follows:

END OF YEAR	INVESTMENT A	INVESTMENT B	INVESTMENT C
1	$10,000		$10,000
2	10,000		
3	10,000		
4	10,000		
5	10,000	$10,000	
6		10,000	50,000
7		10,000	
8		10,000	
9		10,000	
10		10,000	10,000

Assuming a 20 percent discount rate, find the present value of each investment.

5-20. (*Present Value*) The Kumar Corporation is planning on issuing bonds that pay no interest but can be converted into $1,000 at maturity, seven years from their purchase. To price these bonds competitively with other bonds of equal risk, it is determined that they should yield 10 percent, compounded annually. At what price should the Kumar Corporation sell these bonds?

5-21. (*Perpetuities*) What is the present value of the following?

    a. A $300 perpetuity discounted back to the present at 8 percent

    b. A $1,000 perpetuity discounted back to the present at 12 percent

    c. A $100 perpetuity discounted back to the present at 9 percent

    d. A $95 perpetuity discounted back to the present at 5 percent

5-22. (*Solving for n with Nonannual Periods*) About how many years would it take for your investment to grow fourfold if it were invested at 16 percent compounded semiannually?

5-23. (*Complex Present Value*) How much do you have to deposit today so that beginning 11 years from now you can withdraw $10,000 a year for the next five years (periods 11 through 15) plus an *additional* amount of $20,000 in that last year (period 15)? Assume an interest rate of 6 percent.

5-24. (*Loan Amortization*) On December 31, Beth Klemkosky bought a yacht for $50,000, paying $10,000 down and agreeing to pay the balance in 10 equal annual end-of-year installments that include both the principal and 10 percent interest on the declining balance. How big would the annual payments be?

5-25. (*Solving for i of an Annuity*) You lend a friend $30,000, which your friend will repay in five equal annual end-of-year payments of $10,000, with the first payment to be received one year from now. What rate of return does your loan receive?

5-26. (*Solving for i in Compound Interest*) You lend a friend $10,000, for which your friend will repay you $27,027 at the end of five years. What interest rate are you charging your "friend"?

5-27. (*Loan Amortization*) A firm borrows $25,000 from the bank at 12 percent compounded annually to purchase some new machinery. This loan is to be repaid in equal annual installments at the end of each year over the next five years. How much will each annual payment be?

5-28. (*Present Value Comparison*) You are offered $1,000 today, $10,000 in 12 years, or $25,000 in twenty-five years. Assuming that you can earn 11 percent on your money, which should you choose?

5-29. (*Compound Annuity*) You plan on buying some property in Florida five years from today. To do this you estimate that you will need $20,000 at that time for the purchase. You would like to accumulate these funds by making equal annual deposits in your savings account, which pays 12 percent annually. If you make your first deposit at the end of this year and you would like your account to reach $20,000 when the final deposit is made, what will be the amount of your deposits?

5-30. (*Complex Present Value*) You would like to have $50,000 in 15 years. To accumulate this amount you plan to deposit each year an equal sum in the bank, which will earn 7 percent interest compounded annually. Your first payment will be made at the end of the year.

    a. How much must you deposit annually to accumulate this amount?

    b. If you decide to make a large lump-sum deposit today instead of the annual deposits, how large should this lump-sum deposit be? (Assume you can earn 7 percent on this deposit.)

    c. At the end of five years you will receive $10,000 and deposit this in the bank toward your goal of $50,000 at the end of 15 years. In addition to this deposit, how much must you deposit in equal annual deposits to reach your goal? (Again assume you can earn 7 percent on this deposit.)

5-31. (*Comprehensive Present Value*) You are trying to plan for retirement in 10 years, and currently you have $100,000 in a savings account and $300,000 in stocks. In addition you plan on adding to your savings by depositing $10,000 per year in your savings account at the end of each of the next five years and then $20,000 per year at the end of each year for the final five years until retirement.

    a. Assuming your savings account returns 7 percent compounded annually while your investment in stocks will return 12 percent compounded annually, how much will you have at the end of 10 years? (Ignore taxes.)

    b. If you expect to live for 20 years after you retire, and at retirement you deposit all of your savings in a bank account paying 10 percent, how much can you withdraw each year after retirement (20 equal withdrawals beginning one year after you retire) to end up with a zero balance at death?

5-32. (*Loan Amortization*) On December 31, Son-Nan Chen borrowed $100,000, agreeing to repay this sum in 20 equal annual end-of-year installments that include both the principal and 15 percent interest on the declining balance. How large will the annual payments be?

5-33. (*Loan Amortization*) To buy a new house you must borrow $150,000. To do this you take out a $150,000, 30-year, 10 percent mortgage. Your mortgage payments, which are made at the end of each year (one payment each year), include both principal and 10 percent interest on the declining balance. How large will your annual payments be?

5-34. (*Present Value*) The state lottery's million-dollar payout provides for $1 million to be paid over 19 years in $50,000 amounts. The first $50,000 payment is made immediately and the 19 remaining $50,000 payments occur at the end of each of the next 19 years. If 10 percent is the appropriate discount rate, what is the present value of this stream of cash flows? If 20 percent is the appropriate discount rate, what is the present value of the cash flows?

5-35. (*Solving for i in Compound Interest—Financial Calculator Needed*) In September 1963 the first issue of the comic book *X-MEN* was issued. The original price for that issue was 12 cents. By September 1996, 33 years later, the value of this comic book had risen to $4,000. What annual rate of interest would you have earned if you had bought the comic in 1963 and sold it in 1996?

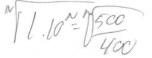

5-36. (*Comprehensive Present Value*) You have just inherited a large sum of money and you are trying to determine how much you should save for retirement and how much you can spend now. For retirement you will deposit today (January 1, 1997) a lump sum in a bank account paying 10 percent compounded annually. You don't plan on touching this deposit until you retire in five years (January 1, 2002), and you plan on living for 20 additional years and then dropping dead on December 31, 2021. During your retirement you would like to receive income of $50,000 per year to be received the first day of each year, with the first payment on January 1, 2002, and the last payment on January 1, 2021. Complicating this objective is your desire to have one final three-year fling during which time you'd like to track down all the original members of "Leave It to Beaver" and "The Brady Bunch" and get their autographs. To finance this you want to receive $250,000 on January 1, 2017, and *nothing* on January 1, 2018, and January 1, 2019, as you will be on the road. In addition, after you pass on (January 1, 2022), you would like to have a total of $100,000 to leave to your children.

   a. How much must you deposit in the bank at 10 percent on January 1, 1997, to achieve your goal? (Use a timeline to answer this question.)

   b. What kinds of problems are associated with this analysis and its assumptions?

COMPREHENSIVE PROBLEM

For your job as the business reporter for a local newspaper, you are given the task of putting together a series of articles that explains the power of the time value of money to your readers. Your editor would like you to address several specific questions in addition to demonstrating for the readership the use of the time value of money techniques by applying them to several problems. What would be your response to the following memorandum from your editor:

TO: Business Reporter

FROM: Perry White, Editor, *Daily Planet*

RE: Upcoming Series on the Importance and Power of the Time Value of Money

In your upcoming series on the time value of money, I would like to make sure you cover several specific points. In addition, before you begin this assignment, I want to make sure we are all reading from the same script, as accuracy has always been the cornerstone of the *Daily Planet*. In this regard, I'd like a response to the following questions before we proceed:

a. What is the relationship between discounting and compounding?

b. What is the relationship between the $PVIF_{i,n}$ and $PVIFA_{i,n}$?

c. (1) What will $5,000 invested for 10 years at 8 percent compounded annually grow to?

   (2) How many years will it take $400 to grow to $1,671, if it is invested at 10 percent compounded annually?

   (3) At what rate would $1,000 have to be invested to grow to $4,046 in 10 years?

d. Calculate the future sum of $1,000, given that it will be held in the bank for five years and earn 10 percent compounded semiannually?

e. What is an annuity due? How does this differ from an ordinary annuity?

f. What is the present value of an ordinary annuity of $1,000 per year for seven years discounted back to the present at 10 percent? What would be the present value if it were an annuity due?

g. What is the future value of an ordinary annuity of $1,000 per year for seven years compounded at 10 percent? What would be the future value if it were an annuity due?

h. You have just borrowed $100,000, and you agree to pay it back over the next 25 years in 25 equal end-of-year annual payments that include the principal payments plus 10 percent compound interest on the unpaid balance. What will be the size of these payments?

i. What is the present value of a $1,000 perpetuity discounted back to the present at 8 percent?

j. What is the present value of a $1,000 annuity for 10 years with the first payment occurring at the end of year 10 (that is, ten $1,000 payments occurring at the end of year 10 through year 19), given an appropriate discount rate of 10 percent?

k. Given a 10 percent discount rate, what is the present value of a perpetuity of $1,000 per year if the first payment does not begin until the end of year 10?

SELF–TEST SOLUTIONS

SS–1.

This is a compound interest problem in which you must first find the future value of $25,000 growing at 8 percent compounded annually for three years and then allow that future value to grow for an additional three years at 10 percent. First, the value of the $25,000 after three years growing at 8 percent is

$$FV_3 = PV(1 + i)^n$$
$$FV_3 = \$25,000(1 + .08)^3$$
$$FV_3 = \$25,000(1.260)$$
$$FV_3 = \$31,500$$

Thus, after three years you have $31,500. Now this amount is allowed to grow for three years at 10 percent. Plugging this into equation (5–6), with $PV = \$31,500$, $i = 10$ percent, and $n = 3$ years, we solve for FV_3:

$$FV_3 = \$31,500(1 + .10)^3$$
$$FV_3 = \$31,500(1.331)$$
$$FV_3 = \$41,926.50$$

Thus, after six years the $25,000 will have grown to $41,926.50.

SS–2.

This loan amortization problem is actually just a present-value-of-an-annuity problem in which we know the values of i, n, and PV and are solving for PMT. In this case the value of i is 13 percent, n is 10 years, and PV is $30,000. Substituting these values into equation (5–9) we find

$$\$30,000 = PMT\left[\sum_{t=1}^{10}\frac{1}{(1 + .13)^t}\right]$$

$$\$30,000 = PMT(5.426)$$

$$\$5,528.93 = PMT$$

Valuation and Characteristics of Bonds

LEARNING OBJECTIVES

After reading this chapter you should be able to

1. Distinguish between different kinds of bonds.
2. Explain the more popular features of bonds.
3. Define the term *value* as used for several different purposes.
4. Describe the basic process for valuing assets.
5. Estimate the value of a bond.
6. Compute a bondholder's expected rate of return.
7. Explain three important relationships that exist in bond valuation.

Types of Bonds • Terminology and Characteristics of Bonds • Definitions of Value • Valuation: An Overview • Valuation: The Basic Process • Bond Valuation • The Bondholder's Expected Rate of Return (Yield to Maturity) • Bond Valuation: Three Important Relationships

D uring 1995, the chief financial officers for IBM and Pacific Bell watched the price of their firms' bonds (a form of debt issued by public corporations) increase by over 20 percent. IBM's bonds were valued at $970 at the beginning of 1995, but sold for $1,180 by year end. Pacific Bell's bonds were selling for $842 in January 1995, but by the end of the year, they were worth $1,060. If you had purchased these bonds at the outset of 1995 and sold them at the end of the year, you would have earned a 30 percent and 33 percent rate of return on the two bonds, respectively (including the interest income you received from the bonds). These investments would have certainly beat a savings account at a bank. However, 1995 was no typical year for bond investors. The rate of returns earned on bonds were unusually attractive in 1995—a 27 percent average return for bonds of large companies. In 1994, however, investors in long-term corporate bonds received a negative 6 percent return. How could the returns be so volatile from year to year, when these aren't even stocks that we usually think of as being risky investments? Read on, and you will find the answer to this puzzle.

Knowing the fair value or price of an asset is no easy matter. The *Maxims* of the French writer La Rouchefoucauld, written over three centuries ago, still speak to us: "The greatest of all gifts is the power to estimate things at their true worth."

Understanding how to value financial securities is essential if managers are to meet the objective of maximizing the value of the firm. If they are to maximize the investor's value, they must know what drives the value of an asset. Specifically, they need to understand how bonds and stocks are valued in the marketplace; otherwise, they cannot act in the best interest of the firm's investors.

A bond is one form of a company's long-term debt. In this chapter, we begin by identifying the different kinds of bonds. We next look at the features or characteristics of most bonds. We then examine the concepts of and procedures for valuing an asset and apply these ideas to valuing bonds, one form of a company's long-term debt.

We now begin our study by considering the different kinds of bonds.

OBJECTIVE 1

TYPES OF BONDS

bond

A **bond** is a *type of debt or long-term promissory note, issued by the borrower, promising to pay its holder a predetermined and fixed amount of interest per year.* However, there are a wide variety of such creatures. Just to mention a few, we have

- Debentures
- Subordinated debentures
- Mortgage bonds
- Eurobonds
- Zero and very low coupon bonds
- Junk bonds

We will briefly explain each of these types of bonds.

Debentures

debenture

The term **debenture** applies to *any unsecured long-term debt.* Because these bonds are unsecured, the earning ability of the issuing corporation is of great concern to the bondholder. They are also viewed as being more risky than secured bonds and as a result must provide investors with a higher yield than secured bonds provide. Often the issuing firm attempts to provide some protection to the holder through the prohibition of any additional encumbrance of assets. This prohibits the future issuance of secured long-term debt that would further tie up the firm's assets and leave the bondholders less protected. To the issuing firm, the major advantage of debentures is that no property has to be secured by them. This allows the firm to issue debt and still preserve some future borrowing power.

Subordinated Debentures

Many firms have more than one issue of debentures outstanding. In this case a hierarchy may be specified, in which some debentures are given *subordinated standing in case of insolvency.* The claims of the **subordinated debentures** are honored only after the claims of secured debt and unsubordinated debentures have been satisfied.

subordinated debentures

Mortgage Bonds

A **mortgage bond** is a *bond secured by a lien on real property.* Typically, the value of the real property is greater than that of the mortgage bonds issued. This provides the mortgage bondholders with a margin of safety in the event the market value of the secured property declines. In the case of foreclosure, the trustees have the power to sell the secured property and use the proceeds to pay the bondholders. In the event that the proceeds from this sale do not cover the bonds, the bondholders become general creditors, similar to debenture bondholders, for the unpaid portion of the debt.

mortgage bond

Eurobonds

Eurobonds are not so much a different type of security as they are securities, in this case *bonds, issued in a country different from the one in whose currency the bond is denominated.* For example, a bond that is issued in Europe or in Asia by an American company and that pays interest and principal to the lender in U.S. dollars would be considered a Eurobond. Thus, even if the bond is not issued in Europe, it merely needs to be sold in a country different from the one in whose currency it is denominated to be considered a Eurobond. The Eurobond market actually had its roots in the 1950s and 1960s as the U.S. dollar became increasingly popular because of its role as the primary international reserve. In recent years as the U.S. dollar has gained a reputation for being one of the most stable currencies, demand for Eurobonds has increased. The primary attractions to borrowers, aside from favorable rates, in the Eurobonds market are the relative lack of regulation (Eurobonds are not registered with the Securities and Exchange Commission, or SEC), less rigorous disclosure requirements than those of the SEC, and the speed with which they can be issued. Interestingly, not only are Eurobonds not registered with the SEC, but U.S. citizens and residents may not be offered them during their initial distribution.

Eurobonds

Zero and Very Low Coupon Bonds

Zero and very low coupon bonds allow the issuing firm to issue *bonds at a substantial discount from their $1,000 face value with a zero or very low coupon rate.* The investor receives a large part (or all on the zero coupon bond) of the return from the appreciation of the bond. For example, in 1983, IntelComm, a telecommunications firm, issued $300 million of debt maturing in 2001 with a zero coupon rate. These bonds were sold at a 71 percent discount from their par value; that is, investors only paid $288 for a bond with a $1,000 par value. Investors who purchased these bonds for $288 and hold them until they mature in 2001 will receive a 13.25 percent yield to maturity, with all of this yield coming from appreciation of the bond. IntelComm, on the other hand, will have no cash outflows until these bonds mature; however, at that time it will have to pay back $300 million even though they only received $86 million when the bonds were first issued.

zero and very low coupon bonds

As with any form of financing, there are both advantages and disadvantages of issuing zero or very low coupon bonds. The disadvantages are, first (as already mentioned), when the bonds mature IntelComm will face an extremely large cash outflow, much greater than the cash inflow it experienced when the bonds were first issued. Second, discount bonds are not callable and can only be retired at maturity. Thus, if interest rates fall, IntelComm cannot benefit by requiring the investors to sell their bonds back to the company. The advantages of zero and low coupon bonds are, first, that annual cash outflows associated with interest payments do not occur with zero coupon bonds and are at a relatively low level with low coupon bonds. Second, because there is relatively strong investor demand for this type of debt, prices tend to be bid up and yields tend to be bid down. That is to say, IntelComm was able to issue zero coupon bonds at about half a percent less than it would have been if they had been traditional coupon bonds. Finally, IntelComm is able to deduct the annual amortization of the discount from taxable income, which will provide a positive annual cash flow to IntelComm.

Junk Bonds (High-Yield Bonds)

Junk bonds (high-yield bonds) **Junk bonds** are high-risk debt with *ratings of BB or below* by Moody's and Standard and Poor's. The lower the rating, the higher the chance of default; the lowest class is CC for Standard & Poor's and Ca for Moody's. Originally, the term was used to describe bonds issued by "fallen angels"; that is, firms with sound financial histories that were facing severe financial problems and suffering from poor credit ratings.

Junk bonds are also called **high-yield bonds** for the high interest rates they pay the investor, typically having an interest rate of between 3 and 5 percent more than AAA grade long-term debt.

Before the mid-1970s, smaller firms simply did not have access to the capital markets because of the reluctance of investors to accept speculative grade bonds. However, by the late 1980s junk bonds became the way to finance hostile takeovers—buying a firm without the management's approval. For example, the purchase of RJR Nabisco for some $20 billion by the investment group KKR was largely accomplished by junk bond financing. However, the eventual bankruptcy of Drexel Burnham Lambert, the investment banker most responsible for developing a large junk bond market, the jailing of the "king of junk bonds" Michael Milken, and increasing interest rates brought an end to the extensive use of junk bonds for financing corporate takeovers. (Michael Milken, a partner at Drexel Burnham Lambert, used to have an annual conference in Beverly Hills, California, nicknamed "The Predator's Ball" for attracting takeover investors and corporate raiders who needed junk bond financing to accomplish their takeovers.)

When corporate takeovers subsided from their highs, most people thought the junk bond was forever dead. By 1990, the junk bond market was virtually nonexistent. Then, in 1992, with investors looking for higher interest rates and a rebounding economy, the junk bond market was revitalized. The following year, new junk bond issues reached a record $62 billion. Also, less than 20 percent of the proceeds from junk bonds in 1995 were used to finance mergers and acquisitions, compared to 60 percent in the 1980s. Also, in 1995, more than 800 companies had issued junk bonds, up from several hundred in the 1980s. The borrowers in the 1990s come from a variety of industries, including manufacturing, media, retailing, consumer products, financial services, and housing. Also, credit quality improved. Only 17 percent of new issues in 1995 fell into the lower ratings of creditworthiness, compared with 66 percent in 1988.

As we look forward to the late 1990s and the next millennium, junk bonds will continue to play an important role in the financing of many middle-sized firms. Mutual funds and pension funds, who owned 40 percent of all junk bonds in 1995, should continue to provide an active market for such securities. So, contrary to the conventional wisdom of the early 1990s, the junk bond market is alive and well.

Now having an understanding of the kinds of bonds firms might issue, let's now look at some of the characteristics and terminology of bonds.

Issuing Junk Bonds: A Case Example

On the matter of junk bonds, Lea Carty, an economist at the bond-rating agency Moody's Investors Service in New York, says, "The junk bond market is here to stay. It's become a very important form of financing for younger, riskier firms." One such young, risky company is CommNet.

CommNet, which went public in 1986 and had yet to make a profit by 1995, is an example of a hot, young company that issued junk bonds. A 10-year-old firm with $90 million in sales was one of the first companies in the cellular telephone industry to use junk bond financing in 1993. The company's first issue raised $100 million to expand CommNet's eight-state rural telephone systems. The company sold more junk bonds in 1995, raising $80 million by selling 10-year notes with an 11.25 percent coupon.

Proceeds from CommNet's second junk sale were used to pay investors of convertible stock. A conventional bank loan wasn't a viable alternative because banks don't allow companies to buy back stock with bank proceeds, he said.

The firm's chief financial officer, Dan Dwyer, remembers the experience this way: "I think it was a combination of the quality of our company and market timing. The company's philosophy chose to sell bonds instead of stock in hopes of increasing value to shareholders."

Dwyer doesn't rule out a third junk bond issue in the future. "If we see an acquisition opportunity out there, we may well be back in the high-yield market," he said.

Source: John Accola, "Junk Is Looking Good: Denver Companies Find Raising Cash with Risky Securities Easy as ATM," *Rocky Mountain News*, Denver: Denver Publishing Company, January 14, 1996, p. 80A.

BACK TO THE FOUNDATIONS

Some have thought junk bonds were fundamentally different from other securities, but they are not. They are bonds with a great amount of risk, and therefore promise high expected returns. Thus, **Axiom 1: The Risk-Return Trade-off—We Won't Take on Additional Risk Unless We Expect to Be Compensated with Additional Return.**

TERMINOLOGY AND CHARACTERISTICS OF BONDS

OBJECTIVE 2

Before applying our valuation expertise to valuing bonds, we first need to understand the terminology related to bonds. Also, we should be apprised of the different types of bonds that exist. Then we will be better prepared to determine the value of a bond.

When a firm or nonprofit institution needs financing, one source is *bonds*. As already noted, this type of financing instrument is simply a long-term promissory note, issued by the borrower, promising to pay its holder a predetermined and fixed amount of interest each year. Some of the more important terms and characteristics that you might hear about bonds are as follows:

- Claims on assets and income
- Par value
- Coupon interest rate
- Maturity
- Indenture
- Current yield
- Bond ratings

Let's consider each in turn.

Claims on Assets and Income

In the case of insolvency, claims of debt in general, including bonds, are honored before those of both common stock and preferred stock. However, different types of debt may also have a hierarchy among themselves as to the order of their claim on assets.

Bonds also have a claim on income that comes ahead of common and preferred stock. In general if interest on bonds is not paid, the bond trustees can classify the firm as insolvent and force it into bankruptcy. Thus, the bondholder's claim on income is more likely to be honored than that of common and preferred stockholders, whose dividends are paid at the discretion of the firm's management.

Par Value

par value of a bond

The **par value of a bond** is its *face value that is returned to the bondholder at maturity*. In general, corporate bonds are issued in denominations of $1,000, although there are some exceptions to this rule. Also, when bond prices are quoted, either by financial managers or in the financial press, prices are generally expressed as a percentage of the bond's par value. For example, a Revlon bond that pays $103.75 per year interest and matures in 2010 was recently quoted in *The Wall Street Journal* as selling for $101\frac{3}{8}$. That does not mean you can buy the bond for $101.38. It means that this bond is selling for $101\frac{3}{8}$ percent of its par value of $1,000. Hence, the market price of this bond is actually $1,013.75. At maturity in 2010, the bondholder will receive the $1,000.

Coupon Interest Rate

coupon interest rate

The **coupon interest rate** on a bond indicates the *percentage of the par value of the bond that will be paid out annually in the form of interest*. Thus, regardless of what happens to the price of a bond with an 8 percent coupon interest rate and a $1,000 par value, it will pay out $80 annually in interest until maturity (.08 × $1,000 = $80).

Maturity

maturity

The **maturity** of a bond indicates *the length of time until the bond issuer returns the par value to the bondholder and terminates or redeems the bond*.

Indenture

indenture

An **indenture** is the *legal agreement between the firm issuing the bonds and the bond trustee who represents the bondholders*. The indenture provides the specific terms of the loan agreement, including a description of the bonds, the rights of the bondholders, the rights of the issuing firm, and the responsibilities of the trustee. This legal document may run 100 pages or more in length, with the majority of it devoted to defining protective provisions for the bondholder. The bond trustee, usually a banking institution or trust company, is then assigned the task of overseeing the relationship between the bondholder and the issuing firm, protecting the bondholder, and seeing that the terms of the indenture are carried out.

Typically, the restrictive provisions included in the indenture attempt to protect the bondholders' financial position relative to that of other outstanding securities. Common provisions involve (1) prohibitions on the sale of accounts receivable, (2) constraints on the issuance of common stock dividends, (3) restrictions on the purchase or sale of fixed assets, and (4) constraints on additional borrowing. Prohibitions on the sale of accounts receivable are specified because such sales would ben-

Bondholders Beware

We have learned that the bond rating attached to a bond when it is issued does not necessarily continue with it until maturity. In fact, with all the debt that corporations piled on in the late 1980s, it seemed that the only direction debt ratings went was down. The ethical question here: Does management have a duty to bondholders to watch out for their interests? Is just living by the letter of the bond covenants—while working hard to evade them—all right?

Let's look at a couple of examples that have infuriated bondholders. In early 1988, Shearson Lehman Hutton helped sell $1 billion of RJR Nabisco bonds. About six months later Shearson helped Kohlberg Kravis Roberts (KKR), an investment banker, buy RJR. The way the purchase was arranged, RJR issued large amounts of new debt, driving the market value of the previously issued bonds down by $100 million. Needless to say, a lot of bondholders were angry.

Texaco is another company that has worked around bond covenants. Several years ago, Pennzoil sued Texaco for $10 billion and won the case. To minimize damage to shareholders as a result of their court battle with Pennzoil, Texaco filed for Chapter 11 bankruptcy protection. The company entered bankruptcy, bond interest payments were passed, and later it emerged from bankruptcy with its credit standing unchanged.

Was what Shearson did unethical—to issue, then destroy? Should Texaco have used bankruptcy to protect its shareholders at the expense of its bondholders? What do you think?

efit the firm's short-run liquidity position at the expense of its future liquidity position. Constraints on common stock dividends generally mean limiting their issuance when the firm's liquidity falls below a specified level, or simply limiting the maximum dividend payout to some fraction, say 50 percent or 60 percent of earnings under any circumstance. Fixed-asset restrictions generally require lender permission before the liquidation of any fixed asset or prohibit the use of any existing fixed asset as collateral on new loans. Constraints on additional borrowing are usually in the form of restrictions or limitations on the amount and type of additional long-term debt that can be issued. All these restrictions have one thing in common: They attempt to prohibit actions that would improve the status of other securities at the expense of bonds and to protect the status of bonds from being weakened by any managerial action.

Current Yield

The **current yield** on a bond refers to the *ratio of the annual interest payment to the bond's current market price.* If, for example, we have a bond with an 8 percent coupon interest rate, a par value of $1,000, and a market price of $700, it would have a current yield of

current yield

$$\text{current yield} = \frac{\text{annual interest payments}}{\text{market price of the bond}} \qquad (6\text{–}1)$$
$$= \frac{.08 \times \$1000}{\$700} = \frac{\$80}{\$700} = 0.114 = 11.4\%$$

Bond Ratings

John Moody first began to rate bonds in 1909; since that time three rating agencies—Moody's, Standard and Poor's, and Fitch Investor Services—have provided ratings on corporate bonds. These ratings involve a judgment about the future risk potential of the bond. Although they deal with expectations, several historical factors seem to play a significant role in their determination.[1] Bond ratings are favorably affected by (1) a greater reliance on equity as opposed to debt in financing the firm, (2) profitable operations, (3) a low variability in past earnings, (4) large firm size, and (5) little use of subordinated debt. In turn, the rating a bond receives affects the rate of return demanded on the bond by the investors. The poorer the bond rating, the higher the rate of return demanded in the capital markets. Table 6–1 provides an example and description of these ratings. Thus, bond ratings are extremely important for the financial manager. They provide an indicator of default risk that in turn affects the rate of return that must be paid on borrowed funds.

BACK TO THE FOUNDATIONS

When we say that a lower bond rating means a higher interest rate charged by the investors (bondholders), we are observing an application of **Axiom 1: The Risk-Return Trade-off—We Won't Take on Additional Risk Unless We Expect to Be Compensated with Additional Return.**

Table 6–1
Standard and Poor's Corporate Bond Ratings

AAA	This is the highest rating assigned by Standard and Poor's for debt obligation and indicates an extremely strong capacity to pay principal and interest.
AA	Bonds rated AA also qualify as high-quality debt obligations. Their capacity to pay principal and interest is very strong, and in the majority of instances they differ from AAA issues only in small degree.
A	Bonds rated A have a strong capacity to pay principal and interest, although they are somewhat more susceptible to the adverse effects of changes in circumstances and economic conditions.
BBB	Bonds rated BBB are regarded as having an adequate capacity to pay principal and interest. Whereas they normally exhibit adequate protection parameters, adverse economic conditions or changing circumstances are more likely to lead to a weakened capacity to pay principal and interest for bonds in this category than for bonds in the A category.
BB B CCC CC	Bonds rated BB, B, CCC, and CC are regarded, on balance, as predominantly speculative with respect to the issuer's capacity to pay interest and repay principal in accordance with the terms of the obligation. BB indicates the lowest degree of speculation and CC the highest. While such bonds will likely have some quality and protective characteristics, these are outweighed by large uncertainties or major risk exposures to adverse conditions.
C	The rating C is reserved for income bonds on which no interest is being paid.
D	Bonds rated D are in default, and payment of principal and/or interest is in arrears.

Plus (+) or Minus (−): To provide more detailed indications of credit quality, the ratings from AA to BB may be modified by the addition of a plus or minus sign to show relative standing within the major rating categories.

Source: Standard and Poor's Fixed Income Investor, Vol. 8 (1980). Reprinted by permission.

---

[1]See Thomas F. Pogue and Robert M. Soldofsky, "What's in a Bond Rating?" *Journal of Financial and Quantitative Analysis*, 4 (June 1969), pp. 201–28; and George E. Pinches and Kent A. Mingo, "A Multivariate Analysis of Industrial Bond Ratings," *Journal of Finance*, 28 (March 1973), pp. 1–18.

We are now ready to think about bond valuation. But, to begin, we must first clarify precisely what we mean by value. Next, we need to understand the basic concepts of valuation and the process for valuing an asset. Then we may apply these concepts to valuing a bond—and in Chapter 7 to valuing stocks.

DEFINITIONS OF VALUE

OBJECTIVE 3

The term *value* is often used in different contexts, depending on its application. Examples of different uses of this term include the following:

Book value is the *value of an asset as shown on a firm's balance sheet.* It represents the historical cost of the asset rather than its current worth. For instance, the book value of a company's preferred stock is the amount the investors originally paid for the stock and therefore the amount the firm received when the stock was issued.

book value

Liquidation value is the *dollar sum that could be realized if an asset were sold individually and not as part of a going concern.* For example, if a firm's operations were discontinued and its assets were divided up and sold, the sales price would represent the asset's liquidation value.

liquidation value

The **market value** of an asset is the *observed value for the asset in the marketplace.* This value is determined by supply and demand forces working together in the marketplace, where buyers and sellers negotiate a mutually acceptable price for the asset. For instance, the market price for Ford common stock on June 20, 1996, was $34. This price was reached by a large number of buyers and sellers working through the New York Stock Exchange. In theory, a market price exists for all assets. However, many assets have no readily observable market price because trading seldom occurs. For instance, the market price for the common stock of Blanks Engraving, a Dallas-based family-owned firm, would be more difficult to establish than the market value of J. C. Penney's common stock.

market value

The **intrinsic or economic value** of an asset—also called the **fair value**—is the *present value of the asset's expected future cash flows.* This value is the amount an investor should be willing to pay, given the amount, timing, and riskiness of future cash flows. Once the investor has estimated the intrinsic value of a security, this value could be compared with its market value when available. If the intrinsic value is greater than the market value, then the security is undervalued in the eyes of the investor. Should the market value exceed the investor's intrinsic value, then the security is overvalued.

intrinsic or economic value
fair value

We hasten to add that if the securities market is working efficiently, the market value and the intrinsic value of a security will be equal. Whenever a security's intrinsic value differs from its current market price, the competition among investors seeking opportunities to make a profit will quickly drive the market price back to its intrinsic value. Thus, we may define an **efficient market** as *one in which the values of all securities at any instant fully reflect all available public information, which results in the market value and the intrinsic value being the same.* If the markets are efficient, it is extremely difficult for an investor to make extra profits from an ability to predict prices.

efficient market

BACK TO THE FOUNDATIONS

The fact that investors have difficulty identifying stocks that are undervalued relates to **Axiom 6: Efficient Capital Markets—The Markets Are Quick and the Prices Are Right.** In an efficient market, the price reflects all available public information about the security, and therefore it is priced fairly.

The idea of market efficiency has been the backdrop for an intense battle between professional investors and university professors. The academic community has con-

Sure, Markets Are Rational, Just Like Life

The idea that the markets are efficient is not without its detractors. The following excerpts are taken from an article appearing in the *Wall Street Journal* that represents just one such example of skepticism.

To mainstream economists, markets are the great citadel of rational man. When buying a car, you and I may indulge a fantasy, or a neurosis. But as participants in impersonal markets, we are cool, calculating and predictable. And be there, somewhere in the land, an investor who succumbs to fantasy and pays an irrational price, then the army of rational soldiers will step into the breach and profit from the error, thereby correcting it (by selling). In this sense, financial markets are different. Even if you think the Land Rover I purchase is overpriced, there is no way you can sell it short. But the presence of other investors will keep me from paying too much for a stock.

This is true, usually. According to economics texts, it is true all the time—a signifi-cant leap. According to the state religion of economics departments and business schools, prices are so uniformly rational that no one can constantly profit from exploiting stocks. Harvard's Michael Jensen long ago deemed this view "accepted as a fact of life."

Indeed it permeates every breath of modern finance. Since beating the stock market is a presumed impossibility, consistently successful investors are dismissed as lucky coin-flippers. Moreover, the assumption of market rationality has perverted the notion of "risk." Since each stock price is assumed to be "right," each bounce of every stock is also assumed to be right, and the amount that any one stock has bounced around has been widely accepted as a proxy for its "riskiness."

There is another interpretation—the stock prices are occasionally silly and many short-term bounces are meaningless, the product of the herd leading to one direction and then another. A small but growing band of economists are coming around. In their view, the human traits that influence behavior—among them fear of ridicule—also affect markets. "One of the biggest errors in human judgment is to pay attention to the crowd," says Robert Shiller, a Yale economist. This explains the crash of 1987, when stocks fell 23% on no news.

Welcome to the school of behavioral economics. It is loosely knit and boasts no grand theory—only that the old theory of pervasive rationality doesn't fit the human actors who actually buy and sell. . . . Such work once was considered heretical. . . . But behavior is now a hot topic, even among statistically oriented economists. No less a sage than Prof. Jensen is studying neurology. "I have been driven by the idea that rationality doesn't describe a whole lot of behavior," the former apostle of rationalism says.

Source: Excerpts from Roger Lowenstein, "Sure, Markets Are Rational, Just Like Life," *Wall Street Journal*, June 13, 1996, p. C1.

---

tended that someone throwing darts at the list of securities in *The Wall Street Journal* could do as well as a professional money manager. Market professionals retort that academicians are grossly mistaken in this view. The war has been intense but also one that the student of finance should find intriguing, and it can be followed each month in *The Wall Street Journal*, where the investment performance of dart throwers and different professional investors are compared. Through May 1996, there had been 72 contests between these rivals. The score: 41 for the professional managers and 31 for the dart throwers. Also, as aptly expressed by one teacher, the real point about efficient markets is that an investor should throw a large wet towel at the *Wall Street Journal*, not a dart. That is, we want to be broadly diversified with a large group of stocks, not just one. The importance of diversification is explained in Chapter 8.

Intrinsic value is the present value of expected future cash flows. This statement is true regardless of what type of asset we are valuing. If you remember only one thing from this chapter, remember that intrinsic value is the present value of expected future cash flows.

VALUATION: AN OVERVIEW

For our purposes, *the value of an asset is its intrinsic value or the present value of its expected future cash flows*, where these cash flows are discounted back to the present using the investor's required rate of return. This statement is true for valuing all assets and serves as the basis of almost all that we do in finance. Thus, value is affected by three elements:

1. The amount and timing of the asset's expected cash flows
2. The riskiness of these cash flows
3. The investor's required rate of return for undertaking the investment

The first two factors are characteristics of the asset; the third one, the required rate of return, is the minimum rate of return necessary to attract an investor to purchase or hold a security, which is determined by *the rates of return available on similar investments*, or what is called the **opportunity cost of funds.** This rate must be high enough to compensate the investor for the risk perceived in the asset's future cash flows. (The required rate of return is explained more fully in Chapter 8.)

opportunity cost of funds

Our discussions should remind us of three of our axioms that help us understand finance:

Axiom 1: The Risk-Return Trade-off—We Won't Take on Additional Risk Unless We Expect to Be Compensated with Additional Return.
Axiom 2: The Time Value of Money—A Dollar Received Today Is Worth More Than a Dollar Received in the Future.
Axiom 3: Cash—Not Profits—Is King.

Determining the economic worth or value of an asset always relies on these three axioms. Without them, we would have no basis for explaining value. With them, we can know that the amount and timing of cash, not earnings, drive value. Also, we must be rewarded for taking risk; otherwise, we will not invest.

Figure 6–1 on page 182 depicts the basic factors involved in valuation. As the figure shows, finding the value of an asset involves:

1. Assessing the asset's characteristics, which include the amount and timing of the expected cash flows and the riskiness of these cash flows;
2. Determining the investor's required rate of return, which embodies the investor's attitude about assuming risk and perception of the riskiness of the asset; and
3. Discounting the expected cash flows back to the present, using the investor's required rate of return as the discount rate.

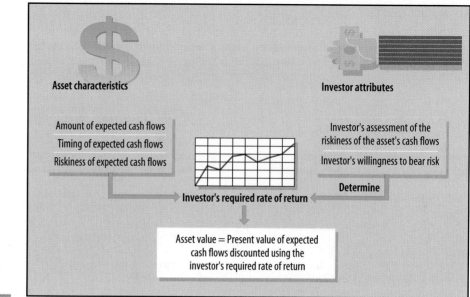

Figure 6–1
Basic Factors Determining an Asset's Value

PAUSE AND REFLECT

Intrinsic value is a function of the cash flows yet to be received, the riskiness of these cash flows, and the investor's required rate of return.

OBJECTIVE 4

VALUATION: THE BASIC PROCESS

The valuation process can be described as follows: It is assigning value to an asset by calculating the present value of its expected future cash flows using the investor's required rate of return as the discount rate. The investor's required rate of return, k, is determined by the level of the risk-free rate of interest and the risk premium that the investor feels is necessary to compensate for the risks assumed in owning the asset. Therefore, a basic security valuation model can be defined mathematically as follows:

$$V = \frac{C_1}{(1 + k)^1} + \frac{C_2}{(1 + k)^2} + \cdots + \frac{C_n}{(1 + k)^n} \qquad (6\text{–}2)$$

or

$$V = \sum_{t=1}^{n} \frac{C_t}{(1 + k)^t}$$

where
C_t = cash flow to be received at time t
V = the intrinsic value or present value of an asset producing expected future cash flows, C_t, in years 1 through n
k = the investor's required rate of return

Using equation (6–2), there are three basic steps in the valuation process:

Step 1: Estimate the C_t in equation (6–2), which is the amount and timing of the future cash flows the security is expected to provide.

Step 2: Determine k, the investor's required rate of return.

Step 3: Calculate the intrinsic value, V, as the present value of expected future cash flows discounted at the investor's required rate of return.

Equation (6–2), which measures the present value of future cash flows, is the basis of the valuation process. It is the most important equation in this chapter, because all the remaining equations in this chapter and in Chapters 7 and 8 are merely reformulations of this one equation. If we understand equation (6–2), all the valuation work we do, and a host of other topics as well, will be much clearer in our minds.

With the foregoing principles of valuation as our foundation, let's now look at how bonds are valued.

BOND VALUATION

The valuation process for a bond, as depicted in Figure 6–2, requires knowledge of three essential elements: (1) the amount of the cash flows to be received by the investor, (2) the maturity date of the loan, and (3) the investor's required rate of return. The amount of cash flows is dictated by the periodic interest to be received and by the par value to be paid at maturity. Given these elements, we can compute the value of the bond, or the present value.

PAUSE AND REFLECT

The value of a bond is the present value both of future interest to be received and the par or maturity value of the bond. Simply list these cash flows, use your required rate of return as the discount rate, and find the value.

EXAMPLE

Consider a bond issued by American Airlines with a maturity date of 2016 and a stated coupon rate of 9 percent.[2] In 1996, with 20 years left to maturity, investors owning the bonds were requiring an 8.4 percent rate of return. We can calculate the value of the bonds to these investors using the following three-step valuation procedure:

Step 1: Estimate the amount and timing of the expected future cash flows. Two types of cash flows are received by the bondholder:
  a. Annual interest payments equal to the coupon rate of interest times the face value of the bond. In this example the bond's coupon interest rate is

(A) Cash Flow Information	Periodic interest payments For example, $65 per year Principal amount or par value For example, $1,000
(B) Term to Maturity	For example, 12 years
(C) Investor's Required Rate of Return	For example, 8 %

Figure 6–2
Data Requirements for Bond Valuation

---

[2]American Airlines remits the interest to its bondholders on a semiannual basis on January 15 and July 15. However, for the moment assume the interest is to be received annually. The effect of semiannual payments will be examined later.

Financial Management in Practice

Reading a Bond Quote in the *Wall Street Journal*

Below is shown a section of the *Wall Street Journal* that gives the quotes on July 1, 1996, for some of the corporate bonds traded on the New York Stock Exchange on that date.

Bonds	Cur Yld	Vol	Close	Net Chg
Caterplnc 6s07	6.8	49	$88\frac{3}{8}$	$+\frac{3}{8}$
ChsCp 8s04	7.9	1	101	$-\frac{5}{8}$
ChsCp $6\frac{1}{8}$08	6.8	8	$89\frac{1}{2}$	$-\frac{1}{2}$
CPWV $7\frac{1}{4}$13	7.8	30	$93\frac{1}{2}$	$-\frac{5}{8}$
Chiquta $10\frac{1}{2}$04	10.5	3	100	-1
ChckFul 7s12	cv	65	84	-1
Chryslr 10.4s99	10.0	61	$104\frac{1}{8}$	$-\frac{3}{8}$
Chryslr 10.95s17	10.0	8	109	...
ChryF $6\frac{1}{2}$98	6.4	6	101	...
Clardge $11\frac{3}{4}$02	13.6	341	$86\frac{3}{8}$	...
ClrkOil $9\frac{1}{2}$04	9.3	51	$102\frac{1}{8}$	$+\frac{1}{8}$
ClevEl $8\frac{3}{4}$05	9.0	25	$97\frac{1}{4}$	$+\frac{1}{4}$

The bonds shown in the list above as "CaterpInc 6s07" were issued by Caterpillar, Inc.; they pay a 6 percent coupon interest rate (indicated by the "6s"), or $60 interest paid annually (actually $30 paid semiannually) on a par value of $1,000; and they mature in 2007 (07 is the last two digits of the year the bonds mature). The closing price of the bonds on July 1, 1996, was $88\frac{3}{8}$, which is stated as a percent of the bond's $1,000 par value; thus, the bond's closing price on July 1 was $883.75 = .88375 × $1,000. The current yield on the bonds is 6.8 percent, calculated as the annual interest divided by the closing price, or $60 ÷ $883.75 = 6.8%. During the trading day, 49 bonds were traded on the exchange, as reflected by the "Vol" heading.[1] Finally, the net change "Net Chg" in the price of the bond from the previous day's close was an increase of $\frac{3}{8}$ of 1 percent.

[1]There may have been a lot more than 49 bonds changing hands on July 1, 1996. Many bond trades are negotiated directly between institutional investors or through bankers and are not listed in the *Wall Street Journal*.

9 percent; thus the annual interest payment is $90 = .09 × $1,000. Assuming that 1996 interest payments have already been made, these cash flows will be received by the bondholder in each of the 20 years before the bond matures (1997 through 2016 = 20 years).

b. The face value of the bond of $1,000 to be received in 2016. To summarize, the cash flows received by the bondholder are as follows:

Years	1	2	3	4	...	19	20
	$90	$90	$90	$90	...	$90	$ 90
							+$1,000
							$1,090

Step 2: Determine the investor's required rate of return by evaluating the riskiness of the bond's future cash flows. An 8.4 percent required rate of return for the bondholders is given. In Chapter 8, we will learn how this rate is determined. For now, simply realize that the investor's required rate of return is equal to a rate earned on a risk-free security plus a risk premium for assuming risk.

Step 3: Calculate the intrinsic value of the bond as the present value of the expected future interest and principal payments discounted at the investor's required rate of return.

The present value of American Airlines bonds is found as follows:

$$\text{bond value} = V_b = \frac{\$ \text{ interest in year 1}}{(1 + \text{required rate of return})^1}$$
$$+ \frac{\$ \text{ interest in year 2}}{(1 + \text{required rate of return})^2}$$
$$+ \cdots + \frac{\$ \text{ interest in year 20}}{(1 + \text{required rate of return})^{20}} \qquad \text{(6–3a)}$$
$$+ \frac{\$ \text{ par value of bond}}{(1 + \text{required rate of return})^{20}}$$

or, summing over the interest payments,

$$Vb = \underbrace{\sum_{t=1}^{20} \frac{\$ \text{ interest in year } t}{(1 + \text{required rate of return})^t}}_{\text{present value of interest}} + \underbrace{\frac{\$ \text{ par value of bond}}{(1 + \text{required rate of return})^{20}}}_{\text{present value of par value}}$$

PAUSE AND REFLECT

The foregoing equation is a restatement in a slightly different form of equation (6–2). Recall that equation (6–2) states that the value of an asset is the present value of future cash flows to be received by the investor.

Using I_t to represent the interest payment in year t, M to represent the bond's maturity (or par) value, and k_b to equal the bondholder's required rate of return, we may express the value of a bond maturing in year n as follows:

$$V_b = \sum_{t=1}^{n} \frac{\$I_t}{(1 + k_b)^t} + \frac{\$M}{(1 + k_b)^n} \qquad \text{(6–3b)}$$

Finding the value of the American Airlines bonds may be represented graphically as follows:

YEAR	0	1	2	3	4	5	6	...	20
Dollars received at end of year		$90	$90	$90	$90	$90	$90	...	$ 90 $1,000 $1,090
Present value	$1,057								

CALCULATOR SOLUTION

DATA INPUT	FUNCTION KEY
20	N
8.4	I/Y
90	PMT
1000	FV

FUNCTION KEY	ANSWER
CPT PV	−1,057

However, because the investor's required rate of return is 8.4 percent, we are unable to use the present value tables at the end of the text to solve the problem. We must therefore rely on a calculator solution. Using the TI BAII Plus, we find the value of the bond to be $1,057, as calculated in the margin.[3] Thus, if investors consider 8.4

---

[3]As noted in Chapter 5, we are using the TI BAII Plus. You may want to return to the Chapter 5 section "Moving Money through Time with the Aid of a Financial Calculator" or Appendix A, to see a more complete explanation of using the TI BAII Plus. For an explanation of other calculators, see the study guide that accompanies this text.

percent to be an appropriate required rate of return in view of the risk level associated with American Airlines bonds, paying a price of $1,057 would satisfy their return requirement. ■

Semiannual Interest Payments

In the preceding American Airlines illustration, the interest payments were assumed to be paid annually. However, companies typically pay interest to bondholders semiannually. For example, consider Alaskan Airlines bonds maturing in 14 years that pay $68.75 per year, but disburses the interest semiannually ($34.375 each January 15 and July 15).

Several steps are involved in adapting equation (6–3b) for semiannual interest payments.[4] First, thinking in terms of *periods* instead of years, a bond with a life of n years paying interest semiannually has a life of $2n$ periods. In other words, a five-year bond ($n = 5$) that remits its interest on a semiannual basis actually makes 10 payments. Yet although the number of periods has doubled, the *dollar* amount of interest being sent to the investors for each period and the bondholders' required rate of return are half of the equivalent annual figures. I_t becomes $I_t/2$ and k_b is changed to $k_b/2$; thus, for semiannual compounding, equation (6–3b) becomes

$$V_b = \sum_{t=1}^{2n} \frac{\$I_t/2}{\left(1 + \frac{k_b}{2}\right)^t} + \frac{\$M}{\left(1 + \frac{k_b}{2}\right)^{2n}} \qquad (6\text{–}4)$$

Alternatively, using the notations introduced in Chapter 5 for discounting cash flows, the above equation may be restated as follows:

$$V_b = (\$I_t \div 2)(PVIFA_{k_b/2,2n}) + \$M(PVIF_{k_b/2,2n}) \qquad (6\text{–}5)$$

Assuming the Alaskan Airlines bondholders' annual required ratio of return is 7.2 percent, we can use the TI BAII Plus calculator in the margin to find the bond value, but now assuming semiannual interest payments. Thus, the value of a bond paying $34.375 in semiannual interest for 14 years, where the investor has a 7.2 percent required rate of return, would be $972.

OBJECTIVE 6

THE BONDHOLDER'S EXPECTED RATE OF RETURN (YIELD TO MATURITY)

Theoretically, each investor could have a different required rate of return for a particular security. However, the financial manager is only interested in the required rate of return that is implied by the market prices of the firm's securities. In other words, the consensus of a firm's investors about the expected rate of return is reflected in the current market price of the stock.

expected rate of return

To measure the bondholder's **expected rate of return,** $\overline{k}_b$, we would find the *discount rate that equates the present value of the future cash flows (interest and maturity value) with the current market price of the bond.*[5] The expected rate of return for a bond is also the *rate of return the investor will earn if the bond is held*

yield to maturity

to maturity, or the **yield to maturity.** Thus, when referring to bonds, the terms *expected rate of return* and *yield to maturity* are often used interchangeably.

---

[4]The logic for calculating the value of a bond that pays interest semiannually is similar to the material presented in Chapter 5, where compound interest with nonannual periods was discussed.

[5]When we speak of computing an expected rate of return, we are not describing the situation very accurately. Expected rates of return are ex ante (before the fact) and are based on "expected and unobservable future cash flows" and, therefore, can only be "estimated."

To illustrate this concept, consider the Brister Corporation's bonds, which are selling for $1,100. The bonds carry a coupon interest rate of 9 percent and mature in 10 years. (Remember, the coupon rate determines the interest payment—coupon rate × par value.)

In determining the expected rate of return ($\bar{k}_b$), implicit in the current market price, we need to find the rate that discounts the anticipated cash flows back to a present value of $1,100, the current market price (P_0) for the bond.

Finding the expected rate of return for a bond using the present value tables is done by trial and error. We have to keep trying new rates until we find the discount rate that results in the present value of the future interest and maturity value of the bond just equaling the current market value of the bond. If the expected rate is somewhere between rates in the present value tables, we then must interpolate between the rates.

For our example, if we try 7 percent, the bond's present value is $1,140.16. Since the present value of $1,140.16 is greater than the market price of $1,100, we should next try a higher rate. Increasing the discount rate, say, to 8 percent gives a present value of $1,066.90. (These computations are shown below.) Now the present value is less than the market price; thus, we know that the investor's expected rate of return is between 7 percent and 8 percent.

| | | 7% | | 8% | |
YEARS	CASH FLOW	PRESENT VALUE FACTORS	PRESENT VALUE	PRESENT VALUE FACTORS	PRESENT VALUE
1–10	$90 per year	7.024	$ 632.16	6.710	$ 603.90
10	$1,000 in year 10	0.508	508.00	0.463	$ 463.00
		Present value at 7%	$1,140.16	Present value at 8%	$1,066.90

The actual expected return for the Brister Corporation bondholders is 7.54 percent, which may be found by using the TI BAII Plus calculator in the margin.

BOND VALUATION: THREE IMPORTANT RELATIONSHIPS

OBJECTIVE 7

We have now learned to find the value of a bond (V_b), given (1) the amount of interest payments (I_t), (2) the maturity value (M), (3) the length of time to maturity (n years), and (4) the investor's required rate of return, k_b. We also know how to compute the expected rate of return ($\bar{k}_b$), which also happens to be the current interest rate on the bond, given (1) the current market value (P_0), (2) the amount of interest payments (I_t), (3) the maturity value (M), and (4) the length of time to maturity (n years). We now have the basics. But let's go further in our understanding of bond valuation by studying several important relationships.

First Relationship

The value of a bond is inversely related to changes in the investor's present required rate of return (the current interest rate). In other words, as interest rates increase (decrease), the value of the bond decreases (increases).

To illustrate, assume that an investor's required rate of return for a given bond is 12 percent. The bond has a par value of $1,000 and annual interest payments of $120, indicating a 12 percent coupon interest rate ($120 ÷ $1,000 = 12%). Assuming a five-year maturity date, the bond would be worth $1,000, computed as follows:

$$V_b = \frac{I_1}{(1 + k_b)^1} + \cdots + \frac{I_n}{(1 + k_b)^n} + \frac{M}{(1 + k_b)^n} \qquad (6\text{--}3)$$

$$= \sum_{t=1}^{n} \frac{I_t}{(1 + k_b)^t} + \frac{M}{(1 + k_b)^n}$$

$$= \sum_{t=1}^{5} \frac{\$120}{(1 + .12)^t} + \frac{\$1{,}000}{(1 + .12)^5}$$

Using present value tables we have:

$$V_b = \$120(PVIFA_{12\%,\ 5\ yr}) + \$1{,}000(PVIF_{12\%,\ 5\ yr})$$
$$V_b = \$120(3.605) + \$1{,}000(.567)$$
$$= \$432.60 + \$567.00$$
$$= \$999.60 \cong \$1{,}000.00$$

If, however, the investor's required rate of return increases from 12 percent to 15 percent, the value of the bond would decrease to $899.24, computed as follows:

$$V_b = \$120(PVIFA_{15\%,\ 5\ yr}) + \$1{,}000(PVIF_{15\%,\ 5\ yr})$$
$$V_b = \$120(3.352) + \$1{,}000(.497)$$
$$= \$402.24 + \$497.00$$
$$= \$899.24$$

On the other hand, if the investor's required rate of return decreases to 9 percent, the bond would increase in value to $1,116.80:

$$V_b = \$120(PVIFA_{9\%,\ 5\ yr}) + \$1{,}000(PVIF_{9\%,\ 5\ yr})$$
$$V_b = \$120(3.890) + \$1{,}000(.650)$$
$$= \$466.80 + \$650.00$$
$$= \$1{,}116.80$$

This inverse relationship between the investor's required rate of return and the value of a bond is presented in Figure 6–3. Clearly, as an investor demands a higher rate of return, the value of the bond decreases. The higher rate of return the investor desires can be achieved only by paying less for the bond. Conversely, a lower required rate of return yields a higher market value for the bond.

Changes in bond prices represent an element of uncertainty for the bond investor. If the current interest rate (required rate of return) changes, the price of the bond also fluctuates. An increase in interest rates causes the bondholder to incur a loss in market value. Since future interest rates and the resulting bond value cannot be predicted with certainty, a bond investor is exposed to the *risk of changing values as interest rates vary*. This risk has come to be known as **interest rate risk.**

interest- rate risk

Second Relationship

The market value of a bond will be less than the par value if the investor's required rate of return is above the coupon interest rate; but it will be valued above par value if the investor's required rate of return is below the coupon interest rate.

Using the previous example, we observed that

1. The bond has a *market* value of $1,000, equal to the par or maturity value, when the investor's required rate of return equals the 12 percent coupon interest rate. In other words, if

$$\text{required rate} = \text{coupon rate, then } \textit{market value} = \textit{par value}$$
$$12\% \quad = \quad 12\% \quad \text{, then} \quad \$1{,}000 \quad = \quad \$1{,}000$$

2. When the required rate is 15 percent, which exceeds the 12 percent coupon rate, the market value falls below par value to $899.24; that is, if

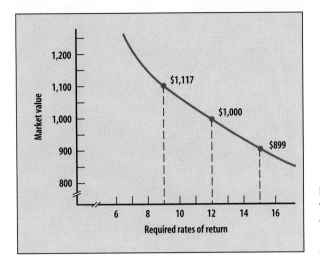

Figure 6–3

Value and Required Rates for a 5-Year Bond at 12 Percent Coupon Rate

required rate > coupon rate, then *market value < par value*
  15%   >   12%   , then $899.24   < $1,000

In this case the *bond sells at a discount below par value;* thus, it is called a **discount bond.**

discount bond

3. When the required rate is 9 percent, or less than the 12 percent coupon rate, the market value, $1,116.80, exceeds the bond's par value. In this instance, if

required rate < coupon rate, then *market value > par value*
   9%   <   12%   , then $1,116.80   > $1,000

The *bond is now selling at a premium above par value;* thus, it is a **premium bond.**

premium bond

Third Relationship

Long-term bonds have greater interest rate risk than do short-term bonds.

As already noted, a change in current interest rates (required rate of return) causes an inverse change in the market value of a bond. However, the impact on value is greater for long-term bonds than it is for short-term bonds.

In Figure 6–3 we observed the effect of interest rate changes on a 5-year bond paying a 12 percent coupon interest rate. What if the bond did not mature until 10 years from today instead of 5 years? Would the changes in market value be the same? Absolutely not. The changes in value would be more significant for the 10-year bond. For example, if we vary the current interest rates (the bondholder's required rate of return) from 9 percent to 12 percent and then to 15 percent, as we did earlier with the 5-year bond, the values for both the 5-year and the 10-year bonds would be as shown below.

	MARKET VALUE FOR A 12% COUPON-RATE BOND MATURING IN	
REQUIRED RATE	**5 YEARS**	**10 YEARS**
9%	$1,116.80	$1,192.16
12	1,000.00	1,000.00
15	899.24	849.28

Figure 6–4

Market Values of a 5-Year and a 10-Year Bond at Different Required Rates

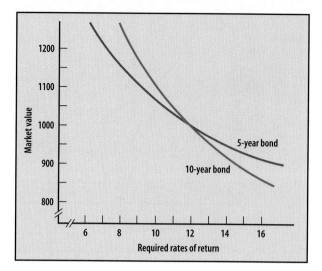

Using these values and the required rates, we can graph the changes in values for the two bonds relative to different interest rates. These comparisons are provided in Figure 6–4. The figure clearly illustrates that the price of a long-term bond (say, 10 years) is more responsive or sensitive to interest rate changes than the price of a short-term bond (say, 5 years).

The reason long-term bond prices fluctuate more than short-term bond prices in response to interest rate changes is simple. Assume an investor bought a 10-year bond yielding a 12 percent interest rate. If the current interest rate for bonds of similar risk increased to 15 percent, the investor would be locked into the lower rate for 10 years. If, on the other hand, a shorter-term bond had been purchased—say, one maturing in 2 years—the investor would have to accept the lower return for only 2 years and not the full 10 years. At the end of year 2, the investor would receive the maturity value of $1,000 and could buy a bond offering the higher 15 percent rate for the remaining 8 years. Thus, interest rate risk is determined, at least in part, by the length of time an investor is required to commit to an investment. However, the holder of a long-term bond may take some comfort from the fact that long-term interest rates are usually not as volatile as short-term rates. If the short-term rate changed 1 percentage point, for example, it would not be unusual for the long-term rate to change only .3 percentage points.

SUMMARY

Valuation is an important issue if we are to manage the company effectively. An understanding of the concepts and how to compute the value of a security underlie much that we do in finance and in making correct decisions for the firm as a whole. Only if we know what matters to our investors can we maximize the firm's value.

OBJECTIVE 1

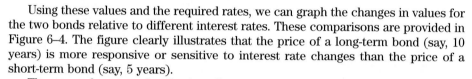

Distinguish between different kinds of bonds

There are a variety of types of bonds, including

- Debentures
- Subordinated debentures
- Mortgage bonds

- Eurobonds
- Zero and very low coupon bonds
- Junk bonds

Explain the more popular features of bonds

OBJECTIVE 2

Some of the more important terms and characteristics that you might hear about bonds include the following:

- Claims on assets and income
- Par value
- Coupon interest rate
- Maturity
- Indenture
- Current yield
- Bond ratings

Define the term *value* as used for several different purposes

OBJECTIVE 3

Value is defined differently depending on the context. But for us, value is the present value of future cash flows expected to be received from an investment discounted at the investor's required rate of return.

Describe the basic process for valuing assets

OBJECTIVE 4

The valuation process can be described as follows: It is assigning value to an asset by calculating the present value of its expected future cash flows using the investor's required rate of return as the discount rate. The investor's required rate of return, k, equals the risk-free rate of interest plus a risk premium to compensate the investor for assuming risk.

Estimate the value of a bond

OBJECTIVE 5

The value of a bond is the present value both of future interest to be received and the par or maturity value of the bond.

Compute a bondholder's expected rate of return

OBJECTIVE 6

To measure the bondholder's expected rate of return, we find the discount rate that equates the present value of the future cash flows (interest and maturity value) with the current market price of the bond. The expected rate of return for a bond is also the rate of return the investor will earn if the bond is held to maturity, or the yield to maturity.

Explain three important relationships that exist in bond valuation

OBJECTIVE 7

Certain key relationships exist in bond valuation, these being

1. A decrease in interest rates (required rates of return) will cause the value of a bond to increase; an interest rate increase will cause a decrease in value. The change in value caused by changing interest rates is called interest rate risk.
2. If the bondholder's required rate of return (current interest rate)
   a. Equals the coupon interest rate, the bond will sell at par, or maturity value.

b. Exceeds the bond's coupon rate, the bond will sell below par value, or at a discount.

c. Is less than the bond's coupon rate, the bond will sell above par value, or at a premium.

3. A bondholder owning a long-term bond is exposed to greater interest rate risk than one owning a short-term bond.

KEY TERMS

Bond, 172

Book Value, 179

Coupon Interest Rate, 176

Current Yield, 177

Debenture, 172

Discount Bond, 189

Efficient Market, 179

Eurobonds, 173

Expected Rate of Return, 186

Fair Value, 179

Indenture, 176

Interest Rate Risk, 188

Intrinsic or Economic Value, 179

Junk Bonds (High-yield Bonds), 174

Liquidation Value, 179

Market Value, 179

Maturity, 176

Mortgage Bond, 173

Opportunity Cost of Funds, 181

Par Value of a Bond, 175

Premium Bond, 189

Subordinated Debentures, 173

Yield to Maturity, 186

Zero and Very Low Coupon Bonds, 173

STUDY QUESTIONS

6-1. Distinguish between debentures and mortgage bonds.

6-2. Define (a) Eurobonds, (b) zero coupon bonds, and (c) junk bonds.

6-3. Describe the bondholder's claim on the firm's assets and income.

6-4. a. How does a bond's par value differ from its market value?

b. Explain the difference between a bond's coupon interest rate, the current yield, and a bondholder's required rate of return.

6-5. What factors determine a bond's rating? Why is the rating important to the firm's manager?

6-6. What are the basic differences between book value, liquidation value, market value, and intrinsic value?

6-7. What is a general definition of the intrinsic value of a security?

6-8. Explain the three factors that determine the intrinsic or economic value of an asset.

6-9. Explain the relationship between an investor's required rate of return and the value of a security.

6-10. Define the bondholder's expected rate of return.

SELF-TEST PROBLEMS

ST-1. (*Bond Valuation*)   Trico bonds have a coupon rate of 8 percent, a par value of $1,000, and will mature in 20 years. If you require a return of 7 percent, what price would you be willing to pay for the bond? What happens if you pay *more* for the bond? What happens if you pay *less* for the bond?

ST-2. (*Bond Valuation*)   Sunn Co.'s bonds, maturing in seven years, pay 8 percent interest on a $1,000 face value. However, interest is paid semiannually. If your required rate of return is 10 percent, what is the value of the bond? How would your answer change if the interest were paid annually?

ST-3. (*Bondholder's Expected Rate of Return*)   Sharp Co. bonds are selling in the market for $1,045. These 15-year bonds pay 7 percent interest annually on a $1,000 par value. If they are purchased at the market price, what is the expected rate of return?

STUDY PROBLEMS

6-1. (*Bond Valuation*)   Calculate the value of a bond that expects to mature in 12 years and has a $1,000 face value. The coupon interest rate is 8 percent and the investor's required rate of return is 12 percent.

6-2. (*Bond Valuation*)   Enterprise, Inc., bonds have a 9 percent coupon rate. The interest is paid semiannually and the bonds mature in eight years. Their par value is $1,000. If your required rate of return is 8 percent, what is the value of the bond? What is its value if the interest is paid annually?

6-3. (*Bondholder's Expected Rate of Return*)   The market price is $900 for a 10-year bond ($1,000 par value) that pays 8 percent interest (4 percent semiannually). What is the bond's expected rate of return?

6-4. (*Bond Valuation*)   Exxon 20-year bonds pay 9 percent interest annually on a $1,000 par value. If bonds sell at $945, what is the bond's expected rate of return?

6-5. (*Bondholder's Expected Rate of Return*)   Zenith Co.'s bonds mature in 12 years and pay 7 percent interest annually. If you purchase the bonds for $1,150, what is your expected rate of return?

6-6. (*Bond Valuation*)   National Steel 15-year, $1,000 par value bonds pay 8 percent interest annually. The market price of the bonds is $1,085, and your required rate of return is 10 percent.
   a. Compute the bond's expected rate of return.
   b. Determine the value of the bond to you, given your required rate of return.
   c. Should you purchase the bond?

6-7. (*Bond Valuation*)   You own a bond that pays $100 in annual interest, with a $1,000 par value. It matures in 15 years. Your required rate of return is 12 percent.
   a. Calculate the value of the bond.
   b. How does the value change if your required rate of return (1) increases to 15 percent or (2) decreases to 8 percent?
   c. Explain the implications of your answers in part b as they relate to interest rate risk, premium bonds, and discount bonds.
   d. Assume that the bond matures in 5 years instead of 15 years. Recompute your answers in part b.
   e. Explain the implications of your answers in part d as they relate to interest rate risk, premium bonds, and discount bonds.

6-8. (*Bond Valuation*)   Arizona Public Utilities issued a bond that pays $80 in annual interest, with a $1,000 par value. It matures in 20 years. Your required rate of return is 7 percent.
   a. Calculate the value of the bond.
   b. How does the value change if your required rate of return (1) increases to 10 percent or (2) decreases to 6 percent?
   c. Explain the implications of your answers in part b as they relate to interest rate risk, premium bonds, and discount bonds.

d. Assume that the bond matures in 10 years instead of 20 years. Recompute your answers in part b.

e. Explain the implications of your answers in part d as they relate to interest rate risk, premium bonds, and discount bonds.

6-9. (*Bond Valuation—Zero Coupon*) The Kumar Corporation is planning on issuing bonds that pay no interest but can be converted into $1,000 at maturity, seven years from their purchase. To price these bonds competitively with other bonds of equal risk, it is determined that they should yield 10 percent, compounded annually. At what price should the Kumar Corporation sell these bonds?

6-10. (*Bond Values*) You are examining three bonds with par value of $1,000 (you receive $1,000 at maturity) and are concerned with what would happen to their market value if interest rates (or the market discount rate) changed. The three bonds are
Bond A—A bond with 3 years left to maturity that pays 10 percent per year compounded semiannually.
Bond B—A bond with 7 years left to maturity that pays 10 percent per year compounded semiannually.
Bond C—A bond with 20 years left to maturity that pays 10 percent per year compounded semiannually.
What would be the value of these bonds if the market discount rate were
  a. 10 percent per year compounded semiannually?
  b. 4 percent per year compounded semiannually?
  c. 16 percent per year compounded semiannually?
  d. What observations can you make about these results?

COMPREHENSIVE PROBLEM

Below you will find data on $1,000 par value bonds issued by Occidental Petroleum, Oryx, and Southwestern Bell at the end of 1996. Assume you are thinking about buying these bonds as of January 1997. Answer the following questions for each of these bonds:

a. Calculate the values of the bonds if your required rates of return are as follows: Occidental Petroleum, 9 percent; Oryx, 10 percent; and Southwestern Bell, 7 percent; where

	OCCIDENTAL PETROLEUM	ORYX	SOUTHWESTERN BELL
Coupon interest rates	10.25%	7.50%	7.375%
Years to maturity	5	10	27

b. At the end of 1996, the bonds were selling for the following amounts:

Occidental Petroleum $1,140
Oryx $880
Southwestern Bell $990

What were the expected rates of return for each bond?

c. How would the values of the bonds change if (1) your required rate of return (k_b) increases 2 percentage points or (2) decreases 2 percentage points?

d. Explain the implications of your answers in part b in terms of interest rate risk, premium bonds, and discount bonds.

e. Should you buy the bonds? Explain.

SS-1.

$$\text{value } (V_b) = \sum_{t=1}^{20} \frac{\$80}{(1.07)^t} + \frac{\$1,000}{(1.07)^{20}}$$

Thus,

$$
\begin{array}{lr}
\text{present value of interest:} & \$80(10.594) = \$847.52 \\
\text{present value of par value:} & \$1,000(0.258) = \underline{\$\ \ 258.00} \\
& \text{value } (V_b) = \underline{\$1,105.52}
\end{array}
$$

If you pay more for the bond, your required rate of return will not be satisfied. In other words, by paying an amount for the bond that exceeds $1,105.52, the expected rate of return for the bond is less than the required rate of return. If you have the opportunity to pay less for the bond, the expected rate of return exceeds the 7 percent required rate of return.

SS-2. If interest is paid semiannually:

$$\text{value } (V_b) = \sum_{t=1}^{14} \frac{\$40}{(1 + 0.05)^t} + \frac{\$1,000}{(1 + 0.05)^{14}}$$

Thus,

$$
\begin{array}{r}
\$40(9.899) = \$395.96 \\
\$1,000(0.505) = \underline{\ \ 505.00} \\
\text{value } (V_b) = \underline{\$900.96}
\end{array}
$$

If interest is paid annually:

$$\text{value } (V_b) = \sum_{t=1}^{7} \frac{\$80}{(1.10)^t} + \frac{\$1,000}{(1.10)^7}$$
$$V_b = \$80(4.868) + \$1,000(0.513)$$
$$V_b = \$902.44$$

SS-3.

$$\$1,045 = \sum_{t=1}^{15} \frac{\$70}{(1 + \bar{k}_b)^t} + \frac{\$1,000}{(1 + \bar{k}_b)^{15}}$$

At 6%: $70(9.712) + $1,000(0.417) = $1,096.84
At 7%: Value must equal $1,000.

Interpolation:

$$\text{Expected rate of return: } \bar{k}_b = 6\% + \frac{\$51.84}{\$96.84}(1\%) = 6.54\%$$

CALCULATOR SOLUTION	
DATA INPUT	**FUNCTION KEY**
15	N
70	+/− PMT
1000	+/− FV
1045	PV
FUNCTION KEY	**ANSWER**
CPT	
I/Y	6.52

Valuation and Characteristics of Stock

Preferred Stock • Common Stock • The Stockholder's Expected Rate of Return

D uring the first half of the 1990s, a record number of privately owned companies issued stock for the first time to the public—often called initial public offerings, or IPOs. Some of the more well known ones included Netscape and Planet Hollywood. However, their stories could be told by many other young firms from cosmetics makers to oil companies, all having one thing in common, a need for additional equity capital for growth. One such firm is FPA Medical Management.

> Dr. Sol Lizerbram heads up FPA Medical Management, a small San Diego company that assembles networks of doctors. A tiny startup just five years ago, FPA did its IPO in October of 1994. Armed with $11.5 million raised at the initial offering and $26 million raised in another offering last fall, Lizerbram hired staff, acquired medical and management services groups, and seeded new startups. From zero earnings, 40 employees, and just $18 million in revenue 18 months ago, FPA now employs nearly 700, reaches throughout California and beyond to six other states, and will pull in an estimated $170 million in revenue this year. "We owe that growth to public capital," says Lizerbram.[1]

The managers of firms wanting to issue stock, whether for the first time or not, need to have a clear understanding of the features of stock and how stock is valued.

---

[1]John Wyatt, "America's Amazing IPO Bonanza," *Fortune*, May 27, 1996, 77.

WHAT'S AHEAD

In Chapter 6, we developed a general concept about valuation, where economic value was defined as the present value of the expected future cash flows generated by the asset. We then applied that concept to valuing bonds.

We continue our study of valuation in this chapter, but we now give our attention to valuing stocks, both preferred stock and common stock. As already noted at the outset of our study of finance, and on several occasions since, the financial manager's objective should be to maximize the value of the firm's common stock. Thus, we need to understand what determines stock value. Also, only with an understanding of valuation can we compute the firm's cost of capital, a concept essential to making effective capital investment decisions—an issue to be discussed in Chapter 11.

PREFERRED STOCK

OBJECTIVE 1

preferred stock

Preferred stock is often referred to as a *hybrid security* because it has *many characteristics of both common stock and bonds.* Preferred stock is similar to common stock in that it has no fixed maturity date, the nonpayment of dividends does not bring on bankruptcy, and dividends are not deductible for tax purposes. On the other hand, preferred stock is similar to bonds in that dividends are limited in amount.

The size of the preferred stock dividend is generally fixed either as a dollar amount or as a percentage of the par value. For example, Texas Utility Electric has preferred stock outstanding that pays an annual dividend of $2.05, while Pacific Telesis has some 7.56 percent preferred stock outstanding. (Pacific Telesis's plans to issue their firm's preferred stock appeared as a news release on their home page and is shown in the Financial Management in Practice box on page 198.) The Pacific Telesis preferred stock has a par value of $25; hence, each share pays 7.56% × $25, or $1.89 in dividends annually. Because the dividends are fixed, preferred stockholders do not share in the residual earnings of the firm but are limited to their stated annual dividend.

In examining preferred stock we will first discuss several features common to almost all preferred stock. Next we will take a brief look at methods of retiring preferred stock. We will close by learning how to value preferred stock.

Features of Preferred Stock

Although each issue of preferred stock is unique, a number of characteristics are common to almost all issues. Some of these more frequent traits include

- Multiple classes of preferred stock
- Preferred stock's claim on assets and income
- Cumulative dividends
- Protective provisions
- Convertibility

FOR IMMEDIATE RELEASE: January 4, 1996

Pacific Telesis to Sell $500 Million of Preferred Securities of Trust

SAN FRANCISCO—Pacific Telesis Group (NYSE: PAC) announced today the sale of $500 million of 7.56% preferred trust securities through Pacific Telesis Financing I, a statutory business trust formed under the laws of the state of Delaware.

The 20 million shares of trust-originated preferred securities, also known as TOPrS, are priced [par value] at $25 per share.

The sale comes after the corporation determined that tax provisions in the Clinton administration's budget proposal would not have a negative impact. The sale had been expected last month, but was delayed while the corporation studied the issue.

Bill Downing, Pacific Telesis chief financial officer, said the corporation intends to use the proceeds to reduce commercial paper outstanding.

The preferred trust securities are expected to be rated "A" by Standard and Poor's Corp. and "a1" by Moody's Investors Service Inc.

They have a 30-year maturity and are callable in five years at par. The settlement date will be Jan. 9, 1996, and the securities will be listed on the New York Stock Exchange under the symbol "PACPRT."

The offering is being managed by Merrill Lynch & Co., Dean Witter Reynolds, Inc., A.G. Edwards & Sons, Inc., Goldman, Sachs & Co., Lehman Brothers Inc., PaineWebber Incorporated, Prudential Securities Incorporated, Salomon Brothers Inc., and Smith Barney Inc.

The offering will be made only by means of a prospectus, copies of which may be obtained from Merrill Lynch or any of the other underwriters.

Pacific Telesis is a diversified telecommunications corporation based in San Francisco.

Source: News release appearing on Pacific Telesis's home page, **http://www.pactcl.com.**

In addition, there are provisions frequently used to retire an issue of preferred stock, including the ability of the firm to call its preferred stock or to use a sinking-fund provision. All these features are presented in the discussion that follows.

Multiple Classes

If a company desires, it can issue more than one series or class of preferred stock, and each class can have different characteristics. In fact, it is quite common for firms that issue preferred stock to issue more than one series. For example, Philadelphia Electric has 13 different issues of preferred stock outstanding. These issues can be further differentiated in that some are convertible into common stock and others are not, and they have varying priority status regarding assets in the event of bankruptcy.

Claim on Assets and Incomes

Preferred stock has priority over common stock with regard to claims on assets in the case of bankruptcy. The preferred stock claim is honored after that of bonds and before that of common stock. Multiple issues of preferred stock may be given an order of priority. Preferred stock also has a claim on income prior to common stock. That is, the firm must pay its preferred stock dividends before it pays common stock dividends. Thus, in terms of risk, preferred stock is safer than common stock because it has a prior claim on assets and income. However, it is riskier than long-term debt because its claims on assets and income come after those of bonds.

Reading a Stock Quote in the *Wall Street Journal*

Below is shown a section of the *Wall Street Journal* that gives the quotes on February 12, 1997 for some of the stocks traded on the New York Stock Exchange on that date.

52 Weeks					Yld		Vol				Net
Hi	Lo	Stock	Sym	Div	%	PE	100s	Hi	Lo	Close	Chg
$107\frac{7}{8}$	$73\frac{5}{8}$	GenElec	GE	2.08	2.0	24	28140	$106\frac{1}{8}$	$104\frac{1}{4}$	$105\frac{7}{8}$	$+1\frac{1}{4}$
$32\frac{7}{8}$	$21\frac{1}{8}$	GenGrowProp	GGP	1.72	5.5	14	1498	$31\frac{1}{2}$	$31\frac{1}{4}$	$31\frac{1}{4}$	$-\frac{1}{4}$
$4\frac{1}{4}$	$2\frac{3}{8}$	GenHost	GH	...	dd	439	$3\frac{1}{2}$	$3\frac{1}{8}$	$3\frac{1}{8}$	$-\frac{1}{4}$
$14\frac{1}{8}$	8	GenHouse	GHW	.32	3.1	dd	65	$10\frac{5}{8}$	$10\frac{3}{8}$	$10\frac{3}{8}$	$-\frac{1}{8}$
$34\frac{3}{8}$	$18\frac{1}{8}$	GenInstrCp	GIC	...	dd	7091	$23\frac{5}{8}$	$23\frac{1}{4}$	$23\frac{1}{2}$	$+\frac{1}{4}$
$68\frac{3}{4}$	52	GenMills	GIS	2.00	2.9	24	5591	$68\frac{1}{4}$	$67\frac{3}{8}$	$67\frac{7}{8}$	$-\frac{3}{4}$
$63\frac{3}{4}$	$45\frac{3}{4}$	GenMotor	GM	2.00f	3.5	10	29880	$57\frac{7}{8}$	$56\frac{3}{4}$	$57\frac{5}{8}$	$+\frac{7}{8}$

The stocks listed above include some familiar companies, such as General Electric (GE), General Mills, and General Motors, that are listed in the *Wall Street Journal* on a daily basis. To help us understand how to read the quotes, consider General Electric:

- The 52 week *high* column shows that General Electric

stock reached a high of $107\frac{7}{8}$ ($107.88) during the past year
- The 52 week *low* column shows that General Electric sold for a low of $73\frac{5}{8}$ ($73.63) during the past year
- The *stock* (GenElec) & *sym* (GE) columns give an abbreviated version of the corporation's name and the ticker symbol, respectively

- *Div*, the dividend column, gives the amount of dividend that General Electric paid its common stockholder's in the last year; $2.08 per share
- *Yld %* (2.0) is the stock's dividend yield—the amount of the dividend divided by the day's closing price ($2.08 ÷ $105.88)
- *PE* (24) gives the current market price ($105\frac{7}{8}$) divided by the firm's earnings per share
- The amount of General Electric stock traded on February 12, 1997 is represented in the *Vol 100s* column, or 2,814,000 shares
- General Electric stock traded at a high price (Hi - $106\frac{1}{8}$) and a low price (Lo - $104\frac{1}{4}$) during the day
- The previous day's closing price is subtracted from the closing price (Close) of $105\frac{7}{8}$ for February 12, 1997 for a net change (Net Chg) of $+1\frac{1}{4}$

Cumulative Feature

Most preferred stocks carry a **cumulative feature** that *requires all past unpaid preferred stock dividends be paid before any common stock dividends are declared.* The purpose is to provide some degree of protection for the preferred shareholder. Without a cumulative feature, there would be no reason why preferred stock dividends would not be omitted or passed when common stock dividends were passed. Because preferred stock does not have the dividend enforcement power of interest from bonds, the cumulative feature is necessary to protect the rights of preferred stockholders.

cumulative feature

Protective Provisions

In addition to the cumulative feature, protective provisions are common to preferred stock. These **protective provisions** generally *allow for voting rights in the event of nonpayment of dividends, or they restrict the payment of common stock divi-*

protective provisions

dends if sinking-fund payments are not met or if the firm is in financial difficulty. In effect, the protective features included with preferred stock are similar to the restrictive provisions included with long-term debt.

To examine typical protective provisions, consider Tenneco Corporation and Reynolds Metals preferred stocks. The Tenneco preferred stock has a protective provision that provides preferred stockholders with voting rights whenever six quarterly dividends are in arrears. At that point the preferred shareholders are given the power to elect a majority of the board of directors. The Reynolds Metals preferred stock includes a protective provision that precludes the payment of common stock dividends during any period in which the preferred stock sinking fund is in default. Both provisions, which yield protection beyond that provided by the cumulative provision and thereby reduce shareholder risk, are desirable. Given these protective provisions for the investor, they reduce the cost of preferred stock to the issuing firm.

Convertibility

convertible preferred stock

Much of the preferred stock that is issued today is **convertible preferred stock;** that is, *at the discretion of the holder the stock can be converted into a predetermined number of shares of common stock.* In fact, today about one-third of all preferred stock issued has a convertibility feature. The convertibility feature is, of course, desirable to the investor and thus reduces the cost of the preferred stock to the issuer.

Retirement Features

Although preferred stock does not have a set maturity associated with it, issuing firms generally provide for some method of retirement. If preferred stock could not be retired, issuing firms could not take advantage of falling interest rates.

call provision

Callable Preferred   Most preferred stock has some type of **call provision** associated with it. A call provision *entitles a company to repurchase its preferred stock (or bonds) from their holders at stated prices over a given time period.* In fact, the Securities and Exchange Commission discourages the issuance of preferred stock without some call provision. The SEC has taken this stance on the grounds that if a method of retirement is not provided, the issuing firm will not be able to replace its preferred stock if interest rates fall.

The call feature on preferred stock usually involves an initial premium above the par value or issuing price of the preferred of approximately 10 percent. Then, over time, the call premium generally falls. By setting the initial call price above the initial issue price and allowing it to decline slowly over time, the firm protects the investor from an early call that carries no premium. A call provision also allows the issuing firm to plan the retirement of its preferred stock at predetermined prices.

sinking-fund provision

Sinking-Fund Provisions   A **sinking-fund provision** *requires the firm periodically to set aside an amount of money for the retirement of its preferred stock.* This money is then used to purchase the preferred stock in the open market or through the use of the call provision, whichever method is cheaper. Although preferred stock does not have a maturity date associated with it, the use of a call provision in addition to a sinking fund can effectively create a maturity date. For instance, the Xerox Corporation has two preferred stock issues, one that has a 10-year sinking-fund provision and another with a 20-year sinking fund. Another firm, the SCANA Corporation, a $4.5 billion energy-based holding company in South Carolina, has preferred stock outstanding that is callable and has a sinking-fund provision. By the terms of the issue, the stock's call premium above its par value is not to exceed the amount of the annual dividend, and the firm is to retire $2.4 million per year from 1996 through the year 2000.

Valuing Preferred Stock

As already explained, the owner of preferred stock generally receives a constant income from the investment in each period. However, the return from preferred stock comes in the form of dividends rather than interest. In addition, while bonds generally have a specific maturity date, most preferred stocks are perpetuities (nonmaturing). In this instance, finding the value (present value) of preferred stock, V_{ps}, with a level cash-flow stream continuing indefinitely, may best be explained by an example.

EXAMPLE

Consider AT&T's preferred stock issue. In similar fashion to valuing bonds in Chapter 6, we will use a three-step valuation procedure.

Step 1: Estimate the amount and timing of the receipt of the future cash flows the preferred stock is expected to provide. AT&T's preferred stock pays an annual dividend of $3.64. The shares do not have a maturity date; that is, they are a perpetuity.

Step 2: Evaluate the riskiness of the preferred stock's future dividends and determine the investor's required rate of return. The investor's required rate of return is assumed to equal 7.28 percent.[2]

Step 3: Calculate the economic or intrinsic value of the share of preferred stock, which is the present value of the expected dividends discounted at the investor's required rate of return. The valuation model for a share of preferred stock, V_{ps}, is therefore defined as follows:

$$V_{ps} = \frac{\text{dividend in year 1}}{(1 + \text{required rate of return})^1}$$ (7-1)

$$+ \frac{\text{dividend in year 2}}{(1 + \text{required rate of return})^2}$$

$$+ \cdots + \frac{\text{dividend in infinity}}{(1 + \text{required rate of return})^\infty}$$

$$= \frac{D_1}{(1 + k_{ps})^1} + \frac{D_2}{(1 + k_{ps})^2} + \cdots + \frac{D_\infty}{(1 + k_{ps})^\infty}$$

$$V_{ps} = \sum_{t=1}^{\infty} \frac{D_t}{(1 + k_{ps})^t}$$

PAUSE AND REFLECT

Equation (7–1) is a restatement in a slightly different form of equation (6–2) in Chapter 6. Recall that equation (6–2) states that the value of an asset is the present value of future cash flows to be received by the investor.

---

[2]For now the required rate of return is given, but in the next chapter we will learn more about measuring an investor's required rate of return. Trust us for now.

Because the dividends in each period are equal for preferred stock, equation (7–1) can be reduced to the following relationship:[3]

$$V_{ps} = \frac{\text{annual dividend}}{\text{required rate of return}} = \frac{D}{k_{ps}} \qquad (7\text{–}2)$$

Equation (7–2) represents the present value of an infinite stream of cash flows, where the cash flows are the same each year. We can determine the value of the AT&T preferred stock, using equation (7–2), as follows:

$$V_{ps} = \frac{D}{k_{ps}} = \frac{\$3.64}{.0728} = \$50$$

PAUSE AND REFLECT

The value of a preferred stock is the present value of all future dividends. But because most preferred stocks are nonmaturing—the dividends continue to infinity—we therefore have to come up with a shortcut for finding value as represented by equation (7–2).

BACK TO THE FOUNDATIONS

Valuing preferred stock relies on three of our axioms presented in Chapter 1, namely:

Axiom 1: The Risk-Return Trade-off—We Won't Take on Additional Risk Unless We Expect to Be Compensated with Additional Return.

Axiom 2: The Time Value of Money—A Dollar Received Today Is Worth More Than a Dollar Received in the Future.

Axiom 3: Cash—Not Profits—Is King.

Determining the economic worth or value of an asset always relies on these three axioms. Without them, we would have no basis for explaining value. With them, we can know that the amount and timing of cash, not earnings, drive value. Also, we must be rewarded for taking risk; otherwise, we will not invest.

---

[3]To verify this result, consider the following equation:

(i)
$$V_{ps} = \frac{D_1}{(1 + k_{ps})^1} + \frac{D_2}{(1 + k_{ps})^2} + \cdots + \frac{D_n}{(1 + k_{ps})^n}$$

If we multiply both sides of this equation by $(1 + k_{ps})$, we have

(ii)
$$V_{ps}(1 + k_{ps}) = D_1 + \frac{D_2}{(1 + k_{ps})} + \cdots + \frac{D_n}{(1 + k_{ps})^{n-1}}$$

Subtracting (i) from (ii) yields

$$V_{ps}(1 + k_{ps} - 1) = D_1 - \frac{D_n}{(1 + k_{ps})^n}$$

As n approaches infinity, $D_n/(1 + k_{ps})$ approaches zero. Consequently,

$$V_{ps}k_{ps} = D_1 \text{ and } V_{ps} = \frac{D_1}{k_{ps}}$$

Since $D_1 = D_2 = \cdots = D_n$, we need not designate the year. Therefore,

(iii)
$$V_{ps} = \frac{D}{k_{ps}}$$

Berkshire Hathaway Issues New Class B Stock

If you look in the *Wall Street Journal* at the shares traded on the New York Stock Exchange, you might be surprised to see that one firm, Berkshire Hathaway, has shares that trade at $32,000 per share (as of June 1996). The firm, founded and operated by Warren Buffett, began as an insurance company in Omaha, Nebraska, and has since grown into a multibillion-dollar enterprise that now owns a portfolio of companies. But few of us could afford to buy very many—if even one—of the shares. So Buffett made a decision to issue some class B shares that would be priced at a small portion of the original shares. The following is a Dow Jones News Service release announcing the new shares.

Berkshire Hathaway Class B Shares Priced at $1,110

OMAHA, Neb. (Dow Jones)—Berkshire Hathaway, Inc.'s (BRK) offer of 450,000 new class B shares was priced at $1,100 each.

In a press release, the company said its class A common shares closed today at $33,400. The company has said the class B shares would come to market at about one-thirtieth of the price of the class A shares.

The offering may be increased to 517,500 shares of the lower-priced stock if the underwriter, Salomon Brothers, Inc., exercises its over-allotment option in full.

Berkshire Hathaway, which is about 40% owned by Warren Buffett, is an insurance holding company.

COMMON STOCK

OBJECTIVE 3

common stock

Common stock is *a certificate that indicates ownership in the corporation.* In effect, bondholders and preferred stockholders can be viewed as creditors, whereas the common stockholders are the true owners of the firm. Common stock does not have a maturity date, but exists as long as the firm does. Nor does common stock have an upper limit on its dividend payments. Dividend payments must be declared by the firm's board of directors before they are issued. In the event of bankruptcy the common stockholders, as owners of the corporation, cannot exercise claims on assets until the firm's creditors, including the bondholders and preferred shareholders, have been satisfied.

In examining common stock, we will look first at several of its features or characteristics. Then we will focus on valuing common stock.

Features or Characteristics of Common Stock

We now examine common stock's claim on income and assets, stockholder voting rights, preemptive rights, and the meaning and importance of its limited-liability feature.

Claim on Income

As the owners of the corporation, the common shareholders have the right to the residual income after bondholders and preferred stockholders have been paid. This income may be paid directly to the shareholders in the form of dividends or retained and reinvested by the firm. Although it is obvious the shareholder benefits immediately from the distribution of income in the form of dividends, the reinvestment of earnings also benefits the shareholder. Plowing back earnings into the firm results in an increase in the value of the firm, in its earning power, and in its future dividends. This action in turn results in an increase in the value of the stock. In effect, residual income is distributed directly to shareholders in the form of dividends or indirectly in the form of capital gains on their common stock.

What Does a Stock Look Like?

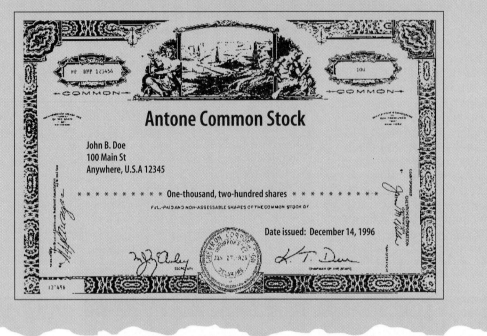

The right to residual income has both advantages and disadvantages for the common stockholder. The advantage is that the potential return is limitless. Once the claims of the most senior securities (bonds and preferred stock) have been satisfied, the remaining income flows to the common stockholders in the form of dividends or capital gains. The disadvantage: If the bond and preferred stock claims on income totally absorb earnings, common shareholders receive nothing. In years when earnings fall, it is the common shareholder who suffers first.

Claim on Assets

Just as common stock has a residual claim on income, it also has a residual claim on assets in the case of liquidation. Only after the claims of debt holders and preferred stockholders have been satisfied do the claims of common shareholders receive attention. Unfortunately, when bankruptcy does occur, the claims of the common shareholders generally go unsatisfied. This residual claim on assets adds to the risk of common stock. Thus, while common stock has historically provided a large return, averaging 10 percent annually since the late 1920s, it also has large risks associated with it.

Voting Rights

The common stock shareholders are entitled to elect the board of directors, and are in general, the only security holders given a vote. Early in this century it was not uncommon for a firm to issue two classes of common stock, which were identical except that only one carried voting rights. For example, both the Parker Pen Co. and the Great Atlantic and Pacific Tea Co. (A&P) had two such classes of common stock. This practice was virtually eliminated by (1) the Public Utility Holding Company Act of 1935, which gave the Securities and Exchange Commission the power to require that newly issued common stock carry voting rights, (2) the New York Stock Exchange's refusal to list common stock without voting privileges, and (3) investor demand for the inclusion of voting rights. However, with the merger boom of the eighties, dual classes of common stock with different voting rights again emerged, this time as a defensive tactic used to prevent takeovers.

Common shareholders not only have the right to elect the board of directors, they also must approve any change in the corporate charter. A typical charter change might involve the authorization to issue new stock or perhaps a merger proposal.

Voting for directors and charter changes occurs at the corporation's annual meeting. While shareholders may vote in person, the majority generally vote by proxy. A **proxy** *gives a designated party the temporary power of attorney to vote for the signee at the corporation's annual meeting.* The firm's management generally solicits proxy votes and, if the shareholders are satisfied with its performance, has little problem securing them. However, in times of financial distress or when management takeovers are threatened, **proxy fights**—*battles between rival groups for proxy votes*—occur.

proxy

proxy fight

While each share of stock carries the same number of votes, the voting procedure is not always the same from company to company. The two procedures commonly used are majority and cumulative voting. Under **majority voting,** *each share of stock allows the shareholder one vote, and each position on the board of directors is voted on separately.* Because each member of the board of directors is elected by a simple majority, a majority of shares has the power to elect the entire board of directors.

majority voting

With **cumulative voting,** *each share of stock allows the shareholder a number of votes equal to the number of directors being elected.* The shareholder can then cast all of his or her votes for a single candidate or split them among the various candidates. The advantage of a cumulative voting procedure is that it gives minority shareholders the power to elect a director.

cumulative voting

PAUSE AND REFLECT

In theory, the shareholders pick the corporate board of directors, generally through proxy voting, and the board of directors in turn picks the management. Unfortunately, in reality the system frequently works the other way around. Management selects both the issues and the board of director nominees and then distributes the proxy ballots. In effect, shareholders are offered a slate of nominees selected by management from which to choose. The end result is that management effectively selects the directors, who then may have more allegiance to the managers than to the shareholders. This in turn sets up the potential for agency problems in which a divergence of interests between managers and shareholders is allowed to exist, with the board of directors not monitoring the managers on behalf of the shareholders as they should.

Preemptive Rights

The **preemptive right** *entitles the common shareholder to maintain a proportionate share of ownership in the firm.* When new shares are issued, common shareholders have the first right of refusal. If a shareholder owns 25 percent of the corporation's stock, then he or she is entitled to purchase 25 percent of the new shares. *Certificates issued to the shareholders giving them an option to purchase a stated number of new shares of stock at a specified price during a 2- to 10-week period* are called **rights.** These rights can be exercised, generally at a price set by management below the common stock's current market price, can be allowed to expire, or can be sold in the open market.

preemptive right

rights

Limited Liability

Although the common shareholders are the actual owners of the corporation, their *liability in the case of bankruptcy is limited to the amount of their investment.* The advantage is that investors who might not otherwise invest their funds in the firm become willing to do so. This **limited liability** feature aids the firm in raising funds.

limited liability

Valuing Common Stock

Like bonds and preferred stock, a common stock's value is equal to the present value of all future cash flows expected to be received by the stockholder. However, in contrast to bonds, common stock does not promise its owners interest income or a maturity payment at some specified time in the future. Nor does common stock entitle the holder to a predetermined constant dividend, as does preferred stock. For common stock, the dividend is based on the profitability of the firm and on management's decision to pay dividends or to retain the profits for reinvestment purposes. As a consequence, dividend streams tend to increase with the growth in corporate earnings. Thus, the growth of future dividends is a prime distinguishing feature of common stock.

The Growth Factor in Valuing Common Stock

What is meant by the term *growth* when used in the context of valuing common stock? A company can grow in a variety of ways. It can become larger by borrowing money to invest in new projects. Likewise, it can issue new stock for expansion. Management could also acquire another company to merge with the existing firm, which would increase the firm's assets. In all these cases, the firm is growing through the use of new financing, by issuing debt or common stock. Although management could accurately say that the firm has grown, the original stockholders may or may not participate in this growth. Growth is realized through the infusion of new capital. The firm size has clearly increased, but unless the original investors increase their investment in the firm, they will own a smaller portion of the expanded business.

internal growth   Another means of growing is **internal growth,** which requires that *management retain some or all of the firm's profits for reinvestment in the firm*, resulting in the growth of future earnings and, hopefully, the value of the common stock. This process underlies the essence of potential growth for the firm's current stockholders and what we can call the only relevant growth for our purposes in valuing a firm's common shares.[4]

EXAMPLE

To illustrate the nature of internal growth, assume that the return on equity for PepsiCo is 16 percent.[5] If PepsiCo's management decides to pay all the profits out in dividends to its stockholders, the firm will experience no growth internally. It might become larger by borrowing more money or issuing new stock, but internal growth will come only through the retention of profits. If, on the other hand, PepsiCo retained all the profits, the stockholders' investment in the firm would grow by the amount of profits retained, or by 16 percent. If, however, management kept only 50 percent of the profits for reinvestment, the common shareholders' investment would increase only by half of the 16 percent return on equity, or by 8 percent. We can express this relationship by the following equation:

$$g = ROE \times r \tag{7-3}$$

where g = the growth rate of future earnings and the growth in the common stockholders' investment in the firm

ROE = the return on equity (net income/common book value)

r = the company's percentage of profits retained, called the profit-retention rate[6]

---

[4]We are not arguing that the existing common stockholders never benefit from the use of external financing; however, such benefit is more evasive if capital markets are efficient.

[5]The return on equity is the percentage return on the common shareholder's investment in the company and is computed as follows:

$$\text{return on equity} = \frac{\text{net income}}{(\text{par value} + \text{paid-in capital} + \text{retained earnings})}$$

[6]The retention rate is also equal to $(1 - \text{the percentage of profits paid out in dividends})$. The percentage of profits paid out in dividends is often called the dividend-payout ratio.

Ethics: Keeping Perspective

Ethical and moral lapses in the business and financial community, academia, politics, and religion fill the daily press. But the rash of insider-trading cases on Wall Street against recent graduates of top business and law schools seems particularly disturbing because the cream of the crop, with six-figure incomes and brilliant careers ahead, is being convicted.

Most appear to have been very bright, highly motivated overachievers, driven by peer rivalries to win a game in which the score had a dollar sign in front of it. While there have been a few big fish, most sold their futures for $20,000 to $50,000 of illicit profits. They missed the point—that life is a marathon, not a sprint.

In fact, most business school graduates become competent executives, managing people and resources for the benefit of society. The rewards—the titles and money—are merely the byproducts of doing a good job.

_____

Source: John S. R. Shad, "Business's Bottom Line: Ethics," *Ethics in American Business: A Special Report*, *Touche Ross & Co.*, 1988, 56.

Therefore, if only 25 percent of the profits were retained by PepsiCo, we would expect the common stockholders' investment in the firm and the value of the stock price to increase or grow by 4 percent; that is,

$$g = 16\% \times .25 = 4\%$$

In summary, common stockholders frequently rely on an increase in the stock price as a source of return. If the company is retaining a portion of its earnings for reinvestment, future profits and dividends should grow. This growth should be reflected in an increased market price of the common stock in future periods, provided that the return on the funds reinvested exceeds the investor's required rate of return. Therefore, both types of return (dividends and price appreciation) are necessary in the development of a valuation model for common stock.

To explain this process, let us begin by examining how an investor might value a common stock that is to be held for only one year.

Common Stock Valuation—Single Holding Period

For an investor holding a common stock for only one year, the value of the stock should equal the present value of both the expected dividend to be received in one year, D_1, and the anticipated market price of the share at year end, P_1. If k_{cs} represents a common stockholder's required rate of return, the value of the security, V_{cs}, would be

$$V_{cs} = \text{present value of dividend in one year } (D_1)$$
$$+ \text{present value of market price in one year } (P_1)$$
$$= \frac{D_1}{(1 + k_{cs})} + \frac{P_1}{(1 + k_{cs})}$$

EXAMPLE

Suppose an investor is contemplating the purchase of RMI common stock at the beginning of this year. The dividend at year end is expected to be $1.64, and the market price by the end of the year is projected to be $22. If the investor's required rate of return is 18 percent, the value of the security would be

$$V_{cs} = \frac{\$1.64}{1 + .18} + \frac{\$22}{1 + .18}$$
$$= \$1.39 + \$18.64$$
$$= \$20.03$$

Promoting Stock on the Internet

The following story reported in the *Wall Street Journal* shows both the potential for communicating with investors and the ethical issues that can arise.

When Todd Bakar, a securities analyst with Hambrecht & Quist, began following Iomega Corp., he considered himself prudent. On the plus side, Iomega has a hot product: an affordable and removable storage disk with far more capacity than conventional floppies. On the other hand, Mr. Bakar observed, the stock price was rich. At $9.50 a share, price had risen a remarkable 17 times in 15 months.

That was in March [1996]. Two months later in May, Iomega had quintupled to $54. All based on one positive earnings report and literally thousands of messages over the *Motley Fool*, an on-line bulletin board on America Online. Some of the messages were informative; some were "financial trash."

According to Iomega and Hambrecht & Quist, some of these cyberscribes, both bulls and bears, have taken liberties with the truth, and as a result, the Securities and Exchange Commission has opened a probe into trading in the stock, as part of which the *Fool* has turned over thousands of postings. Kenneth Israel Jr., the SEC's district administrator in Salt Lake City says, "Obviously there is some concern with what is going on over the Internet generally— not to say there is anything illegal going on—is a new world for everybody." What should the SEC look at? For starters, is aggressive and possibly ma- nipulative promotion—an activity rightly regulated in traditional "public" forums—getting a free ride on the info highway?

David and Tom Gardner, the brothers who run the *Fool*, and who recommend Iomega in their model portfolio, say the *Fool* provides the best research going—and provides it to the little guy. A bulletin board open to thousands can dig up more than any Wall Street firm—or journalist. "The exciting thing now, we have an open environment," Tom Gardner says. "It's a meritocracy." The brothers concede that their service is open to manipulators, but add that they are open to swift refutation.

Source: Roger Lowenstein, "Who's the Fool in Iomega's Skyrocket?" *Wall Street Journal*, May 23, 1996, C1.

Once again we see that valuation is a three-step process. First, we estimate the expected future cash flows from common stock ownership (a $1.64 dividend and a $22 end-of-year expected share price). Second, we estimate the investor's required rate of return after assessing the riskiness of the expected cash flows (assumed to be 18 percent). Finally, we discount the expected dividend and end-of-year share price back to the present at the investor's required rate of return. The result is $20.03.

PAUSE AND REFLECT

The intrinsic value of a common stock, like preferred stock, is the present value of all future dividends. And we have the same problem we had with preferred stock: It is hard to value cash flows that continue in perpetuity. So we must make some assumptions about the expected growth of future dividends. If, for example, we assume that dividends grow at a constant rate forever, we can then calculate the present value of the stock.

Common Stock Valuation—Multiple Holding Periods

multiple-holding-period valuation model

Since common stock has no maturity date and is frequently held for many years, a **multiple-holding-period valuation model** is needed. This model is *an equation used* *to value stock that has no maturity date, but continues in perpetuity (or as long as the firm exists).* The general common stock valuation model can be defined as follows:

$$V_{cs} = \frac{D_1}{(1 + k_{cs})^1} + \frac{D_2}{(1 + k_{cs})^2} + \cdots + \frac{D_n}{(1 + k_{cs})^n} + \cdots + \frac{D_\infty}{(1 + k_{cs})^\infty} \quad (7\text{--}4)$$

PAUSE AND REFLECT

Turn back to Chapter 6, and compare equation (6–2) with equation (7–4). Equation (7–4) is merely a restatement in a slightly different form of equation (6–2). Recall that equation (6–2), which is the basis for our work in valuing securities, states that the value of an asset is the present value of future cash flows to be received by the investor. Equation (7–4) is simply applying equation (6–2) to valuing common stock.

Equation (7–4) indicates that we are discounting the dividend at the end of the first year, D_1, back one year; the dividend in the second year, D_2, back two years; the dividend in the nth year back n years; and the dividend in infinity back an infinite number of years. The required rate of return is k_{cs}. In using equation (7–4), note that the value of the stock is established at the beginning of the year, say January 1, 1998. The most recent past dividend, D_0, would have been paid the previous day, December 31, 1997. Thus, if we purchased the stock on January 1, the first dividend would be received in 12 months, on December 31, 1998, which is represented by D_1.

Fortunately, equation (7–4) can be reduced to a much more manageable form if dividends grow each year at a constant rate, g. The constant-growth common-stock valuation equation may be presented as follows:[7]

$$\text{common stock value} = \frac{\text{dividend in year 1}}{\text{required rate of return} - \text{growth rate}} \quad (7\text{--}7)$$

$$V_{cs} = \frac{D_1}{k_{cs} - g}$$

---

[7]Where common stock dividends grow at a constant rate of g every year, we can express the dividend in any year in terms of the dividend paid at the end of the previous year, D_0. For example, the expected dividend one year hence is simply $D_0(1 + g)$. Likewise, the dividend at the end of t years is $D_0(1 + g)^t$. Using this notation, the common-stock valuation equation in (7–4) can be rewritten as follows:

$$V_{cs} = \frac{D_0(1 + g)^1}{(1 + k_{cs})^1} + \frac{D_0(1 + g)^2}{(1 + k_{cs})^2} + \cdots + \frac{D_0(1 + g)^n}{(1 + k_{cs})^n} + \cdots + \frac{D_0(1 + g)^\infty}{(1 + k_{cs})^\infty} \quad (7\text{--}5)$$

If both sides of equation (7–5) are multiplied by $(1 + k_{cs})/(1 + g)$ and then equation (7–4) is subtracted from the product, the result is

$$\frac{V_{cs}(1 + k_{cs})}{1 + g} - V_{cs} = D_0 - \frac{D_0(1 + g)^\infty}{(1 + k_{cs})^\infty} \quad (7\text{--}6)$$

If $k_{cs} > g$, which normally should hold, $[D_0(1 + g)^\infty/(1 + k_{cs})^\infty]$ approaches zero. As a result,

$$\frac{V_{cs}(1 + k_{cs})}{1 + g} - V_{cs} = D_0$$

$$V_{cs}\left(\frac{1 + k_{cs}}{1 + g}\right) - V_{cs}\left(\frac{1 + g}{1 + g}\right) = D_0$$

$$V_{cs}\left[\frac{(1 + k_{cs}) - (1 + g)}{1 + g}\right] = D_0$$

$$V_{cs}(k_{cs} - g) = D_0(1 + g)$$

$$V_{cs} = \frac{D_1}{k_{cs} - g} \quad (7\text{--}7)$$

Consequently, the intrinsic value (present value) of a share of common stock whose dividends grow at a constant annual rate can be calculated using equation (7–7). Although the interpretation of this equation may not be intuitively obvious, simply remember that it solves for the present value of the future dividend stream growing at a rate, g, to infinity, assuming that k_{cs} is greater than g.

EXAMPLE

Consider the valuation of a share of common stock that paid a $2 dividend at the end of the last year and is expected to pay a cash dividend every year from now to infinity. Each year the dividends are expected to grow at a rate of 10 percent. Based on an assessment of the riskiness of the common stock, the investor's required rate of return is 15 percent. Using this information, we would compute the value of the common stock as follows:

1. Since the $2 dividend was paid last year (actually, yesterday), we must compute the next dividend to be received, that is, D_1, where

$$D_1 = D_0(1 + g)$$
$$= \$2(1 + .10)$$
$$= \$2.20$$

2. Now, using equation (7–7),

$$V_{cs} = \frac{D_1}{k_{cs} - g}$$
$$= \frac{\$2.20}{.15 - .10}$$
$$= \$44$$

We have argued that the value of a common stock is equal to the present value of all future dividends, which is without question a fundamental premise of finance. In practice, however, managers, along with many security analysts, often talk about the relationship between stock value and earnings, rather than dividends. We would encourage you to be very cautious in using earnings to value a stock. Even though it may be a popular practice, the evidence available suggests that investors look to the cash flows generated by the firm, not the earnings, for value. A firm's value truly is the present value of the cash flows it produces.

We now turn to our last issue in stock valuation, that of the stockholder's expected returns, a matter of key importance to the financial manager.

BACK TO THE FOUNDATIONS

Valuing common stock is no different from valuing preferred stock; only the pattern of the cash flows changes, but nothing else. Thus, the valuation of common stock relies on the same three axioms developed in Chapter 1 that were used in valuing preferred stock:

Axiom 1: The Risk-Return Trade-off—We Won't Take on Additional Risk Unless We Expect to Be Compensated with Additional Return.

Axiom 2: The Time Value of Money—A Dollar Received Today Is Worth More Than A Dollar Received in the Future.

Axiom 3: Cash—Not Profits—Is King.

Determining the economic worth or value of an asset always relies on these three axioms. Without them, we would have no basis for explaining value. With them, we can know that the amount and timing of cash, not earnings, drives value. Also, we must be rewarded for taking risk; otherwise, we will not invest.

As stated in Chapter 6, the expected rate of return on a bond is the return the bond-holder expects to receive on the investment by paying the existing market price for the security. This rate of return is of interest to the financial manager because it tells the manager about the investor's expectations. The same can be said for the financial manager needing to know the expected rate of return of the firm's stockholders, which is the topic of this section.

The Preferred Stockholder's Expected Rate of Return

In computing the preferred stockholder's expected rate of return, we use the valuation equation for preferred stock. Earlier, equation (7–2) specified the value of a preferred stock, V_{ps}, as

$$V_{ps} = \frac{\text{annual dividend}}{\text{required rate of return}} = \frac{D}{k_{ps}} \qquad (7\text{--}2)$$

Solving equation (7–2) for k_{ps}, we have

$$k_{ps} = \frac{\text{annual dividend}}{\text{value}} = \frac{D}{V_{ps}} \qquad (7\text{--}8)$$

Thus, a preferred stockholder's *required* rate of return simply equals the stock's annual dividend divided by the intrinsic value. We may also restate equation (7–8) to solve for a preferred stock's *expected* rate of return, $\bar{k}_{ps}$, as follows:[8]

$$\bar{k}_{ps} = \frac{\text{annual dividend}}{\text{market price}} = \frac{D}{P_{ps}} \qquad (7\text{--}9)$$

Note that we have merely substituted the current market price, P_{ps}, for the intrinsic value, V_{ps}. The expected rate of return, $\bar{k}_{ps}$, therefore equals the annual dividend relative to the price the stock is presently selling for, P_{ps}. Thus, the **expected rate of return, $\bar{k}_{ps}$,** is *the rate of return the investor can expect to earn from the investment if bought at the current market price*. For example, if the present market price of preferred stock is $50 and it pays a $3.64 annual dividend, the expected rate of return implicit in the present market price is

expected rate of return

$$\bar{k}_{ps} = \frac{D}{P_{ps}} = \frac{\$3.64}{\$50} = 7.28\%$$

Therefore, investors (who pay $50 per share for a preferred security that is paying $3.64 in annual dividends) are expecting a 7.28 percent rate of return.

The Common Stockholder's Expected Rate of Return

The valuation equation for common stock was defined earlier in equation (7–4) as

$$\text{value} = \frac{\text{dividend in year 1}}{(1 + \text{required rate of return})^1}$$

$$+ \frac{\text{dividend in year 2}}{(1 + \text{required rate of return})^2}$$

$$+ \cdots + \frac{\text{dividend in year infinity}}{(1 + \text{required rate of return})^\infty}$$

---

[8]We will use $\bar{k}$ to represent a security's *expected* rate of return versus k for the investor's *required* rate of return.

Netscape Issues Stock to the Public

Below is the *New York Times* account of Netscape Communications Corporation issuing stock to the public on August 10, 1995—an event that set a new record for a first-day stock offering.

A 15-month-old company that has never made a dime of profit had one of the most stunning debuts in Wall Street history yesterday as investors rushed to pour their money into cyberspace.

Netscape Communications Corporation, founded in April 1994, produces a popular software program that allows users of personal computers and modems to pilot their way through the Internet's World Wide Web.

Netscape became the latest—and hottest—company in the Internet business to list shares on the nation's stock exchanges. Shares of Netscape, which had been priced at $28 before trading began at 11 A.M., opened far higher—at $71. The shares soon surged to as high as $74.75. By noon, money managers at big mutual funds and other institutional investors

fortunate enough to be in on the ground floor could have cashed in profit of more than 150 percent and gone to lunch.

But that left plenty of action for other investors, some of whom racked up losses, during an afternoon of frantic buying and selling. Indeed, many of the 5.75 million available shares—13 percent of the total number of outstanding shares—traded hands more than once yesterday. The volume of trading reached 13.88 million shares by the time the closing bell rang. The price of Netscape shares ended at $58.25 apiece, up $30.25 from the offering price.

It was the best opening day for a stock in Wall Street history for an issue of its size. The overall dollar value of the one-day gain in the stock was $173.9 million. And the total market value of Netscape, including the shares held previously by management and venture capital firms, grew to $2.2 billion.

As a result of the phenomenal demand, some people are riding the Internet wave to

phenomenal wealth—on paper at least. At the company's current valuation, James H. Clark, the company's 50-year-old chairman and largest shareholder, holds a stake worth $566 million. Marc L. Andreessen, Netscape's 24-year-old vice president of technology and an inventor of its prize software, based on yesterday's closing price, is worth more than $58 million.

Still, Netscape's future is by no means assured. Many hot new issues have soared only to come crashing down to earth. The Internet is still considered to be in its infancy and there are many wealthy and powerful competitors. Microsoft, for example, has licensed a rival browser from Spyglass and plans to distribute it along with the Microsoft Windows 95 software later this year.

Ten months later, in June 1996, Netscape was trading for $54.

Source: Laurence Zuckerman, "With Internet Cachet, Not Profit, a New Stock Is Wall St.'s Darling," *New York Times*, August 10, 1995, A1.

$$V_{cs} = \frac{D_1}{(1 + k_{cs})^1} + \frac{D_2}{(1 + k_{cs})^2} + \cdots + \frac{D_\infty}{(1 + k_{cs})^\infty} \qquad (7\text{--}4)$$

$$V_{cs} = \sum_{t=1}^{\infty} \frac{D_t}{(1 + k_{cs})^t}$$

Owing to the difficulty of discounting to infinity, we made the key assumption that the dividends, D_t, increase at a constant annual compound growth rate of g. If this assumption is valid, equation (7–4) was shown to be equivalent to

$$\text{common stock value} = \frac{\text{dividend in year 1}}{\text{required rate of return} - \text{growth rate}} \qquad (7\text{--}7)$$

$$V_{cs} = \frac{D_1}{k_{cs} - g}$$

Thus, V_{cs} represents the maximum value that an investor having a required rate of return of k_{cs} would pay for a security having an anticipated dividend in year 1 of D_1 that is expected to grow in future years at rate g. Solving equation (7–7) for k_{cs}, we can compute the common stockholder's required rate of return as follows:[9]

$$k_{cs} = \left(\frac{D_1}{V_{cs}}\right) + g \qquad \text{(7–10)}$$

$$\underset{\substack{\text{dividend} \\ \text{yield}}}{\uparrow} \qquad \underset{\substack{\text{annual} \\ \text{growth} \\ \text{rate}}}{\uparrow}$$

From this equation, the common stockholder's required rate of return is equal to the dividend yield plus a growth factor. Although the growth rate, g, applies to the growth in the company's dividends, given our assumptions the stock's value may also be expected to increase at the same rate. For this reason, g represents the annual percentage growth in the stock value. In other words, the investor's required rate of return is satisfied by receiving dividends and capital gains, as reflected by the expected percentage growth rate in the stock price.

As was done for preferred stock earlier, we may revise equation (7–10) to measure a common stock's *expected* rate of return, $\bar{k}_{cs}$. Replacing the intrinsic value, V_{cs}, in equation (7–10) with the stock's current market price, P_{cs}, we may express the stock's expected rate of return as follows:

$$\bar{k}_{cs} = \frac{\text{dividend in year 1}}{\text{market price}} + \text{growth} = \frac{D_1}{P_{cs}} + g \qquad \text{(7–11)}$$

EXAMPLE

As an example of computing the expected rate of return for a common stock where dividends are anticipated to grow at a constant rate to infinity, assume that a firm's common stock has a current market price of $44. If the expected dividend at the conclusion of this year is $2.20 and dividends and earnings are growing at a 10 percent annual rate (last year's dividend was $2), the expected rate of return implicit in the $44 stock price is as follows:

$$\bar{k}_{cs} = \frac{\$2.20}{\$44} + 10\% = 15\%$$

As a final note, we should understand that the *expected* rate of return implied by a given market price equals the *required* rate of return for investors at the margin. For these investors, the expected rate of return is just equal to their required rate of return, and therefore they are willing to pay the current market price for the security. These investors' required rate of return is of particular significance to the financial manager, because it represents the cost of new financing to the firm.

BACK TO THE FOUNDATIONS

We have just learned that on average, the expected return will be equal to the investor's required rate of return. This equilibrium condition is achieved by investors paying for an asset only the amount that will exactly satisfy their required rate of return. Thus, finding the expected rate of return based on the current market price for the security relies on two of the axioms given in Chapter 1:

---

[9]At times the expected dividend at year end (D_1) is not given. Instead, we might only know the most recent dividend (paid yesterday), that is, D_0. If so, equation (7–7) must be restated as follows:

$$V_{cs} = \frac{D_1}{(k_{cs} - g)} = \frac{D_0(1 + g)}{(k_{cs} - g)}$$

Comparing Values of the World's Businesses

Numerous business magazines, including *Forbes*, *Business Week*, and *Fortune*, publish rankings of firms. They rank the firms according to sales, assets, return on equity, or a host of other measures. *The Economist*, in conjunction with the London Business School, has attempted to measure the quality of the company by what its editors define as "added value." The following is an excerpt from *The Economist* describing this endeavor and a listing of several countries' "best companies" as measured by "added value relative to sales."

Why bother, one could ask: is not profitability good enough, whether that means return on sales or—which may matter more to shareholders—return on equity? No. Comparisons of profit and profitability are affected both by peculiarities of accounting practice and by (unavoidable) differences in the cost of capital and the way it is accounted for. Added value, in the wider-than-usual sense* developed by John Kay and some colleagues at LBS, tries to do better than this.

To see why, take a real example: a comparison of Bethlehem Steel, an American steel maker, with Colgate-Palmolive, a producer of consumer goods. In 1989 the two companies' profit and turnover figures were much alike. A return-on-sales comparison would rank them side by side. But Bethlehem employed $1\frac{1}{2}$ times as much capital as Colgate. A return-on-capital ranking would show the steel maker well behind.

That, as it happens, would be a fair conclusion. Yet it might not have been. Ranking by return on capital favors labor-intensive companies over capital-intensive ones. Instead of using costly machines, Colgate might have been (under) paying thousands of women to fill toothpaste-tubes by hand.

A return-on-capital measure also favors companies with old capital over those with newer capital. This stems from the historic-cost accounts used by nearly all companies. These value capital equipment at what it cost in the past, not what it would cost now, after years of inflation. And they not only thus understate the capital employed, but also overstate the return it earns, because the depreciation deducted from gross profit is artificially (and in fact misleadingly) low. The return-on-capital ratio is doubly falsified.

The LBS version of added value gets a round most of these problems. It measures how much more a firm's output is worth than all its inputs of materials, labor and capital. It is thus fair as between capital-intensive and labor-intensive companies. It also gets round differences in the ways companies are financed, by treating all alike, as if all were debt-financed at a standard rate of interest on the real value of their capital.

To find out a firm's added value, take its operating profits, adjust for the vagaries of depreciation (the LBS team has a complex formula for this) and then subtract its capital charge. Note that the result, our "added value," is not the same as the "value added" of value-added tax, which is a measure of the company's output, calculated by subtracting all bought-in inputs from turnover. Ours can be thought of as value added for the shareholder. . . .

---

*See Evan Davis, Stephanie Flanders, and Jonathan Star, "Who Are the World's Most Successful Companies?" *Business Strategy Review*, London Business School, Summer 1991.

Source: "The Best Companies: Scrambling to the Top," *The Economist*, September 7, 1991,

Axiom 1: The Risk-Return Trade-off—We Won't Take on Additional Risk Unless We Expect to Be Compensated with Additional Return.

Axiom 2: The Time Value of Money—A Dollar Received Today Is Worth More Than a Dollar Received in the Future.

The Top Five[a] Added Value as a Percentage of Sales 1981–1990

COUNTRY AND COMPANY NAME	INDUSTRY	PERCENTAGE
United States		
1. Autodesk	computer services	33.9
2. UST	tobacco	33.7
3. King World	TV, radio	33.0
4. Community Psychiatric	health care	29.5
5. St. Jude Medical Equipment	medical	29.3
Japan		
1. Fuji Photo Film	photographics	15.5
2. Murata Manufacturing	electronics	14.4
3. Kyocera	electronics	13.9
4. Matsushita Electric	electronics	7.8
5. Pioneer Electronics	electronics	7.5
Germany		
1. Harpener	conglomerate	20.9
2. Contigas	utilities	19.7
3. Leifheit	household	14.4
4. Boss (Hugo)	clothing	11.9
5. Nordcement	cement	11.5
France		
1. LVMH Moet/Vuitton	luxury goods	18.6
2. Legris	construction materials	12.7
3. Legrand	electricals	12.6
4. CGI Informatique	computer services	11.8
5. Salomon	sports goods	11.7
Britain		
1. Glaxo	pharmaceutical	27.8
2. Alexander Proudfoot	financial services	26.7
3. Tiphook	transport	25.2
4. Cable and Wireless	telecoms	23.1
5. McCarthy and Stone	construction	22.7

[a]Only firms that meet certain size criteria were considered.

SUMMARY

Valuation is an important process in financial management. An understanding of valuation, both the concepts and procedures, supports the financial officer's objective of maximizing the value of the firm.

OBJECTIVE 1

Identify the basic characteristics and features of preferred stock

Preferred stock has no fixed maturity date and the dividends are fixed in amount. Some of the more frequent characteristics of preferred stock include the following:

- There are multiple classes of preferred stock.
- Preferred stock has a priority of claim on assets and income over common stock.
- Any dividends, if not paid as promised, must be paid before any common stock dividends may be paid; that is, they are cumulative.
- Protective provisions are included in the contract with the shareholder to reduce the investor's risk.
- Many preferred stocks are convertible into common stock shares.

In addition there are provisions frequently used to retire an issue of preferred stock, such as the ability of the firm to call its preferred stock or to use a sinking-fund provision.

OBJECTIVE 2

Value preferred stock

Value is the present value of future cash flows discounted at the investor's required rate of return. Although the valuation of any security entails the same basic principles, the procedures used in each situation vary. For example, we learned in Chapter 6 that valuing a bond involves calculating the present value of future interest to be received plus the present value of the principal returned to the investor at the maturity of the bond.

For securities with cash flows that are constant in each year but where there is no specified maturity, such as preferred stock, the present value equals the dollar amount of the annual dividend divided by the investor's required rate of return; that is,

$$\frac{\text{preferred}}{\text{stock value}} = \frac{\text{dividend in year 1}}{\text{required rate of return}}$$

OBJECTIVE 3

Identify the basic characteristics and features of common stock

Common stock involves ownership in the corporation. In effect, bondholders and preferred stockholders can be viewed as creditors, while the common stockholders are the owners of the firm. Common stock does not have a maturity date, but exists as long as the firm does. Nor does common stock have an upper limit on its dividend payments. Dividend payments must be declared by the firm's board of directors before they are issued. In the event of bankruptcy, the common stockholders, as owners of the corporation, cannot exercise claims on assets until the firm's creditors, including the bondholders and preferred shareholders, have been satisfied. However, common stockholders' liability is limited to the amount of their investment.

The common stockholders are entitled to elect the board of directors and are in general the only security holders given a vote. Common shareholders have the right to elect the board of directors and to approve any change in the corporate charter. While each share of stock carries the same number of votes, the voting procedure is not always the same from company to company.

The preemptive right entitles the common shareholder to maintain a proportionate share of ownership in the firm.

Value common stock

For common stock where the future dividends are expected to increase at a constant growth rate, value may be given by the following equation:

$$\frac{\text{common}}{\text{stock value}} = \frac{\text{dividend in year 1}}{\text{required rate of return} - \text{growth rate}}$$

Growth here relates to *internal* growth only, where management retains part of the firm's profits to be reinvested and thereby grow the firm—as opposed to growth through issuing of new stock or acquiring another firm.

Growth in and of itself does not mean that we are creating value for the stock-holders. Only if we are reinvesting at a rate of return greater than the investors' required rate of return will growth result in increased value to the firm. In fact, if we are investing at rates less than the required rate of return for investors, the value of the firm will actually decline.

Calculate a stock's expected rate of return

The expected rate of return on a security is the required rate of return of investors who are willing to pay the present market price for the security, but no more. This rate of return is important to the financial manager because it equals the required rate of return of the firm's investors.

The expected rate of return for preferred stock is computed as follows:

$$\frac{\text{expected return,}}{\text{preferred stock}} = \frac{\text{annual dividend}}{\text{market price}}$$

The expected rate of return for common stock is calculated as follows:

$$\frac{\text{expected return,}}{\text{common stock}} = \frac{\text{dividend in year 1}}{\text{market price}} + \frac{\text{dividend}}{\text{growth rate}}$$

KEY TERMS

Call Provision, 200	Multiple-holding Period, 208
Common Stock, 203	Preemptive Right, 205
Convertible Preferred Stock, 200	Preferred Stock, 197
Cumulative Feature, 199	Protective Provisions, 199
Cumulative Voting, 205	Proxy, 205
Expected Rate of Return, 211	Proxy Fight, 205
Internal Growth, 206	Rights, 205
Limited Liability, 205	Sinking-fund Provision, 200
Majority Voting, 205	Valuation Model, 208

STUDY QUESTIONS

7-1. Why is preferred stock referred to as a hybrid security? It is often said to combine the worst features of common stock and bonds. What is meant by this statement?

7-2. Inasmuch as preferred stock dividends in arrears must be paid before common stock dividends, should they be considered a liability and appear on the right-hand side of the balance sheet?

7-3. Why would a preferred stockholder want the stock to have a cumulative dividend feature and protective provisions?

7-4. Why is preferred stock frequently convertible? Why would it be callable?

7-5. Compare valuing preferred stock and common stock.

7-6. Define the investor's expected rate of return.

7-7. State how the investor's required rate of return is computed.

7-8. The common stockholders receive two types of return from their investment. What are they?

SELF-TEST PROBLEMS

ST-1. (*Preferred Stock Valuation*) What is the value of a preferred stock where the dividend rate is 16 percent on a $100 par value? The appropriate discount rate for a stock of this risk level is 12 percent.

ST-2. (*Preferred Stockholder Expected Return*) You own 250 shares of Dalton Resources preferred stock, which currently sells for $38.50 per share and pays annual dividends of $3.25 per share.

a. What is your expected return?

b. If you require an 8 percent return, given the current price, should you sell or buy more stock?

ST-3. (*Preferred Stock Valuation*) The preferred stock of Armlo pays a $2.75 dividend. What is the value of the stock if your required return is 9 percent?

ST-4. (*Common Stock Valuation*) Crosby Corporation common stock paid $1.32 in dividends last year and is expected to grow indefinitely at an annual 7 percent rate. What is the value of the stock if you require an 11 percent return?

ST-5. (*Common Stockholder Expected Return*) Blackburn & Smith common stock currently sells for $23 per share. The company's executives anticipate a constant growth rate of 10.5 percent and an end-of-year dividend of $2.50.

a. What is your expected rate of return?

b. If you require a 17 percent return, should you purchase the stock?

STUDY PROBLEMS

7-1. (*Preferred Stock Valuation*) What is the value of a preferred stock where the dividend rate is 14 percent on a $100 par value? The appropriate discount rate for a stock of this risk level is 12 percent. *116.07*

7-2. (*Preferred Stockholder Expected Return*) Solitron preferred stock is selling for $42.16 and pays $1.95 in dividends. What is your expected rate of return if you purchase the security at the market price? *4.10%*

7-3. (*Preferred Stockholder Expected Return*) You own 200 shares of Somner Resources preferred stock, which currently sells for $40 per share and pays annual dividends of $3.40 per share.

a. What is your expected return? ~~10.1%~~

b. If you require an 8 percent return, given the current price, should you sell or buy more stock? ~~$28.57~~ Buy

7-4. (*Common Stock Valuation*) You intend to purchase Marigo common stock at $50 per share, hold it one year, and sell after a dividend of $6 is paid. How much will the stock price have to appreciate for you to satisfy your required rate of return of 15 percent?

7-5. (*Common Stockholder Expected Return*) Made-It common stock currently sells for $22.50 per share. The company's executives anticipate a constant growth rate of 10 percent and an end-of-year dividend of $2.

a. What is your expected rate of return if you buy the stock for $22.50?

b. If you require a 17 percent return, should you purchase the stock?

7-6. (*Common Stock Valuation*)   Header Motor, Inc., paid a $3.50 dividend last year. At a constant growth rate of 5 percent, what is the value of the common stock if the investors require a 20 percent rate of return? $24.50

7-7. (*Measuring Growth*)   Given that a firm's return on equity is 18 percent and management plans to retain 40 percent of earnings for investment purposes, what will be the firm's growth rate?

7-8. (*Common Stockholder Expected Return*)   The common stock of Zaldi Co. is selling for $32.84. The stock recently paid dividends of $2.94 per share and has a projected constant growth rate of 9.5 percent. If you purchase the stock at the market price, what is your expected rate of return?   19.3% = exp R or R

7-9. (*Common Stock Valuation*)   Honeywag common stock is expected to pay $1.85 in dividends next year, and the market price is projected to be $42.50 by year end. If the investor's required rate of return is 11 percent, what is the current value of the stock?

7-10. (*Common Stockholder Expected Return*)   The market price for Hobart common stock is $43. The price at the end of one year is expected to be $48, and dividends for next year should be $2.84. What is the expected rate of return?

7-11. (*Preferred Stock Valuation*)   Pioneer preferred stock is selling for $33 in the market and pays a $3.60 annual dividend.

a. What is the expected rate of return on the stock?

b. If an investor's required rate of return is 10 percent, what is the value of the stock for that investor?

c. Should the investor acquire the stock?

7-12. (*Common Stock Valuation*)   The common stock of NCP paid $1.32 in dividends last year. Dividends are expected to grow at an 8 percent annual rate for an indefinite number of years.

a. If NCP's current market price is $23.50, what is the stock's expected rate of return?

b. If your required rate of return is 10.5 percent, what is the value of the stock for you?

c. Should you make the investment?

7-13. (*Preferred Stock Valuation*)   Calculate the value of a preferred stock that pays a dividend of $6 per share and your required rate of return is 12 percent.

7-14. (*Measuring Growth*)   Pepperdine, Inc.'s return on equity is 16 percent and the management plans to retain 60 percent of earnings for investment purposes. What will be the firm's growth rate?

COMPREHENSIVE PROBLEM

You are considering three investments. The first is a bond that is selling in the market at $1,100. The bond has a $1,000 par value, pays interest at 13 percent, and is scheduled to mature in 15 years. For bonds of this risk class you believe that a 14 percent rate of return should be required. The second investment that you are analyzing is a preferred stock ($100 par value) that sells for $90 and pays an annual dividend of $13. Your required rate of return for this stock is 15 percent. The last investment is a common stock ($25 par value) that recently paid a $2 dividend. The firm's earnings per share has increased from $3 to $6 in 10 years, which also reflects the expected growth in dividends per share for the indefinite future. The stock is selling for $20, and you think a reasonable required rate of return for the stock is 20 percent.

a. Calculate the value of each security based on your required rate of return.

b. Which investment(s) should you accept? Why?

c. 1. If your required rates of return changed to 12 percent for the bond, 14 percent for the preferred stock, and 18 percent for the common stock, how would your answers change to parts a and b?

2. Assuming again that your required rate of return for the common stock is 20 percent, but the anticipated constant growth rate changes to 12 percent, how would your answers to parts a and b change?

SELF–TEST SOLUTIONS

SS–1

$$\text{value } (V_{ps}) = \frac{.16 \times \$100}{.12}$$
$$= \frac{\$16}{12}$$
$$= \$133.33$$

SS–2

a. Expected return $= \dfrac{\text{dividend}}{\text{market price}} = \dfrac{\$3.25}{\$38.50} = 0.0844 = 8.44\%$

b. Given your 8 percent required rate of return, the stock is worth $40.62 to you:

$$\text{value} = \frac{\text{dividend}}{\text{required rate of return}} = \frac{\$3.25}{0.08} = \$40.62$$

Because the expected rate of return (8.44%) is greater than your required rate of return (8%) or because the current market price ($38.50) is less than $40.62, the stock is undervalued and you should buy.

SS–3

$$\text{value } (V_{ps}) = \frac{\text{dividend}}{\text{required rate of return}} = \frac{\$2.75}{0.09} = \$30.56$$

SS–4

$$\text{value } (V_{cs}) = \left(\frac{\text{last year dividend } (1 + \text{growth rate})}{\text{required rate of return} - \text{growth rate}} \right)$$
$$= \frac{\$1.32(1.07)}{0.11 - 0.07}$$
$$= \$35.31$$

SS–5

a.
$$\begin{aligned} \text{expected rate} \\ \text{of return} \end{aligned} (\bar{k}_{cs}) = \frac{\text{dividend in year 1}}{\text{market price}} + \begin{aligned} \text{growth} \\ \text{rate} \end{aligned}$$
$$\bar{k}_{cs} = \frac{\$2.50}{\$23.00} + 0.105 = .2137$$
$$\bar{k}_{cs} = 21.37\%$$

b.
$$V_{cs} = \frac{\$2.50}{.17 - .105} = \$38.46$$

The expected rate of return exceeds your required rate of return, which means that the value of the security to you is greater than the current market price. Thus, you should buy the stock.

The Meaning and Measurement of Risk and Return

Expected Return Defined and Measured • Risk Defined and Measured • Rates of Return: The Investor's Experience • Risk and Diversification • The Investor's Required Rate of Return • The Fama and French Attack on the CAPM

LEARNING OBJECTIVES

After reading this chapter you should be able to

1. Define and measure the expected rate of return of an individual investment.

2. Define and measure the riskiness of an individual investment.

3. Compare the historical relationship between risk and rates of return in the capital markets.

4. Explain how diversifying investments affects the riskiness and expected rate of return of a portfolio or combination of assets.

5. Explain the relationship between an investor's required rate of return on an investment and the riskiness of the investment.

6. Explain recent criticisms of the capital asset pricing model.

One of the most important concepts in all of finance deals with risk and return, and our first axiom addresses this topic. An understanding of what we mean by *risk* and *return* can begin by telling about Luciano Siracusano.[1]

There are those who buy stocks and put them in a drawer, content to let time do its work. Then there's Luciano Siracusano. Mr. Siracusano is a restless investor, never happier than when he is putting his money into an upstart company with an ingenious product or buying a tiny piece of an established concern that has just plucked a maverick to be its chief executive. "There's nothing that gives you a bigger high," said Mr. Siracusano.

Mr. Siracusano has had some big successes. He "got a triple," as he put it, out of two stocks in recent years, Chrysler and Hanover Direct, a catalogue retailer. He meant that their value had tripled between the time of his purchase and sale.

One of his more painful memories, however, was his involvement with 3DO, a manufacturer of interactive video games. The company went public in the spring of 1993, and Mr. Siracusano gobbled up a few hundred shares at $20. There was no pain at first: the stock shot past $48. Mr. Siracusano thought it might go even higher. But it didn't. In fact, it fell to less than $9.

The episode shows the biggest downside to passionate investing: the higher risk of large losses. "If you're heavily leveraged, it's possible to get wiped out," Mr. Siracusano observes.

Because the stock market generally rises over the long run, "buy and hold" investors usually court less risk than investors who buy and sell quickly. Many passionate investors also focus on untried companies, where risks are higher. And, as Mr. Siracusano suggested, many active investors use techniques like leveraging, which can amplify profits but also enlarge losses.

"There's nothing wrong with stocks," said Mary Frances Nakagama, vice president for the Merrill Lynch Private Client Group in Red Bank, N.J. "It's sort of like fire. Fire can cook your meals and warm your house but it can also burn your house down. So just be careful how you use it."

---

[1]This introductory story is taken from Lisa W. Foderado, "The Ups and Downs of the Avid Investor," *The New York Times*, October 22, 1995, 4.

The need to recognize risk in financial decisions has already been apparent in earlier chapters. In Chapter 2, we referred to the discount rate or the interest rate as the opportunity cost of funds, but we did not look at the causes for why that rate might be high or low. For example, we did not explain why in June 1996 you could buy bonds issued by AT&T that promised to pay a 7.4 percent rate of return, or why you could buy TWA bonds that would give you an 11.6 percent rate of return, provided that both firms make the payments to the investors as promised. Then in Chapters 6 and 7, when valuing bonds, preferred stock, and common stock, we suggested there is a relationship between an investor's required rate of return and the riskiness of the investment, but we gave little if any explanation.

In this chapter, we will learn that risk is an integral force underlying rates of return. To begin our study, we will define expected return and risk and offer suggestions as to how these important concepts of return and risk can be measured quantitatively. We also compare the historical relationship between risk and rates of return. We will then explain how diversifying investments can affect the expected return and riskiness of those investments. We also consider how the riskiness of an investment should affect the required rate of return on an investment. Finally, we look at some recent criticisms of our approach to measuring risk.

Let's begin our study by looking at what we mean by the expected rate of return and how it can be measured.

BACK TO THE FOUNDATIONS

This chapter has one primary objective, that of helping us understand **Axiom 1: The Risk-Return Trade-off—We Won't Take on Additional Risk Unless We Expect to Be Compensated with Additional Return.**

OBJECTIVE 1

EXPECTED RETURN DEFINED AND MEASURED

The expected benefits or returns an investment generates come in the form of cash flows. Cash flows, not accounting profits, is the relevant variable the financial manager uses to measure returns. This principle holds true regardless of the type of security, whether it is a debt instrument, preferred stock, common stock, or any mixture of these (such as convertible bonds).

Accurately measuring expected future cash flows is not easy in a world of uncertainty. To illustrate: Assume you are considering an investment costing $10,000, where the future cash flows from owning the security depend on the state of the economy, as estimated in Table 8–1.

In any given year, the investment could produce any one of three possible cash flows depending on the particular state of the economy. With this information, how should we select the cash flow estimate that means the most for measuring the investment's expected rate of return? One approach is to calculate an *expected* cash flow. The expected cash flow is simply the weighted average of the *possible* cash flow outcomes such that the weights are the probabilities of the occurrence of the various states of the economy. Let X_i designate the ith possible cash flow, n reflect the number of possible states of the economy, and $P(X_i)$ indicate the probability that the ith cash flow or state of economy will occur. The expected cash flow, $\overline{X}$, may then be calculated as follows:

$$\overline{X} = P(X_1)X_1 + P(X_2)X_2 + \ldots + P(X_n)X_n \qquad \textbf{(8–1)}$$

or

$$\overline{X} = \sum_{i=1}^{n} P(X_i)X_i$$

For the present illustration:

$$\overline{X} = (.2)(\$1{,}000) + (.3)(\$1{,}200) + (.5)(\$1{,}400) = \$1{,}260$$

In addition to computing an expected dollar return from an investment, we can also calculate an **expected rate of return** earned on the $10,000 investment. Similar to the expected cash flow, the expected rate of return is *a weighted average of all the possible returns, weighted by the probability that each return will occur.* As the last column in Table 8–1 shows, the $1,400 cash inflow, assuming strong economic growth, represents a 14 percent return ($1,400 ÷ $10,000). Similarly, the $1,200 and $1,000 cash flows result in 12 percent and 10 percent returns, respectively. Using these percentage returns in place of the dollar amounts, the expected rate of return $\overline{k}$, can be expressed as follows:

expected rate of return

$$\overline{k} = P(k_1)k_1 + P(k_2)k_2 + \ldots + P(k_n)k_n \qquad \textbf{(8–2)}$$

or

$$\overline{k} = \sum_{i=1}^{n} {}_i P(k_i)k_i$$

Table 8–1
Measuring the Expected Return

STATE OF THE ECONOMY	PROBABILITY OF THE STATES[a]	CASH FLOWS FROM THE INVESTMENT	PERCENTAGE RETURNS (CASH FLOW ÷ INVESTMENT COST)
Economic recession	20%	$1,000	10% ($1,000 ÷ $10,000)
Moderate economic growth	30%	1,200	12% ($1,200 ÷ $10,000)
Strong economic growth	50%	1,400	14% ($1,400 ÷ $10,000)

[a]The probabilities assigned to the three possible economic conditions have to be determined subjectively, which requires management to have a thorough understanding of both the investment cash flows and the general economy.

In our example:

$$\overline{k} = (.2)(10\%) + (.3)(12\%) + (.5)(14\%) = 12.6\%$$

With our concept and measurement of experienced returns, let's consider the other side of the investment coin: risk.

RISK DEFINED AND MEASURED

Because we live in a world where events are uncertain, the way we see risk is vitally important in almost all dimensions of our life. The Greek poet and statesman Solon, writing in the sixth century B.C., put it this way:

> There is risk in everything that one does, and no one knows where he will make his landfall when his enterprise is at its beginning. One man, trying to act effectively, fails to foresee something and falls into great and grim ruination, but to another man, one who is acting ineffectively, a god gives good fortune in everything and escape from his folly.[2]

Although Solon would have given more of the credit to Zeus than we would for the outcomes of our ventures, his insight reminds us that little is new in this world, including the need to acknowledge and compensate as best we can for the risks we encounter.

In our study of risk, we want to consider three questions:

1. What is risk?
2. How do we know the amount of risk associated with a given investment; that is, how do we measure risk?
3. If we choose to diversify our investments by owning more than one asset, as most of us do, will such diversification reduce the riskiness of our combined portfolio of investments?

What Is Risk?

Without intending to be trite, risk means different things to different people, depending on the context and on how they feel about taking chances. For the student, risk is the possibility of failing an exam, or the chance of not making his or her best grades. For the coal miner or the oil field worker, risk is the chance of an explosion in the mine or at the well site. For the retired person, risk means perhaps not being able to live comfortably on a fixed income. For the entrepreneur, risk is the chance that a new venture will fail.

risk While certainly acknowledging these different kinds of risk, we will limit our attention to the risk inherent in an investment. In this context, **risk** is the *potential variability in future cash flows*. The wider the range of possible events that can occur, the greater the risk. If we think about it, this is a relatively intuitive concept.

To help us grasp the fundamental meaning of risk within this context, consider two possible investments:

1. The first investment is a U.S. Treasury bill, a government security that matures in 90 days and promises to pay an annual return of 6 percent. If we purchase

---

[2]Translated by Arthur W. H. Adkins from the Greek text of Solon's poem "Prosperity, Justice, and the Hazards of Life," in M. L. West, ed., *Iambi et Elegi Gracci ante Alexandrum Canttati*, vol. 2 (Oxford: Clarendon Press, 1972).

and hold this security for 90 days, we are virtually assured of receiving no more and no less than 6 percent. For all practical purposes, the risk of loss is nonexistent.

2. The second investment involves the purchase of the stock of a local publishing company. Looking at the past returns of the firm's stock, we have made the following estimate of the annual returns from the investment:

CHANCE OF OCCURRENCE	RATE OF RETURN ON INVESTMENT
1 chance in 10 (10%)	0%
2 chances in 10 (20%)	5%
4 chances in 10 (40%)	15%
2 chances in 10 (20%)	25%
1 chance in 10 (10%)	30%

Investing in the publishing company could conceivably provide a return as high as 30 percent if all goes well, or no return (0 percent) if everything goes against the firm. However, in future years, both good and bad, we could expect a 15 percent return on average.[3]

$$\overline{k} = (.10)(0\%) + (.20)(5\%) + (.40)(15\%) + (.20)(25\%) + (.10)(30\%)$$
$$= 15\%$$

Comparing the Treasury bill investment with the publishing company investment, we see that the Treasury bills offer an expected 6 percent rate of return, whereas the publishing company has an expected rate of return of 15 percent. However, our investment in the publishing firm is clearly more "risky"—that is, there is greater uncertainty about the final outcome. Stated somewhat differently, there is a greater variation or dispersion of possible returns, which in turn implies greater risk.[4] Figure 8–1 on page 226 shows these differences graphically in the form of discrete probability distributions.

Although the return from investing in the publishing firm is clearly less certain than for Treasury bills, quantitative measures of risk are useful when the difference between two investments is not so evident. The standard deviation (σ) is such a measure. The **standard deviation** is simply the square root of the *weighted average squared deviation of each possible return from the expected return;* that is:

standard deviation

$$\sigma = \sqrt{\sum_{i=1}^{n} (k_i - \overline{k})^2 P(k_i)} \qquad \textbf{(8–3)}$$

where n = the number of possible outcomes or different rates of return on the investment

k_i = the value of the ith possible rate of return

$\overline{k}$ = the expected value of the rates of return

$P(k_i)$ = the chance or probability that the ith outcome or return will occur

---

[3]We assume that the particular outcome or return earned in one year does *not* affect the return earned in the subsequent year. Technically speaking, the distribution of returns in any year is assumed to be independent of the outcome in any prior year.

[4]How can we possibly view variations above the expected return as risk? Should we even be concerned with the positive deviations above the expected return? Some would agree and view risk as the only negative variability in returns from a predetermined minimum acceptable rate of return. However, as long as the distribution of returns is symmetrical, the same conclusions will be reached.

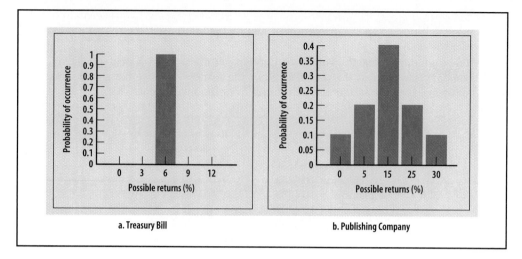

Figure 8–1
Probability Distribution of Returns

For the publishing company, the standard deviation would be 9.22 percent, determined as follows:

$$\sigma = \left[\begin{array}{l} (\ 0\% - 15\%)^2(.10) + (\ 5\% - 15\%)^2(.20) \\ + (15\% - 15\%)^2(.40) + (25\% - 15\%)^2(.20) \\ + (30\% - 15\%)^2(.10) \end{array} \right]$$

$$= \sqrt{85\%} = 9.22\%$$

Although the standard deviation of returns provides us with a quantitative measure of an asset's riskiness, how should we interpret the result? What does it mean? Is the 9.22 percent standard deviation for the publishing company investment good or bad? First, we should remember that statisticians tell us that two-thirds of the time an event will fall within one standard deviation of the expected value (assuming the distribution is normally distributed; that is, it is shaped like a bell). Thus, given a 15 percent expected return and a standard deviation of 9.22 percent for the publishing company investment, we may reasonably anticipate that the actual returns will fall between 5.78 percent and 24.22 percent (15% ± 9.22%) two-thirds of the time—not much certainty with this investment.

A second way of answering the question about the meaning of the standard deviation comes by comparing the investment in the publishing firm against other investments. The attractiveness of a security with respect to its return and risk cannot be determined in isolation. Only by examining other available alternatives can we reach a conclusion about a particular investment's risk. For example, if another investment, say an investment in a firm that owns a local radio station, has the same expected return as the publishing company, 15 percent, but with a standard deviation of 7 percent, we would consider the risk associated with the publishing firm, 9.22 percent, to be excessive. In the technical jargon of modern portfolio theory, the radio company investment is said to "dominate" the publishing firm investment. In commonsense terms, this means that the radio company investment has the same expected return as the publishing company investment but is less risky.

What if we compare the investment in the publishing company with one in a quick oil-change franchise, an investment in which the expected rate of return is an attractive 24 percent but where the standard deviation is estimated at 13 percent?

Now what should we do? Clearly, the oil-change franchise has a higher expected rate of return, but it also has a larger standard deviation. In this example, we see that the real challenge in selecting the better investment comes when one investment has a higher expected rate of return but also exhibits greater risk. *Here the final choice is determined by our attitude toward risk, and there is no single right answer.* You might select the publishing company, while I might choose the oil-change investment, and neither of us would be wrong. We would simply be expressing our tastes and preferences about risk and return.

PAUSE AND REFLECT

The first Chinese symbol shown below represents danger, the second stands for opportunity. The Chinese define risk as the combination of danger and

opportunity. Greater risk, according to the Chinese, means we have greater opportunity to do well, but also greater danger of doing badly.

RATES OF RETURN: THE INVESTOR'S EXPERIENCE

OBJECTIVE 3

In speaking of expected rates of return and risk, we have mostly used hypothetical examples; however, it is also interesting to look at returns that investors have actually received. Such information is readily available. For example, Ibbotson and Sinquefield have provided annual rates of return as far back as 1926.[5] In their results, they summarize, among other things, the annual returns for six portfolios of securities made up of

1. Common stocks of large companies
2. Common stocks of small firms
3. Long-term corporate bonds
4. Long-term U.S. government bonds
5. Intermediate-term U.S. government bonds
6. U.S. Treasury bills

Before comparing these returns, we should think about what to expect. First, we would intuitively expect a Treasury bill to be the least risky of the six portfolios. Because a Treasury bill has a short-term maturity date, the price is less volatile (less

---

[5]Roger G. Ibbotson and Rex A. Sinquefield, *Stocks, Bonds, Bills, and Inflation: 1996 Yearbook* (1926–1995) (Chicago: Dow Jones–Irwin, 1996).

"Figuring Risk: It's Not So Scary"

When we make investments, most of us are risk averse; that is, we dislike risk. We may enjoy taking "small" risks, but if we are investing a significant amount of money, we prefer less risk over more risk. As noted by Pam Black in *Business Week:*

> When it comes to investing, you would rather not hear about it. That's why so much money sits in certificates of deposit or Treasury bills linked to the reassuring phrase "backed by the full faith and credit of the U.S. government." Uncle Sam can keep your investment from credit risk, but what about inflation risk? While the "treacherous" stock market earned 15.2% over the past year, your "safe" 2.2% T-bill return has already been wiped out by 3% inflation.

Thus, even if we want, we cannot avoid risk. While we may avoid the risk of a negative return on an investment, we may lose economic purchasing power because of inflation—another risk the investor must consider. Thus, for the investor, there are numerous dangers (risks) when it comes to investing profitably over the long term.

So what do you need to know? Black continues with the following advice for investors:

> Although such terms as alpha, beta, and standard deviation may be intimidating, they are based on common-sense principles that can help guide your investment choices. "Return is in the hands of the saints," says investment consultant Peter Bernstein. "You only can control how exposed you are."
>
> When it comes to stocks, risk tolerance is a personal choice, but actual risk can be measured. Common investment resources such as the Value Line Composite Index for stocks and Morningstar Inc. for mutual funds evaluate risk using complex statistical formulas such as alpha and beta. There's no need for the average investor to understand the math, but you can benefit from knowing what these numbers mean.
>
> Beta, which measures the volatility of stocks against the S&P 500, is the most widely used assessment of risk. . . . A more universal gauge of volatility is standard deviation. It reveals how much the returns of an asset vacillate around a monthly average return—the higher the number, the more volatile.

How about that, real investors do in fact use all this "stuff" we are talking about in this chapter. It is not just theory for theory's sake.

Source: Pam Black, "Figuring Risk: It's Not So Scary," *Business Week*, November 1, 1993, 154–55.

risky) than the price of an intermediate- or long-term government security. In turn, because there is a chance of default on a corporate bond, which is essentially nonexistent for government securities, a long-term government bond is less risky than a long-term corporate bond. Finally, common stock of large companies is more risky than a corporate bond, with small-company stocks being more risky than the portfolio of large-firm stocks.

With this in mind, we could reasonably expect different rates of return to the holders of these varied securities. If the market rewards an investor for assuming risk, the average annual rates of return should increase as risk increases.

A comparison of the annual rates of return for the six respective portfolios for the years 1926–1995 is provided in Figure 8–2. Four aspects of these returns are included: (1) the nominal average annual rate of return; (2) the standard deviation of the returns, which measures the volatility or riskiness of the portfolio returns; (3) the real average annual rate of return, which is the nominal return less the inflation rate; and (4) the risk premium, which represents the additional return received beyond the risk-free rate (Treasury bill rate) for assuming risk. Also, a frequency distribution of returns is provided. Looking first at the two columns of average annual

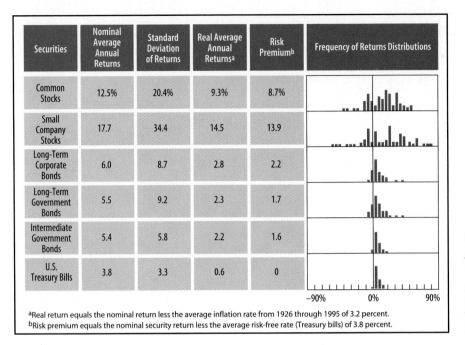

Securities	Nominal Average Annual Returns	Standard Deviation of Returns	Real Average Annual Returns[a]	Risk Premium[b]	Frequency of Returns Distributions
Common Stocks	12.5%	20.4%	9.3%	8.7%	
Small Company Stocks	17.7	34.4	14.5	13.9	
Long-Term Corporate Bonds	6.0	8.7	2.8	2.2	
Long-Term Government Bonds	5.5	9.2	2.3	1.7	
Intermediate Government Bonds	5.4	5.8	2.2	1.6	
U.S. Treasury Bills	3.8	3.3	0.6	0	

[a]Real return equals the nominal return less the average inflation rate from 1926 through 1995 of 3.2 percent.
[b]Risk premium equals the nominal security return less the average risk-free rate (Treasury bills) of 3.8 percent.

Figure 8–2
Annual Rates of Return, 1926–1995

Source: Roger G. Ibbotson and Rex A. Sinquefield, *Stocks, Bonds, Bills and Inflation: 1996 Yearbook* (Chicago: Dow Jones–Irwin, 1996), 32.

returns and standard deviations, we gain a good overview of the risk-return relationships that have existed over the 70 years ending in 1995. For the most part, there has been a positive relationship between risk and return, with Treasury bills being least risky and common stocks being most risky. However, long-term government bonds have been as risky as corporate bonds. This aberration has largely been the result of the five years from 1977 through 1981, a period when interest rates rose to all-time highs, which had a significantly negative impact on bond prices.

The return information in Figure 8–2 clearly demonstrates that only common stock has in the long run served as an inflation hedge and provided any substantial risk premium. However, it is equally apparent that the common stockholder is exposed to sizable risk, as demonstrated by a 20.4 percent standard deviation for large-company stocks and a 34.4 percent standard deviation for small-company stocks. In fact, in the 1926–1995 time frame, common shareholders of large firms received negative returns in 20 of the 70 years, compared with only 1 (1938) in 70 for Treasury bills.

RISK AND DIVERSIFICATION

OBJECTIVE 4

From the preceding discussions, we can define risk as the variability of anticipated returns as measured by the standard deviation. However, more can be said about risk, especially as to its nature, when we own more than one asset in our investment portfolio. Let's consider for the moment how risk is affected if we diversify our investment by holding a variety of securities.

To begin, assume that the date is July 10, 1996. When you awake this morning, you follow your daily routine, which includes reading the *Wall Street Journal*. You always begin by scanning "What's News—Business and Finance," with an eye for anything related to the stocks you own—and there they are. Two of your stocks made the front page, the first being Motorola. The firm announced that profits had

Negotiating a Deal—The Old-Fashioned Way

Warren Buffett is world renowned as an investor. The stock of his firm, Berkshire Hathaway, traded at a price of about $32,000 per share in 1996. His philosophy is to invest in only a small number of companies and then be actively involved with the management. The following is an excerpt from the 1993 Berkshire Hathaway annual report, and gives us a great (and unique) example of a business transaction based not on the technicalities of a long and involved contract, but on trust. Buffett writes:

Mrs. B—Rose Blumkin—had her 100th birthday on December 3, 1993. (The candles cost more than the cake.) That was a day on which the store was scheduled to be open in the evening. Mrs. B, who works seven days a week, for however many hours the store operates, found the proper decision quite obvious: She simply postponed her party until an evening when the store was closed.

Mrs. B's story is well-known but worth telling again. She came to the United States 77 years ago, unable to speak English and devoid of formal schooling. In 1937, she founded the Nebraska Furniture Mart with $500. Last year the store had sales of $200 million, a larger amount by far than that recorded by any other home furnishings store in the United States. Our part in all of this began ten years ago when Mrs. B sold control of the business to Berkshire Hathaway, a deal we completed without obtaining audited financial statements, checking real estate records, or getting any warranties. In short, her word was good enough for us.

Naturally, I was delighted to attend Mrs. B's birthday party. After all, she's promised to attend *my* 100th.

Source: *Berkshire Hathaway, Inc., 1993 Annual Report*, Omaha, Nebraska, 19–20.

declined 32 percent, owing to a cellular-phone price war and the declining demand for computer chips, both products Motorola sells. The result: Motorola's stock fell 15 percent on the announcement. That hurts! The only consolation is the article on Nike, another one of your investments. For Nike, profits were up 38 percent as the result of an unexpected surge in sales. In response, the company's stock increased 4.3 percent—not as much as your loss in Motorola, but it helps. You also notice that these events occurred on a day that the overall market on the New York Stock Exchange increased only one-half of 1 percent.

Clearly, what we have described about Motorola and Nike were events unique to these two companies, and as we would expect, the investors reacted accordingly; that is, the value of the stock changed in light of the new information. While we might have wished we had owned only Nike stock at the time, most of us would prefer to avoid such uncertainties; that is, we are risk averse. Instead, we would like to reduce the risk associated with our investment portfolio, without having to accept a lower expected return. Good news: It is possible by diversifying our portfolio!

Diversifying Away the Risk

If we diversify our investments across different securities rather than invest in only one stock, the variability in the returns of our portfolio should decline. The reduction in risk will occur if the stock returns within our portfolio do not move precisely together over time—that is, if they are not perfectly correlated. Figure 8–3 shows graphically what we may expect to happen to the variability of returns as we add additional stocks to the portfolio. The reduction occurs because some of the volatility in returns of a stock are unique to that security. The unique variability of a single

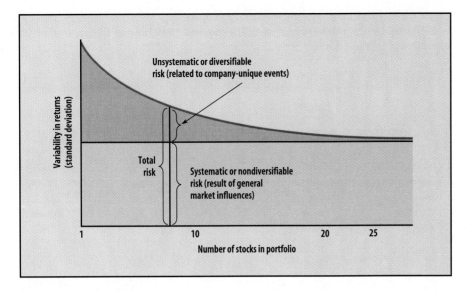

Figure 8–3
Variability of Returns Compared with Size of Portfolio

stock tends to be countered by the uniqueness of another security. However, we should not expect to eliminate all risk from our portfolio. In practice, it would be rather difficult to cancel all the variations in returns of a portfolio, because stock prices have some tendency to move together. Thus, we can divide the total risk (total variability) of our portfolio into two types of risk: (1) **company-unique risk** or **unsystematic risk** and (2) **market risk** or **systematic risk.** Company-unique risk might also be called **diversifiable risk,** in that it *can be diversified away.* Market risk is **nondiversifiable risk;** it *cannot be eliminated through random diversification.* These two types of risk are shown graphically in Figure 8–3. Total risk declines until we have approximately 20 securities, and then the decline becomes very slight.

The remaining risk, which would typically be about 40 percent of the total risk, is the portfolio's systematic or market risk. At this point, our portfolio is highly correlated with all securities in the marketplace. Events that affect our portfolio now are not so much unique events as changes in the general economy, major political events, and sociological changes. Examples include changes in interest rates in the economy, changes in tax legislation that affect all companies, or increasing public concern about the effect of business practices on the environment.

Because we can remove the company-unique or unsystematic risk, there is no reason to believe the market will reward us with additional returns for assuming risk that could be avoided by simply diversifying. Our measure of risk should therefore measure how responsive a stock or portfolio is to changes in a market portfolio, such as the New York Stock Exchange or the S&P 500 Index.[6]

Measuring Market Risk

To help clarify the idea of systematic risk, let's examine the relationship between the common stock returns of McDonald's Corporation and the returns of the S&P 500 Index. The monthly returns for the McDonald's Corporation and the S&P 500

company-unique risk
unsystematic risk

market risk
systematic risk
diversifiable risk
nondiversifiable risk

---

[6]The New York Stock Exchange Index is an index that reflects the performance of all stocks listed on the New York Stock Exchange. The Standard & Poor's (S&P) 500 Index is similarly an index that measures the combined stock-price performance of the companies that constitute the 500 largest companies in the United States, as designated by Standard & Poor's.

holding-period returns

Index for the 24 months ending February 1996 are presented in Table 8–2 and Figure 8–4. These *monthly returns*, or **holding-period returns,** as they are often called, are calculated as follows:[7]

$$k_t = \frac{P_t}{P_{t-1}} - 1 \qquad (8\text{--}4)$$

Table 8–2

Monthly Holding-Period Returns, McDonald's Corporation and the S&P 500 Index, March 1994–February 1996

Month and Year	McDonald's		S&P 500 Index	
	Prices	Returns %	Prices	Returns %
1994				
February	$30.31		$467.14	
March	28.44	−6.19	445.77	−4.57
April	30.00	5.49	450.91	1.15
May	31.00	3.33	456.50	1.24
June	28.88	−6.85	444.27	−2.68
July	27.13	−6.06	458.26	3.15
August	28.25	4.15	475.49	3.76
September	26.38	−6.64	462.69	−2.69
October	28.88	9.48	472.35	2.09
November	28.38	−1.73	453.69	−3.95
December	29.25	3.08	459.27	1.23
1995				
January	32.63	11.54	470.42	2.43
February	33.25	1.92	487.39	3.61
March	34.13	2.63	500.71	2.73
April	35.00	2.56	514.71	2.80
May	37.88	8.21	533.41	3.63
June	39.13	3.30	544.75	2.13
July	38.63	−1.28	562.06	3.18
August	36.50	−5.50	561.88	−0.03
September	38.25	4.79	584.41	4.01
October	41.00	7.19	581.50	−0.50
November	44.63	8.84	605.37	4.10
December	45.13	1.12	615.93	1.74
1996				
January	50.25	11.36	636.02	3.26
February	50.00	−0.50	640.43	0.69
Average monthly return		2.26		1.35
Standard deviation		5.70		2.55

[7]For simplicity's sake, we are ignoring the dividend that the investor receives from the stock as part of the total return. In other words, letting D_t equal the dividend received by the investor in month t, the holding-period return would more accurately be measured as

$$k_t = \frac{P_t + D_t}{P_{t-1}} - 1 \qquad (8\text{--}5)$$

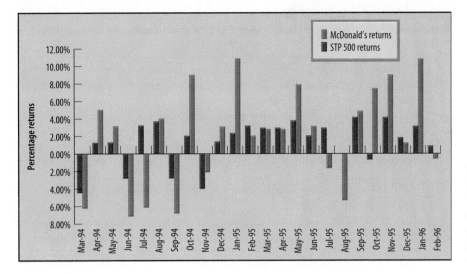

Figure 8–4
Monthly Holding-period
Returns: McDonald's
Corporation and the S&P
500 Index, March 1994–
February 1996

where k_t = the holding-period return in month t for a particular firm like
McDonald's or for a portfolio such as the S&P 500 Index

P_t = a firm's stock price like McDonald's (or the S&P 500 Index) at the
end of month t

For instance, the holding-period return for McDonald's and the S&P 500 Index
for the first month, March 1994, is computed as follows:

$$\text{McDonald's return} = \frac{\text{stock price end of March 1994}}{\text{stock price end of February 1994}} - 1$$

$$= \frac{\$28.44}{\$30.31} - 1 = -.0619 = -6.19\%$$

$$\text{S\&P 500 Index return} = \frac{\text{index value end of March 1994}}{\text{index value end of February 1994}} - 1$$

$$= \frac{\$445.77}{\$467.14} - 1 = -.0457 = -4.57\%$$

At the bottom of Table 8–2, we have also computed the averages of the returns
for the 24 months, both for McDonald's and the S&P 500 Index, and the standard
deviation for these returns. Because we are using historical return data, we assume
each observation has an equal probability of occurrence. Thus, the average return,
$\bar{k}$, is found by summing the returns and dividing by the number of months; that is,

$$\begin{matrix} \text{average} \\ \text{return} \end{matrix} = \bar{k} = \frac{\sum\limits_{t=1}^{n} \text{return in month } t}{\text{number of months}} = \frac{\sum\limits_{t=1}^{n} (k_t)}{n} \quad \textbf{(8-6)}$$

and the standard deviation σ is computed as:

$$\begin{matrix} \text{standard} \\ \text{deviation} \end{matrix} = \sqrt{\frac{\sum\limits_{t=1}^{n} (\text{return in month } t - \text{average return})^2}{\text{number of months} - 1}} \quad \textbf{(8-7)}$$

$$\sigma = \sqrt{\frac{\sum\limits_{t=1}^{n} = (k_t - \bar{k})^2}{n - 1}}$$

In looking at Table 8–2 and Figure 8–4, we notice the following things about McDonald's holding-period returns over the two years ending in February 1996, these being:

1. McDonald's stockholders have had higher average monthly returns than the average stock in the S&P 500 Index, 2.26 percent compared to 1.35 percent. That's the good news.

2. The bad news is McDonald's greater volatility of returns—in other words, greater risk—as evidenced by McDonald's higher standard deviation. As shown at the bottom of Table 8–2, the standard deviation of the returns is 5.70 percent for McDonald's versus 2.55 percent for the S&P 500 Index. McDonald's more volatile returns are also evident in Figure 8–4, where we see the McDonald's returns frequently being higher and lower than the corresponding S&P 500 returns.

3. We should also notice the tendency of McDonald's stock price to increase (decrease) when the value of the S&P 500 Index increases (decreases). In 19 of the 24 months, McDonald's returns were positive (negative) when the S&P 500 Index returns were positive (negative). That is, there is a positive, although not perfect, relationship between McDonald's stock returns and the S&P 500 Index returns.

With respect to our third observation, that there is a relationship between the stock returns for McDonald's and the S&P 500 Index, it is helpful to see this relationship by graphing McDonald's returns against the S&P 500 Index returns. We provide such a graph in Figure 8–5. In the figure, we have plotted McDonald's returns on the vertical axis and the returns for the S&P 500 Index on the horizontal axis. Each of the 24 dots in the figure represent the returns for McDonald's and the S&P 500 Index for a particular month. For instance, the returns for February 1995 for McDonald's and the S&P 500 Index were 1.92 percent and 3.61 percent, respectively, which are noted in the figure.

characteristic line   In addition to the dots in the graph, we have drawn a line of "best fit," which we call the **characteristic line.** *The slope of the characteristic line measures the average relationship between a stock's returns and those of the S&P 500 Index;* or stated differently, *the slope of the line indicates the average movement in a stock's price to a movement in the S&P 500 Index price.* For McDonald's, the slope of the line is 1.35, which simply equals the rise of the line relative to the run of the line.[8] A slope of 1.35, as for McDonald's, means that as the market return (S&P 500 Index returns) increases or decreases one percentage point, the return for McDonald's on average increases or decreases 1.35 percentage points.

beta   We can also think of the 1.35 slope of the characteristic line as indicating that McDonald's returns are 1.35 times as volatile on average as those of the overall market (S&P 500 Index). This slope has come to be called **beta** in investor jargon, and *measures the average relationship between a stock's returns and the market's returns.* It is a term you will see almost anytime you read an article written by a financial analyst about the riskiness of a stock.

Looking once again at Figure 8–5, we see that the dots (returns) are scattered all about the characteristic line—most of the returns do not fit neatly on the characteristic line. That is, the average relationship may be 1.35, but the variation in McDonald's returns is only partly explained by the stock's average relationship with the S&P 500 Index. There are other driving forces unique to McDonald's that also affect the firm's stock returns. (Earlier, we called this company-unique risk.) If we were, however, to diversify our holdings and own, say, 20 stocks with betas of 1.35,

---

[8]Linear regression is the statistical technique used to determine the slope of the line of best fit.

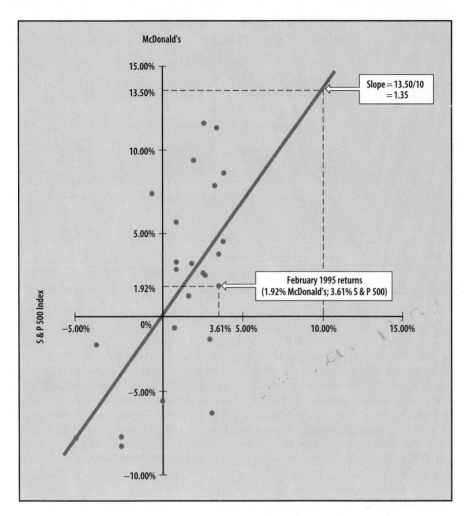

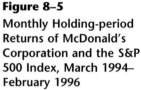

Figure 8–5
Monthly Holding-period Returns of McDonald's Corporation and the S&P 500 Index, March 1994– February 1996

we could essentially eliminate the variation about the characteristic line. That is, we would remove almost all the volatility in returns, except for what is caused by the general market, which is represented by the slope of the line in Figure 8–5. If we plotted the returns of our 20-stock portfolio against the S&P 500 Index, the points in our new graph would fit nicely along a straight line with a slope of 1.35, which means that the beta of the portfolio is also 1.35. The new graph would look something like the one shown in Figure 8–6 on page 236. In other words, by diversifying our portfolio, we can essentially eliminate the variations about the characteristic line, leaving only the variation in returns for a company that comes from variations in the general market returns.

So beta—the slope of the characteristic line—is a measure of a firm's market risk or systematic risk, which is the risk that remains for a company even after we have diversified our portfolio. It is this risk—and only this risk—that matters for any investors who have broadly diversified portfolios.

While we have said that beta is a measure of a stock's systematic risk, how should we interpret a specific beta? For instance, when is a beta considered low and when is it considered high? In general, a stock with a beta of 0 has no systematic risk; a stock with a beta of 1 has systematic or market risk equal to the "typical" stock in the marketplace; and a stock with a beta exceeding 1 has more market risk than the typical stock. Most stocks, however, have betas between 0.60 and 1.60.

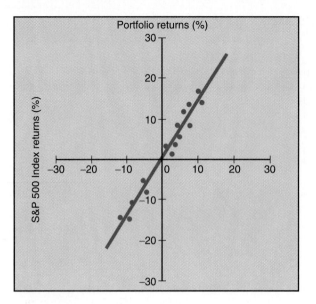

Figure 8–6
Holding-Period Returns:
Hypothetical Portfolio and
the S&P 500 Index

We should also realize that calculating beta is no exact science. The final estimate of a firm's beta is heavily dependent on one's methodology. For instance, it matters whether you use 24 months in your measurement or 60 months, as most professional investment companies do. Take our computation of McDonald's beta. We said McDonald's beta was 1.35, but Standard & Poor's and Value Line, two well-known investment services, have estimated McDonald's beta to be 1.01 and 1.05, respectively. The difference in results can be observed by comparing Standard & Poor's and Value Line's beta estimates for a number of firms as follows:

	STANDARD & POOR'S	VALUE LINE
Coca-Cola	0.88	0.95
Exxon	0.60	0.65
Ford	0.98	1.05
General Electric	1.21	1.15
IBM	0.66	0.95
Merck	1.20	1.00
Nike	1.24	1.20
PepsiCo	1.27	0.95
Wal-Mart	1.07	1.10

Thus, while close in many instances, even the professionals may not agree in their measurement of a given firm's beta.

To this point, we have talked about measuring an individual stock's beta. We will now consider how to measure the beta for a portfolio of stocks.

Measuring a Portfolio's Beta

What if we were to diversify our portfolio, as we have just suggested, but instead of acquiring stocks with the same beta as McDonald's (1.35) we buy 8 stocks with betas of 1.0 and 12 stocks with betas of 1.5. What would the beta of our portfolio become? As it works out, the **portfolio beta** is merely the average of the individual stock betas. Actually, the portfolio beta is a *weighted average of the individual security's betas, with the weights being equal to the proportion of the portfolio invested in each security*. Thus, the beta (β) of a portfolio consisting of *n* stocks is equal to:

portfolio beta

$$\beta_{\text{portfolio}} = \sum_{j=1}^{n} (\text{percentage invested in stock } j) \times (\beta \text{ of stock } j) \quad \textbf{(8–8)}$$

So, assuming we bought equal amounts of each stock in our new 20-stock portfolio, the beta would simply be 1.3, calculated as follows:

$$\text{portfolio beta} = \left(\frac{8}{20} \times 1.0\right) + \left(\frac{12}{20} \times 1.50\right)$$
$$= 1.3$$

Thus, whenever the general market increases or decreases 1 percent, our new portfolio's returns would change 1.3 percent on average, which says that our new portfolio has more systematic or market risk than the market has as a whole.

We can conclude that the beta of a portfolio is determined by the betas of the individual stocks. If we have a portfolio consisting of stocks with low betas, then our portfolio will have a low beta. The reverse is true as well. Figure 8–7 presents these situations graphically.

PAUSE AND REFLECT

We can reduce risk through diversifying our portfolio, but only to a point. What we remove is company-unique or unsystematic risk (also known as diversifiable risk). Systematic or market risk (also termed nondiversifiable risk) cannot be eliminated.

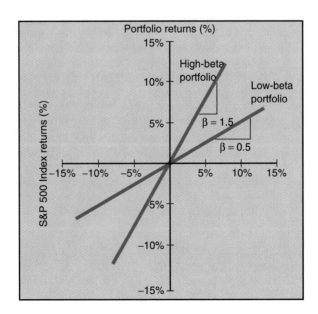

Figure 8–7

Holding-period Returns: High- and Low-Beta Portfolios and the S&P 500 Index

Before leaving the subject of risk and diversification, we want to share a study that demonstrates the effects of diversifying our investments, not just across different stocks, but across different types of securities.

Risk and Diversification Demonstrated[9]

Having described the effect of diversification on risk and returns in a general way, let's now look at some actual numbers to demonstrate how risk and return changes as you diversify your portfolio. As it was earlier in the chapter, our source of information is Ibbotson Associates, a firm that gathers extensive return data on a large group of investments.

To show the effect of diversification on risk and rates of return, Ibbotson compared three portfolios (A, B, and C), consisting of the following investments:

	INVESTMENT MIX IN PORTFOLIO (%)		
TYPES OF SECURITIES	A	B	C
Short-term government securities (Treasury bills)	0	63	34
Long-term government bonds	100	12	14
Large-company stocks	0	25	52
	100	100	100

Figure 8–8 shows the average returns and standard deviations of the three portfolios. The results show that an investor can use diversification to improve the risk-return characteristics of a portfolio. Specifically, we can see that

1. Portfolio A, which consists entirely of long-term government bonds, has an average annual return of 5.5 percent with a standard deviation of 11.3 percent.[10]
2. In portfolio B, we have diversified across all three security types, with the majority of the funds (63%) now invested in Treasury bills and a lesser amount (25%) in stocks. The effects are readily apparent. The average returns of the two portfolios are identical, but the risk associated with portfolio B is almost half that of portfolio A—a standard deviation of 6.1 percent for portfolio B compared to 11.3 percent for portfolio A. Notice that risk has been reduced in portfolio B even though stocks, a far more risky security, have been included in the portfolio. How could this be? Simple: Stocks behave differently than both government bonds and Treasury bills, with the effect being a less risky (lower standard deviation) portfolio.
3. While portfolio B demonstrates how an investor can reduce risk while keeping returns constant, portfolio C, with its increased investment in stocks (52%), shows how an investor can increase average returns while keeping risk constant. This portfolio has a risk level identical to that of long-term government bonds alone (portfolio A), but achieves a higher average return of 8 percent, compared to 5.5 percent for the government bond portfolio.

---

[9]This presentation is taken from material developed by Ibbotson Associates, Chicago. Copyright © 1994.

[10]In this example, Ibbotson Associates use 1970–1993 data to compute the standard deviation for the long-term government bonds; all other computations use the total 1926–1993 time frame.

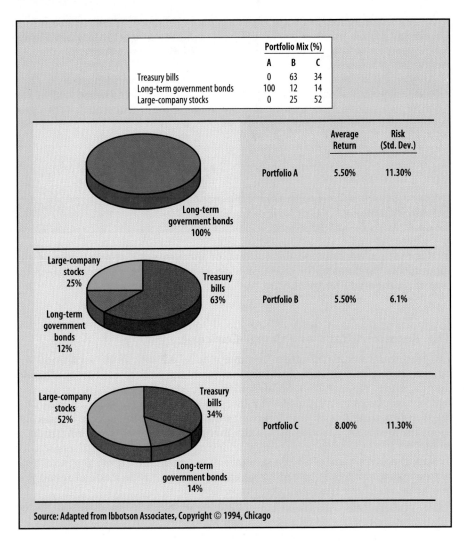

	Portfolio Mix (%)		
	A	B	C
Treasury bills	0	63	34
Long-term government bonds	100	12	14
Large-company stocks	0	25	52

	Average Return	Risk (Std. Dev.)
Portfolio A	5.50%	11.30%
Portfolio B	5.50%	6.1%
Portfolio C	8.00%	11.30%

Source: Adapted from Ibbotson Associates, Copyright © 1994, Chicago

Figure 8–8
The Effect of Diversification on Average Return and Risk
Source: Adapted from Ibbotson Associates, Chicago. Copyright © 1994.

The conclusion to be drawn from the above example is clear. The market rewards diversification. We can indeed lower risk without sacrificing expected returns, and/or we can increase expected returns without having to assume more risk by diversifying our investments.

The above example gives us real-world evidence as to the merits of diversification; however, a clarification is in order. Note that the diversification in the above example is across different asset types—Treasury bills versus long-term government bonds versus common stocks. *Diversifying among different kinds of assets* is called **asset allocation,** as compared to diversification within the different asset classes. The benefit we receive from diversifying is far greater through effective asset allocation than it is from astutely selecting individual stocks to include within an asset category. For instance, Brinson, Singer, and Beebower studied quarterly data from 82 large U.S. pension funds over the period 1977–1987.[11] They found that the asset allocation decision accounted for over 91 percent of the differences among the re-

asset allocation

---

[11]Gary P. Brinson, Ronald F. Singer, and Gilbert L. Beebower, "Determinants of Portfolio Performance," *Financial Analysts Journal*, May–June 1991.

turns of pension funds. Deciding what specific securities to hold accounted for only 4.6 percent of the variation in the different pension returns.[12] The point: Investors in the capital markets should focus more attention on asset allocation than on selecting individual securities.

In the next section, we will complete our study of risk and returns by connecting risk—market or systematic risk, that is—to the investor's *required* rate of return. After all, while risk is an important issue, it is primarily important in its effect on the investor's required rate of return.

OBJECTIVE 5

THE INVESTOR'S REQUIRED RATE OF RETURN

In this section we examine the concept of the investor's required rate of return, especially as it relates to the riskiness of an asset, and then we see how the required rate of return might be measured.

The Required Rate of Return Concept

investor's required rate of return

opportunity cost of funds

The **investor's required rate of return** can be defined as the *minimum rate of return necessary to attract an investor to purchase or hold a security*. This definition considers the investor's **opportunity cost of funds** of making an investment; that is, if an investment is made, the investor must *forgo the return available from the next-best investment*. This forgone return is an opportunity cost of undertaking the investment and consequently is the investor's required rate of return. In other words, we invest with the intention of achieving a rate of return sufficient to warrant making the investment. The investment will be made only if the purchase price is low enough relative to expected future cash flows to provide a rate of return greater than or equal to our required rate of return.

To help us better understand the nature of an investor's required rate of return, we can separate the return into its basic components: the risk-free rate of return plus a risk premium. Expressed as an equation:

$$k = k_{rf} + k_{rp} \tag{8-9}$$

where
k = the investor's required rate of return
k_{rf} = the risk-free rate of return
k_{rp} = the risk premium

risk-free rate of return

The **risk-free rate of return** rewards us for deferring consumption, and not for assuming risk; that is, the risk-free return reflects the basic fact that we invest today so that we can consume more later. By itself, the risk-free rate should be used only as the **required rate of return,** *or discount rate, for riskless investments*. Typically, our measure for the risk-free rate of return is the U.S. Treasury bill rate.

risk premium

The **risk premium,** k_{rp}, is the *additional return we must expect to receive for assuming risk*. As the level of risk increases, we will demand additional expected

---

[12]It is also interesting to know that Brinson, Singer, and Beebower found that timing investments explained a meager 1.8 percent of the variation in pension fund returns. That is, none of the investors of these pension funds were any better than their peers at timing market movements when making investments.

The Investor and Asset Allocation

As suggested in this chapter, how an investor allocates his or her assets is important in terms of the resulting returns and the variability of these returns over time. As we have also noted, stocks are more volatile in their returns than bonds or Treasury bills. The importance of this issue for investors was captured in an article appearing in the *Wall Street Journal*. Some of the author's ideas follow.

Amid the recent market turmoil, maybe you are wondering whether you really have the right mix of investments. Here are a few thoughts to keep in mind:

Taking Stock

If you are a bond investor who is petrified of stocks, the wild price swings of the past few weeks have probably confirmed all your worst suspicions. But the truth is, adding stocks to your bond portfolio could bolster your returns, without boosting your portfolio's overall gyrations.

How can that be? While stocks and bonds often move up and down in tandem, this isn't always the case, and sometimes stocks rise when bonds are tumbling. That happened in this year's [1996] first six months, when U.S. stock-mutual funds soared 10.8% while taxable bonds slipped 0.3%, according to Lipper Analytical Services.

Indeed, Chicago researchers Ibbotson Associates figures a portfolio that's 100% in longer-term government bonds has the same risk profile as a mix that includes 83% in longer-term government bonds and 17% in the blue chip stocks that constitute Standard & Poor's 500 stock index.

But while the risk level is similar, the bond-stock mix had better returns over the past 25 years, gaining 10.2% a year, compared with 9.6% for longer-term government bonds alone. The bottom line?

Everybody should own some stocks. Even cowards.

Same Great Taste, Even More Filling

All right, you will buy a few stocks. But you are sticking strictly to the blue chips. A good move? Here's another fun fact from Ibbotson Associates.

The Chicago firm calculates that a portfolio that's 100% in the S&P 500 is about as risky as a mix that includes 73% S&P500, 6% smaller company stocks and 21% foreign stocks. But the globally diverse portfolio was more rewarding over the past 25 years, climbing 12.9% a year, compared with 12.2% for the S&P 500. If you're going to own stocks, it clearly pays to diversify.

Source: Jonathan Clements, "The Right Mix: Fine-tuning a Portfolio to Make Money and Sleep Soundly," *Wall Street Journal*, July 23, 1996, C1.

returns. Even though we may or may not actually receive this incremental return, we must have reason to expect it; otherwise, why expose ourselves to the chance of losing all or part of our money?

EXAMPLE

Assume you are considering the purchase of a stock that you believe will provide a 14 percent return over the next year. If the expected risk-free rate of return, such as the rate of return for 90-day Treasury bills, is 5 percent, then the risk premium you are demanding to assume the additional risk is 9 percent (14% − 5%). ■

Measuring the Required Rate of Return

We have seen that (1) systematic risk is the only relevant risk—the rest can be diversified away, and (2) the required rate of return, k, equals the risk-free rate, k_{rf}, plus a risk premium, k_{rp}. We may now examine how we actually estimate investors' required rates of return. Looking back at equation (8–9), the really tough task is estimating the risk premium.

The finance profession has had difficulty in developing a practical approach to measure the investor's required rate of return; however, financial managers often use a method called the **capital asset pricing model (CAPM).** The capital asset pricing model is *an equation that equates the expected rate of return on a stock to the risk-free rate plus a risk premium for the stock's systematic risk.* Although certainly not without its critics, the CAPM provides an intuitive approach for thinking about the return that an investor should require on an investment, given the asset's systematic or market risk.

Equation (8–9) provides the natural starting point for measuring the investor's required rate of return and sets us up for using the CAPM. Rearranging this equation to solve for the risk premium (k_{rp}), we have

$$k_{rp} = k - k_{rf} \qquad \textbf{(8–10)}$$

which simply says that the risk premium for a security, k_{rp}, equals the required return, k, less the risk-free rate existing in the market, k_{rf}. For example, if the required return is 15 percent and the risk-free rate is 5 percent, the risk premium is 10 percent. Also, if the required return for the market portfolio, k_m, is 12 percent, and the risk-free rate, k_{rf}, is 5 percent, the risk premium, k_{rp}, for the market would be 7 percent. This 7 percent risk premium would apply to any security having systematic (nondiversifiable) risk equivalent to the general market, or a beta of 1.

In this same market, a security with a beta of 2 should provide a risk premium of 14 percent, or twice the 7 percent risk premium existing for the market as a whole. Hence, in general, the appropriate required rate of return for the jth security, k_j, should be determined by

$$k_j = k_{rf} + \beta_j(k_m - k_{rf}) \qquad \textbf{(8–11)}$$

Equation (8–11) is the CAPM. This equation designates the risk-return trade-off existing in the market, where risk is defined in terms of beta. Figure 8–9 graphs the CAPM as the **security market line.**[13] The security market line is *the graphic representation of the CAPM, where the line shows the appropriate required rate of return given a stock's systematic risk.* As presented in this figure, securities with betas equal to 0, 1, and 2 should have required rates of return as follows:

$$\text{If } \beta_j = 0: k_j = 5\% + 0(12\% - 5\%) = 5\%$$
$$\text{If } \beta_j = 1: k_j = 5\% + 1(12\% - 5\%) = 12\%$$
$$\text{If } \beta_j = 2: k_j = 5\% + 2(12\% - 5\%) = 19\%$$

___

[13]Two key assumptions are made in using the security market line. First, we assume that the marketplace where securities are bought and sold is highly efficient. Market efficiency indicates that the price of an asset responds quickly to new information, thereby suggesting that the price of a security reflects all available information. As a result, the current price of a security is considered to represent the best estimate of its future price. Second, the model assumes that a perfect market exists. A perfect market is one in which information is readily available to all investors at a nominal cost. Also, securities are assumed to be infinitely divisible, with any transaction costs incurred in purchasing or selling a security being negligible. Furthermore, investors are assumed to be single-period wealth maximizers who agree on the meaning and significance of the available information. Finally, within the perfect market, all investors are *price takers*, which simply means that a single investor's actions cannot affect the price of a security. These assumptions are obviously not descriptive of reality. However, from the perspective of positive economics, the mark of a good theory is the accuracy of its predictions, not the validity of the simplifying assumptions that underlie its development.

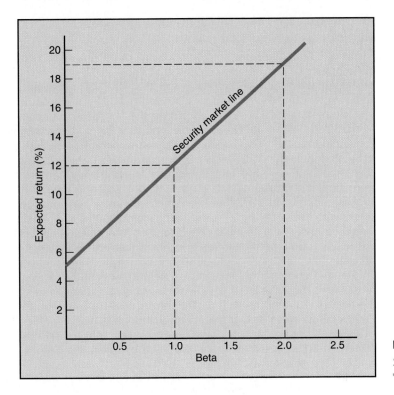

Figure 8–9
Security Market Line

where the risk-free rate, k_{rf}, is 5 percent and the required return for the market portfolio, k_m, is 12 percent.[14]

The conclusion of the matter is that **Axiom 1** is alive and well. It tells us, **We Won't Take on Additional Risk Unless We Expect to Be Compensated with Additional Return.** That is, there is a risk-return trade-off in the market.

THE FAMA AND FRENCH ATTACK ON THE CAPM

OBJECTIVE 6

The primary implication of the capital asset pricing model (CAPM) is that higher returns accrue to securities that have higher levels of nondiversifiable or systematic risk (measured by the security's beta coefficient). However, recent evidence by Fama and French indicates that over the period 1963–1990, differences in beta do not explain differences in the performance (rates of return) of stocks.[15] Further, they found that the total market value of the firm's equity and the ratio of the firm's equity *book*-value to equity *market*-value explain a large portion of the variation in stock returns, much larger than beta! From this evidence they conclude that "beta is dead."

---

[14]For a more in-depth explanation of the CAPM, see B. Rosenberg, "The Capital Asset Pricing Model and the Market Model," *Journal of Portfolio Management* (Winter 1981): 5–16.
[15]Eugene Fama and Kenneth French, "The Cross-section of Expected Stock Returns," *Journal of Finance*, 47, no. 2 (June 1992): 427–65.

The Defense of the CAPM

Two counterarguments have been offered in response to the Fama and French criticisms of CAPM and beta. First, some argue that Fama and French's research methodology was flawed; others contend that Fama and French's contentions are theoretically incomplete. The bottom line is that CAPM is not dead but our faith in its ability to explain the world of risk and return has been shaken.

Two research studies have addressed the "empirical refinement" line of defense of the CAPM. Chan and Lakonishok look at a much longer series of returns than Fama and French.[16] They evaluated the entire period 1926–1991 and found that for the period ended in 1982, higher betas were indeed associated with higher returns. However, for the period after 1982 they found again that beta and stock returns were unrelated. Furthermore, when they looked at the returns of the 10 worst and 10 best months in terms of the stock market's performance, they found that stocks with higher betas did worse in the worst months and better in the best months than their lower-beta counterparts. Thus, we have some limited evidence supporting the basic CAPM prediction that higher betas are associated with higher stock returns.

The second empirical study is by Kothari, Shankin, and Sloan.[17] These authors reexamined the issue as to whether beta explains variations in average returns over the post-1940 period as well as the longer post-1926 period. They, like Fama and French before them, tested the notion that book-to-market value of the firm's equity captures the variation in average returns over a longer period, 1947–1987, using a somewhat different data set than that used by Fama and French. Two of their conclusions are as follows:

- They found a 6 percent risk premium in the sample of stocks used, compared to Fama and French's results indicating there was no risk premium relative to increasing systematic risk.

- Using a different sample of firms in their study, they found that book-to-market value was only weakly related to average stock returns, which sharply disagrees with Fama and French. Based upon this observation they argue that the Fama-French results are limited to their sample of companies and do not necessarily apply to a broader sample of companies.

The theoretical argument against the Fama and French allegations was offered by Roll and Ross.[18] They argue that using an index, such as the S&P 500 Index or the New York Stock Exchange Index, to calculate the market returns may not accurately reflect the returns of the true market portfolio. Since the market portfolio proxy used by Fama and French may not be the correct one, there is no reason to believe that the betas and rates of return should be positively related.[19] Thus, the

---

[16]Louis Chan and Josef Lakonishok, "Are the Reports of Beta's Death Premature?" working paper, University of Illinois, Champaign-Urbana, 1992.

[17]S. P. Kothari, J. Shankin, and R. Sloan, "Another Look at the Cross-section of Expected Stock Returns," *Journal of Finance*, 50, no. 1 (March 1995).

[18]Richard Roll and Stephen A. Ross, "On the Cross-sectional Relation between Expected Returns and Betas," working paper, University of California, Los Angeles, 1992.

[19]Technically, Roll and Ross noted that where the market portfolio is mean-variance efficient, beta and expected returns are exactly linear and positively related. Where the market portfolio is even slightly inefficient, this positive relation no longer holds.

Fama and French results may either be the result of using an incorrect market portfolio proxy or due to a failure of the model to explain any relationship between risk and return. We cannot tell which.

Weighing the Evidence

So what are we to conclude? Is beta dead? At the very least this latest salvo of criticism has forced the academic community to again come to grips with the fundamental shortcomings of the CAPM. The model, like all models that attempt to explain complex real-world phenomena using simplifying assumptions, is an abstraction and does not completely and perfectly "fit the facts" as to the way the world works. Does this mean that the model lacks usefulness? We think not. The model points toward the need to diversify and identifies the source of the risk premium as being tied to the risk of the security which cannot be diversified away. Is the model a complete guide to the underlying determinants of risk premiums? Probably not— we know that insolvency risk is ignored by the CAPM and this risk is a significant fact of life in the way investors evaluate and value securities. Then, just how useful is the model? We are reminded by the Fama and French results that the CAPM is, at best, only a rough approximation to the relationship between risk and return. Thus, we are reminded to treat beta estimates and corresponding risk premium estimates with great care.

The attacks and counterattacks on the effectiveness of the CAPM will, we believe, continue until a more appealing theory comes along that better explains the relationship between risk and returns. In fact, to this point, only one alternative theory has been offered as a substitute, or as a possible complement, for the CAPM. This newer theory, the **arbitrage-pricing model (APM)** considers multiple economic factors when explaining required rates of return, rather than look at systematic risk or general market returns as a single determinant of an investor's required rate of return. The arbitrage-pricing model *maintains that security returns vary from their expected amounts when there are unanticipated changes in basic economic forces.* Such forces would include unexpected changes in industrial production, inflation rates, term structure of interest rates, and the difference between interest rates of high-and-low risk bonds.

arbitrage-pricing model (APM)

SUMMARY

In Chapter 2, we referred to the discount rate as the interest rate or the opportunity cost of funds. At that point, we considered a number of important factors that influence interest rates, including the price of time, expected or anticipated inflation, and risk premium related to maturity (liquidity) and variability of future returns.

In this chapter, we have returned to our study of rates of return, and looked ever so carefully at the relationship between risk and rates of return.

Define and measure the expected rate of return Of an individual investment

OBJECTIVE 1

In a world of uncertainty, we cannot make forecasts with certitude. Thus, we must speak in terms of *expected* events. The expected return on an investment may therefore be stated as a weighted average of all the possible returns, weighted by the probability that each return will occur.

**Define and measure the riskiness
Of an individual investment**

Risk for our purposes is the variability of returns and may be measured by the standard deviation.

**Compare the historical relationship between risk and rates
Of return in the capital markets**

Ibbotson and Sinquefield have provided us with annual rates of return earned on different types of security investments as far back as 1926. They summarize, among other things, the annual returns for six portfolios of securities made up of

1. Common stocks of large companies
2. Common stocks of small firms
3. Long-term corporate bonds
4. Long-term U.S. government bonds
5. Intermediate-term U.S. government bonds
6. U.S. Treasury bills

A comparison of the annual rates of return for these respective portfolios for the years 1926–1993 shows there to be a positive relationship between risk and return, with Treasury bills being least risky and common stocks of small firms being more risky. From the data, we are able to see the benefit of diversification in terms of improving the return-risk relationship. Also, the data clearly demonstrate that only common stock has in the long run served as an inflation hedge, and that risk associated with common stock can be reduced if investors are patient in receiving their returns.

**Explain how diversifying our investments affects the riskiness
and expected rate of return of a portfolio or combination
Of assets**

We made an important distinction between nondiversifiable risk and diversifiable risk. We concluded that the only relevant risk, given the opportunity to diversify our portfolio, is a security's nondiversifiable risk, which we called by two other names: systematic risk and market-related risk.

**Explain the relationship between an investor's required
Rate of return on an investment and the riskiness
Of the investment**

The capital asset pricing model, even with its weaknesses, provides an intuitive framework for understanding the risk-return relationship. The CAPM suggests that investors determine an appropriate required rate of return, depending upon the amount of systematic risk inherent in a security. This minimum acceptable rate of return is equal to the risk-free rate plus a return premium for assuming risk.

Explain recent criticisms of the capital asset pricing model

For several years, the capital asset pricing model (CAPM) was touted as the "new investment technology" and received the blessings of the vast majority of professional investors and finance professors. The model, like any abstract theory, creates some unresolved issues. For example, we might question whether the risk of an asset can be totally captured in a single dimension of sensitivity to the market, as the CAPM proposes. Fama and French, two economists, argue that they have developed evidence that the CAPM does not explain why stock returns differ. Thus, beta, at least according to Fama and French, is not a reasonable way to explain the risk-return relationship in the markets.

KEY TERMS

Arbitrage-pricing Model (APM), 245

Asset Allocation, 239

Beta, 234

Capital Asset Pricing Model (CAPM), 242

Characteristic Line, 234

Company-unique Risk (see Unsystematic Risk), 231

Diversifiable Risk (see Unsystematic Risk), 231

Expected Rate of Return, 225

Company-unique Risk (see Unsystematic Risk), 231

Holding-period Returns, 232

Investor's Required Rate of Return, 240

Market Risk (see Systematic Risk), 231

Nondiversifiable Risk (see Systematic Risk), 231

Opportunity Cost of Funds, 240

Portfolio Beta, 237

Required Rate of Return (see Investor's Required Rate of Return), 240

Risk, 224

Risk Premium, 240

Risk-free Rate of Return, 240

Security Market Line, 242

Standard Deviation, 225

Systematic Risk, 231

Unsystematic Risk, 231

STUDY QUESTIONS

8-1. **a.** What is meant by the investor's required rate of return?

   b. How do we measure the riskiness of an asset?

   c. How should the proposed measurement of risk be interpreted?

8-2. What is (a) unsystematic risk (company-unique or diversifiable risk) and (b) systematic risk (market or nondiversifiable risk)?

8-3. What is the meaning of beta? How is it used to calculate k, the investor's required rate of return?

8-4. Define the security market line. What does it represent?

8-5. How do we measure the beta for a portfolio?

8-6. If we were to graph the returns of a stock against the returns of the S&P 500 Index, and the points did not follow a very ordered pattern, what could we say about that stock? If the stock's returns tracked the S&P 500 returns very closely, then what could we say?

8-7. Over the past six decades, we have had the opportunity to observe the rates of return and variability of these returns for different types of securities. Summarize these observations.

8-8. Describe the potential effect on returns by diversifying your portfolio.

SELF-TEST PROBLEMS

ST-1. (*Expected Return and Risk*) Universal Corporation is planning to invest in a security that has several possible rates of return. Given the following probability distribution of returns what is the expected rate of return on the investment? Also compute the standard deviation of the returns. What do the resulting numbers represent?

PROBABILITY	RETURN
.10	−10%
.20	5%
.30	10%
.40	25%

ST-2. (*Capital Asset Pricing Model*) Using the CAPM, estimate the appropriate required rate of return for the three stocks listed below, given that the risk-free rate is 5 percent and the expected return for the market is 17 percent.

STOCK	BETA
A	.75
B	.90
C	1.40

ST-3. (*Average Expected Return and Risk*) Given the holding-period returns shown below, calculate the average returns and the standard deviations for the Kaifu Corporation and for the market.

MONTH	KAIFU CORP.	MARKET
1	4%	2%
2	6	3
3	0	1
4	2	−1

ST-4. (*Holding-period Returns*) From the price data that follow, compute holding-period returns for periods 2 through 4.

Time	Stock Price
1	$10
2	13
3	11
4	15

ST-5. (*Security Market Line*)

a. Determine the expected return and beta for the following portfolio:

Stock	Percentage of Portfolio	Beta	Expected Return
1	40%	1.00	12%
2	25	0.75	11
3	35	1.30	15

b. Given the information above, draw the security market line and show where the securities fit on the graph. Assume that the risk-free rate is 8 percent and that the expected return on the market portfolio is 12 percent. How would you interpret these findings?

STUDY PROBLEMS

8-1. (*Expected Rate of Return and Risk*) Pritchard Press, Inc., is evaluating a security. One-year Treasury bills are currently paying 9.1 percent. Calculate the investment's expected return and its standard deviation. Should Pritchard invest in this security?

Probability	Return
.15	5%
.30	7%
.40	10%
.15	15%

8-2. *(Expected Rate of Return and Risk)* Syntex, Inc. is considering an investment in one of two common stocks. Given the information that follows, which investment is better, based on risk (as measured by the standard deviation) and return?

COMMON STOCK A		COMMON STOCK B	
PROBABILITY	**RETURN**	**PROBABILITY**	**RETURN**
		.20	−5%
.30	11%	.30	6%
.40	15%	.30	14%
.30	19%	.20	22%

8-3. *(Expected Rate of Return and Risk)* Friedman Manufacturing, Inc. has prepared the following information regarding two investments under consideration. Which investment should be accepted?

COMMON STOCK A		COMMON STOCK B	
PROBABILITY	**RETURN**	**PROBABILITY**	**RETURN**
.2	−2%	.10	4%
.5	18%	.30	6%
.3	27%	.40	10%
		.20	15%

8-4. *(Required Rate of Return Using CAPM)*
   a. Compute a fair rate of return for Intel common stock, which has a 1.2 beta. The risk-free rate is 6 percent and the market portfolio (New York Stock Exchange stocks) has an expected return of 16 percent.
   b. Why is the rate you computed a fair rate?

8-5. *(Estimating Beta)* From the graph below relating the holding-period returns for Aram, Inc. to the S&P 500 Index, estimate the firm's beta.

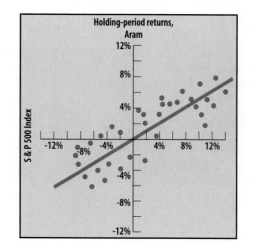

8-6. (*Capital Asset Pricing Model*) Johnson Manufacturing, Inc. is considering several investments. The rate on Treasury bills is currently 6.75 percent, and the expected return for the market is 12 percent. What should be the required rates of return for each investment (using the CAPM)?

[handwritten: b. calculate β for the portfolio?]

Security	Beta
A	1.50
B	.82
C	.60
D	1.15

[handwritten:
$\frac{Inu}{100}A$
$200\,B$
$300\,C$
$600\,D$
$\overline{1200}$

c. What is required 11.9%
of the portfolio? 12%
$\frac{Bp}{}$
A = 14.6%
B = 11.1%   0.98
C = 9.9%
D = 12.8% *]*

8-7. (*Capital Asset Pricing Model*) CSB, Inc. has a beta of .765. If the expected market return is 11.5 percent and the risk-free rate is 7.5 percent, what is the appropriate required return of CSB (using the CAPM)?

8-8. (*Capital Asset Pricing Model*) The expected return for the general market is 12.8 percent, and the risk premium in the market is 4.3 percent. Tasaco, LBM, and Exxos have betas of .864, .693, and .575, respectively. What are the corresponding required rates of return for the three securities?

8-9. (*Computing Holding-Period Returns*)
   a. From the price data below, compute the holding-period returns for Asman and Salinas for periods 2 through 4.

Time	Asman	Salinas
1	$10	$30
2	12	28
3	11	32
4	13	35

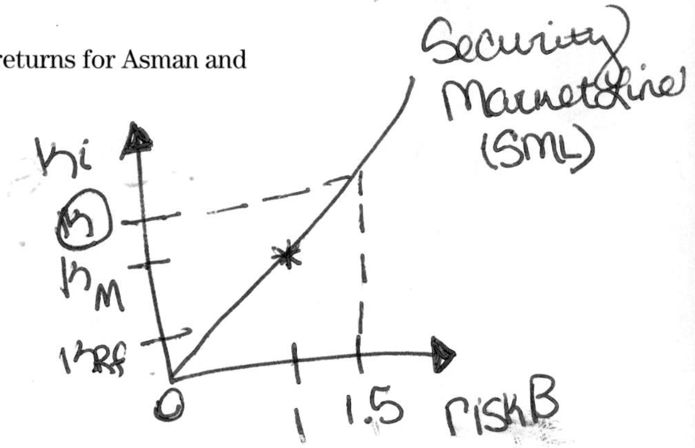

[handwritten graph: Security Market Line (SML); axes labeled k_i, k_m, k_{RF}, horizontal axis riskβ with 1.5 marked]

   b. How would you interpret the meaning of a holding-period return?

8-10. (*Measuring Risk and Rates of Return*)
   a. Given the holding-period returns shown below, compute the average returns and the standard deviations for the Zemin Corporation and for the market.

Month	Zemin Corp.	Market
1	6%	4%
2	3	2
3	−1	1
4	−3	−2
5	5	2
6	0	2

[handwritten:
Treasury Bills = No risk

$y = mx + b$
$y = b + mx$
$k_i = k_{RF} + (k_m - k_{RF})\beta_i$
$k_i = 5.6\% + (12\% - 5.62\%)1.5$ *]*

[handwritten: $k_i = 15.2$]

b. If Zemin's beta is 1.54 and the risk-free rate is 8 percent, what would be an appropriate required return for an investor owning Zemin? (*Note:* Because the above returns are based on monthly data, you will need to annualize the returns to make them compatible with the risk-free rate. For simplicity, you can convert from monthly to yearly returns by multiplying the average monthly returns by 12.)

c. How does Zemin's historical average return compare with the return you believe to be a fair return, given the firm's systematic risk?

8-11. (*Portfolio Beta and Security Market Line*) You own a portfolio consisting of the following stocks:

STOCK	PERCENTAGE OF PORTFOLIO	BETA	EXPECTED RETURN
1	20%	1.00	16%
2	30	0.85	14
3	15	1.20	20
4	25	0.60	12
5	10	1.60	24

The risk-free rate is 7 percent. Also, the expected return on the market portfolio is 15.5 percent.

a. Calculate the expected return of your portfolio.

(*Hint:* The expected return of a portfolio equals the weighted average of the individual stock's expected return, where the weights are the percentage invested in each stock.)

b. Calculate the portfolio beta.

c. Given the information above, plot the security market line on paper. Plot the stocks from your portfolio on your graph.

d. From your plot in part c, which stocks appear to be your winners and which ones appear to be losers?

e. Why should you consider your conclusion in part d to be less than certain?

8-12. (*Expected Return, Standard Deviation, and Capital Asset Pricing Model*) Below you will find the end-of-month prices for both the Standard & Poor's 500 Index and Coca-Cola common stock.

a. Using the data below, calculate the holding-period returns for each of the months.

| MONTH | PRICES | |
AND YEAR	S&P 500	COCA-COLA
1995		
March	$500.71	$56.38
April	514.71	58.13
May	533.41	61.63
June	544.75	63.75
July	562.06	65.63
August	561.88	64.25
September	584.41	69.00
October	581.50	71.88
November	605.37	75.75
December	615.93	74.25
1996		
January	636.02	75.38
February	640.43	80.75
March	645.50	82.75

b. Calculate the average monthly return and the standard deviation of these returns both for the S&P 500 and Coca-Cola.

c. Develop a graph that shows the relationship between the Coca-Cola stock returns and the S&P 500 Index (show the Coca-Cola returns on the vertical axis and the S&P 500 Index returns on the horizontal axis as done in Figure 8–5).

d. From your graph, describe the nature of the relationship between Coca-Cola stock returns and the returns for the S&P 500 Index.

COMPREHENSIVE PROBLEM

Note: Although not absolutely necessary, you are advised to use a computer spreadsheet to work the following problem.

a. Use the price data from the table on the following page for the Standard & Poor's 500 Index, Bristol Myers Squibb, and General Electric to calculate the holding-period returns for the 24 months during 1994 and 1995.

MONTH AND YEAR	PRICES		
	S&P 500	BRISTOL	GE
1993			
December	$466.45	$58.25	$52.44
1994			
January	481.61	57.88	53.88
February	467.14	55.25	52.69
March	445.77	51.50	50.00
April	450.91	53.88	47.63
May	456.50	54.63	49.75
June	444.27	53.63	46.63
July	458.26	52.63	50.38
August	475.49	57.63	49.75
September	462.69	57.38	48.13
October	472.35	58.38	48.88
November	453.69	57.75	46.00
December	459.27	57.88	51.00
1995			
January	470.42	61.50	51.50
February	487.39	61.88	54.75
March	500.71	62.88	54.00
April	514.71	65.12	56.00
May	533.40	66.37	58.00
June	544.75	68.12	56.38
July	562.06	69.25	59.00
August	561.88	68.75	58.88
September	584.41	72.87	63.75
October	581.50	76.25	63.25
November	605.37	80.25	67.12
December	615.93	85.88	72.00

b. Calculate the average monthly holding-period returns and the standard deviation of these returns for the S&P 500 Index, Bristol Myers Squibb, and General Electric.

c. Plot (1) the holding-period returns for Bristol Myers Squibb against the Standard & Poor's 500 Index, and (2) the General Electric holding-period returns against the Standard & Poor's 500 Index. (Use Figure 8–5 as the format for your graph.)

d. From your graphs in part c, describe the nature of the relationship between the Bristol Myers Squibb stock returns and the returns for the S&P 500 Index. Make the same comparison for General Electric.

e. Assume that you have decided to invest one-half of your money in Bristol Myers Squibb and the remaining in General Electric. Calculate the monthly holding-period returns for your two-stock portfolio. (*Hint:* The monthly return for the portfolio is the average of the two stocks' monthly returns.)

f. Plot the returns of your two-stock portfolio against the Standard & Poor's 500 Index as you did for the individual stocks in part c. How does this graph compare to the graphs for the individual stocks? Explain the difference.

g. Below you are provided the returns on an *annualized* basis that were realized from holding long-term government bonds during 1994 and 1995. Calculate the average *monthly* holding-period returns and the standard deviations of these returns. (*Hint:* You will need to convert the annual returns to monthly returns by dividing each return by 12 months.)

Month and Year	Annualized Rate of Return (%)
1994	
January	6.29
February	6.49
March	6.91
April	7.27
May	7.41
June	7.40
July	7.58
August	7.49
September	7.71
October	7.94
November	8.08
December	7.87
1995	
January	7.85
February	7.61
March	7.45
April	7.36
May	6.95
June	6.57
July	6.72
August	6.86
September	6.55
October	6.37
November	6.26
December	6.06

h. Now assuming that you have decided to invest equal amounts of money in Bristol Myers Squibb, General Electric, and long-term government securities, calculate the monthly returns for your three-asset portfolio. What are the average return and the standard deviation?

i. Make a comparison of the average returns and the standard deviations for all the individual assets and the two portfolios that we designed. What conclusions can be reached by your comparison?

j. According to Standard & Poor's, the betas for Bristol Myers Squibb and General Electric are 1.11 and 1.21, respectively. Compare the meaning of these betas relative to the standard deviations calculated above.

k. The Treasury bill rate at the end of 1995 was approximately 5.5 percent. Given the betas for Bristol Myers Squibb and General Electric and using the above data for the S&P 500 Index as a measure for the market portfolio expected return, estimate an appropriate required rate of return given the level of systematic risk for each stock.

SS–1.

(A) **Probability** $P(k_i)$	(B) **Return** (k_i)	**Expected Return** (k) (A) × (B)	**Weighted** **Deviation** $(k_i - \bar{k})^2 P(k_i)$
.10	−10%	−1%	52.9%
.20	5	1	12.8
.30	10	3	2.7
.40	25	10	57.6
		$\bar{k} = 13\%$	$\sigma^2 = 126.0\%$
			$\sigma = 11.22\%$

From our studies in statistics, we know that if the distribution of returns were normal, then Universal could expect a return of 13 percent with a 67 percent possibility that this return would vary up or down by 11.22 percent between 1.78 percent (13% − 11.22%) and 24.22 percent (13% + 11.22%). However, it is apparent from the probabilities that the distribution is not normal.

SS–2.

Stock A   5% + .75(17% − 5%) = 14.0%
Stock B: 5% + .90(17% − 5%) = 15.8
Stock C: 5% + 1.40(17% − 5%) = 21.8

SS–3.

Kaifu

Average return:
$$\frac{4\% + 6\% + 0\% + 2\%}{4} = 3\%$$

Standard deviation:
$$\sqrt{\frac{\begin{array}{c}(4\% - 3\%)^2 \\ +(6\% - 3\%)^2 \\ +(0\% - 3\%)^2 \\ +(2\% - 3\%)^2\end{array}}{4 - 1}} = 2.58\%$$

Market

Average return:
$$\frac{2\% + 3\% + 1\% - 1\%}{4} = 1.25\%$$

Standard deviation:
$$\sqrt{\frac{\begin{array}{c}(2\% - 1.25\%)^2 \\ +(3\% - 1.25\%)^2 \\ +(1\% - 1.25\%)^2 \\ +(-1\% - 1.25\%)^2\end{array}}{4 - 1)}} = 1.71\%$$

SS–4.

TIME	STOCK PRICE	HOLDING-PERIOD RETURN		
1	$10			
2	13	($13 ÷ $10) − 1 =	30.0%
3	11	($11 ÷ $13) − 1 =	−15.4
4	15	($15 ÷ $11) − 1 =	36.4

SS–5.

a. Portfolio expected return:

$$(.4 \times 12\%) + (.25 \times 11\%) + (.35 \times 15\%) = 12.8\%$$

Portfolio beta:

$$(.4 \times 1) + (.25 \times .75) + (.35 \times 1.3) = 1.04$$

b.

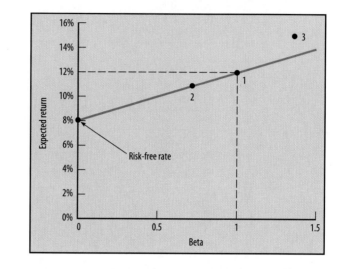

Stocks 1 and 2 seem to be right in line with the security market line, which suggests that they are earning a fair return, given their systematic risk. Stock 3, on the other hand, is earning more than a fair return (above the security market line). We might be tempted to conclude that security 3 is undervalued. However, we may be seeing an illusion; it is possible to misspecify the security market line by using bad estimates in our data.

Capital-Budgeting Techniques and Practice

Finding Profitable Projects • Capital-Budgeting Decision Criteria • Capital Rationing • Problems in Project Ranking— Capital Rationing, Mutually Exclusive Projects, and Problems with the IRR • Ethics in Capital Budgeting • A Glance at Actual Capital-Budgeting Practices

After reading this chapter you should be able to

1. Discuss the difficulty encountered in finding profitable projects in competitive markets and the importance of the search.
2. Determine whether or not a new project should be accepted or rejected using the payback period, the net present value, the profitability index, and the internal rate of return.
3. Explain how the capital-budgeting decision process changes when a dollar limit is placed on the dollar size of the capital budget.
4. Discuss the problems encountered in project ranking.
5. Explain the importance of ethical considerations in capital-budgeting decisions.
6. Discuss the trends in the use of different capital-budgeting criteria.

I n 1988, Ford Motor Company made a decision to reenter the minivan market with a new challenger to Chrysler's Caravan and Voyager. Over the past decade, a number of challengers including Ford Aerostar, GM's APV, and a number of Japanese models had entered the ring against the Chrysler minivan, all with the same result. The Chrysler minivan has scored a knock-out against all comers and has continued to dominate the minivan market by a wide margin.

Given the history of challengers to Chrysler's minivan, it was not an easy decision to challenge the champ. Moreover, the stakes involved are so large that the outcome of this decision will have a major effect on Ford's future. To challenge Chrysler's dominance in this market, Ford committed $1.5 billion, with roughly $500 million going toward design, engineering, and testing. The end result of this is the Ford Winstar, which Ford unveiled in 1994. Whether this was a good decision or a bad decision only time will tell, but early reports indicate that while Ford has come up with a winner, it also faces unexpectedly stiff competition from a new generation of Chrysler minivans.

In this chapter we will look at the process of decision making with respect to investment in fixed assets—that is, should a proposed project be accepted or should it be rejected? We will refer to this process as capital budgeting. Typically, these investments involve rather large cash outlays at the outset and commit the firm to a particular course of action over a relatively long period. Thus, if a capital-budgeting decision is incorrect, reversing it tends to be costly. In evaluating capital investment proposals, we compare the costs and benefits of each in a number of ways. Some of these methods take into account the time value of money; one does not; however, each of these methods is used frequently in the real world. As you will see, our preferred method of analysis will be the net present value (NPV) method, which compares the present value of inflows and outflows.

In this chapter we look first at the difficulties associated with finding profitable projects. Four capital-budgeting criteria are subsequently provided for evaluating capital investments, followed by a discussion of the problems created when the number of projects that can be accepted or the total budget is limited. Chapter 9 closes with an examination of capital budgeting in practice.

FINDING PROFITABLE PROJECTS

capital budgeting

Without question it is easier to *evaluate profitable projects or investments in fixed assets*, a process referred to as **capital budgeting,** than it is to find them. In competitive markets, generating ideas for profitable projects is extremely difficult. The competition is brisk for new profitable projects, and once they have been uncovered competitors generally rush in, pushing down prices and profits. For this reason a firm must have a systematic strategy for generating capital-budgeting projects. Without this flow of new projects and ideas, the firm cannot grow or even survive for long, being forced to live off the profits from existing projects with limited lives. So where do these ideas come from for new products, or for ways to improve existing products or make them more profitable? The answer is from inside the firm—from everywhere inside the firm.

BACK TO THE FOUNDATIONS

The fact that profitable projects are difficult to find relates directly to **Axiom 5: The Curse of Competitive Markets—Why It's Hard to Find Exceptionally Profitable Projects.** When we introduced that axiom we stated that successful investments involve the reduction of competition by creating barriers to entry either through product differentiation or cost advantages. The key to locating profitable projects is to understand how and where they exist.

Typically, a firm has a research and development department that searches for ways of improving on existing products or finding new products. These ideas may come from within the R&D department or be based on referral ideas from executives, sales personnel, or anyone in the firm. For example, at Ford Motor Company prior to the 1980s, ideas for product improvement had typically been generated in Ford's research and development department. Unfortunately, this strategy was not enough to keep Ford from losing much of its market share to the Japanese. In an attempt to cut costs and improve product quality, Ford moved from strict reliance on an R&D department to seeking the input of employees at all levels for new ideas. Bonuses are now provided to workers for their cost-cutting suggestions, and assembly-line personnel who can see the production process from a hands-on point of view are now brought into the hunt for new projects. The effect on Ford has been positive and significant. Although not all suggested projects prove to be profitable, many new ideas generated from within the firm turn out to be good ones. The best way to evaluate new investment proposals is the topic of the remainder of this chapter.

In deciding whether to accept a new project, we will focus on cash flows. Cash flows represent the benefits generated from accepting a capital-budgeting proposal. In this chapter we will assume a given cash flow is generated by a project and work on determining whether that project should be accepted.

We will consider four commonly used criteria for determining acceptability of investment proposals. The first one is the least sophisticated, in that it does not incorporate the time value of money into its calculations; the other three do take it into account. For the time being, the problem of incorporating risk into the capital-budgeting decision is ignored. This issue will be examined in Chapter 10. In addition, we will assume that the appropriate discount rate, required rate of return, or cost of capital is given. The determination of the cost of capital is the topic of Chapter 11.

Payback Period

The **payback period** is the *number of years needed to recover the initial cash outlay.* As this criterion measures how quickly the project will return its original investment, it deals with cash flows rather than accounting profits. It also ignores the time value of money and does not discount these cash flows back to the present. The accept/reject criterion involves whether the project's payback period is less than or equal to the firm's maximum desired payback period. For example, if a firm's maximum desired payback period is three years and an investment proposal requires an initial cash outlay of $10,000 and yields the following set of annual cash flows, what is its payback period? Should the project be accepted?

payback period

Year	After-Tax Cash Flow
1	$2,000
2	4,000
3	3,000
4	3,000
5	1,000

In this case, after three years the firm will have recaptured $9,000 on an initial investment of $10,000, leaving $1,000 of the initial investment to be recouped. During the fourth year a total of $3,000 will be returned from this investment, and, assuming it will flow into the firm at a constant rate over the year, it will take one-third of the year ($1,000/$3,000) to recapture the remaining $1,000. Thus, the payback period on this project is three and a third years, which is more than the desired payback period. Using the payback period criterion, the firm would reject this project.

Although the payback period is used frequently, it does have some rather obvious drawbacks, which can best be demonstrated through the use of an example. Consider two investment projects, A and B, which involve an initial cash outlay of $10,000 each and produce the annual cash flows shown in Table 9–1 on page 262. Both projects have a payback period of two years; therefore, in terms of the payback period criterion both are equally acceptable. However, if we had our choice, it is clear we would select A over B, for at least two reasons. First, regardless of what happens after the payback period, project A returns our initial investment to us earlier within the payback period. Thus, if there is a time value of money, the cash flows occurring within the payback period should not be weighted equally, as they

Finding Profitable Projects in Competitive Markets—Creating Them by Developing a Cost Advantage

As we learned in **Axiom 5: The Curse of Competitive Markets,** it is extremely difficult to find exceptionally profitable projects. We also noted that if you have the ability to produce at a cost below the competition, there is the opportunity for exceptionally large profits. Federal Express is one example of a company that has done exactly this.

Federal Express redefined the production-cost chain for rapid delivery of small parcels. Traditional firms like Emery and Airborne Express operated by collecting freight packages of varying sizes, shipping them to their destination points via air freight and commercial airlines, and then delivering them to the addressee. Federal Express opted to focus only on the market for overnight delivery of small packages and documents. These were collected at local drop points during the late afternoon hours; flown on company-owned planes during early evening hours to a central hub in Memphis, where from 11 p.m. to 3 a.m. each night all parcels were sorted; and then reloaded on company planes and flown during the early morning hours to their destination points, from which they were delivered that morning by company personnel using company trucks. The cost structure thus achieved by Federal Express was low enough to permit guaranteed overnight delivery of a small parcel anywhere in the United States for a price as low as $11. In 1986 Federal Express had a 58 percent market share of the air-express package-delivery market, versus a 15 percent share for UPS, 11 percent for Airborne Express, and 10 percent for Emery/Purolator.

_____

Source: Arthur A. Thompson, Jr., *Economics of the Firm: Theory and Practice* (Englewood Cliffs, NJ: Prentice Hall, 1989), p. 351. Based on information in Michael E. Porter, *Competitive Advantage* (New York: Free Press, 1985), p. 109.

are. In addition, all cash flows that occur after the payback period are ignored. This violates the principle that investors desire more in the way of benefits rather than less—a principle that is difficult to deny, especially when we are talking about money.

Although these deficiencies limit the value of the payback period as a tool for investment evaluation, the payback period has several positive features. First, it deals with cash flows, as opposed to accounting profits, and therefore focuses on the true timing of the project's benefits and costs, even though it does not adjust the cash flows for the time value of money. Second, it is easy to visualize, quickly understood,

Table 9–1
Payback Period Example

	PROJECTS	
	A	**B**
Initial cash outlay	−$10,000	−$10,000
Annual net cash inflows		
Year 1	$ 6,000	$ 5,000
2	4,000	5,000
3	3,000	0
4	2,000	0
5	1,000	0

and easy to calculate. Finally, although the payback period has serious deficiencies, it is often used as a rough screening device to eliminate projects whose returns do not materialize until later years. This method emphasizes the earliest returns, which in all likelihood are less uncertain, and provides for the liquidity needs of the firm. Although its advantages are certainly significant, its disadvantages severely limit its value as a discriminating capital-budgeting criterion.

BACK TO THE FOUNDATIONS

The final three capital-budgeting criteria all incorporate **Axiom 2: The Time Value of Money—A Dollar Received Today Is Worth More Than a Dollar Received in the Future** in their calculations. If we are at all to make rational business decisions we must recognize that money has a time value. In examining the following three capital-budgeting techniques, you will notice that this axiom is the driving force behind each of them.

Net Present Value

The **net present value (NPV)** of an investment proposal is equal to the *present value of its annual net cash flows after taxes less the investment's initial outlay.* The net present value can be expressed as follows:

net present value (NPV)

$$NPV = \sum_{t=1}^{n} \frac{ACF_t}{(1 + k)^t} - IO \qquad \textbf{(9–1)}$$

$$
\begin{aligned}
\text{where } ACF_t &= \text{the annual after-tax cash flow in time period } t \\
&\quad \text{(this can take on either positive or negative values)} \\
k &= \text{the appropriate discount rate; that is, the required} \\
&\quad \text{rate of return or cost of capital}[1] \\
IO &= \text{the initial cash outlay} \\
n &= \text{the project's expected life}
\end{aligned}
$$

The project's net present value gives a measurement of the net value of an investment proposal in terms of today's dollars. Because all cash flows are discounted back to the present, comparing the difference between the present value of the annual cash flows and the investment outlay does not violate the time value of money assumption. The difference between the present value of the annual cash flows and the initial outlay determines the net value of accepting the investment proposal in terms of today's dollars. Whenever the project's NPV is greater than or equal to zero, we will accept the project; and whenever there is a negative value associated with the acceptance of a project, we will reject the project. If the project's net present value is zero, then it returns the required rate of return and should be accepted. This accept/reject criterion is illustrated below:

$$NPV \geq 0.0: \text{accept}$$
$$NPV < 0.0: \text{reject}$$

The following example illustrates the use of net present value as a capital-budgeting criterion.

---

[1]The required rate of return or cost of capital is the rate of return necessary to justify raising funds to finance the project or, alternatively, the rate of return necessary to maintain the firm's current market price per share. These terms will be defined in greater detail in Chapter 11.

Table 9-2
NPV Illustration of Investment in New Machinery

	AFTER-TAX CASH FLOW
Initial outlay	−$40,000
Inflow year 1	15,000
Inflow year 2	14,000
Inflow year 3	13,000
Inflow year 4	12,000
Inflow year 5	11,000

EXAMPLE

A firm is considering new machinery, for which the after-tax cash flows are shown in Table 9–2. If the firm has a 12 percent required rate of return, the present value of the after-tax cash flow is $47,678, as calculated in Table 9–3. Furthermore, the net present value of the new machinery is $7,678. Because this value is greater than zero, the net present value criterion indicates that the project should be accepted.

Note that the worth of the net present value calculation is a function of the accuracy of cash flow predictions. Before the NPV criterion can reasonably be applied, incremental costs and benefits must first be estimated, including the initial outlay, the differential flows over the project's life, and the terminal cash flow.

The NPV criterion is the capital-budgeting decision tool we will find most favorable for several reasons. First of all, it deals with cash flows rather than accounting profits. In this regard it is sensitive to the true timing of the benefits resulting from the project. Moreover, recognizing the time value of money allows comparison of the benefits and costs in a logical manner. Finally, because projects are accepted only if a positive net present value is associated with them, the acceptance of a project using this criterion will increase the value of the firm, which is consistent with the goal of maximizing the shareholders' wealth.

The disadvantage of the NPV method stems from the need for detailed, long-term forecasts of the incremental cash flows accruing from the project's acceptance. De-

Table 9-3
Calculation for NPV Illustration of Investment in New Machinery

	AFTER-TAX CASH FLOW	PRESENT VALUE FACTOR AT 12 PERCENT	PRESENT VALUE
Inflow year 1	15,000	.893	$13,395
Inflow year 2	14,000	.797	11,158
Inflow year 3	13,000	.712	9,256
Inflow year 4	12,000	.636	7,632
Inflow year 5	11,000	.567	6,237
Present value of cash flows			$47,678
Initial outlay			− 40,000
Net present value			$7,678

spite this drawback, the net present value is the most theoretically correct criterion that we will examine. The following example provides an additional illustration of its application.

EXAMPLE

A firm is considering the purchase of a new computer system, which will cost $30,000 initially, to aid in credit billing and inventory management. The incremental after-tax cash flows resulting from this project are provided in Table 9–4. The required rate of return demanded by the firm is 10 percent. To determine the system's net present value, the three-year $15,000 cash flow annuity is first discounted back to the present at 10 percent. From Appendix E in the back of this book, we find that $PVIFA_{10\%, 3\,yr}$ is 2.487. Thus, the present value of this $15,000 annuity is $37,305.

Because the cash inflows have been discounted back to the present, they can now be compared with the initial outlay. This is because both of the flows are now stated in terms of today's dollars. Subtracting the initial outlay ($30,000) from the present value of the cash inflows ($37,305), we find that the system's net present value is $7,305. Because the NPV on this project is positive, the project should be accepted. ■

Profitability Index (Benefit-Cost Ratio)

The **profitability index (PI)**, or **benefit-cost ratio,** is the *ratio of the present value of the future net cash flows to the initial outlay.* Although the net present value investment criterion gives a measure of the absolute dollar desirability of a project, the profitability index provides a relative measure of an investment proposal's desirability—that is, the ratio of the present value of its future net benefits to its initial cost. The profitability index can be expressed as follows:

profitability index (PI or benefit-cost ratio)

$$PI = \frac{\sum_{t=1}^{n} \frac{ACF_t}{(1 + k)^t}}{IO} \qquad (9\text{--}2)$$

where ACF_t = the annual after-tax cash flow in time period t (this can take on either positive or negative values)

k = the appropriate discount rate; that is, the required rate of return or cost of capital

IO = the initial cash outlay

n = the project's expected life

The decision criterion with respect to the profitability index is to accept the project if the PI is greater than or equal to 1.00, and to reject the project if the PI is less than 1.00.

$$PI \geq 1.0: \text{accept}$$
$$PI < 1.0: \text{reject}$$

Table 9–4	
NPV Example Problem of Computer System	
	AFTER-TAX CASH FLOW
Initial outlay	−$30,000
Inflow year 1	15,000
Inflow year 2	15,000
Inflow year 3	15,000

CAPITAL-BUDGETING TECHNIQUES AND PRACTICE **265**

Looking closely at this criterion, we see that it yields the same accept/reject decision as does the net present value criterion. Whenever the present value of the project's net cash flows is greater than its initial cash outlay, the project's net present value will be positive, signaling a decision to accept. When this is true, then the project's profitability index will also be greater than 1, as the present value of the net cash flows (the PI's numerator) is greater than its initial outlay (the PI's denominator). Although these two decision criteria will always yield the same decision, they will not necessarily rank acceptable projects in the same order. This problem of conflicting ranking will be dealt with at a later point.

Because the net present value and profitability index criteria are essentially the same, they have the same advantages over the other criteria examined. Both employ cash flows, recognize the timing of the cash flows, and are consistent with the goal of maximization of shareholders' wealth. The major disadvantage of this criterion, similar to the net present value criterion, is that it requires long, detailed cash flow forecasts.

EXAMPLE

A firm with a 10 percent required rate of return is considering investing in a new machine with an expected life of six years. The after-tax cash flows resulting from this investment are given in Table 9–5. Discounting the project's future net cash flows back to the present yields a present value of $53,667; dividing this value by the initial outlay of $50,000 gives a profitability index of 1.0733, as shown in Table 9–6. This tells us that the present value of the future benefits accruing from this project is 1.0733 times the level of the initial outlay. Because the profitability index is greater than 1.0, the project should be accepted. ■

Internal Rate of Return

internal rate of return (IRR) The **internal rate of return (IRR)** attempts to answer this question: What rate of return does this project earn? For computational purposes, the internal rate of return is defined as *the discount rate that equates the present value of the project's future net cash flows with the project's initial cash outlay*. Mathematically, the internal rate of return is defined as the value *IRR* in the following equation:

$$IO = \sum_{t=1}^{n} \frac{ACF_t}{(1 + IRR)^t} \tag{9-3}$$

Table 9–5
PI Illustration of Investment in New Machinery

	AFTER-TAX CASH FLOW
Initial outlay	−$50,000
Inflow year 1	15,000
Inflow year 2	8,000
Inflow year 3	10,000
Inflow year 4	12,000
Inflow year 5	14,000
Inflow year 6	16,000

Table 9–6

Calculation for PI Illustration of Investment in New Machinery

	After-Tax Cash Flow	Present Value Factor at 10 Percent	Present Value
Initial outlay	−$50,000	1.000	−$50,000
Inflow year 1	15,000	0.909	13,635
Inflow year 2	8,000	0.826	6,608
Inflow year 3	10,000	0.751	7,510
Inflow year 4	12,000	0.683	8,196
Inflow year 5	14,000	0.621	8,694
Inflow year 6	16,000	0.564	9,024

$$PI = \frac{\sum_{t=1}^{n} \frac{ACF_t}{(1+k)^t}}{IO}$$

$$= \frac{\$13,635 + \$6,608 + \$7,510 + \$8,196 + \$8,694 + \$9,024}{\$50,000}$$

$$= \frac{\$53,667}{\$50,000}$$

$$= 1.0733$$

where ACF_t = the annual after-tax cash flow in time period t (this can take on either positive or negative values)

IO = the initial cash outlay

n = the project's expected life

IRR = the project's internal rate of return

In effect, the IRR is analogous to the concept of the yield to maturity for bonds, which was examined in Chapter 6. In other words, a project's internal rate of return is simply the rate of return that the project earns.

The decision criterion associated with the internal rate of return is to accept the project if the internal rate of return is greater than or equal to the required rate of return. We reject the project if its internal rate of return is less than the required rate of return. This accept/reject criterion is illustrated below:

$IRR \geq$ required rate of return: accept
$IRR <$ required rate of return: reject

If the internal rate of return on a project is equal to the shareholders' required rate of return, then the project should be accepted. This is because the firm is earning the rate that its shareholders are requiring. However, the acceptance of a project with an internal rate of return below the investors' required rate of return will decrease the firm's stock price.

If the NPV is positive, then the IRR must be greater than the required rate of return, k. Thus, all the discounted cash flow criteria are consistent and will give similar accept/reject decisions. In addition, because the internal rate of return is another discounted cash flow criterion, it exhibits the same general advantages and disadvantages as both the net present value and profitability index, but has an additional disadvantage of being tedious to calculate if a financial calculator is not available.

Computing the IRR with a Financial Calculator

With today's calculators, the determination of an internal rate of return is merely a matter of a few keystrokes. In Chapter 5, whenever we were solving time value of money problems for i, we were really solving for the internal rate of return. For instance, in the example on page 147, when we solved for the rate that $100 must be compounded annually for it to grow to $179.10 in 10 years, we were actually solving for that problem's internal rate of return. Thus, with financial calculators we need only input the initial outlay, the cash flows and their timing, and then input the function key "I/Y" or the "IRR" button to calculate the internal rate of return. On some calculators it is necessary to input the compute key, CPT, before inputting the function key to be calculated.

Computing the IRR for Even Cash Flows

In this section we are going to put our calculators aside and examine the mathematical process of calculating internal rates of return for a better understanding of the IRR.

The calculation of a project's internal rate of return can either be very simple or relatively complicated. As an example of a straightforward solution, assume that a firm with a required rate of return of 10 percent is considering a project that involves an initial outlay of $45,555. If the investment is taken, the after-tax cash flows are expected to be $15,000 per annum over the project's four-year life. In this case, the internal rate of return is equal to IRR in the following equation:

$$\$45,555 = \frac{\$15,000}{(1 + IRR)^1} + \frac{\$15,000}{(1 + IRR)^2} + \frac{\$15,000}{(1 + IRR)^3} + \frac{\$15,000}{(1 + IRR)^4}$$

From our discussion of the present value of an annuity in Chapter 5, we know that this equation can be reduced to

$$\$45,555 = \$15,000\left[\sum_{t=1}^{4}\frac{1}{(1 + IRR)^t}\right]$$

Appendix E gives values for the $PVIFA_{i,n}$ for various combinations of i and n, which further reduces this equation to

$$\$45,555 = \$15,000\ (PVIFA_{i,\ 4\ yr})$$

Dividing both sides by $15,000, this becomes

$$3.037 = PVIFA_{i,\ 4\ yr}$$

Hence, we are looking for $PVIFA_{i,\ 4\ yr}$ of 3.037 in the four-year row of Appendix E. This value occurs when i equals 12 percent which means that 12 percent is the internal rate of return for the investment. Therefore, since 12 percent is greater than the 10 percent required return, the project should be accepted.

Computing the IRR for Uneven Cash Flows

Unfortunately, although solving for the IRR is quite easy when using a financial calculator or spreadsheet, it can be solved directly in the tables only when the future after-tax net cash flows are in the form of an annuity or a single payment. With a calculator the process is simple: One need only key in the initial cash outlay, the cash flows and their timing, and press the "IRR" button. When a financial calculator is not available and these flows are in the form of an uneven series of flows, a trial-and-error approach is necessary. To do this, we first determine the present value of the future after-tax net cash flows using an arbitrary discount rate. If the present value of the future cash flows at this discount rate is larger than the initial outlay, the rate is increased; if it is smaller than the initial outlay, the discount rate is lowered and the process begins again. This search routine is continued until the present value of the future after-tax cash flows is equal to the initial outlay. The interest rate that creates this situation is the internal rate of return. This is the same basic process that a financial calculator uses to calculate an IRR.

To illustrate the procedure, consider an investment proposal that requires an initial outlay of $3,817 and returns $1,000 at the end of year 1, $2,000 at the end of year 2, and $3,000 at the end of year 3. In this case, the internal rate of return must be determined using trial and error. This process is presented in Table 9–7, in which

Table 9–7
Computing IRR for Uneven Cash Flows without a Financial Calculator

Initial outlay   −$3,817
Inflow year 1   1,000
Inflow year 2   2,000
Inflow year 3   3,000
Solution:

Step 1: Pick an arbitrary discount rate and use it to determine the present value of the inflows.

Step 2: Compare the present value of the inflows with the initial outlay; if they are equal you have determined the IRR.

Step 3: If the present value of the inflows is larger (less than) than the initial outlay, raise (lower) the discount rate.

Step 4: Determine the present value of the inflows and repeat Step 2.

1. TRY i = 15 PERCENT:

	NET CASH FLOWS	PRESENT VALUE FACTOR AT 15 PERCENT	PRESENT VALUE
Inflow year 1	$1,000	.870	$ 870
Inflow year 2	2,000	.756	1,512
Inflow year 3	3,000	.658	1,974
Present value of inflows			$4,356
Initial outlay			−$3,817

2. TRY i = 20 PERCENT:

	NET CASH FLOWS	PRESENT VALUE FACTOR AT 20 PERCENT	PRESENT VALUE
Inflow year 1	$1,000	.833	$ 833
Inflow year 2	2,000	.694	1,388
Inflow year 3	3,000	.579	1,737
Present value of inflows			$3,958
Initial outlay			−3,817

3. TRY i = 22 PERCENT:

	NET CASH FLOWS	PRESENT VALUE FACTOR AT 22 PERCENT	PRESENT VALUE
Inflow year 1	$1,000	.820	$ 820
Inflow year 2	2,000	.672	1,344
Inflow year 3	3,000	.551	1,653
Present value of inflows			$3,817
Initial outlay			−$3,817

an arbitrarily selected discount rate of 15 percent was chosen to begin the process. The trial-and-error technique slowly centers in on the project's internal rate of return of 22 percent. The project's internal rate of return is then compared with the firm's required rate of return, and if the IRR is the larger, the project is accepted.

EXAMPLE

A firm with a required rate of return of 10 percent is considering three investment proposals. Given the information in Table 9–8, management plans to calculate the internal rate of return for each project and determine which projects should be accepted.

Because project A is an annuity, we can easily calculate its internal rate of return by determining the $PVIFA_{i, 4\,yr}$ necessary to equate the present value of the future cash flows with the initial outlay. This computation is done as follows:

$$IO = \sum_{t=1}^{n} \frac{ACF_t}{(1 + IRR)^t}$$

$$\$10,000 = \sum_{t=1}^{4} \frac{\$3,362}{(1 + IRR)^t}$$

$$\$10,000 = \$3,362\ (PVIFA_{i, 4\,yr})$$

$$2.974 = (PVIFA_{i, 4\,yr})$$

We are looking for a $PVIFA_{i, 4\,yr}$ of 2.974, in the four-year row of Appendix E, which occurs in the $i = 13$ percent column. Thus, 13 percent is the internal rate of return. Because this rate is greater than the firm's required rate of return of 10 percent, the project should be accepted.

Project B involves a single future cash flow of $13,605, resulting from an initial outlay of $10,000; thus, its internal rate of return can be determined directly from the present-value table in Appendix C as follows:

$$IO = \frac{ACF_t}{(1 + IRR)^t}$$

$$\$10,000 = \frac{\$13,605}{(1 + IRR)^4}$$

$$\$10,000 = \$13,605\ (PVIF_{i, 4\,yr})$$

$$.735 = (PVIF_{i, 4\,yr})$$

This tells us that we should look for a $PVIF_{i, 4\,yr}$ of .735 in the four-year row of Appendix C, which occurs in the $i = 8$ percent column. We may therefore conclude that 8 percent is the internal rate of return. Because this rate is less than the firm's required rate of return of 10 percent, project B should be rejected.

The uneven nature of the future cash flows associated with project C necessitates the use of the trial-and-error method. The internal rate of return for project C is equal

Table 9–8
Three IRR Investment Proposal Examples

	A	B	C
Initial outlay	−$10,000	−$10,000	−$10,000
Inflow year 1	3,362	0	1,000
Inflow year 2	3,362	0	3,000
Inflow year 3	3,362	0	6,000
Inflow year 4	3,362	13,605	7,000

to the value *IRR* in the following equation:

$$\$10,000 = \frac{\$1,000}{(1 + IRR)^1} + \frac{\$3,000}{(1 + IRR)^2} + \frac{\$6,000}{(1 + IRR)^3} + \frac{\$7,000}{(1 + IRR)^4} \quad (9\text{--}4)$$

Arbitrarily selecting a discount rate of 15 percent and substituting it into equation (9–4) for *IRR* reduces the right-hand side of the equation to $11,090, as shown in Table 9–9. Therefore, because the present value of the future cash flows is larger than the initial outlay, we must raise the discount rate to find the project's internal rate of return. Substituting 20 percent for the discount rate, the right-hand side of equation (9–4) now becomes $9,763. As this is less than the initial outlay of $10,000, we must now decrease the discount rate. In other words, we know that the internal rate of return for this project is between 15 and 20 percent. Because the present value of the future flows discounted back to present at 20 percent was only $237 too low, a discount rate of 19 percent is selected. As shown in Table 9–9, a discount rate of 19 percent reduces the present value of the future inflows down to $10,009, which is approximately the same as the initial outlay. Consequently, project C's in-

Table 9–9
Computing IRR for Project C

TRY *i* = 15 PERCENT:

	NET CASH FLOWS	PRESENT VALUE FACTOR AT 15 PERCENT	PRESENT VALUE
Inflow year 1	$1,000	.870	$ 870
Inflow year 2	3,000	.756	2,268
Inflow year 3	6,000	.658	3,948
Inflow year 4	7,000	.572	4,004
Present value of inflows			$11,090
Initial outlay			−$10,000

TRY *i* = 20 PERCENT:

	NET CASH FLOWS	PRESENT VALUE FACTOR AT 20 PERCENT	PRESENT VALUE
Inflow year 1	$1,000	.833	$ 833
Inflow year 2	3,000	.694	2,082
Inflow year 3	6,000	.579	3,474
Inflow year 4	7,000	.482	3,374
Present value of inflows			$9,763
Initial outlay			−$10,000

TRY *i* = 19 PERCENT:

	NET CASH FLOWS	PRESENT VALUE FACTOR AT 19 PERCENT	PRESENT VALUE
Inflow year 1	$1,000	.840	$ 840
Inflow year 2	3,000	.706	2,118
Inflow year 3	6,000	.593	3,558
Inflow year 4	7,000	.499	3,493
Present value of inflows			$10,009
Initial outlay			−$10,000

ternal rate of return is approximately 19 percent.[6] Because the internal rate of return is greater than the firm's required rate of return of 10 percent, this investment should be accepted. ∎

Complications with IRR: Multiple Rates of Return

Although any project can have only one NPV and one PI, a single project under certain circumstances can have more than one IRR. The reason for this can be traced to the calculations involved in determining the IRR. Equation (9–3) states that the IRR is the discount rate that equates the present value of the project's future net cash flows with the project's initial outlay:

$$IO = \sum_{t=1}^{n} \frac{ACF_t}{(1 + IRR)^t} \qquad \text{(9–3)}$$

However, because equation (9–3) is a polynomial of a degree n, it has n solutions. Now if the initial outlay (IO) is the only negative cash flow and all the annual after-tax cash flows (ACF_t) are positive, then all but one of these n solutions is either a negative or imaginary number and there is no problem. But problems occur when there are sign reversals in the cash flow stream; in fact there can be as many solutions as there are sign reversals. Thus, a normal pattern with a negative initial outlay and positive annual after-tax cash flows after that (−, +, +, +, ..., +) has only one sign reversal, hence only one positive IRR. However, a pattern with more than one sign reversal can have more than one IRR. Consider, for example, the following pattern of cash flows.[7]

	AFTER-TAX CASH FLOW
Initial outlay	−$ 1,600
Inflow year 1	+$10,000
Inflow year 2	−$10,000

In this pattern of cash flows there are two sign reversals, from −$1,600 to +$10,000 and then from +$10,000 to −$10,000, so there can be as many as two positive IRRs that will make the present value of the future cash flows equal to the initial outlay. In fact, two internal rates of return solve this problem, 25 percent and 400 percent. Graphically what we are solving for is the discount rate that makes the project's NPV equal to zero; as Figure 9–1 illustrates, this occurs twice.

---

[6]If desired, the actual rate can be more precisely approximated through interpolation as follows:

DISCOUNT RATE	PRESENT VALUE		
19%	$10,009	difference $9	difference $246
IRR	10,000		
20%	9,763		

Thus, $IRR = 19\% + (\$9/246) \times 1\% = 19.04\%$

[7]This example is taken from James H. Lorie and Leonard J. Savage, "Three Problems in Rationing Capital," *Journal of Business* 28 (October 1955): 229–39.

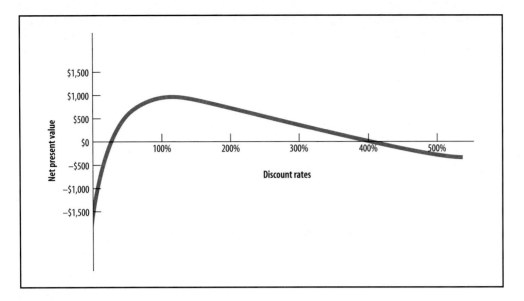

Figure 9–1
Multiple IRRs

Which solution is correct? The answer is that neither solution is valid. Although each fits the definition of IRR, neither provides any insight into the true project returns. In summary, when there is more than one sign reversal in the cash flow stream, the possibility of multiple IRRs exists, and the normal interpretation of the IRR loses its meaning.

CAPITAL RATIONING

The use of our capital-budgeting decision rules developed in this chapter implies that the size of the capital budget is determined by the availability of acceptable investment proposals. However, a firm may *place a limit on the dollar size of the capital budget.* This situation is called **capital rationing.** As we will see, an examination of capital rationing will not only enable us to deal with complexities of the real world better but will serve to demonstrate the superiority of the NPV method over the IRR method for capital budgeting as well.

capital rationing

Using the internal rate of return as the firm's decision rule, a firm accepts all projects with an internal rate of return greater than the firm's required rate of return. This rule is illustrated in Figure 9–2 (see page 274), where projects A through E would be chosen. However, when capital rationing is imposed, the dollar size of the total investment is limited by the budget constraint. In Figure 9–2 the budget constraint of $X precludes the acceptance of an attractive investment, project E. This situation obviously contradicts prior decision rules. Moreover, the solution of choosing the projects with the highest internal rate of return is complicated by the fact that some projects may be indivisible; for example, it is meaningless to recommend that half project D be acquired.

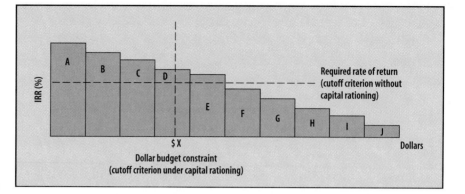

Figure 9–2
Projects Ranked by IRR

PAUSE AND REFLECT

It is always somewhat uncomfortable to deal with problems associated with capital rationing because, under capital rationing, projects with positive net present values are rejected. This is a situation that violates the firm's goal of shareholder wealth maximization. However, in the real world capital rationing does exist, and managers must deal with it. Often when firms impose capital constraints, they are recognizing that they do not have the ability to handle profitably more than a certain number or dollar value of new projects.

Rationale for Capital Rationing

We will first ask why capital rationing exists and whether it is rational. In general, three principal reasons are given for imposing a capital-rationing constraint. First, management may think market conditions are temporarily adverse. In the period surrounding the stock market crash of 1987 this reason was frequently given. At that time interest rates were high, and stock prices were depressed. Second, there may be a shortage of qualified managers to direct new projects; this can happen when projects are of a highly technical nature. Third, there may be intangible considerations. For example, management may simply fear debt, wishing to avoid interest payments at any cost. Or perhaps issuance of common stock may be limited to maintain a stable dividend policy.

Despite strong evidence that capital rationing exists in practice, the question remains as to its effect on the firm. In brief, the effect is negative, and to what degree depends on the severity of the rationing. If the rationing is minor and short-lived, the firm's share price will not suffer to any great extent. In this case capital rationing can probably be excused, although it should be noted that any capital rationing that rejects projects with positive net present values is contrary to the firm's goal of maximization of shareholders' wealth. If the capital rationing is a result of the firm's decision to limit dramatically the number of new projects or to limit total investment to internally generated funds, then this policy will eventually have a significantly negative effect on the firm's share price. For example, a lower share price will eventually result from lost competitive advantage if, owing to a decision to limit arbitrarily its capital budget, a firm fails to upgrade its products and manufacturing processes.

Capital Rationing and Project Selection

If the firm decides to impose a capital constraint on investment projects, the appropriate decision criterion is to select the set of projects with the highest net present value subject to the capital constraint. This guideline may preclude merely taking the highest-ranked projects in terms of the profitability index or the internal rate of return. If the projects shown in Figure 9–2 are divisible, the last project accepted may be only partially accepted. Although partial acceptance may be possible in some cases, the indivisibility of most capital investments prevents it. If a project is a sales outlet or a truck, it may be meaningless to purchase half a sales outlet or half a truck.

To illustrate this procedure, consider a firm with a budget constraint of $1 million and five indivisible projects available to it, as given in Table 9–10. If the highest-ranked projects were taken, projects A and B would be taken first. At that point there would not be enough funds available to take project C; hence, projects D and E would be taken. However, a higher total net present value is provided by the combination of projects A and C. Thus, projects A and C should be selected from the set of projects available. This illustrates our guideline: to select the set of projects that maximizes the firm's net present value.

Project Ranking

In the past, we have proposed that all projects with a positive net present value, a profitability index greater than 1.0, or an internal rate of return greater than the required rate of return be accepted, assuming there is no capital rationing. However, this acceptance is not always possible. In some cases, when two projects are judged acceptable by the discounted cash flow criteria, it may be necessary to select only one of them, as they are mutually exclusive. **Mutually exclusive projects** occur when a *set of investment proposals perform essentially the same task; acceptance of one will necessarily mean rejection of the others.* For example, a company considering the installation of a computer system may evaluate three or four systems, all of which may have positive net present values; however, the acceptance of one system will automatically mean rejection of the others. In general, to deal with mutually exclusive projects, we will simply rank them by means of the discounted cash flow criteria and select the project with the highest ranking. On occasion, however, problems of conflicting ranking may arise. As we will see, in general the net present value method is the preferred decision-making tool because it leads to the selection of the project that increases shareholder wealth the most.

mutually exclusive projects

PROBLEMS IN PROJECT RANKING— CAPITAL RATIONING, MUTUALLY EXCLUSIVE PROJECTS, AND PROBLEMS WITH THE IRR

OBJECTIVE 4

There are three general types of ranking problems: the size disparity problem, the time disparity problem, and the unequal lives problem. Each involves the possibility of conflict in the ranks yielded by the various discounted cash flow capital-budgeting

Table 9–10
Capital-Rationing Example of Five Indivisible Projects

PROJECT	INITIAL OUTLAY	PROFITABILITY INDEX	NET PRESENT VALUE
A	$200,000	2.4	$280,000
B	200,000	2.3	260,000
C	800,000	1.7	560,000
D	300,000	1.3	90,000
E	300,000	1.2	60,000

criteria. As noted previously, when one discounted cash flow criterion gives an accept signal, they will all give an accept signal, but they will not necessarily rank all projects in the same order. In most cases this disparity is not critical; however, for mutually exclusive projects the ranking order is important.

Size Disparity

The size disparity problem occurs when mutually exclusive projects of unequal size are examined. This problem is most easily clarified with an example.

EXAMPLE

Suppose a firm is considering two mutually exclusive projects, A and B; both with required rates of return of 10 percent. Project A involves a $200 initial outlay and cash inflow of $300 at the end of one year, whereas project B involves an initial outlay of $1,500 and a cash inflow of $1,900 at the end of one year. The net present values, profitability indexes, and internal rates of return for these projects are given in Table 9–11.

In this case, if the net present value criterion is used, project B should be accepted, whereas if the profitability index or internal rate of return criterion is used, project A should be chosen. The question now becomes: Which project is better? The answer depends on whether capital rationing exists. Without capital rationing, project B is better because it provides the largest increase in shareholders' wealth; that is, it has a larger net present value. If there is a capital constraint, the problem then focuses on what can be done with the additional $1,300 that is freed if project A is chosen (costing $200, as opposed to $1,500). If the firm can earn more on project A plus the project financed with the additional $1,300 than it can on project B, then project A and the marginal project should be accepted. In effect, we are attempting to select the set of projects that maximize the firm's NPV. Thus, if the marginal project has a net present value greater than $154.50 ($277.10 − $72.70), selecting it plus project A with a net present value of $72.70 will provide a net present value greater than $277.10, the net present value for project B. ■

In summary, whenever the size disparity problem results in conflicting rankings between mutually exclusive projects, the project with the largest net present value will be selected, provided there is no capital rationing. When capital rationing exists, the firm should select the set of projects with the largest net present value.

Table 9–11
Size Disparity Ranking Problem

PROJECT A	PROJECT B
(inflow) $300 ↓	(inflow) $1,900 ↓
1 year	1 year
$200 (outflow)	$1,500 (outflow)
NPV = $72.70	NPV = $227.10
PI = 1.36	PI = 1.15
IRR = 50%	IRR = 27%

Time Disparity

The time disparity problem and the conflicting rankings that accompany it result from the differing reinvestment assumptions made by the net present value and internal rate of return decision criteria. The NPV criterion assumes that cash flows over the life of the project can be reinvested at the required rate of return or cost of capital, whereas the IRR criterion implicitly assumes that the cash flows over the life of the project can be reinvested at the internal rate of return. Again, this problem may be illustrated through the use of an example.

EXAMPLE

Suppose a firm with a required rate of return or cost of capital of 10 percent and with no capital constraint is considering the two mutually exclusive projects illustrated in Table 9–12. The net present value and profitability index indicate that project A is the better of the two, whereas the internal rate of return indicates that project B is the better. Project B receives its cash flows earlier than project A, and the different assumptions made as to how these flows can be reinvested result in the difference in rankings. Which criterion would be followed depends on which reinvestment assumption is used. The net present value criterion is preferred in this case because it makes the most acceptable assumption for the wealth-maximizing firm. It is certainly the most conservative assumption that can be made, because the required rate of return is the lowest possible reinvestment rate. Moreover, as we have already noted, the net present value method maximizes the value of the firm and the shareholders' wealth. ■

Unequal Lives

The final ranking problem to be examined centers on the question of whether it is appropriate to compare mutually exclusive projects with different life spans.

EXAMPLE

Suppose a firm with a 10 percent required rate of return is faced with the problem of replacing an aging machine and is considering two replacement machines, one with a three-year life and one with a six-year life. The relevant cash flow information for these projects is given in Table 9–13 on page 278.

Examining the discounted cash flow criteria, we find that the net present value and profitability index criteria indicate that project B is the better project, whereas the internal rate of return criterion favors project A. This ranking inconsistency is

Table 9–12
Time Disparity Ranking Problem

	PROJECT A				PROJECT B	
$100	$200	$2,000		$650	$650	$650
↓	↓	↓		↓	↓	↓
1	2	3 years		1	2	3 years

$1,000

$$NPV = \$758.10$$
$$PI = 1.758$$
$$IRR = 35\%$$

$1,000

$$NPV = \$616.55$$
$$PI = 1.617$$
$$IRR = 43\%$$

Table 9–13
Unequal Lives Ranking Problem

PROJECT A			PROJECT B					
$500	$500	$500	$300	$300	$300	$300	$300	$300
↓	↓	↓	↓	↓	↓	↓	↓	↓
1	2	3 years	1	2	3	4	5	6 years

$1,000 $1,000

PROJECT A	PROJECT B
NPV = $234.50	NPV = $306.50
PI = 1.2435	PI = 1.306
IRR = 23%	IRR = 20%

caused by the different life spans of the projects being compared. In this case the decision is a difficult one because the projects are not comparable.

The problem of incomparability of projects with different lives arises because future profitable investment proposals may be rejected without being included in the analysis. This can easily be seen in a replacement problem such as the present example, in which two mutually exclusive machines with different lives are being considered. In this case a comparison of the net present values alone on each of these projects would be misleading. If the project with the shorter life were taken, at its termination the firm could replace the machine and receive additional benefits, whereas acceptance of the project with the longer life would exclude this possibility, a possibility that is not included in the analysis. The key question thus becomes: Does today's investment decision include all future profitable investment proposals in its analysis? If not, the projects are not comparable. In this case, if project B is taken, then the project that could have been taken after three years when project A terminates is automatically rejected without being included in the analysis. Thus, acceptance of project B not only forces rejection of project A, but also forces rejection of any replacement machine that might have been considered for years 4 through 6 without including this replacement machine in the analysis.

There are several methods to deal with this situation. The first option is to assume that the cash inflows from the shorter-lived investment will be reinvested at the required rate of return until the termination of the longer-lived asset. Although this approach is the simplest, merely calculating the net present value, it actually ignores the problem at hand—that of allowing for participation in another replacement opportunity with a positive net present value. The proper solution thus becomes the projection of reinvestment opportunities into the future—that is, making assumptions about possible future investment opportunities. Unfortunately, while the first method is too simplistic to be of any value, the second is extremely difficult, requiring extensive cash flow forecasts. The final technique for confronting the problem is to assume that reinvestment opportunities in the future will be similar to the current ones. The two most common ways of doing this are by creating a replacement chain to equalize life spans or calculating the project's equivalent annual annuity (EAA). Using a replacement chain, the present example would call for the creation of a two-chain cycle for project A; that is, we assume that project A can be replaced with a similar investment at the end of three years. Thus, project A would be viewed as two project A's occurring back to back, as illustrated in Figure 9–3. The net present value on this replacement chain is $426.50, which is comparable with project B's net present value. Therefore, project A should be accepted because the net present value of its replacement chain is greater than the net present value of project B.

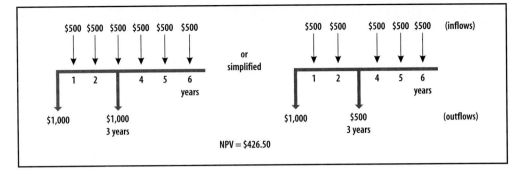

Figure 9–3
Replacement Chain Illustration: Two Project A's Back to Back

One problem with replacement chains is that, depending on the life of each project, it can be quite difficult to come up with equivalent lives. For example, if the two projects had 7- and 13-year lives, a 91-year replacement chain would be needed to establish equivalent lives. In this case it is easier to determine the project's **equivalent annual annuity (EAA).** A project's EAA is simply an *annuity cash flow that yields the same present value as the project's NPV.* To calculate a project's EAA we need only calculate a project's NPV and then divide that number by the $\text{PVIFA}_{i,n}$ to determine the dollar value of an n-year annuity that would produce the same NPV as the project. This can be done in two steps as follows:

equivalent annual annuity (EAA)

Step 1: *Calculate the project's NPV.* In Table 9–13 we determined that project A had an NPV of $234.50, whereas project B had an NPV of $306.50.

Step 2: *Calculate the EAA.* The EAA is determined by dividing each project's NPV by the $\text{PVIFA}_{i,n}$ where i is the required rate of return and n is the project's life. This determines the level of an annuity cash flow that would produce the same NPV as the project. For project A the $\text{PVIFA}_{100\%, 3\text{ yr}}$ is equal to 2.487, whereas the $\text{PVIFA}_{10\%, 6\text{ yr}}$ for project B is equal to 4.355. Dividing each project's NPV by the appropriate $\text{PVIFA}_{i,n}$ we determine the EAA for each project:

$$
\begin{aligned}
EAA_A &= NPV/PVIFA_{i,n} \\
&= \$234.50/2.487 \\
&= \$94.29 \\
EAA_B &= \$306.50/4.355 \\
&= \$70.38
\end{aligned}
$$

How do we interpret the EAA? For a project with an n-year life, it tells us the dollar value of an n-year annual annuity that would provide the same NPV as the project. Thus, for project A a three-year annuity of $94.29 given a discount rate of 10 percent would produce a net present value the same as project A's net present value, which is $234.50. We can now directly compare the equivalent annual annuities to determine which project is better. We can do this because we have found the level of annual annuity that produces an NPV equivalent to the project's NPV. Thus, because they are both annual annuities they are comparable. An easy way to see this is to use the EAAs to create infinite-life replacement chains. To do this we need only calculate the present value of an infinite stream or perpetuity of equivalent annual annuities. This is done by using the present value of an infinite annuity for-

Bad Apple for Baby

As we learned in **Axiom 10: Ethical Behavior Is Doing the Right Thing, and Ethical Dilemmas Are Everywhere in Finance,** unethical behavior eliminates trust and the public's confidence. Once this is gone, it is difficult to recover.

It's a widely held but hard to prove belief that a company gains because it is perceived as more socially responsive than its competitors. Over the years, the three major manufacturers of baby food—Gerber Products, Beech-Nut Nutrition and H. J. Heinz—had, with almost equal success, gone out of their way to build an image of respectability.

Theirs is an almost perfect zero-sum business. They know, at any given time, how many babies are being born. They all pay roughly the same price for their commodities, and their manufacturing and distribution costs are almost identical. So how does one company gain a market share edge over another especially in a stagnant or declining market?

The answer for Beech-Nut was to sell a cheaper, adulterated product. Beginning in 1977, the company began buying a chemical concoction, made up mostly of sugar and water,

and labeling it as apple juice. Sales of that product brought Beech-Nut an estimated $60 million between 1977 and 1982, while reducing material costs about $250,000 annually.

When various investigators tried to do something about it, the company stonewalled. Among other things, they shipped the bogus juice out of a plant in New York to Puerto Rico to put it beyond the jurisdiction of federal investigators, and they even offered the juice as a giveaway to reduce their stocks after they were finally forced to discontinue selling it.

In the end, the company pleaded guilty to 215 counts of introducing adulterated food into commerce and violating the Federal Food Drug and Cosmetic Act. The FDA fined Beech-Nut $2 million.

In addition, Beech-Nut's president, Neils Hoyvald, and its vice president of operations, John Lavery, were found guilty of similar charges. Each was sentenced to a year and one day in jail and fined $100,000. Both are now out on appeal on a jurisdiction technicality.

Why did they do it? The Fort Washington, Pa.-based company will

not comment. But perhaps some portion of motive can be inferred from a report Hoyvald wrote to Nestle, the company that had acquired Beech-Nut in the midst of this coverup. "It is our feeling that we can report safely now that the apple juice recall has been completed. If the recall had been effectuated in early June [when the FDA had first ordered it], over 700,000 cases in inventory would have been affected, due to our many delays, we were only faced with having to destroy 20,000 cases."

One thing is clear: Two executives of a company with an excellent reputation breached a trust and did their company harm.

Since 1987, when the case was brought to a close, Beech-Nut's share of the overall baby food market has fallen from 19.1% to 15.8%. So what was gained in the past has been lost in the present, and perhaps for the future as well.

Source: Stephen Kindel, "Bad Apple for Baby," *Financial World*, June 27, 1989, 48.

mula—that is, simply dividing the equivalent annual annuity by the appropriate discount rate. In this case we find:

$$NPV\infty,_A = \$94.29/.10$$
$$= \$942.90$$
$$NPV\infty,_B = \$70.38/.10$$
$$= \$703.80$$

Here we have calculated the present value of an infinite-life replacement chain. Because the EAA method provides the same results as the infinite-life replacement chain, it really doesn't matter which method you prefer to use. ∎

ETHICS IN CAPITAL BUDGETING

Although it may not seem obvious, ethics has a role in capital budgeting. Beech-Nut provides an example of how these rules have been violated in the past and what the consequences can be. No doubt this project appeared to have a positive net present value associated with it, but in fact, it cost Beech-Nut tremendously. The Ethics in Financial Management article, "Bad Apple for Baby" tells what occurred.

BACK TO THE FOUNDATIONS

Ethics and ethical considerations continually crop up when capital-budgeting decisions are being made. This brings us back to **Axiom 10: Ethical Behavior Is Doing the Right Thing, and Ethical Dilemmas Are Everywhere in Finance.** As the Ethics in Financial Management article, "Bad Apple for Baby" points out, the most damaging event a business can experience is a loss of the public's confidence in the business's ethical standards. In making capital-budgeting decisions we must be aware of this, and that ethical behavior is doing the right thing and is the right thing to do.

A GLANCE AT ACTUAL CAPITAL-BUDGETING PRACTICES

During the past 40 years, the popularity of each of the capital-budgeting methods has shifted rather dramatically. In the 1950s and 1960s, the payback period method dominated capital budgeting; but through the 1970s and 1980s, the internal rate of return and the net present value techniques slowly gained in popularity until they are today used by virtually all major corporations in decision making. Table 9–14 provides the results of a 1992 survey of the 100 largest Fortune 500 firms, showing the popularity of the internal rate of return and net present value methods.

Interestingly, although most firms use the NPV and IRR as their primary techniques, most firms also use the payback period as a secondary decision-making method for capital budgeting. In a sense, they are using the payback period to control for risk. The logic behind this is that, because the payback period dramatically emphasizes early cash flows, which are presumably more certain—that is, have less

Table 9–14
Survey of Capital-Budgeting Practices of the 100 Largest Fortune 500 Industrial Firms

INVESTMENT EVALUATION METHODS USED:	PERCENT OF FIRMS		
	A PRIMARY METHOD	A SECONDARY METHOD	TOTAL USING THIS METHOD
Payback period	24%	59%	83%
Internal rate of return	88%	11%	99%
Net present value	63%	22%	85%
Profitability index	15%	18%	33%

Source: Harold Bierman, Jr., "Capital Budgeting in 1992: A Survey," *Financial Management* (Autumn 1993): 24.

Table 9–15
Project Size and Decision-Making Authority

PROJECT SIZE	TYPICAL BOUNDARIES	PRIMARY DECISION SITE
Very small	Up to $100,000	Plant
Small	$100,000 to $1 million	Division
Medium	$1 million to $10 million	Corporate investment committee
Large	Over $10 million	CEO & board

Source: Marc Ross, "Capital Budgeting Practices of Twelve Large Manufacturers," *Financial Management,* 15 (Winter 1986), pp. 15–22.

risk—than cash flows occurring later in a project's life, managers believe its use will lead to projects with more certain cash flows.

A reliance on the payback period came out even more dramatically in a study of the capital-budgeting practices of 12 large manufacturing firms.[8] Information for this study was gathered from interviews over one to three days in addition to an examination of the records of about 400 projects. This study revealed several points of interest. First, firms were typically found to categorize capital investments as mandatory (regulations and contracts, capitalized maintenance, replacement of antiquated equipment, product quality) or discretionary (expanded markets, new businesses, cost cutting), with the decision-making process being different for mandatory and discretionary projects. Second, it was found that the decision-making process was different for projects of differing size. In fact, approval authority tended to rest in different locations, depending on the size of the project. Table 9–15 provides the typical levels of approval authority.

The study also showed that while the discounted cash flow methods are used at most firms, the simple payback criterion was the measure relied on primarily in one-third of the firms examined. The use of the payback period seemed to be even more common for smaller projects, with firms severely simplifying the discounted cash flow analysis or relying primarily on the payback period. Thus, although discounted cash flow decision-making techniques have become more widely accepted, their use depends to an extent on the size of the project and where within the firm the decision is being made.

SUMMARY

OBJECTIVE 1
OBJECTIVE 2

The process of capital budgeting involves decision making with respect to investment in fixed assets. Before a profitable project can be adopted, it must be identified or found. Unfortunately, coming up with ideas for new products, for ways to improve existing products, or for ways to make existing products more profitable is extremely difficult. In general, the best source of ideas for these new, potentially profitable products is from within the firm. We examine four commonly used criteria for determining the acceptance or rejection of capital-budgeting proposals. The first method, the payback period, does not incorporate the time value of money into its calculations. However, the net present value, profitability index, and internal rate of

---

[8]Marc Ross, "Capital Budgeting Practices of Twelve Large Manufacturers," *Financial Management,* 15 (Winter 1986), pp. 15–22.

return do account for the time value of money. These methods are summarized in Table 9–16 on page 284.

This chapter introduces several complications into the capital-budgeting process. First, we examine capital rationing and the problems it can create by imposing a limit on the dollar size of the capital budget. Although capital rationing does not, in general, lead to the goal of maximization of shareholders' wealth, it does exist in practice. We also discuss problems associated with the evaluation of mutually exclusive projects. Mutually exclusive projects occur when a set of investment proposals perform essentially the same task. In general, to deal with mutually exclusive projects, we rank them by means of the discounted cash flow criteria and select the project with the highest ranking. Conflicting rankings may arise because of the size disparity problem, the time disparity problem, and unequal lives. The problem of incomparability of projects with different life spans is not simply a result of the different life spans; rather, it arises because future profitable investment proposals may be rejected without being included in the analysis. Replacement chains and equivalent annual annuities are presented as possible solutions to this problem. Ethics and ethical decisions continuously crop up in capital budgeting. Just as with all other areas of finance, violating ethical considerations results in a loss of public confidence which can have a significant negative effect on shareholder wealth. Over the past forty years the discounted capital-budgeting techniques have continued to gain in popularity and today dominate in the decision-making process.

OBJECTIVE 3
OBJECTIVE 4
OBJECTIVE 5
OBJECTIVE 6

KEY TERMS

Benefit-Cost Ratio (see Profitability Index), 265

Capital Budgeting, 260

Capital Rationing, 273

Equivalent Annual Annuity (EAA), 279

Internal Rate of Return (IRR), 266

Mutually Exclusive Projects, 275

Net Present Value (NPV), 263

Payback Period, 261

Profitability Index (PI or Benefit-Cost Ratio), 265

Table 9–16
Capital-Budgeting Criteria

1. Payback period = number of years required to recapture the initial investment

Accept if payback ≤ maximum acceptable payback period
Reject if payback > maximum acceptable payback period

Advantages:
- Uses cash flows.
- Is easy to calculate and understand.
- May be used as rough screening device.

Disadvantages:
- Ignores the time value of money.
- Ignores cash flows occurring after the payback period.
- Selection of the maximum acceptable payback period is arbitrary.

2. Net present value = present value of the annual cash flows after taxes less the investment's initial outlay

$$NPV = \sum_{t=1}^{n} \frac{ACF_t}{(1 + k)^t} - IO$$

where ACF_t = the annual after-tax cash flow in time period t (this can take on either positive or negative values)

k = the appropriate discount rate; that is, the required rate of return or the cost of capital

IO = the initial cash outlay

n = the project's expected life

Accept if $NPV \geq 0.0$
Reject if $NPV < 0.0$

Advantages:
- Uses cash flows.
- Recognizes the time value of money.
- Is consistent with the firm goal of shareholder wealth maximization.

Disadvantages:
- Requires detailed long-term forecasts of the incremental benefits and costs.

3. Profitability index = the ratio of the present value of the future net cash flows to the initial outlay

$$PI = \frac{\sum_{t=1}^{n} \frac{ACF_t}{(1 + k)^t}}{IO}$$

Accept if $PI \geq 1.0$
Reject if $PI < 1.0$

Advantages:
- Uses cash flows.
- Recognizes the time value of money.
- Is consistent with the firm goal of shareholder wealth maximization.

Disadvantages:
- Requires detailed long-term forecasts of the incremental benefits and costs.

4. Internal rate of return = the discount rate that equates the present value of the project's future net cash flows with the project's initial outlay

$$IO = \sum_{t=1}^{n} \frac{ACF_t}{(1 + IRR)^t}$$

where IRR = the project's internal rate of return

Accept if $IRR \geq$ required rate of return
Reject if $IRR <$ required rate of return

Advantages:	Disadvantages:
• Uses cash flows. • Recognizes the time value of money. • Is, in general, consistent with the firm goal of shareholder wealth maximization.	• Requires detailed long-term forecasts of the incremental benefits and costs. • Can involve tedious calculations. • Possibility of multiple IRRs.

STUDY QUESTIONS

9-1. Why is the capital-budgeting decision such an important process? Why are capital-budgeting errors so costly?

9-2. What are the criticisms of the use of the payback period as a capital-budgeting technique? What are its advantages? Why is it so frequently used?

9-3. In some countries, expropriation of foreign investments is a common practice. If you were considering an investment in one of those countries, would the use of the payback period criterion seem more reasonable than it otherwise might? Why?

9-4. Briefly compare and contrast the NPV, PI, and IRR criteria. What are the advantages and disadvantages of using each of these methods?

9-5. What are mutually exclusive projects? Why might the existence of mutually exclusive projects cause problems in the implementation of the discounted cash flow capital-budgeting criteria?

9-6. What are common reasons for capital rationing? Is capital rationing rational?

9-7. How should managers compare two mutually exclusive projects of unequal size? Would your approach change if capital rationing existed?

9-8. What causes the time disparity ranking problem? What reinvestment rate assumptions are associated with the net present value and internal rate of return capital-budgeting criteria?

9-9. When might two mutually exclusive projects having unequal lives be incomparable? How should managers deal with this problem?

SELF-TEST PROBLEMS

ST-1. You are considering a project that will require an initial outlay of $54,200. This project has an expected life of five years and will generate after-tax cash flows to the company as a whole of $20,608 at the end of each year over its five-year life. In addition to the $20,608 cash flow from operations during the fifth and final year,

there will be an additional cash inflow of $13,200 at the end of the fifth year asso-
ciated with the salvage value of the machine, making the cash flow in year 5 equal
to $33,808. Thus, the cash flows associated with this project look like this:

	CASH FLOW
Initial outlay	−$54,200
Inflow year 1	20,608
Inflow year 2	20,608
Inflow year 3	20,608
Inflow year 4	20,608
Inflow year 5	33,808

Given a required rate of return of 15 percent, calculate the following:
   a. Payback period
   b. Net present value
   c. Profitability index
   d. Internal rate of return
Should this project be accepted?

STUDY PROBLEMS

9-1. (*IRR Calculation*) Determine the internal rate of return on the following
projects:
   a. An initial outlay of $10,000 resulting in a single cash flow of $17,182 after 8
years
   b. An initial outlay of $10,000 resulting in a single cash flow of $48,077 after 10
years
   c. An initial outlay of $10,000 resulting in a single cash flow of $114,943 after
20 years
   d. An initial outlay of $10,000 resulting in a single cash flow of $13,680 after 3
years

9-2. (*IRR Calculation*) Determine the internal rate of return on the following
projects:
   a. An initial outlay of $10,000 resulting in a cash flow of $1,993 at the end
of each year for the next 10 years
   b. An initial outlay of $10,000 resulting in a cash flow of $2,054 at the end of
each
year for the next 20 years
   c. An initial outlay of $10,000 resulting in a cash flow of $1,193 at the end
of each year for the next 12 years
   d. An initial outlay of $10,000 resulting in a cash flow of $2,843 at the end of
each year for the next 5 years

9-3. (*IRR Calculation*) Determine the internal rate of return to the nearest percent
on the following projects:
   a. An initial outlay of $10,000 resulting in a cash flow of $2,000 at the end of
year 1, $5,000 at the end of year 2, and $8,000 at the end of year 3
   b. An initial outlay of $10,000 resulting in a cash flow of $8,000 at the end of
year 1, $5,000 at the end of year 2, and $2,000 at the end of year 3
   c. An initial outlay of $10,000 resulting in a cash flow of $2,000 at the end of
years 1 through 5 and $5,000 at the end of year 6

9-4. (*NPV, PI, and IRR Calculations*) Fijisawa, Inc., is considering a major expansion of its product line and has estimated the following cash flows associated with such an expansion. The initial outlay associated with the expansion would be $1,950,000 and the project would generate incremental after-tax cash flows of $450,000 per year for six years. The appropriate required rate of return is 9 percent.

    a. Calculate the net present value.
    b. Calculate the profitability index.
    c. Calculate the internal rate of return.
    d. Should this project be accepted?

9-5. (*Payback period, Net Present Value, Profitability Index, and Internal Rate of Return Calculations*) You are considering a project with an initial cash outlay of $80,000 and expected after-tax cash flows of $20,000 at the end of each year for six years. The required rate of return for this project is 10 percent.

    a. What is the project's payback period?
    b. What is the project's NPV?
    c. What is the project's PI?
    d. What is the project's IRR?

9-6. (*Net Present Value, Profitability Index, and Internal Rate of Return Calculations*) You are considering two independent projects, project A and project B. The initial cash outlay associated with project A is $50,000 and the initial cash outlay associated with project B is $70,000. The required rate of return on both projects is 12 percent. The expected annual after-tax cash inflows from each project are as follows:

	PROJECT A	PROJECT B
Initial outlay	−$50,000	−$70,000
Inflow year 1	12,000	13,000
Inflow year 2	12,000	13,000
Inflow year 3	12,000	13,000
Inflow year 4	12,000	13,000
Inflow year 5	12,000	13,000
Inflow year 6	12,000	13,000

Calculate the NPV, PI, and IRR for each project and indicate if the project should be accepted.

9-7. (*Payback Period Calculations*) You are considering three independent projects, project A, project B, and project C. Given the following cash flow information, calculate the payback period for each.

	PROJECT A	PROJECT B	PROJECT C
Initial outlay	−$1,000	−$10,000	−$5,000
Inflow year 1	600	5,000	1,000
Inflow year 2	300	3,000	1,000
Inflow year 3	200	3,000	2,000
Inflow year 4	100	3,000	2,000
Inflow year 5	500	3,000	2,000

If you require a three-year payback before an investment can be accepted, which project(s) would be accepted?

9-8. (*NPV with Varying Required Rates of Return*) Dowling Sportswear is considering building a new factory to produce aluminum baseball bats. This project would require an initial cash outlay of $5,000,000 and will generate annual after-tax cash inflows of $1,000,000 per year for eight years. Calculate the project's NPV given:

a. A required rate of return of 9 percent
b. A required rate of return of 11 percent
c. A required rate of return of 13 percent
d. A required rate of return of 15 percent

9-9. (*Internal Rate of Return Calculations*) Given the following cash flows, determine the internal rate of return for the three independent projects A, B, and C.

	PROJECT A	PROJECT B	PROJECT C
Initial outlay	−$50,000	−$100,000	−$450,000
Cash inflows			
Year 1	$10,000	$25,000	$200,000
Year 2	15,000	25,000	200,000
Year 3	20,000	25,000	200,000
Year 4	25,000	25,000	—
Year 5	30,000	25,000	—

9-10. (*NPV with Varying Required Rates of Return*) Big Steve's, makers of swizzle sticks, is considering the purchase of a new plastic stamping machine. This investment requires an initial outlay of $100,000 and will generate after-tax cash inflows of $18,000 per year for 10 years. For each of the listed required rates of return, determine the project's net present value.

a. The required rate of return is 10 percent.
b. The required rate of return is 15 percent.
c. Would the project be accepted under part (a) or (b)?
d. What is the project's internal rate of return?

9-11. (*Size Disparity Problem*) The D. Dorner Farms Corporation is considering purchasing one of two fertilizer-herbicides for the upcoming year. The more expensive of the two is better and will produce a higher yield. Assume these projects are mutually exclusive and that the required rate of return is 10 percent. Given the following after-tax net cash flows:

	PROJECT A	PROJECT B
Initial outlay	−$500	−$5,000
Inflow year 1	700	6,000

a. Calculate the net present value of each project.
b. Calculate the profitability index of each project.
c. Calculate the internal rate of return of each project.
d. If there is no capital-rationing constraint, which project should be selected? If there is a capital-rationing constraint, how should the decision be made?

9-12. (*Time Disparity Problem*) The State Spartan Corporation is considering two mutually exclusive projects. The cash flows associated with those projects are as follows:

	PROJECT A	PROJECT B
Initial outlay	−$50,000	−$50,000
Inflow year 1	15,625	0
Inflow year 2	15,625	0
Inflow year 3	15,625	0
Inflow year 4	15,625	0
Inflow year 5	15,625	100,000

The required rate of return on these projects is 10 percent.
  a. What is each project's payback period?
  b. What is each project's net present value?
  c. What is each project's internal rate of return?
  d. What has caused the ranking conflict?
  e. Which project should be accepted? Why?

9-13. (*Unequal Lives Problem*) The B. T. Knight Corporation is considering two mutually exclusive pieces of machinery that perform the same task. The two alternatives available provide the following set of after-tax net cash flows:

	EQUIPMENT A	EQUIPMENT B
Initial outflow	−$20,000	−$20,000
Inflow year 1	12,590	6,625
Inflow year 2	12,590	6,625
Inflow year 3	12,590	6,625
Inflow year 4		6,625
Inflow year 5		6,625
Inflow year 6		6,625
Inflow year 7		6,625
Inflow year 8		6,625
Inflow year 9		6,625

Equipment A has an expected life of three years, whereas equipment B has an expected life of nine years. Assume a required rate of return of 15 percent.
  a. Calculate each project's payback period.
  b. Calculate each project's net present value.
  c. Calculate each project's internal rate of return.
  d. Are these projects comparable?
  e. Compare these projects using replacement chains and EAA. Which project should be selected? Support your recommendation.

9-14. (*Equivalent Annual Annuity*) The Andrzejewski Corporation is considering two mutually exclusive projects, one with a three-year life and one with a seven-year life. The after-tax cash flows from the two projects are as follows:

	PROJECT A	PROJECT B
Initial outlay	−$50,000	−$50,000
Inflow year 1	20,000	36,000
Inflow year 2	20,000	36,000
Inflow year 3	20,000	36,000
Inflow year 4	20,000	
Inflow year 5	20,000	
Inflow year 6	20,000	
Inflow year 7	20,000	

a. Assuming a 10 percent required rate of return on both projects, calculate each project's EAA. Which project should be selected?

b. Calculate the present value of an infinite-life replacement chain for each project.

9-15. (*Capital Rationing*) The Cowboy Hat Company of Stillwater, Okla., is considering seven capital investment proposals, for which the funds available are limited to a maximum of $12 million. The projects are independent and have the following costs and profitability indexes associated with them:

PROJECT	COST	PROFITABILITY INDEX
A	$4,000,000	1.18
B	3,000,000	1.08
C	5,000,000	1.33
D	6,000,000	1.31
E	4,000,000	1.19
F	6,000,000	1.20
G	4,000,000	1.18

a. Under strict capital rationing, which projects should be selected?

b. What problems are there with capital rationing?

COMPREHENSIVE PROBLEM

Your first assignment in your new position as assistant financial analyst at Caledonia Products is to evaluate two new capital-budgeting proposals. Since this is your first assignment, you have been asked not only to provide a recommendation, but also to respond to a number of questions aimed at judging your understanding of the capital-budgeting process. This is a standard procedure for all new financial analysts at Caledonia, and will serve to determine whether you are moved directly into the capital-budgeting analysis department or are provided with remedial training. The memorandum you received outlining your assignment follows.

TO: The New Financial Analysts
FROM: Mr. V. Morrison, CEO, Caledonia Products
RE: Capital-Budgeting Analysis

Provide an evaluation of two proposed projects, both with five-year expected lives and identical initial outlays of $110,000. Both of these projects involve additions to Caledonia's highly successful Avalon product line, and as a result, the required rate of return on both projects has been established at 12 percent. The expected after-tax cash flows from each project are as follows:

	PROJECT A	PROJECT B
Initial outlay	−$110,000	−$110,000
Inflow year 1	20,000	40,000
Inflow year 2	30,000	40,000
Inflow year 3	40,000	40,000
Inflow year 4	50,000	40,000
Inflow year 5	70,000	40,000

In evaluating these projects, please respond to the following questions:

a. Why is the capital-budgeting process so important?

b. Why is it difficult to find exceptionally profitable projects?

c. What is the payback period on each project? If Caledonia imposes a three-year maximum acceptable payback period, which of these projects should be accepted?

d. What are the criticisms of the payback period?

e. Determine the net present value for each of these projects. Should they be accepted?

f. Describe the logic behind the net present value.

g. Determine the profitability index for each of these projects. Should they be accepted?

h. Would you expect the net present value and profitability index methods to give consistent accept/reject decisions? Why or why not?

i. What would happen to the net present value and profitability index for each project if the required rate of return increased? If the required rate of return decreased?

j. Determine the internal rate of return for each project. Should they be accepted?

k. How does a change in the required rate of return affect the project's internal rate of return?

l. What reinvestment rate assumptions are implicitly made by the net present value and internal rate of return methods? Which one is better?

You have *also* been asked for your views on three unrelated sets of projects. Each set of projects involves two mutually exclusive projects. These projects follow.

m. Caledonia is considering two investments with one-year lives. The more expensive of the two is the better and will produce more savings. Assume these projects are mutually exclusive and that the required rate of return is 10 percent. Given the following after-tax net cash flows:

	PROJECT A	PROJECT B
Initial outlay	−$195,000	−$1,200,000
Inflow year 1	240,000	1,650,000

1. Calculate the net present value.
2. Calculate the profitability index.
3. Calculate the internal rate of return.
4. If there is no capital-rationing constraint, which project should be selected? If there is a capital-rationing constraint, how should the decision be made?

n. Caledonia is considering two additional mutually exclusive projects. The cash flows associated with these projects are as follows:

	PROJECT A	PROJECT B
Initial outlay	−$10,000	−$100,000
Inflow year 1	32,000	0
Inflow year 2	32,000	0
Inflow year 3	32,000	0
Inflow year 4	32,000	0
Inflow year 5	32,000	200,000

The required rate of return on these projects is 11 percent.
  1. What is each project's payback period?
  2. What is each project's net present value?
  3. What is each project's internal rate of return?
  4. What has caused the ranking conflict?
  5. Which project should be accepted? Why?

o. The final two mutually exclusive projects that Caledonia is considering involves mutually exclusive pieces of machinery that perform the same task. The two alternatives available provide the following set of after-tax net cash flows:

	EQUIPMENT A	EQUIPMENT B
Initial outlay	−$100,000	−$100,000
Inflow year 1	65,000	32,500
Inflow year 2	65,000	32,500
Inflow year 3	65,000	32,500
Inflow year 4		32,500
Inflow year 5		32,500
Inflow year 6		32,500
Inflow year 7		32,500
Inflow year 8		32,500
Inflow year 9		32,500

Equipment A has an expected life of three years, whereas equipment B has an expected life of nine years. Assume a required rate of return of 14 percent.
  1. Calculate each project's payback period.
  2. Calculate each project's net present value.
  3. Calculate each project's internal rate of return.
  4. Are these projects comparable?
  5. Compare these projects using replacement chains and EAAs. Which project should be selected? Support your recommendation.

SS–1.

a. Payback period $= \dfrac{\$54,200}{\$20,608} = 2.630$ years

b. $NPV = \displaystyle\sum_{t=1}^{n} \dfrac{ACF_t}{(1 + k)^t} - IO$

$\quad = \displaystyle\sum_{t=1}^{4} \dfrac{\$20,608}{(1 + .15)^t} + \dfrac{\$33,808}{(1 + .15)^5} - \$54,200$

$\quad = \$20,608(2.855) + \$33,808(.497) - \$54,200$

$\quad = \$58,836 + \$16,803 - \$54,200$

$\quad = \$21,439$

c. $PI = \dfrac{\displaystyle\sum_{t=1}^{n} \dfrac{ACF_t}{(1 + k)^t}}{IO}$

$\quad = \dfrac{\$75,639}{\$54,200}$

$\quad = 1.396$

d. $IO = \displaystyle\sum_{t=1}^{n} \dfrac{ACF_t}{(1 + IRR)^t}$

$\$54,200 = \$20,608\,(PVIFA_{IRR\%,\,4\,yr}) + \$33,808\,(PVIF_{IRR\%,\,5\,yr})$

Try 29 percent:

$\$54,200 = \$20,608(2.203) + \$33,808(.280)$

$\quad\quad\quad = \$45,399 + 9,466$

$\quad\quad\quad = \$54,865$

Try 30 percent:

$\$45,200 = \$20,608(2.166) + \$33,808(.269)$

$\quad\quad\quad = \$44,637 + 9,094$

$\quad\quad\quad = \$53,731$

Thus, the IRR is just below 30 percent and the project should be accepted, because the NPV is positive, the PI is greater than 1.0, and the IRR is greater than the required rate of return of 15 percent.

Cash Flows and Other Topics in Capital Budgeting

Guidelines for Capital Budgeting • Measuring a Project's Benefits and Costs • Risk and the Investment Decision • Incorporating Risk into Capital Budgeting • Examining a Project's Risk through Simulation

LEARNING OBJECTIVES

After reading this chapter you should be able to

1. Identify guidelines by which we measure cash flows.
2. Explain how a project's benefits and costs—that is, its incremental after-tax cash flows—are calculated.
3. Explain what the appropriate measure of risk is for capital-budgeting purposes.
4. Determine the acceptability of a new project using the risk-adjusted discount method of adjusting for risk.
5. Explain the use of simulation for imitating the performance of a project under evaluation.

I n 1994, the Ford Motor Company introduced the Ford Windstar to its lineup of cars, trucks, and minivans. In the introduction to the previous chapter we talked of the importance of this $1.5 billion investment by Ford that was targeted directly at Chrysler's Caravan/Voyager, which has been dominating the minivan market since its beginnings. While this capital-budgeting decision may, on the surface, seem like a relatively simple decision, the forecasting of the expected cash flows associated with the Windstar were, in fact, quite complicated.

To begin with, Ford was introducing a product that competes directly with some of its own products, the Ford Aerostar and the Mercury Villager. Thus, some of the sales of the Windstar would be cannibalizing sales of other Ford products. In addition, Chrysler was in the process of a major redesign of their Caravan/Voyager product line—the first major redesign since its introduction. Given that fact, Ford may have its hands full trying to increase its market share in the minivan market above its current level.

From Ford's point of view, increasing the market share may not be the objective; simply preventing Ford from losing markets share may be all that Ford is looking for from the Windstar. In fact, in many very competitive markets, the evolution and introduction of new products may serve more to preserve market share than to expand it. Certainly, that's the case in the computer market, where Dell, Compaq, and IBM are introducing upgraded models that continually render current models obsolete.

Does competing with yourself just to maintain market share make sense, or is it negative thinking that should be avoided? The answer to this deals with how we estimate a project's future cash flows. In this chapter, we will try to gain an understanding of what a relevant cash flow is. We will evaluate projects relative to their base case—that is, what will happen if the project is not carried out. In the case of the Ford Windstar, we could ask what would have happened to the Ford Aerostar and Mercury Villager sales that were expected to be captured by the Windstar if the Windstar were not introduced? Would they have been lost to a new generation of the Caravan/Voyager if the Windstar were not on the market? It is questions like these, all leading us to an understanding of what are and are not relevant cash flows, that will be addressed in this chapter. Not only will we try to understand the risks Ford faced in making this decision, not knowing exactly how Chrysler and GM would respond, but we will try to understand how our capital-budgeting criterion might be modified to deal with this risk.

WHAT'S AHEAD

This chapter continues our discussion of decision-making rules for deciding when to invest in new projects. First, we will examine what is a relevant cash flow and how to calculate the relevant cash flow. We then turn our attention to the problem of capital budgeting under uncertainty. In discussing capital-budgeting techniques in the preceding chapter, we implicitly assumed the level of risk associated with each investment proposal was the same. In this chapter we lift that assumption and examine various ways in which risk can be incorporated into the capital-budgeting decision.

OBJECTIVE 1 | GUIDELINES FOR CAPITAL BUDGETING

To evaluate investment proposals, we must first set guidelines by which we measure the value of each proposal.

Use Cash Flows Rather Than Accounting Profits

We will use cash flows, not accounting profits, as our measurement tool. The firm receives and is able to reinvest cash flows, whereas accounting profits are shown when they are earned rather than when the money is actually in hand. Unfortunately, a firm's accounting profits and cash flows may not be timed to occur together. For example, capital expenses, such as vehicles and plant and equipment, are depreciated over several years, with their annual depreciation subtracted from profits. Cash flows correctly reflect the timing of benefits and costs—that is, when the money is received, when it can be reinvested, and when it must be paid out.

BACK TO THE FOUNDATIONS

If we are to make intelligent capital-budgeting decisions, we must accurately measure the timing of the benefits and costs, that is, when we receive money and when it leaves our hands. **Axiom 3: Cash—Not Profits—Is King** speaks directly to this. Remember, it is cash inflows that can be reinvested and cash outflows that involve paying out money.

Think Incrementally

Unfortunately, calculating cash flows from a project may not be enough. Decision makers must ask, *What new cash flows will the company as a whole receive if the company takes on a given project?* What if the company does not take on the project? Interestingly, we may find that not all cash flows a firm expects from an investment proposal are incremental in nature. In measuring cash flows, however, the trick is to think incrementally. In doing so, we will see that only **incremental after-tax cash flows** matter. As such, our guiding rule in deciding if a cash flow is incremental will be to look at the company with, versus without, the new product. As you will see in the upcoming sections, this may be easier said than done.

incremental after-tax cash flows

In order to measure the true effects of our decisions, we will analyze the benefits and costs of projects on an incremental basis, which relates directly to **Axiom 4: Incremental Cash Flows—It's Only What Changes That Counts.** In effect, we will ask ourselves what the cash flows will be if the project is taken on versus what they will be if the project is not taken on.

Beware of Cash Flows Diverted from Existing Products

Assume for a moment that we are managers of a firm considering a new product line that might compete with one of our existing products and possibly reduce its sales. In determining the cash flows associated with the proposed project, we should consider only the incremental sales brought to the company as a whole. New-product sales achieved at the cost of losing sales of other products in our line are not considered a benefit of adopting the new product. For example, when General Foods' Post Cereal Division introduced its Dino Pebbles in 1991, the product competed directly with the company's Fruity Pebbles. (In fact, the two were the same product with an addition to the former of dinosaur-shaped marshmallows.) Post meant to target the market niche held by Kellogg's Marshmallow Krispies, but there was no question that sales recorded by Dino Pebbles bit into—literally cannibalized—Post's existing product line.

Remember that we are only interested in the sales dollars to the firm if the project were accepted, as opposed to what the sales dollars would be if the project were rejected. Just moving sales from one product line to a new product line does not bring anything new into the company, but if sales are captured from our competitors or if sales that would have been lost to new competing products are retained, then these are relevant incremental cash flows. In each case these are the incremental cash flows to the firm—looking at the firm as a whole, with the new product versus without the new product.

Look for Incidental or Synergistic Effects

Although in some cases a new project may take sales away from a firm's current projects, in other cases a new effort may actually bring new sales to the existing line. For example, in September 1991 USAir introduced service to Sioux City, Iowa. The new routes connecting this addition to the USAir system not only brought about new ticket sales on those routes, but also fed passengers to connecting routes. If managers were to look at only the revenue from the ticket sales on the Sioux City routes, they would miss the incremental cash flow to USAir as a whole that results from taking on the new route. This is called a synergistic effect. The cash flow comes from any USAir flight that would not have occurred if service to Sioux City had not been available. The bottom line: Any cash flow to any part of the company that may result from the decision at hand must be considered when making that decision.

Work in Working-Capital Requirements

Many times a new project will involve additional investment in working capital. This may take the form of new inventory to stock a sales outlet, additional investment in accounts receivable resulting from additional credit sales, or increased investment in cash to operate cash registers, and more. Working-capital requirements are considered a cash flow even though they do not leave the company. How can investment in inventory be considered a cash outflow when the goods are still in the store? Because the firm does not have access to the inventory's cash value, the firm cannot use the money for other investments. Generally, working-capital requirements are tied up over the life of the project. When the project terminates there is usually an offsetting cash inflow as the working capital is recovered.

Consider Incremental Expenses

Just as cash inflows from a new project are measured on an incremental basis, expenses should also be measured on an incremental basis. For example, if introducing a new product line necessitates training the sales staff, the after-tax cash flow associated with the training program must be considered a cash outflow and charged against the project. If accepting a new project dictates that a production facility be reengineered, the after-tax cash flows associated with that capital investment should be charged against the project. Again, any incremental after-tax cash flow affecting the company as a whole is a relevant cash flow, whether it is flowing in or flowing out.

Remember That Sunk Costs Are Not Incremental Cash Flows

Only cash flows that are affected by the decision making at the moment are relevant in capital budgeting. The manager asks two questions: (1) Will this cash flow occur if the project is accepted? (2) Will this cash flow occur if the project is rejected? Yes to the first question and no to the second equals an incremental cash flow. For example, let's assume you are considering introducing a new taste treat called Puddin' in a Shoe. You would like to do some test-marketing before production. If you are considering the decision to test-market and have not yet done so, the costs associated with the test-marketing are relevant cash flows. Conversely, if you have already test-marketed, the cash flows involved in test-marketing are no longer relevant in project evaluation. It's a matter of timing. Regardless of what you might decide about future production, the cash flows allocated to marketing have already occurred. Cash flows that have already taken place are often referred to as "sunk costs" because they have been sunk into the project and cannot be undone. As a rule, any cash flows that are not affected by the accept/reject criterion should not be included in capital-budgeting analysis.

Account for Opportunity Costs

Now we will focus on the cash flows that are lost because a given project consumes scarce resources that would have produced cash flows if that project had been rejected. This is the opportunity cost of doing business. For example, a product may use valuable floor space in a production facility. Although the cash flow is not obvious, the real question remains: What else could be done with this space? The space could have been rented out, or another product could have been stored there. The key point is that opportunity-cost cash flows should reflect net cash flows that would have been received if the project under consideration were rejected. Again, we are analyzing the cash flows to the company as a whole, with or without the project.

Decide If Overhead Costs Are Truly Incremental Cash Flows

Although we certainly want to include any incremental cash flows resulting in changes from overhead expenses such as utilities and salaries, we also want to make sure that these are truly incremental cash flows. Many times, overhead expenses—heat, light, rent—would occur whether a given project were accepted or rejected. There is often not a single specific project to which these expenses can be allocated. Thus, the question is not whether the project benefits from overhead items but whether the overhead costs are incremental cash flows associated with the project—and relevant to capital budgeting.

Ignore Interest Payments and Financing Flows

In evaluating new projects and determining cash flows, we must separate the investment decision from the financing decision. Interest payments and other financing cash flows that might result from raising funds to finance a project should not be considered incremental cash flows. If accepting a project means we have to raise new funds by issuing bonds, the interest charges associated with raising funds are not a relevant cash outflow. When we discount the incremental cash flows back to the present at the required rate of return, we are implicitly accounting for the cost of raising funds to finance the new project. In essence, the required rate of return reflects the cost of the funds needed to support the project. Managers first determine the desirability of the project and then determine how best to finance it.

MEASURING A PROJECT'S BENEFITS AND COSTS

OBJECTIVE 2

In measuring cash flows, we will be interested only in the incremental, or differential, after-tax cash flows that can be attributed to the proposal being evaluated. That is, we will focus our attention on the difference in the firm's after-tax cash flows with versus without the project. The worth of our decision depends on the accuracy of our cash flow estimates. For this reason, we first examined the question of what cash flows are relevant. Now we will see that, in general, a project's cash flows will fall into one of three categories: (1) the initial outlay, (2) the differential flows over the project's life, and (3) the terminal cash flow.

Initial Outlay

The **initial outlay** involves the *immediate cash outflow necessary to purchase the asset and put it in operating order*. This amount includes the cost of installing the asset (the asset's purchase price plus any expenses associated with shipping or installation) and any nonexpense cash outlays, such as increased working-capital requirements. If we are considering a new sales outlet, there might be additional cash flows associated with investment in working capital in the form of increased inventory and cash necessary to operate the sales outlet. Although these cash flows are not included in the cost of the asset or even expensed on the books, they must be included in our analysis. The after-tax cost of expense items incurred as a result of new investment must also be included as cash outflow—for example, any training expenses or special engineering expenses that would not have been incurred otherwise. Finally, if the investment decision is a replacement decision, the cash inflow associated with the selling price of the old asset, in addition to any tax effects resulting from its sale, must be included.

initial outlay

Determining the initial outlay is a complex matter. Table 10–1 on page 300 summarizes some of the more common calculations involved in determining the initial outlay. This list is by no means exhaustive, but it should help simplify the calculations involved in the example that follows.

PAUSE AND REFLECT

At this point we should realize that the incremental nature of the cash flow is of great importance. In many cases if the project is not accepted, then "status quo" for the firm will simply not continue. In calculating incremental cash flows, we must be realistic in estimating what the cash flows to the company would be if the new project is not accepted. The Financial Management in Practice article "Using the Right Base Case" deals with precisely this question.

1. Installed cost of asset
2. Additional nonexpense outlays incurred (for example, working-capital investments)
3. Additional expenses on an after-tax basis (for example, training expenses)
4. In a replacement decision, the after-tax cash flow associated with the sale of the old machine

Tax Effects—Sale of Old Machine

Potentially one of the most confusing initial outlay calculations is for a replacement project involving the incremental tax payment associated with the sale of an old machine. There are three possible tax situations dealing with the sale of an old asset:

1. The old asset is sold for a price above the depreciated value. Here the difference between the old machine's selling price and its depreciated value is considered a taxable gain and taxed at the marginal corporate tax rate. If, for example, the old machine was originally purchased for $15,000, had a book value of $10,000, and was sold for $17,000, assuming the firm's marginal corporate tax rate is 34 percent, the taxes due from the gain would be ($17,000 − $10,000) × (.34), or $2,380.

2. The old asset is sold for its depreciated value. In this case no taxes result, as there is neither a gain nor a loss in the asset's sale.

3. The old asset is sold for less than its depreciated value. In this case the difference between the depreciated book value and the salvage value of the asset is a taxable loss and may be used to offset ordinary income and thus results in tax savings. For example, if the depreciated book value of the asset is $10,000 and it is sold for $7,000, we have a $3,000 loss. Assuming the firm's marginal corporate tax rate is 34 percent, the cash inflow from tax savings is ($10,000 − $7,000) × (.34), or $1,020.

EXAMPLE

To clarify the calculation of the initial outlay, consider an example of a company in the 34-percent marginal tax bracket. This company is considering the purchase of a new machine for $30,000 to be used in manufacturing. It has a five-year life (according to IRS guidelines) and will be depreciated using the *simplified straight-line method.* (This depreciation method will be explained later.) The useful life of this new machine is also five years. The new machine will replace an existing machine, originally purchased for $30,000 ten years ago, which currently has five more years of expected useful life. The existing machine will generate $2,000 of depreciation expenses for each of the next five years, at which time the book value will be equal to zero. To put the new machine in running order, it is necessary to pay after tax shipping charges of $2,000 and installation charges of $3,000. Because the new machine will work faster than the old one, it will require an increase in goods-in-process inventory of $5,000. Finally, the old machine can be sold to a scrap dealer for $15,000.

Using the Right Base Case

Finance theory assumes that a project will be evaluated against its base case, that is, what will happen if the project is not carried out. Managers tend to explore fully the implications of adopting the project but usually spend less time considering the likely outcome of not making the investment. Yet unless the base case is realistic, the incremental cash flows—the difference between the "with" and the "without" scenarios—will mislead.

Often companies implicitly assume that the base case is simply a continuation of the status quo, but this assumption ignores market trends and competitor behavior. It also neglects the impact of changes the company might make anyway, like improving operations management.

Using the wrong base case is typical of product launches in which the new product will likely erode the market for the company's existing product line. Take Apple Computer's introduction of the Macintosh SE. The new PC had obvious implications for sales of earlier generation Macintoshes. To analyze the incremental cash flows arising from the new product, Apple would have needed to count the lost contribution from sales of its existing products as a cost of the launch.

Wrongly applied, however, this approach would equate the "without" case to the status quo: It would assume that without the SE, sales of existing Macintoshes would continue at their current level. In the competitive PC market, however, nothing stands still. Competitors like IBM would likely innovate and take market share away from the earlier generation Macintoshes—which a more realistic base case would have reflected. Sales of existing products would decline even in the base case.

Consider investments in the marketing of existing brands through promotions, media budgets, and the like. They are often sold as if they were likely to lead to ever-increasing market share. But competitors will also be promoting their brands, and market shares across the board still have to add up to 100 percent. Still, such an investment is not necessarily wasted. It may just need a more realistic justification: Although the investment is unlikely to increase sales above existing levels, it may prevent sales from falling. Marketers who like positive thinking may not like this defensive argument, but it is the only argument that makes economic sense in a mature market.

In situations like this, when the investment is needed just to maintain market share, the returns may be high in comparison with the base case, but the company's reported profits may still go down. Senior managers are naturally puzzled at apparently netting only 5 percent return.[*] Without the investment, however, the profit picture would have looked even worse, especially in the long term.

[*]Joseph L. Bower, *Managing the Resource Allocation Process* (Boston: Harvard Business School Press, 1986), 13.

Source: Reprinted by permission of *Harvard Business Review*. An excerpt from "Must Finance and Strategy Clash?" by Patrick Barwise, Paul R. Marsh, and Robin Wensley, *Harvard Business Review* (September–October, 1989). Copyright © 1989 by The President and Fellows of Harvard College. All rights reserved.

The installed cost of the new machine would be the $30,000 cost plus $2,000 shipping and $3,000 installation fees, for a total of $35,000. Additional outflows are associated with taxes incurred on the sale of the old machine and with increased investment in inventory. Although the old machine has a book value of $10,000, it could be sold for $15,000. The increased taxes from gain on the sale will be equal to the selling price of the old machine less its depreciated book value times the firm's marginal tax rate, or ($15,000 − $10,000) × (.34), or $1,700. The increase in goods-in-process inventory of $5,000 must also be considered part of the initial outlay, with an offsetting inflow of $5,000 corresponding to the recapture of this inventory occurring at the termination of the project. In effect, the firm invests $5,000 in inventory now, resulting in an initial cash outlay, and liquidates this inventory in five years, resulting in a cash inflow at the end of the project. The total outlays associated with the new machine are $35,000 for its installed cost, $1,700 in increased taxes, and $5,000 in investment in inventory, for a total of $41,700. This is somewhat offset by the sale of the old machine for $15,000. Thus, the net initial outlay associated with this project is $26,700. These calculations are summarized in Table 10–2. ▪

Differential Flows over Project's Life

The differential cash flows over the project's life involve the incremental after-tax cash flows resulting from increased revenues, plus labor or material savings and reductions in selling expenses. Overhead items, such as utilities, heat, light, and executive salaries, are generally not affected. However, any resultant change in any of these categories must be included. Any increase in interest payments incurred as a result of issuing bonds to finance the project should *not* be included, as the costs of funds needed to support the project are implicitly accounted for by discounting the project back to the present using the required rate of return. Finally, an adjustment for the incremental change in taxes should be made, including any increase in taxes that might result from increased profits or any tax savings from an increase in depreciation expenses. Increased depreciation expenses affect tax-related cash flows by reducing taxable income and thus lowering taxes. Table 10–3 lists some of the factors that might be involved in determining a project's differential cash flows. However, before looking at an example, we will briefly examine the calculation of depreciation.

PAUSE AND REFLECT

Depreciation plays an important role in the calculation of cash flows. Although it is not a cash flow item, it lowers profits, which in turn lowers taxes. For students developing a foundation in corporate finance, it is the concept of depreciation, not the calculation of it, that is important. The reason the calculation of depreciation is deemphasized is that it is extremely complicated, and its calculation changes every few years as Congress enacts new tax laws. Through all this bear in mind that although depreciation is not a cash flow item, it does affect cash flows by lowering the level of profits on which taxes are calculated.

Table 10–2
Calculation of Initial Outlay for Example Problem

Outflows:		
Purchase price	$30,000	
Shipping fee	2,000	
Installation fee	3,000	
Installed cost of machine		$35,000
Increased taxes from sale of old machine		
($15,000 − $10,000)(.34)		1,700
Increased investment in inventory		5,000
Total outflows		$41,700
Inflows:		
Salvage value of old machine		15,000
Net initial outlay		$26,700

Depreciation, the Tax Reform Act of 1986, and the Revenue Reconciliation Act of 1993

The Revenue Reconciliation Act of 1993 largely left intact the modified version of the Accelerated Cost Recovery System introduced in the Tax Reform Act of 1986. Although this was examined in Chapter 1, a review is appropriate here. This modified version of the old Accelerated Cost Recovery System (ACRS) is used for most depreciable tangible property placed in service beginning in 1987. Under this method, the life of the asset is determined according to the asset's class life, which is assigned by the IRS; for example, most computer equipment has a five-year asset life. It also allows for only a half year's deduction in the first year and a half year's deduction in the year after the recovery period. The asset is then depreciated using the 200 percent declining balance method or an optional straight-line method.

Depreciation Calculation—Simplified Straight-Line Depreciation Method

Depreciation is calculated using a simplified straight-line method. This simplified process ignores the half-year convention that allows only a half-year's deduction in the year the project is placed in service and a half-year's deduction in the first year after the recovery period. By ignoring the half-year convention and assuming a zero salvage value, we are able to calculate annual depreciation by taking the project's initial depreciable value and dividing by its depreciable life as follows:

$$\text{annual depreciation using the simplified straight-line method} = \frac{\text{initial depreciable value}}{\text{depreciable life}}$$

The initial depreciable value is equal to the cost of the asset plus any expenses necessary to get the new asset into operating order.

This is not how depreciation would actually be calculated. The reason we have simplified the calculation is to allow you to focus directly on what should and should not be included in the cash flow calculations. Moreover, because the tax laws change rather frequently, we are more interested in recognizing the tax implications of depreciation than in understanding the specific depreciation provisions of the current tax laws.

Our concern with depreciation is to highlight its importance in generating cash flow estimates and to indicate that the financial manager must be aware of the current tax provisions when evaluating capital-budgeting proposals.

Differential Flows over Project's Life

Extending the earlier example, which illustrated the calculations of the initial outlay, suppose that purchasing the machine is expected to reduce salaries by $10,000 per year and fringe benefits by $1,000 annually, because it will take only one part-time

Table 10–4
Calculation of Depreciation for Example Problem Using Simplified Straight-Line Method

New machine purchase price	$30,000
Shipping fee	2,000
Installation fee	3,000
Total depreciable value	$35,000
Divided by depreciable life	$35,000/5
Equals: Annual depreciation	$7,000

person to operate, whereas the old machine requires two part-time operators. In addition, the cost of defects will fall from $8,000 per year to $3,000. However, maintenance expenses will increase by $4,000 annually. The annual depreciation on this new machine is $7,000 per year, whereas the depreciation expense lost with the sale of the old machine is $2,000 for each of the next five years. Annual depreciation on the new machine is calculated using the simplified straight-line method just described—that is, taking the cost of the new machine plus any expenses necessary to put it in operating order and dividing by its depreciable life. For the new machine these calculations are reflected in Table 10–4.

Because the depreciation on the old machine is $2,000 per year, the increased depreciation will be from $2,000 per year to $7,000 per year, or an increase of $5,000 per year. Although this increase in depreciation expenses is not a cash flow item, it does affect cash flows by reducing book profits, which in turn reduces taxes.

To determine the annual net cash flows resulting from the acceptance of this project, the net savings *before* taxes using both book profit and cash flows must be found. The additional taxes are then calculated based on the before-tax book profit. For this example, Table 10–5 shows the determination of the differential cash flows on an after-tax basis. Thus, the differential cash flows over the project's life are $9,620.

Terminal Cash Flow

The calculation of the terminal cash flow is in general quite a bit simpler than the preceding two calculations. Flows associated with the project's termination generally include the salvage value of the project plus or minus any taxable gains or losses associated with its sales.

Table 10–5
Calculation of Differential Cash Flows for Example Problem

		BOOK PROFIT		CASH FLOW
Savings:	Reduced salary	$10,000		$10,000
	Reduced fringe benefits	1,000		1,000
	Reduced defects ($8,000 − $3,000)	5,000		5,000
Costs:	Increased maintenance expense	−4,000		−4,000
	Increased depreciation expense			
	($7,000 − $2,000)	−5,000		
Net savings before taxes		$ 7,000		$12,000
Taxes (34%)		−2,380	→	−2,380
Net cash flow after taxes				$ 9,620

Table 10–6
Summary of Calculation of Terminal Cash Flow on After-Tax Basis

1. The after-tax salvage value of the project
2. Cash outlays associated with the project's termination
3. Recapture of nonexpense outlays that occurred at the project's initiation (for example, working-capital investments)

Under the current tax laws, in most cases there will be tax payments associated with the salvage value at termination. This is because the current laws allow all projects to be depreciated to zero, and if a project has a book value of zero at termination and a positive salvage value, then that salvage value will be taxed. The tax effects associated with the salvage value of the project at termination are determined exactly like the tax effects on the sale of the old machine associated with the initial outlay. The salvage value proceeds are compared with the depreciated value, in this case zero, to determine the tax.

In addition to the salvage value, there may be a cash outlay associated with the project termination. For example, at the close of a strip-mining operation, the mine must be refilled in an ecologically acceptable manner. Finally, any working-capital outlay required at the initiation of the project—for example, increased inventory needed for the operation of a new plant—will be recaptured at the termination of the project. In effect the increased inventory required by the project can be liquidated when the project expires. Table 10–6 provides a sample list of some of the factors that might affect a project's terminal cash flow.

Extending the example to termination, the depreciated book value and salvage value of the machine at the termination date will be equal to zero. However, there will be a cash flow associated with the recapture of the initial outlay of work-in-process inventory of $5,000. This flow is generated from the liquidation of the $5,000 investment in work-in-process inventory. Therefore, the expected total terminal cash flow equals $5,000.

If we were to construct a cash flow diagram from this example (Figure 10–1), it would have an initial outlay of $26,700, differential cash flows during years 1 through 5 of $9,620, and an additional terminal cash flow at the end of year 5 of $5,000. The cash flow occurring in year 5 is $14,620: the sum of the differential cash flow in year 5 of $9,620 and the terminal cash flow of $5,000.

Cash flow diagrams similar to Figure 10–1 will be used through the remainder of this chapter with arrows above the time line indicating cash inflows and arrows below the time line denoting outflows.

Although the preceding calculations for determining the incremental after-tax net cash flows do not cover all possible cash flows, they do set up a framework in which almost any situation can be handled. To simplify this framework and to provide an overview of the calculations, Table 10–7 on page 306 summarizes the rules in Tables 10–1, 10–3, and 10–6.

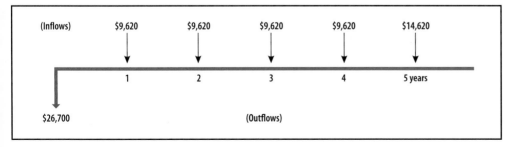

Figure 10–1
Example Cash Flow Diagram

Table 10–7
Summary of Calculation of Incremental After-Tax Cash Flows

A. Initial Outlay
  1. Installed cost of asset
  2. Additional nonexpense outlays incurred (for example, working-capital investment)
  3. Additional expenses, on an after-tax basis (for example, training expenses)
  4. In a replacement decision, the after-tax flow associated with the sale of the old machine
B. Differential Cash Flows over the Project's Life
  1. Added revenue offset by increased expenses
  2. Labor and material savings
  3. Increase in overhead incurred
  4. Tax savings from an increase in depreciation if the new project is accepted.
  5. Do not include interest expenses if the project is financed by issuing debt, as this is accounted for in the required rate of return.
C. Terminal Cash Flow
  1. The after-tax salvage value of the project
  2. Cash outlays associated with the project's termination
  3. Recapture of nonexpense outlays that occurred at the project's initiation (for example, working-capital investments)

Discounted Cash Flow Criteria: Comprehensive Example

To demonstrate further the computations for the discounted cash flow techniques, assume that a manufacturing firm in the electronic components field is in the 34 percent marginal tax bracket with a 15 percent required rate of return or cost of capital. Management is considering replacing a hand-operated assembly machine with a fully automated assembly operation. Given the information in Table 10–8, we want to determine the cash flows associated with this proposal, the project's net present value, profitability index, and internal rate of return, and then to apply the appropriate decision criteria.

First, the initial outlay is determined to be $44,680, as reflected in Table 10–9. Next, the differential cash flows over the project's life are calculated as shown in Table 10–10 on page 308, yielding an estimated $15,008 cash flow per annum. In making these computations, the incremental change in depreciation was determined by first calculating the original depreciable value, which is equal to the cost of the new machine ($50,000) plus any expense charges necessary to get the new machine in operating order (shipping fee of $1,000 plus the installation fee of $5,000). This depreciable amount was then divided by five years. The annual depreciation lost with the sale of the old machine was then subtracted out ($10,000/5 = $2,000 per year for the old machine's remaining five years of life). Once the change in taxes is determined from the incremental change in book profit, it is subtracted from the net cash flow savings before taxes, yielding the $15,008 net cash flow after taxes.

Finally, the terminal cash flow associated with the project has to be determined. In this case, because the new machine is expected to have a zero salvage value, there will be no terminal cash flow. The cash flow diagram associated with this project is shown in Figure 10–2 on page 308.

The net present value for this project is calculated as follows:

$$NPV = \sum_{t=1}^{n} \frac{ACF_t}{(1 + k)^t} - IO \qquad (10\text{–}1)$$

Table 10–8

Comprehensive Capital-Budgeting Example

Existing situation:	One part-time operator—salary $12,000
	Variable overtime—$1,000 per year
	Fringe benefits—$1,000 per year
	Cost of defects—$6,000 per year
	Current book value—$10,000
	Expected life—15 years
	Expected salvage value—$0
	Age—10 years
	Annual depreciation—$2,000 per year
	Current salvage value of old machine—$12,000
	Annual maintenance—$0
	Marginal tax rate—34 percent
	Required rate of return—15 percent
Proposed situation:	Fully automated operation—no operator necessary
	Cost of machine—$50,000
	After tax shipping fee—$1,000
	After tax installation costs—$5,000
	Expected economic life—5 years
	Depreciation method—simplified straight-line over 5 years
	Salvage value after 5 years—$0
	Annual maintenance—$1,000
	Cost of defects—$1,000

$$= \sum_{t=1}^{5} \frac{\$15,008}{(1 + .15)^t} - \$44,680$$

$$= \$15,008(PVIFA_{15\%,\ 5\ yr}) - \$44,680$$

$$= \$15,008(3.352) - \$44,680$$

$$= \$50,307 - \$44,680$$

$$= \$5,627$$

Because its net present value is greater than zero, the project should be accepted. The profitability index, which gives a measure of relative desirability of a project, is calculated as follows:

Table 10–9

Calculation of Initial Outlay for Comprehensive Example

Outflows:	Cost of new machine	$50,000
	Shipping fee	1,000
	Installation cost	5,000
	Increased taxes on sale of old machine	680
	($12,000 − $10,000)(.34)	
Inflows:	Salvage value—old machine	−12,000
	Net initial outlay	$44,680

Table 10–10

Calculation of Differential Cash Flows for Comprehensive Example

		Book Profit	Cash Flow
Savings:	Reduced salary	$12,000	$12,000
	Reduced variable overtime	1,000	1,000
	Reduced fringe benefits	1,000	1,000
	Reduced defects ($6,000 − $1,000)	5,000	5,000
Costs:	Increased maintenance expense	−1,000	−1,000
	Increased depreciation expense ($11,200 − $2,000)	−9,200	
	Net savings before taxes	$ 8,800	$18,000
	Taxes (34%)	−2,992 →	−2,992
	Net cash flow after taxes		$15,008

$$PI = \frac{\sum_{t=1}^{n} \frac{ACF_t}{(1+k)^t}}{IO} \qquad (10\text{--}2)$$

$$= \frac{\$50,307}{\$44,680}$$

$$= 1.13$$

Because the project's PI is greater than 1, the project should be accepted.

The internal rate of return can be determined directly from the PVIFA table, as follows:

$$IO = \sum_{t=1}^{n} \frac{ACF_t}{(1+IRR)^t} \qquad (10\text{--}3)$$

$$\$44,680 = \$15,008 \, (PVIFA_{i,\,5\text{ yr}})$$

$$2.977 = PVIFA_{i,\,5\text{ yr}}$$

Looking for the value of the $PVIFA_{i,\,5\text{ yr}}$ in the 5-year row of the table in Appendix E, we find that the value of 2.977 occurs between the 20 percent column (2.991) and the 21 percent column (2.926). As a result, the project's internal rate of return is between 20 percent and 21 percent, and the project should be accepted.

Applying the decision criteria to this example, we find that each of them indicates the project should be accepted, as the net present value is positive, the profitability index is greater than 1.0, and the internal rate of return is greater than the firm's required rate of return of 15 percent.

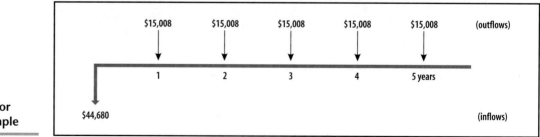

Figure 10–2

Cash Flow Diagram for Comprehensive Example

Up to this point we have ignored risk in capital budgeting; that is, we have discounted expected cash flows back to the present and ignored any uncertainty that there might be surrounding that estimate. In reality the future cash flows associated with the introduction of a new sales outlet or a new product are estimates of what is expected to happen in the future, not necessarily what will happen in the future. For example, when the Ford Motor Company made its decision to introduce the Edsel, you can bet that the expected cash flows it based its decision on were nothing like the cash flows it realized. The cash flows we have discounted back to the present have only been our best estimate of the expected future cash flows. A cash flow diagram based on the possible outcomes of an investment proposal rather than the expected values of these outcomes appears in Figure 10–3.

In this section we will assume that under conditions of risk we do not know beforehand what cash flows will actually result from a new project. However, we do have expectations concerning the possible outcomes and are able to assign probabilities to these outcomes. Stated another way, although we do not know what the cash flows resulting from the acceptance of a new project will be, we can formulate the probability distributions from which the flows will be drawn.

As we learned in Chapter 8, risk occurs when there is some question as to the future outcome of an event. We will now proceed with an examination of the logic behind this definition. Again, risk is defined as the potential variability in future cash flows.

The fact that variability reflects risk can easily be shown with a coin toss. Consider the possibility of flipping a coin—heads you win, tails you lose—for 25 cents with your finance professor. Most likely you would be willing to take on this game, because the utility gained from winning 25 cents is about equal to the utility lost if you lose 25 cents. Conversely, if the flip is for $1,000, you may be willing to play only if you are offered more than $1,000 if you win—say, you win $1,500 if it turns out heads and lose $1,000 if it turns out tails. In each case the probability of winning and losing is the same; that is, there is an equal chance that the coin will land heads or tails. In each case, however, the width of the dispersion changes, which is why the second coin toss is more risky and why you may not take the chance unless the payoffs are altered. The key here is the fact that only the dispersion changes; the probability of winning or losing is the same in each case. Thus, the potential variability in future returns reflects the risk.

The final question to be addressed is whether individuals are in fact risk averse. Although we do see people gambling where the odds of winning are against them, it should be stressed that monetary return is not the only possible return they may re-

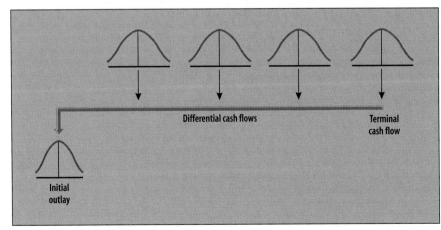

Figure 10–3
Example Cash Flow Diagram Based on Possible Outcome

ceive. A nonmonetary, psychological reward accrues to some gamblers, allowing them to fantasize that they will break the bank, never have to work again, and retire to some offshore island. Actually, the heart of the question is how wealth is measured. Although gamblers appear to be acting as risk seekers, they actually attach an additional nonmonetary return to gambling; the risk is in effect its own reward. When this is considered, their actions seem totally rational. It should also be noted that although gamblers appear to be pursuing risk on one hand, on the other hand they are eliminating some risk by purchasing insurance and diversifying their investments.

In the remainder of this chapter we assume that although future cash flows are not known with certainty, the probability distribution from which they come is known. Also, because we have illustrated that the dispersion of possible outcomes reflects risk, we are prepared to use a measure of dispersion or variability later in the chapter when we quantify risk.

In the pages that follow, remember that there are only two basic issues that we address: (1) What is risk in terms of capital-budgeting decisions, and how should it be measured? (2) How should risk be incorporated into capital-budgeting analysis?

What Measure of Risk Is Relevant in Capital Budgeting

Before we begin our discussion of how to adjust for risk, it is important to determine just what type of risk we are to adjust for. In capital budgeting, a project's risk can be looked at on three levels. First, there is the **project standing alone risk,** which is a *project's risk ignoring the fact that much of this risk will be diversified away as the project is combined with the firm's other projects and assets.* Second, we have the project's **contribution-to-firm risk,** which is the *amount of risk that the project contributes to the firm as a whole; this measure considers the fact that some of the project's risk will be diversified away as the project is combined with the firm's other projects and assets, but ignores the effects of diversification of the firm's shareholders.* Finally, there is **systematic risk,** which is the *risk of the project from the viewpoint of a well-diversified shareholder; this measure takes into account that some of a project's risk will be diversified away as the project is combined with the firm's other projects, and, in addition, some of the remaining risk will be diversified away by shareholders as they combine this stock with other stocks in their portfolios.* Graphically, this is shown in Figure 10–4.

Should we be interested in the project standing alone risk? The answer is no. Perhaps the easiest way to understand why not is to look at an example. Let's take the case of research and design projects at Johnson & Johnson. Each year Johnson & Johnson takes on hundreds of new R&D projects, knowing that they only have about a 10 percent probability of being successful. If they are successful, the profits can be enormous; if they fail, the investment is lost. If the company has only one project, and it is an R&D project, the company would have a 90 percent chance of failure. Thus, if we look at these R&D projects individually and measure their stand alone risk, we would have to judge them to be enormously risky. However, if we consider the effect of the diversification that comes about from taking on several hundred independent R&D projects a year, all with a 10 percent chance of success, we can see that these R&D projects do not add much risk to Johnson & Johnson. In short, because much of a project's risk is diversified away within the firm, the project stand alone risk is an inappropriate measure of the meaningful level of risk of a capital-budgeting project.

Should we be interested in the project's contribution-to-firm risk? Once again, at least in theory the answer is no, provided investors are well diversified and there is no chance of bankruptcy. From our earlier discussion of risk in Chapter 8 we saw that as shareholders, if we combined an individual security with other securities to form a diversified portfolio, much of the risk of the individual security would be diversified away. In short, all that affects the shareholders is the systematic risk of the project, and as such is all that is theoretically relevant for capital budgeting.

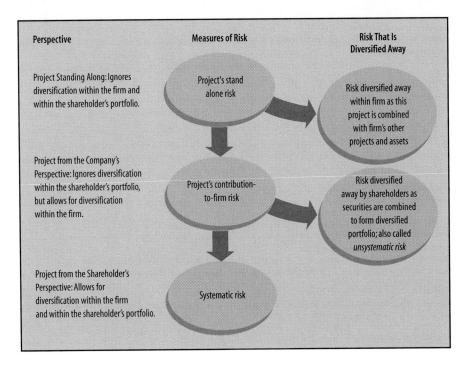

Perspective	Measures of Risk	Risk That Is Diversified Away
Project Standing Along: Ignores diversification within the firm and within the shareholder's portfolio.	Project's stand alone risk	Risk diversified away within firm as this project is combined with firm's other projects and assets
Project from the Company's Perspective: Ignores diversification within the shareholder's portfolio, but allows for diversification within the firm.	Project's contribution-to-firm risk	Risk diversified away by shareholders as securities are combined to form diversified portfolio; also called *unsystematic risk*
Project from the Shareholder's Perspective: Allows for diversification within the firm and within the shareholder's portfolio.	Systematic risk	

Figure 10–4

Looking at Three Measures of a Project's Risk

Measuring Risk for Capital-Budgeting Purposes with a Dose of Reality—Is Systematic Risk All There Is?

According to the CAPM, systematic risk is the only relevant risk for capital-budgeting purposes; however, reality complicates this somewhat. In many instances a firm will have undiversified shareholders, including owners of small corporations. Because they are not diversified, for those shareholders the relevant measure of risk is the project's contribution-to-firm risk.

The possibility of bankruptcy also affects our view of what measure of risk is relevant. As you recall in developing the CAPM, we made the assumption that bankruptcy costs were zero. Because the project's contribution-to-firm risk can affect the possibility of bankruptcy, this may be an appropriate measure of risk if there are costs associated with bankruptcy. Quite obviously, in the real world there is a cost associated with bankruptcy. First, if a firm fails, its assets, in general, cannot be sold for their true economic value. Moreover, the amount of money actually available for distribution to stockholders is further reduced by liquidation and legal fees that must be paid. Finally, the opportunity cost associated with the delays related to the legal process further reduces the funds available to the shareholder. Therefore, because costs are associated with bankruptcy, reduction of the chance of bankruptcy has a very real value associated with it.

Indirect costs of bankruptcy also affect other areas of the firm, including production, sales, and the quality and efficiency of management. For example, firms with a higher probability of bankruptcy may have a more difficult time recruiting and retaining quality managers because jobs with that firm are viewed as being less secure. Suppliers also may be less willing to sell on credit. Finally, customers may lose confidence and fear that the firm may not be around to honor the warranty or to supply spare parts for the product in the future. As a result, as the probability of bankruptcy increases, the eventual bankruptcy may become self-fulfilling as potential customers and suppliers flee. The end result is that because the project's contribution-to-firm risk affects the probability of bankruptcy for the firm, it is a relevant risk measure for capital budgeting.

Finally, problems in measuring a project's systematic risk make its implementation extremely difficult. It is much easier talking about a project's systematic risk than it is measuring it.

Given all this, what do we use? The answer is that we will give consideration to both measures. We know in theory systematic risk is correct. We also know that bankruptcy costs and undiversified shareholders violate the assumptions of the theory, which brings us back to the concept of a project's contribution-to-firm risk. Still, the concept of systematic risk holds value for capital-budgeting decisions, because that is the risk that shareholders are compensated for assuming. Therefore, we will concern ourselves with both the project's contribution-to-firm risk and the project's systematic risk, and not try to make any specific allocation of importance between the two for capital-budgeting purposes.

INCORPORATING RISK INTO CAPITAL BUDGETING

In the preceding chapter we ignored any risk differences between projects. This approach is simple but not valid; different investment projects do in fact contain different levels of risk. We will now look at the risk-adjusted discount rate, which is based on the notion that investors require higher rates of return on more risky projects.

BACK TO THE FOUNDATIONS

All the methods used to compensate for risk in capital budgeting find their roots in **Axiom 1: The Risk-Return Trade-off—We Won't Take on Additional Risk Unless We Expect to Be Compensated with Additional Return.** In fact, the risk-adjusted discount method puts this concept directly into play.

Risk-Adjusted Discount Rates

risk-adjusted discount rate

The use of **risk-adjusted discount rates** is based on the concept that investors demand higher returns for more risky projects. This is the basic principle behind **Axiom 1** and the CAPM, and this relationship between risk and return is illustrated graphically in Figure 10–5.

As we know from **Axiom 1,** the expected rate of return on any investment should include compensation for delaying consumption equal to the risk-free rate of return, plus compensation for any risk taken on. Under the risk-adjusted discount rate approach, if the risk associated with the investment is greater than the risk involved in

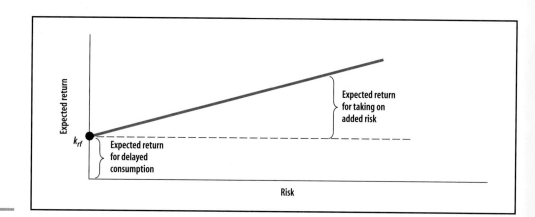

Figure 10–5
Risk-Return Relationship

a typical endeavor, the discount rate is adjusted upward to compensate for this added risk. Once the firm determines the appropriate required rate of return for a project with a given level of risk, the cash flows are discounted back to the present at the risk-adjusted discount rate. Then the normal capital-budgeting criteria are applied, except in the case of the internal rate of return. For the IRR, the hurdle rate with which the project's internal rate of return is compared now becomes the risk-adjusted discount rate. Expressed mathematically, the net present value using the risk-adjusted discount rate becomes

$$NPV = \sum_{t=1}^{n} \frac{ACF_t}{(1 + k^*)^t} - IO \qquad\qquad (10\text{--}4)$$

where ACF_t = the annual after-tax cash flow expected in time period t

IO = the initial cash outlay

k^* = the risk-adjusted discount rate

n = the project's expected life

The logic behind the risk-adjusted discount rate stems from the idea that if the level of risk in a project is different from that of the typical firm project, then management must incorporate the shareholders' probable reaction to this new endeavor into the decision-making process. If the project has more risk than a typical project, then a higher required rate of return should apply. Otherwise, marginal projects will lower the firm's share price—that is, reduce shareholders' wealth. This will occur as the market raises its required rate of return on the firm to reflect the addition of a more risky project, whereas the incremental cash flows resulting from the acceptance of the new project are not large enough to offset this change fully. By the same logic, if the project has less than normal risk, a reduction in the required rate of return is appropriate. Thus, the risk-adjusted discount method attempts to apply more stringent standards—that is, require a higher rate of return— to projects that will increase the firm's risk level. This is because these projects will lead shareholders to demand a higher required rate of return to compensate them for the higher risk level of the firm. If this adjustment is not made, the marginal projects containing above-average risk could actually lower the firm's share price.

EXAMPLE

A toy manufacturer is considering the introduction of a line of fishing equipment with an expected life of five years. In the past, this firm has been quite conservative in its investment in new products, sticking primarily to standard toys. In this context, the introduction of a line of fishing equipment is considered an abnormally risky project. Management thinks that the normal required rate of return for the firm of 10 percent is not sufficient. Instead, the minimum acceptable rate of return on this project should be 15 percent. The initial outlay would be $110,000, and the expected cash flows from this project are given below:

YEAR	EXPECTED CASH FLOW
1	$30,000
2	30,000
3	30,000
3	30,000
4	30,000
5	30,000

Discounting this annuity back to the present at 15 percent yields a present value of the future cash flows of $100,560. Because the initial outlay on this project is $110,000, the net present value becomes −$9,440, and the project should be rejected. If the normal required rate of return of 10 percent had been used as the discount rate, the project would have been accepted with a net present value of $3,730. ◼

In practice, when the risk-adjusted discount rate is used, projects are generally grouped according to purpose, or risk class; then the discount rate preassigned to that purpose or risk class is used. For example, a firm with a required rate of return of 12 percent might use the following rate-of-return categorization:

Project	Required Rate of Return
Replacement decision	12%
Modification or expansion of existing product line	15
Project unrelated to current operations	18
Research and development operations	25

The purpose of this categorization of projects is to make their evaluation easier, but it also introduces a sense of the arbitrary into the calculations that makes the evaluation less meaningful. The trade-offs involved in the classification above are obvious; time and effort are minimized, but only at the cost of precision.

Risk-Adjusted Discount Rate and Measurement of a Project's Systematic Risk

When we initially talked about systematic risk or the beta, we were talking about measuring it for the entire firm. As you recall, although we could estimate a firm's beta using historical data, we did not have complete confidence in our results. As we will see, estimating the appropriate level of systematic risk for a single project is even more fraught with difficulties. To truly understand what it is we are trying to do and the difficulties we will encounter, let us step back a bit and examine systematic risk and the risk adjustment for a project.

What we are trying to do is use the CAPM to determine the level of risk and the appropriate risk-return trade-offs for a particular project. We will then take the expected return on this project and compare it to the required return suggested by the CAPM to determine whether the project should be accepted. If the project appears to be a typical one for the firm, using the CAPM to determine the appropriate risk-return trade-offs and then judging the project against them may be a warranted approach. But if the project is not a typical project, what do we do? Historical data generally do not exist for a new project. In fact, for some capital investments—for example, a truck or a new building—historical data would not have much meaning. What we need to do is make the best of a bad situation. We either (1) fake it—that is, use historical accounting data, if available, to substitute for historical price data in estimating systematic risk—or (2) we attempt to find a substitute firm in the same industry as the capital-budgeting project and use the substitute firm's estimated systematic risk as a proxy for the project's systematic risk.

Beta Estimation Using Accounting Data

When we are dealing with a project that is identical to the firm's other projects, we need only estimate the level of systematic risk for the firm and use that estimate as

Incorporating Risk into Capital Budgeting at Merck

The risks that pharmaceutical firms face in product development are great. It takes $359 million and 10 years, on average, to bring a new drug to market. Then, once the drug has reached the market, 70 percent of the time it is unprofitable. To allow for this risk, Merck uses a simulation approach and sensitivity analysis. In this way they are able to identify key variables that affect the project's outcome.

Last year Merck and Co., Inc., invested well over $2 billion in R&D and capital expenditures combined. The company spent much of the money on risky, long-term projects that are notoriously difficult to evaluate. Indeed, the critics of modern finance would argue that such projects should not be subjected to rigorous financial analysis, because such analysis fails to

reflect the strategic value of long-term investments. Yet at Merck, it is those projects with the longest time horizon that receive the most intense and financially sophisticated analyses. In fact, Merck's financial function is active and influential with a highly quantitative, analytical orientation. The company is seldom, if ever, criticized for being shortsighted.

Why doesn't all this analysis choke off long-term investing, as critics of modern finance theory say it should? In part because Merck is a leader in building financial models of scientific and commercial processes and in using those models to improve business decisions. Rather than relying on static, single-point forecasts, Merck's models use probability distributions for numerous variables

and come up with a range of possible outcomes that both stimulate discussion and facilitate decision making.

For example, Merck's Research Planning Model, now ten years old, and its Revenue Hedging Model, now four years old, integrate economics, finance, statistics, and computer science to produce disciplined, quantitative analyses of specific elements of Merck's business. These models do not make decisions. Instead, they provide Merck executives with cogent information both about risks and returns and about financial performance for specific projects and activities.

Source: Reprinted by permission of *Harvard Business Review:* An excerpt from "Financial Engineering at Merck" by Timothy A. Luehrman, *Harvard Business Review* (January–February 1994): 93. Copyright © 1994 by The President and Fellows of Harvard College. All rights reserved.

---

a proxy for the project's risk. Unfortunately, when projects are not typical of the firm, this approach does not work. For example, when R. J. Reynolds introduces a new food through one of its food products divisions, this new product most likely carries with it a different level of systematic risk from what is typical for Reynolds as a whole.

To get a better approximation of the systematic risk level on this project, we will estimate the level of systematic risk for the food division and use that as a proxy for the project's systematic risk. Unfortunately, historical stock price data are available only for the company as a whole, and as you recall historical stock return data are generally used to estimate a firm's beta. Thus, we are forced to use accounting return data rather than historical stock return data for the division to estimate the division's systematic risk. To estimate a project's beta using accounting data we need only run a time-series regression of the division's return on assets (net income/total assets) on the market index (the S&P 500). The regression coefficient from this equation would be the project's accounting beta and would serve as an approximation for the project's true beta or measure of systematic risk. Alternatively, a multiple regression model based on accounting data could be developed to explain betas. The results of this model could then be applied to firms that are not publicly traded to estimate their betas.

How good is the accounting beta technique? It certainly is not as good as a direct calculation of the beta. In fact, the correlation between the accounting beta and the beta calculated on historical stock return data is only about 0.6; however, better luck has been experienced with multiple regression models used to predict betas. Unfortunately, in many cases there may not be any realistic alternative to the calculation of the accounting beta. Owing to the importance of adjusting for a project's risk, the accounting beta method is much preferred to doing nothing.

The Pure Play Method for Estimating a Project's Beta

pure play method

Whereas the accounting beta method attempts to directly estimate a project or division's beta, the **pure play method** attempts to identify publicly traded firms that are engaged solely in the same business as the project or division. Once the proxy or pure play firm is identified, its systematic risk is determined and then used as a proxy for the project or division's level of systematic risk. What we are doing is *looking for a publicly traded firm on the outside that looks like our project and using that firm's required rate of return to judge our project.* In doing so we are presuming that the systematic risk and the capital structure of the proxy firm are identical to those of the project.

In using the pure play method it should be noted that a firm's capital structure is reflected in its beta. When the capital structure of the proxy firm is different from that of the project's firm, some adjustment must be made for this difference. Although not a perfect approach, it does provide some insights as to the level of systematic risk a project might have.

OBJECTIVE 5

EXAMINING A PROJECT'S RISK THROUGH SIMULATION

Simulation: Explained and Illustrated

simulation

Another method for evaluating risk in the investment decision is through the use of **simulation.** The certainty equivalent and risk-adjusted discount rate approaches provided us with a single value for the risk-adjusted net present value, whereas a simulation approach gives us a probability distribution for the investment's net present value or internal rate of return. Simulation *involves the process of imitating the performance of the project under evaluation. This is done by randomly selecting observations from each of the distributions that affect the outcome of the project, combining those observations to determine the final output of the project, and continuing with this process until a representative record of the project's probable outcome is assembled.*

The easiest way to develop an understanding of the computer simulation process is to follow through an example simulation for an investment project evaluation. Suppose a chemical producer is considering an extension to its processing plant. The simulation process is portrayed in Figure 10–6. First, the probability distributions are determined for all the factors that affect the project's returns; in this case, let us assume there are nine such variables:

1. Market size
2. Selling price
3. Market growth rate

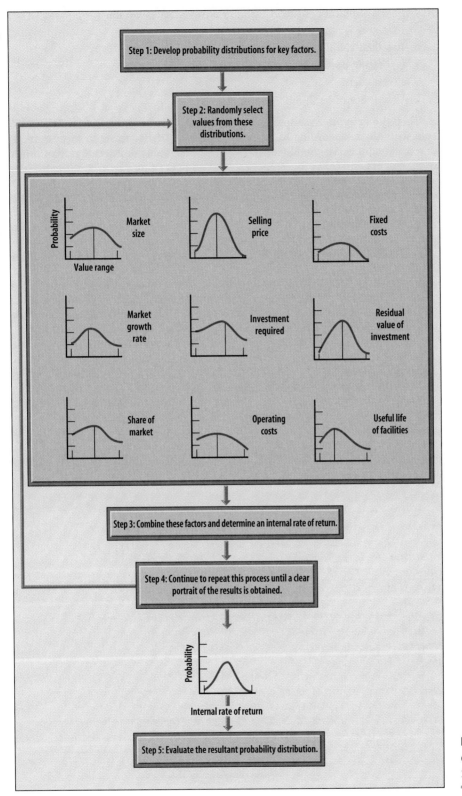

Figure 10–6
Capital-Budgeting
Simulation

4. Share of market (which results in physical sales volume)
5. Investment required
6. Residual value of investment
7. Operating costs
8. Fixed costs
9. Useful life of facilities

Then the computer randomly selects one observation from each of the probability distributions, according to its chance of actually occurring in the future. These nine observations are combined, and a net present value or internal rate of return figure is calculated. This process is repeated as many times as desired, until a representative distribution of possible future outcomes is assembled. Thus, the inputs to a simulation include all the principal factors affecting the project's profitability, and the simulation output is a probability distribution of net present values or internal rates of return for the project. The decision maker bases the decision on the full range of possible outcomes. The project is accepted if the decision maker feels that enough of the distribution lies above the normal cutoff criteria ($NPV \geq 0$, $IRR \geq$ required rate of return).

Suppose the output from the simulation of a chemical producer's project is as given in Figure 10–7. This output provides the decision maker with the probability of different outcomes occurring in addition to the range of possible outcomes. Sometimes called **scenario analysis,** this *examination identifies the range of possible outcomes under the worst, best, and most likely case.* The firm's management will examine the distribution to determine the project's level of risk and then make the appropriate adjustment.

You'll notice that although the simulation approach helps us to determine the amount of total risk a project has, it does not differentiate between systematic and unsystematic risk. Because systematic risk cannot be diversified away for free, the simulation approach does not provide a complete method of risk assessment. However, it does provide important insights as to the total risk level of a given investment project. Now we will look briefly at how the simulation approach can be used to perform sensitivity analysis.

scenario analysis

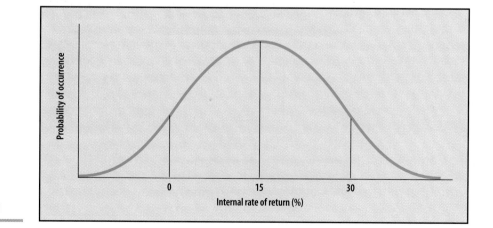

Figure 10–7
Output from Simulation

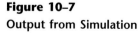

Sensitivity Analysis through Simulation Approach

Sensitivity analysis involves *determining how the distribution of possible net present values or internal rates of return for a particular project is affected by a change in one particular input variable.* This is done by changing the value of one input variable while holding all other input variables constant. The distribution of possible net present values or internal rates of return that is generated is then compared with the distribution of possible returns generated before the change was made to determine the effect of the change. For this reason sensitivity analysis is commonly called *what-if analysis.*

For example, the chemical producer that was considering a possible expansion to its plant may wish to determine the effect of a more pessimistic forecast of the anticipated market growth rate. After the more pessimistic forecast replaces the original forecast in the model, the simulation is rerun. The two outputs are then compared to determine how sensitive the results are to the revised estimate of the market growth rate.

SUMMARY

In this chapter, we examine the measurement of incremental cash flows associated with a firm's investment proposals which are used to evaluate those proposals. Relying on **Axiom 3: Cash—Not Profits—Is King,** and **Axiom 4: Incremental Cash Flows—It's Only What Changes That Counts,** we focus only on the incremental or differential after-tax cash flows attributed to the investment proposal. Care is taken to beware of cash flows diverted from existing products, look for incidental or synergistic effects, consider working capital requirements, consider incremental expenses, ignore sunk costs, account for opportunity costs, examine overhead costs carefully, and ignore interest payments and financing flows.

OBJECTIVE 1

In general, a project's cash flows fall into one of three categories: (1) the initial outlay, (2) the differential flows over the project's life, and (3) the terminal cash flow. A summary of the typical entries in each of these categories appears in Table 10–7.

OBJECTIVE 2

We also cover the problem of incorporating risk into the capital-budgeting decision. First, we explore just what type of risk to adjust for: the project's stand alone risk, the project's contribution-to-firm risk, or the project's systematic risk. In theory, systematic risk is the appropriate risk measure, but bankruptcy costs and the issue of undiversified shareholders also give weight to considering a project's contribution-to-firm risk as the appropriate risk measure. Both measures of risk are valid, and we avoid making any specific allocation of importance between the two in capital budgeting.

OBJECTIVE 3

Two commonly used methods for incorporating risk into capital budgeting are (1) risk-adjusted discount rates and (2) simulation. The risk-adjusted discount rate involves an upward adjustment of the discount rate to compensate for risk. This method is based on the concept that investors demand higher returns for riskier projects. The simulation method is used to provide information as to the location and shape of the distribution of possible outcomes. Decisions could be based directly on this method, or it could be used to determine input into either certainty equivalent or risk-adjusted discount rate method approaches.

OBJECTIVE 4
OBJECTIVE 5

KEY TERMS

STUDY QUESTIONS

10-1. Why do we focus on cash flows rather than accounting profits in making our capital-budgeting decisions? Why are we interested only in incremental cash flows rather than total cash flows?

10-2. If depreciation is not a cash flow expense, does it affect the level of cash flows from a project in any way? Why?

10-3. If a project requires additional investment in working capital, how should this be treated in calculating cash flows?

10-4. How do sunk costs affect the determination of cash flows associated with an investment proposal?

10-5. In the preceding chapter we examined the payback period capital-budgeting criterion. Often this capital-budgeting criterion is used as a risk-screening device. Explain the rationale behind its use.

10-6. The use of the risk-adjusted discount rate assumes that risk increases over time. Justify this assumption.

10-7. Explain how simulation works. What is the value in using a simulation approach?

SELF-TEST PROBLEMS

ST-1. The Scotty Gator Corporation of Meadville, Pa., maker of Scotty's electronic components, is considering replacing one of its current hand-operated assembly machines with a new fully automated machine. This replacement would mean the elimination of one employee, generating salary and benefit savings. Given the following information, determine the cash flows associated with this replacement.

Existing situation:	One full-time machine operator—salary and benefits, $25,000 per year
	Cost of maintenance—$2,000 per year
	Cost of defects—$6,000
	Original depreciable value of old machine—$50,000
	Annual depreciation—$5,000 per year
	Expected life—10 years
	Age—five years old
	Expected salvage value in five years—$0
	Current salvage value—$5,000
	Marginal tax rate—34 percent

Proposed situation:	Fully automated machine
	Cost of machine—$60,000
	After tax installation fee—$3,000
	After tax shipping fee—$3,000
	Cost of maintenance—$3,000 per year
	Cost of defects—$3,000 per year
	Expected life—five years
	Salvage value—$20,000
	Depreciation method—simplified
	straight-line method over five years

STUDY PROBLEMS

10-1. (*Capital Gains Tax*) The J. Harris Corporation is considering selling one of its old assembly machines. The machine, purchased for $30,000 five years ago, had an expected life of 10 years and an expected salvage value of zero. Assume Harris uses simplified straight-line depreciation, creating depreciation of $3,000 per year, and could sell this old machine for $35,000. Also assume a 34 percent marginal tax rate.

   a. What would be the taxes associated with this sale?

   b. If the old machine were sold for $25,000, what would be the taxes associated with this sale?

   c. If the old machine were sold for $15,000, what would be the taxes associated with this sale?

   d. If the old machine were sold for $12,000, what would be the taxes associated with this sale?

10-2. (*Cash Flow Calculations*) The Winky Corporation, maker of cow-grooming equipment, is considering replacing a hand-operated machine used in the manufacturer of grooming components with a new fully automated machine. Given the following information, determine the cash flows associated with this replacement.

Existing situation:	Two full-time machine operators—
	salaries $10,000 each per year
	Cost of maintenance—$5,000 per year
	Cost of defects—$5,000
	Original cost of old machine—$30,000
	Expected life—10 years
	Age—five years old
	Expected salvage value—$0
	Depreciation method—simplified
	straight-line over 10 years,
	$3,000 per year
	Current salvage value—$10,000
	Marginal tax rate—34 percent

Proposed situation:	Fully automated machine
	Cost of machine—$55,000
	After tax installation fee—$5,000
	Cost of maintenance—$6,000 per year
	Cost of defects—$2,000 per year
	Expected life—five years
	Salvage value—$0
	Depreciation method—simplified
	straight-line method over five years

10-3. (*Capital-Budgeting Calculation*) Given the cash flow information in problem 10-2 and a required rate of return of 15 percent, compute the following for the automated machine:

    a. Payback period

    b. Net present value

    c. Profitability index

    d. Internal rate of return

Should this project be accepted?

10-4. (*Cash Flow and New Project Analysis*) The Chung Chemical Corporation is considering the purchase of a chemical analysis machine. Although the machine being considered will not produce any increase in sales revenues, it will result in a before-tax reduction in labor costs of $35,000 per year. The machine has a purchase price of $100,000, and it would cost an additional $5,000 after tax to install this machine properly. In addition, to operate this machine properly, inventory must be increased by $5,000. This machine has an expected life of 10 years, after which it will have no salvage value. Also, assume simplified straight-line depreciation and that this machine is being depreciated down to zero, a 34 percent marginal tax rate, and a required rate of return of 15 percent.

    a. What is the initial outlay associated with this project?

    b. What are the annual after-tax cash flows associated with this project for years 1 through 9?

    c. What is the terminal cash flow in year 10 (i.e., what is the annual after-tax cash flow in year 10 plus any additional cash flows associated with termination of the project)?

    d. Should this machine be purchased?

10-5. (*Cash Flow and New Project Analysis*) Raymobile Motors is considering the purchase of a new production machine for $500,000. Although the purchase of this machine will not produce any increase in sales revenues, it will result in a before-tax reduction of labor costs by $150,000 per year. To operate this machine properly, workers would have to go through a brief training session that would cost $25,000 after tax. In addition, it would cost $5,000 after tax to install this machine properly. Also, because this machine is extremely efficient, its purchase would necessitate an increase in inventory of $30,000. This machine has an expected life of 10 years, after which it will have no salvage value. Assume simplified straight-line depreciation and that this machine is being depreciated down to zero, a 34 percent marginal tax rate, and a required rate of return of 15 percent.

    a. What is the initial outlay associated with this project?

    b. What are the annual after-tax cash flows associated with this project for years 1 through 9?

c. What is the terminal cash flow in year 10 (i.e., what is the annual after-tax cash flow in year 10 plus any additional cash flows associated with termination of the project)?

d. Should this machine be purchased?

10-6. (*Cash Flow and Capital-Budgeting Calculation*) The Jabot Cosmetics Corporation is considering replacing a 10-year-old machine that originally cost $30,000, has a current book value of $10,000 with five years of expected life left, and is being depreciated using the simplified straight-line method over its 15-year expected life down to a terminal value of zero in five years, generating depreciation of $2,000 per year. The replacement machine being considered would cost $80,000 and have a five-year expected life over which it would be depreciated using the simplified straight-line method down to zero. At termination in five years the new machine would have a salvage value of $40,000. Material efficiencies resulting from the replacement would result in savings of $30,000 per year before depreciation and taxes. Currently, the old machine could be sold for $15,000. Assuming simplified straight-line depreciation, a 34 percent marginal tax rate, and a required rate of return of 20 percent, calculate

a. The payback period

b. The net present value

c. The profitability index

d. The internal rate of return

10-7. (*Risk-Adjusted NPV*) The Hokie Corporation is considering two mutually exclusive projects. Both require an initial outlay of $10,000 and will operate for five years. Project A will produce expected cash flows of $5,000 per year for years 1 through 5, while Project B will produce expected cash flows of $6,000 per year for years 1 through 5. Because project B is the riskier of the two projects, the management of Hokie Corporation has decided to apply a required rate of return of 15 percent to its evaluation but only a 12 percent required rate of return to project A. Determine each project's risk-adjusted net present value.

10-8. (*Risk-Adjusted Discount Rates and Risk Classes*) The G. Wolfe Corporation is examining two capital-budgeting projects with five-year lives. The first, project A, is a replacement project; the second, project B, is a project unrelated to current operations. The G. Wolfe Corporation uses the risk-adjusted discount rate method and groups projects according to purpose, and then uses a required rate of return or discount rate that has been preassigned to that purpose or risk class. The expected cash flows for these projects are given below:

	PROJECT A	PROJECT B
Initial investment:	−$250,000	−$400,000
Cash inflows:		
Year 1	$ 30,000	$135,000
Year 2	40,000	135,000
Year 3	50,000	135,000
Year 4	90,000	135,000
Year 5	130,000	135,000

The purpose/risk classes and preassigned required rates of return are as follows:

PURPOSE	REQUIRED RATE OF RETURN
Replacement decision	12%
Modification or expansion of existing product line	15
Project unrelated to current operations	18
Research and development operations	20

Determine the project's risk-adjusted net present value.

COMPREHENSIVE PROBLEM

It's been two months since you took a position as an assistant financial analyst at Caledonia Products. While your boss has been pleased with your work, he is still a bit hesitant about unleashing you without supervision. Your next assignment involves both the calculation of the cash flows associated with a new investment under consideration and the evaluation of several risky projects. Given your lack of tenure at Caledonia, you have been asked not only to provide a recommendation, but also to respond to a number of questions aimed at judging your understanding of the capital-budgeting process. The memorandum you received outlining your assignment follows:

TO: The Financial Analyst

FROM: Mr. V. Morrison, CEO, Caledonia Products

RE: Cash Flow Analysis and Capital Budgeting

We are currently considering the purchase of a new fully automated machine to replace an older, manually operated one. The machine being replaced, now five years old, originally had an expected life of 10 years. It was being depreciated using the simplified straight-line method from $20,000 down to zero, thus generating $2,000 in depreciation per year, and could be sold for $25,000. The old machine took one operator, who earned $15,000 per year in salary and $2,000 per year in fringe benefits. Since the new machine is fully automated, this worker would no longer be needed. The annual costs of maintenance and defects associated with the old machine were $7,000 and $3,000, respectively. The replacement machine being considered had a purchase price of $50,000, a salvage value after five years of $10,000, and would be depreciated over five years using the simplified straight-line depreciation method down to zero. To get the automated machine in running order, there would be a $2,000 shipping fee and a $2,000 installation charge, both on an after tax basis. In addition, because the new machine would work faster than the old one, investment in raw materials and goods-in-process inventories would need to be increased by a total of $5,000. The annual costs of maintenance and defects on the new machine would be $2,000 and $4,000, respectively. The new machine also requires maintenance workers to be specially trained; fortunately, a similar machine was purchased three months ago, and at that time the maintenance workers went through the $5,000 after tax training program needed to familiarize themselves with the new equipment. Caledonia's management is uncertain whether or not to charge half of this $5,000 training fee toward the new project. Finally, to purchase the new machine, it appears the firm would have to borrow an additional $20,000 at 10 percent interest from its local bank, resulting in additional interest payments of $2,000 per year. The required rate of return on projects of this kind is 20 percent and Caledonia is in the 34 percent marginal tax bracket. Please provide a written response to the following questions:

a. Should Caledonia focus on cash flows or accounting profits in making our capital-budgeting decisions? Should we be interested in incremental cash flows, incremental profits, total cash flows, or total profits?
b. How does depreciation affect cash flows?
c. How do sunk costs affect the determination of cash flows?
d. What is the project's initial outlay?
e. What are the differential cash flows over the project's life?
f. What is the terminal cash flow?
g. Draw a cash flow diagram for this project.
h. What is its net present value?
i. What is its internal rate of return?
j. Should the project be accepted? Why or why not?
k. In capital budgeting, risk can be measured from three perspectives. What are those three measures of a project's risk?
l. According to the CAPM, which measurement of a project's risk is relevant? What complications does reality introduce into the CAPM view of risk, and what does that mean for our view of the relevant measure of a project's risk?
m. Explain how simulation works. What is the value in using a simulation approach?
n. What is sensitivity analysis and what is its purpose?

SELF–TEST SOLUTIONS

SS–1.
Step 1: First calculate the initial outlay.

Initial outlay	
Outflows:	
Cost of machine	$60,000
Installation fee	3,000
Shipping fee	3,000
Inflows:	
Salvage value—old machine	−5,000
Tax savings on sale of old machine	
($22,000 − $5,000)(.34)	−6,800
	$54,200

Step 2: Calculate the differential cash flows over the project's life.

		BOOK PROFIT	CASH FLOW
Savings:	Reduced salary	$25,000	$25,000
	Reduced defects	3,000	3,000
Costs:	Increased maintenance	−1,000	−1,000
	Increased depreciation		
	($13,200 − $5000)[a]	−8,200	
Net savings before taxes		$18,800	$27,000
Taxes (.34)		−6,392	−6,392
Annual net cash flow after taxes			$20,608

[a]Annual depreciation on the new machine is equal to the cost of the new machine ($60,000) plus any expenses necessary to get it in operating order (the shipping fee of $3,000 plus the installation fee of $3,000) divided by the depreciable life (five years).

Step 3: Calculate the terminal cash flow.

Salvage value—new machine	$20,000
Less: Taxes—recapture of depreciation ($20,000 × .34)	6,800
	$13,200

Thus, the cash flow in the final year will be equal to the annual net cash flow in that year of $20,608 plus the terminal cash flow of $13,200 for a total of $33,808.

Cost of Capital

The Cost of Capital: Key Definitions and Concepts •
Determining Individual Costs of Capital • The Weighted Average
Cost of Capital • Calculating Divisional Costs of Capital:
PepsiCo, Inc. • Using a Firm's Cost of Capital to Evaluate New
Capital Investments

T he Morristown division of Amorite Manufacturing Inc. is faced with an
investment opportunity that requires the expenditure of $75 million to
renovate a production facility that will provide after-tax savings of $25 mil-
lion per year for the next four years. Should the investment be undertaken?
When we addressed capital-budgeting problems in Chapter 9, we learned
that projects should be undertaken only if their net present value (NPV) is
positive. To calculate the NPV we must estimate both the project's cash
flows and the appropriate discount rate. In Chapter 9 we referred to the appropriate discount rate as the cost of capital, and it was always given or assumed to be known. In this chapter we learn how to estimate the appropriate discount rate or cost of capital for use in evaluating investment
opportunities like that faced by Amorite.

LEARNING OBJECTIVES

After reading this chapter you
should be able to

1. Describe the concepts underlying the firm's cost of capital
   (technically its weighted average cost of capital) and the
   purpose for its calculation.

2. Calculate the after-tax cost of
   debt, preferred stock, and
   common equity.

3. Calculate a firm's weighted
   average cost of capital.

4. Describe the procedure used
   by PepsiCo to estimate the
   cost of capital for a multiple
   division firm.

5. Use the cost of capital to evaluate new investment opportunities.

Having studied the linkage between risk and rates of return for securities (Chapter 8) and the valuation of bonds and stocks (Chapters 6 and 7), we are prepared to consider the firm's cost of capital. A firm's cost of capital serves as the linkage between the firm's financing decisions and its investment decisions. The cost of capital becomes the hurdle rate that must be achieved by an investment before it will increase shareholder wealth. The term *cost of capital* is frequently used interchangeably with the firm's required rate of return, the hurdle rate for new investments, the discount rate for evaluating a new investment, and the firm's opportunity cost of funds. Regardless of the term used, the basic concept is the same. The cost of capital is that rate which must be earned on an investment project if the project is to increase the value of the common stockholder's investment in the project.

In this chapter we will discuss the fundamental determinants of a firm's cost of capital as well as the rationale for its calculation and use. This will entail developing the logic for estimating the cost of debt capital, preferred stock, and common stock. Chapter 12 takes up consideration of the impact of the firm's financing mix on the cost of capital.

THE COST OF CAPITAL: KEY DEFINITIONS AND CONCEPTS

Investor Opportunity Costs, Required Rates of Return, and the Cost of Capital

In Chapter 9 we referred to the discount rate used in calculating NPV simply as the appropriate discount rate. In this chapter we define what we mean by this term. Specifically, the appropriate discount rate primarily reflects the **investor's required rate of return.** In Chapter 8 we defined the investor's required rate of return for a security as the *minimum rate of return necessary to attract an investor to purchase or hold a security.* This rate of return considers the investor's opportunity cost of making an investment; that is, if an investment is made, the investor must forgo the return available on the next-best investment. This forgone return is the opportunity cost of undertaking the investment and, consequently, is the investor's required rate of return.

Is the investor's required rate of return the same thing as the cost of capital? Not exactly. Two basic considerations drive a wedge between the investor's required rate of return and the cost of capital to the firm. First, there are taxes. When a firm borrows money to finance the purchase of an asset, the interest expense is deductible for federal income tax calculations. Consider a firm that borrows at 9 percent and then deducts its interest expense from its revenues before paying taxes at a rate of 34 percent. For each dollar of interest it pays, the firm reduces its taxes by $.34. Consequently, the actual cost of borrowing to the firm is only 5.94% [.09 − (.34 × .09) = .09(1 − .34) = 0.0594 = 5.94%]. The second thing that causes the firm's cost of capi-

investor's required rate of return

tal to differ from the investor's required rate of return is any *transaction costs incurred when a firm raises funds by issuing a particular type of security*, sometimes called **flotation costs**. For example, if a firm sells new shares for $25 per share but incurs transaction costs of $5 per share, then the cost of capital for the new common equity is increased. Assume that the investor's required rate of return is 15 percent for each $25 share, then .15 × $25 = $3.75 must be earned each year to satisfy the investor's required return. However, the firm has only $20 to invest, so the cost of capital (k) is calculated as the rate of return that must be earned on the $20 net proceeds, which will produce a dollar return of $3.75; that is,

$$\$20k = \$25 \times .15 = \$3.75$$

$$k = \frac{\$3.75}{\$20.00} = .1875 = 18.75\%$$

We will have more to say about both these considerations as we discuss the costs of the individual sources of capital to the firm.

Financial Policy and the Cost of Capital

A firm's **financial policy**—that is, the *policies regarding the sources of finances it plans to use and the particular mix (proportions) in which they will be used*, governs its use of debt and equity financing. The particular mixture of debt and equity that the firm utilizes can impact the firm's cost of capital. However, in this chapter we will assume that the firm maintains a fixed financial policy that is reflected in a fixed debt-equity ratio. Determination of the target mix of debt and equity financing is the subject of Chapter 12.

The firm's overall cost of capital will reflect the combined costs of all the sources of financing used by the firm. We will refer to this overall cost of capital as the firm's **weighted average cost of capital.** The weighted average cost of capital is *the average of the after-tax costs of each of the sources of capital used by a firm to finance a project where the weights reflect the proportion of total financing raised from each source.* Consequently, the weighted average cost of capital is the rate of return that the firm must earn on its investments so that it can compensate both its creditors and stockholders with their individual required rates of return. Let's now turn to a discussion of how the costs of debt and equity can be estimated.

flotation costs

financial policy

weighted average cost of capital

DETERMINING INDIVIDUAL COSTS OF CAPITAL

OBJECTIVE 2

In order to attract new investors, companies have created a wide variety of financing instruments or securities. In this chapter we will stick to three basic types of financing instruments: debt, preferred stock, and common stock. In calculating the respective cost of financing from each of these types of financing instruments, we estimate the investor's required rate of return properly adjusted for any transaction or flotation costs associated with each funding source. In addition, since we will be discounting after-tax cash flows, we should adjust our cost of capital for any influence of corporate taxes. In summary, the cost of a particular source of capital is equal to the investor's required rate of return after adjusting for the effects of both flotation costs and corporate taxes.

The Cost of Debt

The investor's required rate of return on debt is simply the return that creditors demand on new borrowing. In Chapter 6 we estimated this required rate of return by solving the following bond valuation equation:

$$P_d = \sum_{t=1}^{n} \frac{\text{interest paid in period } t \ (I_t)}{(1 + \text{bondholder's required rate of return } (k_d))^t} +$$

$$\frac{\text{maturity value of the debt } (\$M)}{(1 + \text{bondholder's required rate of return } (k_d))^n}$$

(11–1)

where P_d is the market price of the debt security and n is the number of periods to maturity. Should the firm incur flotation costs such as brokerage commissions and legal and accounting fees in issuing the debt, then the cost of debt capital, k_d, is found as follows:

$$\frac{\text{net proceeds}}{\text{per bond } (NP_d)} = \sum_{t=1}^{n} \frac{\$I_t}{(1 + k_d)^t} + \frac{\$M}{(1 + k_d)^n}$$

(11–2)

The adjustment for flotation costs simply involves replacing the market price of the bond with the net proceeds per bond (NP_d) received by the firm after paying these costs. The result of this adjustment is that the discount rate that solves equation (11–2) is now the firm's cost of debt financing before adjusting for the effect of corporate taxes—that is, the before-tax cost of debt (k_d). The final adjustment we make is to account for the fact that interest is tax deductible. Thus, the after-tax cost of debt capital is simply $k_d(1 - T_c)$, where T_c is the corporate tax rate.

As we learned in Chapter 6, the interest payments on bonds are generally the same for each period. Under these conditions, equation (11–2) can be restated using the interest factors in the present value tables in Appendices B and C as follows:

$$NP_d = \$I_t(PVIFA_{k_d, n}) + \$M(PVIF_{k_d, n})$$

(11–2a)

BACK TO THE FOUNDATIONS

When we calculate the bondholder's required rate of return, we rely on the observed market price of the firm's bonds to be an accurate reflection of their worth. Buyers and sellers only stop trading when they are convinced that the price properly reflects all available information. **Axiom 6: Efficient Capital Markets—The Markets Are Quick and the Prices Are Right.** What we mean here, very simply, is that investors are ever vigilant and quickly act on information that affects the riskiness and, consequently, the price of a firm's bonds and other securities.

EXAMPLE: THE COST OF DEBT CAPITAL

Synopticom Inc. plans a bond issue for the near future and wants to estimate its current cost of debt capital. After talking with the firm's investment banker, the firm's chief financial officer has determined that a 20-year maturity bond with a $1,000 face value and 8 percent coupon (paying 8% × $1,000 = $80 per year in interest) can be sold to investors for $908.32. Equation (11–1) can be used to solve for the investor's required rate of return as we illustrated on page 187 of Chapter 6. In this case Synopticom's creditors require a 9 percent rate of return. The cost of capital to the firm is higher than 9 percent, however, since the firm will have to pay flotation costs of $58.32 per bond when it issues the securities. The flotation costs reduce the net proceeds to Synopticom to $850. Substituting into equation (11–2) we find that the before-tax cost of capital for the bond issue is 9.75 percent. Once again we can solve equation (11–2) using a financial calculator as we illustrate in the margin.

One final adjustment is necessary to obtain the firm's after-tax cost of debt capital. Assuming that Synopticom is in the 34 percent corporate income tax bracket, we estimate the after-tax cost of debt capital as follows:

after-tax cost of debt $= k_d(1 - T_c)$
after-tax cost of debt $= 9.75\%(1 - .34) = 6.435\%$

CALCULATOR SOLUTION

DATA INPUT	FUNCTION KEY
20	N
850	+/− PV
80	PMT
1000	FV

FUNCTION KEY	ANSWER
CPT	
I/Y	9.73*

*The difference between 9.75 percent and 9.73 percent is simply the result of rounding.

The tax deductibility of interest expense makes debt financing less costly to the firm. This is an example of **Axiom 8: Taxes Bias Business Decisions.** The tax deductibility of interest, other things remaining constant, serves to encourage firms to use more debt in their capital structure than they might otherwise use.

The Cost of Preferred Stock

Determining the cost of preferred stock is very straightforward because of the simple nature of the cash flows paid to the holders of preferred shares. You will recall from Chapter 7 that the value of a preferred stock is simply

$$\text{Price of preferred stock } (P_{ps}) = \frac{\text{preferred stock dividend}}{\text{required rate of return for preferred stockholder}} \qquad \textbf{(11--3)}$$

where P_{ps} is the current market price of the preferred shares. Solving for the preferred stockholder's required rate of return we get the following:

$$\text{Required rate of return for preferred stockholder} = \frac{\text{preferred stock dividend}}{\text{price of preferred stock}} \qquad \textbf{(11--4)}$$

Once again, where flotation costs are incurred when new preferred shares are sold, the investor's required rate of return is less than the cost of preferred capital to the firm. To calculate the cost of preferred stock, we must adjust the required rate of return to reflect these flotation costs. We replace the price of a preferred share in equation (11–4) with the net proceeds per share from the sale of new preferred shares (NP_{ps}), and the resulting formula can be used to calculate the cost of preferred stock to the firm.

$$\text{cost of preferred stock } (k_{ps}) = \frac{\text{preferred stock dividend}}{\text{net proceeds per preferred share}} \qquad \textbf{(11--5)}$$

What about corporate taxes? In the case of preferred stock, no tax adjustment must be made since preferred dividends are not tax deductible.

EXAMPLE: **THE COST OF PREFERRED STOCK**

On January 10, 1996, AmaxGold had an issue of preferred stock that traded on the NYSE. The issue paid an annual dividend of $3.75 per share and the preferred stock price closed at $60.375. Assume that if the firm were to sell an issue of preferred stock with the same characteristics as its outstanding issue, it would incur flotation costs of $2.375 per share and the shares would sell for their January 10, 1996, closing price. What is AmaxGold's cost of preferred stock?

Substituting into equation (11–5) we get the following cost of preferred stock for AmaxGold:

$$k_{ps} = \frac{\$3.75}{(\$60.375 - \$2.375)} = .06465 \text{ or } 6.465\%$$

Note that there is no adjustment for taxes, as preferred dividends are not tax deductible—that is, preferred dividends are paid after corporate taxes, unlike bond interest which is paid with before-tax dollars. ■

The Cost of Common Equity

Common equity is unique in two respects. First, the cost of common equity is more difficult to estimate than the cost of debt or preferred stock since the common stockholder's required rate of return is not observable. This results from the fact that common stockholders are the residual owners of the firm, which means that their return is equal to what is left of the firm's earnings after paying the firm's bondholders their contractually set interest and principal payments and the preferred stockholders their promised dividends. Second, common equity can be obtained from either the retention of firm earnings or through the sale of new shares. The cost associated with each of these sources is different from one another since the firm does not incur any flotation costs when it retains earnings but does when it sells new common shares.

We discuss two methods for estimating the common stockholder's required rate of return, which is the foundation for our estimate of the firm's cost of equity capital. These methods are based on the dividend growth model and the capital asset pricing model, which were both discussed earlier in Chapter 8 where we discussed stock valuation.

The Dividend Growth Model

Recall from Chapter 7 that the value of a firm's common stock is equal to the present value of all future dividends. Where dividends are expected to grow at a rate g forever and this rate g is less than the investor's required rate of return, k_c, then the value of a share of common stock, P_{cs}, can be written as:

$$P_{cs} = \frac{D_1}{k_c - g} \qquad (11\text{--}6)$$

where D_1 is the dividend expected to be received by the firm's common shareholders one year hence. The expected dividend is simply equal to the current dividend multiplied by 1 plus the annual rate of growth in dividends (i.e., $D_1 = D_0(1 + g)$). The investor's required rate of return then is found by solving equation (11–6) for k_{cs}.

$$k_{cs} = \frac{D_1}{P_{cs}} + g \qquad (11\text{--}7)$$

Note that k_{cs} is the investor's required rate of return for investing in the firm's stock. It also serves as our estimate of the cost of equity capital, where new equity capital is obtained by retaining a part of the firm's current period earnings. Recall that common equity financing can come from one of two sources: the retention of earnings (i.e., earnings not paid out in dividends to the common stockholders) or from the sale of new common shares. When the firm retains earnings, it doesn't incur any flotation costs, thus the investor's required rate of return is the same as the firm's cost of new equity capital in this instance.

If the firm issues new shares to raise equity capital, then it incurs flotation costs. Once again we adjust the investor's required rate of return for flotation costs by substituting the net proceeds per share, NP_{cs}, for the stock price, P_{cs}, in equation (11–7) to estimate the cost of new common stock, k_{ncs}.

$$k_{ncs} = \frac{D_1}{NP_{cs}} + g \qquad (11\text{--}8)$$

EXAMPLE: ESTIMATING THE COST OF COMMON STOCK USING THE DIVIDEND GROWTH MODEL

The Talbot Corporation's common shareholders anticipate receiving a $2.20 per share dividend next year based on the fact that they received $2 last year and expect dividends to grow 10 percent next year. Furthermore, analysts predict that dividends will continue to grow at a rate of 10 percent into the foreseeable future. Given that the firm's stock is trading for $50 per share, we can calculate the investor's required rate of return (and the cost of retained earnings) as follows:

$$k_{cs} = \frac{D_1}{P_{cs}} + g = \frac{\$2.20}{\$50.00} + .10 = .144 \text{ or } 14.4\%$$

Should Talbot decide to issue new common stock, then it would incur a cost of $7.50 per share, or 15 percent of the current stock price. The resulting cost of new common equity capital would be:

$$k_{ncs} = \frac{D_1}{NP_{cs}} + g = \frac{\$2.20}{\$50 - 7.50} + .10 = .1518 \text{ or } 15.18\%$$

Thus, Talbot faces two costs of capital with respect to common equity. If it retains earnings, then the cost of capital to the firm is 14.4 percent, and if it issues new common stock, the corresponding cost is 15.18 percent. This difference will prove to be important later when we calculate the overall or weighted average cost of capital for the firm. ■

BACK TO THE FOUNDATIONS

The dividend growth model for common stock valuation relies on three of the fundamental axioms of finance. First, stock value is equal to the present value of expected future dividends. This reflects **Axiom 2: The Time Value of Money—A Dollar Received Today Is Worth More Than a Dollar Received in the Future.** Furthermore, dividends represent actual cash receipts to stockholders and are incorporated into the valuation model in a manner that reflects the timing of their receipt. This attribute of the dividend growth model reflects **Axiom 3: Cash—Not Profits—Is King.** Finally, the rate used to discount the expected future dividends back to the present reflects the riskiness of the dividends. The higher the riskiness of the dividend payments, the higher the investor's required rate of return. This reflects **Axiom 1: The Risk-Return Trade-off—We Won't Take On Additional Risk Unless We Expect to Be Compensated with Additional Return.**

Issues in Implementing the Dividend Growth Model

The principal advantage of the dividend growth model is its simplicity. To estimate an investor's required rate of return, the analyst need only observe the current dividend and stock price and estimate the rate of growth in future dividends. The primary drawback relates to the applicability or appropriateness of the valuation model. That is, the dividend growth model is based on the fundamental assumption that dividends are expected to grow at a constant rate g forever. To avoid this assumption, analysts frequently utilize more complex valuation models in which dividends are expected to grow for, say, five years at one rate and then grow at a lower rate from year 6 forward. We will not consider these more complex models here.

Even if the constant growth rate assumption is acceptable, we must arrive at an estimate of that growth rate. We could estimate the rate of growth in historical dividends ourselves or go to published sources of growth rate expectations. Investment advisory services such as Merrill Lynch and Value Line provide their own analysts' estimates of earnings growth rates (generally spanning up to five years), and the Institutional Brokers' Estimate System (I/B/E/S) collects and publishes earnings per share forecasts made by over 1,000 analysts for a broad list of stocks. These estimates are helpful but still require the careful judgment of the analyst in their use, since they relate to earnings (not dividends) and only extend five years into the future (not forever, as required by the dividend growth model). Nonetheless, these estimates provide a useful guide to making your initial dividend growth rate estimate.

We do have some scientific evidence regarding the usefulness of analysts' earnings growth rate estimates in the estimation of investors' required rates of return on common stocks. Although the period covered by the study is dated (1982–1984) it provides some interesting insights into investors' required rates of return for common stocks.

Robert Harris studied the use of analysts' forecasts in conjunction with the dividend growth model to compute required rates of return for the stocks in the Standard & Poor's 500 Index.[1] In his study Harris calculated an average of the analysts' forecasts of five-year growth rates in earnings for all stocks in the S&P 500 Index for each quarter during 1982–1984. He then used these averages as proxies for the growth rates in dividends for each quarter. Second, using the dividend growth model, found in equation (11–7), he estimated an average cost of equity for all 500 stocks for each quarter in his study period. These costs of equity capital estimates were compared to the average yield on U.S. government bonds to calculate the implied risk premium for the average stock in the index. (Recall that a risk premium is simply the difference in the rate of return on a risky security such as a share of common stock and a less risky security such as a U.S. government bond.) The results, presented in Table 11–1, suggest that common stockholders had a required rate of return of 17.26 percent to 20.08 percent for the average stock in the S&P 500 Index throughout this time period. The average cost of equity capital over the entire period was 18.41 percent, and the average risk premium averaged 6.16 percent (ranging from 4.78 percent to 7.16 percent). These figures give us some insight into the basic magnitudes of the cost of equity capital for the very large and established companies that comprise the Standard & Poor's 500 Index and the corresponding risk premiums.

Table 11–1
Required Rates of Return and Risk Premiums (%)

	GOVERNMENT BOND YIELD	S&P 500 REQUIRED RETURN	S&P 500 RISK PREMIUM
1982			
Quarter 1	14.27	20.81	6.54
Quarter 2	13.74	20.68	6.94
Quarter 3	12.94	20.23	7.29
Quarter 4	10.72	18.58	7.86
Average	12.92	20.08	7.16
1983			
Quarter 1	10.87	18.07	7.20
Quarter 2	10.80	17.76	6.96
Quarter 3	11.79	17.90	6.11
Quarter 4	11.90	17.81	5.91
Average	11.34	17.88	6.54
1984			
Quarter 1	12.09	17.22	5.13
Quarter 2	13.21	17.42	4.21
Quarter 3	12.83	17.34	4.51
Quarter 4	11.78	17.05	5.27
Average	12.48	17.26	4.78
Average 1982–1984	12.25	18.41	6.16

Source: Robert Harris, "Using Analysts' Forecasts to Estimate Shareholder Required Returns," *Financial Management* (Spring 1986): 62. Used by permission.

---

[1] Robert Harris, "Using Analysts' Forecasts to Estimate Shareholder Required Returns," *Financial Management* (Spring 1986): 510–67.

The Capital Asset Pricing Model

Recall from Chapter 8 that the capital asset pricing model (CAPM) provides a basis for determining the investor's expected or required rate of return from investing in common stock. The model depends on three things:

1. the risk-free rate, k_{rf},
2. the systematic risk of the common stock's returns relative to the market as a whole or the stock's beta coefficient, β; and
3. the market risk premium, which is equal to the difference in the expected rate of return for the market as a whole; that is, the expected rate of return for the "average security" minus the risk-free rate, or in symbols, $k_m - k_{rf}$.

Using the CAPM, the investor's required rate of return can be written as follows:

$$k_c = k_{rf} + \beta(k_m - k_{rf}) \tag{11-9}$$

EXAMPLE: ESTIMATING THE COST OF COMMON STOCK USING THE CAPM

The Talbot Corporation's common stock has a beta coefficient of 0.82. Furthermore, the risk-free rate is currently 7 percent and the expected rate of return on the market portfolio of all risky assets is 16 percent. Using the CAPM from equation (11–9), we can estimate Talbot's cost of capital as follows:

$$k_c = k_{rf} + \beta(k_m - k_{rf})$$
$$= 7\% + .82(16\% - 7\%) = .144 \text{ or } 14.4\%$$

Note that the required rate of return we have estimated is the cost of internal common equity since no transaction costs are considered. ◾

Issues in Implementing the CAPM

The CAPM approach has two primary advantages. First, the model is simple and easy to understand and implement. The model variables are readily available from public sources with the possible exception of beta coefficients for small and/or non–publicly traded firms. Second, since the model does not rely on dividends or any assumption about the growth rate in dividends, it can be applied to companies that do not currently pay dividends or are not expected to experience a constant rate of growth in dividends.

Using the CAPM requires that we obtain estimates of each of the three model variables—k_{rf}, β, and $(k_m - k_{rf})$. Let's consider each in turn. First, the analyst has a wide range of U.S. government securities upon which to base an estimate of the risk-free rate. Treasury securities with maturities from 30 days to 20 years are readily available, but the CAPM offers no guidance as to the appropriate choice. In fact, the model itself assumes that there is but one risk-free rate and it corresponds to a one-period return (the length of the period is not specified, however). Consequently, we are left to our own judgment as to which maturity we should use to represent the risk-free rate. For applications of the cost of capital involving long-term capital expenditure decisions, it seems reasonable to select a risk-free rate of comparable maturity. So, if we are calculating the cost of capital to be used as the basis for evaluating investments that will provide returns over the next 20 years, it seems appropriate to use a risk-free rate corresponding to a U.S. Treasury bond of comparable maturity.

Second, estimates of security beta coefficients are available from a wide variety of investment advisory services, including Merrill Lynch and Value Line, among others. Alternatively, we could collect historical stock market returns for the company of interest as well as a general market index (such as the Standard & Poor's 500 Index) and estimate the stock's beta as the slope of the relationship between the two return series—as we did in Chapter 8. However, since beta estimates are widely available for a large majority of publicly traded firms, analysts frequently rely on published sources for betas.

Finally, estimation of the market risk premium can be accomplished by looking at the history of stock returns and the premium earned over (under) the risk-free rate of interest. In Chapter 8 we reported a summary of the historical returns earned on risk-free securities and common stocks in Figure 8–2. We saw that on average over the last 70 years, common stocks have earned a premium of roughly 7 percent over long-term government bonds. Thus, for our purposes we will utilize this estimate of the market risk premium ($k_m - k_{rf}$) when estimating the investor's required rate of return on equity using the CAPM.

BACK TO THE FOUNDATIONS

The capital asset pricing model, or CAPM, is a formal representation of **Axiom 1: The Risk-Return Trade-off—We Won't Take On Additional Risk Unless We Expect to Be Compensated with Additional Return.** By formal we mean that the specific method of calculating the additional returns needed to compensate for additional risk is specified in the form of an equation—the CAPM. The added risk is measured in terms of systematic or nondiversifiable risk as measured by the beta coefficient. The additional return required to compensate for risk is then calculated as the product of the beta coefficient and the market risk premium.

OBJECTIVE 3

THE WEIGHTED AVERAGE COST OF CAPITAL

Now that we have calculated the individual costs of capital for each of the sources of financing the firm might use, we now turn to the combination of these capital costs into a single weighted average cost of capital. To estimate the weighted average cost of capital, we need to know the cost of each of the sources of capital used and the capital structure mix. We use the term **capital structure** to refer to *the proportions of each source of financing used by the firm*. Although a firm's capital structure can be quite complex, we will focus our examples on the three basic sources of capital: bonds, preferred stock, and common equity.

capital structure

Capital Structure Weights

We opened this chapter with a description of an investment opportunity faced by the Morristown division of Amorite Manufacturing Inc. A critical element in the analysis of that investment was an estimate of the cost of capital—the discount rate—to be used to calculate the NPV for the project. The reason we calculate a cost of capital is that it enables us to evaluate one or more of the firm's investment opportunities. Remember that the cost of capital should reflect the riskiness of the project being evaluated, so a firm may calculate multiple costs of capital where it makes investments in multiple divisions or business units having different risk characteristics. Thus, for the calculated cost of capital to be meaningful, it must correspond directly to the riskiness of the particular project being analyzed. That is, in theory the cost of capital should reflect the particular way in which the funds are raised (the capital structure used) and the systematic risk characteristics of the project. Consequently, the correct way to calculate capital struc-

How Do Managers Resolve Ethical Decisions?

What makes a managerial choice an ethical one? Brief et al. (1991) suggest that if the decision entails reflection on the moral significance of the choice, then the choice is an ethical one. How do managers resolve ethical dilemmas? There is some evidence suggesting that two factors come to bear on ethical choices: values and accountability.

We will consider two social value systems that are present in Western society, which are particularly relevant to the study of finance. These are the Smithian and Humanitarian value systems. The Smithian system is derived from the writings of the 19th-century moral philosopher and political economist Adam Smith. This value system is reflected in the current-day teachings of economists such as Milton Friedman (1962). Briefly, this system holds that when individuals pursue their own self-interest in the marketplace, they contribute to the good of society. At the firm level this system provides the basis for the market system and is used as the basis for corporate self-interest. In contrast, the Humanitarian system is based on the funda-

mental premise of the equality of individuals in society. This system seeks to protect individuals from the harshness of the market system and to promote equality of opportunity.

Personal value systems are not the only influence on managerial decisions that have ethical implications. Managers are influenced by their perception of the value systems of the individuals to whom they are held accountable. That is, ethical choices made by managers are influenced by the values they believe are held by the person to whom they are accountable. Arendt (1951, 1977) provides evidence that suggests that the effects of accountability may be more profound than those of the individual manager's values. Consequently, the potentially overpowering effects of hierarchical accountability may lead individual managers not to construe the moral significance attached to the choices they make. They may see no choice but to comply with the higher authority. Brief et al. (1991) provide empirical evidence bearing on the question of the relative importance of personal values versus accountability in the choices

made by individuals. Using a set of experiments involving 135 M.B.A. students, they concluded that personal values may not be related to how an individual chooses to resolve ethical dilemmas when the choices (values) of the higher authority are known explicitly.

Note that we have not addressed the normative issue: How should ethical dilemmas be resolved? Instead we have addressed the positive question, How do managers actually deal with ethical choices? The principal finding of the studies we have reviewed is that the *perceived values of one's superiors* have a profound impact on the way in which a subordinate resolves ethical dilemmas. So choose your superior carefully.

Sources: H. Arendt, *The Origins of Totalitarianism* (New York: Harcourt Brace, 1951); H. Arendt, *Eichmann in Jerusalem* (New York: Penguin Books, 1977); A. Brief, J. M. Dukerich, and L. I. Doran, "Resolving Ethical Dilemmas in Management: Experimental Investigations of Values, Accountability and Choice," *Journal of Applied Social Psychology* 21 (1991): 380–96; M. Friedman, *Capitalism and Freedom* (Chicago: University of Chicago Press, 1962).

ture weights is to use the actual dollar amounts of the various sources of capital actually used by the firm.[2]

In practice firms seldom raise funds using a mix of debt and equity. Instead they raise funds from one source this year and another the next. For example, if a firm finances a particular investment wholly with debt, this means that it will have to use more equity at a later date if it is to maintain its capital structure mix. Consequently,

---

[2]There are instances when we will want to calculate the cost of capital for the firm as a whole. In this case the appropriate weights to use are based upon the market value of the various capital sources used by the firm. Market values rather than book values properly reflect the sources of financing used by a firm at any particular point in time. However, where a firm is privately owned, it is not possible to get market values of its securities, and book values are often used.

Table 11–2
Calculating the Weighted Average Cost of Capital

Source of Capital	Capital Structure Weights	×	Cost of Capital	=	Product
Bonds	w_d		$k_d(1 - T_c)$		$w_d \cdot k_d(1 - T_c)$
Preferred stock	w_p		k_p		$w_p \cdot k_p$
Common equity					
Retained earnings	w_c		k_c		$w_c k_c$
Common stock	w_{ns}		k_{ns}		$w_{ns} k_{ns}$
Sum =	100%				k_{wacc}

target capital structure mix

the weights used to calculate the cost of capital should be the firm's **target capital structure mix.** This target mix is the *mix of financing sources that the firm plans to maintain through time.*

Calculating the Weighted Average Cost of Capital

The weighted average cost of capital, k_{wacc}, is simply a weighted average of all the capital costs incurred by the firm. Table 11–2 illustrates the procedure used to estimate k_{wacc} for a firm that has debt, preferred stock, and common equity in its target capital structure mix.

EXAMPLE: **ESTIMATING THE WEIGHTED AVERAGE COST OF CAPITAL**

Ash Inc.'s capital structure and estimated capital costs are found in Table 11–3. Note that the sum of the capital structure weights must equal 100% if we have properly accounted for all sources of financing and in the correct amounts. For example, Ash plans to invest a total of $3 million in common equity into the $5 million investment. However, $1 million of the common equity will come from the retention of earnings, whereas $2 million will come from the sale of new common shares.

We calculate the weighted average cost of capital following the procedure laid out in Table 11–2 and using the information found in Table 11–3. As shown in Table 11–4, Ash Inc.'s weighted average cost of capital is 13.5 percent.

We have estimated the average cost to Ash Inc. of raising $5 million. In this situation, some authors recommend that we calculate two costs of capital: One for the first $1.6667 million of capital and another for more than $1.6667 million up to $5 million. The importance of the $1.6667 million figure relates to the fact that the firm has $1 million in retained earnings which is equal to 60 percent of $1.6667 million (i.e., $1.6667 million = $1 million ÷ .60). Thus the firm can raise the entire equity compo-

Table 11–3
Capital Structure and Capital Costs for Ash Inc.

Source of Capital	Amount of Funds Raised	Percentage of Total	Cost of Capital
Bonds	$1,750,000	35%	7%
Preferred stock	250,000	5%	13%
Common equity			
Retained earnings	1,000,000	20%	16%
Common stock	2,000,000	40%	18%
Total	$5,000,000	100%	

Table 11–4
Weighted Average Cost of Capital for Ash, Inc.

SOURCE OF CAPITAL	CAPITAL STRUCTURE WEIGHTS	×	COST OF CAPITAL	=	PRODUCT
Bonds	35%		7%		2.45%
Preferred stock	5%		13%		0.65%
Common equity					
Retained earnings	20%		16%		3.2%
Common stock	40%		18%		7.2%
Total	100%		k_{wacc}	=	13.5%

nent needed for $1.6667 million using only retained earnings. The resulting weighted average cost of capital for up to $1.6667 million in capital would be 12.7 percent since the cost of internally generated equity is only 16 percent. The corresponding weighted average cost of capital for more than $1.6667 million and up to $5 million is 13.90 percent since the cost of common equity raised through the sale of new common stock is 18 percent. We do not recommend that these additional calculations be made for two reasons: First, our ability to estimate the cost of equity capital is imprecise (see Eugene F. Fama and Kenneth R. French, 1997, Industry costs of equity, *Journal of Financial Economics* 43, 153–193). Second, we know that firms infrequently issue new equity and in this situation would probably increase their use of debt financing to account for the $2 million in equity financing not available from retained earnings. At some point in the future the firm would then rebalance its capital structure to reflect the desired 60 percent equity financing by making a sizable new equity offering or through the retention of earnings. Thus, for our purposes we calculate a single cost of capital for the entire $5 million and use this as the hurdle rate for investing these funds. ■

Survey of Firm Costs of Capital

Since a firm's cost of capital is an internal calculation made by the firm's analysts, there is very limited evidence available concerning actual firm costs of capital. One such study was performed by Blume, Friend, and Westerfield, in which they surveyed the 100 largest corporations listed on the NYSE.[3] In the survey, managers were asked to indicate their estimated cost of capital for debt and common equity. The results of the survey are reported in Table 11–5 (see page 340) and reflect the responses of 10 public utilities and 20 nonutility industrial firms.

Although the study was completed some time ago and the levels of the rates reported would obviously be quite different today, it does illustrate a number of important points. First, we see that utilities, which are generally thought to face lower risk than other industrial firms due to their regulated status, do indeed face a lower cost of capital than nonutilities. This is evidenced by the fact that the average cost of capital rises to 13.1 percent from 12.4 percent when utilities are excluded from the average. Using a bit of algebra we can use these two averages to solve for the average cost of capital for the 10 public utilities. The result is 11 percent. So the difference in capital costs for public utilities and other industrial firms is sizable.

---

[3]Marshall E. Blume, Irwin Friend, and Randolph Westerfield, "Impediments to Capital Formation: Summary Report of a Survey of Nonfinancial Corporations," working paper, Wharton School, University of Pennsylvania, Philadelphia, 1980.

Table 11–5
Average Costs of Capital and Investment Cutoff Rates for Plant and Equipment

| | **BEFORE-TAX COST-OF-DEBT (%)** | **AFTER-TAX COST (%)** | | | | **AFTER-TAX CUTOFF RATE FOR PLANT AND EQUIPMENT INVESTMENTS (%)** | |
		NEW COMMON EQUITY	**RETAINED EARNINGS**	**DEBT**	**WEIGHTED COST**	**LEAST RISKY**	**MOST RISKY**
All industries	12.5	17.2	16.6	6.4	12.4	12.9	19.6
All industries except public utilities	12.5	17.8	17.0	6.3	13.1	13.1	20.3

Source: Adapted from Marshall E. Blume, Irwin Friend, and Randolph Wester field, "Impediments to Capital Formation: Summary Report of a Survey of Nonfinancial Corporations," working paper, Wharton School, University of Pennsylvania, Philadelphia, 1980, 6.

The second observation we can make based upon the results found in Table 11–5 is that new common stock is indeed slightly more expensive than retained earnings, as we discussed earlier. Third, the required rate of return for common equity is about 5 percent higher than the before-tax cost of debt: 17.2 percent compared to 12.5 percent. Although this premium probably varies with general market conditions and the business cycle, we see that there is clear evidence of a risk premium to the holders of the more risky security.

Our final observation concerning Table 11–5 relates to the disparity between the cost of capital and the required rates of return used for risky projects. The weighted average cost of capital is at the low end of the range of required rates of return on investments in new plant and equipment. This indicates that the cost of capital is an appropriate rate of discount for low-risk projects but is too low for higher-risk projects. Note that the weighted average cost of capital provided here reflects the firm's estimated cost of capital for their existing asset portfolio and capital structure mix. This cost of capital would be the appropriate discount rate for evaluating projects that reflect the firm's existing assets. If the responding firms perceive their existing asset investments as low risk, then the cost of capital for the firm is the appropriate discount rate for low-risk investments. Since the required rates of return on the most risky investments greatly exceed the firm's weighted average cost of capital, these investments must be viewed as having substantially more risk than the firm's existing asset investments.

OBJECTIVE 4

CALCULATING DIVISIONAL COSTS OF CAPITAL: PEPSICO, INC.

An increasing number of firms are seriously engaged in the process of trying to focus their decisions on increasing shareholder value. This means accepting only those investment opportunities that offer a rate of return higher than the cost of capital. PepsiCo is one such firm. PepsiCo goes to great lengths to estimate the cost of capital for each of its three major operating divisions (restaurants, snack foods, and beverages).[4] We will briefly summarize the basic elements of the calculations involved

---

[4]PepsiCo spun off its restaurants division in February 1997. However, the example used here was based on the pre-spinoff company.

Table 11–6
Estimating PepsiCo's Cost of Debt

	Treasury Rate	+	Spread to Treasuries	+	Pretax Cost of Debt	×	(1 − Tax Rate)	After-Tax Cost of Debt
Restaurants	7.28%	+	1.65%	=	8.93%	×	.62	5.54%
Snack foods	7.28%	+	1.15%	=	8.43%	×	.62	5.23%
Beverages	7.28%	+	1.23%	=	8.51%	×	.62	5.28%

in these estimates, including the cost of debt financing, the cost of common equity, the target capital structure weights, and the weighted average cost of capital.

Table 11–6 contains the estimates of the after-tax cost of debt for each of PepsiCo's three divisions. PepsiCo's analysts use a simple risk premium method for estimating the cost of debt whereby they add a premium called *spread to Treasuries* to the current Treasury rate for long-term bonds. PepsiCo's analysts adjust the spread for each operating division to reflect what it feels is an appropriate premium for the operating and financial risks of each division. For example, the restaurants division is assigned a higher premium over Treasuries than the other two divisions (i.e., 1.65 percent) based on the risk attributes of the business and the fact that the target debt-to-assets ratio in this division is 30 percent compared to 20 percent for snack foods and 26 percent for beverages.

Table 11–7 contains the estimates of the cost of equity capital for each of PepsiCo's three operating divisions using the CAPM. We will not explain the intricacies of their method for estimating divisional betas except to say that they make use of beta estimates for a number of competitor firms from each of the operating divisions, which involves making appropriate adjustments for differences in the use of financial leverage across the competitor firms used in the analysis.[5]

The weighted average cost of capital for each of the divisions is estimated in Table 11–8 on page 342 using the capital costs estimated in Tables 11–6 and 11–7 and using PepsiCo's target capital structure weights for each operating division. Note that the weighted average costs of capital for all three divisions fall within a very narrow range, between 10.08 percent and 10.29 percent.

Table 11–7
Cost of Equity Capital for PepsiCo's Operating Divisions

	Risk-Free Rate	+	Beta	Expected Market Return	−	Risk-Free Rate	=	Cost of Equity
Restaurants	7.28%	+	1.17	(11.48%	−	7.28%)	=	12.20%
Snack foods	7.28%	+	1.02	(11.48%	−	7.28%)	=	11.56%
Beverages	7.28%	+	1.07	(11.48%	−	7.28%)	=	11.77%

---

[5]This method of using betas from comparable firms is sometimes referred to as the pure play method, since the analyst seeks independent beta estimates for firms engaged in only one business (i.e., restaurants or beverages). The betas for these pure play companies are then used to estimate the beta for a business or division.

Table 11–8

PepsiCo's Weighted Average Cost of Capital for Each of Its Operating Divisions

	Cost of Equity Times the Target Equity Ratio	+	Cost of Debt Times the Target Debt Ratio	=	Weighted Average Cost of Capital
Restaurants	(12.20%)(0.70)	+	(5.54%)(0.30)	=	10.20%
Snack foods	(11.56%)(0.80)	+	(5.23%)(0.20)	=	10.29%
Beverages	(11.77%)(0.74)	+	(5.28%)(0.26)	=	10.08%

OBJECTIVE 5

USING A FIRM'S COST OF CAPITAL TO EVALUATE NEW CAPITAL INVESTMENTS

Now that we have learned the principles used to estimate a firm's cost of capital, it is tempting to use this capital cost to evaluate all the firm's investment opportunities. This can produce some very expensive mistakes. Recall that the cost of capital depends primarily on the use of the funds, not their source. Consequently, the appropriate cost of capital for individual investment opportunities should, in theory and practice, reflect the individual risk characteristics of the investment. With this principle in mind, we reason that the firm's weighted average cost of capital is the appropriate discount rate for estimating a project's NPV only when the project has similar risk characteristics to the firm. This would be true, for example, where the investment involves expanding an existing facility but would not be true where the investment involves entering into a completely new business with different risk characteristics.

What does it mean to say that a firm and an investment opportunity have similar risk characteristics? We can think of an investment's risk characteristics as coming from two sources: business risk and financial risk. By **business risk** we mean *the potential variability in the firm's expected earnings before interest and taxes (EBIT)*. In Chapter 8 we learned that investors should not be worried about total variability but should only be concerned about systematic variability. **Financial risk** refers to *the added variability in earnings available to a firm's shareholders, and the added chance of insolvency caused by the use of securities bearing a limited rate of return in the firm's financial structure*. For example, in Chapter 3 we learned that firms that use higher levels of financial leverage also experience higher volatility in earnings available to the common stockholders. This higher volatility leads investors to require higher rates of return, which means a higher cost of capital for the project.

In summary, the firm's weighted average cost of capital is the appropriate discount rate for evaluating the NPV of investments whose business and financial risks are similar to those of the firm as a whole. See Table 11–9 for a summary of the formulas involved in estimating the weighted average cost of capital. If either of these sources of project risk is different from the risks of the firm, then the analyst must alter the estimate of the cost of capital to reflect these differences. If financial risk is different, then this calls for the use of different financial mix ratios when calculating the weighted average cost of capital, as well as estimates of individual capital costs that properly reflect these financial risks. If operating-risk characteristics differ, then once again capital costs must be adjusted to reflect this difference. In our discussion of PepsiCo we saw that it estimates three different weighted average costs of capital to reflect what it feels are meaningful differences in the operating and financial risk characteristics of its three operating divisions.

business risk

financial risk

Table 11–9
Summary of Cost of Capital Formulas

1. The After-Tax Cost of Debt, $k_d(1 - T_c)$
   a. Calculate the before-tax cost of debt, k_d, as follows:

$$NP_d = \sum_{t=1}^{n} \frac{\$I_t}{(1 + k_d)^t} + \frac{\$M}{(1 + k_d)^n} \qquad \textbf{(11–2)}$$

   where NP_d is the net proceeds received by the firm from the sale of each bond; $\$I_t$ is the dollar amount of interest paid to the investor in period t for each bond; $\$M$ is the maturity value of each bond paid in period n; k_d is the before-tax cost of debt to the firm; and n is the number of periods to maturity.

   b. Calculate the after-tax cost of debt as follows:

$$\text{after-tax cost of debt} = k_d(1 - T_c)$$

   where T_c is the corporate tax rate.

2. The Cost of Preferred Stock, k_p

$$k_{ps} = \frac{\text{preferred stock dividend}}{NP_{ps}} \qquad \textbf{(11–5)}$$

   where NP_0 is the net proceeds per share of new preferred stock sold after flotation costs.

3. The Cost of Common Equity
   a. Method 1: dividend growth model
   Calculate the cost of internal common equity (retained earnings), k_c, as follows:

$$k_{cs} = \frac{D_1}{P_{cs}} + g \qquad \textbf{(11–7)}$$

   where D_1 is the expected dividend for the next year, P_0 is the current price of the firm's common stock, and g is the rate of growth in dividends per year.
   Calculate the cost of external common equity (new stock offering), k_{ns}, as follows:

$$k_{ncs} = \frac{D_1}{NP_{cs}} + g \qquad \textbf{(11–8)}$$

   where NP_0 is the net proceeds to the firm after flotation costs per share of stock sold.

   b. Method 2: capital asset pricing model, k_c

$$k_c = k_{rf} + \beta(k_m - k_{rf}) \qquad \textbf{(11–9)}$$

   where the risk-free rate is k_{rf}; the systematic risk of the common stock's returns relative to the market as a whole or the stock's beta coefficient is β; and the market risk premium, which is equal to the difference in the expected rate of return for the market as a whole (i.e., the expected rate of return for the "average security" minus the risk-free rate), is $k_m - k_{rf}$.

4. The Weighted Average Cost of Capital

$$k_{wacc} = w_d \cdot k_d(1 - T_c) + w_p \cdot k_p + w_{cs}k_{cs} + w_{ncs}k_{ncs} \qquad \textbf{(11–10)}$$

   where the w_i terms represent the market value weights associated with the firm's use of each of its sources of financing. Note that we are simply calculating a weighted average of the costs of each of the firm's sources of capital where the weights reflect the firm's relative use of each source.

This practice reflects PepsiCo's adherence to the principle that the cost of capital is primarily a function of the use of the capital (i.e., the riskiness of the different operating divisions).

BACK TO THE FOUNDATIONS

The firm's weighted average cost of capital provides the appropriate discount rate for evaluating new projects only where the projects offer the same riskiness as the firm as a whole. This limitation of the usefulness of the firm's weighted average cost of capital is a direct extension of **Axiom 1: The Risk-Return Trade-off—We Won't Take On Additional Risk Unless We Expect to Be Compensated with Additional Return.** If project risk differs from that of the firm, then the firm's cost of capital (which reflects the risk of the firm's investment portfolio) is no longer the appropriate cost of capital for the project. For this reason firms that invest in multiple divisions or business units that have different risk characteristics should calculate a different cost of capital for each division. In theory each individual investment opportunity has its own unique risk attributes and correspondingly should have a unique cost of capital. However, given the impreciseness with which we estimate the cost of capital, we generally calculate the cost of capital for each operating division of the firm, not each project.

SUMMARY

OBJECTIVE 1

We opened our discussion of this chapter by discussing the investment opportunity facing the Morristown division of Amorite Manufacturing Inc. The investment required that the firm invest $75 million to renovate a production facility that will provide after-tax savings to the firm of $25 million per year over the next five years. In Chapter 9 we learned that the proper way to evaluate whether or not to undertake the investment involves calculating its net present value (NPV). To calculate NPV we must estimate both project cash flows and an appropriate discount rate. In this chapter we have learned that the proper discount rate is a weighted average of the after-tax costs of all the firm's sources of financing. In addition, we have learned that the cost of capital for any source of financing is estimated by first calculating the investor's required rate of return, then making appropriate adjustments for flotation costs and corporate taxes (where appropriate). If Morristown's weighted average cost of capital is 10 percent, then the NPV of the plant renovation is $4,250 and the investment should be made. The reason is that the project is expected to increase the wealth of Amorite's shareholders by $4,250. Very simply, the project is expected to return a present value amount of $4,250 more than Amorite's sources of capital require, and since the common stockholders get any residual value left after returning the promised return to each of the other sources of capital, they receive the NPV.

OBJECTIVE 2

Calculating the after-tax cost of debt capital

To calculate the after-tax cost of debt capital we must first calculate the before-tax cost of capital using the following formula:

$$NP_d = \sum_{t=1}^{n} \frac{\$I_t}{(1 + k_d)^t} + \frac{\$M}{(1 + k_d)^n} \qquad (11\text{--}2)$$

where NP_d = the net proceeds received by the firm from the sale of each bond

$$\$I_t = \text{the dollar amount of interest paid to the investor}$$
in period t for each bond

$$\$M = \text{the maturity value of each bond paid in period } n$$

$$k_d = \text{the before-tax cost of debt to the firm}$$

$$n = \text{the number of periods to maturity}$$

Next, we adjust for the effects of corporate taxes since the bond interest is deducted from the firm's taxable income.

$$\text{after-tax cost of debt} = k_d(1 - \text{corporate tax rate})$$

Estimating the cost of preferred stock

The cost of preferred stock is relatively easy to calculate. We simply calculate the dividend yield on the preferred issue using net proceeds from the sale of each new share as follows:

$$\text{cost of preferred stock} = \frac{\text{preferred stock dividend}}{\text{net proceeds per preferred share}} \qquad \textbf{(11–5)}$$

Note that no adjustment is made for corporate taxes since preferred stock dividends, unlike bond interest, are paid with after-tax earnings.

Estimating the cost of common equity

Common equity can be obtained by the firm in one of two ways. First, the firm can retain a portion of its net income after paying common dividends. The retention of earnings constitutes a means of raising common-equity financing internally—that is, no capital market issuance of securities is involved. Second, the firm can also raise equity capital through the sale of a new issue of common stock.

We discussed two methods for estimating the cost of common equity. The first involved using the dividend growth model:

$$k_{cs} = \frac{D_1}{P_{cs}} + g \qquad \textbf{(11–7)}$$

where g is the rate at which dividends are expected to grow forever, k_c is the investor's required rate of return, and P_0 is the current price of a share of common stock. When a new issue of common shares is issued, the firm incurs flotation costs. These costs reduce the amount of funds the firm receives per share. Consequently, the cost of external common equity using the dividend growth model requires that we substitute the new proceeds per share, NP_0, for share price:

$$k_{ncs} = \frac{D_1}{NP_{cs}} + g \qquad \textbf{(11–8)}$$

The second method for estimating the cost of common equity involves the use of capital asset pricing model (CAPM), which we first discussed in Chapter 8. There we learned that the CAPM provides a basis for evaluating investor's required rates of return on common equity, k_c, using three variables:

1. the risk-free rate, k_{rf};
2. the systematic risk of the common stock's returns relative to the market as a whole or the stock's beta coefficient, β; and
3. the market risk premium which is equal to the difference in the expected rate of return for the market as a whole—that is, the expected rate of return for the "average security" minus the risk-free rate, $k_m - k_{rf}$.

The CAPM is written as follows:

$$k_c = k_{rf} + \beta(k_m - k_{rf})$$ **(11–9)**

We found that all of the variables on the right-hand side of equation (11–9) could be obtained from public sources for larger, publicly traded firms. However, for non–publicly traded firms the CAPM is more difficult to apply in the estimation of investor-required rates of return.

OBJECTIVE 3

Calculating a firm's weighted average cost of capital

The firm's weighted average cost of capital, k_{wacc}, can be defined as follows:

$$k_{wacc} = w_d \cdot k_d(1 - T_c) + w_{ps} \cdot k_{ps} + w_{cs}k_{cs} + w_{ncs}k_{ncs}$$

where the w_i terms represent the market value weights associated with the firm's use of each of its sources of financing. Note that we are simply calculating a weighted average of the costs of each of the firm's sources of capital where the weights reflect the firm's relative use of each source.

The weights used to calculate k_{wacc} should theoretically reflect the market values of each capital source as a fraction of the total market value of all capital sources (i.e., the market value of the firm). However, the analyst frequently finds the use of market value weights is impractical, either because the firm's securities are not publicly traded or because all capital sources are not used in proportion to their makeup of the firm's target capital structure in every financing episode. In these instances we found that the weights should be the firm's long-term target financial mix.

OBJECTIVE 4
OBJECTIVE 5

Limitations of the firm's weighted average cost of capital

The firm's weighted average cost of capital will reflect the operating or business risk of the firm's present set of investments and the financial risks attendant upon the way in which those assets are financed. Therefore, this cost of capital estimate is useful only for evaluating new investment opportunities that have similar business and financial risks. Remember that the primary determinant of the cost of capital for a particular investment is the risk of the investment itself, not the source of the capital. Multidivision firms such as PepsiCo resolve this problem by calculating a different cost of capital for each of their major operating divisions.

KEY TERMS

Business Risk, 342	Flotation Costs, 329
Capital Structure, 336	Investor's Required Rate of Return, 328
Financial Policy, 329	Target Capital Structure Mix, 338
Financial Risk, 342	Weighted Average Cost of Capital, 329

STUDY QUESTIONS

11-1. Define the term *cost of capital.*

11-2. Why do we calculate a firm's weighted average cost of capital?

11-3. In computing the cost of capital, which sources of capital do we consider?

11-4. How does a firm's tax rate affect its cost of capital? What is the effect of the flotation costs associated with a new security issue?

11-5. a. Distinguish between internal common equity and new common stock.

b. Why is a cost associated with internal common equity?

c. Describe the two approaches that could be used in computing the cost of common equity.

11-6. What might we expect to see in practice in the relative costs of different sources of capital?

SELF-TEST PROBLEMS

ST-1. (*Individual Costs of Capital*) Compute the cost for the following sources of financing:

a. A $1,000 par value bond with a market price of $970 and a coupon interest rate of 10 percent. Flotation costs for a new issue would be approximately 5 percent. The bonds mature in 10 years and the corporate tax rate is 34 percent.

b. A preferred stock selling for $100 with an annual dividend payment of $8. If the company sells a new issue, the flotation cost will be $9 per share. The company's marginal tax rate is 30 percent.

c. Internally generated common stock totaling $4.8 million. The price of the common stock is $75 per share, and the dividend per share was $9.80 last year. The dividend is not expected to change in the future.

d. New common stock where the most recent dividend was $2.80. The company's dividends per share should continue to increase at an 8 percent growth rate into the indefinite future. The market price of the stock is currently $53; however, flotation costs of $6 per share are expected if the new stock is issued.

ST-2. (*Weighted Average Cost of Capital*) The capital structure for the Carion Corporation is provided below. The company plans to maintain its debt structure in the future. If the firm has a 5.5 percent after-tax cost of debt, a 13.5 percent cost of preferred stock, and an 18 percent cost of common stock, what is the firm's weighted average cost of capital?

CAPITAL STRUCTURE ($000)	
Bonds	$1,083
Preferred stock	268
Common stock	3,681
	$5,032

STUDY PROBLEMS

11-1. (*Individual or Component Costs of Capital*) Compute the cost for the following sources of financing

a. A bond that has a $1,000 par value (face value) and a contract or coupon interest rate of 11 percent. A new issue would have a flotation cost of 5 percent of the $1,125 market value. The bonds mature in 10 years. The firm's average tax rate is 30 percent and its marginal tax rate is 34 percent.

b. A new common stock issue that paid a $1.80 dividend last year. The par value of the stock is $15, and earnings per share have grown at a rate of 7 percent per year. This growth rate is expected to continue into the foreseeable future. The company maintains a constant dividend-earnings ratio of 30 percent. The price of this stock is now $27.50, but 5 percent flotation costs are anticipated.

c. Internal common equity where the current market price of the common stock is $43. The expected dividend this coming year should be $3.50, increasing thereafter at a 7 percent annual growth rate. The corporation's tax rate is 34 percent.

d. A preferred stock paying a 9 percent dividend on a $150 par value. If a new issue is offered, flotation costs will be 12 percent of the current price of $175.

e. A bond selling to yield 12 percent after flotation costs, but prior to adjusting for the marginal corporate tax rate of 34 percent. In other words, 12 percent is the rate that equates the net proceeds from the bond with the present value of the future cash flows (principal and interest).

11-2. (*Individual or Component Costs of Capital*) Compute the cost for the following sources of financing:

a. A bond selling to yield 8 percent after flotation costs, but prior to adjusting for the marginal corporate tax rate of 34 percent. In other words, 8 percent is the rate that equates the net proceeds from the bond with the present value of the future cash flows (principal and interest).

b. A new common stock issue that paid a $1.05 dividend last year. The par value of the stock is $2, and the earnings per share have grown at a rate of 5 percent per year. This growth rate is expected to continue into the foreseeable future. The company maintains a constant dividend-earnings ratio of 40 percent. The price of this stock is now $25, but 9 percent flotation costs are anticipated.

c. A bond that has a $1,000 par value and a contract or coupon interest rate of 12 percent. A new issue would net the company 90 percent of the $1,150 market value. The bonds mature in 20 years, the firm's average tax rate is 30 percent, and its marginal tax rate is 34 percent.

d. A preferred stock paying a 7 percent dividend on a $100 par value. If a new issue is offered, the company can expect to net $85 per share.

e. Internal common equity where the current market price of the common stock is $38. The expected dividend this forthcoming year should be $3, increasing thereafter at a 4 percent annual growth rate. The corporation's tax rate is 34 percent.

11-3. (*Cost of Equity*) Salte Corporation is issuing new common stock at a market price of $27. Dividends last year were $1.45 and are expected to grow at an annual rate of 6 percent forever. Flotation costs will be 6 percent of market price. What is Salte's cost of equity?

11-4. (*Cost of Debt*) Belton is issuing a $1,000 par value bond that pays 7 percent annual interest and matures in 15 years. Investors are willing to pay $958 for the bond. Flotation costs will be 11 percent of market value. The company is in an 18 percent tax bracket. What will be the firm's after-tax cost of debt on the bond?

11-5. (*Cost of Preferred Stock*) The preferred stock of Walter Industries sells for $36 and pays $2.50 in dividends. The net price of the security after issuance costs is $32.50. What is the cost of capital for the preferred stock?

11-6. (*Cost of Debt*) The Zephyr Corporation is contemplating a new investment to be financed 33 percent from debt. The firm could sell new $1,000 par value bonds at a net price of $945. The coupon interest rate is 12 percent, and the bonds would mature in 15 years. If the company is in a 34 percent tax bracket, what is the after-tax cost of capital to Zephyr for bonds?

11-7. (*Cost of Preferred Stock*) Your firm is planning to issue preferred stock. The stock sells for $115; however, if new stock is issued, the company would receive only $98. The par value of the stock is $100 and the dividend rate is 14 percent. What is the cost of capital for the stock to your firm?

11-8. (*Cost of Internal Equity*) Pathos Co.'s common stock is currently selling for $21.50. Dividends paid last year were $.70. Flotation costs on issuing stock will be 10 percent of market price. The dividends and earnings per share are projected to have an annual growth rate of 15 percent. What is the cost of internal common equity for Pathos?

11-9. (*Cost of Equity*) The common stock for the Bestsold Corporation sells for $58. If a new issue is sold, the flotation costs are estimated to be 8 percent. The company pays 50 percent of its earnings in dividends, and a $4 dividend was recently paid. Earnings per share five years ago were $5. Earnings are expected to continue to grow at the same annual rate in the future as during the past five years. The firm's marginal tax rate is 34 percent. Calculate the cost of (a) internal common and (b) external common.

11-10. (*Cost of Debt*) Sincere Stationery Corporation needs to raise $500,000 to improve its manufacturing plant. It has decided to issue a $1,000 par value bond with a 14 percent annual coupon rate and a 10-year maturity. The investors require a 9 percent rate of return.

   a. Compute the market value of the bonds.

   b. What will the net price be if flotation costs are 10.5 percent of the market price?

   c. How many bonds will the firm have to issue to receive the needed funds?

   d. What is the firm's after-tax cost of debt if its average tax rate is 25 percent and its marginal tax rate is 34 percent?

11-11. (*Cost of Debt*)

   a. Rework problem 11-10 assuming a 10 percent coupon rate. What effect does changing the coupon rate have on the firm's after-tax cost of capital?

   b. Why is there a change?

COMPREHENSIVE PROBLEM

(*Weighted Average Cost of Capital*) The capital structure for Nealon, Inc., is provided below. Flotation costs are (a) 15 percent of market value for a new bond issue, (b) $1.21 per share for common stock, and (c) $2.01 per share for preferred stock. The dividends for common stock were $2.50 last year and are projected to have an annual growth rate of 6 percent. The firm is in a 34 percent tax bracket. What is the weighted average cost of capital if the firm finances are in the proportions shown below? Market prices are $1,035 for bonds, $19 for preferred stock, and $35 for common stock. There will be $500,000 of internal common equity funding (i.e., retained earnings) available.

Nealon, Inc., Balance Sheet

TYPE OF FINANCING	PERCENTAGE OF FUTURE FINANCING
Bonds (8%, $1,000 par, 16-year maturity)	38%
Preferred stock (5,000 shares outstanding,	
$50 par, $1.50 dividend)	15
Common stock	47
Total	100%

SELF–TEST SOLUTIONS

The following notations are used in this group of problems:

k_d = the before-tax cost of debt
k_{ps} = the cost of preferred stock
k_{cs} = the cost of internal common stock
k_{ncs} = the cost of new common stock
t = the marginal tax rate

D_t = the dollar dividend per share, where D_0 is the most recently paid dividend and D_1 is the forthcoming dividend

P_0 = the value (present value) of a security

NP_0 = the value of a security less any flotation costs incurred in issuing the security

SS–1.

a.

$$\$921.50 = \sum_{t=1}^{n} \frac{\$100}{(1 + k_d)^t} + \frac{\$1,000}{(1 + k_d)^{10}}$$

RATE	VALUE
11%	$940.90
k_d%	$921.50
12%	$887.00

$\}\ \$19.40$ $\}\ \$53.90$

$$k_d = 0.11 + \left(\frac{\$19.40}{\$53.90}\right)0.01 = .1136 = 11.36\%$$

$$k_{d(1 - t)} = 11.36\% (1 - 0.34) = 7.50\%$$

b.

$$k_{ps} = \frac{D}{NP_0}$$

$$k_{ps} = \frac{\$8}{\$100 - \$9} = .0879 = 8.79\%$$

c.

$$k_{cs} = \frac{D_1}{P_0} + g$$

$$k_{cs} = \frac{\$9.80}{\$75} + 0\% = .1307 = 13.07\%$$

d.

$$k_{ncs} = \frac{D_1}{NP_0} + g$$

$$k_{ncs} = \frac{\$2.80(1 + 0.08)}{\$53 - \$6} + 0.08 = .1443 = 14.43\%$$

SS–2.

Carion Corporation—Weighted Cost of Capital

	CAPITAL STRUCTURE	WEIGHTS	INDIVIDUAL COSTS	WEIGHTED COSTS
Bonds	$1,083	0.2152	5.5%	1.18%
Preferred stock	268	0.0533	13.5%	0.72%
Common stock	3,681	0.7315	18.0%	13.17%
	$5,032	1.0000		15.07%

Determining the Financing Mix

Business and Financial Risk • Breakeven Analysis • Operating Leverage • Financial Leverage • Combination of Operating and Financial Leverage • Planning the Financing Mix • A Quick Look at Capital Structure Theory • Basic Tools of Capital Structure Management • A Glance at Actual Capital Structure Management

In 1993 the Coca-Cola Company enjoyed a sales increase of 6.8 percent over the level of reported sales for 1992. This firm's change in net income, however, rose greater than 30.8 percent over the same one-year period. Such disparity in the relationship between sales fluctuations and net income fluctuations is not peculiar to Coca-Cola.

Consider that over the same year Phillips Petroleum saw its sales rise by only 3.2 percent, yet its net income rose by a whopping 35 percent. Further, Archer Daniels Midland experienced a sales rise of 6.3 percent and a 12.7 percent increase in net income.

We know that sales fluctuations are not always in the positive direction. Over this 1992–1993 time frame Chevron Corp., the large integrated oil company, endured a 3.6 percent contraction in sales revenues; yet its net income contracted by a larger and more painful 19.4 percent.

What is it about the nature of business that causes changes in sales revenues to translate into larger variations in net income and finally the earnings available to the common shareholders? It would actually be a good planning tool for management to be able to decompose such fluctuations into those policies associated with the operating side of the business as distinct from those policies associated with the financing side of the business.

This chapter will show you how to do just that—and more. Consider that the United States was recession free from November 1982 until July 1990. Then a general business contraction did occur that officially lasted until the end of February 1991. The nation's labor markets never regained full speed until the first half of 1994. Essentially, business enterprises were going through a once-in-a-lifetime global realignment. This time period was an essentially challenging one for many American business firms that had loaded their balance sheets with debt over the "good times."

Financial executives had to delicately manage cash flows to service existing debt contracts or face bankruptcy. These same executives had to give considerable thought as to how to finance the next (i.e., incremental) capital project.

Phillips Petroleum, mentioned earlier, paid explicit attention to managing its financing mix over this lengthy period of business cycle expansion and the "short recession" of 1990–1991. Phillips piled up almost $9.0 billion in debt obligations in the process of fending off two hostile takeover attempts during the mid-1980s. As a direct result of these management policies, the firm's debt-to-equity ratio, a measure of financial leverage use, hit a peak of about 77 percent. The firm's reputation among major investors drooped, and so did its stock price.

By mid-April 1996, however, management policies were reversed and the debt-to-equity ratio for Phillips moved downward toward 47 percent, and the absolute amount of debt on the balance sheet was pulled back to about $3.1 billion. This gain in "financial flexibility" allowed Phillips to more aggressively pursue high expected net present value projects. Examples include expanded drilling projects and added investment in basic gas stations. Investors apparently looked with approval on the new policies, as the firm's stock price began to appreciate. Moreover, financial analysts published positive recommendations on Phillips stock as an investment.

If you understand the material and analytical processes in this chapter, you will be able to make positive contributions to company strategies that deal with the firm's financing mix. You will be able to formulate a defensible answer to the question, Should we finance the next capital project with a new issue of bonds or a new issue of common stock? You can also help a lot of firms avoid making serious financial errors, the consequences of which last for several years—because financing decisions typically impact the firm for several years.

Our work in Chapters 6, 7, 8, and 11 allowed us to develop an understanding of how financial assets are valued in the marketplace. Drawing on the tenets of valuation theory, we presented various approaches to measuring the cost of funds to the business organization. This chapter presents concepts that relate to the valuation process and the cost of capital; it also discusses the crucial problem of planning the firm's financing mix.

The cost of capital provides a direct link between the formulation of the firm's asset structure and its financial structure. This is illustrated in Figure 12–1. Recall that the cost of capital is a basic input to the time-adjusted capital-budgeting models. It therefore affects the capital-budgeting, or asset-selection, process. The cost of capital is affected, in turn, by the composition of the right-hand side of the firm's balance sheet—that is, its financial structure.

This chapter examines tools that can be useful aids to the financial manager in determining the firm's proper financial structure. First, we review the technique of breakeven analysis. This provides the foundation for the relationships to be highlighted in the remainder of the chapter. We then examine the

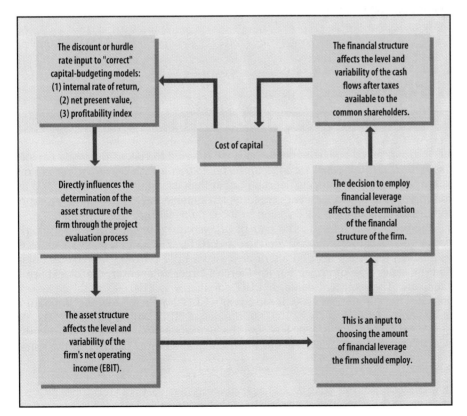

Figure 12–1
Cost of Capital As a Link between Firm's Asset Structure and Financial Structure

concept of operating leverage, some consequences of the firm's use of financial leverage, and the impact on the firm's earnings stream when operating and financial leverage are combined in various patterns. With the foundation in place whereby we can effectively analyze the variability in the firm's earnings streams, we move on to a discussion of capital structure theory and the basic tools of capital structure management. Actual capital structure practices are also placed in perspective. Our immediate tasks are to distinguish two types of risk that confront the firm and to clarify some key terminology that will be used throughout this chapter.

PAUSE AND REFLECT

In this chapter, we become more precise in assessing the causes of variability in the firm's expected revenue streams. It is useful to think of business risk as induced by the firm's investment decisions. That is, the composition of the firm's assets determines its exposure to business risk. In this way, business risk is a direct function of what appears on the left-hand side of the company's balance sheet. Financial risk is properly attributed to the manner in which the firm's managers have decided to arrange the right-hand side of the company's balance sheet. The choice to use more financial leverage means that the firm will experience greater exposure to financial risk. The tools developed here will help you quantify the firm's business and financial risk. A solid understanding of these tools will make you a better financial manager.

OBJECTIVE 1

BUSINESS AND FINANCIAL RISK

risk

In studying capital-budgeting techniques we referred to **risk** as the *likely variability associated with expected revenue or income streams*. As our attention is now focused on the firm's financing decision rather than its investment decision, it is useful to separate the income stream variations attributable to (1) the company's exposure to business risk and (2) its decision to incur financial risk.

business risk

Business risk refers to the *relative dispersion (variability) in the firm's expected earnings before interest and taxes* (**EBIT**).[1] Figure 12–2 shows a subjectively estimated probability distribution of next year's EBIT for the Pierce Grain Company and the same type of projection for Pierce's larger competitor, the Blackburn Seed Company. The expected value of EBIT for Pierce is $100,000, with an associated standard deviation of $20,000. If next year's EBIT for Pierce fell one standard deviation short of the expected $100,000, the actual EBIT would equal $80,000. Blackburn's expected EBIT is $200,000, and the size of the associated standard deviation is $20,000. The standard deviation for the expected level of EBIT is the same for

---

[1]If what accountants call "other income" and "other expenses" are equal to zero, then EBIT is equal to net operating income. These terms will be used interchangeably.

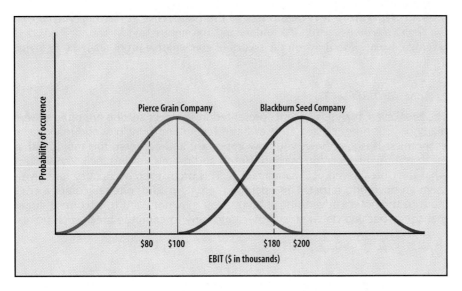

Figure 12–2
Subjective Probability Distribution of Next Year's EBIT

both firms. We would say that Pierce's degree of business risk exceeds Blackburn's because of its larger coefficient of variation of expected EBIT, as follows:

$$\text{Pierce's coefficient of variation of expected } EBIT = \frac{\$20,000}{\$100,000} = .20$$

$$\text{Blackburn's coefficient of variation of expected } EBIT = \frac{\$20,000}{\$200,000} = .10$$

The relative dispersion in the firm's EBIT stream, measured here by its expected coefficient of variation, is the *residual* effect of several causal influences. Dispersion in operating income does not *cause* business risk; rather, this dispersion, which we call business risk, is the *result* of several influences. The company's cost structure, product demand characteristics, and intraindustry competitive position all affect its business risk exposure. Such business risk is a direct result of the firm's investment decision. It is the firm's asset structure, after all, that gives rise to both the level and variability of its operating profits.

Financial risk, conversely, is a direct result of the firm's financing decision. In the context of selecting a proper financing mix, this risk applies to *(1) the additional variability in earnings available to the firm's common shareholders and (2) the additional chance of insolvency borne by the common shareholder caused by the use of financial leverage.*[2] **Financial leverage** means *financing a portion of the firm's assets with securities bearing a fixed (limited) rate of return* in hopes of increasing the ultimate return to the common stockholders. The decision to use debt or preferred stock in the financial structure of the corporation means that those who own the common shares of the firm are exposed to financial risk. Any given level of variability in EBIT will be magnified by the firm's use of financial leverage, and such additional variability will be embodied in the variability of earnings available to the common stockholder and earnings per share. If these magnifications are negative, the common stockholder has a higher chance of insolvency than would have existed had the use of fixed-charge securities (debt and preferred stock) been avoided.

In the rest of this chapter we study techniques that permit a precise assessment of the earnings stream variability caused by (1) operating leverage and (2) financial

financial risk

financial leverage

---

[2]Note that the concept of financial risk used here differs from that used in our examination of cash and marketable securities management in Chapter 15.

leverage. **Operating leverage** refers to the *incurrence of fixed operating costs in the firm's income stream.* To understand the nature and importance of operating leverage, we need to draw on the basics of cost-volume-profit analysis, or *breakeven analysis.*

PAUSE AND REFLECT

The breakeven analysis concepts presented in the next section are often covered in many of your other classes, such as basic accounting principles and managerial economics. This just shows you how important and accepted this tool is within the realm of business decision making. Hotels and motels, for instance, know exactly what their break-even occupancy rate is. This break-even occupancy rate gives them an operating target. This operating target, in turn, often becomes a crucial input to the hotel's advertising strategy. You may not want to become a financial manager—but you do want to understand how to compute break-even points.

OBJECTIVE 2 · **BREAKEVEN ANALYSIS**

The technique of breakeven analysis is familiar to legions of businesspeople. It is usefully applied in a wide array of business settings, including both small and large organizations. This tool is widely accepted by the business community for two reasons: It is based on straightforward assumptions, and companies have found that the information gained from the breakeven model is beneficial in decision-making situations.

Objective and Uses

The objective of breakeven analysis is to determine the break-even quantity of output by studying the relationships among the firm's cost structure, volume of output, and profit. Alternatively, the firm ascertains the break-even level of sales dollars that corresponds to the beak-even quantity of output. We will develop the fundamental relationships by concentrating on units of output and then extend the procedure to permit direct calculation of the break-even sales level.

What is meant by the break-even quantity of output? It is that quantity of output, denominated in units, that results in an EBIT level equal to zero. Use of the break-even model, therefore, enables the financial officer (1) to determine the quantity of output that must be sold to cover all operating costs, as distinct from financial costs, and (2) to calculate the EBIT that will be achieved at various output levels.

Essential Elements of the Breakeven Model

To implement the breakeven model, we must separate the production costs of the company into two mutually exclusive categories: fixed costs and variable costs. You will recall from your study of basic economics that in the long run all costs are variable. Breakeven analysis, therefore, is a short-run concept.

Assumed Behavior of Costs

Fixed Costs

Fixed costs, also referred to as **indirect costs,** *do not vary in total amount as sales volume or the quantity of output changes* over some relevant range of output. Total fixed costs are independent of the quantity of product produced and equal

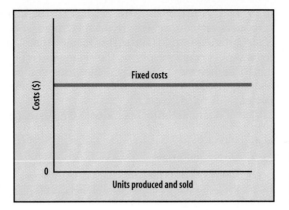

Figure 12–3
Fixed-Cost Behavior over
Relevant Range of Output

some constant dollar amount. As production volume increases, fixed cost per unit of product falls, as fixed costs are spread over larger and larger quantities of output. Figure 12–3 graphs the behavior of total fixed costs with respect to the company's relevant range of output. This total is shown to be unaffected by the quantity of product that is manufactured and sold. Over some other relevant output range, the amount of total fixed costs might be higher or lower for the same company.

In a manufacturing setting, some specific examples of fixed costs are

1. Administrative salaries
2. Depreciation
3. Insurance
4. Lump sums spent on intermittent advertising programs
5. Property taxes
6. Rent

Variable Costs

Variable costs are sometimes referred to as **direct costs.** Variable costs are *fixed per unit of output but vary in total as output changes.* Total variable costs are computed by taking the variable cost per unit and multiplying it by the quantity produced and sold. The breakeven model assumes proportionality between total variable costs and sales. Thus, if sales rise by 10 percent, it is assumed that variable costs will rise by 10 percent. Figure 12–4 graphs the behavior of total variable costs with respect to the company's relevant range of output. Total variable costs are seen

variable costs
direct costs

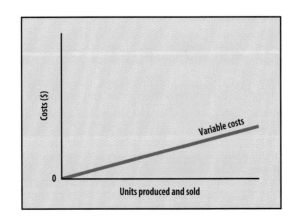

Figure 12–4
Variable-Cost Behavior over
Relevant Range of Output

to depend on the quantity of product that is manufactured and sold. Notice that if zero units of the product are manufactured, then variable costs are zero, but fixed costs are greater than zero. This implies that some contribution to the coverage of fixed costs occurs as long as the selling price per unit exceeds the variable cost per unit. This helps explain why some firms will operate a plant even when sales are temporarily depressed—that is, to provide some increment of revenue toward the coverage of fixed costs.

For a manufacturing operation, some examples of variable costs include

1. Direct labor
2. Direct materials
3. Energy costs (fuel, electricity, natural gas) associated with the production area
4. Freight costs for products leaving the plant
5. Packaging
6. Sales commissions

More on Behavior of Costs

No one really believes that *all* costs behave as neatly as we have illustrated the fixed and variable costs in Figures 12–3 and 12–4. Nor does any law or accounting principle dictate that a certain element of the firm's total costs always be classified as fixed or variable. This will depend on each firm's specific circumstances. In one firm energy costs may be predominantly fixed, whereas in another they may vary with output.[3]

Furthermore, some costs may be fixed for a while, then rise sharply to a higher level as a higher output is reached, remain fixed, and then rise again with further increases in production. Such costs may be termed either (1) *semivariable*, or (2) *semifixed*. The label is your choice, because both are used in industrial practice. An example might be the salaries paid production supervisors. Should output be cut back by 15 percent for a short period, the management of the organization is not likely to lay off 15 percent of the supervisors. Similarly, commissions paid to salespeople often follow a stepwise pattern over wide ranges of success. This sort of cost behavior is shown in Figure 12–5.

To implement the breakeven model and deal with such a complex cost structure, the financial manager must (1) identify the most relevant output range for planning purposes and then (2) approximate the cost effect of semivariable items over this range by segregating a portion of them to fixed costs and a portion to variable costs. In the actual business setting this procedure is not fun. It is not unusual for the analyst who deals with the figures to spend considerably more time allocating costs to fixed and variable categories than in carrying out the actual breakeven calculations.

Total Revenue and Volume of Output

total revenue

Besides fixed and variable costs, the essential elements of the breakeven model include total revenue from sales and volume of output. **Total revenue** means *total sales dollars* and is equal to the selling price per unit multiplied by the quantity sold.

---

[3]In a greenhouse operation, where plants are grown (manufactured) under strictly controlled temperatures, heat costs will tend to be fixed whether the building is fully or only half full of seedlings. In a metal stamping operation, where levers are being produced, there is no need to heat the plant to as high a temperature when the machines are stopped and the workers are not there. In this latter case, the heat costs will tend to be variable.

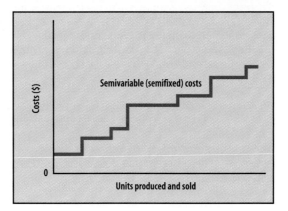

Figure 12–5
Semivariable Cost Behavior over the Relevant Range of Output

The **volume of output** refers to the *firm's level of operations* and may be *indicated either as a unit quantity or as sales dollars.*

volume of output

Finding the Break-Even Point

Finding the break-even point in terms of units of production can be accomplished in several ways. All approaches require the essential elements of the breakeven model just described. The breakeven model is a simple adaptation of the firm's income statement expressed in the following analytical format:

$$\text{sales} - (\text{total variable cost} + \text{total fixed cost}) = \text{profit} \quad \textbf{(12–1)}$$

On a units-of-production basis, it is necessary to introduce (1) the price at which each unit is sold and (2) the variable cost per unit of output. Because the profit item studied in breakeven analysis is EBIT, we will use that acronym instead of the word "profit." In terms of units, the income statement shown in equation (12–1) becomes the breakeven model by setting EBIT equal to zero:

$$\left(\begin{array}{c}\text{sales price} \\ \text{per unit}\end{array}\right)\left(\begin{array}{c}\text{units} \\ \text{sold}\end{array}\right) - \left[\left(\begin{array}{c}\text{variable cost} \\ \text{per unit}\end{array}\right)\left(\begin{array}{c}\text{units} \\ \text{sold}\end{array}\right) + \left(\begin{array}{c}\text{total fixed} \\ \text{cost}\end{array}\right)\right] = EBIT = \$0 \quad \textbf{(12–2)}$$

Our task now becomes finding the number of units that must be produced and sold in order to satisfy equation (12–2)—that is, to arrive at EBIT = $0. This can be done by (1) contribution margin analysis or (2) algebraic analysis. Each approach will be illustrated using the same set of circumstances.

Problem Situation

Even though the Pierce Grain Company manufactures several different products, it has observed over a lengthy period that its product mix is rather constant. This allows management to conduct its financial planning by use of a "normal" sales price per unit and "normal" variable cost per unit. The "normal" sales price and variable cost per unit are calculated from the constant product mix. It is like assuming that the product mix is one big product. The selling price is $10 and the variable cost is $6. Total fixed costs for the firm are $100,000 per year. What is the break-even point in units produced and sold for the company during the coming year?

Contribution Margin Analysis

The contribution margin technique permits direct computation of the break-even quantity of output. The **contribution margin** is the *difference between the unit selling price and unit variable costs,* as follows:

unit sales price
− unit variable cost
= unit contribution margin

The use of the word *contribution* in the present context means contribution to the coverage of fixed operating costs. For the Pierce Grain Company, the unit contribution margin is

unit sales price	$10
unit variable cost	−6
unit contribution margin	$ 4

If the annual fixed costs of $100,000 are divided by the unit contribution margin of $4, we find the break-even quantity of output for Pierce Grain is 25,000 units. Figure 12–6 portrays the contribution-margin technique for finding the break-even point.

Algebraic Analysis

To explain the algebraic method for finding the break-even output level, we need to adopt some notation. Let

$$Q = \text{the number of units sold}$$
$$Q_B = \text{the break-even level of } Q$$
$$P = \text{the unit sales price}$$
$$F = \text{total fixed costs anticipated over the planning period}$$
$$V = \text{the unit variable cost}$$

Equation (12–2), the breakeven model, is repeated on the following page as equation (12–2a) with the model symbols used in place of words. The breakeven model is then solved for Q, the number of units that must be sold in order that EBIT will

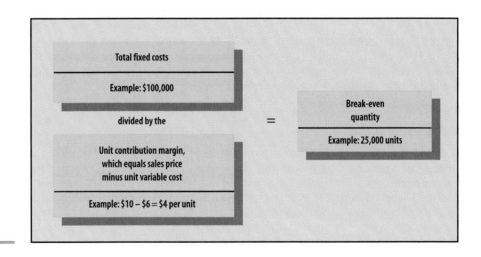

Figure 12–6

Contribution Margin Approach to Breakeven Analysis

equal $0. We label the break-even point quantity Q_B.

$$(P \cdot Q) - [(V \cdot Q) + (F)] = EBIT = \$0$$
$$(P \cdot Q) - (V \cdot Q) - F = \$0 \quad \quad \textbf{(12-2a)}$$
$$Q(P - V) = F$$
$$Q_B = \frac{F}{P - V} \quad \quad \textbf{(12-3)}$$

Observe that equation (12–3) says: Divide total fixed operating costs, F, by the unit contribution margin, $P - V$, and the break-even level of output, Q_B, will be obtained. The contribution margin analysis is nothing more than equation (12–3) in different garb.

Application of equation (12–3) permits direct calculation of Pierce Grain's break-even point, as follows:

$$Q_B = \frac{F}{P - V} = \frac{\$100,000}{\$10 - \$6} = 25,000 \text{ units}$$

Break-Even Point in Sales Dollars

In dealing with the multiproduct firm, it is convenient to compute the break-even point in terms of sales dollars rather than units of output. Sales, in effect, become a common denominator associated with a particular product mix. Furthermore, an outside analyst may not have access to internal unit cost data. He or she may, however, be able to obtain annual reports for the firm. If the analyst can separate the firm's total costs as identified from its annual reports into their fixed and variable components, he or she can calculate a general break-even point in sales dollars.

We will illustrate the procedure using the Pierce Grain Company's cost structure. Suppose that the reported financial information is arranged in the format shown in Table 12–1. We will refer to this type of financial statement as an *analytical income statement*. This distinguishes it from audited income statements published, for example, in the annual reports of public corporations. If we are aware of the simple mathematical relationships on which cost-volume-profit analysis is based, we can use Table 12–1 to find the break-even point in sales dollars for the Pierce Grain Company.

First, let us explore the logic of the process. Recall from equation (12–1) that

sales − (total variable cost + total fixed cost) = *EBIT*

If we let total sales = S, total variable cost = VC, and total fixed cost = F, the preceding relationship becomes

$$S - (VC + F) = EBIT$$

Table 12–1	
Pierce Grain Company Analytical Income Statement	
Sales	$300,000
Less: Total variable costs	180,000
Revenue before fixed costs	$120,000
Less: Total fixed costs	100,000
EBIT	$20,000

Because variable cost per unit of output and selling price per unit are *assumed* constant over the relevant output range in breakeven analysis, the ratio of total variable costs to sales, *VC/S*, is a constant for any level of sales. This permits us to rewrite the previous expression as

$$S - \left[\left(\frac{VC}{S} \right) S \right] - F = EBIT$$

and

$$S \left(1 - \frac{VC}{S} \right) - F = EBIT$$

At the break-even point, however, EBIT = 0, and the corresponding break-even level of sales can be represented as S^*. At the break-even level of sales, we have

$$S^* \left(1 - \frac{VC}{S} \right) - F = 0$$

or

$$S^* \left(1 - \frac{VC}{S} \right) = F$$

Therefore,

$$S^* = \frac{F}{1 - \dfrac{VC}{S}} \qquad\qquad (12\text{–}4)$$

The application of equation (12–4) to Pierce Grain's analytical income statement in Table 12–1 permits the break-even sales level for the firm to be directly computed, as follows:

$$S^* = \frac{\$100,000}{1 - \dfrac{\$180,000}{\$300,000}}$$

$$= \frac{\$100,000}{1 - .60} = \$250,000$$

OBJECTIVE 3   **OPERATING LEVERAGE**

If *fixed* operating costs are present in the firm's cost structure, so is operating leverage. Fixed operating costs do *not* include interest charges incurred from the firm's use of debt financing. Those costs will be incorporated into the analysis when financial leverage is discussed.

So operating leverage arises from the firm's use of fixed operating costs. But what is operating leverage? *Operating leverage* is the responsiveness of the firm's EBIT to fluctuations in sales. By continuing to draw on our data for the Pierce Grain Company, we can illustrate the concept of operating leverage. Table 12–2 contains data for a study of a possible fluctuation in the firm's sales level. It is assumed that Pierce Grain is currently operating at an annual sales level of $300,000. This is referred to in the tabulation as the base sales level at t (time period zero). The question is, How will Pierce Grain's EBIT level respond to a positive 20 percent change in sales? A sales volume of $360,000, referred to as the forecast sales level at $t + 1$,

Table 12–2
Concept of Operating Leverage: Increase in Pierce Grain Company Sales

ITEM	BASE SALES LEVEL, t	FORECAST SALES LEVEL, $t + 1$
Sales	$300,000	$360,000
Less: Total variable costs	180,000	216,000
Revenue before fixed costs	$120,000	$144,000
Less: Total fixed costs	100,000	100,000
EBIT	$ 20,000	$ 44,000

reflects the 20 percent sales rise anticipated over the planning period. Assume that the planning period is one year.

Operating leverage relationships are derived within the mathematical assumptions of cost-volume-profit analysis. In the present example, this means that Pierce Grain's variable cost-to-sales ratio of .6 will continue to hold during time period $t + 1$, and the fixed costs will hold steady at $100,000.

Given the forecasted sales level for Pierce Grain and its cost structure, we can measure the responsiveness of EBIT to the upswing in volume. Notice in Table 12–2 that EBIT is expected to be $44,000 at the end of the planning period. The percentage change in EBIT from t to $t + 1$ can be measured as follows:

$$\text{percentage change in } EBIT = \frac{\$44,000_{t+1} - \$20,000_t}{\$20,000_t}$$
$$= \frac{\$24,000}{\$20,000}$$
$$= 120\%$$

We know that the projected fluctuation in sales amounts to 20 percent of the base period, t, sales level. This is verified below:

$$\text{percentage change in sales} = \frac{\$360,000_{t+1} - \$300,000_t}{\$300,000_t}$$
$$= \frac{\$60,000}{\$300,000}$$
$$= 20\%$$

By relating the percentage fluctuation in EBIT to the percentage fluctuation in sales, we can calculate a specific measure of operating leverage. Thus, we have

$$\text{degree of operating leverage from the base sales level(s)} = DOL_s = \frac{\text{percentage change in } EBIT}{\text{percentage change in sales}} \quad \textbf{(12–5)}$$

Applying equation (12–5) to our Pierce Grain data gives

$$DOL_{\$300,000} = \frac{120\%}{20\%} = 6 \text{ times}$$

Unless we understand what the specific measures of operating leverage tells us, the fact that we may know it is equal to six times is nothing more than sterile information. For Pierce Grain, the inference is that for *any* percentage fluctuation in sales from the base level, the percentage fluctuation in EBIT will be six times as great. If Pierce Grain expected only a 5 percent rise in sales over the coming period, a 30 percent rise in EBIT would be anticipated as follows:

$$\text{(percentage change in sales)} \times (DOL_s) = \text{percentage change in } EBIT$$
$$(5\%) \times (6) = 30\%$$

We will now return to the postulated 20 percent change in sales. What if the direction of the fluctuation is expected to be negative rather than positive? What is in store for Pierce Grain? Unfortunately for Pierce Grain, but fortunately for the analytical process, we will see that the operating leverage measure holds in the negative direction as well. This situation is displayed in Table 12–3.

At the $240,000 sales level, which represents the 20 percent decrease from the base period, Pierce Grain's EBIT is expected to be −$4,000. How sensitive is EBIT to this sales change? The magnitude of the EBIT fluctuation is calculated as

$$\text{percentage change in } EBIT = \frac{-\$4,000_{t+1} - \$20,000_t}{\$20,000_t}$$
$$= \frac{-\$24,000}{\$20,000}$$
$$= -120\%$$

Making use of our knowledge that the sales change was equal to −20 percent permits us to compute the specific measure of operating leverage as

$$DOL_{\$300,000} = \frac{-120\%}{-20\%} = 6 \text{ times}$$

What we have seen, then, is that the degree of operating leverage measure works in the positive or negative direction. A negative change in production volume and sales can be magnified severalfold when the effect on EBIT is calculated.

To this point our calculations of the degree of operating leverage have required two analytical income statements: one for the base period and a second for the subsequent period that incorporates the possible sales alteration. This cumbersome process can be simplified. If unit cost data are available to the financial manager, the relationship can be expressed directly in the following manner:

$$DOL_S = \frac{Q(P - V)}{Q(P - V) - F} \tag{12–6}$$

Observe in equation (12–6) that the variables were all previously defined in our algebraic analysis of the breakeven model. Recall that Pierce sells its product at $10 per unit, the unit variable cost is $6, and total fixed costs over the planning horizon are $100,000. Still assuming that Pierce is operating at a $300,000 sales volume, which means output (Q) is 30,000 units, we can find the degree of operating leverage by application of equation (12–6):

$$DOL_{\$300,000} = \frac{30,000(\$10 - \$6)}{30,000(\$10 - \$6) - \$100,000} = \frac{\$120,000}{\$20,000} = 6 \text{ times}$$

Table 12–3
Concept of Operating Leverage: Decrease in Pierce Grain Company Sales

Item	Base Sales Level, t	Forecast Sales Level, $t + 1$
Sales	$300,000	$240,000
Less: Total variable costs	180,000	144,000
Revenue before fixed costs	$120,000	$ 96,000
Less: Total fixed costs	100,000	100,000
EBIT	$ 20,000	$ −4,000

Whereas equation (12–6) requires us to know unit cost data to carry out the computations, the next formulation we examine does not. If we have an analytical income statement for the base period, then equation (12–7) can be employed to find the firm's degree of operating leverage:

$$DOL_s = \frac{\text{revenue before fixed costs}}{EBIT} = \frac{S - VC}{S - VC - F} \qquad \textbf{(12–7)}$$

Use of equation (12–7) in conjunction with the base period data for Pierce Grain shown in Table 12–3 gives

$$DOL_{\$300,000} = \frac{\$120,000}{\$20,000} = 6 \text{ times}$$

The three versions of the operating leverage measure all produce the same result. Data availability will sometimes dictate which formulation can be applied. The crucial consideration, though, is that you grasp what the measurement tells you. For Pierce Grain, a 1 percent change in sales will produce a 6 percent change in EBIT.

PAUSE AND REFLECT

Before we complete our discussion of operating leverage and move on to the subject of financial leverage, ask yourself, "Which type of leverage is more under the control of management?" You will probably (and correctly) come to the conclusion that the firm's managers have less control over the operating cost structure and almost complete control over its financial structure. What the firm actually produces, for example, will determine to a significant degree the division between fixed and variable costs. There is more room for substitution among the various sources of financial capital than there is among the labor and real capital inputs that enable the firm to meet its production requirements. Thus, you can anticipate more arguments over the choice to use a given degree of financial leverage than the corresponding choice over operating leverage use.

Implications

As the firm's scale of operations moves in a favorable manner above the break-even point, the degree of operating leverage at each subsequent (higher) sales base will decline. In short, the greater the sales level, the lower the degree of operating leverage. As long as some fixed operating costs are present in the firm's cost structure, however, operating leverage exists, and the degree of operating leverage (DOL_s) will exceed 1.00. Operating leverage is present, then, whenever the firm faces the following situation:

$$\frac{\text{percentage change in } EBIT}{\text{percentage change in sales}} > 1.00$$

The greater the firm's degree of operating leverage, the more its profits will vary with a given percentage change in sales. Thus, operating leverage is definitely an attribute of the business risk that confronts the company. We know that the degree of operating leverage falls as sales increase past the firm's break-even point. The sheer size and operating profitability of the firm, therefore, affect and can lessen its business risk exposure.

The manager considering an alteration in the firm's cost structure will benefit from an understanding of the operating leverage concept. It might be possible to replace part of the labor force with capital equipment (machinery). A possible result is an increase in fixed costs associated with the new machinery and a reduction in variable costs attributable to a lower labor bill. This conceivably could raise the firm's degree of operating leverage at a specific sales base. If the prospects for future sales increases are high, then increasing the degree of operating leverage might be a prudent decision. The opposite conclusion will be reached if sales prospects are unattractive.

PAUSE AND REFLECT

As you are introduced to the topic of financial leverage, remember that this is one of the most crucial policy areas on which a financial executive spends his or her time. We describe and measure here what happens to the firm's earnings per share when financial risk is assumed. Try to understand this effect. We demonstrate how actually to measure this effect in the next section. By now you should be realizing that variability of all types—be it in an earnings stream or in stock returns—is a central element of financial thought and the practice of financial management.

FINANCIAL LEVERAGE

We have defined *financial leverage* as the practice of financing a portion of the firm's assets with securities bearing a fixed rate of return in hope of increasing the ultimate return to the common shareholders. In the present discussion we focus on the responsiveness of the company's earnings per share to changes in its EBIT. For the time being, then, the return to the common stockholder being concentrated on is earnings per share. We are *not* saying that earnings per share is the appropriate criterion for all financing decisions. In fact, the weakness of such a contention will be examined later. Rather, the use of financial leverage produces a certain type of *effect*. This effect can be illustrated clearly by concentrating on an earnings-per-share criterion.

Let us assume that the Pierce Grain Company is in the process of getting started as a going concern. The firm's potential owners have calculated that $200,000 is needed to purchase the necessary assets to conduct the business. Three possible financing plans have been identified for raising the $200,000; they are presented in Table 12–4. In plan A no financial risk is assumed: The entire $200,000 is raised by selling 2,000 common shares, each with a $100 par value. In plan B a moderate amount of financial risk is assumed: 25 percent of the assets are financed with a debt issue that carries an 8 percent annual interest rate. Plan C would use the most financial leverage: 40 percent of the assets would be financed with a debt issue costing 8 percent.

Table 12–5 on page 368 presents the impact of financial leverage on earnings per share associated with each fund-raising alternative. If EBIT should increase from $20,000 to $40,000, then earnings per share would rise by 100 percent under plan A. The same positive fluctuation in EBIT would occasion an earnings-per-share rise of 125 percent under plan B, and 147 percent under plan C. In plans B and C the 100 percent increase in EBIT (from $20,000 to $40,000) is magnified to a greater than 100 percent increase in earnings per share. The firm is employing financial leverage and exposing its owners to financial risk when the following situation exists:

$$\frac{\text{percentage change in earnings per share}}{\text{percentage change in } EBIT} > 1.00$$

By following the same general procedures that allowed us to analyze the firm's use of operating leverage, we can lay out a precise measure of financial leverage. Such a measure deals with the sensitivity of earnings per share to EBIT fluctuations.

Table 12–4
Pierce Grain Company Possible Capital Structures

PLAN A: 0% DEBT

		Total debt	$ 0
		Common equity	200,000[a]
Total assets	$200,000	Total liabilities and equity	$200,000

PLAN B: 25% DEBT AT 8% INTEREST RATE

		Total debt	$ 50,000
		Common equity	150,000[b]
Total assets	$200,000	Total liabilities and equity	$200,000

PLAN C: 40% DEBT AT 8% INTEREST RATE

		Total debt	$ 80,000
		Common equity	120,000[c]
Total assets	$200,000	Total liabilities and equity	$200,000

[a]2,000 common shares outstanding
[b]1,500 common shares outstanding
[c]1,200 common shares outstanding

The relationship can be expressed as

$$\text{degree of financial leverage } (DFL) \text{ from base } EBIT \text{ level} = DFL_{EBIT} = \frac{\text{percentage change in earnings per share}}{\text{percentage change in EBIT}} \quad \textbf{(12–8)}$$

Use of equation (12–8) with each of the financing choices outlined for Pierce Grain is shown subsequently. The base EBIT level is $20,000 in each case.

Plan A: $\quad DFL_{\$20,000} = \dfrac{100\%}{100\%} = 1.00 \text{ time}$

Plan B: $\quad DFL_{\$20,000} = \dfrac{125\%}{100\%} = 1.25 \text{ times}$

Plan C: $\quad DFL_{\$20,000} = \dfrac{147\%}{100\%} = 1.47 \text{ times}$

Like operating leverage, the *degree of financial leverage* concept performs in the negative direction as well as the positive. Should EBIT fall by 10 percent, the Pierce Grain Company would suffer a 12.5 percent decline in earnings per share under plan B. If plan C were chosen to raise the necessary financial capital, the decline in earnings would be 14.7 percent. Observe that the greater the DFL, the greater the fluctuations (positive or negative) in earnings per share. The common stockholder is required to endure greater variations in returns when the firm's management chooses to use more financial leverage rather than less. The DFL measure allows the variation to be quantified.

Rather than take the time to compute percentage changes in EBIT and earnings per share, the DFL can be found directly, as follows:

$$DFL_{EBIT} = \frac{EBIT}{EBIT - I} \quad \textbf{(12–9)}$$

Table 12–5

Table 12–5
Pierce Grain Company Analysis of Financial Leverage at Different EBIT Levels

(1)	(2)	(3) = (1) − (2)	(4) = (3) × .5	(5) = (3) − (4)	(6)	
				NET INCOME	**EARNINGS**	
EBIT	**INTEREST**	**EBT**	**TAXES**	**TO COMMON**	**PER SHARE**	
PLAN A: 0% DEBT; $200,000 COMMON EQUITY; 2,000 SHARES						
$ 0	$ 0	$ 0	$ 0	$ 0	$ 0	
20,000	0	20,000	10,000	10,000	5.00 ⎫	
40,000	0	40,000	20,000	20,000	10.00 ⎬	100%
60,000	0	60,000	30,000	30,000	15.00	
80,000	0	80,000	40,000	40,000	20.00	
PLAN B: 25% DEBT; 8% INTEREST RATE; $150,000 COMMON EQUITY; 1,500 SHARES						
$ 0	$4,000	$(4,000)	$(2,000)[a]	$(2,000)	$(1.33) ⎫	
20,000	4,000	16,000	8,000	8,000	5.33 ⎬	
40,000	4,000	36,000	18,000	18,000	12.00 ⎭	125%
60,000	4,000	56,000	28,000	28,000	18.67	
80,000	4,000	76,000	38,000	38,000	25.33	
PLAN C: 40% DEBT; 8% INTEREST RATE; $120,000 COMMON EQUITY; 1,200 SHARES						
$ 0	$6,400	$(6,400)	$(3,200)[a]	$(3,200)	$(2.67) ⎫	
20,000	6,400	13,600	6,800	6,800	5.67 ⎬	
40,000	6,400	33,600	16,800	16,800	14.00 ⎭	147%
60,000	6,400	53,600	26,800	26,800	22.33	
80,000	6,400	73,600	36,800	36,800	30.67	

[a]The negative tax bill recognizes the credit arising from the carryback and carryforward provision of the tax code.

In equation (12–9) the variable, I, represents the total interest expense incurred on *all* the firm's contractual debt obligations. If six bonds are outstanding, I is the sum of the interest expense on all six bonds. If the firm has preferred stock in its financial structure, the dividend on such issues must be inflated to a before-tax basis and included in the computation of I.[4] In this latter instance, I is in reality the sum of all fixed financing costs.

Equation (12–9) has been applied to each of Pierce Grain's financing plans (Table 12–5) at a base EBIT level of $20,000. The results are as follows:

$$\text{Plan A:} \quad DFL_{\$20,000} = \frac{\$20,000}{\$20,000 - 0} = 1.00 \text{ time}$$

$$\text{Plan B:} \quad DFL_{\$20,000} = \frac{\$20,000}{\$20,000 - \$4,000} = 1.25 \text{ times}$$

$$\text{Plan C:} \quad DFL_{\$20,000} = \frac{\$20,000}{\$20,000 - \$6,400} = 1.47 \text{ times}$$

---

[4]Suppose (1) preferred dividends of $4,000 are paid annually by the firm and (2) it faces a 40 percent marginal tax rate. How much must the firm earn *before taxes* to make the $4,000 payment out of after-tax earnings? Because preferred dividends are not tax deductible to the paying company, we have $4,000/(1 − .40) = $6,666.67.

Corporate Financial Policies

The fact that financial leverage effects can be measured provides management with the opportunity to shape corporate policy formally around the decision to use or avoid the use of leverage-inducing financial instruments (primarily debt issues). One company with very specific policies on the use of financial leverage is the Coca-Cola Company. The following discussion is from that firm's 1990 *Annual Report*.

Note how several of the key concepts and techniques presented throughout this book are mentioned in this excerpt. For example, mention is made of (1) the firm's primary objective, (2) its weighted average cost of capital, (3) investment risk characteristics, (4) the prudent use of debt capital, and (5) borrowing capacity.

Management's primary objective is to increase shareholder value over time. To accomplish this objec-tive, the Coca-Cola Company and subsidiaries (the Company) have developed a comprehensive business strategy that emphasizes maximizing long-term cash flow by expanding its global business systems, increasing gallon sales, improving margins, investing in areas offering attractive returns and maintaining an appropriate capital structure.

Management seeks investments that strategically enhance existing operations and offer long-term cash returns that exceed the Company's weighted average cost of capital. For investments with risk characteristics similar to the soft drink industry and assuming a net-debt-to-capital ratio ceiling of 35 percent, that cost of capital is estimated by management to be approximately 12 percent after taxes.

The Company utilizes prudent amounts of debt to lower its overall cost of capital and increase its total return to shareholders. The Company has established a net-debt-to-net-capital ratio ceiling of 35 percent. Net debt is defined as total debt less excess cash, cash equivalents and current marketable securities. Excluding the Company's finance subsidiary, net debt represented 22.8 percent of net capital at December 31, 1990.

Additional borrowing capacity within the 35 percent debt ceiling was approximately $940 million at December 31, 1990, excluding the Company's finance subsidiary. The Company anticipates using this additional borrowing capacity principally to fund investment opportunities that meet its strategic and financial objectives and, as a second priority, to fund the share repurchase program.

Source: The Coca-Cola Company, *Annual Report*, 1990, 32–34.

As you probably suspected, the measures of financial leverage shown previously are identical to those obtained by use of equation (12–8). This will always be the case.

COMBINATION OF OPERATING AND FINANCIAL LEVERAGE

OBJECTIVE 4

Changes in sales revenues cause greater changes in EBIT. Additionally, changes in EBIT translate into larger variations in both earnings per share (EPS) and total earnings available to the common shareholders (EAC), if the firm chooses to use financial leverage. It should be no surprise, then, to find out that combining operating and financial leverage causes rather large variations in earnings per share. This entire process is visually displayed in Figure 12–7 on page 370.

Because the risk associated with possible earnings per share is affected by the use of combined or total leverage, it is useful to quantify the effect. For an illustration, we refer once more to the Pierce Grain Company. The cost structure identified for Pierce Grain in our discussion of breakeven analysis still holds. Furthermore,

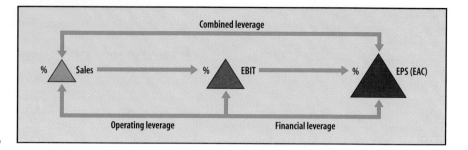

Figure 12–7
Leverage and Earnings
Fluctuations

assume that plan B, which carried a 25 percent debt ratio, was chosen to finance the company's assets. Turn your attention to Table 12–6.

In Table 12–6 an increase in output for Pierce Grain from 30,000 to 36,000 units is analyzed. This increase represents a 20 percent rise in sales revenues. From our earlier discussion of operating leverage and the data in Table 12–6, we can see that this 20 percent increase in sales is magnified into a 120 percent rise in EBIT. From this base sales level of $300,000 the degree of operating leverage is six times.

The 120 percent rise in EBIT induces a change in earnings per share and earnings available to the common shareholders of 150 percent. The degree of financial leverage is therefore 1.25 times.

The upshot of the analysis is that the 20 percent rise in sales has been magnified

Table 12–6
Pierce Grain Company Combined Leverage Analysis

Item	Base Sales Level, t	Forecast Sales Level, $t + 1$	Selected Percentage Changes
Sales	$300,000	$360,000	+20
Less: Total variable costs	180,000	216,000	
Revenue before fixed costs	$120,000	$144,000	
Less: Total fixed costs	100,000	100,000	
EBIT	$ 20,000	$ 44,000	+120
Less: Interest expense	4,000	4,000	
Earnings before taxes (EBT)	$ 16,000	$ 40,000	
Less: Taxes at 50%	8,000	20,000	
Net income	$ 8,000	$ 20,000	+150
Less: Preferred dividends	0	0	
Earnings available to common (EAC)	$ 8,000	$ 20,000	+150
Number of common shares	1,500	1,500	
Earnings per share (EPS)	$ 5.33	$ 13.33	+150

$$\text{Degree of operating leverage} = DOL_{\$300,000} = \frac{120\%}{20\%} = 6 \text{ times}$$

$$\text{Degree of financial leverage} = DFL_{\$20,000} = \frac{150\%}{120\%} = 1.25 \text{ times}$$

$$\text{Degree of combined leverage} = DCL_{\$300,000} = \frac{150\%}{20\%} = 7.50 \text{ times}$$

to 150 percent, as reflected by the percentage change in earnings per share. The formal measure of combined leverage can be expressed as follows:

$$\begin{pmatrix} \text{degree of combined} \\ \text{leverage from the} \\ \text{base sales level} \end{pmatrix} = DCL_s = \left(\cfrac{\text{percentage change in earnings per share}}{\text{percentage change in sales}} \right) \quad \textbf{(12–10)}$$

This equation was used in the bottom portion of Table 12–6 to determine that the degree of combined leverage from the base sales level of $300,000 is 7.50 times. Pierce Grain's use of both operating and financial leverage will cause any percentage change in sales (from the specific base level) to be magnified by a factor of 7.50 when the effect on earnings per share is computed. A 1 percent change in sales, for example, will result in a 7.50 percent change in earnings per share.

Notice that the degree of combined leverage is actually the product (not the simple sum) of the two independent leverage measures. Thus, we have

$$(DOL_s) \times (DFL_{EBIT}) = DCL_s \quad \textbf{(12–11)}$$

or

$$(6) \times (1.25) = 7.50 \text{ times}$$

It is possible to ascertain the degree of combined leverage in a direct fashion, without determining any percentage fluctuations or the separate leverage values. We need only substitute the appropriate values into equation (12–12):[5]

The variable definitions in equation (12–12) are the same ones that have been employed throughout this chapter. Use of equation (12–12) with the information in Table 12–6 gives

$$\begin{aligned} DCL_{\$300,000} &= \frac{30,000(\$10 - \$6)}{30,000(\$10 - \$6) - \$100,000 - \$4,000} \\ &= \frac{\$120,000}{\$16,000} \\ &= 7.5 \text{ times} \end{aligned}$$

Implications

The total risk exposure the firm assumes can be managed by combining operating and financial leverage in different degrees. Knowledge of the various leverage measures aids the financial officer in determining the proper level of overall risk that should be accepted. If a high degree of business risk is inherent in the specific line of commercial activity, then a low posture regarding financial risk would minimize additional earnings fluctuations stemming from sales changes. Conversely, the firm that by its very nature incurs a low level of fixed operating costs might choose to use a high degree of financial leverage in the hope of increasing earnings per share and the rate of return on the common equity investment. Table 12–7 on page 372 summarizes the salient concepts and calculation formats discussed thus far in this chapter.

---

[5]As was the case with the degree of financial leverage metric, the variable I in the combined leverage measure must include the before-tax equivalent of any preferred dividend payments when preferred stock is in the financial structure.

$$DCL_s = \frac{Q(P - V)}{Q(P - V) - F - I} \quad \textbf{(12–12)}$$

Table 12–7

Summary of Leverage Concepts and Calculations

TECHNIQUE	DESCRIPTION OR CONCEPT	CALCULATION	TEXT REFERENCE
BREAKEVEN ANALYSIS			
1. Break-even point quantity	Total fixed costs divided by the unit contribution margin	$Q_B = \dfrac{F}{P - V}$	(12–3)
2. Break-even sales level	Total fixed costs divided by 1 minus the ratio of total variable costs to the associated level of sales	$S^* = \dfrac{F}{1 - \dfrac{VC}{S}}$	(12–4)
OPERATING LEVERAGE			
3. Degree of operating leverage	Percentage change in EBIT divided by the percentage change in sales; or revenue before fixed costs divided by revenue after fixed costs	$DOL_s = \dfrac{Q(P - V)}{Q(P - V) - F}$	(12–6)
FINANCIAL LEVERAGE			
4. Degree of financial leverage	Percentage change in earnings per share divided by the percentage change in EBIT; or EBIT divided by EBT[a]	$DFL_{EBIT} = \dfrac{EBIT}{EBIT - I}$	(12–9)
COMBINED LEVERAGE			
5. Degree of combined leverage	Percentage change in earnings per share divided by the percentage change in sales; or revenue before fixed costs divided by EBT[a]	$DCL_s = \dfrac{Q(P - V)}{Q(P - V) - F - I}$	(12–12)

[a]The use of EBT here presumes no preferred dividend payments. In the presence of preferred dividend payments replace EBT with earnings available to common stock (EAC).

PLANNING THE FINANCING MIX

financial structure

capital structure

Given our understanding of both operating and financial leverage we now direct our attention to the determination of an appropriate financing mix for the firm. First, we must distinguish between financial structure and capital structure. **Financial structure** is the *mix of all items that appear on the right-hand side of the company's balance sheet.* **Capital structure** is the *mix of the long-term sources of funds used by the firm.* The relationship between financial and capital structure can be expressed in equation form:

$$(\text{financial structure}) - (\text{current liabilities}) = \text{capital structure} \quad \textbf{(12–13)}$$

Prudent financial structure design requires answers to the following two questions:

1. What should be the maturity composition of the firm's sources of funds; in other words, how should a firm best divide its total fund sources between short- and long-term components?

2. In what proportions relative to the total should the various forms of permanent financing be utilized?

The major influence on the maturity structure of the financing plan is the nature of the assets owned by the firm. A company heavily committed to real capital investment, represented primarily by fixed assets on its balance sheet, should finance those assets with permanent (long-term) types of financial capital. Furthermore, the permanent portion of the firm's investment in current assets should likewise be financed with permanent capital. Alternatively, assets held on a temporary basis are to be financed with temporary sources. The present discussion assumes that the bulk of the company's current liabilities are comprised of temporary capital.

OBJECTIVE 5

This hedging concept is discussed in Chapter 14. Accordingly, our focus in this chapter is on answering the second of the two questions noted previously—this process is usually called *capital structure management.*

The objective of capital-structure management is to mix the permanent sources of funds used by the firm in a manner that will maximize the company's common stock price. Alternatively, this objective may be viewed as a search for the *funds mix that will minimize the firm's composite cost of capital.* We can call this proper mix of funds sources the **optimal capital structure.**

optimal capital structure

Table 12–8 looks at equation (12–13) in terms of a simplified balance sheet format. It helps us visualize the overriding problem of capital structure management. The sources of funds that give rise to financing fixed costs (long-term debt and preferred equity) must be combined with common equity in the proportions most suitable to the investment marketplace. If that mix can be found, then holding all other factors constant, the firm's common stock price will be maximized.

Although equation (12–13) quite accurately indicates that the corporate capital structure may be viewed as an absolute dollar amount, the real capital structure problem is one of balancing the array of funds sources in a proper manner. Our use of the term *capital structure* emphasizes this latter problem of relative magnitude, or proportions.

The rest of this chapter will cover three main areas. First, we briefly discuss the theory of capital structure to provide a perspective. Second, we examine the basic tools of capital structure management. We conclude with a real-world look at actual capital structure management.

PAUSE AND REFLECT

It pays to understand the essential components of capital structure theory. The assumption of excessive financial risk can put the firm into bankruptcy proceedings. Some argue that the decision to use little financial leverage results in an undervaluation of the firm's shares in the marketplace. The effective financial manager must know how to find the area of optimum financial leverage use—this will enhance share value, all other considerations held constant. Thus, grasping the theory will make you better able to formulate a sound financial structure policy.

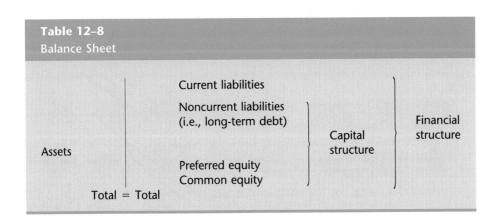

Table 12–8
Balance Sheet

Assets	Current liabilities		
	Noncurrent liabilities (i.e., long-term debt)	Capital structure	Financial structure
	Preferred equity Common equity		
Total = Total			

A QUICK LOOK AT CAPITAL STRUCTURE THEORY

An enduring controversy within financial theory concerns the effect of financial leverage on the overall cost of capital to the enterprise. The heart of the argument may be stated in the form of a question:

Can the firm affect its overall cost of funds, either favorably or unfavorably, by varying the mixture of financing sources used?

This controversy has taken many elegant forms in the finance literature. Most of these presentations appeal more to academics than financial management practitioners. To emphasize the ingredients of capital structure theory that have practical applications for business financial management, we will pursue an intuitive, or non-mathematical, approach to reach a better understanding of the underpinnings of this cost of capital-capital structure argument.

The Importance of Capital Structure

It makes economic sense for the firm to strive to minimize the cost of using financial capital. Both capital costs and other costs, such as manufacturing costs, share a common characteristic in that they potentially reduce the size of the cash dividend that could be paid to common stockholders.

We saw in Chapters 7 and 8 that the ultimate value of a share of common stock depends in part on the returns investors expect to receive from holding the stock. Cash dividends comprise all (in the case of an infinite holding period) or part (in the case of a holding period less than infinity) of these expected returns. Now, hold constant all factors that could affect share price except capital costs. If these capital costs could be kept at a minimum, the dividend stream flowing to the common stockholders would be maximized. This, in turn, would maximize the firm's common stock price.

If the firm's cost of capital can be affected by its capital structure, then capital structure management is clearly an important subset of business financial management.

Analytical Setting

The essentials of the capital structure controversy are best highlighted within a framework that economists would call a "partial equilibrium analysis." In a partial equilibrium analysis changes that do occur in several factors and have an impact on a certain key item are ignored to study the effect of changes in a main factor on that same item of interest. Here, two items are simultaneously of interest: (1) K_o, the firm's composite cost of capital, and (2) P_0, the market price of the firm's common stock. The firm's use of financial leverage is the main factor that is allowed to vary in the analysis. This means that important financial decisions, such as investing policy and dividend policy, are held constant throughout the discussion. We are only concerned with the effect of changes in the financing mix on share price and capital costs.

Consider a rarified economic world where

1. Corporate income is not subject to taxation,
2. Capital structures consist only of stock and bonds,
3. Investors make homogeneous forecasts of net operating income (what we earlier called "EBIT"), and
4. Securities are traded in perfect or efficient markets.

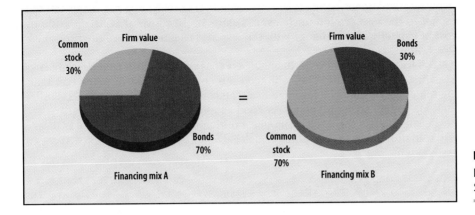

Figure 12–8
Firm Value and Capital Structure Design

In this market setting the direct answer to our question, "Can the firm affect its overall cost of funds, either favorably or unfavorably, by varying the mixture of financing sources used?" would be no. This view of capital structure importance was put into rather elegant form back in 1958 by two well-known financial economists, Franco Modigliani and Merton Miller, both of whom have been awarded the Nobel Prize in economics.

The Modigliani and Miller hypothesis, or the MM view, puts forth that within the perfect economic world described above, the total market value of the firm's outstanding securities will be *unaffected* by the manner in which the right-hand side of the balance sheet is arranged. This means the sum of the market value of outstanding common stock will always be the same regardless of how much or little debt is actually used by the company. This MM view is sometimes called the *independence hypothesis*, as firm value is independent of capital structure design.[6]

The crux of this position on financing choice is illustrated in Figure 12–8. Here the firm's asset mix (i.e., the left-hand side of the balance sheet) is held constant. All that is different is the way the assets are financed. Under financing mix A, the firm funds 30 percent of its assets with common stock and the other 70 percent with bonds. Under financing mix B, the firm reverses this mix and funds 70 percent of the assets with common stock and only 30 percent with bonds. From our earlier discussions we know that financing mix A is the more heavily levered plan.

Notice, however, that the size of each "pie" in Figure 12–8 is exactly the same. The pie represents firm value—the total market value of the firm's outstanding securities. Thus, total firm value associated with financing mix A equals that associated with financing mix B. Firm value is *independent* of the actual financing mix that has been chosen.

This implication is taken further in Figures 12–9 and 12–10 (see page 376). They display how (1) the firm's cost of funds and (2) common stock price, P_0, relate to the firm's financing mix. In Figure 12–9 we see that the firm's overall cost of capital, K_0, is unaffected by an increased use of financial leverage. If more debt is used with a cost of K_d in the capital structure, the cost of common equity, k_c, will rise at the

---

[6]See Franco Modigliani and Merton H. Miller, "The Cost of Capital, Corporation Finance, and the Theory of Investment," *American Economic Review* 48 (June 1958): 261–97; Modigliani and Miller, "Corporate Income Taxes and the Cost of Capital: A Correction," *American Economic Review* 53 (June 1963): 433–43; and Merton H. Miller, "Debt and Taxes," *Journal of Finance* 32 (May 1977): 261–75.

same rate additional earnings are generated. This will keep the composite cost of capital to the corporation unchanged. Figure 12–10 shows that because the overall cost of capital will not change with the leverage use, neither will the firm's common stock price.

The lesson of this view on financing choices is that debt financing is not as cheap as it first appears to be. This will keep the composite cost of funds constant over the full range of financial leverage use. The stark implication for financial officers is that one capital structure is just as good as any other.

Recall, though, the strict economic world in which this viewpoint was developed. We will turn next to a market and legal environment that relaxes the extreme assumptions.

BACK TO THE FOUNDATIONS

The suggestion from capital structure theory that one capital structure is just as good as any other within a perfect ("pure") market framework relies directly on **Axiom 1: The Risk-Return Trade-off—We Won't Take On Added Risk Unless We Expect to Be Compensated with Additional Return.** This means that using more debt in the capital structure will not be ignored by investors in the financial markets. These rational investors will require a higher return on com-

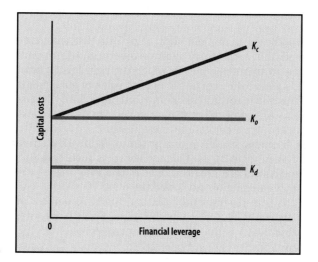

Figure 12–9
Capital Costs and Financial Leverage: No Taxes— Independence Hypothesis

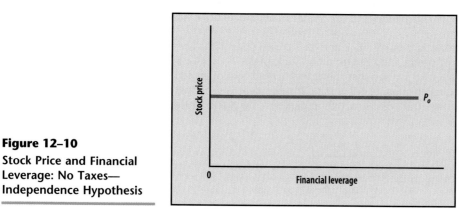

Figure 12–10
Stock Price and Financial Leverage: No Taxes— Independence Hypothesis

mon stock investments in the firm that uses more leverage (rather than less), to compensate for the increased uncertainty stemming from the addition of the debt securities in the capital structure.

Moderate Position: Corporate Income Is Taxed and Firms May Fail

We turn now to a description of the cost of capital–capital structure relationship that has rather wide appeal to both business practitioners and academics. This moderate view (1) admits to the fact that interest expense is tax deductible and (2) acknowledges that the probability of the firm's suffering bankruptcy costs is directly related to the company's use of financial leverage.

Tax Deductibility of Interest Expense

This portion of the analysis recognizes that corporate income is subject to taxation. Furthermore, we assume that interest expense is tax deductible for purposes of computing the firm's tax bill. In this environment the use of debt financing should result in a higher total market value for the firm's outstanding securities. We will see why subsequently.

Table 12–9 illustrates this important element of the U.S. system of corporate taxation. It is assumed that Skip's Camper Manufacturing Company has an expected level of net operating income (EBIT) of $2 million and faces a corporate tax rate (made simple for example purposes) of 50 percent. Two financing plans are analyzed. The first is an unlevered capital structure. The other assumes that Skip's Camper has $8 million of bonds outstanding that carry an interest rate of 6 percent per year.

Notice that if corporate income is *not* taxed, then earnings before taxes of $2 million per year could be paid to shareholders in the form of cash dividends or to bond investors in the form of interest payments, or any combination of the two. This means that the *sum* of the cash flows that Skip's Camper could pay to its contributors of debt or equity is *not* affected by its financing mix.

When corporate income is taxed by the government, however, the sum of the cash flows made to all contributors of financial capital *is affected* by the firm's financing mix. Table 12–9 illustrates this point.

If Skip's Camper chooses the levered capital structure, the total payments to equity and debt holders will be $240,000 *greater* than under the all-common-equity capitalization. Where does this $240,000 come from? The government's take, through

Table 12–9
Skip's Camper Cash Flows to All Investors—The Case of Taxes

	UNLEVERED CAPITAL STRUCTURE	LEVERED CAPITAL STRUCTURE
Expected level of net operating income	$2,000,000	$2,000,000
Less: Interest expense	0	480,000
Earnings before taxes	$2,000,000	$1,520,000
Less: Taxes at 50%	1,000,000	760,000
Earnings available to common stockholders	$1,000,000	$ 760,000
Expected payments to *all* security holders	$1,000,000	$1,240,000

taxes collected, is lower by that amount. This *difference, which flows to the* Skip's Camper *security holders*, is called the **tax shield** on interest. In general, it may be calculated by equation (12–14), where r_d is the interest rate paid on the debt, M is the principal amount of the debt, and t is the firm's marginal tax rate:

tax shield

$$\text{tax shield} = r_d\,(M)(t) \tag{12–14}$$

The moderate position on the importance of capital structure presumes that the tax shield must have value in the marketplace. Accordingly, this tax benefit will increase the total market value of the firm's outstanding securities relative to the all-equity capitalization. Financial leverage does affect firm value. Because the cost of capital is just the other side of the valuation coin, financial leverage also affects the firm's composite cost of capital. Can the firm increase firm value indefinitely and lower its cost of capital continuously by using more and more financial leverage? Common sense would tell us no! So would most financial managers and academicians. The acknowledgment of bankruptcy costs provides one possible rationale.

BACK TO THE FOUNDATIONS

The section above on the "Tax Deductibility of Interest Expense" is a compelling example of **Axiom 8: Taxes Bias Business Decisions.** We have just seen that corporations have an important incentive provided by the tax code to finance projects with debt securities rather than new issues of common stock. The interest expense on the debt issue will be tax deductible. The common stock dividends will not be tax deductible. So firms can indeed increase their total after-tax cash flows available to all investors in their securities by using financial leverage. This element of the U.S. tax code should also remind you of **Axiom 3: Cash—Not Profits—Is King.**

The Likelihood of Firm Failure

The probability that the firm will be unable to meet the financial obligations identified in its debt contracts increases as more debt is employed. The highest costs would be incurred if the firm actually went into bankruptcy proceedings. Here, assets would be liquidated. If we admit that these assets might sell for something less than their perceived market values, both equity investors and debt holders could suffer losses. Other problems accompany bankruptcy proceedings. Lawyers and accountants have to be hired and paid. Managers must spend time preparing lengthy reports for those involved in the legal action.

Milder forms of financial distress also have their costs. As their firm's financial condition weakens, creditors may take action to restrict normal business activity. Suppliers may not deliver materials on credit. Profitable capital investments may have to be foregone, and dividend payments may even be interrupted. At some point the expected cost of default will be large enough to outweigh the tax shield advantage of debt financing. The firm will turn to other sources of financing, mainly common equity. At this point the real cost of debt is thought to be higher than the real cost of common equity.

OBJECTIVE 7

Moderate View: Saucer-Shaped Cost of Capital Curve

This moderate view of the relationship between financing mix and the firm's cost of capital is depicted in Figure 12–11. The result is a saucer-shaped (or U-shaped) average cost of capital curve, K_o. The firm's average cost of equity, K_c, is seen to rise over all positive degrees of financial leverage use. For a while the firm can borrow

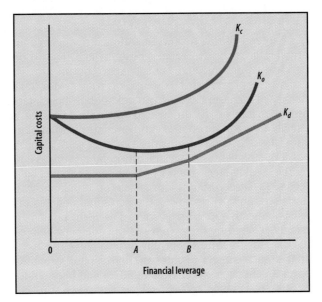

Figure 12–11
Capital Costs and Financial Leverage: The Moderate View, Considering Taxes and Financial Distress

funds at a relatively low after-tax cost of debt, K_d. Even though the cost of equity is rising, it does not rise at a fast enough rate to offset the use of the less expensive debt financing. Thus, between points 0 and A on the financial-leverage axis, the average cost of capital declines and stock price rises.

Eventually, the threat of financial distress causes the cost of debt to rise. In Figure 12–11 this increase in the cost of debt shows up in the after-tax average cost of debt curve, K_d, at point A. Between points A and B, mixing debt and equity funds produces an average cost of capital that is (relatively) flat. The firm's **optimal range of financial leverage** lies between points A and B. *All capital structures between these two points are optimal because they produce the lowest composite cost of capital.* As we said earlier in this chapter, finding this optimal range of financing mixes is the objective of capital structure management.

Point B signifies the firm's debt capacity. **Debt capacity** is the *maximum proportion of debt the firm can include in its capital structure and still maintain its lowest composite cost of capital.* Beyond point B, additional fixed-charge capital can be attracted only at very costly interest rates. At the same time, this excessive use of financial leverage would cause the firm's cost of equity to rise at a faster rate than previously. The composite cost of capital would then rise quite rapidly, and the firm's stock price would decline.

optimal range of financial leverage

debt capacity

PAUSE AND REFLECT

Given the same task or assignment, it is quite likely that you will do it better for yourself than for someone else. If you are paid well enough, you might do the job about as effectively for that other person. Once you receive compensation, your work will be evaluated by someone. This process of evaluation is called "monitoring" within most discussions on agency costs.

This describes the heart of what is called the "agency problem." As American businesses have grown, the owners and managers have become (for the most part) separate groups of individuals. An inherent conflict exists, therefore, between managers and shareholders for whom managers act as agents in carrying out their objectives (for example, corporate goals). The following discussion relates the agency problem to the financial decision-making process of the firm.

Firm Value and Agency Costs

In Chapter 1 of this text we mentioned the agency problem. Recall that the agency problem gives rise to agency costs, which tend to occur in business organizations because ownership and management control are often separate. Thus, the firm's managers can properly be thought of as agents for the firm's stockholders.[7] To ensure that agent-managers act in the stockholders' best interests requires that (1) they have proper incentives to do so and (2) their decisions are monitored. The incentives usually take the form of executive compensation plans and perquisites. The perquisites, though, might be a bloated support staff, country club memberships, luxurious corporate planes, or other amenities. Monitoring requires that certain costs be borne by the stockholders, such as (1) bonding the managers, (2) auditing financial statements, (3) structuring the organization in unique ways that limit useful managerial decisions, and (4) reviewing the costs and benefits of management perquisites. This list is indicative, not exhaustive. The main point is that monitoring costs are ultimately covered by the owners of the company—its common stockholders.

Capital structure management also gives rise to agency costs. Agency problems stem from conflicts of interest, and capital structure management encompasses a natural conflict between stockholders and bondholders. Acting in the stockholders' best interests might cause management to invest in extremely risky projects. Existing investors in the firm's bonds could logically take a dim view of such an investment policy. A change in the risk structure of the firm's assets would change the business risk exposure of the firm. This could lead to a downward revision of the bond rating the firm currently enjoys. A lowered bond rating in turn would lower the current market value of the firm's bonds. Clearly, bondholders would be unhappy with this result.

To reduce this conflict of interest, the creditors (bond investors) and stockholders may agree to include several protective covenants in the bond contract. These bond covenants are discussed in more detail in Chapter 6, but essentially they may be thought of as restrictions on managerial decision making. Typical covenants restrict payment of cash dividends on common stock, limit the acquisition or sale of assets or limit further debt financing. To make sure management complies with the protective covenants means that monitoring costs are incurred. Like all monitoring costs, they are borne by common stockholders. Furthermore, like many costs, they involve the analysis of an important trade-off.

Figure 12–12 displays some of the trade-offs involved with the use of protective bond covenants. Note (in the left panel of Figure 12–12) that the firm might be able to sell bonds that carry no protective covenants only by incurring very high interest rates. With no protective covenants, there are no associated monitoring costs. Also, there are no lost operating efficiencies, such as being able to move quickly to acquire a particular company in the acquisitions market. Conversely, the willingness to submit to several covenants could reduce the explicit cost of the debt contract, but would involve incurring significant monitoring costs and losing some operating efficiencies (which also translates into higher costs). When the debt issue is first sold,

---

[7]Economists have studied the problems associated with control of the corporation for decades. An early, classic work on this topic was A. A. Berle, Jr., and G. C. Means, *The Modern Corporation and Private Property* (New York: Macmillan, 1932). The recent emphasis in corporate finance and financial economics stems from the important contribution of Michael C. Jensen and William H. Meckling, "Theory of the Firm: Managerial Behavior, Agency Costs, and Ownership Structure," *Journal of Financial Economics* 3 (October 1976): 305–60. Professors Jensen and Clifford Smith have analyzed the bondholder–stockholder conflict in a very clear style. See Michael C. Jensen and Clifford W. Smith, Jr., "Stockholder, Manager, and Creditor Interests: Applications of Agency Theory," in Edward I. Altman and Marti G. Subrahmanyam, eds., *Recent Advances in Corporate Finance* (Homewood, IL: Irwin, 1985), 93–131.

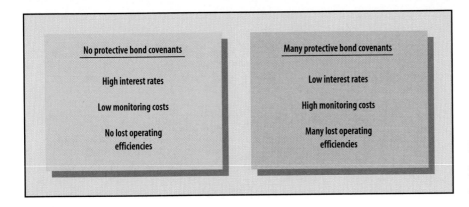

Figure 12–12
Agency Costs of Debt:
Trade-offs

then a trade-off will be arrived at among incurring monitoring costs, losing operating efficiencies, and enjoying a lower explicit interest cost.

Next, we have to consider the presence of monitoring costs at low and higher levels of leverage. When the firm operates at a low debt-to-equity ratio, there is little need for creditors to insist on a long list of bond covenants. The financial risk is just not there to require that type of activity. The firm will likewise benefit from low explicit interest rates when leverage is low. When the debt-to-equity ratio is high, however, it is logical for creditors to demand a great deal of monitoring. This increase in agency costs will raise the implicit cost (the true total cost) of debt financing. It seems logical, then, to suggest that monitoring costs will rise as the firm's use of financial leverage increases. Just as the likelihood of firm failure (financial distress) raises a company's overall cost of capital (K_o), so do agency costs. On the other side of the coin, this means that total firm value (the total market value of the firm's securities) will be *lower* owing to the presence of agency costs. Taken together, the presence of agency costs and the costs associated with financial distress argue in favor of the concept of an *optimal* capital structure for the individual firm.

This discussion can be summarized by introducing equation (12–15) for the market value of the levered firm.

$$\begin{array}{l} \text{market value of} \\ \text{levered firm} \end{array} = \begin{array}{l} \text{market value of} \\ \text{unlevered firm} \end{array} + \begin{array}{l} \text{present value} \\ \text{of tax shields} \end{array} \\ \qquad\qquad - \left(\begin{array}{l} \text{present value} \\ \text{of financial} \\ \text{distress costs} \end{array} + \begin{array}{l} \text{present value} \\ \text{of agency} \\ \text{costs} \end{array} \right) \quad \textbf{(12–15)}$$

The relationship expressed in equation (12–15) is presented graphically in Figure 12–13 on page 382. There we see that the tax shield effect is dominant until point A is reached. After point A, the rising costs of the likelihood of firm failure (financial distress) and agency costs cause the market value of the levered firm to decline. The objective for the financial manager here is to find point B by using all of his or her analytical skill; this must also include a good dose of seasoned judgment. At point B the actual market value of the levered firm is maximized, and its composite cost of capital (K_o) is at a minimum. The implementation problem is that the precise costs of financial distress and monitoring can only be estimated by subjective means; a definite mathematical solution is not available. Thus, planning the firm's financing mix always requires good decision-making and management judgment.

Agency Costs, Free Cash Flow, and Capital Structure

In 1986, Professor Michael C. Jensen further extended the concept of agency costs into the area of capital structure management. The contribution revolves around a concept that Jensen labels "free cash flow."

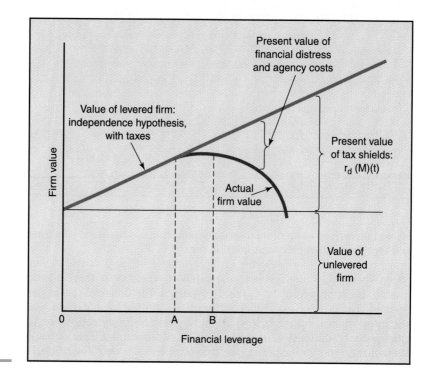

Jensen defines free cash flow as follows:

> Free cash flow is cash flow in excess of that required to fund all projects that have positive net present values when discounted at the relevant cost of capital.[8]

Jensen then proposes that substantial free cash flow can lead to misbehavior by managers and poor decisions that are not in the best interests of the firm's common stockholders. In other words, managers have an incentive to hold on to the free cash flow and have "fun" with it, rather than "disgorge" it, say, in the form of higher cash dividend payments.

But all is not lost. This leads to what Jensen calls his "control hypothesis" for debt creation. This means that by levering up, the firm's shareholders will enjoy increased control over their management team. For example, if the firm issues new debt and uses the proceeds to retire outstanding common stock, then management is obligated to pay out cash to service the debt—this simultaneously reduces the amount of free cash flow available to management with which to have fun.

We can also refer to this motive for financial leverage use as the "threat hypothesis." Management works under the threat of financial failure; therefore, according to the "free cash flow theory of capital structure," it works more efficiently. This is supposed to reduce the agency costs of free cash flow, which will in turn be recognized by the marketplace in the form of greater returns on the common stock.

---

[8]Michael C. Jensen, "Agency Costs of Free Cash Flow, Corporate Finance, and Takeovers," *American Economic Review* 76 (May 1986): 323–29.

The discussions on agency costs, free cash flow, and the control hypothesis for debt creation return us to **Axiom 7: The Agency Problem—Managers Won't Work for the Owners Unless It's in Their Best Interest.** The control hypothesis put forth by Jensen suggests that managers will work harder for shareholder interests when they have to "sweat it out" to meet contractual interest payments on debt securities. But we also learned that managers and bond investors can have a conflict that leads to agency costs associated with using debt capital. Thus, the theoretical benefits that flow from minimizing the agency costs of free cash flow by using more debt will cease when the rising agency costs of debt exactly offset those benefits. You can see how very difficult it is, then, for financial managers to identify precisely their true optimal capital structure.

Note that the free cash flow theory of capital structure does not give a theoretical solution to the question of just how much financial leverage is enough. Nor does it suggest how much leverage is too much leverage. It is a way of thinking about why shareholders and their boards of directors might use more debt to control management behavior and decisions. The basic decision tools of capital structure management still have to be utilized. They will be presented later in this chapter.

Managerial Implications

Where does our examination of capital structure theory leave us? The upshot is that the determination of the firm's financing mix is centrally important to the financial manager. The firm's stockholders are affected by capital structure decisions.

At the very least, and before bankruptcy costs and agency costs become detrimental, the tax shield effect will cause the shares of a levered firm to sell at a higher price than they would if the company had avoided debt financing. Owing to both the risk of failure and agency costs that accompany the excessive use of leverage, the financial manager must exercise caution in the use of fixed-charge capital. This problem of searching for the optimal range of use of financial leverage is our next task.[9]

You have now developed a workable knowledge of capital structure theory. This makes you better equipped to search for your firm's optimal capital structure. Several tools are available to help you in this search process and simultaneously help you make prudent financing choices. These tools are decision oriented. They assist us in answering the question, The next time we need $20 million, should we issue common stock or sell long-term bonds?

---

[9]The relationship between capital structure and enterprise valuation by the marketplace continues to stimulate considerable research output. The complexity of the topic is reviewed in Stewart C. Myers, "The Capital Structure Puzzle," *Journal of Finance* 39 (July 1984): 575–92. Ten useful papers are contained in Benjamin M. Friedman, ed., *Corporate Capital Structures in the United States* (Chicago: National Bureau of Economic Research and The University of Chicago Press, 1985).

BASIC TOOLS OF CAPITAL STRUCTURE MANAGEMENT

Recall from our earlier work that the use of financial leverage has two effects on the earnings stream flowing to the firm's common stockholders. For clarity of exposition Tables 12–4 and 12–5 are repeated here as Tables 12–10 and 12–11. Three possible financing mixes for the Pierce Grain Company are contained in Table 12–10, and an analysis for the corresponding financial leverage effects is displayed in Table 12–11.

The first financial leverage effect is the added variability in the earnings-per-share stream that accompanies the use of fixed-charge securities in the company's capital structure. By means of the degree-of-financial-leverage measure (DFL_{EBIT}) we explained how this variability can be quantified. The firm that uses more financial leverage (rather than less) will experience larger relative changes in its earnings per share (rather than smaller) following EBIT fluctuations. Assume that Pierce Grain elected financing plan C rather than plan A. Plan C is highly levered and plan A is unlevered. A 100 percent increase in EBIT from $20,000 to $40,000 would cause earnings per share to rise by 147 percent under plan C, but only 100 percent under plan A. Unfortunately, the effect would operate in the negative direction as well. A given change in EBIT is *magnified* by the use of financial leverage. This magnification is reflected in the variability of the firm's earnings per share.

The second financial leverage effect concerns the level of earnings per share at a given EBIT under a given capital structure. Refer to Table 12–11. At the EBIT level of $20,000, earnings per share would be $5, $5.33, and $5.67 under financing arrangements A, B, and C, respectively. Above a critical level of EBIT, the firm's earnings per share will be higher if greater degrees of financial leverage are employed. Conversely, below some critical level of EBIT, earnings per share will suffer at greater degrees of financial leverage. Whereas the first financial-leverage effect is quantified

---

Table 12–10
Pierce Grain Company Possible Capital Structures

PLAN A: 0% DEBT

		Total debt	$ 0
		Common equity	200,000[a]
Total assets	$200,000	Total liabilities and equity	$200,000

PLAN B: 25% DEBT AT 8% INTEREST RATE

		Total debt	$ 50,000
		Common equity	150,000[b]
Total assets	$200,000	Total liabilities and equity	$200,000

PLAN C: 40% DEBT AT 8% INTEREST RATE

		Total debt	$ 80,000
		Common equity	120,000[c]
Total assets	$200,000	Total liabilities and equity	$200,000

[a]2,000 common shares outstanding
[b]1,500 common shares outstanding
[c]1,200 common shares outstanding

Table 12-11
Pierce Grain Company Analysis of Financial Leverage at Different EBIT Levels

(1)	(2)	(3) = (1) − (2)	(4) = (3) × .5	(5) = (3) − (4)	(6)	
				NET INCOME	EARNINGS	
EBIT	INTEREST	EBT	TAXES	TO COMMON	PER SHARE	
PLAN A: 0% DEBT; $200,000 COMMON EQUITY; 2,000 SHARES						
$ 0	$ 0	$ 0	$ 0	$ 0	$ 0	
20,000	0	20,000	10,000	10,000	5.00	100%
40,000	0	40,000	20,000	20,000	10.00	
60,000	0	60,000	30,000	30,000	15.00	
80,000	0	80,000	40,000	40,000	20.00	
PLAN B: 25% DEBT; 8% INTEREST RATE; $150,000 COMMON EQUITY; 1,500 SHARES						
$ 0	$4,000	$(4,000)	$(2,000)[a]	$(2,000)	$(1.33)	
20,000	4,000	16,000	8,000	8,000	5.33	125%
40,000	4,000	36,000	18,000	18,000	12.00	
60,000	4,000	56,000	28,000	28,000	18.67	
80,000	4,000	76,000	38,000	38,000	25.33	
PLAN C: 40% DEBT; 8% INTEREST RATE; $120,000 COMMON EQUITY; 1,200 SHARES						
$ 0	$6,400	$(6,400)	$(3,200)[a]	$(3,200)	$(2.67)	
20,000	6,400	13,600	6,800	6,800	5.67	147%
40,000	6,400	33,600	16,800	16,800	14.00	
60,000	6,400	53,600	26,800	26,800	22.33	
80,000	6,400	73,600	36,800	36,800	30.67	

[a]The negative tax bill recognizes the credit arising from the carryback and carryforward provision of the tax code.

by the degree-of-financial-leverage measure (DFL_{EBIT}), the second is quantified by what is generally referred to as EBIT-EPS analysis. (EPS refers, of course, to earnings per share.) The rationale underlying this sort of analysis is simple. Earnings is one of the key variables that influences the market value of the firm's common stock. The effect of a financing decision on EPS, then, should be understood because the decision will probably affect the value of the stockholders' investment.

EBIT-EPS Analysis
EXAMPLE

Assume that plan B in Table 12–11 is the existing capital structure for the Pierce Grain Company. Furthermore, the asset structure of the firm is such that EBIT is expected to be $20,000 per year for a very long time. A capital investment is available to Pierce Grain that will cost $50,000. Acquisition of this asset is expected to raise the projected EBIT level to $30,000, permanently. The firm can raise the needed cash by (1) selling 500 shares of common stock at $100 each or (2) selling new bonds that will net the firm $50,000 and carry an interest rate of 8.5 percent. These capital structures and corresponding EPS amounts are summarized in Table 12–12.

At the projected EBIT level of $30,000, the EPS for the common stock and debt alternatives are $6.50 and $7.25, respectively. Both are considerably above the $5.33 that would occur if the new project were rejected and the additional financial capital were not raised. Based on a criterion of selecting the financing plan that will provide the highest EPS, the bond alternative is favored. But what if the basic business risk

Table 12–12
Pierce Grain Company Analysis of Financing Choices

PART A: CAPITAL STRUCTURES

EXISTING CAPITAL STRUCTURE		WITH NEW COMMON STOCK FINANCING		WITH NEW DEBT FINANCING	
Long-term debt at 8%	$ 50,000	Long-term debt at 8%	$ 50,000	Long-term debt at 8%	$ 50,000
Common stock	150,000	Common stock	200,000	Long-term debt at 8.5%	50,000
				Common stock	150,000
Total liabilities and equity	$200,000	Total liabilities and equity	$250,000	Total liabilities and equity	$250,000
Common shares outstanding	1,500	Common shares outstanding	2,000	Common shares outstanding	1,500

PART B: PROJECTED EPS LEVELS

	EXISTING CAPITAL STRUCTURE	WITH NEW COMMON STOCK FINANCING	WITH NEW DEBT FINANCING
EBIT	$20,000	$30,000	$30,000
Less: Interest expense	4,000	4,000	8,250
Earnings before taxes (EBT)	$16,000	$26,000	$21,750
Less: Taxes at 50%	8,000	13,000	10,875
Net income	$ 8,000	$13,000	$10,875
Less: Preferred dividends	0	0	0
Earnings available to common	$ 8,000	$13,000	$10,875
EPS	$ 5.33	$ 6.50	$ 7.25

to which the firm is exposed causes the EBIT level to vary over a considerable range? Can we be sure that the bond alternative will *always* have the higher EPS associated with it? The answer, of course, is no. When the EBIT level is subject to uncertainty, a graphic analysis of the proposed financing plans can provide useful information to the financial manager.

Graphic Analysis

The EBIT-EPS analysis chart allows the decision maker to visualize the impact of different financing plans on EPS over a range of EBIT levels. The relationship between EPS and EBIT is linear. All we need, therefore, to construct the chart is two points for each alternative. Part B of Table 12–12 already provides us with one of these points. The answer to the following question for each choice gives us the second point: At what EBIT level will the EPS for the plan be exactly zero? If the EBIT level *just covers* the plan's financing costs (on a before-tax basis), then EPS will be zero. For the stock plan, an EPS of zero is associated with an EBIT of $4,000. The $4,000 is the interest expense incurred under the existing capital structure. If the bond plan is elected, the interest costs will be the present $4,000 plus $4,250 per year arising from the new debt issue. An EBIT level of $8,250, then, is necessary to provide a zero EPS with the bond plan.

The EBIT-EPS analysis chart representing the financing choices available to the Pierce Grain Company is shown as Figure 12–14. EBIT is charted on the horizontal axis and EPS on the vertical axis. The intercepts on the horizontal axis represent

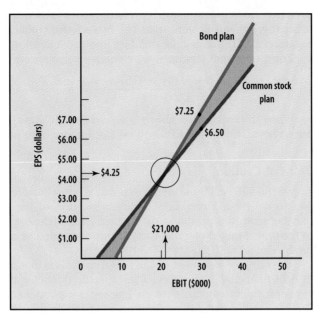

Figure 12–14
EBIT-EPS Analysis Chart

the before-tax equivalent financing charges related to each plan. The straight lines for each plan tell us the EPS amounts that will occur at different EBIT amounts.

Notice that the bond-plan line has a *steeper slope* than the stock-plan line. This ensures that the lines for each financing choice will *intersect*. Above the intersection point, EPS for the plan with greater leverage will exceed that for the plan with lesser leverage. The intersection point, encircled in Figure 12–14, occurs at an EBIT level of $21,000 and produces EPS of $4.25 for each plan. When EBIT is $30,000, notice that the bond plan produces EPS of $7.25, and the stock plan, $6.50. Below the intersection point, EPS with the stock plan will *exceed* that with the more highly levered bond plan. The steeper slope of the bond-plan line indicates that with greater leverage, EPS is more sensitive to EBIT changes.

Computing Indifference Points

The point of intersection in Figure 12–14 is called the **EBIT-EPS indifference point.** It identifies the *EBIT level at which the EPS will be the same regardless of the financing plan chosen by the financial manager.* This indifference point, some-times called the break-even point, has major implications for financial planning. At EBIT amounts in excess of the EBIT indifference level, the more heavily levered financing plan will generate a higher EPS. At EBIT amounts below the EBIT indifference level, the financing plan involving less leverage will generate a higher EPS. It is important, then, to know the EBIT indifference level.

EBIT-EPS indifference point

We can find it graphically, as in Figure 12–14. At times it may be more efficient, though, to calculate the indifference point directly. This can be done by using the following equation:

$$\underset{\text{EPS: Stock Plan}}{\underbrace{\frac{(EBIT - I)(1 - t) - P}{S_s}}} = \underset{\text{EPS: Bond Plan}}{\underbrace{\frac{(EBIT - I)(1 - t) - P}{S_b}}} \qquad \textbf{(12–16)}$$

where S_s and S_b are the number of common shares outstanding under the stock and bond plans, respectively, I is interest expense, t is the firm's income tax rate, and P is preferred dividends paid. In the present case P is zero, because there is no preferred stock outstanding. If preferred stock is associated with one of the financing alternatives, keep in mind that the preferred dividends, P, are not tax deductible. Equation (12–16) does take this fact into consideration.

For the present example, we calculate the indifference level of EBIT as

$$\frac{(EBIT - \$4,000)(1 - 0.5) - 0}{2,000} = \frac{(EBIT - \$8,250)(1 - 0.5) - 0}{1,500}$$

When the expression above is solved for EBIT, we obtain $21,000. If EBIT turns out to be $21,000, then EPS will be $4.25 under both plans.

Word of Caution

Above the EBIT-EPS indifference point, a more heavily levered financial plan promises to deliver a larger EPS. Strict application of the criterion of selecting the financing plan that produces the highest EPS might have the firm issuing debt most of the time it raised external capital. Our discussion of capital structure theory taught us the dangers of that sort of action.

The primary weakness of EBIT-EPS analysis is that it disregards the implicit costs of debt financing. The effect of the specific financing decision on the firm's cost of common equity capital is totally ignored. Investors should be concerned with both the level and variability of the firm's expected earnings stream. EBIT-EPS analysis considers only the level of the earnings stream and ignores the variability (riskiness) inherent in it. Thus, this type of analysis must be used in conjunction with other basic tools in reaching the objective of capital structure management.

Comparative Leverage Ratios

In Chapter 3 we explored the overall usefulness of financial ratio analysis. Leverage ratios, are one of the categories of financial ratios identified in that chapter. We emphasize here that the computation of leverage ratios is one of the basic tools of capital structure management.

Two types of leverage ratios must be computed when a financing decision faces the firm. We call these *balance-sheet leverage ratios* and *coverage ratios*. The firm's balance sheet supplies inputs for computing the balance sheet leverage ratios. In various forms these balance sheet metrics compare the firm's use of funds supplied by creditors with those supplied by owners.

Inputs to the coverage ratios generally come from the firm's income statement. At times the external analyst may have to consult balance sheet information to construct some of these needed estimates. On a privately placed debt issue, for example, some fraction of the current portion of the firm's long-term debt might have to be used as an estimate of that issue's sinking fund. Coverage ratios provide estimates of the firm's ability to service its financing contracts. High coverage ratios, compared with a standard, imply unused debt capacity.

In reality we know that EBIT might be expected to vary over a considerable range of outcomes. For this reason the coverage ratios should be calculated several times, each at a different level of EBIT. If this is accomplished over all possible values of EBIT, a probability distribution for each coverage ratio can be constructed. This provides the financial manager with much more information than simply calculating the coverage ratios based on the expected value of EBIT.

Industry Norms

The comparative leverage ratios calculated have additional utility to the decision maker if they can be compared with some standard. Generally, corporate financial analysts, investment bankers, commercial bank loan officers, and bond-rating agencies rely on industry classes from which to compute "normal" ratios. Although industry groupings may actually contain firms whose basic business risk exposure differs widely, the practice is entrenched in American business behavior. At the very least, then, the financial officer must be interested in industry standards because almost everybody else is.

Several published studies indicate that capital structure ratios vary in a significant manner among industry classes.[10] For example, random samplings of the common equity ratios of large retail firms seem to differ statistically from those of major steel producers. The major steel producers use financial leverage to a lesser degree than do the large retail organizations. On the whole, firms operating in the *same* industry tend to exhibit capital structure ratios that cluster around a central value which we call a norm. Business risk will vary from industry to industry. As a consequence, the capital structure norms will vary from industry to industry.

This is not to say that all companies in the industry will maintain leverage ratios "close" to the norm. For instance, firms that are very profitable may display high coverage ratios and high balance-sheet leverage ratios. The moderately profitable firm, though, might find such a posture unduly risky. Here the usefulness of industry-normal leverage ratios is clear. If the firm chooses to deviate in a material manner from the accepted values for the key ratios, it must have a sound reason.

A GLANCE AT ACTUAL CAPITAL STRUCTURE MANAGEMENT

We now examine some opinions and practices of financial executives that reinforce an emphasis on the importance of capital structure management.

Target Debt Ratios

Selected comments from financial executives point to the widespread use of target debt ratios. A vice-president and treasurer of the American Telephone and Telegraph Company (AT&T) described his firm's debt ratio policy in terms of a range:

> All of the foregoing considerations led us to conclude, and reaffirm for a period of many years, that the proper range of our debt was 30% to 40% of total capital. Reasonable success in meeting financial needs under the diverse market and economic conditions that we have faced attests to the appropriateness of this conclusion.[11]

A frequently mentioned influence on the level of the target debt ratio is ability to meet financing charges. Other factors identified by executives as affecting the target are (1) maintaining a desired bond rating, (2) providing an adequate borrowing reserve, and (3) exploiting the advantages of financial leverage.

---

[10]See, for example, Eli Schwartz and J. Richard Aronson, "Some Surrogate Evidence in Support of the Concept of Optimal Financial Structure," *Journal of Finance* 22 (March 1967): 10–18; David F. Scott, Jr., "Evidence on the Importance of Financial Structure," *Financial Management* 1 (Summer 1972): 45–50; and David F. Scott, Jr., and John D. Martin, "Industry Influence on Financial Structure," *Financial Management* 4 (Spring 1975): 67–73.

[11]John J. Scanlon, "Bell System Financial Policies," *Financial Management* 1 (Summer 1972): 16–26.

Table 12–13
Setting Target Financial Structure Ratios

	RANK	
TYPE OF INFLUENCE	1	2
Internal management and staff analysts	85%	7%
Investment bankers	3	39
Commercial bankers	0	9
Trade creditors	1	0
Security analysts	1	4
Comparative industry ratios	3	23
Other	7	18
Total	100%	100%

Source: David F. Scott, Jr., and Dana J. Johnson, "Financing Policies and Practices in Large Corporations," *Financial Management* 11 (Summer 1982): 53.

Who Sets Target Debt Ratios?

We know that firms do use target debt ratios in arriving at financing decisions. But who sets or influences these target ratios? This and other questions concerning corporate financing policy were investigated in one study published in 1982.[12] This survey of the 1,000 largest industrial firms in the United States (as ranked by total sales dollars) involved responses from 212 financial executives.

In one portion of this study the participants were asked to rank several possible influences on their target leverage (debt) ratios. Table 12–13 displays the percentage of responses ranked either number one or number two in importance. Ranks past the second are omitted in that they were not very significant. Notice that the most important influence is the firm's own management group and staff of analysts. This item accounted for 85 percent of the responses ranked number one. Of the responses ranked number two in importance, investment bankers dominated the outcomes and accounted for 39 percent of such replies. Also notice that comparisons with ratios of industry competitors and commercial bankers have some impact on the determination of leverage targets.

Debt Capacity

Previously in this chapter we noted that the firm's debt capacity is the maximum proportion of debt that it can include in its capital structure and still maintain its lowest composite cost of capital. But how do financial executives make the concept of debt capacity operational? Table 12–14 is derived from the same 1982 survey, involving 212 executives, mentioned above. These executives defined debt capacity in a wide variety of ways. The most popular approach was as a target percentage of total capitalization. Twenty-seven percent of the respondents thought of debt capacity in this manner. Forty-three percent of the participating executives remarked that debt capacity is defined in terms of some balance sheet–based financial ratio (see the first three items in Table 12–14). Maintaining a specific bond rating was also indicated to be a popular approach to implementing the debt capacity concept.

---

[12]David F. Scott, Jr., and Dana J. Johnson, "Financing Policies and Practices in Large Corporations," *Financial Management* 11 (Summer 1982): 51–59.

Table 12–14
Definitions of Debt Capacity in Practice

STANDARD OR METHOD	1,000 LARGEST CORPORATIONS (PERCENT USING)
Target percent of total capitalization (long-term debt to total capitalization)	27%
Long-term debt to net worth ratio (or its inverse)	14
Long-term debt to total assets	2
Interest (or fixed charge) coverage ratio	6
Maintain bond ratings	14
Restrictive debt covenants	4
Most adverse cash flow	4
Industry standard	3
Other	10
No response	16
Total	100%

Source: Derived from David F. Scott, Jr., and Dana J. Johnson, "Financing Policies and Practices in Large Corporations," *Financial Management* 11 (Summer 1982): 51–59.

Business Risk

The single most important factor that should affect the firm's financing mix is the underlying nature of the business in which it operates. In this chapter we defined business risk as the relative dispersion in the firm's expected stream of EBIT. If the nature of the firm's business is such that the variability inherent in its EBIT stream is high, then it would be unwise to impose a high degree of financial risk on top of this already uncertain earnings stream.

The AT&T financial officer referred to earlier has commented on the relationship between business risk and financial risk:

> In determining how much debt a firm can safely carry, it is necessary to consider the basic risks inherent in that business. This varies considerably among industries and is related essentially to the nature and demand for an industry's product, the operating characteristics of the industry, and its ability to earn an adequate return in an unknown future.[13]

It appears clear that the firm's capital structure cannot be properly designed without a thorough understanding of its commercial strategy.

SUMMARY

In this chapter we study the process of arriving at an appropriate financial structure for the firm and examine tools that can assist the financial manager in this task. We are concerned with assessing the variability in the firm's residual earnings stream (either earnings per share or earnings available to the common shareholders) in-

---

[13]Scanlon, "Bell System Financial Policies," 19.

duced by the use of operating and financial leverage. This assessment builds on the tenets of breakeven analysis.

OBJECTIVE 1

We then deal with the design of the firm's financing mix, particularly emphasizing management of the firm's permanent sources of funds—that is, its capital structure. The objective of capital structure management is to arrange the company's sources of funds so that its common stock price will be maximized, all other factors held constant.

OBJECTIVE 2

Breakeven analysis

Breakeven analysis permits the financial manager to determine the quantity of output or the level of sales that will result in an EBIT level of zero. This means the firm has neither a profit nor a loss before any tax considerations. The effect of price changes, cost structure changes, or volume changes on profits (EBIT) can be studied. To make the technique operational, it is necessary that the firm's costs be classified as fixed or variable. Not all costs fit neatly into one of these two categories. Over short planning horizons, though, the preponderance of costs can be assigned to either the fixed or variable classification. Once the cost structure has been identified, the break-even point can be found by use of contribution margin analysis or algebraic analysis.

OBJECTIVE 3

Operating leverage

Operating leverage is the responsiveness of the firm's EBIT to changes in sales revenues. It arises from the firm's use of fixed operating costs. When fixed operating costs are present in the company's cost structure, changes in sales are magnified into even greater changes in EBIT. The firm's degree of operating leverage from a base sales level is the percentage change in EBIT divided by the percentage change in sales. All types of leverage are two-edged swords. When sales decrease by some percentage, the negative impact on EBIT will be even larger.

OBJECTIVE 4

Financial leverage

A firm employs financial leverage when it finances a portion of its assets with securities bearing a fixed rate of return. The presence of debt and/or preferred stock in the company's financial structure means that it is using financial leverage. When financial leverage is used, changes in EBIT translate into larger changes in earnings per share. The concept of the degree of financial leverage dwells on the sensitivity of earnings per share to changes in EBIT. The DFL from a base EBIT level is defined as the percentage change in earnings per share divided by the percentage change in EBIT. All other things equal, the more fixed-charge securities the firm employs in its financial structure, the greater its degree of financial leverage. Clearly, EBIT can rise or fall. If it falls, and financial leverage is used, the firm's shareholders endure negative changes in earnings per share that are larger than the relative decline in EBIT. Again, leverage is a two-edged sword.

Combining operating and financial leverage

Firms use operating and financial leverage in various degrees. The joint use of operating and financial leverage can be measured by computing the degree of combined leverage, defined as the percentage change in earnings per share divided by the percentage change in sales. This measure allows the financial manager to ascertain the effect on total leverage caused by adding financial leverage on top of operating leverage. Effects can be dramatic, because the degree of combined leverage is the product of the degrees of operating and financial leverage.

Capital structure theory

OBJECTIVE 5
OBJECTIVE 6
OBJECTIVE 7

Can the firm affect its composite cost of capital by altering its financing mix? Attempts to answer this question have comprised a significant portion of capital structure theory for over three decades. Extreme positions show that the firm's stock price is either unaffected or continually affected as the firm increases its reliance on leverage-inducing funds. In the real world, an operating environment where interest expense is tax deductible and market imperfections operate to restrict the amount of fixed-income obligations a firm can issue, most financial officers and financial academics subscribe to the concept of an optimal capital structure. The optimal capital structure minimizes the firm's composite cost of capital. Searching for a proper range of financial leverage, then, is an important financial management activity.

OBJECTIVE 8

Complicating the manager's search for an optimal capital structure are conflicts that lead to agency costs. A natural conflict exists between stockholders and bondholders (the agency costs of debt). To reduce excessive risk taking by management on behalf of stockholders, it may be necessary to include several protective covenants in bond contracts that serve to restrict managerial decision making.

Another type of agency cost is related to "free cash flow." Managers, for example, have an incentive to hold on to free cash flow and enjoy it, rather than pay it out in the form of higher cash-dividend payments. This conflict between managers and stockholders leads to the concept of the *free cash flow theory of capital structure*. This same theory is also known as the *control hypothesis* and the *threat hypothesis*. The ultimate resolution of these agency costs affects the specific form of the firm's capital structure.

Tools of capital structure management

OBJECTIVE 9

The decision to use senior securities in the firm's capitalization causes two types of financial leverage effects. The first is the added variability in the earnings-per-share stream that accompanies the use of fixed-charge securities. We explain how this can be quantified by the use of the degree of financial leverage metric. The second financial leverage effect relates to the level of earnings per share (EPS) at a given EBIT under a specific capital structure. We rely on EBIT-EPS analysis to measure this second effect. Through EBIT-EPS analysis the decision maker can inspect the impact of alternative financing plans on EPS over a full range of EBIT levels.

A second tool of capital structure management is the calculation of comparative leverage ratios. Balance-sheet leverage ratios and coverage ratios can be computed according to the contractual stipulations of the proposed financing plans. Comparison of these ratios with industry standards enables the financial officer to determine if the firm's key ratios are materially out of line with accepted practice.

Capital structure practices

Surveys indicate that most financial officers in large firms believe in the concept of an optimal capital structure. The optimal capital structure is approximated by the identification of target debt ratios. The targets reflect the firm's ability to service fixed financing costs and also consider the business risk to which the firm is exposed.

Survey studies have provided information on who sets or influences the firm's target leverage ratios. The firm's own management group and staff of analysts are the major influence, followed in importance by investment bankers. Studies also show that executives put the concept of debt capacity in operation in many ways. The most popular approach is to define debt capacity in terms of a target long-term debt to total capitalization ratio. Maintaining a specific bond rating (such as Aa or A) is also a popular approach to implementing the debt capacity concept.

KEY TERMS

Business Risk, 354

Capital Structure, 372

Contribution Margin, 360

Debt Capacity, 379

Direct Costs (see Variable Costs), 357

EBIT-EPS Indifference Point, 387

Financial Leverage, 355

Financial Risk, 355

Financial Structure, 372

Fixed Costs, 356

Indirect Costs (see Fixed Costs), 356

Operating Leverage, 356

Optimal Capital Structure, 373

Optimal Range of Financial Leverage, 379

Risk, 354

Tax Shield, 378

Total Revenue, 358

Variable Costs, 357

Volume of Output, 359

STUDY QUESTIONS

12-1. Distinguish between business risk and financial risk. What gives rise to, or causes, each type of risk?

12-2. Define the term *financial leverage*. Does the firm use financial leverage if preferred stock is present in the capital structure?

12-3. Define the term *operating leverage*. What type of effect occurs when the firm uses operating leverage?

12-4. A manager in your firm decides to employ breakeven analysis. Of what shortcomings should this manager be aware?

12-5. If a firm has a degree of combined leverage of 3.0 times, what does a negative sales fluctuation of 15 percent portend for the earnings available to the firm's common stock investors?

12-6. Breakeven analysis assumes linear revenue and cost functions. In reality these linear functions over large output and sales levels are highly improbable. Why?

12-7. Define the following terms:
   a. Financial structure
   b. Capital structure
   c. Optimal capital structure
   d. Debt capacity

12-8. What is the primary weakness of EBIT-EPS analysis as a financing decision tool?

12-9. What is the objective of capital structure management?

12-10. Distinguish between (a) balance-sheet leverage ratios and (b) coverage ratios. Give two examples of each and indicate how they would be computed.

12-11. Why might firms whose sales levels change drastically over time choose to use debt only sparingly in their capital structures?

12-12. What condition would cause capital structure management to be a meaningless activity?

12-13. What does the term *independence hypothesis* mean as it applies to capital structure theory?

12-14. Who have been the foremost advocates of the independence hypothesis?

12-15. A financial manager might say that the firm's composite cost of capital is saucer-shaped or U-shaped. What does this mean?

12-16. Define the EBIT-EPS indifference point.

12-17. Explain how industry norms might be used by the financial manager in the design of the company's financing mix.

12-18. Define the term *free cash flow*.

12-19. What is meant by the *free cash flow theory of capital structure?*

12-20. In almost every instance, what funds source do managers use first in the financing of their capital budgets?

SELF-TEST PROBLEM

ST-1. (*Fixed Costs and the Break-even Point*) Bonaventure Manufacturing expects to earn $210,000 next year after taxes. Sales will be $4 million. The firm's single plant is located on the outskirts of Olean, N.Y. The firm manufactures a combined bookshelf and desk unit used extensively in college dormitories. These units sell for $200 each and have a variable cost per unit of $150. Bonaventure experiences a 30 percent tax rate.
   a. What are the firm's fixed costs expected to be next year?
   b. Calculate the firm's break-even point in both units and dollars.

12-1. (*Leverage Analysis*) You have developed the following analytical income statement for the Hugo Boss Corporation. It represents the most recent year's operations, which ended yesterday.

Sales	$50,439,375
Variable costs	(25,137,000)
Revenue before fixed costs	$25,302,375
Fixed costs	(10,143,000)
EBIT	$15,159,375
Interest expense	(1,488,375)
Earnings before taxes	$13,671,000
Taxes at 50%	(6,835,500)
Net income	$ 6,835,500

Your supervisor in the controller's office has just handed you a memorandum asking for written responses to the following questions:

a. At this level of output, what is the degree of operating leverage?

b. What is the degree of financial leverage?

c. What is the degree of combined leverage?

d. What is the firm's break-even point in sales dollars?

e. If sales should increase by 30 percent, by what percent would earnings before taxes (and net income) increase?

12-2. (*EBIT-EPS Analysis*) Four recent liberal arts graduates have interested a group of venture capitalists in backing a new business enterprise. The proposed operation would consist of a series of retail outlets to distribute and service a full line of vacuum cleaners and accessories. These stores would be located in Dallas, Houston, and San Antonio. Two financing plans have been proposed by the graduates. Plan A is an all-common-equity structure. Two million dollars would be raised by selling 100,000 shares of common stock. Plan B would involve the use of long-term debt financing. One million dollars would be raised by marketing bonds with an effective interest rate of 8 percent. Under this alternative, another $1 million would be raised by selling 50,000 shares of common stock. With both plans, then, $2 million is needed to launch the new firm's operations. The debt funds raised under plan B are considered to have no fixed maturity date, in that this portion of financial leverage is thought to be a permanent part of the company's capital structure. The fledgling executives have decided to use a 30 percent tax rate in their analysis, and they have hired you on a consulting basis to do the following:

a. Find the EBIT indifference level associated with the two financing proposals.

b. Prepare an analytical income statement that proves EPS will be the same regardless of the plan chosen at the EBIT level found in part a above.

12-3. (*Leverage Analysis*) You have developed the following analytical income statement for your corporation. It represents the most recent year's operations, which ended yesterday.

Sales	$45,750,000
Variable costs	22,800,000
Revenue before fixed costs	$22,950,000
Fixed costs	9,200,000
EBIT	$13,750,000
Interest expense	1,350,000
Earnings before taxes	$12,400,000
Taxes at 50%	6,200,000
Net income	$ 6,200,000

Your supervisor in the controller's office has just handed you a memorandum asking for written responses to the following questions:

a. At this level of output, what is the degree of operating leverage?

b. What is the degree of financial leverage?

c. What is the degree of combined leverage?

d. What is the firm's break-even point in sales dollars?

e. If sales should increase by 25 percent, by what percent would earnings before taxes (and net income) increase?

12-4. (*Break-even Point and Operating Leverage*) Footwear, Inc., manufacturers a complete line of men's and women's dress shoes for independent merchants. The average selling price of its finished product is $85 per pair. The variable cost for this same pair of shoes is $58. Footwear, Inc., incurs fixed costs of $170,000 per year.

a. What is the break-even point in pairs of shoes for the company?

b. What is the dollar sales volume the firm must achieve to reach the break-even point?

c. What would be the firm's profit or loss at the following units of production sold: 7,000 pairs of shoes? 9,000 pairs of shoes? 15,000 pairs of shoes?

d. Find the degree of operating leverage for the production and sales levels given in part c above.

12-5. (*Break-even Point and Profit Margin*) Mary Clark, a recent graduate of Clarion South University, is planning to open a new wholesaling operation. Her target operating profit margin is 26 percent. Her unit contribution margin will be 50 percent of sales. Average annual sales are forecast to be $3,250,000.

a. How large can fixed costs be for the wholesaling operation and still allow the 26 percent operating profit margin to be achieved?

b. What is the break-even point in dollars for the firm?

12-6. (*Leverage Analysis*) You have developed the following analytical income statement for your corporation. It represents the most recent year's operations, which ended yesterday.

Sales	$30,000,000
Variable costs	13,500,000
Revenue before fixed costs	$16,500,000
Fixed costs	8,000,000
EBIT	$ 8,500,000
Interest expense	1,000,000
Earnings before taxes	$ 7,500,000
Taxes at 50%	3,750,000
Net income	$ 3,750,000

Know for test!

Your supervisor in the controller's office has just handed you a memorandum asking for written responses to the following questions:

a. At this level of output, what is the degree of operating leverage?

b. What is the degree of financial leverage?

c. What is the degree of combined leverage?

d. What is the firm's break-even point in sales dollars?

e. If sales should increase by 25 percent, by what percent would earnings before taxes (and net income) increase?

12-7. (*Break-even Point and Selling Price*) Parks Castings, Inc., will manufacture and sell 200,000 units next year. Fixed costs will total $300,000, and variable costs will be 60 percent of sales.

a. The firm wants to achieve an earnings before interest and taxes level of $250,000. What selling price per unit is necessary to achieve this result?

b. Set up an analytical income statement to verify your solution to part a.

12-8. (*Operating Leverage*) Rocky Mount Metals Company manufacturers an assortment of woodburning stoves. The average selling price for the various units is $500. The associated variable cost is $350 per unit. Fixed costs for the firm average $180,000 annually.

a. What is the break-even point in units for the company?

b. What is the dollar sales volume the firm must achieve to reach the break-even point?

c. What is the degree of operating leverage for a production and sales level of 5,000 units for the firm? (Calculate to three decimal places.)

d. What will be the projected effect on earnings before interest and taxes if the firm's sales level should increase by 20 percent from the volume noted in part c above?

12-9. (*Sales Mix and Break-even Point*) Toledo Components produces four lines of auto accessories for the major Detroit automobile manufacturers. The lines are known by the code letters A, B, C, and D. The current sales mix for Toledo and the contribution margin ratio (unit contribution margin divided by unit sales price) for these product lines are as follows:

PRODUCT LINE	PERCENT OF TOTAL SALES	CONTRIBUTION MARGIN RATIO
A	33⅓%	40%
B	41⅔	32
C	16⅔	20
D	8⅓	60

Total sales for next year are forecast to be $120,000. Total fixed costs will be $29,400.

    a. Prepare a table showing (1) sales, (2) total variable costs, and (3) the total contribution margin associated with each product line.

    b. What is the aggregate contribution margin ratio indicative of this sales mix?

    c. At this sales mix, what is the break-even point in dollars?

12-10. (*Sales Mix and Break-even Point*) Because of production constraints, Toledo Components (see problem 12-9) may have to adhere to a different sales mix for next year. The alternative plan is outlined below.

PRODUCT LINE	PERCENT OF TOTAL SALES
A	25%
B	36⅔
C	33⅓
D	5

    a. Assuming all other facts in problem 12-9 remain the same, what effect will this different sales mix have on Toledo's break-even point in dollars?

    b. Which sales mix will Toledo's management prefer?

12-11. (*EBIT-EPS Analysis*) A group of retired college professors has decided to form a small manufacturing corporation. The company will produce a full line of traditional office furniture. Two financing plans have been proposed by the investors. Plan A is an all-common-equity alternative. Under this agreement, 1 million common shares will be sold to net the firm $20 per share. Plan B involves the use of financial leverage. A debt issue with a 20-year maturity period will be privately placed. The debt issue will carry an interest rate of 10 percent, and the principal borrowed will amount to $6 million. The corporate tax rate is 50 percent.

    a. Find the EBIT indifference level associated with the two financing proposals.

    b. Prepare an analytical income statement that proves EPS will be the same regardless of the plan chosen at the EBIT level found in part a.

    c. Prepare an EBIT-EPS analysis chart for this situation.

    d. If a detailed financial analysis projects that long-term EBIT will always be close to $2.4 million annually, which plan will provide for the higher EPS?

12-12. (*EBIT-EPS Analysis*) Four recent liberal arts graduates have interested a group of venture capitalists in backing a new business enterprise. The proposed operation would consist of a series of retail outlets to distribute and service a full line of vacuum cleaners and accessories. These stores would be located in Dallas, Houston, and San Antonio. Two financing plans have been proposed by the grad-uat4es. Plan A is an all-common-equity structure. Two million dollars would be raised by selling 80,000 shares of common stock. Plan B would involve the use of long-term debt financing. One million dollars would be raised by marketing bonds with an effective interest rate of 12 percent. Under this alternative, another $1 million would be raised by selling 40,000 shares of common stock. With both plans, then, $2 million is needed to launch the new firm's operations. The debt funds raised under plan B are considered to have no fixed maturity date, in that this portion of financial lever-age is thought to be a permanent part of the company's capital structure. The fledging executives have decided to use a 40 percent tax rate in their analysis, and they have hired you on a consulting basis to do the following:

    a. Find the EBIT indifference level associated with the two financing proposals.

    b. Prepare an analytical income statement that proves EPS will be the same regardless of the plan chosen at the EBIT level found in part a.

12-13. (*Assessing Leverage Use*) Some financial data for three corporations are displayed below.

MEASURE	FIRM A	FIRM B	FIRM C	INDUSTRY NORM
Debt ratio	20%	25%	40%	20%
Times burden covered	8 times	10 times	7 times	9 times
Price-earnings ratio	9 times	11 times	6 times	10 times

a. Which firm appears to be excessively levered?

b. Which firm appears to be employing financial leverage to the most appropriate degree?

c. What explanation can you provide for the higher price-earnings ratio enjoyed by firm B as compared with firm A?

COMPREHENSIVE PROBLEM

Imagine that you were hired recently as a financial analyst for a relatively new, highly leveraged ski manufacturer located in the foothills of Colorado's Rocky Mountains. Your firm manufacturers only one product, a state-of-the-art snow ski. The company has been operating up to this point without much quantitative knowledge of the business and financial risks it faces.

Ski season just ended, however, so the president of the company has started to focus more on the financial aspects of managing the business. He has set up a meeting for next week with the CFO, Maria Sanchez, to discuss matters such as the business and financial risks faced by the company. Accordingly, Maria has asked you to prepare an analysis to assist her in her discussions with the president.

As a first step in your work, you compiled the following information regarding the cost structure of the company:

Output level	80,000 units
Operating assets	$4,000,000
Operating asset turnover	8 times
Return on operating assets	32%
Degree of operating leverage	6 times
Interest expense	$600,000
Tax rate	35%

As the next step, you need to determine the break-even point in units of output for the company. One of your strong points has been that you always prepare supporting work papers, which show how you arrive at your conclusions. You know Maria would like to see such work papers for this analysis to facilitate her review of your work.

Therefore, you will have the information you require to prepare an analytical income statement for the company. You are sure that Maria would like to see this statement; in addition, you know that you need it to be able to answer the following questions. You also know Maria expects you to prepare, in a format that is presentable to the president, answers to the following questions to serve as a basis for her discussions with the president.

a. What is the degree of financial leverage?

b. What is the degree of combined leverage?

c. What is the firm's break-even point in sales dollars?

d. If sales should increase by 30 percent (as the president expects), by what percent would EBT (earnings before taxes) and net income increase?

e. Prepare another analytical income statement, this time to verify the calculations from part d above.

SELF–TEST SOLUTION

SS–1.

a.

$$
\begin{aligned}
[(P \cdot Q) - [(V \cdot Q) + (F)]](1 - T) &= \$210{,}000 \\
[(\$4{,}000{,}000) - (\$3{,}000{,}000) - F](.7) &= \$210{,}000 \\
(\$1{,}000{,}000 - F)(.7) &= \$210{,}000 \\
\$700{,}000 - .7F &= \$210{,}000 \\
.7F &= \$490{,}000 \\
F &= \underline{\underline{\$700{,}000}}
\end{aligned}
$$

Fixed costs next year, then, are expected to be $700,000.

b.

$$
Q_B = \frac{F}{P - V} = \frac{\$700{,}000}{\$50} = \underline{\underline{14{,}000 \; units}}
$$

$$
S^* = \frac{F}{1 - \dfrac{VC}{S}} = \frac{\$700{,}000}{1 - .75} = \frac{\$700{,}000}{.25} = \underline{\underline{\$2{,}800{,}000}}
$$

The firm will breakeven (EBIT = 0) when it sells 14,000 units. With a selling price of $200 per unit, the break-even sales level is $2,800,000.

Dividend Policy and Internal Financing

Key Terms • Does Dividend Policy Affect Stock Price? • The Dividend Decision in Practice • Dividend Payment Procedures • Stock Dividends and Stock Splits • Stock Repurchases

In May 1994, the FPL Group, the parent company of Florida Power & Light, announced a 32 percent reduction in its dividend—a decision never before made by a profitable utility company. (Reducing the dividend to its shareholders when the firm is not experiencing financial problems is a rare event indeed.) At the same time it announced the dividend cut, FPL also announced its intent to repurchase up to 10 million shares of its common stock. (A firm can either pay dividends or repurchase its own stock as a way to distribute profits to the investors.)

Although the firm's stock price declined immediately after the announcement, it then outperformed the stock prices of most other utility firms by a significant margin in the two years following the announcement. Also, within six weeks of the dividend cut, at least 15 major stock brokerage firms had added the stock to their recommended "buy" lists.

Although few utilities have followed FPL's example, a remarkable number of companies are now choosing stock repurchases in place of larger dividend increases. As we will see later in this chapter, repurchasing the firm's stock saves the investors some taxes.[1]

---

[1]Donald H. Chew, "A Message from the Editor," *Journal of Applied Corporate Finance* 9, no. 1 (Spring 1996): 2.

WHAT'S AHEAD

As already noted at numerous times in our studies thus far, the primary goal or objective of the firm should be to maximize the value, or price, of a firm's common stock. The success or failure of management's decisions can be evaluated only in light of their impact on the firm's common stock price. We observed that the company's investments (Chapters 9 and 10) and financing decisions (Chapter 12) can increase the value of the firm. As we look at the firm's policies regarding dividends and internal financing (how much of the company's financing comes from cash flows generated internally), we return to the same basic question: Can management influence the price of the firm's stock, in this case through its dividend policies? After addressing this important question, we then look at the practical side of the question: What practices do managers commonly follow in making decisions about paying or not paying a dividend to the firm's stockholders?

PAUSE AND REFLECT

Given what we have studied in earlier chapters, we would certainly expect that dividends, and therefore the firm's dividend policy, would be important to stockholders. However, when we consider the whole scheme of things, whether a firm pays a dividend may not matter much to investors, in terms of affecting the firm's stock price. In fact, we have difficulty explaining a firm's actions in regard to paying dividends. Yet chief financial officers, from time immemorial, have acted as if dividend policy is important. In this chapter, we will try to resolve this question, but not as completely as we would honestly like.

KEY TERMS

OBJECTIVE 1

Before taking up the particular issues relating to dividend policy, we must understand several key terms and interrelationships.

A firm's dividend policy includes two basic components. First, the **dividend payout ratio** indicates the *amount of dividends paid relative to the company's earnings.* For instance, if the dividend per share is $2 and the earnings per share is $4, the payout ratio is 50 percent ($2/$4). The second component is the stability of the dividends over time. As will be observed later in the chapter, dividend stability may be almost as important to the investor as the amount of dividends received.

In formulating a dividend policy, the financial manager faces trade-offs. Assuming that management has already decided how much to invest and chosen its debt-equity mix for financing these investments, the decision to pay a large dividend means simultaneously deciding to retain little, if any, profits; this in turn results in a greater reliance on external equity financing. Conversely, given the firm's investment and financing decisions, a small dividend payment corresponds to high profit retention with less need for externally generated equity funds. These trade-offs, which are fundamental to our discussion, are illustrated in Figure 13–1 on page 404.

dividend payout ratio

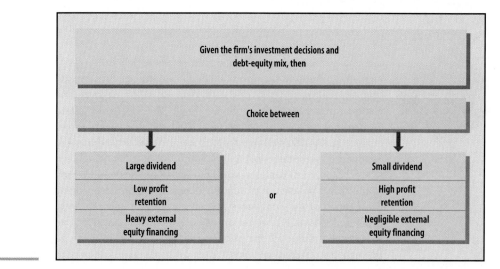

Figure 13–1
Dividend Retention/
Financing Trade-offs

OBJECTIVE 2

DOES DIVIDEND POLICY AFFECT STOCK PRICE?[2]

The fundamental question to be resolved in our study of the firm's dividend policy may be stated simply as, What is a sound rationale or motivation for dividend payments? If we believe our objective should be to maximize the value of the common stock, we may restate the question as, Given the firm's capital-budgeting and borrowing decisions, what is the effect of the firm's dividend policies on the stock price? *Does a high dividend payment decrease stock value, increase it, or make no real difference?*

At first glance, we might reasonably conclude that a firm's dividend policy is important. We have already (Chapter 7) defined the value of a stock to be equal to the present value of future dividends. How can we now suggest that dividends are not important? Why do so many companies pay dividends, and why is a page in the *Wall Street Journal* devoted to dividend announcements? Based on intuition, we could quickly conclude that dividend policy is important. However, we might be surprised to learn that the dividend question has been a controversial issue for well over three decades. Fischer Black, some 20 years ago, called it the "dividend puzzle." In his words:

> Why do corporations pay dividends? Why do investors pay attention to dividends? Perhaps the answers to these questions are obvious. Perhaps the answers are not so obvious. I claim the answers to these questions are not obvious at all. The harder we look at the dividend picture, the more it seems like a puzzle, with pieces that just don't fit together. What should the individ-

---

[2]The concepts of this section draw heavily from Donald H. Chew, Jr., ed., "Do Dividends Matter? A Discussion of Corporate Dividend Policy," in *Six Roundtable Discussions of Corporate Finance with Joel Stern* (New York: Quorum Books, 1986), 67–101; and a book of readings edited by Joel M. Stern and Donald H. Chew, Jr., *The Revolution in Corporate Finance* (New York: Basil Blackwell, 1986). For a more recent discussion on the firm's dividend policy, but with the same conclusions as the other articles just listed, see Michael J. Barclay, Clifford W. Smith, and Ross L. Watts, "The Determinants of Corporate Leverage and Dividend Policies," *Journal of Applied Corporate Finance* 7, no. 4 (Winter 1995): 4–19.

ual investor do about dividends in his portfolio? We don't know. What should the corporation do about dividend policy? We don't know.[3]

Twenty years later, in 1996, Peter Bernstein reexamined the "puzzle that fascinated Fischer Black."[4] His conclusion about the role of dividend policy in creating shareholder value: It is still very much a puzzle.

Three Basic Views

Some would argue that the amount of the dividend is irrelevant and any time spent on the decision is a waste of energy. Others contend that a high dividend will result in a high stock price. Still others take the view that dividends actually hurt the stock value. Let us look at these three views in turn.

View 1: Dividend Policy Is Irrelevant

Much of the controversy about the dividend issue is based in the time-honored disagreements between the academic and professional communities. Experienced practitioners perceive stock price changes as resulting from dividend announcements and therefore see dividends as important. Professors who argue that dividends are irrelevant see a failure to carefully define dividend policy and argue that the relationship between dividends and stock price may be an illusion.[5]

The position that dividends are not important rests on two preconditions. First, we assume that investment and borrowing decisions have already been made and that these decisions will not be altered by the amount of any dividend payments. Second, **perfect capital markets** are assumed to exist, which means that *(1) investors can buy and sell stocks without incurring any transaction costs, such as brokerage commissions; (2) companies can issue stocks without any cost of doing so; (3) there are no corporate or personal taxes; (4) complete information about the firm is readily available; (5) there are no conflicts of interest between managements and stockholders; and (6) financial distress and bankruptcy costs are nonexistent.*

The first assumption—that we have already made the investment and financing decisions—simply keeps us from confusing the issues. We want to know the effect of dividend decisions on a stand-alone basis, without mixing in other decisions. The second assumption, that of perfect markets, also allows us to study the effect of dividend decisions in isolation, much as a physicist studies motion in a vacuum to avoid the influence of friction.

Given these assumptions, the effect of a dividend decision on share price may be stated unequivocally: *There is no relationship between dividend policy and stock value.* One dividend policy is as good as another. In the aggregate, investors are concerned only with *total* returns from investment decisions; they are indifferent whether these returns come from capital gains or dividend income. They also recognize that the dividend decision, given the investment policy, is really a choice of financing strategy. That is, to finance growth, the firm (a) may choose to issue stock, allowing internally generated funds (profits) to be used to pay dividends; or (b) it may use internally generated funds to finance its growth, while paying less in dividends but not having to issue stock. In the first case, shareholders receive dividend

perfect capital markets

---

[3]Fischer Black, "The Dividend Puzzle," *Journal of Portfolio Management* 2 (Winter 1976): 5–8.

[4]Peter L. Bernstein, "Dividends: The Puzzle," *Journal of Applied Corporate Finance* 9, no. 1 (Spring 1996): 16–22.

[5]For an excellent presentation of this issue, see Merton Miller, "Can Management Use Dividends to Influence the Value of the Firm?" in Stern and Chew, eds., *The Revolution in Corporate Finance*, 299–305.

income; in the second case, the value of their stock should increase, providing capital gains. The nature of the return is the only difference; total returns should be about the same. Thus, to argue that paying dividends can make shareholders better off is to argue that paying out cash with one hand and taking it back with the other hand is a worthwhile activity for management.

The firm's dividend payout could affect stock price if the shareholder has no other way to receive income from the investment. However, assuming the capital markets are relatively efficient, a stockholder who needs current income could always sell shares. If the firm pays a dividend, the investor could eliminate any dividend received, in whole or in part, by using the dividend to purchase stock. The investor can thus personally create any desired dividend stream, no matter what dividend policy is in effect.

View 2: High Dividends Increase Stock Value

The belief that a firm's dividend policy is unimportant implicitly assumes that an investor is indifferent between income that comes through capital gains or through dividends. However, dividends are more predictable than capital gains; management can control dividends, but it cannot dictate the price of the stock. Investors are less certain of receiving income from capital gains than from dividends. The incremental risk associated with capital gains relative to dividend income implies a higher required rate for discounting a dollar of capital gains than for discounting a dollar of dividends. In other words, we would value a dollar of expected dividends more highly than a dollar of expected capital gains. We might, for example, require a 14 percent rate of return for a stock that pays its entire return from dividends, but a 20 percent return for a high-growth stock that pays no dividend. In so doing, we would give a higher value to the dividend income than we would to the capital gains. This view, which says *dividends are more certain than capital gains*, has been called the **bird-in-the-hand dividend theory.**

bird-in-the-hand dividend theory

The position that dividends are less risky than capital gains, and should therefore be valued differently, is not without its critics. If we hold to our basic decision not to let the firm's dividend policy influence its investment and capital-mix decisions, the company's operating cash flows, both in expected amount and variability, are unaffected by its dividend policy. Because the dividend policy has no impact on the volatility of the company's overall cash flows, it has no impact on the riskiness of the firm.

Increasing a firm's dividend does not reduce the basic riskiness of the stock; rather, if a dividend payment requires management to issue new stock, it only transfers risk *and* ownership from the current owners to new owners. We would have to acknowledge that the current investors who receive the dividend trade an uncertain capital gain for a "safe" asset (the cash dividend). However, if risk reduction is the only goal, the investor could have kept the money in the bank and not bought the stock in the first place.

We might find fault with this bird-in-the-hand dividend theory, but there is still a strong perception among many investors and professional investment advisers that dividends are important. They frequently argue their case based on their own personal experience. As expressed by one investment adviser:

> In advising companies on dividend policy, we're absolutely sure on one side that the investors in companies like the utilities and the suburban banks want dividends. We're absolutely sure on the other side that . . . the high-technology companies should have no dividends. For the high earners—the ones that have a high rate of return like 20 percent or more than their cost of capital—we think they should have a low payout ratio. We think a typical industrial company which earns its cost of capital—just earns its cost of

capital—probably should be in the average [dividend payout] range of 40 to 50 percent.[6]

View 3: Low Dividends Increase Stock Value

The third view of how dividends affect stock price argues that dividends actually hurt the investor. This belief has largely been based on the difference in tax treatment for dividend income and capital gains. Contrary to the perfect-markets assumption of no taxes, most investors do pay income taxes. For these taxpayers, the objective is to maximize the *after-tax* return on investment relative to the risk assumed. This objective is realized by *minimizing* the effective tax rate on the income and, whenever possible, by *deferring* the payment of taxes.

Beginning in 1993, the tax rates for married couples filing jointly range from 15 percent at the low end (the tax rate on taxable income less than $39,600) and 39.6 percent at the high end (the tax rate on $250,000 or more of income). However, for a gain from the sale of investments held more than one year, the tax rate is not to exceed 28 percent, which is a lower rate for any income above $89,000. Thus, investors in the higher income tax brackets are taxed at a lower rate on a dollar of capital gains than on a dollar of dividend income. Also, taxes on dividend income are paid when the dividend is received, while taxes on price appreciation (capital gains) are deferred until the stock is actually sold. Thus, when it comes to tax considerations, most investors would prefer the retention of a firm's earnings as opposed to the payment of cash dividends. If earnings are retained within the firm, the stock price increases, but the increase is not taxed until the stock is sold.

Although the majority of investors are subject to taxes, certain investment companies, trusts, and pension plans are exempt on their dividend income. Also, for tax purposes a corporation may generally exclude 70 percent of the dividend income received from another corporation. In these cases, investors may prefer dividends over capital gains.

To summarize, when it comes to taxes, we want to maximize our *after*-tax return, as opposed to the *before*-tax return. Investors try to defer taxes whenever possible. Stocks that allow tax deferral (low dividends–high capital gains) will possibly sell at a premium relative to stocks that require current taxation (high dividends–low capital gains). In this way, the two stocks may provide comparable *after-tax* returns. This suggests that a policy of paying low dividends will result in a higher stock price. Again, we are reminded of the fundamental **Axiom 8: Taxes Bias Business Decisions** with the tax benefits associated with capital gains as opposed to dividend income supporting a low-dividend policy.

Improving Our Thinking

We have now looked at three views on dividend policy. Which is right? The argument that dividends are irrelevant is difficult to refute, given the perfect market assumptions. However, in the real world, it is not always easy to feel comfortable with such an argument. Conversely, the high-dividend philosophy, which measures risk by how we split the firm's cash flows between dividends and retention, is not particularly appealing when studied carefully. The third view, which is essentially a tax argument against high dividends, is persuasive. Even today, although the preferential tax rate for capital gains is limited, its "deferral advantage" is still alive and well. However, if low dividends are so advantageous and generous dividends are so hurtful, why do

---

[6]From a discussion by John Childs, an investment adviser at Kidder Peabody, in Chew, ed., "Do Dividends Matter?" 83–84.

Excerpts from "Do Dividends Matter? A Discussion of Corporate Dividend Policy"

The discussion on dividend policy that follows involved a number of individuals, both from the academic community and from the business world. However, we have included only the moderator's introduction and the remarks of Joel Stern, one of the participants. These two individuals capture the essence of what is known or not known about the relationship between a firm's dividend policy and the preference of investors for dividend income.

Joseph T. Willett, Moderator: I would like to welcome the participants and guests to this discussion, the subject of which is Corporate Dividend Policy. The general questions we want to address are these: Does dividend policy matter? And if so, why and how does it matter? Certain people argue that the theory of finance, combined with the treatment

of dividends under U.S. tax law, would suggest that low dividends benefit investors. Others argue that because of the demand by some investors for current income, high dividends benefit investors. In the presence of these widely held views, I think it is fair to say that most carefully executed research has revealed no consistent relationship between dividends and share prices. From these studies, the market collectively appears to be "dividend neutral." That is, while individual investors may have preferences between dividends and capital gains, the results suggest neither a preference for nor an aversion to dividends. Which, of course, doesn't satisfy either the pro-dividend or anti-dividend group. Amid all this confusion, one observation stands

out: nearly all successful firms pay dividends. And, furthermore, dividend policy is an important concern of most chief financial officers and financial managers generally. These facts of corporate practice, in light of all the evidence on the subject, present us with a puzzle—one which has continued to baffle the academic finance profession. In a paper written in 1976, entitled "The Dividend Puzzle," Fischer Black of MIT—one of the most widely respected researchers in the field—posed the question: "What should the individual investor do about dividends in his portfolio? What should the corporation do about dividend policy?"

Joel Stern: I'd like to point out that the major reason why people like Fischer Black believe they don't know the an-

companies continue to pay dividends? It is difficult to believe that managers would forgo such an easy opportunity to benefit their stockholders. What are we missing?

The need to find the missing elements in our "dividend puzzle" has not been ignored. When we need to understand better an issue or phenomenon, we have two options: improving our thinking or gathering more evidence about the topic. Scholars and practitioners have taken both approaches. Although no single definitive answer has yet been found that is acceptable to all, several plausible extensions have been developed. Some of the more popular additions include (1) the residual dividend theory, (2) the clientele effect, (3) the information effect, (4) agency costs, and (5) expectations theory.

The Residual Dividend Theory

In perfect markets, we assume there is no cost to the firm when it issues new securities. However, in reality the process is quite expensive, and the flotation costs associated with a new offering may be as much as 20 percent of the dollar issue size. Thus, if management chooses to issue stock rather than retain profits to finance new investments, a larger amount of securities is required to receive the amount

swer to the question of the appropriate dividend policy is this: the evidence that has been accumulated in the academic community by serious researchers—by people that we have a lot of respect for, who are on the faculties of the premiere business schools—almost without exception, these academics find that there is no evidence to suggest that investors at the margin, where prices are set, have any preference for dividends over capital gains. This supports the point of view that the price-setting, marginal investor is "dividend-neutral," which means that a dollar of dividends gained is equal to a dollar of capital gains returned, while being indifferent how that return was divided between dividends and price appreciation. There is a second point of view, that has been expressed recently in research, which shows that investors who receive dividends cannot undo the harmful tax consequences of receiving that dividend. And, as a result, the market is actually "dividend averse," marking down prices of shares that pay cash dividends, so that the pretax returns that investors earn are high enough such that, post-tax, the returns are what they would have been had the company not paid cash dividends in the first place. But there is no creditable evidence that I am aware of—none that has been accepted by the academic finance community—that shows that investors prefer dividends over capital gains.

If the evidence that has been published to date says that investors are dividend neutral or dividend averse, then how is it that somebody with the esteem of Fischer Black can come along and say: "We don't know what the right dividend policy is." The problem is that he is what we call a "positive economist." That doesn't mean that he is an economist who is positive about things. It means that he says the job of the economist is to account for what we see around us. He believes that markets behave in a sensible fashion at the margin; that under the guidance of the dominant price-setting investors, the market behaves in a rational manner, making the right choices for itself. Therefore, he is saying that there must be a reason why almost all companies for all time have been paying cash dividends. If a few companies paid dividends for all time, or almost all companies paid dividends only occasionally, then one could make the case that it is possible dividends are really not important. But, if we find that almost all companies pay dividends for almost all time, there must be a good reason why they are paying the dividends. Therefore, who are we, as financial advisers, to say to a company, "No, don't pay cash dividends. After all, it won't harm you very much despite the fact that almost all companies are paying cash dividends"? That wouldn't make very much sense.

Source: Donald H. Chew, Jr., ed., "Do Dividends Matter? A Discussion of Corporate Dividend Policy," in *Six Roundtable Discussions of Corporate Finance with Joel Stern* (New York: Quorum Books, 1986), 67–101.

needed for the investment. For example, if $300,000 is needed to finance proposed investments, an amount exceeding the $300,000 will have to be issued to offset flotation costs incurred in the sale of the new stock issue. This means, very simply, that new equity capital raised through the sale of common stock will be more expensive than capital raised through the retention of earnings.

In effect, flotation costs eliminate our indifference between financing by internal capital and by new common stock. Given these costs, *dividends would be paid only if profits are not completely used for investment purposes;* that is, only when there are "residual earnings" after the financing of new investments. This policy is called the **residual dividend theory.**[7]

residual dividend theory

Given the existence of flotation costs, the firm's dividend policy should now be as follows:

1. Accept an investment if the net present value is positive; that is, the expected rate of return exceeds the cost of capital.

---

[7]The residual dividend theory is consistent with the "pecking order" theory of finance as described by Stewart Myers, "The Capital Structure Puzzle," *The Journal of Finance* (July 1984): 575–92.

2. Finance the equity portion of new investments *first* by internally generated funds. Only after this capital is fully utilized should the firm issue new common shares.

3. If any internally generated funds still remain after making all investments, pay dividends to the investors. However, if all internal capital is needed for financing the equity portion of proposed investments, pay no dividend.

Thus, dividend policy is influenced by (1) the company's investment opportunities, and (2) the availability of internally generated capital, where dividends are paid *only* after all acceptable investments have been financed. According to this concept, dividend policy is totally passive in nature, having by itself no direct influence on the market price of the common stock.

The Clientele Effect

What if the investors do not like the dividend policy chosen by management? In perfect markets, where we have no costs in buying or selling stock, there is no problem. The investors may simply satisfy their personal income preferences by purchasing or selling securities when the dividends received do not satisfy their current needs for income. If an investor does not view the dividends received in any given year to be sufficient, he or she can simply sell a portion of stock, thereby "creating a dividend." In addition, if the dividend is larger than the investor desired, he or she will purchase stock with the "excess cash" created by the dividend. However, once we remove the assumption of perfect markets, we find that buying or selling stock is not cost free. Brokerage fees are incurred, ranging approximately from 1 percent to 10 percent. Even more costly is that the investor who buys the stock with cash received from a dividend will have to pay taxes before reinvesting the cash. And when a stock is bought or sold, it must first be reevaluated. Acquisition of the information for decision making also may be time-consuming and costly. Finally, aside from the cost of buying or selling part of the stock, some institutional investors, such as university endowment funds, are precluded from selling stock and "spending" the proceeds.

As a result of these considerations, investors may not be too inclined to buy stocks that require them to "create" a dividend stream more suitable to their purposes. Rather, if investors do in fact have a preference between dividends and capital gains, we could expect them to seek firms that have a dividend policy consistent with these preferences. They would, in essence, "sort themselves out" by buying stocks that satisfy their preferences for dividends and capital gains. Individuals and institutions that need current income would be drawn to companies that have high dividend payouts. Other investors, such as wealthy individuals, would much prefer to avoid taxes by holding securities that offer no or small dividend income but large

clientele effect

capital gains. In other words, there would be a **clientele effect:** *Firms draw a given clientele, given their stated dividend policy.*

The possibility that clienteles of investors exist might lead us to believe that the firm's dividend policy matters. However, unless there is a greater aggregate demand for a particular policy than the market can satisfy, dividend policy is still unimportant; one policy is as good as the other. The clientele effect only warns firms to avoid making capricious changes in their dividend policy. Given that the firm's investment decisions are already made, the level of the dividend is still unimportant. The change in the policy matters only when it requires clientele to shift to another company.

The Information Effect

The investor in the world of perfect markets would argue with considerable persuasion that a firm's value is determined strictly by its investment and financing decisions and that the dividend policy has no impact on value. Yet we know from experience that a large, unexpected change in dividends can have a significant impact on the stock price. For instance, in November 1990 Occidental Petroleum cut its dividend from $2 to $1. In response, the firm's stock price went from about $32 to $17. How can we suggest that dividend policy matters little, when we can cite numerous such examples of a change in dividend affecting the stock price, especially when the change is negative?

Despite such "evidence," we are not looking at the real cause and effect. It may be that investors use a change in dividend policy as a *signal* about the firm's financial condition, especially its earning power. Thus, a dividend increase that is larger than expected might signal to investors that management expects significantly higher earnings in the future. Conversely, a dividend decrease, or even a less than expected increase, might signal that management is forecasting less favorable future earnings.

Some would claim that management frequently has inside information about the firm that it cannot make available to investors. This *difference in accessibility to information between management and investors*, called **information asymmetry,** *may result in a lower stock price than would occur under conditions of certainty.* This reasoning says that, by regularly increasing dividends, management is making a commitment to continue these cash flows to the stockholders for the foreseeable future. So in a risky marketplace, dividends become a means to minimize any "drag" on the stock price that might come from differences in the level of information available to managers and investors.

information asymmetry

Dividends may therefore be important only as a communication tool; management may have no other credible way to inform investors about future earnings, or at least no convincing way that is less costly.

Agency Costs

Up to this point, we have not allowed for separation between management and owners. However, with only a superficial look at the real world, we know that managers and investors are typically not the same people. Moreover, they do not have access to the same information about the firm; nor at times do they even have the same incentives.

If the two groups are not the same, we must then assume that management is dedicated to the same goals as its owners. That is, we are making a presupposition that the behavior of companies with separate owners and managers will not differ from the behavior of owner-managed firms.

BACK TO THE FOUNDATIONS

Axiom 7 warned us there may be a conflict between management and owners, especially in large firms where managers and owners have different incentives. That is, **Managers Won't Work for the Owners Unless It Is in Their Best Interest** to do so. As we shall see in this section, the dividend policy may be one way to reduce this problem.

In reality, however, conflicts may still exist, and the stock price of a company owned by investors who are separate from management may be less than the stock value of a closely held firm. This potential difference in price is the *cost of the conflict to the owners*, which has come to be called **agency costs.**[8]

agency costs

Recognizing the possible problem, management, acting independently or at the insistence of the board of directors, frequently takes action to minimize the cost

---

[8]See M. C. Jensen and W. H. Meckling, "Theory of the Firm: Managerial Behavior, Agency Costs, and Ownership Structure," *Journal of Financial Economics* (October 1976): 305–60.

associated with the separation of ownership and management control. Such action, which in itself is costly, includes auditing by independent accountants, assigning supervisory functions to the company's board of directors, creating covenants in lending agreements that restrict management's powers, and providing incentive compensation plans for management that help "bond" management with the owners.

A firm's dividend policy may be perceived by owners as a tool to minimize agency costs. Assuming that the payment of a dividend requires management to issue stock to finance new investments, new investors may be attracted to the company only if management provides convincing information that the capital will be used profitably. Thus, the payment of dividends indirectly results in a closer monitoring of management's investment activities. In this case, dividends may make a meaningful contribution to the value of the firm.

Expectations Theory[9]

A common thread through much of our discussion of dividend policy, particularly as it relates to information effects, is the word *expected*. We should not overlook the significance of this word when we are making any financial decision within the firm. *No matter what the decision area, how the market price responds to management's actions is not determined entirely by the action itself; it is also affected by investors' expectations about the ultimate decision to be made by management.* This concept or idea is called the **expectations theory.**

expectations theory

As the time approaches for management to announce the amount of the next dividend, investors form expectations as to how much that dividend will be. These expectations are based on several factors internal to the firm, such as past dividend decisions, current and expected earnings, investment strategies, and financing decisions. They also consider such things as the condition of the general economy, the strength or weakness of the industry at the time, and possible changes in government policies.

When the actual dividend decision is announced, the investor compares the actual decision with the expected decision. If the amount of the dividend is as expected, even if it represents an increase from prior years, the market price of the stock will remain unchanged. However, if the dividend is higher or lower than expected, investors will reassess their perceptions of the firm. They will question the meaning of the *unexpected* change in the dividend. They may use the unexpected dividend decision as a clue about unexpected changes in earnings; that is, the unexpected dividend change has information content about the firm's earnings and other important factors. In short, management's actual decision about the firm's dividend policy may not be terribly significant, unless it departs from investors' expectations. If there is a difference between actual and expected dividends, we will more than likely see a movement in the stock price.

The Empirical Evidence

Our search for an answer to the question of dividend relevance has been less than successful. We have given it our best thinking, but still no single definitive position has emerged. Maybe we could gather evidence to show the relationship between dividend practices and security prices. We might also inquire into the perceptions of financial managers who make decisions about dividend policies, with the idea that their beliefs affect their decision making. Then we could truly know that dividend policy is important or that it does not matter.

---

[9]Much of the thinking in this section came from Miller, "Can Management Use Dividends to Influence the Value of the Firm?" 299–303.

To test the relationship between dividend payments and security prices, we could compare a firm's dividend yield (dividend/stock price) and the stock's total return. The question is, Do stocks that pay high dividends provide higher or lower returns to investors? Such tests have been conducted with the use of highly sophisticated statistical techniques. Despite the use of these extremely powerful analytical tools, which involve intricate and complicated procedures, the results have been mixed.[10] However, over long periods, the results have given a slight advantage to the low-dividend stocks; that is, stocks that pay lower dividends appear to have higher prices. More recently, researchers have found some modest relationships between a firm's dividend policy and share price, but still nothing convincing either way.[11] Thus, the findings are far from conclusive, however, owing to the relatively large standard errors of the estimates. (The apparent differences may be the result of random sampling error and not real differences.) We simply have been unable to disentangle the effect of dividend policy from other influences.

Several reasons may be given for our inability to arrive at conclusive results. First, to be accurate, we would need to know the amount of dividends investors *expected* to receive. Because these expectations cannot be observed, we can only use historical data, which may or may not relate to current expectations. Second, most empirical studies have assumed a linear relationship between dividend payments and stock prices. The actual relationship may be nonlinear, possibly even discontinuous. Whatever the reasons, the evidence to date is inconclusive and the jury is still out.

Because our statistical prowess does not provide any conclusive evidence, let's turn to our last hope. What do the financial managers of the world believe about the relevance of dividend policy? Although we may not conclude that a manager's opinion is necessarily the "final word in the matter," having these insights is helpful. If financial managers believe that dividends matter and act consistently in accordance with that conviction, they could influence the relationship between stock value and dividend policy. As stated by one group of researchers:[12]

> In the matter of dividend policy, designing broad-based tests of actual corporate decision-making that would allow us to distinguish among these theories has proven to be quite difficult. The dearth of reliable empirical evidence on this topic has forced proponents of each theory to rely largely on anecdotes to buttress their arguments.

To help us gain some understanding of managements' perceptions, let's turn to a study by Baker, Farrelly, and Edelman, which surveyed financial executives at 318 firms listed on the New York Stock Exchange.[13] The study favors the relevance of dividend policy, but not overwhelmingly so. For the most part, managers are divided between (a) believing that dividends are important or (b) having no opinion about the matter.

Regarding the question about the price-dividend relationship, Baker et al. asked the financial managers straight up, "Does the firm's dividend policy affect the price of the common stock?" Slightly more than 60 percent of the responses were affirm-

[10]See F. Black and M. Scholes, "The Effects of Dividend Yield and Dividend Policy on Common Stock Prices and Returns," *Journal of Financial Economics*, 1 (May 1974): 1–22; and M. H. Miller and M. Scholes, "Dividends and Taxes: Some Empirical Evidence," *Journal of Political Economy*, 90 (1982): 1118–41.

[11]Clifford Smith and Ross Watts, "The Investment Opportunity Set and Corporate Financing, Dividend, and Compensation Policies," *Journal of Financial Economics* 32 (1992): 263–92.

[12]Barclay, Smith, and Watts, "The Determinants of Corporate Leverage and Dividend Policies," 4.

[13]H. Kent Baker, Gail E. Farrelly, and Richard B. Edelman, "A Survey of Management Views on Dividend Policy," *Financial Management* 14 (Autumn 1985): 78–84.

ative, which is significant, but there were still almost 40 percent who had no opinion or disagreed. Thus, we could conclude that most managers think that dividends matter, but they have no mandate. Similarly, when asked if dividends provide informational content about the firm's future, the managers are basically split between no opinion and agreement. When asked about the trade-off between dividends and capital gains, almost two-thirds of the managers thought stockholders have a preference either for dividends or capital gains, with a lesser number (56 percent) believing that investors perceive the relative riskiness of capital gains and dividends to be different. Interestingly enough, though, almost half of the managers felt no clear responsibility to be responsive to stockholders' preferences.

What Are We to Conclude?

We have now looked carefully at the importance of a firm's dividend policy as management seeks to increase the shareholders' wealth. We have gone to great lengths to gain insight and understanding from our best thinking. We have even drawn from the empirical evidence on hand to see what the findings suggest.

A reasonable person cannot reach a definitive conclusion; nevertheless, management is left with no choice. A firm must develop a dividend policy, based, it is hoped, on the best available knowledge. Although we can give advice with some reservation, the following conclusions would appear reasonable:

1. As a firm's investment opportunities increase, the dividend payout ratio should decrease. In other words, an inverse relationship should exist between the amount of investments with an expected rate of return that exceeds the cost of capital (positive *NPV*s) and the dividends remitted to investors. Because of flotation costs associated with raising external capital, the retention of internally generated equity financing is preferable to selling stock (in terms of the wealth of the current common shareholders).

2. The firm's dividend policy appears to be important; however, appearances may be deceptive. The real issue may be the firm's *expected* earning power and the riskiness of these earnings. Investors may be using the dividend payment as a source of information about the company's *expected* earnings. Management's actions regarding dividends may carry greater weight than a statement by management that earnings will be increasing.

3. If dividends influence stock price, this is probably based on the investor's desire to minimize and defer taxes, and from the role of dividends in minimizing agency costs.

4. If the expectations theory has merit, which we believe it does, management should avoid surprising investors when it comes to the firm's dividends decision. The firm's dividend policy might effectively be treated as a *long-term residual*. Rather than project investment requirements for a single year, management could anticipate financing needs for several years. Based on the expected investment opportunities during the planning horizon, the firm's debt-equity mix, and the funds generated from operations, a *target* dividend payout ratio could be established. If internal funds remained after projection of the necessary equity financing, dividends would be paid. However, the planned dividend stream should distribute residual capital evenly to investors over the planning period. Conversely, if over the long term the entire amount of internally generated capital is needed for reinvestment in the company, then no dividend should be paid.

In setting a firm's dividend policy, financial managers must work in the world of reality with the concepts we have set forth so far in this chapter. Again, although these concepts do not provide an equation that explains the key relationships, they certainly give us a more complete view of the finance world, which can only help us make better decisions. Other considerations of a more practical nature also appear as part of the firm's decision making about its dividend policy.

Other Practical Considerations

Many considerations may influence a firm's decision about its dividends, some of them unique to that company. Some of the more general considerations are given here.

Legal Restrictions

Certain legal restrictions may limit the amount of dividends a firm may pay. These legal constraints fall into two categories. First, *statutory restrictions* may prevent a company from paying dividends. While specific limitations vary by state, generally a corporation may not pay a dividend (1) if the firm's liabilities exceed its assets, (2) if the amount of the dividend exceeds the accumulated profits (retained earnings), and (3) if the dividend is being paid from capital invested in the firm.

The second type of legal restriction is unique to each firm and results from restrictions in debt and preferred stock contracts. To minimize their risk, investors frequently impose restrictive provisions on management as a condition to their investment in the company. These constraints may include the provision that dividends may not be declared prior to the debt being repaid. Also, the corporation may be required to maintain a given amount of working capital. Preferred stockholders may stipulate that common dividends may not be paid when any preferred dividends are delinquent.

Liquidity Position

Contrary to common opinion, the mere fact that a company shows a large amount of retained earnings in the balance sheet does not indicate that cash is available for the payment of dividends. The firm's current position in liquid assets, including cash, is basically independent of the retained earnings account. Historically, a company with sizable retained earnings has been successful in generating cash from operations. Yet these funds are typically either reinvested in the company within a short period or used to pay maturing debt. Thus, a firm may be extremely profitable and still be *cash poor*. Because dividends are paid with cash, *and not with retained earnings*, the firm must have cash available for dividends to be paid. Hence, the firm's liquidity position has a direct bearing on its ability to pay dividends.

Absence or Lack of Other Sources of Financing

As already noted, a firm may (1) retain profits for investment purposes or (2) pay dividends and issue new debt or equity securities to finance investments. For many small or new companies, this second option is not realistic. These firms do not have access to the capital markets, so they must rely more heavily on internally generated funds. As a consequence, the dividend payout ratio is generally much lower for a small or newly established firm than for a large, publicly owned corporation.

Earnings Predictability

A company's dividend payout ratio depends to some extent on the predictability of a firm's profits over time. If earnings fluctuate significantly, management cannot rely on internally generated funds to meet future needs. When profits are realized, the firm may retain larger amounts to ensure that money is available when needed. Conversely, a firm with a stable earnings trend will typically pay out a larger portion of its earnings in dividends. This company has less concern about the availability of profits to meet future capital requirements.

Ownership Control

For many large corporations, control through the ownership of common stock is not an issue. However, for many small and medium-sized companies, maintaining voting control takes a high priority. If the current common stockholders are unable to participate in a new offering, issuing new stock is unattractive, in that the control of the current stockholder is diluted. The owners might prefer that management finance new investments with debt and through profits rather than by issuing new common stock. This firm's growth is then constrained by the amount of debt capital available and by the company's ability to generate profits.

Inflation

Before the late 1970s, inflationary pressures had not been a significant problem for either consumers or businesses. However, during much of the 1980s, the deterioration of the dollar's purchasing power had a direct impact on the replacement of fixed assets. In a period of inflation, as fixed assets become worn and obsolete, the funds generated from depreciation ideally are used to finance the replacements. As the cost of equivalent equipment continues to increase, the depreciation funds become insufficient. This requires a greater retention of profits, which implies that dividends have to be adversely affected. In the 1990s, however, inflation has not been a primary concern for most companies.

OBJECTIVE 4

Alternative Dividend Policies

Regardless of a firm's long-term dividend policy, most firms choose one of several year-to-year dividend payment patterns.

constant dividend payout ratio

1. **Constant dividend payout ratio.** In this policy, the *percentage of earnings paid out in dividends is held constant.* Although the dividend-to-earnings ratio is stable, the dollar amount of the dividend naturally fluctuates from year to year as profits vary.

stable dollar dividend per share

2. **Stable dollar dividend per share.** This policy *maintains a relatively stable dollar dividend over time.* An increase in the dollar dividend usually does not occur until management is convinced that the higher dividend level can be maintained in the future. Management also will not reduce the dollar dividend until the evidence clearly indicates that a continuation of the current dividend cannot be supported.

small, regular dividend plus a year-end extra

3. **Small, regular dividend plus a year-end extra.** A corporation following this policy *pays a small regular dollar dividend plus a year-end* extra dividend *in prosperous years.* The extra dividend is declared toward the end of the fiscal year, when the company's profits for the period can be estimated. Management's objective is *to avoid the connotation of a permanent dividend.*

However, this purpose may be defeated if *recurring* extra dividends come to be expected by investors.

Of the three dividend policies, the stable dollar dividend is by far the most common. Figure 13–2 graphs the general tendency of companies to pay stable, but increasing, dividends, even though the profits fluctuate significantly. In one study, corporate managers were found to be reluctant to change the dollar amount of the dividend in response to temporary fluctuations in earnings from year to year. This aversion was particularly evident when it came to decreasing the amount of the dividend from the previous level.[14] One explanation for the stable dividend is the **increasing-stream hypothesis of dividend policy** which suggests that *dividend stability is essentially a smoothing of the dividend stream to minimize the effect of other types of company reversals.*[15] Thus, corporate managers make every effort to avoid a dividend cut, attempting instead to develop a gradually increasing dividend series over the long-term future. However, if a dividend reduction is absolutely necessary, the cut should be large enough to reduce the probability of future cuts.

increasing-stream hypothesis of dividend policy

As an example of a stable dividend policy, Figure 13–3 on page 418 compares W. R. Grace & Company's earnings per share and dividends per share for 1980 through 1995. Ignoring some of the outliers—most recently 1995—the firm has paid out around 50 percent to 60 percent of its earnings in dividends. This percentage, however, has varied from 33 percent in 1981 to 140 percent in 1992. Thus, the historical dividends and earnings patterns for the firm clearly demonstrate management's hesitancy to change dividends in response to short-term fluctuations in earnings. Profits have been highly volatile since 1981; however, the dollar dividends have been held constant until a slight decrease in 1995. On the other hand, when profits rose sharply in 1981 and again in 1993, dividends were increased only slightly if at all.

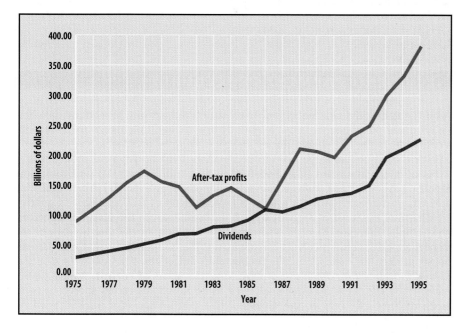

Figure 13–2
Corporate Earnings and Dividends

[14]John Lintner, "Distribution of Income of Corporations among Dividends, Retained Earnings, and Taxes," *American Economic Review* 46 (May 1956): 97–113.

[15]Keith V. Smith, "Increasing-Stream Hypothesis of Corporate Dividend Policy," *California Management Review* 15 (Fall 1971): 56–64.

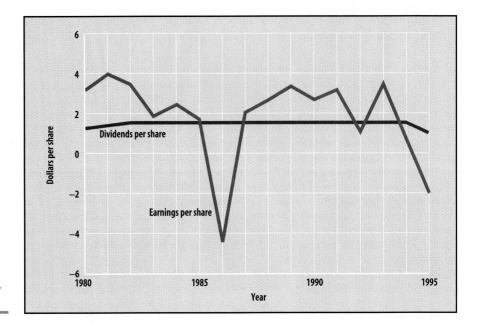

Figure 13–3
Earnings per Share and
Dividends per Share: W. R.
Grace & Company

PAUSE AND REFLECT

We don't with certitude know much about dividend policy and its effect on the firm's stock price, but we do know quite a lot about dividend practices, including that managers fear the thought of cutting the dividend. It usually will be done only as a last resort. Count on it.

OBJECTIVE 5

DIVIDEND PAYMENT PROCEDURES

After the firm's dividend policy has been structured, several procedural details must be arranged. For instance, how frequently are dividend payments to be made? If a stockholder sells the shares during the year, who is entitled to the dividend? To answer these questions, we need to understand dividend payment procedures.

Generally, companies pay dividends on a quarterly basis. To illustrate, General Electric pays $6.72 per share in annual dividends. However, the firm actually issues a $1.68 quarterly dividend for a total yearly dividend of $6.72 ($1.68 × 4 quarters).

The final approval of a dividend payment comes from the board of directors. As an example, Emerson Electric on August 5, 1996, announced that holders of record as of August 16 would receive a $.49 dividend. The dividend payment was to be made

declaration date
date of record

on September 10. August 5 is the **declaration date**—the *date when the dividend is formally declared by the board of directors.* The **date of record,** August 16, designates *when the stock transfer books are to be closed.* Investors shown to own the stock on this date receive the dividend. If a notification of a transfer is recorded subsequent to August 16, the new owner is not entitled to the dividend. However, a problem could develop if the stock were sold on August 15, one day prior to the record date. Time would not permit the sale to be reflected on the stockholder list by the August 16 date of record. To avoid this problem, *stock brokerage companies have uniformly decided to terminate the right of ownership to the dividend two*

ex-dividend date

working days prior to the date of record. This prior date is the **ex-dividend date.**

Dividend Payouts: Different Practices in Different Countries

How much of earnings do most firms pay out in dividends? It depends on the country. As shown in the accompanying graph, British firms pay out a lot more than German and Japanese companies.

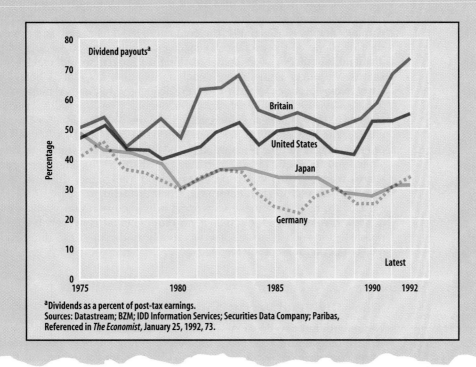

Therefore, any acquirer of Emerson Electric stock on August 14 or thereafter does not receive the dividend. Finally, the *company mails the dividend check to each investor* on September 10, the **payment date.** These events may be diagrammed as follows:

payment date

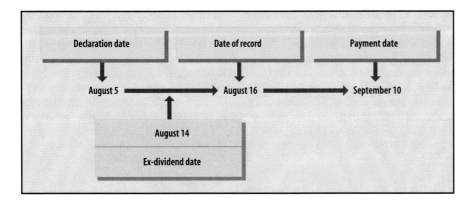

STOCK DIVIDENDS AND STOCK SPLITS

An integral part of dividend policy is the use of stock dividends and stock splits. Both involve issuing new shares of stock on a pro rata basis to the current shareholders, while the firm's assets, its earnings, the risk assumed, and the investors' percentage of ownership in the company remain unchanged. The only definite result from either a stock dividend or a stock split is the increase in the number of shares of stock outstanding.

To illustrate the effect of a stock dividend, assume that the Katie Corporation has 100,000 shares outstanding.[16] The firm's after-tax profits are $500,000, or $5 in earnings per share. Currently, the company's stock is selling at a price-earnings multiple of 10, or $50 per share. Management is planning to issue a 20 percent stock dividend, so that a stockholder owning 10 shares would receive two additional shares. We might immediately conclude that this investor is being given an asset (two shares of stock) worth $100; consequently, his or her personal worth should increase by $100. This conclusion is erroneous. The firm will be issuing 20,000 new shares (100,000 shares × 20 percent). Since the $500,000 in after-tax profits does not change, the new earnings per share will be $4.167 ($500,000/120,000 shares). If the price-earnings multiple remains at 10, the market price of the stock after the dividend should fall to $41.67 ($4.167 earnings per share × 10). The investor now owns 12 shares worth $41.67, which provides a $500 total value; thus, he or she is neither better nor worse off than before the stock dividend.

This example may make us wonder why a corporation would even bother with a stock dividend or stock split if no one benefits. However, before we study the rationale for such distributions, we should understand the differences between a stock split and a stock dividend.

Stock Dividend versus Split

The only difference between a stock dividend and a stock split relates to their respective accounting treatment. Stated differently, *there is absolutely no difference on an economic basis between a stock dividend and a stock split.* Both represent a proportionate distribution of additional shares to the current stockholders. However, *for accounting purposes* the **stock split** has been defined as a *stock dividend exceeding 25 percent.* Thus, a **stock dividend** is conventionally defined as a *distribution of shares up to 25 percent of the number of shares currently outstanding.*

The accounting treatment for a stock dividend requires the issuing firms to capitalize the "market value" of the dividend. In other words, the dollar amount of the dividend is transferred from retained earnings to the capital accounts (par and paid-in capital). This procedure may best be explained by an example. Assume that the L. Bernard Corporation is preparing to issue a 15 percent stock dividend. Table 13–1 presents the equity portion of the firm's balance sheet prior to the distribution. The market price for the stock has been $14. Thus, the 15 percent stock dividend increases the number of shares by 150,000 (1,000,000 shares × 15 percent). The "market value" of this increase is $2,100,000 (150,000 shares × $14 market price). To record this transaction, $2,100,000 would be transferred from retained earnings, resulting in a $300,000 increase in total par value (150,000 shares × $2 par value) and a $1,800,000 increment to paid-in capital. The $1,800,000 is the residual difference between $2,100,000 and $300,000. Table 13–2 shows the revised balance sheet.

---

[16]The logic of this illustration is equally applicable to a stock split.

Table 13–1

L. Bernard Corporation Balance Sheet before Stock Dividend

Common stock	
Par value (1,000,000 shares outstanding; $2 par value)	$2,000,000
Paid-in capital	8,000,000
Retained earnings	15,000,000
Total equity	$25,000,000

Table 13–2

L. Bernard Corporation Balance Sheet after Stock Dividend

Common stock	
Par value (1,150,000 shares outstanding; $2 par value)	$2,300,000
Paid-in capital	9,800,000
Retained earnings	12,900,000
Total equity	$25,000,000

Table 13–3

L. Bernard Corporation Balance Sheet after Stock Split

Common stock	
Par value (2,000,000 shares outstanding; $1 par value)	$2,000,000
Paid-in capital	8,000,000
Retained earnings	15,000,000
Total equity	$25,000,000

What if the management of L. Bernard Corporation changed the plan and decided to split the stock two for one? In other words, a 100 percent increase in the number of shares would result. In accounting for the split, the changes to be recorded are (1) an increase in the number of shares and (2) a decrease in the per-share par value from $2 to $1. The dollar amounts of each account do not change. Table 13–3 reveals the new balance sheet.

Thus, for a stock dividend, an amount equal to the market value of the stock dividend is transferred from retained earnings to the capital stock accounts. When stock is split, only the number of shares changes, and the par value of each share is decreased proportionately. Despite this dissimilarity in accounting treatment, remember that no real economic difference exists between a split and a dividend.

Rationale for a Stock Dividend or Split

Although *stock* dividends and splits occur far less frequently than *cash* dividends, a significant number of companies choose to use these share distributions either with or in lieu of cash dividends. The extent of stock splits and stock dividends over the years can be made clear by a little price comparison. In 1926, a ticket to the movies cost 25 cents—and even much less in the rural communities. At the same time, the average share price on the New York Stock Exchange was $35. Today, if we want to

August 6, 1996, Announcement by Hershey Foods Corporation to Split Stock

The following announcement appeared in the *Wall Street Journal:*

Hershey Foods Corp., Hershey, Pa., declared 2-for-1 splits of its common stock and Class B common stock to holders of record Aug. 23. The company said that splitting the common stock, which has been trading at around $80, will put it "in a more popular price range and should enhance trading liquidity." The board also increased the quarterly dividend on the common stock on a pre-split basis by 11% to 40 cents a share from 35 cents. In addition, the board increases the quarterly dividend on the Class B common stock on a presplit basis by 11% to 36 cents a share from 32.5 cents. The dividends are payable Sept. 13 to stockholders of record Aug. 23. In New York Stock Exchange composite trading, the common shares rose 37.5 cents to $84.25.

Source: "Corporate Dividend News," *Wall Street Journal*, August 7, 1996, p. C11.

go to a new movie, we can pay $7 or more. However, the average share price is still about $35. The relatively constant share price is the result of the shares being split over and over again. We can only conclude that investors apparently like it that way. But why do they, if no economic benefit results to the investor from doing so?

Proponents of stock dividends and splits frequently maintain that stockholders receive a key benefit because the price of the stock will not fall precisely in proportion to the share increase. For a two-for-one split, the price of the stock might not decrease a full 50 percent, and the stockholder is left with a higher total value. There are two reasons for this disequilibrium. First, many financial executives believe that an optimal price range exists. Within this range the total market value of the common stockholders is thought to be maximized. As the price exceeds this range, fewer investors can purchase the stock, thereby restraining the demand. Consequently, downward pressure is placed on its price. For instance, Hershey Foods Corporation announced a two-for-one split on its shares that were trading for $80. The reason given: The split would put it "in a more popular price range and should enhance trading liquidity. ("Liquidity" in this context means that more shares would be bought and sold by investors.) You can read the full announcement of this decision, as reported in the *Wall Street Journal*, in the Financial Management in Practice article shown here.

The second explanation relates to the *informational content* of the dividend-split announcement. Stock dividends and splits have generally been associated with companies with growing earnings. The announcement of a stock dividend or split has therefore been perceived as favorable news. The empirical evidence, however, fails to verify these conclusions. Most studies indicate that investors are perceptive in identifying the true meaning of a share distribution. If the stock dividend or split is not accompanied by a positive trend in earnings and increases in cash dividends, price increases surrounding the stock dividend or split are insignificant.[17] Therefore, we should be suspicious of the assertion that a stock dividend or split can help increase investors' net worth.

A second reason for stock dividends or splits is the conservation of corporate cash. If a company is encountering cash problems, it may substitute a stock dividend for a cash dividend. However, as before, investors will probably look beyond the dividend to ascertain the underlying reason for conserving cash. If the stock dividend is an effort to conserve cash for attractive investment opportunities, the shareholder may bid up the stock price. If the move to conserve cash relates to financial difficulties within the firm, the market price will most likely react adversely.

STOCK REPURCHASES

OBJECTIVE 7

A **stock repurchase** (**stock buyback**) is when *a firm repurchases its own stock, resulting in a reduction in the number of shares outstanding.* For well over three decades, corporate managements have been active in repurchasing their own equity securities. The growing significance of share repurchases over the past 20 years is shown in Figure 13–4. Also, if you were to look at the balance sheet of a firm like the McDonald's Corporation, you would see that the firm's treasury stock—the amount paid for repurchasing its own stock—is severalfold the amount of the total amount originally invested by the stockholders. This situation is not unusual for many large companies. Several reasons have been given for *stock repurchases.* Examples of such benefits include

stock repurchase
stock buyback

1. Means for providing an internal investment opportunity
2. Approach for modifying the firm's capital structure
3. Favorable impact on earnings per share

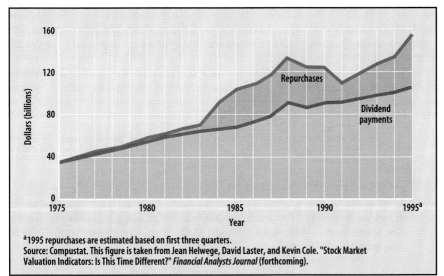

ª1995 repurchases are estimated based on first three quarters.
Source: Compustat. This figure is taken from Jean Helwege, David Laster, and Kevin Cole. "Stock Market Valuation Indicators: Is This Time Different?" *Financial Analysts Journal* (forthcoming).

Figure 13–4
Dividends and Share Repurchases, 1975–1995

ª1995 repurchases are estimated based on first three quarters.

Source: Compustat. This figure is taken from Jean Helwege, David Laster, and Kevin Cole, "Stock Market Valuation Indicators: Is This Time Different?" *Financial Analysts Journal* (forthcoming).

---

[17]See James A. Millar and Bruce D. Fielitz, "Stock Split and Stock-Dividend Decisions," *Financial Management* 2 (Winter 1973): 35–45; and Eugene Fama, Lawrence Fisher, Michael Jensen, and Richard Roll, "The Adjustment of Stock Prices to New Information," *International Economic Review* (February 1969): 1–21.

4. Elimination of a minority ownership group of stockholders

5. Minimization of the dilution in earnings per share associated with mergers

6. Reduction in the firm's costs associated with servicing small stockholders

Also, from the shareholders' perspective, a stock repurchase, as opposed to a cash dividend, has a potential tax advantage.

Share Repurchase as a Dividend Decision

Clearly, the payment of a common stock dividend is the conventional method for distributing a firm's profits to its owners. However, it need not be the only way. Another approach is to repurchase the firm's stock. The concept may best be explained by an example.

EXAMPLE

Telink, Inc. is planning to pay $4 million ($4 per share) in dividends to its common stockholders. The following earnings and market price information is provided for Telink:

Net income	$7,500,000
Number of shares	1,000,000
Earnings per share	$7.50
Price-earnings ratio	8
Expected market price per share after dividend payment	$60

In a recent meeting several board members, who are also major stockholders, question the need for a dividend payment. They maintain that they do not need the income, so why not allow the firm to retain the funds for future investments? In response, management contends that the available investments are not sufficiently profitable to justify retention of the income. That is, the investor's required rates of return exceed the expected rates of return that could be earned with the additional $4 million in investments.

Because management opposes the idea of retaining the profits for investment purposes, one of the firm's directors has suggested that the $4 million be used to repurchase the company's stock. In this way, the value of the stock should increase. This result may be demonstrated as follows:

1. Assume that shares are repurchased by the firm at the $60 market price (ex-dividend price) plus the contemplated $4 dividend per share, or for $64 per share.

2. Given a $64 price, 62,500 shares would be repurchased ($4 million ÷ $64 price).

3. If net income is not reduced, but the number of shares declines as a result of the share repurchase, earnings per share would increase from $7.50 to $8, computed as follows:

$$\text{earnings per share} = \text{net income/outstanding shares}$$
$$(\text{before repurchase}) = \$7,500,000/1,000,000$$
$$= \$7.50$$
$$(\text{after repurchase}) = \$7,500,000/(1,000,000 - 62,500)$$
$$= \$8$$

4. Assuming that the price-earnings ratio remains at 8, the new price after the repurchase would be $64, up from $60, where the increase exactly equals the amount of the forgone dividend. ■

"Many Concerns Use Excess Cash to Repurchase Their Shares"

Mattel, Inc. and General Dynamics are two firms, among many, who are repurchasing their own shares. These events, along with the rationale for the decision to repurchase their shares, are told in this *Wall Street Journal* article.

Stock buybacks are back. Faced with the prospect of only modest economic growth, many companies are using excess cash to buy their own shares rather than build new plants.

Consider the case of Mattel Inc., the El Segundo, Calif., toy maker. It just announced plans to buy 10 million shares during the next four years, even though its stock, priced at $24, is selling at a healthy 16.6 times its past 12-month earnings. The reason: Plant capacity is sufficient to handle current sales growth of 10% to 12% yearly and excess cash is building up at the rate of $200 million a year.

"We don't need the cash to grow so we've decided to give it back," says James Eskridge, Mattel's chief financial officer. Actually, Mattel plans to use about half of the $200 million each year for buybacks and dividends and the rest for growth.

The effect [of a stock repurchase] on individual stocks can be significant, says Robert Giordano, director of economic research at Goldman Sachs & Co. A case in point is General Dynamics Corp., which last summer began selling some divisions and using the proceeds to buy its stock when shares were trading at about $65 each. After nearly $1 billion in buybacks, the stock has gained about 37%, closing yesterday at $89\frac{1}{2}$.

"The market reacts positively to purchases, and it appreciates a firm that does not squander excess cash," says Columbia Business School professor Gailen Hite.

Some of the buybacks have come from companies whose stock prices have been hurt. Drug makers, for example, have seen their stocks pummeled by fears that health-care reform will sap profits. As a result, pharmaceutical companies have been big players in the buyback game.

But economists and analysts are much more intrigued by companies that are awash in cash, thanks to improving sales and several years of cost-cutting and debt reduction. At this stage of an economic recovery, many such companies would be investing heavily in plant and equipment. Not this time.

"Companies are throwing off more cash than they can ever hope to invest in plant, equipment or inventories," says Charles Clough, chief investment strategist for Merrill Lynch Capital Markets. Companies already have pared down debt, and now they're turning to equity, he says. His prediction: "He who shrinks his balance sheet the fastest wins in the '90s."

Leslie Schism, "Many Concerns Use Excess Cash to Repurchase Their Shares," *Wall Street Journal*, September 2, 1993, pp. C1, C10.

In this example, Telink's stockholders are essentially provided the same value, whether a dividend is paid or stock is repurchased. If management pays a dividend, the investor will have a stock valued at $60 plus $4 received from the dividend. Conversely, if stock is repurchased in lieu of the dividend, the stock will be worth $64. These results were based on assuming (1) the stock is being repurchased at the exact $64 price, (2) the $7,500,000 net income is unaffected by the repurchase, and (3) the price-earnings ratio of 8 does not change after the repurchase. Given these assumptions, however, the stock repurchase serves as a perfect substitute for the dividend payment to the stockholders.

The Investor's Choice

Given the choice between a stock repurchase and a dividend payment, which would an investor prefer? In perfect markets, where there are no taxes, no commissions when buying and selling stock, and no informational content assigned to a dividend, the investor would be indifferent with regard to the choices. The investor could create a dividend stream by selling stock when income is needed.

If market imperfections exist, the investor may have a preference for one of the two methods of distributing the corporate income. First, the firm may have to pay too high a price for the repurchased stock, which is to the detriment of the remaining stockholders. If a relatively large number of shares are being bought, the price may be bid up too high, only to fall after the repurchase operation. Second, as a result of the repurchase the market may perceive the riskiness of the corporation as increasing, which would lower the price-earnings ratio and the value of the stock.

Financing or Investment Decision

Repurchasing stock when the firm has excess cash may be regarded as a dividend decision. However, a stock repurchase may also be viewed as a financing decision. By issuing debt and then repurchasing stock, a firm can immediately alter its debt-equity mix toward a higher proportion of debt. Rather than choose how to distribute cash to the stockholders, management is using stock repurchase as a means to change the corporation's capital structure.

In addition to dividend and financing decisions, many managers consider stock repurchase an investment decision. When equity prices are depressed in the marketplace, management may view the firm's own stock as being materially undervalued and representing a good investment opportunity. While the firm's management may be wise to repurchase stock at unusually low prices, this decision cannot and should not be viewed in the context of an investment decision. Buying its own stock cannot provide expected returns as other investments do. No company can survive, much less prosper, by investing only in its own stock.

The Repurchase Procedure

If management intends to repurchase a block of the firm's outstanding shares, it should make this information public. All investors should be given the opportunity to work with complete information. They should be told the purpose of the repurchase, as well as the method to be used to acquire the stock.

Three methods for stock repurchase are available. First, the shares could be bought in the open market. Here the firm acquires the stock through a stockbroker at the going market price. This approach may place upward pressure on the stock price until the stock is acquired. Also, commissions must be paid to the stockbrokers as a fee for their services.

tender offer   The second method is to make a tender offer to the firm's shareholders. A **tender offer** is a *formal offer by the company to buy a specified number of shares at a predetermined and stated price. The tender price is set above the current market price in order to attract sellers.* A tender offer is best when a relatively large number of shares are to be bought, since the company's intentions are clearly known and each shareholder has the opportunity to sell the stock at the tendered price.

The third and final method for repurchasing stock entails the purchase of the stock from one or more major stockholders. These purchases are made on a negotiated basis. Care should be taken to ensure a fair and equitable price. Otherwise, the remaining stockholders may be hurt as a result of the sale.

Describe the trade-off between paying dividends and retaining the profits within the company

A company's dividend decision has an immediate impact upon the firm's financial mix. If the dividend payment is increased, less funds are available internally for financing investments. Consequently, if additional equity capital is needed, the company has to issue new common stock.

Explain the relationship between a corporation's dividend policy and the market price of its common stock

In trying to understand the effect of the dividend policy on a firm's stock price, we must realize the following:

- In perfect markets, the choice between paying or not paying a dividend does not matter. However, when we realize in the real world that there are costs of issuing stock, we have a preference to use internal equity to finance our investment opportunities. Here the dividend decision is simply a residual factor, where the dividend payment should equal the remaining internal capital after financing the equity portion of investments.
- Other market imperfections that may cause a company's dividend policy to affect the firm's stock price include (1) the tax benefit of capital gains, (2) agency costs, (3) the clientele effect, and (4) the informational content of a given policy.

Describe practical considerations that may be important to the firm's dividend policy

Other practical considerations that may affect a firm's dividend payment decision include

- Legal restrictions
- The firm's liquidity position
- The company's accessibility to capital markets
- The stability of earnings
- The desire of investors to maintain control of the company
- Inflation rates

Distinguish between the types of dividend policy corporations frequently use

In practice, managers have generally followed one of three dividend policies:

- Constant dividend payout ratio, where the percentage of dividends to earnings is held constant
- Stable dollar dividend per share, where a relatively stable dollar dividend is maintained over time
- Small, regular dividend plus a year-end extra, where the firm pays a small, regular dollar dividend plus a year-end extra dividend in prosperous years

Of the three dividend policies, the stable dollar dividend is by far the most common.

Specify the procedures a company follows in administering the dividend payment

Generally, companies pay dividends on a quarterly basis. The final approval of a dividend payment comes from the board of directors. The critical dates in this process are as follows:

- Declaration date—the date when the dividend is formally declared by the board of directors
- Date of record—the date when the stock transfer books are closed to determine who owns the stock
- Ex-dividend date—two working days prior to the date of record, after which the right to receive the dividend no longer goes with the stock
- Payment date—the date the dividend check is mailed to the stockholders

Describe why and how a firm might pay noncash dividends (stock dividends and stock splits) instead of cash dividends

Stock dividends and stock splits have been used by corporations either in lieu of or to supplement cash dividends. At the present, no empirical evidence identifies a relationship between stock dividends and splits and the market price of the stock. Yet a stock dividend or split could conceivably be used to keep the stock price within an optimal trading range. Also, if investors perceive that the stock dividend contains favorable information about the firm's operations, the price of the stock could increase.

Explain the purpose and procedures related to stock repurchases

As an alternative to paying a dividend, management can repurchase stock. In perfect markets, an investor would be indifferent between receiving a dividend or a share repurchase. The investor could simply create a dividend stream by selling stock when income is needed. If, however, market imperfections exist, the investor may have a preference for one of the two methods of distributing the corporate income. A stock repurchase may also be viewed as a financing decision. By issuing debt and then repurchasing stock, a firm can immediately alter its debt-equity mix toward a higher proportion of debt. Also, many managers consider a stock repurchase an investment decision—buying the stock when they believe it to be undervalued.

KEY TERMS

Agency Costs, 411

Bird-in-the-Hand Dividend Theory, 406

Clientele Effect, 410

Constant Dividend Payout Ratio, 416

Date of Record, 418

Declaration Date, 418

STUDY QUESTIONS

13-1. What is meant by the term *dividend payout ratio*?

13-2. Explain the trade-off between retaining internally generated funds and paying cash dividends.

13-3. a. What are the assumptions of a perfect market?
   b. What effect does dividend policy have on the share price in a perfect market?

13-4. What is the impact of flotation costs on the financing decision?

13-5. a. What is the *residual dividend theory*?
   b. Why is this theory operational only in the long term?

13-6. Why might investors prefer capital gains to the same amount of dividend income?

13-7. What legal restrictions may limit the amount of dividends to be paid?

13-8. How does a firm's liquidity position affect the payment of dividends?

13-9. How can ownership control constrain the growth of a firm?

13-10. a. Why is a stable dollar dividend policy popular from the viewpoint of the corporation?
   b. Is it also popular with investors? Why?

13-11. Explain declaration date, date of record, and ex-dividend date.

13-12. What are the advantages of a stock split or dividend over a cash dividend?

13-13. Why would a firm repurchase its own stock?

SELF-TEST PROBLEMS

ST-1. (*Dividend Growth Rate*) Schulz, Inc. maintains a constant dividend payout ratio of 35 percent. Earnings per share last year were $8.20 and are expected to grow indefinitely at a rate of 12 percent. What will be the dividend per share this year? In five years?

ST-2. (*Stock Split*) The debt and equity section of the Robson Corporation balance sheet is shown below. The current market price of the common shares is $20. Reconstruct the financial statement assuming that (a) a 15 percent stock dividend is issued and (b) a two-for-one stock split is declared.

Debt	$1,800,000
Common	
Par ($2; 100,000 shares)	200,000
Paid-in capital	400,000
Retained earnings	900,000
	$3,300,000

STUDY PROBLEMS

13-1. (*Flotation Costs and Issue Size*) Your firm needs to raise $10 million. Assuming that flotation costs are expected to be $15 per share and that the market price of the stock is $120, how many shares would have to be issued? What is the dollar size of the issue?

13-2. (*Flotation Costs and Issue Size*) If flotation costs for a common stock issue are 18 percent, how large must the issue be so that the firm will net $5,800,000? If the stock sells for $85 per share, how many shares must be issued?

13-3. (*Stock Dividend*) RCB has 2 million shares of common stock outstanding. Net income is $550,000, and the P/E ratio for the stock is 10. Management is planning a 20 percent stock dividend.
   a. What will be the price of the stock after the stock dividend?
   b. If an investor owns 100 shares prior to the stock dividend, does the total value of his or her shares change? Explain.

13-4. (*Stock Split*) You own 5 percent of Trexco Corporation's common stock, which most recently sold for $98 prior to a planned two-for-one stock split announcement. Before the split there are 25,000 shares of common stock outstanding.
   a. Relative to now, what will be your financial position after the stock split? (Assume the stock price falls proportionately.)
   b. The executive vice-president in charge of finance believes the price will only fall 40 percent after the split because she feels the price is above the optimal price range. If she is correct, what will be your net gain?

13-5. (*Dividend Policies*) The earnings for Crystal Cargo, Inc. have been predicted for the next five years and are listed below. There are 1 million shares outstanding. Determine the yearly dividend per share to be paid if the following policies are enacted:
   a. Constant dividend payout ratio of 50 percent.
   b. Stable dollar dividend targeted at 50 percent of the earnings over the five-year period.
   c. Small, regular dividend of $.50 per share plus a year-end extra when the profits in any year exceed $1,500,000. The year-end extra dividend will equal 50 percent of profits exceeding $1,500,000.

YEAR	PROFITS AFTER TAXES
1	$1,400,000
2	2,000,000
3	1,860,000
4	900,000
5	2,800,000

13-6. (*Repurchase of Stock*) The Dunn Corporation is planning to pay dividends of $500,000. There are 250,000 shares outstanding, with an earnings per share of $5. The stock should sell for $50 after the ex-dividend date. If instead of paying a dividend, management decides to repurchase stock

   a. What should be the repurchase price?

   b. How many shares should be repurchased?

   c. What if the repurchase price is set below or above your suggested price in part a?

   d. If you own 100 shares, would you prefer that the company pay the dividend or repurchase stock?

13-7. (*Flotation Costs and Issue Size*) D. Butler, Inc. needs to raise $14 million. Assuming that the market price of the firm's stock is $95 and flotation costs are 10 percent of the market price, how many shares would have to be issued? What is the dollar size of the issue?

13-8. (*Stock Split*) You own 20 percent of Rainy Corp., which recently sold for $86 before a planned two-for-one split announcement. Before the split there are 80,000 shares of common stock outstanding.

   a. What is your financial position before the split, and what will it be after the stock split? (Assume the stock price falls proportionately.)

   b. Your stockbroker believes the market will react positively to the split and that the price will fall only 45 percent after the split. If she is correct, what will be your net gain?

COMPREHENSIVE PROBLEM

The following article appeared in the July 2, 1995, issue of the *Dallas Morning News.* Scott Burns, the author, argues the case for the importance of dividends.

Let us now praise the lowly dividend.

Insignificant to some. Small potatoes to others. An irksome sign of tax liability to many. However characterized, dividends are experiencing yet another round of defamation on Wall Street.

Why pay out dividends, the current argument goes, when a dollar of dividend can be retained as a dollar of book value that the market will value at two, three or four dollars? With the average stock now selling at more than three times book value, investors should prefer companies that retain earnings rather than pay them out, even if they do nothing more with the money than repurchase shares.

The New Wisdom

Instead, the New Wisdom says, the investor should go for companies that retain earnings, reinvest them and try to maximize shareholder value. Dividends should be avoided in the pursuit of long-term capital gains.

The only problem with this reasoning is that we've heard it before. And always at market tops.

- We heard it in the late 1960s as stock prices soared and dividend yields fell.

- We heard it again in the early '70s as investors fixated on the "Nifty Fifty" and analysts calmly projected that with growth companies yielding 1 percent or less, the most important part of the return was the certainty of 20 percent annual earnings growth.

- And we're hearing it now, with stock prices hitting new highs each day. The Standard & Poor's 500 Index, for instance, is up 19.7 percent since Dec. 31, the equivalent of more than seven years of dividends at the current yield of 2.6 percent.

Tilting the Yield

Significantly, we didn't hear that dividends were irrelevant in the late '70s, as stock valuations moved to new lows. At that time, portfolio managers talked about "yield tilt"—running a portfolio with a bias toward dividend return to offset some of the risk of continuing stock market decline. Indeed, many of the best performing funds in the late '70s were Equity-Income funds, the funds that seek above-average dividend income.

You can understand how much dividends contribute to long-term returns by taking a look at the performance of a major index, with and without dividend reinvestment. If you had invested $10,000 in the S&P's 500 Index in January 1982 and taken all dividends in cash, your original investment would have grown to $37,475 by the end of 1994.

It doesn't get much better than that.

The gain clocks a compound annual return of 10.7 percent, and total gain of $27,475. During the same period you would have collected an additional $14,244 in dividends.

Not a trivial sum, either.

In other words, during one of the biggest bull markets in history, unreinvested dividend income accounted for more than one-third of your total return.

If you had reinvested those dividends in additional stock, the final score would be even better: $60,303. The appreciation of your original investment would have been $27,475 while the growth from reinvested dividends would have been $22,828. Nearly half—45 percent—of your total return came from reinvested dividends. And this happened during a stellar period of rising stock prices.

Now consider the same investment during a period of misery. If you had invested $10,000 in the S&P's Index stocks in January 1968, your investment would have grown to only $14,073 over the next 13 years, a gain of only $4,073. During much of that time, the value of your original investment would have been less than $10,000. Dividends during the period would have totaled $7,088—substantially more than stock appreciation. Reinvested, the same dividends would have grown to $9,705, helping your original investment grow to $23,778.

In a period of major ups and downs that many investors don't like to remember, dividends accounted for 70 percent of total return (see accompanying chart).

We could fiddle with these figures any number of ways. We could reduce the value of dividends by calculating income taxes. We could raise it by starting with the Dow Jones industrial average stocks, which tendto have higher dividends. But the point here is very simple: Whether you spend them or reinvest them, dividends are always an important part of the return on common stock.

A Close Look at Dividends in Two Markets

Anatomy of the bull market of 1982–1994

Original investment		$10,000
Gain on original investment		$27,475
Total dividends	$14,244	
Gain on reinvested dividends	$8,584	
Total gain from dividends		$22,828
Total		**$60,303**

Compound annualized return equals 14.8%; 45% from dividends.

Anatomy of a bear market, 1968–1980

Original investment		$10,000
Gain on original investment		$4,073
Total dividends	$7,088	
Gain on reinvested dividends	$2,617	
Total gain from dividends		$9,705
Total		**$23,778**

Compound annualized return equals 6.9%; 70% from dividends.

Source: Franklin/Templeton Group Hypothetical Illustration Program.

Based on your reading of this chapter, evaluate what Burns is saying. Do you agree or disagree with him? Why?

Source: Scott Burns, "Those Lowly Dividends," *Dallas Morning News*, July 2, 1995, pp. 1H.

SELF-TEST SOLUTIONS

SS–1.

$$\text{Dividend per share} = 35\% \times \$8.20 = \$2.87$$

Dividends:

$$1\text{ year} = \$2.87(1 + 0.12) = \$3.21$$

$$5\text{ years} = \$2.87(1 + 0.12)^5 = \$2.87(1.762) = \$5.06$$

SS–2.

a. If a 15 percent stock dividend is issued, the financial statement would appear as follows:

Debt	$1,800,000
Common	
Par ($2 par; 115,000 shares)	230,000
Paid-in capital	670,000
Retained earnings	600,000
	$3,300,000

b. A two-for-one split would result in a 100 percent increase in the number of shares. Because the total par value remains at $200,000, the new par value per share is $1 ($200,000/200,000 shares). The new financial statement would be as follows:

Debt	$1,800,000
Common	
Par ($1 par; 200,000 shares)	200,000
Paid-in capital	400,000
Retained earnings	900,000
	$3,300,000

Introduction to Working-Capital Management

LEARNING OBJECTIVES

After reading this chapter you should be able to

1. Describe the risk-return trade-off involved in managing a firm's working capital.

2. Explain the determinants of net working capital.

3. Calculate the effective cost of short-term credit.

4. List and describe the basic sources of short-term credit.

Managing Current Assets and Liabilities • Appropriate Level of Working Capital • Estimation of the Cost of Short-Term Credit • Sources of Short-Term Credit

On average, U.S. companies invest more than 15 cents in working capital from each $1 of sales. In 1990, American Standard fit into this mold very well with over $735 million invested in working capital. By the mid-1990s American Standard had revenues totaling $4.2 billion but had reduced its net working capital roughly by half.

In 1990, American Standard had three primary product lines: plumbing supplies, air conditioners, and brakes for trucks and buses. The firm faced static sales and huge interest payments (the result of a $3.1 billion junk bond issue used to stave off a hostile takeover attempt by Black & Decker in 1989). To improve the firm's operating performance, its chairman, Emmanuel Kampouris, introduced a strategy aimed at reducing the firm's $735 million in net working capital to zero by the late 1990s. This is feasible if the company can reduce its inventories so low that they can be financed without borrowing. The idea is to deliver goods and bill customers more rapidly so that customer payments are sufficient to pay for minimal stocks of inventories. Kampouris sought to accomplish this ambitious goal through implementation of a lean manufacturing system known as *demand flow technology*. Under this system, plants manufacture products as customers order them. Suppliers deliver straight to the assembly line, thus reducing stocks of parts, and plants ship the products as soon as they are completed. The system dramatically reduces inventories of both parts and finished goods. To date, American Standard has reduced its inventories by more than one-half, down to $326 million since 1990. Thus, American Standard invests only 5 cents out of each sales dollar in working capital, compared to the norm of 15 cents. By saving interest payments on supplies, the company has increased its cash flow by $60 million a year.

WHAT'S AHEAD

working capital
net working capital

Chapter 14 addresses two related topics: It introduces the related concepts involved in managing a firm's investment in working capital, and it presents a discussion of short-term financing. Traditionally, **working capital** is defined as the *firm's total investment in current assets.* **Net working capital,** on the other hand, is the *difference between the firm's current assets and its current liabilities.*

net working capital = current assets − current liabilities **(14–1)**

Throughout this chapter, the term *working capital* will refer to net working capital. In managing the firm's net working capital, we are concerned with *managing the firm's liquidity.* This entails managing two related aspects of the firm's operations: (1) investment in current assets, and (2) use of short-term or current liabilities.

Short-term sources of financing include all those forms that have maturities of one year or less, that is, current liabilities. There are two major issues involved in analyzing a firm's use of short-term financing: (1) How much short-term financing should the firm use? and (2) What specific sources of short-term financing should the firm select? We will use the hedging principle of working-capital management to address the first of these questions. We will then address the second issue by considering three basic factors: (1) the effective cost of credit, (2) the availability of credit in the amount needed and for the period that financing is required, and (3) the influence of the use of a particular credit source on the cost and availability of other sources of financing.

This chapter provides the basic principles underlying the analysis of all of these aspects.

OBJECTIVE 1   **MANAGING CURRENT ASSETS AND LIABILITIES**

Other things remaining the same, the greater the firm's investment in current assets, the greater its liquidity. As a means of increasing its liquidity, the firm may choose to invest additional funds in cash or marketable securities. Such action involves a trade-off, however, because such assets earn little or no return. The firm thus finds that it can reduce its risk of illiquidity only by reducing its overall return on invested funds, and vice versa.

Working-Capital Management and the Risk-Return Trade-off

The risk-return trade-off involved in managing the firm's working capital involves a trade-off between the firm's liquidity and its profitability. By maintaining a large investment in current assets like cash and inventory, the firm reduces the chance of production stoppages and lost sales from inventory shortages and the inability to pay bills on time, which might in turn result in credit-rating problems. However, as the firm increases its investment in working capital, there is not a corresponding increase in its returns. This means that the firm's return on investment drops because profits are unchanged, while the investment in assets increases.

Many of the working-capital decisions made by financial managers involve risk-return trade-offs between liquidity and profitability. The principles that guide these decisions are the same ones set out in **Axiom 1: The Risk-Return Trade-off—We Won't Take On Additional Risk Unless We Expect to Be Compensated with Additional Return.** The more current assets held and the more long-term financing used, the less the risk and the less the return.

The firm's use of current versus long-term debt also involves a risk-return trade-off. *Other things remaining the same, the greater the firm's reliance on short-term debt or current liabilities in financing its asset investments, the greater the risk of illiquidity.* On the other hand, the use of current liabilities offers some very real advantages in that they can be less costly than long-term financing and they provide the firm with a flexible means of financing its fluctuating needs for assets. However, if for some reason the firm has problems raising short-term funds or needs funds for longer than expected, there can be real trouble. Thus, a firm can reduce its risk of illiquidity through the use of long-term debt at the expense of a reduction in its return on invested funds. Once again we see that the risk-return trade-off involves an increased risk of illiquidity versus increased profitability.

Advantages of Current Liabilities: The Return

Flexibility

Current liabilities offer the firm a flexible source of financing. They can be used to match the timing of a firm's needs for short-term financing. If, for example, a firm needs funds for a three-month period during each year to finance a seasonal expansion in inventories, then a three-month loan can provide substantial cost savings over a long-term loan (even if the interest rate on short-term financing should be higher). The use of long-term debt in this situation involves borrowing for the entire year rather than for the period when the funds are needed, which increases the amount of interest the firm must pay. This brings us to the second advantage generally associated with the use of short-term financing.

Interest Cost

In general, interest rates on short-term debt are lower than on long-term debt for a given borrower. This relationship was introduced in Chapter 2 and is referred to as the term structure of interest rates. For a given firm, the term structure might appear as follows.

LOAN MATURITY	INTEREST RATE
3 months	4.00%
6 months	4.60
1 year	5.30
3 years	5.90
5 years	6.75
10 years	7.50
30 years	8.25

Note that this term structure reflects the rates of interest applicable to a given borrower at a particular time, it would not, for example, describe the rates of interest available to another borrower or even those applicable to the same borrower at a different time.

Disadvantages of Current Liabilities: The Risk

The use of current liabilities or short-term debt as opposed to long-term debt subjects the firm to a greater risk of illiquidity for two reasons. First, short-term debt, due to its very nature, must be repaid or rolled over more often, and so it increases the possibility that the firm's financial condition might deteriorate to a point where the needed funds might not be available.[1]

A second disadvantage of short-term debt is the uncertainty of interest costs from year to year. For example, a firm borrowing during a six-month period each year to finance a seasonal expansion in current assets might incur a different rate of interest each year. This rate reflects the current rate of interest at the time of the loan, as well as the lender's perception of the firm's riskiness. If fixed-rate long-term debt were used, the interest cost would be known for the entire period of the loan agreement.

OBJECTIVE 2 **APPROPRIATE LEVEL OF WORKING CAPITAL**

Managing the firm's net working capital (its liquidity) has been shown to involve simultaneous and interrelated decisions regarding investment in current assets and use of current liabilities. Fortunately, a guiding principle exists that can be used as a benchmark for the firm's working-capital policies: the hedging principle, or principle of self-liquidating debt. This principle provides a guide to the maintenance of a level of liquidity sufficient for the firm to meets its maturing obligations on time.[2]

PAUSE AND REFLECT

In Chapter 12 we discussed the firm's financing decision in terms of the choice between debt and equity sources of financing. There is, however, yet another critical dimension of the firm's financing decision. This relates to the maturity structure of the firm's debt. How should the decision be made as to whether to use short-term or current debt or longer-maturity debt? This is one of the fundamental questions addressed in this chapter and one that is critically important to the financial success of the firm. Basically, the hedging principle is one possible rule of thumb for guiding a firm's debt-maturity financing decisions. This principle states that financing maturity should follow the cash flow–producing characteristics of the asset being financed. For example, an asset that is expected to provide cash flows over an extended period such as five years should, in accordance with the hedging principle, be financed with debt with a pat-

---

[1]The dangers of such a policy are readily apparent in the experiences of firms that have been forced into bankruptcy. Penn Central, for example, went bankrupt when it had $80 million in short-term debt that it was unable to refinance (roll over).

[2]A value-maximizing approach to the management of the firm's liquidity involves assessing the value of the benefits derived from increasing the firm's investment in liquid assets and weighing them against the added costs to the firm's owners resulting from investing in low-yield current assets. Unfortunately, the benefits derived from increased liquidity relate to the expected costs of bankruptcy to the firm's owners, and these costs are "unmeasurable" by existing technology. Thus, a "valuation" approach to liquidity management exists only in the theoretical realm.

How Firms Manage Their Working Capital

	ELECTRONIC COMPUTERS[a]		BOOK PUBLISHING[b]		AIR TRANS- PORTATION[c]		OIL AND GAS EXPLORATION[d]		GASOLINE STATIONS[e]		RESTAU- RANTS[f]	
Current assets (%)	72	73	68	70	46	39	48	33	45	48	25	25
Current liabilities (%)	40	38	43	53	37	43	40	31	38	39	36	38
Long-term debt (%)	12	11	17	14	23	26	27	28	27	22	32	33

The above table provides aggregate percent of assets numbers for six different industries and two time periods.* The first column of percentages under each industry reflects the average for 1990–1991, and the second column reflects the 1986–1987 average.

Averaged across all industries for both years current assets were 49 percent of total assets, while current liabilities averaged 40 percent and long-term debt was only 23 percent. There is substantial variation in the relative importance of current assets across industries, with electronic computers and book publishing having the highest percent of assets invested in current assets, and restaurants having the lowest. Note also the relationship between current liabilities and long-term debt. With the exception of the restaurant industry, current liabilities are anywhere from two to four times as large as long-term debt.

So what can we conclude? First, current assets are a major component of a firm's investments and can constitute as much as 70 percent of firm assets. Second, most firms maintain current ratios (i.e., current assets/current liabilities) greater than 1, although this relationship varies both across industries and over time. Finally, long-term debt is frequently a less important source of financing (measured in terms of its percent of assets) than are current liabilities. The message is this: Working-capital management is extremely important to the firm's financial well-being and deserves serious consideration!

* Robert Morris Associates (RMA) cautions that the Studies be regarded only as a general guideline and not as an absolute industry norm. This is due to limited samples within categories, the categorization of companies by their primary Standard Industrial Classification (SIC) number only, and different methods of operations by companies within the same industry. For these reasons, RMA recommends that the figures be used only as general guidelines in addition to other methods of financial analysis.

[a]Manufacturers—Electronic Computers SIC #3571.
[b]Manufacturers—Books: Publishing, or Publishing and Printing SIC #2731.
[c]Services—Air Transportation, Scheduled SIC #4512.
[d]Contractors—Oil and Gas Well Drilling SIC #1381.
[e]Retailers—Gasoline Service Stations SIC #5541.
[f]Retailers—Restaurants SIC #5812.

Source: Copyright © 1991 by Robert Morris Associates, Philadelphia, PA. Reprinted with permission.

tern of similar cash flow requirements. Note that when the hedging principle is followed, the firm's debt will "self-liquidate" because the assets being financed will generate sufficient cash to retire the debt as it comes due.

Hedging Principle

Very simply, the **hedging principle,** or **principle of self-liquidating debt,** involves *matching the cash flow–generating characteristics of an asset with the maturity of the source of financing used to finance its acquisition.* For example, a seasonal expansion in inventories, according to the hedging principle, should be financed with a short-term loan or current liability. The rationale underlying the rule is straightforward. Funds are needed for a limited period, and when that time has passed, the cash needed to repay the loan will be generated by the sale of the extra inventory items.

hedging principle
principle of self-liquidating debt

Obtaining the needed funds from a long-term source (longer than one year) would mean that the firm would still have the funds after the inventories they helped finance had been sold. In this case the firm would have "excess" liquidity, which it either holds in cash or invests in low-yield marketable securities until the seasonal increase in inventories occurs again and the funds are needed. The result of all this would be an overall lowering of firm profits.

Consider an example in which a firm purchases a new conveyor belt system, which is expected to produce cash savings to the firm by eliminating the need for two laborers and, consequently, their salaries. This amounts to an annual savings of $24,000, whereas the conveyor belt costs $250,000 to install and will last 20 years. If the firm chooses to finance this asset with a 1-year note, then it will not be able to repay the loan from the $24,000 cash flow generated by the asset. In accordance with the hedging principle, the firm should finance the asset with a source of financing that more nearly matches the expected life and cash flow–generating characteristics of the asset. In this case, a 15- to 20-year loan would be more appropriate.

Permanent and Temporary Assets

The notion of maturity matching in the hedging principle can be most easily understood when we think in terms of the distinction between permanent and temporary investments in assets. As opposed to the more traditional fixed and current asset categories. **Permanent investments** in an asset are *investments that the firm expected to hold for a period longer than one year*. Note that we are referring to the period the firm plans to hold an investment, not the useful life of the asset. For example, permanent investments are made in the firm's minimum level of current assets, as well as in its fixed assets. **Temporary investments,** on the other hand, are composed of *current assets that will be liquidated and not replaced within the current year*. Thus, some part of the firm's current assets is permanent and the remainder is temporary. For example, a seasonal increase in level of inventories is a temporary investment; the buildup in inventories will be eliminated when it is no longer needed.

margin: permanent investments

margin: temporary investments

Temporary, Permanent, and Spontaneous Source of Financing

Since total assets must always equal the sum of temporary, permanent, and spontaneous sources of financing, the hedging approach provides the financial manager with the basis for determining the sources of financing to use at any point.

Now, what constitutes a temporary, permanent, or spontaneous source of financing? Temporary sources of financing consist of current liabilities. Short-term notes payable constitute the most common example of a temporary source of financing. Examples of notes payable include unsecured bank loans, commercial paper, and loans secured by accounts receivable and inventories. Permanent sources of financing include intermediate-term loans, long-term debt, preferred stock, and common equity.

Spontaneous sources of financing consist of trade credit and other accounts payable that arise *spontaneously* in the firm's day-to-day operations. For example, as the firm acquires materials for its inventories, **trade credit** is often *made available spontaneously or on demand from the firm's suppliers. Trade credit appears on the firm's balance sheet as accounts payable,* and the size of the accounts-payable balance varies directly with the firm's purchases of inventory items. In turn, inventory purchases are related to anticipated sales. Thus, part of the financing needed by the firm is spontaneously provided in the form of trade credit.

margin: trade credit

In addition to trade credit, wages and salaries payable, accrued interest, and accrued taxes also provide valuable sources of spontaneous financing. These expenses accrue throughout the period until they are paid. For example, if a firm has a wage expense of $10,000 a week and pays its employees monthly, then its employees ef-

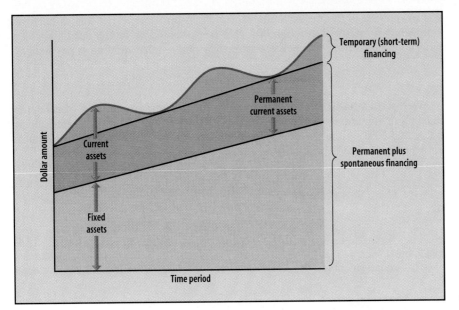

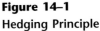

Figure 14–1
Hedging Principle

fectively provide financing equal to $10,000 by the end of the first week following a payday, $20,000 by the end of the second week, and so forth, until the workers are paid. Since these expenses generally arise in direct conjunction with the firm's on-going operations, they too are referred to as spontaneous.

Hedging Principle: Graphic Illustration

The hedging principle can now be stated very succinctly: *Asset needs of the firm not financed by spontaneous sources should be financed in accordance with this rule: Permanent asset investments are financed with permanent sources, and temporary investments are financed with temporary sources.*

The hedging principle is depicted in Figure 14–1. Total assets are broken down into temporary and permanent asset investment categories. The firm's permanent investment in assets is financed by the use of permanent sources of financing (intermediate- and long-term debt, preferred stock, and common equity) or spontaneous sources (trade credit and other accounts payable). For illustration purposes spontaneous sources of financing are treated as if their amount were fixed. In practice, of course, spontaneous sources of financing fluctuate with the firm's purchases and its expenditures for wages, salaries, taxes, and other items that are paid on a delayed basis. Its temporary investment in assets is financed with temporary (short-term) debt.

ESTIMATION OF THE COST OF SHORT-TERM CREDIT   O B J E C T I V E   3

Approximate Cost-of-Credit Formula

The procedure for estimating the cost of short-term credit is a very simple one and relies on the basic interest equation:

$$\text{interest} = \text{principal} \times \text{rate} \times \text{time} \qquad \textbf{(14–2)}$$

where *interest* is the dollar amount of interest on a *principal* that is borrowed at some annual *rate* for a fraction of a year (represented by *time*). For example, a six-month loan for $1,000 at 8 percent interest would require an interest payment of $40.

$$\text{interest} = \$1{,}000 \times .08 \times \frac{1}{2} = \$40$$

We use this basic relationship to solve for the cost of a source of short-term financing or the annual percentage rate (APR) where the interest amount, the principal sum, and the time period for financing are known. Thus, solving the basic interest equation for APR produces[3]

$$APR = \frac{\text{interest}}{\text{principal} \times \text{time}} \qquad \textbf{(14–3)}$$

or

$$APR = \frac{\text{interest}}{\text{principal}} \times \frac{1}{\text{time}} \qquad \textbf{(14–3a)}$$

This equation, called the APR calculation, is clarified with the following example.

EXAMPLE

The SKC Corporation plans to borrow $1,000 for a 90-day period. At maturity the firm will repay the $1,000 principal amount plus $30 interest. The effective annual rate of interest for the loan can be estimated using the APR equation, as follows:

$$APR = \frac{\$30}{\$1{,}000} \times \frac{1}{90/360}$$

$$= .03 \times \frac{360}{90} = .12 = 12\%$$

The effective annual cost of funds provided by the loan is therefore 12 percent. ∎

Annual Percentage Yield Formula

The simple APR calculation does not consider compound interest. To account for the influence of compounding, we can use the following equation:

$$APY = \left(1 + \frac{i}{m}\right)^m - 1 \qquad \textbf{(14–4)}$$

where *APY* is the annual percentage yield, *i* is the nominal rate of interest per year (12 percent in the above example), and *m* is the number of compounding periods within a year [$m = 1/\text{time} = 1/(90/360) = 4$ in the preceding example]. Thus, the effective rate of interest on the loan in the example problem, considering compounding, is

$$APY = \left(1 + \frac{.12}{4}\right)^4 - 1 = .126 = 12.6\%$$

Compounding effectively raises the cost of short-term credit. Because the differences between APR and APY are usually small, we use the simple interest values of APR to compute the cost of short-term credit.

---

[3]For ease of computation we will assume a 30-day month and 360-day year in this chapter.

Short-term credit sources can be classified into two basic groups: unsecured and se-cured. **Unsecured loans** include all those *sources that have as their security only the lender's faith in the ability of the borrower to repay the funds when due.* Major sources of unsecured short-term credit include accrued wages and taxes, trade credit, unsecured bank loans, and commercial paper. **Secured loans** involve the *pledge of specific assets as collateral in the event the borrower defaults in payment of prin-cipal or interest.* Commercial banks, finance companies, and factors are the primary suppliers of secured credit. The principal sources of collateral include accounts re-ceivable and inventories.

unsecured loans

secured loans

Unsecured Sources: Accrued Wages and Taxes

Because most businesses pay their employees only periodically (weekly, biweekly, or monthly), firms accrue a wages-payable account that is, in essence, a loan from their employees. For example, if the wage expense for the Appleton Manufacturing Com-pany is $450,000 per week and it pays its employees monthly, then by the end of a four-week month the firm will owe its employees $1.8 million in wages for services they have already performed during the month. Consequently, the employees finance their own efforts through waiting a full month for payment.

Similarly, firms generally make quarterly income tax payments for their estimated quarterly tax liability. This means that the firm has the use of the tax moneys it owes based on quarterly profits up through the end of the quarter. In addition, the firm pays sales taxes and withholding (income) taxes for its employees on a deferred basis. The longer the period that the firm holds the tax payments, the greater the amount of fi-nancing they provide.

Note that these sources of financing *rise and fall spontaneously* with the level of firm sales. That is, as the firm's sales increase, so do its labor expense, sales taxes collected, and income tax. Consequently, these accrued expense items provide the firm with automatic or spontaneous sources of financing.

Unsecured Sources: Trade Credit

Trade credit provides one of the most flexible sources of short-term financing available to the firm. We previously noted that trade credit is a primary source of spontaneous, or on-demand, financing. That is, trade credit arises spontaneously with the firm's pur-chases. To arrange for credit the firm need only place an order with one of its suppli-ers. The supplier checks the firm's credit and, if it is good, sends the merchandise. The purchasing firm then pays for the goods in accordance with the supplier's credit terms.

Credit Terms and Cash Discounts

Very often the credit terms offered with trade credit involve a cash discount for early payment. For example, a supplier might offer terms of 2/10, net 30, which means that a 2 percent discount is offered for payment within 10 days or the full amount is due in 30 days. Thus, a 2 percent penalty is involved for not paying within 10 days, or for delaying payment from the tenth to the thirtieth day (that is, for 20 days). The effec-tive annual cost of not taking the cash discount can be quite severe. Using a $1 in-voice amount, the effective cost of passing up the discount period using the preced-ing credit terms and our APR equation can be estimated.

$$APR = \frac{\$.02}{\$.98} \times \frac{1}{20/360} = .3673 = 36.73\%$$

Note that the 2 percent cash discount is the *interest* cost of extending the payment period an *additional* 20 days. Note also that the principal amount of the credit is $.98. This amount constitutes the full principal amount as of the tenth day of the credit period, after which time the cash discount is lost. The effective cost of passing up the 2 percent discount for 20 days is quite expensive: 36.73 percent. Furthermore, once the discount period has passed, there is no reason to pay before the final due date (the thirtieth day). Table 14–1 lists the effective annual cost of a number of alternative credit terms. Note that the cost of trade credit varies directly with the size of the cash discount and inversely with the length of time between the end of the discount period and the final due date.

Stretching of Trade Credit

Some firms that use trade credit engage in a practice called *stretching of trade accounts*. This practice involves delaying payments beyond the prescribed credit period. For example, a firm might purchase materials under credit terms of 3/10, net 60; however, when faced with a shortage of cash, the firm might extend payment to the eightieth day. Continued violation of trade terms can eventually lead to a loss of credit. However, for short periods, and at infrequent intervals, stretching offers the firm an emergency source of short-term credit.

Advantages of Trade Credit

As a source of short-term financing, trade credit has a number of advantages. First, trade credit is conveniently obtained as a normal part of the firm's operations. Second, no formal agreements are generally involved in extending credit. Furthermore, the amount of credit extended expands and contracts with the needs of the firm; this is why it is classified as a spontaneous, or on-demand, source of financing.

Unsecured Sources: Bank Credit

Commercial banks provide unsecured short-term credit in two basic forms: lines of credit and transaction loans (notes payable). Maturities of both types of loans are usually one year or less, with rates of interest depending on the creditworthiness of the borrower and the level of interest rates in the economy as a whole.

Line of Credit

line of credit

A **line of credit** is *generally an informal agreement or understanding between the borrower and the bank as to the maximum amount of credit that the bank will provide the borrower at any one time.* Under this type of agreement there is no *legal*

Table 14–1 Effective Rates of Interest on Selected Trade Credit Terms	
Credit Terms	**Effective Rates**
2/10, net 60	14.69%
2/10, net 90	9.18
3/20, net 60	27.84
6/10, net 90	28.72

commitment on the part of the bank to provide the stated credit. In a **revolving credit agreement,** which is a variant of this form of financing, a *legal obligation is involved.* The line of credit agreement generally covers a period of one year corresponding to the borrower's *fiscal* year. Thus, if the borrower is on a July 31 fiscal year, its lines of credit will be based on the same annual period.

revolving credit agreement

Credit Terms   Lines of credit generally do not involve fixed rates of interest; instead they state that credit will be extended at $\frac{1}{2}$ *percent over prime* or some other spread over the bank's prime rate.[4] Furthermore, the agreement usually does not spell out the specific use that will be made of the funds beyond a general statement, such as *for working-capital purposes.*

Lines of credit usually require that the borrower maintain a *minimum balance in the bank throughout the loan period*, called a **compensating balance.** This required balance (which can be stated as a percent of the line of credit or the loan amount) increases the effective cost of the loan to the borrower, unless a deposit balance equal to or greater than this balance requirement is ordinarily maintained in the bank.

compensating balance

The effective cost of short-term bank credit can be estimated using the APR equation. Consider the following example.

EXAMPLE

M & M Beverage Company has a $300,000 line of credit that requires a compensating balance equal to 10 percent of the loan amount. The rate paid on the loan is 12 percent per annum, $200,000 is borrowed for a six-month period, and the firm does not currently have a deposit with the lending bank. The dollar cost of the loan includes the interest expense and, in addition, the opportunity cost of maintaining an idle cash balance equal to the 10 percent compensating balance. To accommodate the cost of the compensating-balance requirement, assume that the added funds will have to be borrowed and simply left idle in the firm's checking accounts. Thus, the amount actually borrowed (B) will be larger than the $200,000 needed. In fact, the needed $200,000 will constitute 90 percent of the total borrowed funds because of the 10 percent compensating-balance requirement, hence $.90B = \$200,000$, such that $B = \$222,222$. Thus, interest is paid on a $222,222 loan ($222,222 \times .12 \times \frac{1}{2} = \$13,333.32$), of which only $200,000 is available for use by the firm.[5] The effective annual cost of credit, therefore, is

$$APR = \frac{\$13,333.32}{\$200,000} \times \frac{1}{180/360} = .1333 = 13.33\%$$

In the M & M Beverage Company example, the loan required the payment of principal ($222,222) plus interest ($13,333.32) at the end of the six-month loan period. Frequently, bank loans will be made on a discount basis. That is, the loan interest will be deducted from the loan amount before the funds are transferred to the borrower. Extending the M & M Beverage Company example to consider discounted interest involves reducing the loan proceeds ($200,000) in the previous example by the amount

---

[4]The *prime rate of interest* is the rate that a bank charges its most creditworthy borrowers.

[5]The same answer would have been obtained by assuming a total loan of $200,000, of which only 90 percent, or $180,000, was available for use by the firm; that is,

$$APR = \frac{\$12,000}{\$180,000} \times \frac{1}{180/360} = 13.3$$

Interest is now calculated on the $200,000 loan amount ($12,000 = \$200,000 \times .12 \times \frac{1}{2}$).

of interest for the full six months ($13,333.32). The effective rate of interest on the loan is now

$$APR = \frac{\$13{,}333.32}{\$200{,}000 - \$13{,}333.32} \times \frac{1}{180/360}$$

$$= .1429 = 14.29\%$$

The effect of discounting interest was to raise the cost of the loan from 13.33 percent to 14.29 percent. This results from the fact that the firm pays interest on the same amount of funds as before ($222,222); however, this time it gets the use of $13,333.32 less, or $200,000 − $13,333.32 = $186,666.68.[6] ■

Transaction Loans

Still another form of unsecured short-term bank credit can be obtained in the form of **transaction loans.** Here the loan is *made for a specific purpose.* This is the type of loan that most individuals associate with bank credit and is obtained by signing a promissory note.

Unsecured transaction loans are very similar to a line of credit regarding cost, term to maturity, and compensating-balance requirements. In both instances commercial banks often require that the borrower *clean up* its short-term loans for a 30- to 45-day period during the year. This means, very simply, that the borrower must be free of any bank debt for the stated period. The purpose of such a requirement is to ensure that the borrower is not using short-term bank credit to finance a part of its permanent needs for funds.

Unsecured Sources: Commercial Paper

commercial paper

Only the largest and most creditworthy companies are able to use **commercial paper,** which is simply a *short-term promise to pay that is sold in the market for short-term debt securities.*

Credit Terms

The maturity of the credit source is generally six months or less, although some issues carry 270-day maturities. The interest rate on commercial paper is generally slightly lower ($\frac{1}{2}$ to 1 percent) than the prime rate on commercial bank loans. Also, interest is usually discounted, although sometimes interest-bearing commercial paper is available.

New issues of commercial paper are either placed directly (sold by the issuing firm directly to the investing public) or dealer placed. Dealer placement involves the use of a commercial paper dealer, who sells the issue for the issuing firm. Many ma-

---

[6]If M&M needs the use of a full $200,000, then it will have to borrow more than $222,222 to cover both the compensating-balance requirement *and* the discounted interest. In fact, the firm will have to borrow some amount B such that

$$B - .10B - (.12 \times \tfrac{1}{2})B = \$200{,}000$$
$$.84B = \$200{,}000$$

$$B = \frac{\$200{,}000}{.84} = \$238{,}095$$

The cost of credit remains the same at 14.29 percent, as we see below:

$$APR = \frac{\$14{,}285.70}{\$238{,}095 - \$23{,}810 - \$14{,}285.70} \times \frac{1}{180/360}$$

$$= .1429 = 14.29\%$$

jor finance companies, such as General Motors Acceptance Corporation, place their commercial paper directly. The volume of direct versus dealer placements is roughly 4 to 1 in favor of direct placements. Dealers are used primarily by industrial firms that either make only infrequent use of commercial paper market or, owing to their small size, would have difficulty placing the issue without the help of a dealer.

Commercial Paper as a Source of Short-Term Credit

Several advantages accrue to the user of commercial paper.

1. **Interest rate.** Commercial paper rates are generally lower than rates on bank loans and comparable sources of short-term financing.
2. **Compensating-balance requirement.** No minimum balance requirements are associated with commercial paper. However, issuing firms usually find it desirable to maintain line-of-credit agreements sufficient to back up their short-term financing needs in the event that a new issue of commercial paper cannot be sold or an outstanding issue cannot be repaid when due.
3. **Amount of credit.** Commercial paper offers the firm with very large credit needs a single source for all its short-term financing. Because of loan restrictions placed on the banks by the regulatory authorities, obtaining the necessary funds from a commercial bank might require dealing with a number of institutions.[7]
4. **Prestige.** Because it is widely recognized that only the most creditworthy borrowers have access to the commercial paper market, its use signifies a firm's credit status.

Using commercial paper for short-term financing, however, involves a very important risk. That is, the commercial paper market is highly impersonal and denies even the most creditworthy borrower any flexibility in terms of repayment. When bank credit is used, the borrower has someone with whom he or she can work out any temporary difficulties that might be encountered in meeting a loan deadline. This flexibility simply does not exist for the user of commercial paper.

Estimation of the Cost of Commercial Paper

The cost of commercial paper can be estimated using the simple effective cost-of-credit equation (APR). The key points to remember are that commercial paper interest is usually discounted and that if a dealer is used to place the issue, a fee is charged. Even if a dealer is not used, the issuing firm will incur costs associated with preparing and placing the issue, and these costs must be included in estimating the cost of credit.

EXAMPLE

The EPG Manufacturing Company uses commercial paper regularly to support its needs for short-term financing. The firm plans to sell $100 million in 270-day-maturity paper on which it expects to have to pay discounted interest at a rate of 12 percent per annum ($9 million). In addition, EPG expects to incur a cost of approximately $100,000 in dealer placement fees and other expenses of issuing the paper. The effective cost of credit to EPG can be calculated as follows:

$$APR = \frac{\$9,000,000 + \$100,000}{\$100,000,000 - \$100,000 - \$9,000,000} \times \frac{1}{270/360}$$

$$= .1335 = 13.35\%$$

---

[7]Member banks of the Federal Reserve System are limited to 10 percent of their total capital, surplus, and undivided profits when making loans to a single borrower. Thus, when a corporate borrower's needs for financing are very large, it may have to deal with a group of participating banks to raise the needed funds.

where the interest cost is calculated as $\$100,000,000 \times .12 \times [270/360] = \$9,000,000$ plus the $\$100,000$ dealer placement fee. Thus, the effective cost of credit to EPG is 13.35 percent. ■

Secured Sources: Accounts-Receivable Loans

Secured sources of short-term credit have certain assets of the firm pledged as collateral to secure the loan. Upon default of the loan agreement, the lender has first claim to the pledged assets in addition to its claim as a general creditor of the firm. Hence, the secured credit agreement offers an added margin of safety to the lender.

Generally, a firm's receivables are among its most liquid assets. For this reason they are considered by many lenders to be prime collateral for a secured loan. Two basic procedures can be used in arranging for financing based on receivables: pledging and factoring.

Pledging Accounts Receivable

pledging accounts receivable

Under the **pledging accounts receivable** arrangement, the *borrower simply pledges accounts receivable as collateral for a loan obtained from either a commercial bank or a finance company.* The amount of the loan is stated as a percent of the face value of the receivables pledged. If the firm provides the lender with a *general line* on its receivables, then all of the borrower's accounts are pledged as security for the loan. This method of pledging is simple and inexpensive. However, because the lender has no control over the quality of the receivables being pledged, it will set the maximum loan at a relatively low percent of the total face value of the accounts, generally ranging downward from a maximum of around 75 percent.

Still another approach to pledging involves the borrower's presenting specific invoices to the lender as collateral for a loan. This method is somewhat more expensive because the lender must assess the creditworthiness of each individual account pledged; however, given this added knowledge the lender should be willing to increase the loan as a percent of the face value of the invoices. In this case the loan might reach as high as 85 or 90 percent of the face value of the pledged receivables.

Credit Terms Accounts-receivable loans generally carry an interest rate 2 to 5 percent higher than the bank's prime lending rate. Finance companies charge an even higher rate. In addition, the lender will usually charge a handing fee stated as a percent of the face value of the receivables processed, which may be as much as 1 to 2 percent of the face value.

EXAMPLE

The A. B. Good Company sells electrical supplies to building contractors on terms of net 60. The firm's average monthly sales are $\$100,000$; thus, given the firm's two-month credit terms, its average receivables balance is $\$200,000$. The firm pledges all its receivables to a local bank, which in turn advances up to 70 percent of the face value of the receivables at 3 percent over prime and with a 1 percent processing charge on *all* receivables pledged. A. B. Good follows a practice of borrowing the maximum amount possible, and the current prime rate is 10 percent.

The APR of using this source of financing for a full year is computed as follows:

$$APR = \frac{\$18,200 + \$12,000}{\$140,000} \times \frac{1}{360/360} = .2157 = 21.57\%$$

where the total dollar cost of the loan consists of both the annual interest expense (.13 × .70 × $200,000 = $18,200) and the annual processing fee (.01 × $100,000 × 12 months = $12,000). The amount of credit extended is .70 × $200,000 = $140,000. Note that the processing charge applies to *all* receivables pledged. Thus, the A. B. Good Company pledges $100,000 each month, or $1,200,000 during the year, on which a 1 percent fee must be paid, for a total annual charge of $12,000.

One more point: The lender, in addition to making advances or loans, may be providing certain credit services to the borrower. For example, the lender may provide billing and collection services. The value of these services should be considered in computing the cost of credit. In the preceding example, A. B. Good Company may *save* credit department expenses of $10,000 per year by pledging all its accounts and letting the lender provide those services. In this case, the cost of short-term credit is only

$$APR = \frac{\$18,200 + \$12,000 - \$10,000}{\$140,000} \times \frac{1}{360/360} = .1443 = 14.43\%$$

Advantages and Disadvantages of Pledging

The primary advantage of pledging as a source of short-term credit is the flexibility it provides the borrower. Financing is available on a continuous basis. The new accounts created through credit sales provide the collateral for the financing of new production. Furthermore, the lender may provide credit services that eliminate or at least reduce the need for similar services within the firm. The primary disadvantage associated with this method of financing is its cost, which can be relatively high compared with other sources of short-term credit, owing to the level of the interest rate charged on loans and the processing fee on pledged accounts.

Factoring Accounts Receivable

Factoring accounts receivable involves the *outright sale of a firm's accounts to a financial institution called a factor.* A **factor** is a *firm that acquires the receivables of other firms.* The factoring institution may be a commercial finance company that engages solely in the factoring of receivables (known as an *old-line factor*) or it may be a commercial bank. The factor, in turn, bears the risk of collection and, for a fee, services the accounts. The fee is stated as a percent of the face value of all receivables factored (usually 1 to 3 percent).

The factor firm typically does *not* make payment for factored accounts until the accounts have been collected or the credit terms have been met. Should the firm wish to receive immediate payment for its factored accounts, it can borrow from the factor, using the factored accounts as collateral. The maximum loan the firm can obtain is equal to the face value of its factored accounts less the factor's fee (1 to 3 percent) less a reserve (6 to 10 percent) less the interest on the loan. For example, if $100,000 in receivables is factored, carrying 60-day credit terms, a 2 percent factor's fee, a 6 percent reserve, and interest at 1 percent per month on advances, then the maximum loan or advance the firm can receive is computed as follows:

Face amount of receivables factored	$100,000
Less: Fee (.02 × $100,000)	(2,000)
Reserve (.06 × $100,000)	(6,000)
Interest (.01 × $92,000 × 2 months)	(1,840)
Maximum advance	$90,160

(margin glossary terms) factoring accounts receivable

factor

Note that interest is discounted and calculated based on a maximum amount of funds available for advance ($92,000 = $100,000 − $2,000 − $6,000). Thus, the effective cost of credit can be calculated as follows:

$$APR = \frac{\$1,840 + \$2,000}{\$90,160} \times \frac{1}{60/360}$$

$$= .2555 = 25.55\%$$

Secured Sources: Inventory Loans

Inventory loans, or *loans secured by inventories,* provide a second source of security for short-term credit. The amount of the loan that can be obtained depends on both the marketability and perishability of the inventory. Some items, such as raw materials (grains, oil, lumber, and chemicals), are excellent sources of collateral, because they can easily be liquidated. Other items, such as work-in-process inventories, provide very poor collateral because of their lack of marketability.

There are several methods by which inventory can be used to secure short-term financing. These include a floating or blanket lien, chattel mortgage, field warehouse receipt, and terminal warehouse receipt.

floating lien agreement

Under a **floating lien agreement,** the *borrower gives the lender a lien against all its inventories.* This provides the simplest but least secure form of inventory collateral. The borrowing firm maintains full control of the inventories and continues to sell and replace them as it sees fit. Obviously, this lack of control over the collateral greatly dilutes the value of this type of security to the lender.

chattel mortgage agreement

Under a **chattel mortgage agreement,** the *inventory is identified* (by serial number or otherwise) *in the security agreement and the borrower retains title to the inventory but cannot sell the items without the lender's consent.*

field warehouse–financing agreement

Under a **field warehouse–financing agreement,** *inventories used as collateral are physically separated from the firm's other inventories, and placed under the control of a third-party field-warehousing firm.*

terminal warehouse agreement

The **terminal warehouse agreement** differs from the field warehouse agreement in only one respect. Here the *inventories pledged as collateral are transported to a public warehouse that is physically removed from the borrower's premises.* The lender has an added degree of safety or security because the inventory is totally removed from the borrower's control. Once again the cost of this type of arrangement is increased because the warehouse firm must be paid by the borrower; in addition, the inventory must be transported to and, eventually, from the public warehouse.

SUMMARY

OBJECTIVE 1

Working-capital management involves managing the firm's liquidity, which in turn involves managing (1) the firm's investment in current assets and (2) its use of current liabilities. Each of these problems involves risk–return trade-offs. Investing in current assets reduces the firm's risk of illiquidity at the expense of lowering its overall rate of return on its investment in assets. Furthermore, the use of long-term sources of financing enhances the firm's liquidity while reducing its rate of return on assets.

OBJECTIVE 2

The hedging principle, or principle of self-liquidating debt, is a benchmark for working-capital decisions. Basically, this principle involves matching the cash flow–generating characteristics of an asset with the cash flow requirements of the source of funds used to finance its acquisition.

Three basic factors provide the key considerations in selecting a source of short-term financing: (1) the effective cost of credit, (2) the availability of financing in the amount and for the time needed, and (3) the effect of the use of credit from a particular source on the cost and availability of other sources of credit.

The various sources of short-term credit can be categorized into two groups: unsecured and secured. Unsecured credit offers no specific assets as security for the loan agreement. The primary sources include trade credit, lines of credit, unsecured transaction loans from commercial banks, and commercial paper. Secured credit is generally provided to business firms by commercial banks, finance companies, and factors. The most popular sources of security involve the use of accounts receivable and inventories. Loans secured by accounts receivable include pledging agreements, in which a firm pledges its receivables as security for a loan, and factoring agreements, in which the firm sells the receivables to a factor. A primary difference in these two arrangements relates to the ability of the lender to seek payment from the borrower in the event the accounts used as collateral become uncollectible. In a pledging arrangement the lender retains the right of recourse in the event of default, whereas in factoring, a lender is generally without recourse.

Loans secured by inventories can be made using one of several types of security arrangements. Among the most widely used are the floating lien, chattel mortgage, field warehouse agreement, and terminal warehouse agreement. The form of agreement used will depend on the type of inventories pledged as collateral and the degree of control the lender wishes to exercise over the loan collateral.

KEY TERMS

Chattel Mortgage Agreement, 450

Commercial Paper, 446

Compensating Balance, 445

Factor, 449

Factoring Accounts Receivable, 449

Field Warehouse–Financing Agreement, 450

Floating Lien Agreement, 450

Hedging Principle, 439

Inventory Loans, 450

Line of Credit, 444

Net Working Capital, 436

Permanent Investments, 440

Pledging Accounts Receivable, 448

Principle of Self-liquidating Debt (see Hedging Principle), 439

Revolving Credit Agreement, 445

Secured Loans, 443

Temporary Investments, 440

Terminal Warehouse Agreement, 450

Trade Credit, 440

Transaction Loans, 446

Unsecured Loans, 443

Working Capital, 436

STUDY QUESTIONS

14-1. Define and contrast the terms *working capital* and *net working capital.*

14-2. Discuss the risk-return relationship involved in the firm's asset investment decisions as that relationship pertains to working-capital management.

14-3. What advantages and disadvantages are generally associated with the use of short-term debt? Discuss.

14-4. Explain what is meant by the statement "The use of current liabilities as opposed to long-term debt subjects the firm to a greater risk of illiquidity."

OBJECTIVE 3

OBJECTIVE 4

14-5. Define the hedging principle. How can this principle be used in the management of working capital?

14-6. Define the following terms:

    a. Permanent asset investments

    b. Temporary asset investments

    c. Permanent sources of financing

    d. Temporary sources of financing

    e. Spontaneous sources of financing

14-7. What distinguishes short-term, intermediate-term, and long-term debt?

14-8. What considerations should be used in selecting a source of short-term credit? Discuss each.

14-9. How can the formula "interest = principal × rate × time" be used to estimate the effective cost of short-term credit?

14-10. How can we accommodate the effects of compounding in our calculation of the effective cost of short-term credit?

14-11. There are three major sources of unsecured short-term credit other than accrued wages and taxes. List and discuss the distinguishing characteristics of each.

14-12. What is meant by the following trade credit terms: 2/10, net 30? 4/20, net 60? 3/15, net 45?

14-13. Define the following:

    a. Line of credit   **c.** Compensating balance

    b. Commercial paper   **d.** Prime rate

14-14. List and discuss four advantages of the use of commercial paper.

14-15. What risk is involved in the firm's use of commercial paper as a source of short-term credit? Discuss.

14-16. List and discuss the distinguishing features of the principal sources of secured credit based on accounts receivable.

SELF-TEST PROBLEMS

ST-1. (*Analyzing the Cost of a Commercial Paper Offering*) The Marilyn Sales Company is a wholesale machine tool broker that has gone through a recent expansion of its activities, resulting in a doubling of its sales. The company has determined that it needs an additional $200 million in short-term funds to finance peak season sales during roughly six months of the year. Marilyn's treasurer has recommended that the firm use a commercial paper offering to raise the needed funds. Specifically, he has determined that a $200 million offering would require 10 percent interest (paid in advance or discounted) plus a $125,000 placement fee. The paper would carry a six-month (180-day) maturity. What is the effective cost of credit?

ST-2. (*Analyzing the Cost of Short-Term Credit*) The treasurer of the Lights-a-Lot Manufacturing Company is faced with three alternative bank loans. The firm wishes to select the one that minimizes its cost of credit on a $200,000 note that it plans to issue in the next 10 days. Relevant information for the three loan configurations is found below:

    a. An 18 percent rate of interest with interest paid at year-end and no compensating-balance requirement.

b. A 16 percent rate of interest but carrying a 20 percent compensating-balance requirement. This loan also calls for interest to be paid at year-end.

c. A 14 percent rate of interest that is discounted, plus a 20 percent compensating-balance requirement.

Analyze the cost of each of these alternatives. You may assume the firm would not normally maintain any bank balance that might be used to meet the 20 percent compensating-balance requirements of alternatives (b) and (c).

STUDY PROBLEMS

14-1. (*Estimating the Cost of Bank Credit*) Paymaster Enterprises has arranged to finance its seasonal working-capital needs with a short-term bank loan. The loan will carry a rate of 12 percent per annum with interest paid in advance (discounted). In addition, Paymaster must maintain a minimum demand deposit with the bank of 10 percent of the loan balance throughout the term of the loan. If Paymaster plans to borrow $100,000 for a period of three months, what is the effective cost of the banking loan?

$$APR = \frac{\$i}{(P - CB - i)} \times \frac{1}{t}$$

$$13.79\% \quad \frac{3,000}{(100,000 - 10,000 - 3,000)} \times \frac{1}{90/360} =$$

14-2. (*Estimating the Cost of Commercial Paper*) On February 3, 199X, the Burlington Western Company plans a commercial paper issue of $20 million. The firm has never used commercial paper before but has been assured by the firm placing the issue that it will have no difficulty raising the funds. The commercial paper will carry a 270-day maturity and will require interest based on a rate of 11 percent per annum. In addition, the firm will have to pay fees totaling $200,000 in order to bring the issue to market and place it. What is the effective cost of the commercial paper to Burlington Western?

14-3. (*Cost of Trade Credit*) Calculate the effective cost of the following trade credit terms where payment is made on the net due date.

    a. 2/10, net 30   36.7%
    b. 3/15, net 30   74.2%
    c. 3/15, net 45   37.1%
    d. 2/15, net 60   16.3%

14-4. (*Annual Percentage Yield*) Compute the cost of the trade credit terms in problem 14-3 using the compounding formula, or annual percentage yield.

14-5. (*Cost of Short-Term Financing*) The R. Morin Construction Company needs to borrow $100,000 to help finance the cost of a new $150,000 hydraulic crane used in the firm's commercial construction business. The crane will pay for itself in one year, and the firm is considering the following alternatives for financing its purchase:

Alternative A—The firm's bank has agreed to lend the $100,000 at a rate of 14 percent. Interest would be discounted, and a 15 percent compensating-balance would be required. However, the compensating balance requirement would not be binding on R. Morin because the firm normally maintains a minimum demand deposit (checking account) balance of $25,000 in the bank.

Alternative B—The equipment dealer has agreed to finance the equipment with a one-year loan. The $100,000 loan would require payment of principal and interest totaling $116,300.

    a. Which alternative should R. Morin select?

    b. If the bank's compensating-balance requirement were to necessitate idle demand deposits equal to 15 percent of the loan, what effect would this have on the cost of the bank loan alternative?

Alt A 16.28%

Alt B 16.3%

19.7%

14-6. (*Cost of Short-term Bank Loan*) On July 1, 199X, the Southwest Forging Corporation arranged for a line of credit with the First National Bank of Dallas. The terms of the agreement called for a $100,000 maximum loan with interest set at 1 percent over prime. In addition, the firm has to maintain a 20 percent compensating balance in its demand deposit account throughout the year. The prime rate is currently 12 percent.

a. If Southwest normally maintains a $20,000 to $30,000 balance in its checking account with FNB of Dallas, what is the effective cost of credit through the line-of-credit agreement where the maximum loan amount is used for a full year?

b. Recompute the effective cost of trade to Southwest if the firm will have to borrow the compensating balance and it borrows the maximum possible under the loan agreement. Again, assume the full amount of the loan is outstanding for a whole year.

14-7. (*Cost of Commercial Paper*) Tri-State Enterprises plans to issue commercial paper for the first time in the firm's 35-year history. The firm plans to issue $500,000 in 180-day maturity notes. The paper will carry a $10\frac{1}{4}$ percent rate with discounted interest and will cost Tri-State $12,000 (paid in advance) to issue.

a. What is the effective cost of credit to Tri-State?

b. What other factors should the company consider in analyzing whether to issue the commercial paper?

14-8. (*Cost of Accounts Receivable*) Johnson Enterprises, Inc., is involved in the manufacture and sale of electronic components used in small AM/FM radios. The firm needs $300,000 to finance an anticipated expansion in receivables due to increased sales. Johnson's credit terms are net 60, and its average monthly credit sales are $200,000. In general, the firm's customers pay within the credit period; thus the firm's average accounts receivable balance is $400,000. Chuck Idol, Johnson's comptroller, approached the firm's bank with a request for a loan for the $300,000, using the firm's accounts receivable as collateral. The bank offered to make a loan at a rate of 2 percent over prime plus a 1 percent processing charge on all receivables pledged ($200,000 per month). Furthermore, the bank agreed to lend up to 75 percent of the face value of the receivables pledged.

a. Estimate the cost of the receivables loan to Johnson where the firm borrows the $300,000. The prime rate is currently 11 percent.

b. Idol also requested a line of credit for $300,000 from the bank. The bank agreed to grant the necessary line of credit at a rate of 3 percent over prime and required a 15 percent compensating balance. Johnson currently maintains an average demand deposit of $80,000. Estimate the cost of the line of credit to Johnson.

c. Which source of credit should Johnson select? Why?

14-9. (*Cost of Factoring*) MDM, Inc., is considering factoring its receivables. The firm has credit sales of $400,000 per month and has an average receivables balance of $800,000 with 60-day credit terms. The factor has offered to extend credit equal to 90 percent of the receivables factored less interest on the loan at a rate of $1\frac{1}{2}$ percent per month. The 10 percent difference in the advance and the face value of all receivables factored consists of a 1 percent factoring fee plus a 9 percent reserve, which the factor maintains. In addition, if MDM, Inc., decides to factor its receivables, it will sell them all, so that it can reduce its credit department costs by $1,500 a month.

a. What is the cost of borrowing the maximum amount of credit available to MDM, Inc., through the factoring agreement?

b. What considerations other than cost should be accounted for by MDM, Inc., in determining whether to enter the factoring agreement?

14-10. (*Cost of Secured Short-Term Credit*) The Sean-Janeow Import Co. needs $500,000 for the three-month period ending September 30, 199X. The firm has explored two possible sources of credit.

1. S-J has arranged with its bank for a $500,000 loan secured by accounts receivable. The bank has agreed to advance S-J 80 percent of the value of its pledged receivables at a rate of 11 percent plus a 1 percent fee based on all receivables pledged. S-J's receivables average a total of $1 million year-round.

2. An insurance company has agreed to lend the $500,000 at a rate of 9 percent per annum, using a loan secured by S-J's inventory of salad oil. A field warehouse agreement would be used, which would cost S-J $2,000 a month. Which source of credit should S-J select? Explain.

14-11. (*Cost of Short-Term Financing*) You plan to borrow $20,000 from the bank to pay for inventories for a gift shop you have just opened. The bank offers to lend you the money at 10 percent annual interest for the six months the funds will be needed.

a. Calculate the effective rate of interest on the loan.

b. In addition, the bank requires you to maintain a 15 percent compensating balance in the bank. Because you are just opening your business, you do not have a demand deposit account at the bank that can be used to meet the compensating balance requirement. This means that you will have to put 15 percent of the loan amount from your own personal money (which you had planned to use to help finance the business) in a checking account. What is the cost of the loan now?

c. In addition to the compensating-balance requirement in part (b), you are told that interest will be discounted. What is the effective rate of interest on the loan now?

14-12. (*Cost of Factoring*) A factor has agreed to lend the JVC Corporation working capital on the following terms. JVC's receivables average $100,000 per month and have a 90-day average collection period. (Note that JVC's credit terms call for payment in 90 days, and accounts receivable average $300,000 because of the 90-day average collection period.) The factor will charge 12 percent interest on any advance (1 percent per month paid in advance), will charge a 2 percent processing fee on all receivables factored, and will maintain a 20 percent reserve. If JVC undertakes the loan, it will reduce its own credit department expenses by $2,000 per month. What is the annual effective rate of interest to JVC on the factoring arrangement? Assume that the maximum advance is taken.

SELF–TEST SOLUTIONS

SS–1.

The discounted interest cost of the commercial paper issue is calculated as follows:

$$\text{interest expense} = .10 \times \$200,000,000 \times 180/360 = \$10,000,000$$

The effective cost of credit can now be calculated as follows:

$$APR = \frac{\$10,000,000 + \$125,000}{\$200,000,000 - \$125,000 - \$10,000,000} \times \frac{1}{180/360}$$

$$= .1066 = 10.66\%$$

SS–2.

a.
$$APR = \frac{.18 \times \$200,000}{\$200,000} \times \frac{1}{1}$$

$$= .18 = 18\%$$

b.
$$APR = \frac{.16 \times \$200{,}000}{\$200{,}000 - (.20 \times \$200{,}000)} \times \frac{1}{1}$$

$$= .20 = 20\%$$

c.
$$APR = \frac{.14 \times \$200{,}000}{\$200{,}000 - (.14 \times \$200{,}000) - (.2 \times \$200{,}000)} \times \frac{1}{1}$$

$$= .2121 = 21.21\%$$

Alternative (a) offers the lowest-cost service of financing, although it carries the highest stated rate of interest. The reason for this is that there is no compensating-balance requirement, nor is interest discounted for this alternative.

Liquid Asset Management

Why a Company Holds Cash • Cash Management Objectives and Decisions • Collection and Disbursement Procedures • Evaluation of Costs of Cash Management Services • Composition of Marketable-Securities Portfolio • Accounts-Receivable Management • Inventory Management • Just-in-Time Inventory Control

A t the end of 1995, General Motors (GM) held 5.1 percent of its total assets, amounting to just over $217.1 billion, in the form of cash and short-term marketable securities. The marketable securities in this instance had original maturities of 90 days or less. During 1995 this largest of U.S. corporations generated sales revenues of $168.8 billion. Based on a 365-day year, this means GM "produced" $462,465,753 in sales revenues *each day.*

If GM could have freed up only one day's worth of sales and invested it in three-month U.S. Treasury bills in January 1996 yielding 5.05 percent, then the firm's before-tax profits would have jumped by $23.35 million. That is a tidy sum and demonstrates why firms like to have efficient treasury management departments in place. Shareholders enjoy the added profits.

If GM's management felt that its shareholders could stand the excitement and bear a little more risk, then the freed-up cash might be invested in bank certificates of deposit (CDs) of a similar three-month maturity. At the same time in January 1996, the CDs of major money-center commercial banks were yielding 5.44 percent to investors.

That difference of 39 basis points (i.e., 5.44 percent versus 5.05 percent) may not seem like much, but when put to work on an investment of over $462 million, it produces a considerable outcome. In this case, the increased before-tax profits would total $25.16 million. By investing the excess cash in CDs rather than Treasury bills, GM's before-tax profits would be $1.81 million greater (i.e., $25.16 million versus $23.35 million).

Managing the cash and marketable-securities portfolio are important tasks for the financial executive. This chapter will teach you about sophisticated cash management systems and about prudent places to "park" the firm's excess cash balances so they earn a positive rate of return and are liquid at the same time. We will also explore sound management techniques that relate to the other asset components of the firm's working capital—accounts receivable and inventory.

457

Chapter 14 provided an introduction and overview of the concept of working-capital management. In this chapter, we will explore in more depth management of the asset components of the working-capital equation. Accordingly, we will focus on the alternatives available to managers for increasing shareholder wealth with respect to the most important types of current assets: (1) cash, (2) marketable securities, (3) accounts receivable, and (4) inventory. These are listed in order of declining liquidity.

Such alternatives will include (1) techniques available to management for favorably influencing cash receipt and disbursement patterns, (2) investments that allow a firm to employ excess cash balances productively, (3) critical decision formulas for determining the appropriate amount of investment in accounts receivable, and (4) methods, such as those pertaining to order quantity and order point issues, for evaluating most suitable levels of inventory.

These issues are important to the financial manager for several reasons. For example, judicious management of cash and near-cash assets allows the firm to hold the minimum amount of cash necessary to meet the firm's obligations in a timely manner. As a result, the firm is able to take advantage of the opportunity to earn a return on its liquid assets and increase its profitability.

Wise management of accounts receivable and inventory is important because these two classes of assets generally constitute a large portion of a firm's total assets. Using GM again as an example, taken together, this firm's investment in accounts receivable and inventory represented 9.9 percent of its total assets at the end of 1995. On an absolute basis, GM held $21.5 billion in receivables and inventory at that time. This is serious stuff and a major challenge to the organization and its financial management abilities. Any changes in assets of such magnitude to the firm will affect its profitability. An increase in accounts receivable, for example, not only results in higher sales through extension of additional trade credit, but also increases the need for financing to support the additional investment. The costs of credit investigation and collection also are increased, as could be bad debt expense. Likewise, a larger investment in inventory, by allowing more efficient production and speedier delivery to customers, leads to increased sales. At the same time, additional financing is required to support the increased level of inventory and the concomitant handling and carrying costs.

With such significance in mind, we begin the study of current asset management by exploring the various aspects of the management of cash and marketable securities. Afterward, we will turn to an analysis of the important issues related to the management of accounts receivable and inventory.

Before proceeding to our discussion of cash management, it will be helpful to distinguish among several terms. **Cash** is the currency and coin the firm has on hand in petty cash drawers, in cash registers, or in checking accounts (i.e., demand deposit accounts) at the various commercial banks. **Marketable securities,** also called near cash or near-cash assets, are *security investments that the firm can quickly convert into cash balances.* Generally, firms hold marketable securities with very short maturity periods—less than one year. Together, cash and marketable securities constitute the most liquid assets of a firm.

cash

marketable securities

PAUSE AND REFLECT

It is useful to think of the firm's cash balance as a reservoir that rises with cash inflows and falls with cash outflows. Any nonfinancial firm (in other words, any company that manufactures products, such as Ford Motor Company) desires to minimize its cash balances consistent with meeting its financial obligations in a timely manner.

Holding too much cash—what analysts tend to call "excess cash"—results in a loss of profitability to the firm. The auto manufacturer, for example, is not in business to build up its cash reservoir. Rather, it wants to manage its cash balance in order to maximize its financial returns because this will enhance shareholder wealth.

WHY A COMPANY HOLDS CASH

OBJECTIVE 1

A thorough understanding of why and how a firm holds cash requires an accurate conception of how cash flows into and through the enterprise. Figure 15–1 depicts the process of cash generation and disposition in a typical manufacturing setting. The arrows designate the direction of the flow—that is, whether the cash balance increases or decreases.

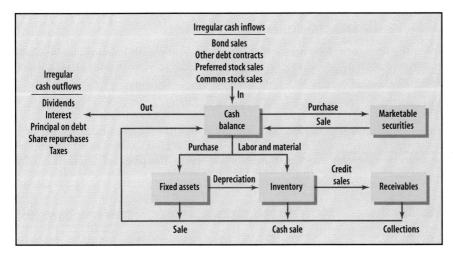

Figure 15–1
The Cash Generation and Disposition Process

Cash Flow Process

The irregular increases in the firm's cash holdings can come from several external sources. Funds can be obtained in the financial markets from the sale of securities, such as bonds, preferred stock, and common stock, or the firm can enter into non-marketable-debt contracts with lenders such as commercial banks. These irregular cash inflows do not occur on a daily basis. The reason is that external financing contracts or arrangements usually involve huge sums of money stemming from a major need identified by the company's management, and these needs do not occur every day. For example, a new product might be in the launching process, or a plant expansion might be required to provide added productive capacity.

In most organizations the financial officer responsible for cash management also controls the transactions that affect the firm's investment in marketable securities. As excess cash becomes temporarily available, marketable securities are purchased. When cash is in short supply, a portion of the marketable-securities portfolio is liquidated.

Whereas the irregular cash inflows are from external sources, the other main sources of cash arise from internal operations and occur on a more regular basis. Over long periods, the largest receipts come from accounts-receivable collections and to a lesser extent from direct cash sales of finished goods. Many manufacturing concerns also generate cash on a regular basis through the liquidation of scrap or obsolete inventory. At various times fixed assets may also be sold, thereby generating some cash inflow.

Apart from the investment of excess cash in near-cash assets, the cash balance experiences reductions for three key reasons. First, on an irregular basis, withdrawals are made to (1) pay cash dividends on preferred and common stock shares, (2) meet interest requirements on debt contracts, (3) repay the principal borrowed from creditors, (4) buy the firm's own shares in the financial markets for use in executive compensation plans or as an alternative to paying a cash dividend, and (5) pay tax bills. Again, by an *irregular basis* we mean items *not* occurring on a daily or frequent schedule. Second, the company's capital expenditure program designates that fixed assets be acquired at various intervals. Third, inventories are purchased on a regular basis to ensure a steady flow of finished goods off the production line. Note that the arrow linking the investment in fixed assets with the inventory account is labeled *depreciation*. This indicates that a portion of the cost of fixed assets is charged against the products coming off the assembly line. This cost is subsequently recovered through the sale of the finished-goods inventory, because the product's selling price will be set by management to cover all the costs of production, including depreciation.

Motives for Holding Cash

The influences described above that affect the firm's cash balance can be classified in terms of the three motives put forth by John Maynard Keynes: (1) the transactions motive, (2) the precautionary motive, and (3) the speculative motive.[1]

The Transactions Motive

Balances held for transaction purposes allow the firm to meet cash needs that arise in the ordinary course of doing business. In Figure 15–1, transaction balances would be used to meet the irregular outflows as well as the planned acquisition of fixed assets and inventories.

---

[1]John Maynard Keynes, *The General Theory of Employment, Interest, and Money* (New York: Harcourt Brace Jovanovich, 1936).

The relative amount of cash needed to satisfy transaction requirements is affected by a number of factors, such as the industry in which the firm operates. It is well-known that utilities can forecast cash receipts quite accurately, because of stable demand for their services. Computer software firms, however, have a more difficult time predicting their cash flows. New products are brought to market at a rapid pace, thereby making it difficult to project cash flows and balances precisely.

The Precautionary Motive

Precautionary balances are a buffer stock of liquid assets. This motive for holding cash relates to the maintenance of balances to be used to satisfy possible, but as yet indefinite, needs.

Cash flow predictability also has a material influence on the firm's demand for cash through this precautionary motive. The airline industry provides a typical illustration. Air passenger carriers are plagued with a high degree of cash flow uncertainty. The weather, rising fuel costs, and continual strikes by operating personnel make cash forecasting difficult for any airline. The upshot of this problem is that because of all the things that *might* happen, the minimum cash balances desired by the management of the air carriers tend to be large.

In actual business practice, the precautionary motive is met to a large extent by the holding of a portfolio of *liquid assets*, not just cash. Notice in Figure 15–1 the two-way flow of funds between the company's holdings of cash and marketable securities. In large corporate organizations, funds may flow either into or out of the marketable-securities portfolio on a daily basis.

The Speculative Motive

Cash is held for speculative purposes in order to take advantage of potential profit-making situations. Construction firms that build private dwellings will at times accumulate cash in anticipation of a significant drop in lumber costs. If the price of building supplies does drop, the companies that built up their cash balances stand to profit by purchasing materials in large quantities. This will reduce their cost of goods sold and increase their net profit margin. Generally, the speculative motive is the least important component of a firm's preference for liquidity. The transactions and precautionary motives account for most of the reasons why a company holds cash balances.

PAUSE AND REFLECT

Any company can benefit from a properly designed cash management system. If you identify what you believe to be a superbly run business organization, the odds are that the firm has in place a sound cash management system. Before we explore several cash management techniques, it is necessary to introduce (1) the risk-return trade-off, (2) the objectives, and (3) the decisions that comprise the center of the cash management process. Keep in mind that the billion-dollar company will save millions each year by grasping these concepts, and the small and midsized organizations may actually enhance their overall chances of survival.

CASH MANAGEMENT OBJECTIVES AND DECISIONS

The Risk-Return Trade-off

A companywide cash management program must be concerned with minimizing the firm's risk of insolvency. In the context of cash management, the term **insolvency** describes the *situation where the firm is unable to meet its maturing liabilities on time.* In such a case the company is *technically insolvent* in that it lacks the necessary liquidity to make prompt payment on its current debt obligations. A firm could avoid this problem by carrying large cash balances to pay the bills that come due.

The financial manager must strike an acceptable balance between holding too much cash and too little cash. This is the focal point of the risk-return trade-off. A large cash investment minimizes the chances of insolvency, but penalizes company profitability. A small cash investment frees excess balances for investment in both marketable securities and longer-lived assets; this enhances company profitability and the value of the firm's common shares, but increases the chances of running out of cash.

BACK TO THE FOUNDATIONS

The dilemma faced by the financial manager is a clear application of **Axiom 1: The Risk-Return Trade-off—We Won't Take On Additional Risk Unless We Expect to Be Compensated with Additional Return.** To accept the risk of not having sufficient cash on hand, the firm must be compensated with a return on the cash that is invested. Moreover, the greater the risk of the investment in which the cash is placed, the greater the return the firm demands.

The Objectives

The risk-return trade-off can be reduced to two prime objectives for the firm's cash management system.

1. Enough cash must be on hand to meet the disbursal needs that arise in the course of doing business.
2. Investment in idle cash balances must be reduced to a minimum.

Evaluation of these operational objectives, and a conscious attempt on the part of management to meet them, gives rise to the need for some typical cash management decisions.

The Decisions

Two conditions or ideals would allow the firm to operate for extended periods with cash balances near or at a level of zero: (1) a completely accurate forecast of net cash flows over the planning horizon and (2) perfect synchronization of cash receipts and disbursements.

Cash flow forecasting is the initial step in any effective cash management program. Given that the firm will, as a matter of necessity, invest in some cash balances, certain types of decisions related to the size of those balances dominate the cash management process. These include decisions that answer the following questions:

1. What can be done to speed up cash collections and slow down or better control cash outflows?
2. What should be the composition of a marketable-securities portfolio?

PAUSE AND REFLECT

Although the sheer number of cash collection and payment techniques is large, the concepts on which those techniques rest are simple. Controlling the cash inflow and outflow is a major theme of treasury management. But, within the confines of ethical management, the cash manager is always thinking, (1) "How can I speed up the firm's cash receipts?" and (2) "How can I slow down the firm's cash payments and not irritate too many important constituencies, such as suppliers?"

The critical point is that cash saved becomes available for investment elsewhere in the company's operations, and at a positive rate of return this will increase total profitability. Grasping the elements of cash management requires that you understand the concept of cash float. We address the concept of float and float reduction early in the discussion on collection and disbursement procedures.

COLLECTION AND DISBURSEMENT PROCEDURES

OBJECTIVE 3

The efficiency of the firm's cash management program can be enhanced by knowledge and use of various procedures aimed at (1) accelerating cash receipts and (2) improving the methods used to disburse cash. We will see that greater opportunity for corporate profit improvement lies with the cash receipts side of the funds flow process, although it would be unwise to ignore opportunities for favorably affecting cash disbursement practices.

Managing the Cash Inflow

The reduction of float lies at the center of the many approaches employed to speed up cash receipts. **Float** (or total float), which is *the length of time from when a check is written until the actual recipient can draw upon or use the "good funds,"* has four elements as follows:

float

1. **Mail float** is caused by the time lapse from the moment a customer mails a remittance check until the firm begins to process it.
2. **Processing float** is caused by the time required for the firm to process remittance checks before they can be deposited in the bank.
3. **Transit float** is caused by the time necessary for a deposited check to clear through the commercial banking system and become usable funds to the company. Credit is deferred for a maximum of two business days on checks that are cleared through the Federal Reserve System.
4. **Disbursing float** derives from the fact that funds are available in the company's bank account until its payment check has cleared through the banking system.

We will use the term *float* to refer to the total of its four elements just described. Float reduction can yield considerable benefits in terms of usable funds released for company use and returns produced on such freed-up balances. As an example, for

1995 the Walt Disney Company reported total revenues of $12.112 billion. The amount of usable funds that would be released if Disney could achieve a one-day reduction in float can be approximated by dividing annual revenues (sales) by the number of days in a year. In this case one day's freed-up balances would be

$$\frac{\text{annual revenues}}{\text{days in year}} = \frac{\$12,112,000,000}{365} = \$33,183,562$$

If these released funds, which represent one day's sales of approximately $33.2 million, could be invested to return 6 percent a year, then the annual value of the one-day float reduction would be

$$(\text{sales per day}) \times (\text{assumed yield}) = \$33,183,562 \times .06 = \$1,991,014$$

It is clear that effective cash management can yield impressive opportunities for profit improvement. Let us look now at specific techniques for reducing float.

EXAMPLE

The positive operating profit effects that stem from the use of wise cash management techniques that result in float reduction can be dramatic when large total revenues are involved. Our analysis above showed that the value of a one-day float reduction for the Walt Disney Company could approach $2 million for the year when money-market yields are in the vicinity of 6 percent annually.

Suppose now that we want to estimate the value of a one-day float reduction for IBM, which has annual total revenues far in excess of the entertainment giant Disney. Incidentally, for 1995, Disney's sales revenues ranked 102 on the well-known Fortune 500 list. IBM's ranked number 6 out of 500.

IBM's 1995 sales revenues were reported at $71.94 billion. Again, let's assume that prudent investment in money-market securities will earn 6 percent annually. We ask, What is the estimated value of a one-day float reduction to IBM? Following the procedures outlined above, you will find that one day's freed-up balances for IBM will be $197,095,890, or in excess of $197 million. Then we find the annual (before-tax) value of the float reduction as

$$(\text{sales per day}) \times (\text{assumed yield}) = \$197,095,890 \times .06 = \$11,825,753$$

Such prospective gains in operating profits make it worthwhile for the firm and its treasury management function to closely evaluate the cash management services offered by commercial banks—even when the bank fees can also be quite costly. We will learn how to make decisions of this nature later in the chapter. ■

The Lockbox Arrangement

The lockbox system is the most widely used commercial banking service for expediting cash gathering. Banks have offered this service since 1946. Such a system speeds up the conversion of receipts into usable funds by reducing both mail and processing float. In addition, it is possible to reduce transit float if lockboxes are located near Federal Reserve Banks and their branches. For large corporations that receive checks from all parts of the country, float reductions of two to four days are not unusual.

Figure 15–2 illustrates an elementary, but typical, cash collection system for a hypothetical firm. It also shows the origin of mail float, processing float, and transit float. The numbers represent the steps in this system. First, the customer places his or her remittance check in the U.S. mail, which is then delivered to the firm's headquarters. This causes the mail float. On the check's arrival at the firm's headquarters (or local collection center), general accounting personnel must go through the book-keeping procedures needed to prepare them for local deposit. The checks are then

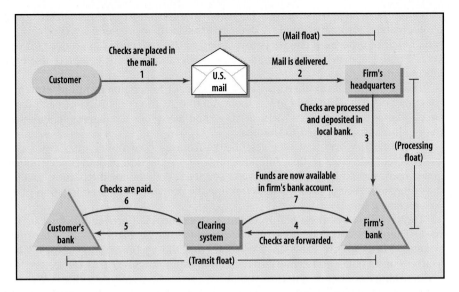

Figure 15–2
Ordinary Cash Collection System

deposited. This causes the processing float. The checks are then forwarded for payment through the commercial bank clearing mechanism. The checks will be charged against the customer's own bank account. At this point the checks are said to be "paid" and become "good" funds available for use by the company that received them. This bank clearing procedure represents transit float and, as we said earlier, can amount to a delay of up to two business days.

The lockbox arrangement shown in Figure 15–3 is based on a simple procedure. The firm's customers are instructed to mail their remittance checks not to company headquarters or regional offices, but to a numbered post office box. The bank that is providing the lockbox service is authorized to open the box, collect the mail, process the checks, and deposit the checks directly into the company's account.

Typically a large bank will collect payments from the lockbox at one- to two-hour intervals, 365 days of the year. During peak business hours, the bank may pick up mail every 30 minutes.

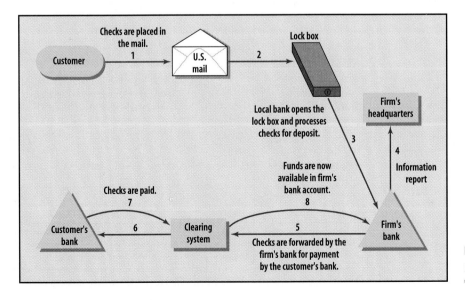

Figure 15–3
Simple Lockbox System

Once the mail is received at the bank, the checks will be examined, totaled, photocopied, and microfilmed. A deposit form is then prepared by the bank, and each batch of processed checks is forwarded to the collection department for clearance. Funds deposited in this manner are usually available for company use in one business day or less.

The bank can notify the firm via some type of telecommunications system the same day deposits are made about their amount. At the conclusion of each day, all check photocopies, invoices, deposit slips, and any other documents included with the remittances are mailed to the firm.

Note that the firm that receives checks from all over the country will have to use several lockboxes to take full advantage of a reduction in mail float. The firm's major bank should be able to offer as a service a detailed lockbox study, analyzing the company's receipt patterns to determine the proper number and location of lockbox receiving points.

The two systems described by Figures 15–2 and 15–3 are summarized in Table 15–1. There, the step numbers refer to those shown in Figure 15–2 (the ordinary system). Furthermore, Table 15–1 assumes that the customer and the firm's headquarters or its collection center are located in different cities. This causes the lag of two working days before the firm actually receives the remittance check. We notice at the bottom of Table 15–1 that the installation of the lockbox system can result in

Table 15–1
Comparison of Ordinary Cash Collection System with Simple Lockbox System

Steps	Ordinary System and Time		Advantage of Lockbox
1	Customer writes check and places it in the mail.	1 day	
2	Mail is delivered to firm's headquarters.	2 days	Mail will not have to travel as far. Result: Save 1 day.
3	Accounting personnel process the checks and deposit them in the firm's local bank.	2 days	Bank personnel prepare checks for deposit. Result: Save 2 days.
4 and 5	Checks are forwarded for payment through the clearing mechanism.	1 day	As the lockboxes are located near Federal Reserve Banks or branches, transit float can be reduced.
6 and 7	The firm receives notice from its bank that the checks have cleared and the funds are now "good."	1 day	Result: Save 1 day.
	Total working days	7 days	Overall result: Save 4 working days.

funds being credited to the firm's bank account a full *four* working days *faster* than is possible under the ordinary collection system.

Previously in this chapter we calculated the 1995 sales per day for Disney to be $33.2 million and assumed the firm could invest its excess cash in marketable securities to yield 6 percent annually. If Disney could speed up its cash collections by four days, as the hypothetical firm did in Table 15–1, the results would be startling. The gross annual savings to Disney (apart from operating the lockbox system) would amount to $7.96 million, as follows:

$$\text{(sales per day)} \times \text{(days of float reduction)} \times \text{(assumed yield)}$$
$$= \$33,183,562 \times (4) \times .06 = \$7,964,055$$

As you might guess, the prospects for generating revenues of this magnitude are important not only to the firms involved, but also to commercial banks that offer lockbox services.

In summary, the benefits of a lockbox arrangement are these:

1. **Increased working cash.** The time required for converting receivables into available funds is reduced. This frees up cash for use elsewhere in the enterprise.

2. **Elimination of clerical functions.** The bank takes over the tasks of receiving, endorsing, totaling, and depositing checks. With less handling of receipts by employees, better audit control is achieved and the chance of documents becoming lost is reduced.

3. **Early knowledge of dishonored checks.** Should a customer's check be uncollectible because of lack of funds, it is returned, usually by special handling, to the firm.

These benefits are not free. Usually, the bank levies a charge for each check processed through the system. The benefits derived from the acceleration of receipts must exceed the incremental costs of the lockbox system, or the firm would be better off without it. Later in this chapter a straightforward method for assessing the desirability of a specific cash management service, such as the lockbox arrangement, will be illustrated.

Preauthorized Checks (PACs)

Whereas the lockbox arrangement can often reduce total float by two to four days, for some firms the use of preauthorized checks (PACs) can be an even more effective way of converting receipts into working cash. A PAC resembles the ordinary check, but it does not contain or require the signature of the person on whose account it is being drawn. A PAC is created only with the individual's legal authorization.

The PAC system is advantageous when the firm regularly receives a large volume of payments of a fixed amount from the same customers. This type of cash management service has proved useful to insurance companies, savings and loan associations, consumer credit firms, leasing enterprises, and charitable and religious organizations. The objective of this system is to reduce both mail and processing float. Notice, in relation to either the typical cash collection system (Figure 15–2) or the lockbox system (Figure 15–3), that the customer no longer (1) physically writes his or her own check nor (2) deposits such check in the mail.

The operation of a PAC system is illustrated in Figure 15–4 on page 468. It involves the following sequence of events:

1. The firm's customers authorize it to draw checks on their respective demand deposit accounts.

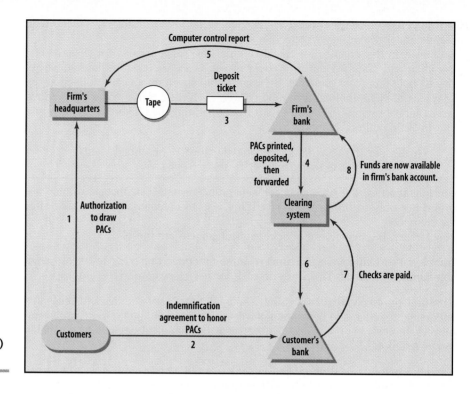

Figure 15–4
Preauthorized Check (PAC)
System

2. Indemnification agreements are signed by the customers and forwarded to the banks where they maintain their demand deposit accounts. These agreements authorize the banks to honor the PACs when they are presented for payment through the commercial bank clearing system.

3. The firm prepares a magnetic tape that contains all appropriate information about the regular payments.

4. At each processing cycle (monthly, weekly, semimonthly) the corporation retains a hard-copy listing of all tape data for control purposes. Usually, the checks that are about to be printed will be deposited in the firm's demand deposit account, so a deposit ticket will also be forwarded to the bank.

5. Upon receipt of the tape the bank will produce the PACs, deposit them to the firm's account, forward them for clearing through the commercial banking system, and return a control report to the firm.

For firms that can take advantage of a PAC system, the benefits include the following:

1. **Highly predictable cash flows.**

2. **Reduced expenses.** Billing and postage costs are eliminated, and the clerical processing of customer payments is significantly reduced.

3. **Customer preference.** Many customers prefer not to be bothered with a regular billing. With a PAC system the check is actually written for the customer and the payment made even if he or she is on vacation or otherwise out of town.

4. **Increased working cash.** Mail float and processing float can be dramatically reduced in comparison with other payment-processing systems.

Depository Transfer Checks (DTCs)

Both depository transfer checks and wire transfers are used in conjunction with what is known as **concentration banking.** A concentration bank is one *where the firm maintains a major disbursing account.*

concentration banking

In an effort to accelerate collections, many companies have established multiple collection centers. Regional lockbox networks are one type of approach to strategically located collection points. Even without lockboxes, firms may have numerous sales outlets throughout the country and collect cash over the counter. This requires many local bank accounts to handle daily deposits. Rather than have funds sitting in these multiple bank accounts in different geographic regions of the country, most firms will regularly transfer the surplus balances to one or more concentration banks. Centralizing the firm's pool of cash provides the following benefits:

1. **Lower levels of excess cash.** Desired cash-balance target levels are set for each regional bank. These target levels consider both compensating balance requirements and necessary working levels of cash. Cash in excess of the target levels can be transferred regularly to concentration banks for deployment by the firm's top-level management.

2. **Better control.** With more cash held in fewer accounts, stricter control over available cash is achieved. Quite simply, there are fewer problems. The concentration banks can prepare sophisticated reports that detail corporatewide movements of funds into and out of the central cash pool.

3. **More efficient investments in near-cash assets.** The coupling of information from the firm's cash forecast with data on available funds supplied by the concentration banks allows the firm quickly to transfer cash to the marketable-securities portfolio.

Depository transfer checks (DTCs) provide a *means for moving funds from local bank accounts to concentration bank accounts.* The depository transfer check itself is an *unsigned, nonnegotiable instrument.* It is payable only to the bank of deposit (the concentration bank) for credit to the firm's specific account. The firm files an authorization form with each bank from which it might withdraw funds. This form instructs the bank to pay the depository transfer checks without any signature. The movement of cash through the use of depository transfer checks can operate with a conventional mail system or an automated system.

depository transfer checks (DTCs)

When the mail system is used, a company employee deposits the day's receipts in a local bank and fills out a preprinted depository transfer check for the exact amount of the deposit. The company then mails the depository transfer check to the firm's concentration bank. While this document is traveling in the mails, the checks just deposited at the local bank are being cleared. As soon as the concentration bank receives the depository transfer check, the firm's account is credited for the designated amount. The funds credited to the concentration account are not available for the firm's use, of course, until the document has been cleared with the local depository bank for payment.

If the firm's depository banks are geographically dispersed so that the mail will take several days in reaching the concentration bank, then *no* float reduction might be achieved through this system. In an attempt to reduce the mail float associated with conventional depository transfer check systems, some banks have initiated a type of special mail handling of these instruments that can cut as much as one full day off regular mail delivery schedules.

An innovation in speeding cash into concentration bank accounts is the **automated depository transfer check (DTC) system.** In this system the *mail float involved in moving the transfer document from the local bank to the concentration bank is eliminated.* This system is depicted in Figure 15–5 on page 470.

automated depository transfer check (DTC) system

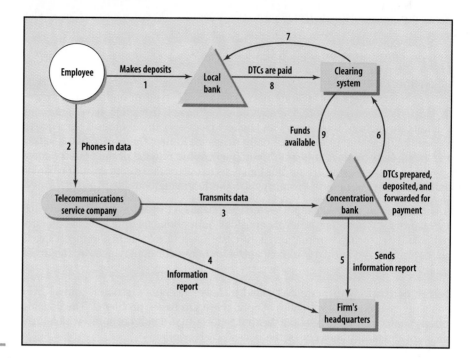

Figure 15–5

Automated Depository Transfer Check (DTC) System

The local company employee makes the daily deposit as usual. This employee does *not*, however, manually fill out the preprinted depository transfer check (DTC); instead, he or she telephones the deposit information to a regional data collection center. Usually, the center is operated for a fee by a firm, such as National Data Corporation. Various data collection centers will accumulate information throughout the day on the firm's regional deposits. Then, at specified cutoff times the deposit information from all local offices is transmitted to the concentration bank.

At this point the concentration bank prepares the depository transfer check and credits it to the company's account. The transfer checks are placed into the commercial bank check-clearing process and presented to the firm's local bank for payment. When paid by the local bank, the funds become available in the concentration bank account for company use. Major banks claim that funds transferred by use of the automated depository transfer check system can become available for company use in one business day or less.

Wire Transfers

The fastest way to move cash between banks is by use of **wire transfers,** which *eliminate transit float.* Funds moved in this manner, then, immediately become usable funds or "good funds" to the firm at the receiving bank. The following two major communication facilities are used to accommodate wire transfers:

1. **Bank Wire.** Bank Wire is a private wire service used and supported by approximately 250 banks in the United States for transferring funds, exchanging credit information, or effecting securities transactions.

2. **Federal Reserve Wire System.** The Fed Wire is directly accessible to commercial banks that are members of the Federal Reserve System. A commercial bank that is not on the Bank Wire or is not a member of the Federal Reserve System can use the wire transfer through its correspondent bank.

Wire transfers are often initiated on a standing-order basis. By means of a written authorization from company headquarters, a local depository bank might be instructed to transfer funds regularly to the firm's concentration bank.

As might be expected, wire transfers are a relatively expensive method of marshaling funds through a firm's money management system. Generally, the movement of small amounts does not justify the use of wire transfers.

Management of Cash Outflow

Significant techniques and systems for improving the firm's management of cash disbursements include (1) zero balance accounts, (2) payable-through drafts, and (3) remote disbursing. The first two offer markedly better control over companywide payments, and as a secondary benefit they *may* increase disbursement float. The last technique, remote disbursing, aims solely to increase disbursement float.

Zero Balance Accounts (ZBAs)

Large corporations that operate multiple branches, divisions, or subsidiaries often maintain numerous bank accounts (in different banks) for the purpose of making timely operating disbursements. It does make good business sense for payments for purchased parts that go into, say, an automobile transmission to be made by the Transmission and Chassis Division of the auto manufacturer rather than its central office. The Transmission and Chassis Division originates such purchase orders, receives and inspects the shipment when it arrives at the plant, authorizes payment, and writes the appropriate check. To have the central office involved in these matters would be a waste of company time.

What tends to happen, however, is that with several divisions utilizing their own disbursal accounts, excess cash balances build up in outlying banks and rob the firm of earning assets. Zero balance accounts are used to alleviate this problem. The objectives of a zero balance account system for the firm are (1) to achieve better control over its cash payments, (2) to reduce excess cash balances held in regional banks for disbursing purposes, and (3) to increase disbursing float.

Zero balance accounts (ZBAs) *permit centralized control (at the headquarters level) over cash outflows while maintaining divisional disbursing authority.* Under this system the firm's authorized employees, representing their various divisions, continue to write checks on their individual accounts. Note that the numerous individual disbursing accounts are now *all* located in the same concentration bank. Actually, these separate accounts contain no funds at all, thus their appropriate label, "zero balance." These accounts have all the characteristics of regular demand deposit accounts including separate titles, numbers, and statements.

Figure 15–6 on page 472 presents a schematic of a zero balance account (ZBA) cash disbursement system. The firm is assumed to have three operating divisions, each with its own ZBA. The system works as follows: The firm's authorized agents write their payment checks as usual against their specific accounts. These checks clear through the banking system in the usual way. On a daily basis checks are presented to the firm's concentration bank (the drawee bank) for payment. As the checks are paid by the bank, negative (debit) balances build up in the proper disbursing accounts. At the end of each day the negative balances are restored to a zero level by means of credits to the zero balance accounts; a corresponding reduction of funds is made against the firm's concentration (master) demand deposit account. Each morning a report is electronically forwarded to corporate headquarters reflecting the balance in the master account as well as the previous day's activity in each zero balance account. Using the report, the financial officer in charge of near-cash investments is ready to initiate appropriate transactions.

zero balance accounts (ZBAs)

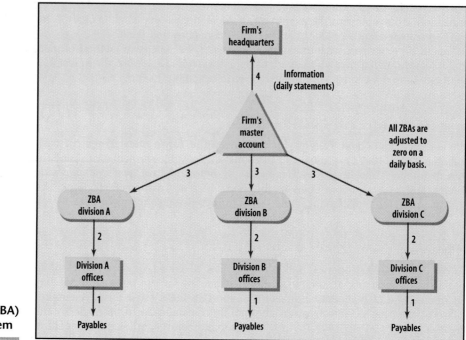

Figure 15–6

Zero Balance Account (ZBA)
Cash Disbursement System

Managing the cash outflow through use of a ZBA system offers the following benefits to the firm with many operating units:

1. Centralized control over disbursements is achieved, even though payment authority continues to rest with operating units.
2. Management time spent on superficial cash management activities is reduced. Exercises such as observing the balances held in numerous bank accounts, transferring funds to those accounts short of cash, and reconciling the accounts demand less attention.
3. Excess balances held in outlying accounts can be reduced.
4. The costs of cash management can be reduced, as wire transfers to build up funds in outlying disbursement accounts are eliminated.
5. Funds may be made available for company use through an increase in disbursement float. When local bank accounts are used to pay nearby suppliers, the checks clear rapidly. The same checks, if drawn on a ZBA located in a more distant concentration bank, will take more time to clear against the disbursing firm's account.

Payable-Through Drafts

Payable-through drafts (PTDs) are *legal instruments that have the physical appearance of ordinary checks but are not drawn on a bank. Instead, payable-through drafts are drawn on and payment is authorized by the issuing firm against its demand deposit account.* Figure 15–7 illustrates a payable-through draft system.

Like checks, the drafts are cleared through the banking system and are presented to the issuing firm's bank. The bank serves as a collection point and passes the drafts on to the firm. The corporate issuer usually has to return by the following business day all drafts it does not wish to cover (pay). Those documents not returned to the bank are automatically paid. The firm inspects the drafts for validity by checking

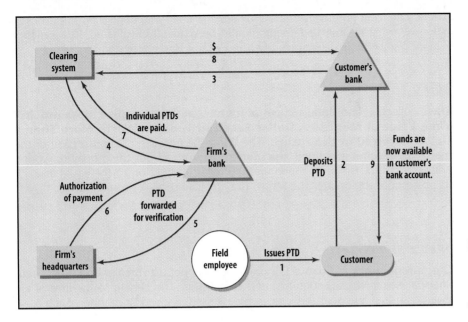

Figure 15–7
Payable-Through Draft (PTD) Cash Disbursement System

signatures, amounts, and dates. Stop-payment orders can be initiated by the company on any drafts considered inappropriate.

The main purpose of using a payable-through draft system is *to provide for effective control over field payments*. Central office control over payments begun by regional units is provided as the drafts are reviewed in advance of final payment. Payable-through drafts, for example, are used extensively in the insurance industry. The claims agent does not typically have check-signing authority against a corporate disbursement account. This agent can issue a draft, however, for quick settlement of a claim.

The Federal Reserve System requires transfer of available or "good" funds upon presentation of drafts to the payable-through bank. The payable-through bank will cover drafts but will be reluctant to absorb the float that would occur until the issuing firm authorizes payment the next business day. Therefore, the drafts presented for payment will usually be charged *in total* against the corporate master demand deposit account. That is for purposes of measuring usable funds available to the firm on that day. Legal payment of the *individual drafts* will still take place after their review and approval by the firm.

Remote Disbursing

A few banks will provide the corporate customer with a cash management service specifically designed to extend disbursing float. The firm's concentration bank may have a correspondent relationship with a smaller bank located in a distant city. In that remote city the Federal Reserve System is unable to maintain frequent clearings of checks drawn on local banks. For example, a firm that is located in Dallas and maintains its master account there may open an account with a bank situated in, say, Amarillo, Texas. The firm will write the bulk of its payment checks against the account in the Amarillo bank. The checks will probably take at least one business day longer to clear, so the firm can "play the float" to its advantage.

A firm must use this technique of remote disbursing with extreme care. If a key supplier of raw materials located in Dallas has to wait the extra day for funds drawn on the Amarillo account, the possibility of incurring ill will might outweigh the apparent gain from an increase in the disbursing float. The impact on the firm's reputation of using remote disbursing should be explicitly evaluated. The practice of remote disbursing is discouraged by the Federal Reserve System.

BACK TO THE FOUNDATIONS

These collection and disbursement procedures are an illustration of **Axiom 2: The Time Value of Money—A Dollar Received Today Is Worth More Than a Dollar Received in the Future.** The faster the firm can take possession of the money to which it is entitled, the sooner the firm can put the money to work generating a return. Similarly, the longer the firm can hold on to the liquid assets in its possession, the greater the return the firm can receive on such funds.

PAUSE AND REFLECT

Our previous work in Chapter 12 presented the popular breakeven model used by financial executives, accountants, and economists. The benefit to the firm of a given cash management service can be assessed in a similar manner. Such a model follows. More complicated methods can be presented (some that involve use of an appropriate company discount rate), but the model below is used by managers and is easily explained to them. The important point is: Cash management services are not free.

OBJECTIVE 4

EVALUATION OF COSTS OF CASH MANAGEMENT SERVICES

A form of breakeven analysis can help the financial officer decide whether a particular collection or disbursement service will provide an economic benefit to the firm. The evaluation process involves a very basic relationship in microeconomics:

$$\text{added costs} = \text{added benefits} \tag{15-1}$$

If equation (15–1) holds exactly, then the firm is no better or worse off for having adopted the given service. We will illustrate this procedure in terms of the desirability of installing an additional lockbox. Equation (15–1) can be restated on a per unit basis as follows:

$$P = (D)(S)(i) \tag{15-2}$$

where P = increases in per check processing cost if the new system is adopted
D = days saved in the collection process (float reduction)
S = average check size in dollars
i = the daily, before-tax opportunity cost (rate of return) of carrying cash

Assume that check processing cost P will rise by $.18 a check if the lockbox is used. The firm has determined that the average check size, S, that will be mailed to the lockbox location will be $900. If funds are freed by use of the lockbox, they will be invested in marketable securities to yield an *annual* before-tax return of 6 percent. With these data it is possible to determine the reduction in check collection time

D required to justify the use of the lockbox. That level of D is found to be

$$\$.18 = (D)(\$900)\left(\frac{.06}{365}\right)$$
$$1.217 \text{ days} = D$$

Thus, the lockbox is justified if the firm can speed up its collections by *more* than 1.217 days. This same style of analysis can be adapted to analyze the other tools of cash management.

Before moving on to a discussion of the firm's marketable-securities portfolio, it will be helpful to draw together the preceding material. Table 15–2 summarizes the salient features of the cash collection and disbursal techniques we have considered here.

Table 15–2

Features of Selected Cash Collection and Disbursal Techniques: A Summary

TECHNIQUE	OBJECTIVE	HOW ACCOMPLISHED
Cash Collection Techniques		
1. Lockbox system	Reduce (1) mail float, (2) processing float, and (3) transit float.	Strategic location of lockboxes to reduce mail float and transit float. Firm's commercial bank has access to lockbox to reduce processing float.
2. Preauthorized checks	Reduce (1) mail float and (2) processing float.	The firm writes the checks (the PACs) *for* its customers to be charged against their demand deposit accounts.
3. (Ordinary) Depository transfer checks	Eliminate excess funds in regional banks.	Used in conjunction with concentration banking whereby the firm maintains several collection centers. The transfer check authorizes movement of funds from a local bank to the concentration bank.
4. Automated depository transfer checks	Eliminate the mail float associated with the ordinary transfer check.	Telecommunications company transmits deposit data to the firm's concentration bank.
5. Wire transfers	Move funds immediately between banks. This eliminates transit float in that only "good funds" are transferred.	Use of Bank Wire or the Federal Reserve Wire System.
Cash Disbursal Techniques		
1. Zero balance accounts	(1) Achieve better control over cash payments, (2) reduce excess cash balances held in regional banks, and, possibly, (3) increase disbursing float.	Establish zero balance accounts for all of the firm's disbursing units. These accounts are all in the same concentration bank. Checks are drawn against these accounts, with the balance in each account never exceeding $0. Divisional disbursing authority is thereby maintained at the local level of management.
2. Payable-through drafts	Achieve effective central-office control over field-authorized payments.	Field office issues drafts rather than checks to settle up payables.
3. Remote disbursing	Extend disbursing float.	Write checks against demand deposit accounts held in distant banks.

COMPOSITION OF MARKETABLE-SECURITIES PORTFOLIO

Once the design of the firm's cash receipts and payments system has been determined, the financial manager faces the task of selecting appropriate financial assets for inclusion in the firm's marketable-securities portfolio.

General Selection Criteria

Certain criteria can provide the financial manager with a useful framework for selecting a proper marketable-securities mix. These considerations include evaluation of the (1) financial risk, (2) interest rate risk, (3) liquidity, (4) taxability, and (5) yields among different financial assets. We will briefly delineate these criteria from the investor's viewpoint.

Financial Risk

Financial risk here refers to the uncertainty of expected returns from a security attributable to possible changes in the financial capacity of the security issuer to make future payments to the security owner. If the chance of default on the terms of the instrument is high (or low), then the financial risk is said to be high (or low).

In both financial practice and research, when estimates of risk-free returns are desired, the yields available on Treasury securities are consulted and the safety of other financial instruments is weighed against them.

Interest Rate Risk

Interest rate risk refers to the uncertainty of expected returns from a financial instrument attributable to changes in interest rates. Of particular concern to the corporate treasurer is the price volatility associated with instruments that have long, as opposed to short, terms to maturity. An illustration can help clarify this point.

Suppose the financial officer is weighing the merits of investing temporarily available corporate cash in a new offering of U.S. Treasury obligations that will mature in either (1) 3 years or (2) 20 years from the date of issue. The purchase price of the 3-year notes or 20-year bonds is at their par value of $1,000 per security. The maturity value of either class of security is equal to par, $1,000, and the coupon rate (stated interest rate) is set at 7 percent, compounded annually.

If after one year from the date of purchase prevailing interest rates rise to 9 percent, the market prices of these currently outstanding Treasury securities will fail to bring their yields to maturity in line with what investors could obtain by buying a new issue of a given instrument. The market prices of *both* the 3-year and 20-year obligations will decline. The price of the 20-year instrument will decline by a greater dollar amount, however, than that of the 3-year instrument.

One year from the date of issue the price obtainable in the marketplace for the original 20-year instrument, which now has 19 years to go to maturity, can be found by computing P as follows:

$$P = \sum_{t=1}^{19} \frac{\$70}{(1+.09)^t} + \frac{\$1,000}{(1+.09)^{19}} = \$821.01$$

In the previous expression (1) t is the year in which the particular return, either interest or principal amount, is received; (2) $70 is the annual interest payment; and (3) $1,000 is the contractual maturity value of the bond. The rise in interest rates has forced the market price of the bond down to $821.01.

What will happen to the price of the note that has two years remaining to maturity? In a similar manner, we can compute its price, P:

$$P = \sum_{t=1}^{2} \frac{\$70}{(1 + .09)^t} + \frac{\$1,000}{(1 + .09)^2} = \$964.84$$

The market price of the shorter-term note will decline to $964.84. Table 15–3 shows that the market value of the shorter-term security was penalized much less by the given rise in the general level of interest rates.

If we extended the illustration, we would see that, in terms of market price, a 1-year security would be affected less than a 2-year security, a 91-day security less than a 182-day security, and so on. Equity securities would exhibit the largest price changes because of their infinite maturity periods. To hedge against the price volatility caused by interest rate risk, the firm's marketable-securities portfolio will tend to be composed of instruments that mature over short periods.

Liquidity

In the present context of managing the marketable-securities portfolio, *liquidity* refers to the ability to transform a security into cash. Should an unforeseen event require that a significant amount of cash be immediately available, then a sizable portion of the portfolio might have to be sold. The financial manager will want the cash quickly and will not want to accept a large price concession in order to convert the securities. Thus, in the formulation of preferences for the inclusion of particular instruments in the portfolio, the manager must consider (1) the period needed to sell the security and (2) the likelihood that the security can be sold at or near its prevailing market price.

Taxability

The tax treatment of the income a firm receives from its security investments does not affect the ultimate mix of the marketable-securities portfolio as much as the criteria mentioned earlier. This is because the interest income from most instruments suitable for inclusion in the portfolio is taxable at the federal level. Still, some corporate treasurers seriously evaluate the taxability of interest income and capital gains.

The interest income from only one class of securities escapes the federal income tax. That class of securities is generally referred to as *municipal obligations*, or more simply as *municipals*. Because of the tax-exempt feature of interest income from state and local government securities, municipals sell at lower yields to maturity in the market than do securities that pay taxable interest. The after-tax yield on a

Table 15–3
Market Price Effect of Rise in Interest Rates

ITEM	THREE-YEAR INSTRUMENT	TWENTY-YEAR INSTRUMENT
Original price	$1,000.00	$1,000.00
Price after one year	964.84	821.01
Decline in price	$ 35.16	$ 178.99

Table 15–4
Comparison of After-Tax Yields

	TAX-EXEMPT DEBT ISSUE (6% COUPON)	TAXABLE DEBT ISSUE (8% COUPON)
Interest income	$ 60.00	$ 80.00
Income tax (.34)	0.00	27.20
After-tax interest income	$ 60.00	$ 60.00
After-tax yield	$ 60.00 = 6%	$ 52.80 = 5.28%
	$1,000.00	$1,000.00

Derivation of equivalent before-tax yield on a taxable debt issue:

$$r = \frac{r^*}{1 - T} = \frac{.06}{1 - .34} = 9.901\%$$

where r = equivalent before-tax yield
    r^* = after-tax yield on tax-exempt security
    T = firm's marginal income tax rate

Proof: Interest income [$1,000 × .09091]	$90.91
Income tax (.34)	30.91
After-tax interest income	$60.00

municipal obligation, however, could be higher than the yield from a non–tax-exempt security. This would depend mainly on the purchasing firm's tax situation.

Consider Table 15–4. A firm is assumed to be analyzing whether to invest in a one-year tax-free debt issue yielding 6 percent on a $1,000 outlay or a one-year taxable issue that yields 8 percent on a $1,000 outlay. The firm pays federal taxes at the rate of 34 percent. The yields quoted in the financial press and in the prospectuses that describe debt issues are *before-tax* returns. The actual *after-tax* return enjoyed by the investor depends on his or her tax bracket. Notice that the actual after-tax yield received by the firm is only 5.28 percent on the taxable issue versus 6 percent on the tax-exempt obligation. The lower portion of Table 15–4 shows that the fully taxed bond must yield 9.091 percent to make it comparable with the tax-exempt issue.

Yields

The final selection criterion that we mention is a significant one—the yields that are available on the different financial assets suitable for inclusion in the near-cash portfolio. By now it is probably obvious that the factors of (1) financial risk, (2) interest rate risk, (3) liquidity, and (4) taxability all influence the available yields on financial instruments. The yield criterion involves an evaluation of the risks and benefits inherent in all of these factors. If a given risk is assumed, such as lack of liquidity, a higher yield may be expected on the nonliquid instrument.

Figure 15–8 summarizes our framework for designing the firm's marketable-securities portfolio. The four basic considerations are shown to influence the yields available on securities. The financial manager must focus on the risk-return trade-offs identified through analysis. Coming to grips with these trade-offs will enable the

Considerations	→	Influence	→	Focus Upon	→	Determine
Financial risk Interest rate risk Liquidity Taxability		Yields		Risk vs. return preferences		Marketable- securities mix

Figure 15–8
Designing the Marketable-Securities Portfolio

financial manager to determine the proper marketable-securities mix for the company. Let us look now at the marketable securities prominent in firms' near-cash portfolios.

Marketable-Security Alternatives

U.S. Treasury Bills

U.S. Treasury bills are the best-known and most popular short-term investment outlet among firms. A Treasury bill is a direct obligation of the U.S. government sold on a regular basis by the U.S. Treasury. New Treasury bills are issued in denominations of $10,000, $15,000, $50,000, $100,000, $500,000, and $1 million. In effect, therefore, one can buy bills in multiples of $5,000 above the smallest purchase price of $10,000 by combining $10,000 bills and $15,000 bills to reach the desired sum.

Bills currently are regularly offered with maturities of 91, 182, and 365 days. The three-month and six-month bills are auctioned weekly by the Treasury, and the one-year bills are offered every four weeks. Bids (orders to purchase) are accepted by the various Federal Reserve Banks and their branches, which perform the role of agents for the Treasury. Each Monday, bids are received until 1:30 P.M.; after that time they are opened, tabulated, and forwarded to the Treasury for allocation (filling the purchase orders).

Treasury bills are sold on a discount basis; for that reason the investor does not receive an actual interest payment. The return is the difference between the purchase price and the face (par) value of the bill.

Of prime importance to the corporate treasurer is the fact that a very active secondary market exists for bills. After a bill has been acquired by the firm, should the need arise to turn it into cash, a group of securities dealers stand ready to purchase it. This highly developed secondary market for bills not only makes them extremely liquid, but also allows the firm to buy bills with maturities of a week or even less.

As bills have the full financial backing of the U.S. government, they are, for all practical purposes, risk free. This negligible financial risk and high degree of liquidity makes the yields lower than those obtainable on other marketable securities. The income from Treasury bills is subject to federal income taxes, but *not* to state and local income taxes.

Federal Agency Securities

Federal agency securities are debt obligations of corporations and agencies that have been created to effect the various lending programs of the U.S. government. Five such government-sponsored corporations account for the majority of outstanding agency debt. The "big five" agencies are

1. The Federal National Mortgage Association (FNMA)
2. The Federal Home Loan Banks (FHLB)

3. The Federal Land Banks
4. The Federal Intermediate Credit Banks
5. The Banks for Cooperatives

It is not true that the "big five" federally sponsored agencies are owned by the U.S. government and that the securities they issue are fully guaranteed by the government. The "big five" agencies are now entirely owned by their member associations or the general public. In addition, the issuing agency, not the federal government, stands behind its promises to pay.

These agencies sell their securities in a variety of denominations. The entry barrier caused by the absolute dollar size of the smallest available Treasury bill—$10,000—is not as severe in the market for agencies. A wide range of maturities is also available. Obligations can at times be purchased with maturities as short as 30 days or as long as 15 years.

Agency debt usually sells on a coupon basis and pays interest to the owner on a semiannual schedule, although there are exceptions. Some issues have been sold on a discount basis, and some had paid interest only once a year.

The income from agency debt that the investor receives is subject to taxation at the federal level. Of the "big five" agencies, only the income from FNMA issues is taxed at the state and local level.

The yields available on agency obligations will always exceed those of Treasury securities of similar maturity. This yield differential is attributable to lesser marketability and greater default risk. The financial officer might keep in mind, however, that none of these agency issues has ever gone into default.

Bankers' Acceptances

Bankers' acceptances are one of the least-understood instruments suitable for inclusion in the firm's marketable-securities portfolio. Their part in U.S. commerce today is largely concentrated in the financing of foreign transactions. Generally, an acceptance is a draft (order to pay) drawn on a specific bank by an exporter in order to obtain payment for goods shipped to a customer, who maintains an account with that specific bank.

Because acceptances are used to finance the acquisition of goods by one party, the document is not "issued" in specialized denominations; its dollar size is determined by the cost of the goods being purchased. Usual sizes, however, range from $25,000 to $1 million. The maturities on acceptances run from 30 to 180 days, although longer periods are available from time to time. The most common period is 90 days.

Acceptances, like Treasury bills, are sold on a discount basis and are payable to the bearer of the paper. A secondary market for the acceptances of large banks does exist.

The income generated from investing in acceptances is fully taxable at the federal, state, and local levels. Because of their greater financial risk and lesser liquidity, acceptances provide investors a yield advantage over Treasury bills and agency obligations. In fact, the acceptances of major banks are a very safe investment, making the yield advantage over Treasuries worth looking at from the firm's vantage point.

Negotiable Certificates of Deposit

A *negotiable certificate of deposit (CD)* is a marketable receipt for funds that have been deposited in a bank for a fixed period. The deposited funds earn a fixed rate of interest. These are not to be confused with ordinary passbook savings accounts or nonmarketable time deposits offered by all commercial banks. CDs are offered by major money-center banks. We are talking here about "corporate" CDs—not those offered to individuals.

CDs are offered by key banks in a variety of denominations running from $25,000 to $10 million. The popular sizes are $100,000, $500,000, and $1 million. The original maturities on CDs can range from 1 to 18 months.

CDs are offered by banks on a basis different from Treasury bills; that is, they are not sold at a discount. Rather, when the certificate matures, the owner receives the full amount deposited plus the earned interest.

A secondary market for CDs does exist, the heart of which is found in New York City. Whereas CDs may be issued in registered or bearer form, the latter facilitates transactions in the secondary market and thus is the more common.

Even though the secondary market for CDs of large banks is well organized, it does not operate as smoothly as the aftermarket in Treasuries. CDs are more heterogeneous than Treasury bills. Treasury bills have similar rates, maturity periods, and denominations; more variety is found in CDs. This makes it harder to liquidate large blocks of CDs, because a more specialized investor must be found. The securities dealers who "make" the secondary market in CDs mainly trade in $1 million units. Smaller denominations can be traded, but they will bring a relatively lower price.

The income received from an investment in CDs is subject to taxation at all government levels. In recent years CD yields have been above those available on bankers' acceptances.

Commercial Paper

Commercial paper refers to short-term, unsecured promissory notes sold by large businesses to raise cash. These are sometimes described in the popular financial press as short-term corporate IOUs. Because they are unsecured, the issuing side of the market is dominated by large corporations, which typically maintain sound credit ratings. The issuing (borrowing) firm can sell the paper to a dealer who will in turn sell it to the investing public; if the firm's reputation is solid, the paper can be sold directly to the ultimate investor.

The denominations in which commercial paper can be bought vary over a wide range. At times paper can be obtained in sizes from $5,000 to $5 million, or even more.

Commercial paper can be purchased with maturities that range from 3 to 270 days. Notes with maturities exceeding 270 days are very rare, because they would have to be registered with the Securities and Exchange Commission—a task firms avoid, when possible, because it is time-consuming and costly.

These notes are *generally* sold on a discount basis in bearer form, although sometimes paper that is interest bearing and made payable to the order of the investor is available.

The next point is of considerable interest to the financial officer responsible for management of the firm's near-cash portfolio. For practical purposes, there is *no* active trading in a secondary market for commercial paper. This distinguishes commercial paper from all the previously discussed short-term investment vehicles. On occasion, a dealer or finance company (the borrower) will redeem a note prior to its contract maturity date, but this is not a regular procedure. Thus, when the corporation evaluates commercial paper for possible inclusion in its marketable-securities portfolio, it should plan to hold it to maturity.

The return on commercial paper is fully taxable to the investor at all levels of government. Because of its lack of marketability, commercial paper in past years consistently provided a yield advantage over other near-cash assets of comparable maturity. The lifting of interest rate ceilings in 1973 by the Federal Reserve Board on certain large CDs, however, allowed commercial banks to make CD rates fully competitive in the attempt to attract funds. Over any time period, then, CD yields *may* be slightly above the rates available on commercial paper.

Repurchase Agreements

Repurchase agreements (repos) are legal contracts that involve the actual sale of securities by a *borrower* to the *lender*, with a commitment on the part of the borrower to *repurchase* the securities at the contract price plus a stated interest charge. The securities sold to the lender are U.S. government issues or other instruments of the money market such as those described above. The borrower is either a major financial institution—most important, a commercial bank—or a dealer in U.S. government securities.

Why might the corporation with excess cash prefer to buy repurchase agreements rather than a given marketable security? There are two major reasons. First, the original maturities of the instruments being sold can, in effect, be adjusted to suit the particular needs of the investing corporation. Funds available for very short periods, such as one or two days, can be productively employed. The second reason is closely related to the first. The firm could, of course, buy a Treasury bill and then resell it in the market in a few days when cash is required. The drawback here would be the risk involved in liquidating the bill at a price equal to its earlier cost to the firm. The purchase of a repo removes this risk. The contract price of the securities that make up the arrangement is *fixed* for the duration of the transaction. The corporation that buys a repurchase agreement, then, is protected against market price fluctuations throughout the contract period. This makes it a sound alternative investment for funds that are freed up for only very short periods.

These agreements are usually executed in sizes of $1 million or more. The maturities may be for a specified time period or may have no fixed maturity date. In the latter case either lender or borrower may terminate the contract without advance notice.

The returns the lender receives on repurchase agreements are taxed at all government levels. Because the interest rates are set by direct negotiation between lender and borrower, no regular published series of yields is available for direct comparison with the other short-term investments. The rates available on repurchase agreements, however, are closely related to, but generally *less* than, Treasury bill rates of comparable maturities.

Money-Market Mutual Funds

The money-market mutual funds sell their shares to raise cash, and by pooling the funds of large numbers of small savers, they can build their liquid-asset portfolios. Many of these funds allow the investor to start an account with as little as $1,000. This small initial investment, coupled with the fact that some liquid-asset funds permit subsequent investments in amounts as small as $100, makes this type of outlet for excess cash suited to the small firm and even the individual. Furthermore, the management of a small enterprise may not be highly versed in the details of short-term investments. By purchasing shares in a liquid-asset fund, the investor is also buying managerial expertise.

Money-market mutual funds typically invest in a diversified portfolio of short-term, high-grade debt instruments such as those described above. Some such funds, however, will accept more interest rate risk in their portfolios and acquire some corporate bonds and notes. Money-market mutual funds offer the investing firm a high degree of liquidity. By redeeming (selling) shares, the investor can obtain cash quickly. Procedures for liquidation vary among the funds, but shares can usually be redeemed by means of (1) special redemption checks supplied by the fund, (2) tele-

Table 15–5
Annual Yields (Percent) on Selected Three-Month Marketable Securities

Year	T-Bills	Acceptances	Commercial Paper	CDs
1980	11.51	12.72	12.66	13.07
1981	14.03	15.32	15.32	15.91
1982	10.69	11.89	11.89	12.27
1983	8.61	8.90	8.88	9.07
1984	9.52	10.14	10.10	10.37
1985	7.48	7.92	7.95	8.05
1986	5.98	6.38	6.49	6.51
1987	5.82	6.75	6.82	6.87
1988	6.68	7.56	7.66	7.73
1989	8.12	8.87	8.99	9.09
1990	7.51	7.93	8.06	8.15
1991	5.42	5.70	5.87	5.83
1992	3.45	3.62	3.75	3.68
1993	3.02	3.13	3.22	3.17
1994	4.29	4.56	4.66	4.63
1995	5.51	5.81	5.93	5.92

Source: *Federal Reserve Statistical Release* G.13 (415), various issues.

phone instructions, (3) wire instructions, or (4) a letter. When liquidation is ordered by telephone or wire, the mutual fund can remit to the investor by the next business day.

The returns earned from owning shares in a money-market mutual fund are taxable at all government levels. The yields follow the returns the investor could receive by purchasing the marketable securities directly.

The Yield Structure of Marketable Securities

What type of return can the financial manager expect on a marketable securities portfolio? This is a reasonable question. Some insight can be obtained by looking at the past, although we must realize that future returns are not guided by past experience. It is also useful to have some understanding of how the returns on one type of instrument stack up against another. The behavior of yields on short-term debt instruments over the 1980–1995 period is shown in Table 15–5.

The discussion in this chapter on designing the firm's marketable-securities portfolio touched on the essential elements of several near-cash assets. At times it is difficult to sort out the distinguishing features among these short-term investments. To alleviate that problem, Table 15–6 on pages 484–485 draws together their principal characteristics.

ACCOUNTS-RECEIVABLE MANAGEMENT

OBJECTIVE 6

We now turn from the most liquid of the firm's current assets (cash and marketable securities) to those which are less liquid—accounts receivable and inventories. All firms by their very nature are involved in selling either goods or services. Although some of these sales will be for cash, a large portion will involve credit. Whenever a

Table 15–6
Features of Selected Money-Market Instruments

INSTRUMENTS	DENOMINATIONS	MATURITIES
U.S. Treasury bills—direct obligations of the U.S. government	$10,000 15,000 50,000 100,000 500,000 1,000,000	91 days 182 days 365 days 9-month not presently issued
Federal agency securities— obligations of corporations and agencies created to effect the federal government's lending programs	Wide variation; from $1,000 to $1 million	5 days (Farm Credit consolidated system-wide discount notes) to more than 10 years
Bankers' acceptances— drafts accepted for future payment by commercial banks	No set size; typically range from $25,000 to $1 million	Predominantly from 30 to 180 days
Negotiable certificates of deposit—marketable receipts for funds deposited in a bank for a fixed time period	$25,000 to $10 million	1 to 18 months
Commercial paper—short-term unsecured promissory notes	$5,000 to $5 million; $1,000 and $5,000 multiples above the initial offering size are sometimes available.	3 to 270 days
Repurchase agreements— legal contracts between a borrower (security seller) and lender (security buyer). The borrower will repurchase at the contract price plus an interest charge.	Typical sizes are $500,000 or more.	According to terms of contract
Money-market mutual funds—holders of diversified portfolios of short-term, high-grade debt instruments	Some require an initial investment as small as $1,000.	Shares can be sold at any time

BASIS	LIQUIDITY	TAXABILITY
Discount	Excellent secondary market	Exempt from state and local income tax
Discount or coupon; usually on coupon	Good for issues of "big five" agencies	Generally exempt at local level; FNMA issues are *not* exempt
Discount	Good for acceptances of large "money-market" banks	Taxed at all levels of government
Accrued interest	Fair to good	Taxed at all levels of government
Discount	Poor; no active secondary market in usual sense	Taxed at all levels of government
Not applicable	Fixed by the agreement; that is, borrower will repurchase	Taxed at all levels of government
Net asset value	Good; provided by the fund itself	Taxed at all levels of government

sale is made on credit, it increases the firm's accounts receivable. Thus, the importance of how a firm manages its accounts receivable depends on the degree to which the firm sells on credit.

Accounts receivable typically comprise over 25 percent of a firm's assets. In effect, when we discuss management of accounts receivable, we are discussing the management of one-quarter of the firm's assets. Moreover, because cash flows from a sale cannot be invested until the account is collected, control of receivables takes on added importance; efficient collection determines both profitability and liquidity of the firm.

Size of Investment in Accounts Receivable

The size of the investment in accounts receivable is determined by several factors. First, the percentage of credit sales to total sales affects the level of accounts receivable held. Although this factor certainly plays a major role in determining a firm's investment in accounts receivable, it generally is not within the control of the financial manager. The nature of the business tends to determine the blend between credit sales and cash sales. A large grocery store tends to sell exclusively on a cash basis, whereas most construction-lumber supply firms make their sales primarily with credit.

The level of sales is also a factor in determining the size of the investment in accounts receivable. Very simply, the more sales, the greater accounts receivable. It is not a decision variable for the financial manager, however.

The final determinants of the level of investment in accounts receivable are the credit and collection policies—more specifically, the terms of sale, the quality of customer, and collection efforts. These policies *are* under the control of the financial manager. The terms of sale specify both the time period during which the customer must pay and the terms, such as penalties for late payments or discounts for early payments. The type of customer or credit policy also affects the level of investment in accounts receivable. For example, the acceptance of poorer credit risks and their subsequent delinquent payments may lead to an increase in accounts receivable. The strength and timing of the collection efforts can affect the period for which past-due accounts remain delinquent, which in turn affects the level of accounts receivable. Collection and credit policy decisions may further affect the level of investment in accounts receivable by causing changes in the sales level and the ratio of credit sales to total sales. The factors that determine the level of investment in accounts receivable are displayed in Figure 15–9.

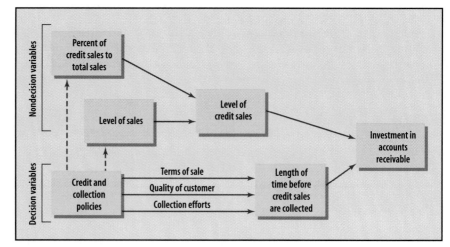

Figure 15–9
Determinants of Investment in Accounts Receivable

As we examine the credit decision, try to remember that our goal is not to minimize losses but to maximize profits. Although we will spend a good deal of time trying to sort out those customers with the highest probability of default, this analysis is only an input into a decision based on maximization of shareholder wealth. Essentially a firm with a high profit margin can tolerate a more liberal credit policy than a firm with a low profit margin.

Terms of Sales—Decision Variable

The **terms of sale** *identify the possible discount for early payment, the discount period, and the total credit period.* They are generally stated in the form *a/b* net *c*, indicating that the customer can deduct *a* percent if the account is paid within *b* days; otherwise, the account must be paid within *c* days. Thus, for example, trade credit terms of 2/10, net 30, indicate that a 2 percent discount can be taken if the account is paid within 10 days; otherwise it must be paid within 30 days. Failure to take the discount represents a cost to the customer. For instance, if the terms are 2/10, net 30, the annualized opportunity cost of passing up this 2 percent discount in order to withhold payment for an additional 20 days is 36.73 percent. This is determined as follows:

terms of sale

$$\begin{pmatrix} \text{annualized opportunity cost} \\ \text{of foregoing the discount} \end{pmatrix} = \frac{a}{1 - a} \times \frac{360}{c - b} \qquad \textbf{(15–3)}$$

Substituting the values from the example, we get

$$36.73\% = \frac{.02}{1 - .02} \times \frac{360}{30 - 10}$$

In industry the typical discount ranges anywhere from 1/2 to 10 percent, whereas the discount period is generally 10 days and the total credit period varies from 30 to 90 days. Although the terms of credit vary radically from industry to industry, they tend to remain relatively uniform within any particular industry. Moreover, the terms tend to remain relatively constant over time, and they do not appear to be used frequently as a decision variable.

Type of Customer—Decision Variable

A second decision variable involves determining the *type of customer* who is to qualify for trade credit. Several costs always are associated with extending credit to less creditworthy customers. First, as the probability of default increases, it becomes more important to identify which of the possible new customers would be a poor risk. When more time is spent investigating the less creditworthy customer, the costs of credit investigation increase.

Default costs also vary directly with the quality of the customer. As the customer's credit rating declines, the chance that the account will not be paid on time increases. In the extreme case, payment never occurs. Thus, taking on less-creditworthy customers results in increases in default costs.

Collection costs also increase as the quality of the customer declines. More delinquent accounts force the firm to spend more time and money collecting them. Overall, the decline in customer quality results in increased costs of credit investigation, collection, and default.

In determining whether to grant credit to an individual customer, we are primarily interested in the customer's short-run welfare. Thus, liquidity ratios, other obligations, and the overall profitability of the firm become the focal point in this analysis. Credit-rating services, such as Dun & Bradstreet, provide information on the financial status, operations, and payment history for most firms. Other possible sources of information would include credit bureaus, trade associations, Chambers of Commerce, competitors, bank references, public financial statements, and, of course, the firm's past relationship with the customer.

One way in which both individuals and firms are often evaluated as credit risks credit scoring is through the use of credit scoring. **Credit scoring** involves the *numerical evaluation of each applicant*. An applicant receives a score based on his or her answers to a simple set of questions. This score is then evaluated according to a predetermined standard, its level relative to the standard determining whether credit should be extended. The major advantage of credit scoring is that it is inexpensive and easy to perform. For example, once the standards are set, a computer or clerical worker without any specialized training could easily evaluate any applicant.

The techniques used for constructing credit-scoring indexes range from the simple approach of adding up default rates associated with the answers given to each question, to sophisticated evaluations using multiple discriminate analysis (MDA). MDA is a statistical technique for calculating the appropriate importance to assign each question used in evaluating the applicant.

Another model that could be used for credit scoring has been provided by Edward Altman, who used multiple discriminant analysis to identify businesses that might go bankrupt. In his landmark study Altman used financial ratios to predict which firms would go bankrupt over the period 1946–1965. Using multiple discriminant analysis, Altman came up with the following index:

$$Z = 3.3\left(\frac{\text{EBIT}}{\text{total assets}}\right) + 1.0\left(\frac{\text{sales}}{\text{total assets}}\right) + 0.6\left(\frac{\text{market value of equity}}{\text{book value of debt}}\right)$$
$$+ 1.4\left(\frac{\text{retained earnings}}{\text{total assets}}\right) + 1.2\left(\frac{\text{working capital}}{\text{total assets}}\right)$$

(15–4)

Altman found that of the firms that went bankrupt over this time period, 94 percent had Z scores of less than 2.7 one year prior to bankruptcy and only 6 percent had scores above 2.7 percent. Conversely, of those firms that did not go bankrupt, only 3 percent had Z scores below 2.7 and 97 percent had scores above 2.7.

PAUSE AND REFLECT

It is tempting to look at the credit decision as a single yes or no decision based on some simple formula. However, simply to look at the immediate future in making a credit decision would be a mistake. If extending a customer credit means the customer may become a regular customer in the future, it may be appropriate to take a risk that otherwise would not be prudent. Our goal is to ensure that all cash flows affected by the decision at hand are considered, not simply the most immediate cash flows.

Collection Efforts—Decision Variable

The key to maintaining control over collection of accounts receivable is the fact that the probability of default increases with the age of the account. Thus, control of accounts receivable focuses on the control and elimination of past-due receivables. One common way of evaluating the current situation is *ratio analysis*. The financial manager can determine whether accounts receivables are under control by examining the average collection period, the ratio of receivables to assets, the ratio of credit sales to receivables (called the accounts-receivable turnover ratio), and the amount of bad debts relative to sales over time. In addition, the manager can perform what is called an aging of accounts receivable to provide a breakdown in both dollars and percentages of the proportion of receivables that are past due. Comparing the current aging of receivables with past data offers even more control.

Once the delinquent accounts have been identified, the firm's accounts-receivable group makes an effort to collect them. For example, a past-due letter, called a *dunning letter*, is sent if payment is not received on time, followed by an additional dunning letter in a more serious tone if the account becomes 3 weeks past due, followed after 6 weeks by a telephone call. Finally, if the account becomes 12 weeks past due, it might be turned over to a collection agency. Again, a direct trade-off exists between collection expenses and lost goodwill on one hand and noncollection of accounts on the other, and this trade-off is always part of making the decision.

INVENTORY MANAGEMENT

OBJECTIVE 7

Inventory management involves the *control of the assets that are produced to be sold in the normal course of the firm's operations*. The general categories of inventory include raw-materials inventory, work-in-process inventory, and finished-goods inventory. The importance of inventory management to the firm depends on the extent of the inventory investment. For an average firm, approximately 4.88 percent of all assets are in the form of inventory. However, the percentage varies widely from industry to industry. Thus, the importance of inventory management and control varies from industry to industry also. For example, it is much more important in the automotive dealer and service station trade, where inventories make up 49.72 percent of total assets, than in the hotel business, where the average investment in inventory is only 1.56 percent of total assets.

inventory management

Purposes and Types of Inventory

The purpose of carrying inventories is to uncouple the operations of the firm—that is, to make each function of the business independent of each other function—so that delays or shutdowns in one area do not affect the production and sale of the final product. Because production shutdowns result in increased costs, and because delays in delivery can lose customers, the management and control of inventory are important duties of the financial manager.

Decision making in investment in inventory involves a basic trade-off between risk and return. The risk is that if the level of inventory is too low, the various functions of business do not operate independently, and delays in product and customer delivery can result. The return results because reduced inventory investment saves money. As the size of inventory increases, storage and handling costs as well as the required return on capital invested in inventory rise. Therefore, as the inventory a firm holds is increased, the risk of running out of inventory is lessened, but inventory expenses rise.

Raw-Materials Inventory

Raw-materials inventory consists of *basic materials purchased from other firms to be used in the firm's production operations*. These goods may include steel, lumber, petroleum, or manufactured items such as wire, ball bearings, or tires that the firm does not produce itself. Regardless of the specific form of the raw-materials

raw-materials inventory

inventory, all manufacturing firms by definition maintain a raw-materials inventory. Its purpose is to uncouple the production function from the purchasing function—that is, to make these two functions independent of each other—so that delays in shipment of raw materials do not cause production delays. In the event of a delay in shipment, the firm can satisfy its need for raw materials by liquidating its inventory.

Work-in-Process Inventory

work-in-process inventory

Work-in-process inventory consists of *partially finished goods requiring additional work before they become finished goods.* The more complex and lengthy the production process, the larger the investment in work-in-process inventory. The purpose of work-in-process inventory is to uncouple the various operations in the production process so that machine failures and work stoppages in one operation will not affect the other operations. Assume, for example, there are 10 different production operations, each one involving the piece of work produced in the previous operation. If the machine performing the first production operation breaks down, a firm with no work-in-process inventory will have to shut down all 10 production operations. Yet if a firm has such inventory, the remaining 9 operations can continue by drawing the input for the second operation from inventory.

Finished-Goods Inventory

finished-goods inventory

Finished-goods inventory consists of *goods on which production has been completed but that are not yet sold.* The purpose of a finished-goods inventory is to uncouple the production and sales functions so that it is not necessary to produce the goods before a sale can occur—sales can be made directly out of inventory. In the auto industry, for example, people would not buy from a dealer who made them wait weeks or months when another dealer could fill the order immediately.

Stock of Cash

Although we have already discussed cash management at some length, it is worthwhile to mention cash again in the light of inventory management. This is because the *stock of cash* carried by a firm is simply a special type of inventory. In terms of uncoupling the various operations of the firm, the purpose of holding a stock of cash is to make the payment of bills independent of the collection of accounts due. When cash is kept on hand, bills can be paid without prior collection of accounts.

Inventory Management Techniques

The importance of effective inventory management is directly related to the size of the investment in inventory. Effective management of these assets is essential to the goal of maximizing shareholder wealth. To control the investment in inventory, management must solve two problems: the order quantity problem and the order point problem.

Order Quantity Problem

order quantity problem

The **order quantity problem** involves *determining the optimal order size for an inventory item given its expected usage, carrying costs, and ordering costs.*

The economic order quantity (EOQ) model attempts to determine the order size that will minimize total inventory costs. It assumes that

$$\text{total inventory costs} = \text{total carrying costs} + \text{total ordering costs} \qquad (15\text{--}5)$$

Assuming that inventory is allowed to fall to zero and then is immediately replenished (this assumption will be lifted when we discuss the order point problem), the average inventory becomes $Q/2$, where Q is inventory order size in units. This can be seen graphically in Figure 15–10.

If the average inventory is $Q/2$ and the carrying cost per unit is C, then carrying costs become

$$\begin{matrix} \text{total} \\ \text{carrying costs} \end{matrix} = \begin{pmatrix} \text{average} \\ \text{inventory} \end{pmatrix} \begin{pmatrix} \text{carrying cost} \\ \text{per unit} \end{pmatrix} \qquad \textbf{(15–6)}$$

$$= \left(\frac{Q}{2}\right) C \qquad \textbf{(15–6a)}$$

where Q = the inventory order size in units
C = carrying costs per unit

The carrying costs on inventory include the required rate of return on investment in inventory, in addition to warehouse or storage costs, wages for those who operate the warehouse, and costs associated with inventory shrinkage. Thus, carrying costs include both real cash flows and opportunity costs associated with having funds tied up in inventory.

The ordering costs incurred are equal to the ordering costs per order times the number of orders. If we assume total demand over the planning period is S we order in lots sizes of Q, then S/Q represents the number of orders over the planning period. If the ordering cost per order is O, then

$$\begin{matrix} \text{total} \\ \text{ordering costs} \end{matrix} = \begin{pmatrix} \text{number} \\ \text{of orders} \end{pmatrix} \begin{pmatrix} \text{ordering cost} \\ \text{per order} \end{pmatrix} \qquad \textbf{(15–7)}$$

$$= \left(\frac{S}{Q}\right) O \qquad \textbf{(15–7a)}$$

where S = total demand in units over the planning period
O = ordering cost per order

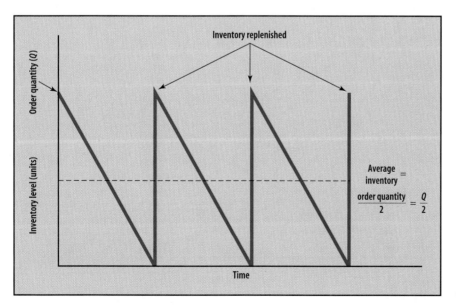

Figure 15–10

Inventory Level and the Replenishment Cycle

Thus, total costs in equation (15–5) become

$$\text{total costs} = \left(\frac{Q}{2}\right) C + \left(\frac{S}{Q}\right) O \tag{15–8}$$

Figure 15–11 illustrates this equation graphically.

What we are looking for is the ordering size Q^*, which provides the minimum total costs. By manipulating equation (15–8), we find that the optimal value of Q—that is, the economic ordering quantity (EOQ)—is

$$Q^* = \sqrt{\frac{2SO}{C}} \tag{15–9}$$

The use of the EOQ model can best be illustrated through an example.

EXAMPLE

Suppose a firm expects total demand (S) for its product over the planning period to be 5,000 units, whereas the ordering cost per order (O) is $200 and the carrying cost per unit (C) is $2. Substituting these values into equation (15–9) yields

$$Q^* = \sqrt{\frac{2 \cdot 5,000 \cdot 200}{2}} = \sqrt{1,000,000} = 1,000 \text{ units}$$

Thus, if this firm orders in 1,000-unit lot sizes, it will minimize its total inventory costs. ∎

Examination of EOQ Assumptions

Despite the fact that the EOQ model tends to yield quite good results, there are weaknesses in the EOQ model associated with several of its assumptions. When its assumptions have been dramatically violated, the EOQ model can generally be modified to accommodate the situation. The model's assumptions are as follows:

1. **Constant or uniform demand.** Although the EOQ model assumes constant demand, demand may vary from day to day. If demand is stochastic—that is, not

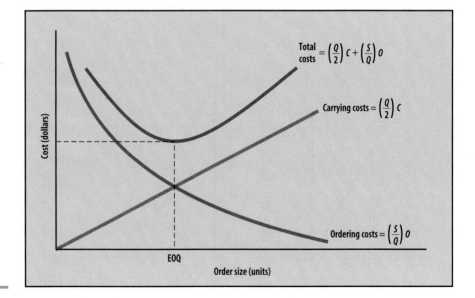

Figure 15–11

Total Cost and EOQ
Determination

known in advance—the model must be modified through the inclusion of a safety stock.

2. **Constant unit price.** The inclusion of variable prices resulting from quantity discounts can be handled quite easily through a modification of the original EOQ model, redefining total costs and solving for the optimum order quantity.

3. **Constant carrying costs.** Unit carrying costs may vary substantially as the size of the inventory rises, perhaps decreasing because of economies of scale or storage efficiency or increasing as storage space runs out and new warehouses have to be rented. This situation can be handled through a modification in the original model similar to the one used for variable unit price.

4. **Constant ordering costs.** Although this assumption is generally valid, its violation can be accommodated by modifying the original EOQ model in a manner similar to the one used for variable unit price.

5. **Instantaneous delivery.** If delivery is not instantaneous, which is generally the case, the original EOQ model must be modified through the inclusion of a safety stock, that is, the inventory held to accommodate any unusually large and unexpected usage during the delivery time.

6. **Independent orders.** If multiple orders result in cost savings by reducing paperwork and transportation cost, the original EOQ model must be further modified. Although this modification is somewhat complicated, special EOQ models have been developed to deal with it.

These assumptions illustrate the limitations of the basic EOQ model and the ways in which it can be modified to compensate for them. An understanding of the limitations and assumptions of the EOQ model provides the financial manager with more of a base for making inventory decisions.

Order Point Problem

The two most limiting assumptions—those of constant or uniform demand and instantaneous delivery—are dealt with through the inclusion of **safety stock,** which is the *inventory held to accommodate any unusually large and unexpected usage during delivery time.* The *decision on how much safety stock to hold* is generally referred to as the **order point problem;** that is, how low should inventory be depleted before it is reordered?

Two factors go into the determination of the appropriate order point: (1) the procurement or delivery-time stock and (2) the safety stock desired. Figure 15–12 on page 494 graphs the process involved in order point determination. We observe that the order point problem can be decomposed into its two components, the **delivery-time stock**—that is, the *inventory needed between the order date and the receipt of the inventory ordered*—and the safety stock. Thus, the order point is reached when inventory falls to a level equal to the delivery-time stock plus the safety stock.

$$\begin{matrix} \text{inventory order point} \\ \text{[order new inventory} \\ \text{when the level of inventory} \\ \text{falls to this level]} \end{matrix} = \begin{pmatrix} \text{delivery-time} \\ \text{stock} \end{pmatrix} + \begin{pmatrix} \text{safety} \\ \text{stock} \end{pmatrix} \quad \textbf{(15–10)}$$

As a result of constantly carrying safety stock, the average level of inventory increases. Whereas before the inclusion of safety stock the average level of inventory was equal to EOQ/2, now it will be

$$\text{average inventory} = \frac{\text{EOQ}}{2} + \text{safety stock} \quad \textbf{(15–11)}$$

safety stock

order point problem

delivery-time stock

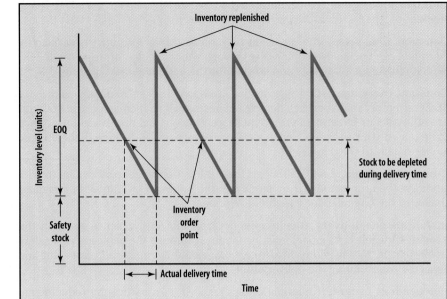

Figure 15–12
Order Point Determination

In general, several factors simultaneously determine how much delivery-time stock and safety stock should be held. First, the efficiency of the replenishment system affects how much delivery-time stock is needed. Because the delivery-time stock is the expected inventory usage between ordering and receiving inventory, efficient replenishment of inventory would reduce the need for delivery-time stock.

The uncertainty surrounding both the delivery time and the demand for the product affects the level of safety stock needed. The more certain the patterns of these inflows and outflows from the inventory, the less safety stock required. In effect, if these inflows and outflows are highly predictable, then there is little chance of any stock-out occurring. However, if they are unpredictable, it becomes necessary to carry additional safety stock to prevent unexpected stock-outs.

The safety margin desired also affects the level of safety stock held. If it is a costly experience to run out of inventory, the safety stock held will be larger than it would be otherwise. If running out of inventory and the subsequent delay in supplying customers result in strong customer dissatisfaction and the possibility of lost future sales, then additional safety stock is necessary. A final determinant is the cost of carrying additional inventory, in terms of both the handling and storage costs and the opportunity cost associated with the investment in additional inventory. Very simply, the greater the costs, the smaller the safety stock.

Over the past decade or so, a different technique aimed at reducing the firm's investment in inventory has been adopted by numerous companies. It is known as 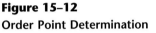 the **just-in-time inventory control system.** The aim is to operate with the *lowest average level of inventory possible.* Within the EOQ model the basics are to reduce (1) ordering costs and (2) safety stocks. This is achieved by attempting to receive an almost continuous flow of deliveries of component parts. The result is to actually have about two to four hours' worth of inventory on hand. In effect, trucks, railroads, and airplanes become the firm's warehouses. This system has spawned a new emphasis on the dual relationship between the firm and its suppliers.

Inflation and EOQ

Inflation affects the EOQ model in two major ways. First, although the EOQ model can be modified to assume constant price increases, often major price increases occur only once or twice a year and are announced ahead of time. If this is the case, the EOQ model may lose its applicability and may be replaced with **anticipatory buying**—that is, *buying in anticipation of a price increase to secure the goods at a lower cost.* Of course, as with most decisions, there are trade-offs. The costs are the added carrying costs associated with the inventory. The benefits, of course, come from buying at a lower price. The second way inflation affects the EOQ model is through increased carrying costs. As inflation pushes interest rates up, the cost of carrying inventory increases. In our EOQ model this means that C increases, which results in a decline in Q^*, the optimal economic order quantity.

anticipatory buying

$$\downarrow Q^* = \sqrt{\frac{2SO}{C\uparrow}} \qquad\qquad (15\text{--}12)$$

SUMMARY

As you recall, several of the axioms that form the foundations of financial management relate to the importance of cash and cash flows. In this chapter, we have developed many of the tools that a financial manager needs to manage the firm's cash and other current assets with the overall objective of ensuring that the firm has an appropriate level of liquidity or net working capital to carry out the goal of maximizing shareholder wealth.

OBJECTIVE 1

The firm experiences both regular and irregular cash flows. Once cash is obtained, the firm will have three motives for holding cash rather than invest it: to satisfy transactions, precautionary, and speculative liquidity needs. To a certain extent, such needs can be satisfied by holding readily marketable securities rather than cash. A significant challenge of cash management, then, is dealing with the trade-off between the firm's need to have cash on hand to pay liabilities that arise in the course of doing business and the objective of maximizing wealth by reducing to a minimum idle cash balances that earn no return.

OBJECTIVE 2
OBJECTIVE 3

Various procedures exist to improve the efficiency of a firm's cash management. Such procedures focus not only (although primarily) on accelerating the firm's cash receipts, but also on improving the methods for disbursing cash. Generally, at the heart of attempts to accelerate cash receipts is a significant effort to reduce the mail, processing, and transit elements of the float. Often used in conjunction with concentration banking and a lockbox arrangement are depository transfer checks and wire transfers.

On the cash disbursements side, firms try to prolong the time cash stays in their own accounts by increasing the disbursement float through the use of zero balance accounts, payable-through drafts, and, especially, remote disbursing. The first two of these methods also offer much better central-office control over disbursements. Before any collection or disbursement procedure is introduced, however, a careful analysis should be performed to ensure that expected benefits outweigh the expected costs of such procedures.

OBJECTIVE 4
OBJECTIVE 5

Because idle cash earns no return, a financial manager will look for opportunities to invest such cash until it is required in the operations of the company. A variety of different readily marketable securities, which are described in the chapter, are available in the market today. The yields on such securities vary depending on four factors: the (1) financial risk, (2) interest rate risk, (3) liquidity, and (4) taxability of the security. By simultaneously taking into account these factors and the desired rate of return, the financial manager is able to determine the most suitable mix of cash and marketable securities for the firm.

OBJECTIVE 6

When we consider that accounts receivable constitute approximately 25 percent of total assets for the typical firm, the importance of accounts-receivable management becomes even more apparent. The size of a firm's investment in accounts receivable depends on three factors: the percentage of credit sales to total sales, the level of sales, and the credit and collection policies of the firm. The financial manager, however, generally only has control over the terms of sale, the quality of customer, and the collection of efforts.

OBJECTIVE 7

Although the level of investment in inventories by the typical firm is less than the investment in accounts receivable, inventory management and control remains an important function of the financial manager because inventories play a significant role in the operations of the firm. The purpose of holding inventory is to make each function of the business independent of the other functions. The primary issues related to inventory management are (1) How much inventory should be ordered? and (2) When should the order be placed? The EOQ model is used to answer the first of these questions. The order point model, which depends on the desired levels of delivery-time stock and safety stock, is applied to answer the second question. The relatively new just-in-time approach to inventory control is growing in popularity as an attempt to obtain additional cost savings by reducing the level of inventory a firm needs to have on hand. Instead of depending solely on its own inventories, the firm relies on its vendors to furnish supplies "just in time" to satisfy the firm's production requirements.

KEY TERMS

Anticipatory Buying, 495

Automated Depository Transfer Check (DTC) System, 469

Cash, 459

Concentration Banking, 469

Credit Scoring, 488

Delivery-Time Stock, 493

Depository Transfer Checks (DTCs), 469

Finished-Goods Inventory, 490

Float, 463

Insolvency, 462

Inventory Management, 489

Just-in-Time Inventory Control System, 494

Marketable Securities, 459

Order Point Problem, 493

Order Quantity Problem, 490

Payable-Through Drafts (PTDs), 472

Raw-Materials Inventory, 489

Safety Stock, 493

Terms of Sale, 487

Wire Transfers, 470

Work-in-Process Inventory, 490

Zero Balance Accounts (ZBAs), 471

STUDY QUESTIONS

15-1. What is meant by the cash flow process?

15-2. Identify the principal motives for holding cash and near-cash assets. Explain the purpose of each motive.

15-3. What is concentration banking and how may it be of value to the firm?

15-4. What are the two major objectives of the firm's cash management system?

15-5. What three decisions dominate the cash management process?

15-6. Within the context of cash management, what are the key elements of (total) float? Briefly define each element.

15-7. Distinguish between financial risk and interest rate risk as these terms are commonly used in discussions of cash management.

15-8. Your firm invests in only three different classes of marketable securities: commercial paper, Treasury bills, and federal agency securities. Recently, yields on these money-market instruments of three months' maturity were quoted at 6.10, 6.25, and 5.90 percent. Match the available yields with the types of instruments your firm purchases.

15-9. What key factors might induce a firm to invest in repurchase agreements rather than a specific security of the money market?

15-10. What factors determine the size of the investment a firm makes in accounts receivable? Which of these factors are under the control of the financial manager?

15-11. If a credit manager experienced no bad debt losses over the past year, would this be an indication of proper credit management? Why or why not?

15-12. What are the risk-return trade-offs associated with adopting a more liberal trade credit policy?

15-13. What is the purpose of holding inventory? Name several types of inventory and describe their purpose.

15-14. Can cash be considered a special type of inventory? If so, what functions does it attempt to uncouple?

15-15. What are the major assumptions made by the EOQ model?

15-16. How might inflation affect the EOQ model?

SELF-TEST PROBLEMS

ST-1. (*Buying and Selling Marketable Securities*) Mountaineer Outfitters has $2 million in excess cash that it might invest in marketable securities. To buy and sell the securities, however, the firm must pay a transaction fee of $45,000.

    a. Would you recommend purchasing the securities if they yield 12 percent annually and are held for

        1. One month?
        2. Two months?
        3. Three months?
        4. Six months?
        5. One year?

    b. What minimum required yield would the securities have to return for the firm to hold them for three months? (What is the break-even yield for a three-month holding period?)

ST-2. (*EOQ Calculations*) Consider the following inventory information and relationships for the F. Beamer Corporation:

        1. Orders can be placed only in multiples of 100 units.
        2. Annual unit usage is 300,000. (Assume a 50-week year in your calculations.)
        3. The carrying cost is 30 percent of the purchase price of the goods.
        4. The purchase price is $10 per unit.
        5. The ordering cost is $50 per order.

6. The desired safety stock is 1,000 units. (This does not include delivery-time stock.)

7. Delivery time is two weeks.

Given this information

    a. What is the optimal EOQ level?

    b. How many orders will be placed annually?

    c. At what inventory level should a reorder be made?

STUDY PROBLEMS

15-1. (*Concentration Banking*) Byron Sporting Goods operates in Miami, Florida. The firm produces and distributes a full line of athletic equipment on a nationwide basis. The firm currently uses a centralized billing system. Byron Sporting Goods has annual credit sales of $438 million. Austin National Bank has presented an offer to operate a concentration-banking system for the company. Byron already has an established line of credit with Austin. Austin says it will operate the system on a flat-fee basis of $200,000 per year. The analysis done by the bank's cash-management services division suggests that three days in mail float and one day in processing float can be eliminated.

Because Byron borrows almost continuously from Austin National, the value of the float reduction would be applied against the line of credit. The borrowing rate on the line of credit is set at an annual rate of 8 percent. Furthermore, because of the reduction in clerical help, the new system will save the firm $66,000 in processing costs. Byron uses a 365-day year in analyses of this sort. Should Byron accept the bank's offer to install the new system?

15-2. (*Concentration Banking*) Byron Sporting Goods operates in Miami, Florida. The firm produces and distributes a full line of athletic equipment on a nationwide basis. The firm currently uses a centralized billing system. Byron Sporting Goods has annual credit sales of $362 million. Austin National Bank has presented an offer to operate a concentration banking system for the company. Byron already has an established line of credit with Austin. Austin says it will operate the system on a flat-fee basis of $175,000 per year. The analysis done by the bank's cash-management services division suggests that three days in mail float and one day in processing float can be eliminated.

Because Byron borrows almost continuously from Austin National, the value of the float reduction would be applied against the line of credit. The borrowing rate on the line of credit is set at an annual rate of 7 percent. Furthermore, because of the reduction in clerical help, the new system will save the firm $57,500 in processing costs. Byron uses a 365-day year in analyses of this sort. Should Byron accept the bank's offer to install the new system?

15-3. (*Buying and Selling Marketable Securities*) Miami Dice & Card Company has generated $800,000 in excess cash that it could invest in marketable securities. In order to buy and sell the securities, the firm will pay total transaction fees of $20,000.

    a. Would you recommend purchasing the securities if they yield 10.5 percent annually and are held for

        1. One month?

        2. Two months?

        3. Three months?

        4. Six months?

        5. One year?

b. What minimum required yield would the securities have to return for the firm to hold them for two months? (What is the break-even yield for a two-month holding period?)

15-4. (*Costs of Services*) Mustang Ski-Wear, Inc., is investigating the possibility of adopting a lockbox system as a cash receipts acceleration device. In a typical year this firm receives remittances totaling $12 million by check. The firm will record and process 6,000 checks over this same period. The Colorado Springs Second National Bank has informed the management of Mustang that it will expedite checks and associated documents through the lockbox system for a unit cost of $.20 per check. Mustang's financial manager has projected that cash freed up by adoption of the system can be invested in a portfolio of near-cash assets that will yield an annual before-tax return of 7 percent. Mustang financial analysts use a 365-day year in their procedures.

a. What reduction in check collection time is necessary for Mustang to be neither better nor worse off for having adopted the proposed system?

b. How would your solution to part a be affected if Mustang could invest the freed-up balances only at an expected annual return of 4.5 percent?

c. What is the logical explanation for the difference in your answers to part a and part b?

15-5. (*Lockbox System*) Penn Steelworks is a distributor of cold-rolled steel products to the automobile industry. All its sales are on a credit basis, net 30 days. Sales are evenly distributed over its 10 sales regions throughout the United States. Delinquent accounts are no problem. The company has recently undertaken an analysis aimed at improving its cash management procedures. Penn determined that it takes an average of 3.2 days for customers' payments to reach the head office in Pittsburgh from the time they are mailed. It takes another full day in processing time prior to depositing the checks with a local bank. Annual sales average $4.8 million for each regional office. Reasonable investment opportunities can be found yielding 7 percent per year. To alleviate the float problem confronting the firm, the use of a lockbox system in each of the 10 regions is being considered. This would reduce mail float by 1.2 days. One day in processing float would also be eliminated, plus a full day in transit float. The lockbox arrangement would cost each region $250 per month.

a. What is the opportunity cost to Penn Steelworks of the funds tied up in mailing and processing? Use a 365-day year.

b. What would the net cost or savings be from use of the proposed cash acceleration technique? Should Penn adopt the system?

15-6. (*Cash Receipts Acceleration System*) Peggy Pierce Designs, Inc., is a vertically integrated, national manufacturer and retailer of women's clothing. Currently, the firm has no coordinated cash management system. A proposal, however, from the First Pennsylvania Bank aimed at speeding up cash collections is being examined by several of Pierce's corporate executives.

The firm currently uses a centralized billing procedure, which requires that all checks be mailed to the Philadelphia head office for processing and eventual deposit. Under this arrangement all the customers' remittance checks take an average of five business days to reach the head office. Once in Philadelphia, another two days are required to process the checks for ultimate deposit at the First Pennsylvania Bank.

The firm's daily remittances average $1 million. The average check size is $2,000. Pierce Designs currently earns 6 percent annually on its marketable-securities portfolio.

The cash acceleration plan proposed by officers of First Pennsylvania involves both a lockbox system and concentration banking. First Pennsylvania would be the firm's only concentration bank. Lockboxes would be established in (1) San Francisco, (2) Dallas, (3) Chicago, and (4) Philadelphia. This would reduce funds tied up by mail float to three days, and processing float will be eliminated. Funds would then be transferred twice each business day by means of automated depository transfer checks from local banks in San Francisco, Dallas, and Chicago to the First Pennsylvania Bank. Each DTC costs $15. These transfers will occur all 270 business days of the year. Each check processed through the lockbox system will cost $.18.

a. What amount of cash balances will be freed-up if Pierce Designs, Inc., adopts the system suggested by First Pennsylvania?

b. What is the opportunity cost of maintaining the current banking setup?

c. What is the projected annual cost of operating the proposed system?

d. Should Pierce adopt the new system? Compute the net annual gain or loss associated with adopting the system.

15-7. (*Marketable-Securities Portfolio*) The Alex Daniel Shoe Manufacturing Company currently pays its employees on a weekly basis. The weekly wage bill is $500,000. This means that on average the firm has accrued wages payable of ($500,000 + $0)/2 = $250,000.

Alex Daniel, Jr., works as the firm's senior financial analyst and reports directly to his father, who owns all of the firm's common stock. Alex Daniel, Jr., wants to move to a monthly wage payment system. Employees would be paid at the end of every fourth week. The younger Daniel is fully aware that the labor union representing the company's workers will not permit the monthly payments system to take effect unless the workers are given some type of fringe benefit compensation. A plan has been worked out whereby the firm will make a contribution to the cost of life insurance coverage for each employee. This will cost the firm $35,000 annually. Alex Daniel, Jr., expects the firm to earn 7 percent annually on its marketable-securities portfolio.

a. Based on the projected information, should Daniel Shoe Manufacturing move to the monthly wage-payment system?

b. What annual rate of return on the marketable-securities portfolio would enable the firm to just break even on this proposal?

15-8. (*Valuing Float Reduction*) The Cowboy Bottling Company will generate $12 million in credit sales next year. Collection of these credit sales will occur evenly over this period. The firm's employees work 270 days a year. Currently, the firm's processing system ties up four days' worth of remittance checks. A recent report from a financial consultant indicated procedures that will enable Cowboy Bottling to reduce processing float by two full days. If Cowboy invests the released funds to earn 6 percent, what will be the annual savings?

15-9. (*Accounts Payable Policy and Cash Management*) Bradford Construction Supply Company is suffering from a prolonged decline in new construction in its sales area. In an attempt to improve its cash position, the firm is considering changes in its accounts-payable policy. After careful study it has determined that the only alternative available is to slow disbursements. Purchases for the coming year are expected to be $37.5 million. Sales will be $65 million, which represents about a 20 percent drop from the current year. Currently, Bradford discounts approximately 25 percent of its payments at 3 percent, 10 days, net 30, and the balance of accounts is paid in 30 days. If Bradford adopts a policy of payment in 45 days or 60 days, how much can the firm gain if the annual opportunity cost of investment is 12 percent? What will be the result if this action causes Bradford Construction suppliers to increase their prices to the company by ½ percent to compensate for the 60-day extended term of payment? In your calculations use a 365-day year and ignore any compounding effects related to expected returns.

15-10. (*Interest Rate Risk*) Two years ago your corporate treasurer purchased for the firm a 20-year bond at its par value of $1,000. The coupon rate on this security is 8 percent. Interest payments are made to bondholders once a year. Currently, bonds of this particular risk class are yielding investors 9 percent. A cash shortage has forced you to instruct your treasurer to liquidate his bond.

a. At what price will your bond be sold? Assume annual compounding.

b. What will be the amount of your gain or loss over the original purchase price?

c. What would be the amount of your gain or loss had the treasurer originally purchased a bond with a 4-year rather than a 20-year maturity? (Assume all characteristics of the bonds are identical except their maturity periods.)

d. What do we call this type of risk assumed by your corporate treasurer?

15-11. (*Comparison of After-Tax Yields*) The corporate treasurer of Aggieland Fireworks is considering the purchase of a BBB-rated bond that carries a 9 percent coupon. The BBB-rated security is taxable, and the firm is in the 46 percent marginal tax bracket. The face value of this bond is $1,000. A financial analyst who reports to the corporate treasurer has alerted him to the fact that a municipal obligation is coming to the market with a 5½ percent coupon. The par value of this security is also $1,000.

a. Which one of the two securities do you recommend the firm purchase? Why?

b. What must the fully taxed bond yield before tax to make it comparable with the municipal offering?

15-12. (*Trade Credit Discounts*) Determine the effective annualized cost of forgoing the trade credit discount on the following terms:

a. 1/10, net 20

b. 2/10, net 30

c. 3/10, net 30

d. 3/10, net 60

e. 3/10, net 90

f. 5/10, net 60

15-13. (*Altman Model*) The following ratios were supplied by six loan applicants. Given this information and the credit-scoring model developed by Altman (equation [15-4]), which loans have a high probability of defaulting next year?

	$\dfrac{\text{EBIT}}{\text{TOTAL ASSETS}}$	$\dfrac{\text{SALES}}{\text{TOTAL ASSETS}}$	$\dfrac{\text{MARKET VALUE OF EQUITY}}{\text{BOOK VALUE OF DEBT}}$	$\dfrac{\text{RETAINED EARNINGS}}{\text{TOTAL ASSETS}}$	$\dfrac{\text{WORKING CAPITAL}}{\text{TOTAL ASSETS}}$
Applicant 1	.2	.2	1.2	.3	.5
Applicant 2	.2	.8	1.0	.3	.8
Applicant 3	.2	.7	.6	.3	.4
Applicant 4	.1	.4	1.2	.4	.4
Applicant 5	.3	.7	.5	.4	.7
Applicant 6	.2	.5	.5	.4	.4

15-14. (*Ratio Analysis*) Assuming a 360-day year, calculate what the average investment in inventory would be for a firm, given the following information in each case.

a. The firm has sales of $600,000, a gross profit margin of 10 percent, and an inventory turnover ratio of 6.

b. The firm has a cost-of-goods-sold figure of $480,000 and an average age of inventory of 40 days.

c. The firm has a cost-of-goods-sold figure of $1.15 million and an inventory turnover rate of 5.

d. The firm has a sales figure of $25 million, a gross profit margin of 14 percent, and an average age of inventory of 45 days.

15-15. (*EOQ Calculations*) A downtown bookstore is trying to determine the optimal order quantity for a popular novel just printed in paperback. The store feels that the book will sell at four times its hardback figures. It would therefore sell approximately 3,000 copies in the next year at a price of $1.50. The store buys the book at a wholesale figure of $1. Costs for carrying the book are estimated at $.10 a copy per year, and it costs $10 to order more books.

    a. Determine the EOQ.

    b. What would be the total costs for ordering the books 1, 4, 5, 10, and 15 times a year?

    c. What questionable assumptions are being made by the EOQ model?

15-16. (*Comprehensive EOQ Calculations*) Knutson Products, Inc., is involved in the production of airplane parts and has the following inventory, carrying, and storage costs:

    1. Orders must be placed in round lots of 100 units.

    2. Annual unit usage is 250,000. (Assume a 50-week year in your calculations.)

    3. The carrying cost is 10 percent of the purchase price.

    4. The purchase price is $10 per unit.

    5. The ordering cost is $100 per order.

    6. The desired safety stock is 5,000 units. (This does not include delivery-time stock.)

    7. The delivery time is one week.

Given the above information:

    a. Determine the optimal EOQ level.

    b. How many orders will be placed annually?

    c. What is the inventory order point? (That is, at what level of inventory should a new order be placed?)

    d. What is the average inventory level?

    e. What would happen to the EOQ if annual unit sales doubled (all other unit costs and safety stocks remaining constant)? What is the elasticity of EOQ with respect to sales? (That is, what is the percent change in EOQ dividend by the percent change in sales?)

    f. If carrying costs double, what would happen to the EOQ level? (Assume the original sales level of 250,000 units.) What is the elasticity of EOQ with respect to carrying costs?

    g. If the ordering costs double, what would happen to the level of EOQ? (Again assume original levels of sales and carrying costs.) What is the elasticity of EOQ with respect to ordering costs?

    h. If the selling price doubles, what would happen to EOQ? What is the elasticity of EOQ with respect to selling price?

COMPREHENSIVE PROBLEM

New Wave Surfing Stuff, Inc. is a manufacturer of surfboards and related gear that sells to exclusive surf shops located in several Atlantic and Pacific mainland coastal towns as well as several Hawaiian locations. The company's headquarters are located in Carlsbad, California, a small southern California coastal town. True to form, the company's officers, all veteran surfers, have been somewhat laid back about various critical areas of financial management. With an economic downturn in California adversely affecting their business, however, the officers of the company have decided to focus intently on ways to improve New Wave's cash flows. The CFO, Willy Bonik, has been requested to forgo any more daytime surfing jaunts until he has wrapped up a plan to accelerate New Wave's cash flows.

In an effort to ensure his quick return to the surf, Willy has decided to focus on what he believes is one of the easiest methods of improving New Wave's cash collections, namely, adoption of a cash receipts acceleration system that includes a lockbox system and concentration banking. Willy is well aware that New Wave's current system leaves much room for improvement. The company's accounts-receivable system currently requires that remittances from customers be mailed to the headquarters office for processing and then deposited in the local branch of the Bank of the U.S. Such an arrangement takes a considerable amount of time. The checks take an average of five days to reach the Carlsbad headquarters. Then, depending on the surf conditions, processing within the company takes anywhere from two to four days, with the average from the day of receipt by the company to the day of deposit at the bank being three days.

Willy feels pretty certain that such delays are costly. After all, New Wave's average daily collections are $150,000. The average remittance size is $750. If Willy could get these funds into his marketable-securities account more quickly, he could earn an annual rate of 5 percent on such funds. In addition, if he could arrange for someone else to do the processing. Willy could save $55,000 per year in costs related to clerical staffing.

New Wave's banker was pleased to provide Willy with a proposal for a combination of a lockbox system and a concentration-banking system. Bank of the U.S. would be New Wave's concentration bank. Lockboxes would be established in Honolulu, Newport Beach, and Daytona Beach. Each check processed through the lockbox system would cost New Wave $0.30. This arrangement, however, would reduce mail float by an average 2.5 days. The funds so collected would be transferred twice each day, 270 days a year, using automated depository transfer checks (DTCs) from each of the local lockbox banks to Bank of the U.S. Each DTC would cost $0.35. The combination of lockbox system and concentration banking would eliminate the time it takes the company to process cash collections, thereby making the funds available for short-term investment.

a. What would be the average amount of cash made available if New Wave were to adopt the system proposed by Bank of the U.S.?

b. What is the annual opportunity cost of maintaining the current cash collection and deposit system?

c. What is the expected annual cost of the complete system proposed by Bank of the U.S.?

d. What is the net gain or loss that is expected to result from the proposed new system? Should New Wave adopt the new system?

SELF-TEST SOLUTIONS

SS-1.

a. Here we must calculate the dollar value of the estimated return for each holding period and compare it with the transaction fee to determine if a gain can be made by investing in the securities. Those calculations and the resultant recommendations follow.

	RECOMMENDATION
1. $\$2,000,000(.12)(1/12)$ = $\$20,000 < \$45,000$	No
2. $\$2,000,000(.12)(2/12)$ = $\$40,000 < \$45,000$	No
3. $\$2,000,000(.12)(3/12)$ = $\$60,000 > \$45,000$	Yes
4. $\$2,000,000(.12)(6/12)$ = $\$120,000 > \$45,000$	Yes
5. $\$2,000,000(.12)(12/12)$ = $\$240,000 > \$45,000$	Yes

b. Let (%) be the required yield. With $2 million to invest for three months we have

$\$2,000,000(\%)(3/12) = \$45,000$

$\$2,000,000(\%) \qquad = \$180,000$

$\qquad\qquad\qquad = \$180,000/2,000,000 = 9\%$

The break-even yield, therefore, is 9%.

SS–2.

a.

$$EOQ = \sqrt{\frac{2SO}{C}}$$

$$= \sqrt{\frac{2(300,000)(50)}{3}}$$

$= 3,162$ units, but because orders must be placed in 100-unit lots, the effective EOQ becomes 3,200 units

b. $\dfrac{\text{total usage}}{\text{EOQ}} = \dfrac{300,000}{3,200} = 93.75$ orders per year

c. Inventory order point = delivery time + safety stock

$$= \frac{2}{50} \times 300,000 + 1,000$$

$$= 12,000 + 1,000$$

$$= 13,000 \text{ units}$$

International Business Finance

The Globalization of Product and Financial Markets • Exchange Rates • Interest-Rate Parity Theory • Purchasing-Power Parity Theory • Exposure to Exchange Rate Risk • Multinational Working-Capital Management • International Financing and Capital Structure Decisions • Direct Foreign Investment

LEARNING OBJECTIVES

After reading this chapter you should be able to

1. Discuss the internationalization of business.
2. Explain why foreign exchange rates in two different countries must be in line with each other.
3. Discuss the concept of interest rate parity.
4. Explain the purchasing-power parity theory and the law of one price.
5. Explain what exchange rate risk is and how it can be controlled.
6. Identify working-capital management techniques that are useful for international businesses to reduce exchange rate risk and potentially increase profits.
7. Explain how the financing sources available to multinational corporations differ from those available to domestic firms.
8. Discuss the risks involved in direct foreign investment.

Today, international economic boundaries no longer exist. In financial management, when we ask, Where can funds be raised least expensively? Where can this new product be produced least expensively? Where will our major competition come from? the answer will quite likely involve a foreign country. If we are going to be successful in business, we must have an international perspective in our decision making.

The case of the biotechnology industry typifies how the internationalization of business coupled with recent technological breakthroughs have created both competition and opportunities for U.S. firms. Here, we as financial managers must be able to look at new projects and see both their potential and risks from an international perspective.

One business battle presently being fought in the international arena is for dominance in biotechnology products. Not only are the profits from success going to come from sales around the world, but the competition is also international in perspective. The United States has been at the forefront of biotechnology, but Japanese companies are quickly gaining ground. Drawing on a strategy that has served them well in other industries, the Japanese are heavily relying on "piggybacking." The key to this strategy is to use their considerable financial assets to supply needed cash to biotechnology laboratories around the world, which then grant the Japanese access to technological breakthroughs. By riding piggyback on basic research conducted in other countries, the Japanese companies, in effect, augment their own research budgets, freeing resources for perfecting products that have the best chance of dominating markets around the world. Takeda, for example, which has a joint venture with Abbott Labs and alliances in West Germany, France, and Italy, funds research at Harvard University.

Today, the United States is spending three times the Japanese investment per year on biotech R&D and still holds a considerable lead in most areas of research. However, only time will tell how this will all turn out. What is important to us is that we recognize that businesses are no longer bound by international boundaries, and that we must be able to apply our trade around the world.

WHAT'S AHEAD

This chapter highlights the complications that an international business faces when it deals in multiple currencies. Effective strategies for the reduction of foreign exchange risk are discussed. Working-capital management and capital structure decisions in the international context are also covered. For the international firm, direct foreign investment is a capital-budgeting decision—with some additional complexities.

THE GLOBALIZATION OF PRODUCT AND FINANCIAL MARKETS

World trade has grown much faster over the last few decades than world aggregate output (global gross national product or GNP). The dollar value of world exports has grown from $129.5 billion in 1962 to $4.2 *trillion* in 1994. This remarkable increase in international trade is reflected in the increased openness of almost all national economies to international influences. For example, the proportion of U.S. GNP accounted for by exports and imports (about one-fifth) is now double what it was two decades ago, and is even higher for manufactured goods (see Figure 16–1). The U.S. Department of Commerce estimates that the United States exports about one-fifth of its industrial production and that about 70 percent of all U.S. goods compete directly with foreign goods.

Some industries and states are highly dependent on the international economy. For example, the electronic consumer products and automobile industries are widely considered to be global industries. Ohio ranks fourth in terms of manufactured exports, and more than half of Ohio workers are employed by firms that depend to some extent on exports.

There has also been a rise in the global level of international portfolio and direct investment. Both direct and portfolio investment in the United States have been increasing faster than U.S. investment overseas. Direct investment occurs when the **multinational corporation (MNC),** *a corporation with holdings and/or operations in more than one country,* has control over the investment, such as when it builds an offshore manufacturing facility. Portfolio investment involves financial assets with maturities greater than one year, such as the purchase of foreign stocks and bonds. Total foreign investment in the U.S. now exceeds such U.S. investment overseas.

A major reason for long-run overseas investments of United States companies is the high rates of return obtainable from these investments. The amount of U.S. *direct foreign investment (DFI)* abroad is large and growing. Significant amounts of the total assets, sales, and profits of American MNCs are attributable to foreign investments and foreign operations. Direct foreign investment is not limited to American firms. Many European and Japanese firms have operations abroad, too. During the last decade, these firms have been increasing their sales and setting up production facilities abroad, especially in the United States.

Capital flows between countries for international financial investment have also been increasing. Many firms, investment companies, and individuals invest in the capital markets in foreign countries. The motivation is twofold; to obtain returns higher than those obtainable in the domestic capital markets, and to reduce portfolio risk

multinational corporation (MNC)

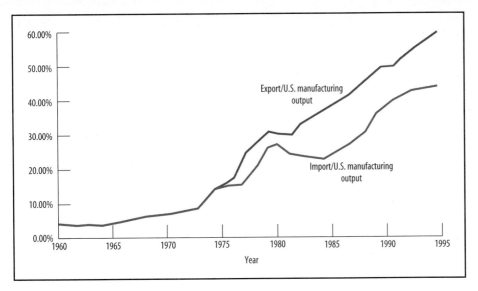

Figure 16–1
U.S. Trade As a Share of U.S. Manufacturing Output

through international diversification. The increase in world trade and investment activity is reflected in the recent globalization of financial markets. The Eurodollar market is larger than any domestic financial market. U.S. companies are increasingly turning to this market for funds. Even companies and public entities that have no overseas presence are beginning to rely on this market for financing.

In addition, most national financial markets are becoming more integrated with global markets because of the rapid increase in the volume of interest rate and currency swaps. Because of the widespread availability of these swaps, the currency denomination and the source country of financing for many globally integrated companies are dictated by accessibility and relative cost consideration regardless of the currency ultimately needed by the firm.

The foreign exchange markets have also grown rapidly, and the weekly trading volume in these globally integrated markets, between $3 and $5 trillion, exceeds the annual trading volume on the world's securities markets. Even a *purely domestic firm* that buys all its inputs and sells all its output in its home country is not immune to foreign competition, nor can it totally ignore the workings of the international financial markets.

EXCHANGE RATES   OBJECTIVE 2

Recent History of Exchange Rates

Between 1949 and 1970, the exchange rates between the major currencies were fixed. All countries were required to set a specific *parity rate* for their currency vis-à-vis the U.S. dollar. For example, consider the German currency, the deutsche mark (DM). In 1949, the parity rate was set at DM4.0 per dollar (DM4.0/$). The actual exchange rate prevailing on any day was allowed to lie within a narrow band around the parity rate. The DM was allowed to fluctuate between DM4.04 and DM3.96/$. A country could effect a major adjustment in the exchange rate by changing its parity rate with respect to the dollar. When the currency was made cheaper with respect to the dollar, this adjustment was called a *devaluation*. A *revaluation* resulted when a currency became more expensive with respect to the dollar. In 1969, the DM parity rate was adjusted to DM3.66/$. This adjustment was a revaluation of the DM parity by 9.3 percent. The new bands around the parity were DM3.7010 and DM3.6188/$. The DM strengthened against the dollar since fewer DM were needed to buy a dollar.

Since 1973, a **floating-rate international currency system,** *a system in which exchange rates between different national currencies are allowed to fluctuate with supply and demand conditions,* has been operating. For most currencies, there are no parity rates and no bands within which the currencies fluctuate.[1] Most major currencies, including the U.S. dollar, fluctuate freely, depending upon their values as perceived by the traders in foreign exchange markets. The country's relative economic strengths, its level of exports and imports, the level of monetary activity, and the deficits or surpluses in its balance of payments (BOP) are all important factors in the determination of exchange rates.[2] Short-term, day-to-day fluctuations in exchange rates are caused by changing supply and demand conditions in the foreign exchange market.

The Foreign Exchange Market

The foreign exchange market provides a mechanism for the transfer of purchasing power from one currency to another. This market is not a physical entity like the New York Stock Exchange; it is a network of telephone and computer connections among banks, foreign exchange dealers, and brokers. The market operates simultaneously at three levels. At the first level, customers buy and sell foreign exchange (that is, foreign currency) through their banks. At the second level, banks buy and sell foreign exchange from other banks in the same commercial center. At the last level, banks buy and sell foreign exchange from banks in commercial centers in other countries. Some important commercial centers for foreign exchange trading are New York, London, Zurich, Frankfurt, Hong Kong, Singapore, and Tokyo.

An example will illustrate this multilevel trading. A trader in Texas may buy foreign exchange (pounds) from a bank in Houston for payment to a British supplier against some purchase made. The Houston bank, in turn, may purchase the foreign currency (pounds) from a New York bank. The New York bank may buy the pounds from another bank in New York or from a bank in London.

Because this market provides transactions in a continuous manner for a very large volume of sales and purchases, the currency markets are efficient: In other words, it is difficult to make a profit by shopping around from one bank to another. Minute differences in the quotes from different banks are quickly eliminated. Because of the arbitrage mechanism, simultaneous quotes to different buyers in London and New York are likely to be the same.

Two major types of transactions are carried out in the foreign exchange markets: spot and forward transactions.

Spot Exchange Rates

A typical spot transaction involves an American firm buying foreign currency from its bank and paying for it in dollars. *The price of foreign currency in terms of the domestic currency* is the **exchange rate.** Another type of spot transaction is when

---

[1]The system of floating rates is referred to as the "floating-rate regime."

[2]The balance of payments for the United States reflects the difference between the import and export of goods (the trade balance) and services. Capital inflows and outflows are tabulated in the capital account.

an American firm receives foreign currency from abroad. The firm typically would sell the foreign currency to its bank for dollars. These are both **spot transactions** because *one currency is traded for another currency today.* The actual exchange rate quotes are expressed in several different ways, as discussed later. To allow time for the transfer of funds, the *value date* when the currencies are actually exchanged is two days after the spot transaction occurs. Four banks could easily be involved in the transactions: the local banks of the buyer and seller of the foreign exchange, and the money-center banks that handle the purchase and sale in the interbank market. Perhaps the buyer or seller will have to move the funds from one of its local banks to another, bringing even more banks into the transaction. A forward transaction entails an agreement today to deliver a specified number of units of a currency on a future date in return for a specified number of units of another currency.

spot transactions

On the spot exchange market, contrasted with the over-the-counter market, the quoted exchange rate is typically called a direct quote. A **direct quote** *indicates the number of units of the home currency required to buy one unit of the foreign currency.* That is, in New York the typical exchange-rate quote indicates the number of dollars needed to buy one unit of a foreign currency: dollars per pound, dollars per mark, and so on. The spot rates in columns 2 and 3 of Table 16–1 are the direct exchange quotes taken from the *Wall Street Journal* on January 24, 1996. To buy £1 on January 23, 1996, $1.5145 was needed. To buy FF1 and DM1, $.1975 and $.6761 were needed, respectively. The quotes in the spot market in Paris are given in terms of francs and those in Frankfurt in terms of deutsche marks.

direct quote

$ .01 / peso

An **indirect quote** *indicates the number of units of a foreign currency that can be bought for one unit of the home currency.* This reads as francs per dollar, marks per dollar, and so forth. An indirect quote is the general method used in the over-the-counter market. Exceptions to this rule include British pounds, Irish punts, Australian dollars, and New Zealand dollars, which are quoted via direct quote for historical reasons. Indirect quotes are given in the last two columns of Table 16–1.

indirect quote

peso / $ .01

In summary, a direct quote is the dollar/foreign currency rate ($/FC), and an indirect quote is the foreign currency/dollar (FC/$). Therefore, an indirect quote is the reciprocal of a direct quote and vice versa. The following example illustrates the computation of an indirect quote from a given direct quote.

Table 16–1
Foreign Exchange Rates Reported on January 24, 1996

COUNTRY	U.S. $ EQUIV.		CURRENCY PER U.S. $	
	TUE	MON	TUE	MON
Argentina (Peso)	1.0007	1.0007	.9992	.9993
Australia (Dollar)	.7334	.7323	1.3635	1.3656
Austria (Schilling)	.09654	.09613	10.358	10.403
Bahrain (Dinar)	2.6532	2.6532	.3769	.3769
Belgium (Franc)	.03305	.03289	30.260	30.400
Brazil (Real)	1.0288	1.0288	.9720	.9720
Britain (Pound)	1.5145	1.5117	.6603	.6615
30-Day Forward	1.5134	1.5106	.6608	.6620
90-Day Forward	1.5116	1.5088	.6616	.6628
180-Day Forward	1.5088	1.5061	.6628	.6640
Canada (Dollar)	.7309	.7298	1.3681	1.3701

Country	U.S. $ EQUIV.		CURRENCY PER U.S. $	
	Tue	Mon	Tue	Mon
30-Day Forward	.7309	.7298	1.3682	1.3702
90-Day Forward	.7308	.7297	1.3684	1.3705
180-Day Forward	.7302	.7291	1.3696	1.3715
Chile (Peso)	.002439	.002429	409.95	411.65
China (Renminbl)	.1202	.1206	8.3170	8.2928
Colombia (Peso)	.0009820	.0009818	1018.33	1018.50
Czech. Rep. (Koruna)	...	...	...	...
Commercial rate	.03683	.03666	27.154	27.276
Denmark (Krone)	.1756	.1749	5.6948	5.7187
Ecuador (Sucre)	...	...	...	...
Floating rate	.0003455	.0003455	2894.50	2894.50
Finland (Markka)	.2214	.2208	4.5167	4.5285
France (Franc)	.1975	.1980	5.0630	5.0512
30-Day Forward	.1977	.1980	5.0589	5.0510
90-Day Forward	.1979	.1984	5.0528	5.0395
180-Day Forward	.1982	.1988	5.0465	5.0313
Germany (Mark)	.6761	.6768	1.4790	1.4775
30-Day Forward	.6773	.6779	1.4765	1.4751
90-Day Forward	.6794	.6801	1.4718	1.4703
180-Day Forward	.6827	.6834	1.4649	1.4634
Greece (Drachma)	.004117	.004104	242.90	243.67
Hong Kong (Dollar)	.1294	.1293	7.7280	7.7331
Hungary (Forint)	.006974	.006965	143.39	143.57
India (Rupee)	.02790	.02792	35.842	35.820
Indonesia (Ruplah)	.0004359	.0004369	2294.00	2289.00
Ireland (Punt)	1.5735	1.5691	.6355	.6373
Israel (Shekel)	.3199	.3199	3.1260	3.1257
Italy (Lira)	.0006270	.0006285	1595.00	1591.00
Japan (Yen)	.009465	.009454	105.65	105.78
30-Day Forward	.009508	.009497	105.18	105.30
90-Day Forward	.009585	.009574	104.33	104.45
180-Day Forward	.009698	.009686	103.12	103.25
Jordan (Dinar)	1.4104	1.4104	.7090	.7090
Kuwait (Dinar)	3.3322	3.3325	.3001	.3001
Lebanon (Pound)	.0006279	.0006279	1592.50	1592.50
Malaysia (Ringglt)	.3917	.3916	2.5530	2.5534
Malta (Lira)	2.7809	2.7682	.3596	.3612
Mexico (Peso)	...	...	...	...
Floating rate	.1347	.1365	7.4250	7.3250
Netherlands (Guilder)	.6038	.6045	1.6561	1.6543
New Zealand (Dollar)	.6614	.6647	1.5119	1.5044
Norway (Krone)	.1548	.1544	6.4599	6.4774
Pakistan (Rupee)	.02920	.02920	34.247	34.250
Peru (new Sol)	.4292	.4292	2.3299	2.3300
Philippines (Peso)	.03820	.03821	26.178	26.170
Poland (Zloty)	.3948	.3948	2.5330	2.5330
Portugal (Escudo)	.006553	.006533	152.60	153.07

Table 16–1
Foreign Exchange Rates Reported on January 24, 1996 *(continued)*

COUNTRY	U.S. $ EQUIV.		CURRENCY PER U.S. $	
	TUE	MON	TUE	MON
Russia (Ruble) (a)	.0002128	.0002132	4700.00	4691.00
Saudi Arabia (Riyal)	.2666	.2666	3.7509	3.7503
Singapore (Dollar)	.7052	.7027	1.4180	1.4230
Slovak Rep. (Koruna)	.03322	.03321	30.098	30.108
South Africa (Rand)	.2742	.2741	3.6467	3.6480
South Korea (Won)	.001270	.001267	787.40	789.20
Spain (Peseta)	.008055	.008020	124.15	124.69
Sweden (Krona)	.1460	.1467	6.8493	6.8168
Switzerland (Franc)	.8413	.8414	1.1886	1.1885
30-Day Forward	.8441	.8442	1.1847	1.1846
90-Day Forward	.8491	.8491	1.1777	1.1777
180-Day Forward	.8565	.8564	1.1675	1.1677
Taiwan (Dollar)	.03646	.03646	27.430	27.430
Thailand (Baht)	.03959	.03959	25.259	25.260
Turkey (Lira)	.00001632	.00001636	61279.50	61113.00
United Arab (Dirham)	.2724	.2724	3.6711	3.6710
Uruguay (New Peso)	...	...	...	...
Financial	.1387	.1393	7.2100	7.1788
Venezuela (Bolivar)	.003448	.003448	290.00	290.00
Brady Rate	.002740	.002740	365.00	365.00
SDR	1.4626	1.4588	.6837	.6855
ECU	1.2428	1.2458		

[a]Exchange rates: Tuesday, January 23, 1996. The New York foreign exchange selling rates apply to trading among banks in amounts of $1 million and more, as quoted at 3 P.M. Eastern time by Dow Jones Telerate Inc. and other sources. Retail transactions provide fewer units of foreign currency per dollar.
[b]Special Drawing Rights (SDR) are based on exchange rates for the U.S, German, British, French, and Japanese currencies. Source: International Monetary Fund.
[c]European Currency Unit (ECU) is based on a basket of community currencies.
a-fixing, Moscow Interbank Currency Exchange

EXAMPLE

Suppose you want to compute the indirect quotes from the direct quotes of spot rates for pounds, francs, and marks given in column 2 of Table 16–1. The direct quotes are pound, 1.5145; French franc, .1975; and deutsch mark, .6761. The related indirect quotes are calculated as the *reciprocal* of the direct quote as follows:

$$\text{indirect quote} = \frac{1}{\text{direct quote}}$$

Thus,

pounds
$$\frac{1}{\$1.5145/\pounds} = \pounds.6603/\$$$

francs
$$\frac{1}{\$.1975/FF} = FF5.0630/\$$$

deutsche marks
$$\frac{1}{\$.6761/DM} = DM1.4790/\$$$

Notice that the above direct quotes and indirect quotes are identical to those shown in columns 2 and 4 of Table 16–1. ▨

Direct and indirect quotes are useful in conducting international transactions, as the following examples show.

▨ EXAMPLE ▨

An American business must pay DM1,000 to a German firm on January 23, 1996. How many dollars will be required for this transaction?

$.6761/DM × DM1,000 = $676.10 ▨

▨ EXAMPLE ▨

An American business must pay $2,000 to a British resident on January 23, 1996. How many pounds will the British resident receive?

£.6603/$ × $2,000 = £1520.60 ▨

Exchange Rates and Arbitrage

The foreign exchange quotes in two different countries must be in line with each other. The direct quote for U.S. dollars in London is given in pounds per dollar. Because the foreign exchange markets are efficient, the direct quotes for the per U.S. dollar in London, on January 23, 1996, must be very close to the indirect rate of £.6603/$ prevailing in New York on that date.

If the exchange rate quotations between the London and New York spot exchange markets were *out of line*, then an *enterprising trader could make a profit by buying in the market where the currency was cheaper and selling it in the other.* Such a buy-and-sell strategy would involve a zero net investment of funds and no risk bearing yet would provide a sure profit. Such a person is called an **arbitrageur,** and the process of buying and selling in more than one market to make a riskless profit is called arbitrage. Spot exchange markets are efficient in the sense that arbitrage opportunities do not persist for any length of time. That is, the exchange rates between two different markets are quickly brought *in line*, aided by the arbitrage process. **Simple arbitrage** *eliminates exchange rate differentials across the markets for a single currency,* as in the preceding example for the New York and London quotes. **Triangular arbitrage** does the *same across the markets for all currencies.* **Covered-interest arbitrage** *eliminates differentials across currency and interest rate markets.*

Suppose that London quotes £.6700/$ instead of £.6603/$. If you simultaneously bought a pound in New York for £.6603/$ and sold a pound in London for £.6700/$, you would have (1) taken a zero net investment position since you bought £1 and sold £1, (2) locked in a sure profit of £.0097/$ *no matter which way* the pound subsequently moves, and (3) set in motion the forces that will eliminate the different quotes in New York and London. As others in the marketplace learn of your transaction, they will attempt to make the same transaction. The increased demand to buy pounds in New York will lead to a higher quote there and the increased supply of pounds will lead to a lower quote in London. The workings of the market will produce a new spot rate that lies between £.6603/$ and £.6700/$ and is the same in New York and in London.

Asked and Bid Rates

Two types of rates are quoted in the spot exchange market: the asked and the bid rates. The **asked rate** is the *rate the bank or the foreign exchange trader "asks" the*

arbitrageur

simple arbitrage

triangular arbitrage
covered-interest arbitrage

asked rate

customer to pay in home currency for foreign currency when the bank is selling and the customer is buying. The asked rate is also known as the **selling rate** or the *offer rate.* The **bid rate** is *the rate at which the bank buys the foreign currency from the customer by paying in home currency.* The bid rate is also known as the **buying rate.** Note that Table 16–1 contains only the selling, offer, or asked rates, not the buying rate.

selling rate
bid rate
buying rate

bid = buy
ask = sell

The bank sells a unit of foreign currency for more than it pays for it. Therefore, the direct asked quote ($/FC) is greater than the direct bid quote. The *difference between the asked quote and the bid quote* is known as the **bid-asked spread.** When there is a large volume of transactions and the trading is continuous, the spread is small and can be less than -1% (.001) for the major currencies. The spread is much higher for infrequently traded currencies. The spread exists to compensate the banks for holding the risky foreign currency and for providing the service of converting currencies.

bid-asked spread

how a country makes a profit

Cross Rates

A **cross rate** is *the computation of an exchange rate for a currency from the exchange rates of two other currencies.* The following example illustrates how this works.

cross rate

EXAMPLE

Taking the dollar/pound and the mark/dollar rates from columns 2 and 4 of Table 16–1, determine the mark/pound and pound/mark exchange rates. We see that

$$(\$/\pounds) \times (DM/\$) = (DM/\pounds)$$

or

$$1.5145 \times 1.4790 = DM2.2399$$

Thus, the pound/mark exchange rate is

$$1/2.2399 = \pounds.4464/DM$$

Cross-rate computations make it possible to use quotations in New York to compute the exchange rate between pounds, marks, and francs. Arbitrage conditions hold in cross rates, too. For example, the pound exchange rate in Frankfurt (the direct quote marks/pound) must be 2.2399. The mark exchange rate in London must be .4464 pounds/mark. If the rates prevailing in Frankfurt and London were different from the computed cross rates, using quotes from New York, a trader could use three different currencies to lock in arbitrage profits through a process called triangular arbitrage.

Forward Exchange Rates

A **forward exchange contract** *requires delivery, at a specified future date, of one currency for a specified amount of another currency.* The exchange rate for the forward transaction is agreed on today; the actual payment of one currency and the receipt of another currency take place at the future date. For example, a 30-day contract on March 1 is for delivery on March 31. Note that the forward rate is not the same as the spot rate that will prevail in the future. The actual spot rate that will prevail is not known today; only the forward rate is known. The actual spot rate will depend on the market conditions at that time; it may be more or less than today's forward rate. **Exchange rate risk** is the *risk that tomorrow's exchange rate will differ from today's rate.*

forward exchange contract

exchange rate risk

As indicated earlier, it is extremely unlikely that the future spot rate will be exactly the same as the forward rate quoted today. Assume that you are going to receive a payment denominated in pounds from a British customer in 30 days. If you wait for 30 days and exchange the pounds at the spot rate, you will receive a dollar amount reflecting the exchange rate 30 days hence (that is, the future spot rate). As of today, you have no way of knowing the exact dollar value of your future pound receipts. Consequently, you cannot make precise plans about the use of these dollars. If, conversely, you buy a future contract, then you know the exact dollar value of your future receipts, and you can make precise plans concerning their use. The forward contract, therefore, can reduce your uncertainty about the future, and the major advantage of the forward market is that of risk reduction.

Forward contracts are usually quoted for periods of 30, 90, and 180 days. A contract for any intermediate date can be obtained, usually with the payment of a small premium. Forward contracts for periods longer than 180 days can be obtained by special negotiations with banks. Contracts for periods greater than one year can be costly.

Forward rates, like spot rates, are quoted in both direct and indirect form. The direct quotes for the 30-day and 90-day forward contracts on pounds, francs, and marks are given in column 2 of Table 16–1. The indirect quotes for forward contracts, like spot rates, are reciprocals of the direct quotes. The indirect quotes are indicated in column 4 of Table 16–1. The direct quotes are the dollar/foreign currency rate, and the indirect quotes are the foreign currency/dollar rate similar to the spot exchange quotes.

The 30-day forward quote for pounds is $1.5134 per pound. This means that if one purchases the contract for forward pounds on January 23, 1996, the bank will deliver £1 against the payment of $1.5134 on January 22, 1996. The bank is contractually bound to deliver £1 at this price, and the buyer of the contract is legally obligated to buy it at this price on February 22, 1996. Therefore, this is the price the customer must pay regardless of the actual spot rate prevailing on February 22, 1996. If the spot price of the pound is less than $1.5134, then the customer pays *more* than the spot price. If the spot price is greater than $1.5234, then the customer pays *less* than the spot price.

The forward rate is often quoted at a premium to or discount from the existing spot rate. For example, the 30-day forward rate for the pound may be quoted as a .0011 premium (1.5134 forward rate − 1.5145 spot rate). If the forward contract is selling for more dollars than the spot—that is, a larger direct quote—the pound is said to be selling at a discount, which means the dollar is selling at a premium to the pound. Consider another example: If the indirect spot and forward quotes for the mark are 1.4790 and 1.4800, respectively, the mark is selling at a premium to the dollar and the dollar at a discount to the mark. When the forward contract sells for fewer dollars than the spot—a smaller direct quote—the pound is said to be at a discount from the dollar. Notice in column 2 of Table 16–1 that the forward contracts are selling at a discount for pounds a premium for French francs. This premium or discount forward-spot differential is also called the **forward-spot differential.**

Notationally, the relationship may be written

$$F - S = \text{premium } (F > S) \text{ or discount } (S > F) \qquad \textbf{(16–1)}$$

where
F = the forward rate, direct quote
S = the spot rate, direct quote

The premium or discount can also be expressed as an annual percentage rate, computed as follows:

$$\frac{F - S}{S} \times \frac{12}{n} \times 100 = \text{annualized percentage} \qquad \textbf{(16–2)}$$

premium $(F > S)$ or discount $(S > F)$

where n = the number of months of the forward contract

Table 16–2
Percent-per-Annum (Discount)

	30-Day	90-Day
British pound	−0.87%	−0.77%
French franc	−1.22%	−0.81%

EXAMPLE

Compute the percent-per-annum premium on the 30-day pound.

Step 1: Identify F, S, and n.

$$F = 1.5134, \ S = 1.5145, \ n = 1 \text{ month}$$

Step 2: Because S is greater than F, we compute the annualized percentage discount:

$$D = \frac{1.5134 - 1.5145}{1.5145} \times \frac{12 \text{ months}}{1 \text{ month}} \times 100$$

$$= -0.87\%$$

The percent-per-annum discount on the 30-day pound is −0.87%. The percent-per-annum discount on the 30-day and 90-day pound and franc contracts are computed similarly. The results are given in Table 16–2.　■

Examples of Exchange Rate Risk

The concept of exchange rate risk applies to all types of international business. The measurement of these risks, and the type of risk, may differ among businesses. Let us see how exchange rate risk affects international trade contracts, international portfolio investments, and direct foreign investments.

Exchange Rate Risk in International Trade Contracts

The idea of exchange rate risk in trade contracts is illustrated in the following situations.

Case I. An American automobile distributor agrees to buy a car from the manufacturer in Detroit. The distributor agrees to pay $6,500 on delivery of the car, which is expected to be 30 days from today. The car is delivered on the thirtieth day and the distributor pays $6,500. Notice that from the day this contract was written until the day the car was delivered, the buyer knew the *exact dollar amount* of the liability. There was, in other words, *no uncertainty* about the value of the contract.

Case II. An American automobile distributor enters into a contract with a British supplier to buy a car from Britain for £3,500. The amount is payable on the delivery of the car, 30 days from today. From Figure 16–2 on page 516 we see the range of spot rates that we believe can occur on the date the contract is consummated. On the thirtieth day, the American importer will pay some amount in the range of $4,600.75 (3,500 × 1.3145) to $6,000.75 (3,500 × 7.7145) for the car. Today, the American firm is not certain what its future dollar outflow will be 30 days hence. That is, the *dollar value of the contract is uncertain*.

These two examples help illustrate the idea of foreign exchange risk in international trade contracts. In the domestic trade contract (Case I), the exact dollar amount of the future dollar payment is known today with certainty. In the case of the international trade contract (Case II), where the *contract is written in the foreign currency*, the exact dollar amount of the contract is not known. The variability of the exchange rate induces variability in the future cash flow.

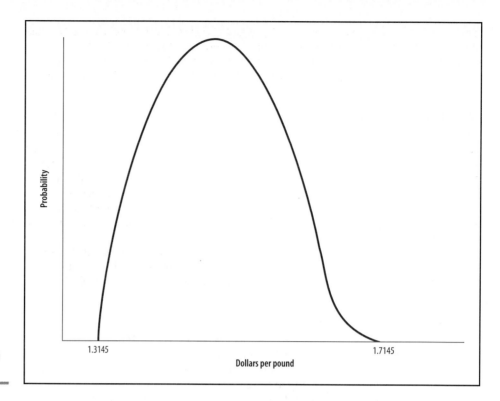

Figure 16–2

A Subjective Probability Distribution of the Pound Exchange Rate, 30 Days in the Future

Exchange rate risk exists when the contract is written in terms of the foreign currency or *denominated* in foreign currency. There is no direct exchange rate risk if the international trade contract is written in terms of the domestic currency. That is, in Case II, if the contract were written in dollars, the American importer would face *no* direct exchange rate risk. With the contract written in dollars, the British exporter would bear *all* the exchange rate risk because the British exporter's future pound receipts would be uncertain. That is, the British exporter would receive payment in dollars, which would have to be converted into pounds at an unknown (as of today) pound/dollar exchange rate. In international trade contracts of the type discussed here, at least one of the two parties to the contract *always* bears the exchange rate risk.

Certain types of international trade contracts are denominated in a third currency, different from either the importer's or the exporter's domestic currency. In Case II, the contract might have been denominated in, say, the deutsche mark. With a mark contract, both importer and exporter would be subject to exchange rate risk.

Exchange rate risk is not limited to the two-party trade contracts; it exists also in foreign portfolio investments and direct foreign investments.

Exchange Rate Risk in Foreign Portfolio Investments

Let us look at an example of exchange rate risk in the context of portfolio investments. An American investor buys a German security. The exact return on the investment in the security is unknown. Thus, the security is a risky investment. The investment return in the holding period of, say, three months stated in marks could be anything from −2 to +8 percent. In addition, the mark/dollar exchange rate may depreciate by 4 percent or appreciate by 6 percent in the three-month period during which the investment is held. The return to the American investor, in dollars, will therefore be in the range of −6 to +14 percent.[3] Notice that the return to a German investor. In marks, is in the range of −2 to +8 percent. Clearly, for the American investor, the exchange factor induces a greater variability in the dollar rate of return. Hence, the exchange rate fluctuations may increase the riskiness of the investments.

Exchange Rate Risk in Direct Foreign Investment

The exchange rate risk of a direct foreign investment (DFI) is more complicated. In a DFI, the parent company invests in assets denominated in a foreign currency. That is, the balance sheet and the income statement of the subsidiary are written in terms of the foreign currency. The parent company receives the repatriated profit stream in dollars. Thus, the exchange rate risk concept applies to fluctuations in the dollar value of the assets located abroad as well as to the fluctuations in the home currency–denominated profit stream. Exchange risk not only affects immediate profits, it may affect the future profit stream as well.

Although exchange rate risk can be a serious complication in international business activity, remember the principle of the risk-return trade-off: Traders and corporations find numerous reasons that the returns from international transactions outweigh the risks.

BACK TO THE FOUNDATIONS

In international transactions, just as in domestic transactions, the key to value is the timing and amounts of cash flow spent and received. However, economic transactions across international borders add an element of risk because cash flows are denominated in the currency of the country in which business is being transacted. Consequently, the dollar value of the cash flows will depend on the exchange rate that exists at the time the cash changes hands. The fact remains, however, that it's cash spent and received that matters. This is the point of Axiom 3: **Cash—Not Profits—Is King.**

INTEREST-RATE PARITY THEORY

OBJECTIVE 3

Forward rates generally entail a premium or a discount relative to current spot rates. However, these forward premiums and discounts differ between currencies and maturities (see Table 16–2). These differences depend solely on the difference in the level of interest rates between the two countries, called the *interest rate differential.* The value of the premium or discount can be theoretically computed from the **interest-rate parity (IRP) theory.** This theory states that *(except for the effects of small transaction costs) the forward premium or discount should be equal and opposite in size to the difference in the national interest rates for securities of the same maturity.*

interest-rate parity (IRP) theory

Stated very simply, what does all this mean? It means that because of arbitrage, the interest rate differential between two countries must be equal to the difference between the forward and spot exchange rates. If this were not true, arbitrageurs would buy in the forward market and sell in the spot market (or vice versa) until prices were back in line and there were no profits left to be made. For example, if prices in the

---

[3]Example: Assume the spot exchange rate is $.50/DM. In three months, the exchange rate would be .50 × (1 − .04) = .48 to .50 × (1 + .06) = .53. A $50 investment today is equivalent to a DM100 investment. The DM100 investment would return DM98 to DM108 in three months. The return, in the worst case is DM98 × .48 = $47.04. The return, in the best case, is DM108 × .53 = $57.24. The holding-period return, on the $50 investment, will be between −6 percent ($47.04 − $50)/$50) and +14 percent ($57.24 − $50)/$50).

"Traders Say Dollar May Have Hit Bottom"

LONDON—The dollar's latest ten-day rally, following its stunning declines earlier this year, has foreign-exchange experts struggling to determine whether the U.S. currency has finally hit bottom.

A sustained dollar recovery isn't considered likely until other ingredients are present. Besides investor confidence that the Clinton administration wants a stable dollar, a broad rally would require higher U.S. interest rates, lower German rates, and settlement of the U.S. trade dispute with Japan, analysts say.

The interest rate outlook, at least, does seem to promise some relief for the dollar. Short-term German rates are currently higher than their U.S. equivalents, a difference that contributes to the mark's strength. But Hermann Remsperger, chief economist at Berlin Handles & Frankfurter Bank in Frankfurt, expects that to be reversed by year end as the Fed raises rates to damp U.S. inflation and lower German inflation possibly allows the Bundesbank to cut rates.

Economists add that further Fed tightening could stabilize the U.S. bond market, which would further draw back investors, lending further support to the dollar. "For the dollar to strengthen in the long run, there must be the expectation that capital gains in the U.S. are in the offing—especially for foreign investors" says Remsperger.

The U.S.-Japan trade front is more problematic. While many economists and traders are skeptical that U.S.-Japanese tensions will ease sufficiently enough to allow a resolution soon, "Sentiment can't turn fully positive for the dollar until the Clinton administration achieves satisfaction from the Japanese government on measures to stimulate domestic demand in Japan and to afford greater access to U.S. exports."

Meanwhile, a strong yen is hurting the competitiveness of Japan's exports, and weighing down the country's already weak economy. "The very strong yen is a burden for the Japanese economy," says Mr. Remsperger. "If you look at the trade account in yen terms, you see that this burden has ready been shown in the figures—in other words they are exporting less." But the weak Japanese economy is also cutting Japanese demand for U.S. imports.

forward market were too low, arbitrageurs would enter the market, increase the demand for the forward foreign currency, and drive up the prices in the forward market until those prices obeyed the interest-rate parity theory.

OBJECTIVE 4 | **PURCHASING-POWER PARITY THEORY**

purchasing-power parity (PPP) theory

Long-run changes in exchange rates are influenced by international differences in inflation rates and the purchasing power of each nation's currency. Exchange rates of countries with high rates of inflation will tend to decline. According to the **purchasing-power parity (PPP) theory,** *in the long run, exchange rates adjust so that the purchasing power of each currency tends to be the same. Thus, exchange rate changes tend to reflect international differences in inflation rates. Countries with high rates of inflation tend to experience declines in the value of their currency.* Thus, if Britain experiences a 10 percent rate of inflation in a year that Germany experiences only a 6 percent rate, the UK currency (the pound) will be expected to decline in value approximately by 3.77 percent (1.10/1.06) against the German currency (the deutsche mark). More accurately, according to the PPP

$$\text{expected spot rate} = \text{current spot rate} \times \text{expected difference in inflation rate}$$

$$\begin{matrix} \text{expected spot rate} \\ \text{(domestic currency} \\ \text{per unit of foreign} \\ \text{currency)} \end{matrix} = \begin{matrix} \text{current spot rate} \\ \text{(domestic currency} \\ \text{per unit of foreign} \\ \text{currency)} \end{matrix} \times \frac{(1 + \text{expected domestic inflation rate})}{(1 + \text{expected foreign inflation rate})}$$

Thus, if the beginning value of the mark were £.40, with a 6 percent inflation rate in Germany and a 10 percent inflation rate in Britain, according to the PPP, the expected value of the deutsche mark at the end of that year will be £.40 × [1.10/1.06], or £.4151.

Stated very simply, what does this mean? It means that a dollar should have the same purchasing power anywhere in the world—well, at least on average. Obviously, this is not quite true. However, what the purchasing-power parity theory tells us is that we should expect, on average, that differences in inflation rates between two countries should be reflected in changes in the exchange rates. In effect, the best forecast of the difference in inflation rates between two countries should also be the best forecast of the change in the spot rate of exchange.

The Law of One Price

Underlying the PPP relationship is the **law of one price.** This law is actually *a proposition that in competitive markets where there are no transportation costs or barriers to trade, the same goods sold in different countries sells for the same price if all the different prices are expressed in terms of the same currency.* The idea is that the worth, in terms of marginal utility, of a good does not depend on where it is bought or sold. Because inflation will erode the purchasing power of any currency, its exchange rate must adhere to the PPP relationship if the law of one price is to hold over time.

law of one price

There are enough obvious exceptions to the concept of purchasing-power parity that it may, at first glance, seem difficult to accept. For example, in the Spring of 1996, a Big Mac cost $2.36 in the United States, and given the then existing exchange rates, it cost an equivalent of $2.02 in Mexico, $2.70 in Japan, and $3.22 in Germany. On the surface this might appear to violate the purchasing-power parity theory and the law of one price; however, we must remember that this theory is based upon the concept of arbitrage. In the case of a Big Mac, it's pretty hard to imagine buying Big Macs in Mexico for $2.02, shipping them to Germany, and reselling them for $3.22. But for commodities like gold and other items that are relatively inexpensive to ship and do not have to be consumed immediately, the law of one price holds much better.

International Fisher Effect

According to the domestic Fisher effect (FE), nominal interest rates reflect the expected inflation rate and a real rate of return. In other words,

$$\begin{matrix} \text{nominal} \\ \text{interest rate} \end{matrix} = \begin{matrix} \text{expected} \\ \text{inflation rate} \end{matrix} + \begin{matrix} \text{real rate} \\ \text{of interest} \end{matrix}$$

inflation makes a difference

While there is mixed empirical support for the international Fisher effect (IFE), it is widely thought that, for the major industrial countries, the real rate of interest is about 3 percent when a long-term period is considered. In such a case, with the previous assumption regarding inflation rates, interest rates in Britain and Germany would be (.10 + .03 + .003) or 13.3 percent and (.06 + .03 + .0018) or 9.18 percent, respectively.

In effect, the IFE states that the real interest rate should be the same all over the world, with the difference in nominal or stated interest rates simply resulting from the difference in expected inflation rates. As we look at interest rates around the world, this tells us that we should not necessarily send our money to a bank account in the country with the highest interest rates. That course of action might only result in sending our money to a bank in the country with the highest expected level of inflation.

EXPOSURE TO EXCHANGE RATE RISK

An asset denominated or valued in terms of foreign-currency cash flows will lose value if that foreign currency declines in value. It can be said that such an asset is exposed to exchange rate risk. However, this possible decline in asset value may be offset by the decline in value of any liability that is also denominated or valued in terms of that foreign currency. Thus, a firm would normally be interested in its net exposed position (exposed assets − exposed liabilities) for each period in each currency.

While expected changes in exchange rates can often be included in the cost-benefit analysis relating to such transactions, in most cases there is an unexpected component in exchange rate changes and often the cost-benefit analysis for such transactions does not fully capture even the expected change in the exchange rate. For example, price increases for the foreign operations of many MNCs often have to be less than those necessary to fully offset exchange rate changes, owing to the competitive pressures generated by local businesses, as the Japanese automakers found in 1988 for their U.S. sales.

Three measures of foreign exchange exposure are translation exposure, transactions exposure, and economic exposure. Translation exposure arises because the foreign operations of MNCs have accounting statements denominated in the local currency of the country in which the operation is located. For U.S. MNCs, the *reporting currency* for its consolidated financial statements is the dollar, so the assets, liabilities, revenues, and expenses of the foreign operations must be translated into dollars. International transactions often require a payment to be made or received in a foreign currency in the future, so these transactions are exposed to exchange rate risk. Economic exposure exists over the long term because the value of future cash flows in the reporting currency (that is, the dollar) from foreign operations are exposed to exchange rate risk. Indeed, the whole stream of future cash flows is exposed. The Japanese automaker situation highlights the effect of economic exposure on an MNC's revenue stream. The three measures of exposure now are examined more closely.

Translation Exposure

Foreign currency assets and liabilities are considered exposed if their foreign currency value for accounting purposes is to be translated into the domestic currency using the currency exchange rate—the exchange rate in effect on the balance sheet date. Other assets and liabilities and equity amounts that are translated at the historic exchange rate—the rate in effect when these items were first recognized in the company's accounts—are not considered to be exposed. The rate (current or historic) used to translate various accounts depends on the translation procedure used.

While transaction exposure can result in exchange rate change–related losses and gains that are realized and have an impact on both reported and taxable income, translation exposure results in exchange rate losses and gains that are reflected in the company's accounting books, but are unrealized and have little or no impact on taxable income. Thus, if financial markets are efficient and managerial goals are consistent with owner wealth maximization, a firm should not have to waste real resources hedging against possible paper losses caused by translation exposure. However, if there are significant agency or information costs or if markets are not efficient, a firm may indeed find it economical to hedge against translation losses or gains.

Transaction Exposure ◀━━

Receivables, payables, and fixed-price sales or purchase contracts are examples of foreign currency transactions whose monetary value was fixed at a time different from the time when these transactions are actually completed. **Transaction exposure** is a term that *describes the net contracted foreign currency transactions for which the settlement amounts are subject to changing exchange rates.* A company normally must set up an additional reporting system to track transaction exposure, because several of these amounts are not recognized in the accounting books of the firm.

transaction exposure

Exchange rate risk may be neutralized or hedged by a change in the asset and liability position in the foreign currency. An exposed asset position (such as an account receivable) can be hedged or covered by creating a liability of the same amount and maturity denominated in the foreign currency (such as a forward contract to sell the foreign currency). An exposed liability position (such as an account payable) can be covered by acquiring assets of the same amount and maturity in the foreign currency (such as a forward contract to buy the foreign currency). The objective is to have a zero net asset position in the foreign currency. This eliminates exchange rate risk, since the loss (gain) in the liability (asset) is exactly offset by the gain (loss) in the value of the asset (liability) when the foreign currency appreciates (depreciates). Two popular forms of hedge are the money-market hedge and the exchange-market or forward-market hedge. In both types of hedge the amount and the duration of the asset (liability) positions are matched. Note as you read the next two subsections how IRP theory assures that each hedge provides the same cover.

Money-Market Hedge

In a money-market hedge, the exposed position in a foreign currency is offset by borrowing or lending in the money market. Consider the case of the American firm with a net liability position (that is, the amount it owes) of £3,000. The firm knows the exact amount of its pound liability in 30 days, but it does not know the liability in dollars. Assume that the 30-day money-market rates in both the United States and Britain are, respectively, 1 percent for lending and 1.5 percent for borrowing. The American business can take the following steps:

Step 1: Calculate the present value of the foreign currency liability (£3,000) that is due in 30 days. Use the money-market rate applicable for the foreign country (1 percent in the United Kingdom). The present value of £3,000 is £2,970.30, computed as follows: 3,000/(1 + .01).

Step 2: Exchange dollars on today's spot market to obtain the £2,970.30. The dollar amount needed today is $4,498.52 (2,970.30 × 1.5145).

Step 3: Invest £2,970.30 in a United Kingdom one-month money-market instrument. This investment will compound to exactly £3,000 in one month. The future liability of £3,000 is covered by the £2,970.30 investment.[4]

Note: If the American business does not own this amount today, it can borrow $4,498.52 from the U.S. money market at the going rate of 1.5 percent. In 30 days the American business will need to repay $4,566.00 [$4,498.52 × (1 + .015)].

Assuming that the American business borrows the money, its management may base its calculations on the knowledge that the British goods, on delivery in 30 days, will cost it $4,566.00. The British business will receive £3,000. The American business need not wait for the future spot exchange rate to be revealed. On today's date, the future dollar payment of the contract is known with certainty. This certainty helps the American business in making its pricing and financing decisions.

---

[4]Observe that £2,970.30 × (1 + .01) = £3,000.

Many businesses hedge in the money market. The firm needs to borrow (creating a liability) in one market, lend or invest in the other money market, and use the spot exchange market on today's date. The mechanics of covering a net asset position in the foreign currency are the exact reverse of the mechanics of covering the liability position. With a net asset position in pounds: Borrow in the United Kingdom money market in pounds, convert to dollars on the spot exchange market, invest in the U.S. money market. When the net assets are converted into pounds (i.e., when the firm receives what it is owed), pay off the loan and the interest. The cost of hedging in the money market is the cost of doing business in three different markets. Information about the three markets is needed, and analytical calculations of the type indicated here must be made.

Many small and infrequent traders find the cost of the money-market hedge prohibitive, owing especially to the need for information about the market. These traders use exchange-market or forward-market hedge, which has very similar hedging benefits.

The Forward-Market Hedge

The forward market provides a second possible hedging mechanism. It works as follows: A net asset (liability) position is covered by a liability (asset) in the forward market. Consider again the case of the American firm with a liability of £3,000 that must be paid in 30 days. The firm may take the following steps to cover its liability position:

Step 1: Buy a forward contract today to purchase £3,000 in 30 days. The 30-day forward rate is $1.5134/£.

Step 2: On the thirtieth day pay the banker $4,540.20 (3,000 × $1.5134) and collect £3,000. Pay these pounds to the British supplier.

By the use of the forward contract the American business knows the exact worth of the future payment in dollars ($4,540.20). The exchange rate risk in pounds is totally eliminated by the net asset position in the forward pounds. In the case of a net asset exposure, the steps open to the American firm are the exact opposite: Sell the pounds forward, and on the future day receive and deliver the pounds to collect the agreed-on dollar amount.

The use of the forward market as a hedge against exchange rate risk is simple and direct. That is, match the liability or asset position against an offsetting position in the forward market. The forward-market hedge is relatively easy to implement. The firm directs its banker that it needs to buy or sell a foreign currency on a future date, and the banker gives a forward quote.

The forward-market hedge and the money-market hedge give an identical future dollar payment (or receipt) if the forward contracts are priced according to the interest-rate parity theory. The alert student may have noticed that the dollar payments in the money-market hedge and the forward-market hedge examples were, respectively, $4,566.00 and $4,540.20. Recall from our previous discussions that in efficient markets, the forward contracts do indeed conform to IRP theory. However, the numbers in our example are not identical because the forward rate used in the forward-market hedge is not exactly equal to the interest rates in the money-market hedge.

Currency-Futures Contracts and Options

The forward-market hedge is not adequate for some types of exposure. If the foreign currency asset or liability position occurs on a date for which forward quotes are not available, the forward-market hedge cannot be accomplished. In certain cases the forward-market hedge may cost more than the money-market hedge. In these cases, a corporation with a large amount of exposure may prefer the money-market hedge. In addition to forward-market and money-market hedges, a company can also hedge its exposure by buying (or selling) some relatively new instruments—foreign currency futures contracts and foreign currency options. Although futures contracts are similar to forward contracts in that they provide fixed prices for the required delivery of foreign currency at maturity, exchange traded options permit fixed (strike) price foreign currency transactions anytime before maturity. Futures contracts and options differ from forward contracts in that, unlike forward contracts, which are customized regarding amount and maturity date, futures and options are traded in standard amounts with standard maturity dates. In addition, although forward contracts are written by banks, futures and options are traded on organized exchanges, and individual traders deal with the exchange-based clearing organization rather than with each other. The purchase of futures requires the fulfillment of margin requirements (about 5 to 10 percent of the face amount), whereas the purchase of forward contracts requires only good credit standing with a bank. The purchase of options requires an immediate outlay that reflects a premium above the strike price and an outlay equal to the strike price when and if the option is executed.

Economic Exposure

The economic value of a company can vary in response to exchange rate changes. This change in value may be caused by a rate change–induced decline in the level of expected cash flows and/or by an increase in the riskiness of these cash flows. *Economic exposure* refers to the overall impact of exchange rate changes on the value of the firm and includes not only the strategic impact of changes in competitive relationships that arise from exchange rate changes, but also the economic impact of transactions exposure, and if any, translation exposure.

Economic exposure to exchange rate changes depends on the competitive structure of the markets for a firm's inputs and outputs and how these markets are influenced by changes in exchange rates. This influence, in turn, depends on several economic factors, including price elasticities of the products, the degree of competition from foreign markets, and direct (through prices) and indirect (through incomes) impact of exchange rate changes on these markets. Assessing, the economic exposure faced by a particular firm thus depends on the ability to understand and model the structure of the markets for its major inputs (purchases) and outputs (sales).

A company need not engage in any cross-border business activity to be exposed to exchange rate changes, because product and financial markets in most countries are related and influenced to a large extent by the same global forces. The output of a company engaged in business activity only within one country may be competing with imported products, or it may be competing for its inputs with other domestic and foreign purchasers. For example, a Canadian chemical company that did no cross-border business nevertheless found that its profit margin depended directly on the U.S. dollar/Japanese yen exchange rate. The company used coal as an input in its production process, and the Canadian price of coal was heavily influenced by the extent to which the Japanese bought U.S. coal, which in turn depended on the dollar/yen exchange rate.

Although translation exposure need not be managed, it might be useful for a firm to manage its transaction and economic exposures because they affect firm value directly. In most companies, transaction exposure is generally tracked and managed by the office of the corporate treasurer. Economic exposure is difficult to define in operating terms, and very few companies manage it actively. In most companies, economic exposure is generally considered part of the strategic planning process, rather than a treasurer's or finance function.

MULTINATIONAL WORKING-CAPITAL MANAGEMENT

The basic principles of working-capital management for a multinational corporation are similar to those for a domestic firm. However, tax and exchange rate factors are additional considerations for the MNC. For an MNC with subsidiaries in many countries, the optimal decisions in the management of working capital are made by considering the market as a whole. The global or centralized financial decisions for an MNC is superior to the set of independent optimal decisions for the subsidiaries. This is the control problem of the MNC. If the individual subsidiaries make decisions that are best for them individually, the consolidation of such decisions may not be best for the MNC as a whole. To effect global management, sophisticated computerized models—incorporating many variables for each subsidiary—are solved to provide the best overall decision for the MNC.

Before considering the components of working-capital management, we examine two techniques that are useful in the management of a wide variety of working-capital components.

Leading and Lagging

Two important risk-reduction techniques for many working-capital problems are called leading and lagging. Often forward-market and money-market hedges are not available to eliminate exchange risk. Under such circumstances, leading and lagging may be used to reduce exchange risk.

Recall that a net asset (long) position is not desirable in a weak or potentially depreciating currency. If a firm has a net asset position in such a currency, it should expedite the disposal of the asset. The firm should get rid of the asset earlier than it otherwise would have, or *lead*, and convert the funds into assets in a relatively stronger currency. By the same reasoning, the firm should *lag*, or delay the collection against a net asset position in a strong currency. If the firm has a net liability (short) position in the weak currency, then it should delay the payment against the liability, or lag, until the currency depreciates. In the case of an appreciating or strong foreign currency and a net liability position, the firm should lead the payments—that is, reduce the liabilities earlier than it would otherwise have.

These principles are useful in the management of working capital of an MNC. They cannot, however, eliminate the foreign exchange risk. When exchange rates change continuously, it is almost impossible to guess whether or when the currency will depreciate or appreciate. This is why the risk of exchange rate changes cannot be eliminated. Nevertheless, the reduction of risk, or the increased gain from exchange rate changes, via the lead and lag is useful for cash management, accounts-receivable management, and short-term liability management.

Cash Management and Positioning of Funds

Positioning of funds takes on an added importance in the international context. Funds may be transferred from a subsidiary of the MNC in country A to another subsidiary in country B such that the foreign exchange exposure and the tax liability of the MNC as a whole are minimized. It bears repeating that, owing to the global strategy of the MNC, the tax liability of the subsidiary in country A may be greater than it would otherwise have been, but the overall tax payment for all units of the MNC is minimized.

transfer price   The transfer of funds among subsidiaries and the parent company is done by royalties, fees, and transfer pricing. A **transfer price** is the *price a subsidiary or a parent company charges other companies that are part of the MNC for its goods or ser-*

vices. A parent that wishes to transfer funds from a subsidiary in a depreciating-currency country may charge a higher price on the goods and services sold to this subsidiary by the parent or by subsidiaries from strong-currency countries.

INTERNATIONAL FINANCING AND CAPITAL STRUCTURE DECISIONS

OBJECTIVE 7

An MNC has access to many more financing sources than a domestic firm. It can tap not only the financing sources in its home country that are available to its domestic counterparts, but also sources in the foreign countries in which it operates. Host countries often provide access to low-cost subsidized financing to attract foreign investment. In addition, the MNC may enjoy preferential credit standards because of its size and investor preference for its home currency. An MNC may be able to access third-country capital markets—countries in which it does not operate but which may have large, well-functioning capital markets. Finally, an MNC can also access external currency markets: Eurodollar, Eurocurrency, or Asian dollar markets. These external markets are unregulated, and because of their lower spread, can offer very attractive rates for financing *and* for investments. With the increasing availability of interest rate and currency swaps, a firm can raise funds in the lowest-cost maturities and currencies and swap them into funds with the maturity and currency denomination it requires. Because of its ability to tap a larger number of financial markets, the MNC may have a lower cost of capital; and because it may be better able to avoid the problems or limitations of any one financial market, it may have a more continuous access to external finance compared to a domestic company.

Access to national financial markets is regulated by governments. For example, in the United States, access to capital markets is governed by SEC regulations. Access to Japanese capital markets is governed by regulations issued by the Ministry of Finance. Some countries have extensive regulations; other countries have relatively open markets. These regulations may differ depending on the legal residency terms of the company raising funds. A company that cannot use its local subsidiary to raise funds in a given market will be treated as foreign. In order to increase their visibility in a foreign capital market, a number of MNCs are now listing their equities on the stock exchanges of many of these countries.

The external currency markets are predominantly centered in Europe, and about 80 percent of their value is denominated in terms of the U.S. dollar. Thus most external currency markets can be characterized as Eurodollar markets. Such markets consist of an active short-term money market and an intermediate-term capital market with maturities ranging up to 15 years and averaging about 7 to 9 years. The intermediate-term market consists of the Eurobond and the Syndicated Eurocredit markets. Eurobonds are usually issued as unregistered bearer bonds and generally tend to have higher flotation costs but lower coupon rates compared to similar bonds issued in the United States. A Syndicated Eurocredit loan is simply a large-term loan that involves contributions by a number of lending banks.

In arriving at its capital structure decisions, an MNC has to consider a number of factors. First, the capital structure of its local affiliates is influenced by local norms regarding capital structure in that industry and in that country. Local norms for companies in the same industry can differ considerably from country to country. Second, the local affiliate capital structure must also reflect corporate attitudes toward exchange rate and political risk in that country, which would normally lead to higher levels of local debt and other local capital. Third, local affiliate capital structure must reflect home country requirements with regard to the company's consolidated capital structure. Finally, the optimal MNC capital structure should reflect its wider access to financial markets, its ability to diversify economic and political risks, and its other advantages over domestic companies.

BACK TO THE FOUNDATIONS

Investment across international boundaries gives rise to special risks not encountered when investing domestically. Specifically, political risks and exchange rate risk are unique to international investing. Once again, **Axiom 1: The Risk-Return Trade-off—We Won't Take On Additional Risk Unless We Expect to Be Compensated with Additional Return** provides a rationale for evaluating these considerations. Where added risks are present, added rewards are necessary to induce investment.

DIRECT FOREIGN INVESTMENT

An MNC often makes direct foreign investments abroad in the form of plants and equipment. The decision process for this type of investment is very similar to the capital-budgeting decision in the domestic context—with some additional twists. Most real-world capital-budgeting decisions are made with uncertain future outcomes. Recall that a capital-budgeting decision has three major components: the estimation of the future cash flows (including the initial cost of the proposed investment), the estimation of the risk in these cash flows, and the choice of the proper discount rate. We will assume that the NPV criterion is appropriate as we examine (1) the risks associated with direct foreign investment and (2) factors to be considered in making the investment decision that may be unique to the international scene.

Risks in Direct Foreign Investment

Risks in domestical capital budgeting arise from two sources: business risk and financial risk. The international capital-budgeting problem incorporates these risks as well as political risk and exchange risk.

Business Risk and Financial Risk

International business risk is due to the response of business to economic conditions in the foreign country. Thus the U.S. MNC needs to be aware of the business climate in both the United States and the foreign country. Additional business risk is due to competition from other MNCs, local businesses, and imported goods. Financial risk refers to the risks introduced in the profit stream by the firm's financial structure. The financial risks of foreign operations are not very different from those of domestic operations.

Political Risk

Political risk arises because the foreign subsidiary conducts its business in a political system different from that of the home country. Many foreign governments, especially those in the Third World, are less stable than the U.S. government. A change in a country's political setup frequently brings a change in policies with respect to businesses—and especially with respect to foreign businesses. An extreme change in policy might involve nationalization or even outright expropriation of certain busi-

"Ukraine: Not for the Fainthearted"

KIEV, UKRAINE—S.C. Johnson & Son Inc., the $3 billion family-owned company that makes clothes, floor wax, furniture cleaners, bug killers, and air fresheners, has traditionally been challenged by new frontiers.

When the company opened a plant in Britain 80 years ago, it was one of the first American corporations to go abroad. At the end of the cold war, it trailblazed again this time into the uncertain precincts of the Ukraine.

Johnson Wax's experience since 1990—when the company started to make and bottle detergents and furniture polish in a renovated corner of a ramshackle factory on the outskirts of Kiev—helps explain the reluctance of other consumer-products companies to jump in.

A few months after Ukraine joined Russia and Belarus in leaving the crumbling Soviet Union, it introduced a coupon currency to replace the ruble. In relatively short order, the coupons became all but worthless. By late last year, inflation had reached about 100 percent a month, from almost zero two years before. A fierce credit squeeze by the government left wholesalers little money to by Johnson's products. And a government that had initially promised to create a friendly environment for Western investors became encrusted with old style—many say corrupt—former Communists.

Last year, Johnson Wax halved its production from that of 1992. And almost half of 1993's 10 million bottles that came off the assembly line had to be sold in Russia, where the economy, however turbulent, is far stronger than Ukraine's.

A major attraction for Western manufacturers here is low wages. Johnson would like to raise the pay of some workers above the monthly $150 that the best get, but a 92 percent tax rate on earned income above $150 makes it impossible to do so.

Some improvements in everyday life make the difficulty of doing business here a little easier. To make an overseas telephone call took two days several years ago. Now they can be made on the spot. And there are more flights in and out of the country.

But unpredictability prevails. In the last six months, the Ukrainian government has raised or lowered the value-added tax rate three times. Now there are worries that the government might impose an excise tax on supplies coming across the border from Russia. And still another currency is expected, prompting further headaches.

nesses. These are the political risks of conducting business abroad. A business with no investment in plant and equipment is less susceptible to these risks. Some examples of political risk are listed below:

1. Expropriation of plant and equipment without compensation.
2. Expropriation with minimal compensation that is below actual market value.
3. Nonconvertibility of the subsidiary's foreign earnings into the parent's currency—the problem of *blocked funds*.
4. Substantial changes in the laws governing taxation.
5. Governmental controls in the foreign country regarding the sale price of the products, wages, and compensation to personnel, hiring of personnel, making of transfer payments to the parent, and local borrowing.
6. Some governments require certain amounts of local equity participation in the business. Some require that the majority of the equity participation belong to their country.

All these controls and governmental actions introduce risks in the cash flows of the investment to the parent company. These risks must be considered before making the foreign investment decision. The MNC may decide against investing in countries with risks of types 1 and 2. Other risks can be borne—provided that the returns from the foreign investments are high enough to compensate for them. Insurance against some types of political risks may be purchased from private insurance companies or from the U.S. government Overseas Private Investment Corporation. It should be noted that although an MNC cannot protect itself against all foreign political risks, political risks are also present in domestic business.

Exchange Rate Risk

The exposure of the fixed assets is best measured by the effects of the exchange rate changes on the firm's future earnings stream: that being economic exposure rather than translation exposure. For instance, changes in the exchange rate may adversely affect sales by making competing imported goods cheaper. Changes in the cost of goods sold may result if some components are imported and their price in the foreign currency changes because of exchange rate fluctuations. The thrust of these examples is that the effect of exchange rate changes on income statement items should be properly measured to evaluate exchange rate risk. Finally, exchange rate risk affects the dollar-denominated profit stream of the parent company, whether or not it affects the foreign-currency profits.

SUMMARY

OBJECTIVE 1

The growth of our global economy, the increasing number of multinational corporations, and the increase in foreign trade itself underscore the importance of the study of international finance.

OBJECTIVE 2

Exchange rate mechanics are discussed in the context of the prevailing floating rates. Under this system, exchange rates between currencies vary in an apparently random fashion in accordance with the supply and demand conditions in the exchange market. Important economic factors affecting the level of exchange rates include the relative economic strengths of the countries involved, the balance-of-payments mechanism, and the countries' monetary policies. Several important exchange rate terms are introduced. These include the asked and the bid rates, which represent the selling and buying rates of currencies. The direct quote is the units of home currency per unit of foreign currency, and the indirect quote is the reciprocal of the direct quote. Cross-rate computations reflect the exchange rate between two foreign currencies.

OBJECTIVE 3
OBJECTIVE 4

The forward exchange market provides a valuable service by quoting rates for the delivery of foreign currencies in the future. The foreign currency is said to sell at a discount (premium) forward from the spot rate when the forward rate is greater (less) than the spot rate, in direct quotation. In addition, the influences of purchasing-power parity (PPP) and the international Fisher effect (IFE) in determining the exchange rate are discussed. In rational and efficient markets, forward rates are unbiased forecasts of future spot rates that are consistent with the PPP.

OBJECTIVE 5

Exchange rate risk exists because the exact spot rate that prevails on a future date is not known with certainty today. The concept of exchange rate risk is applicable to a wide variety of businesses, including export-import firms and firms involved in making direct foreign investments or international investments in securities. Exchange exposure is a measure of exchange rate risk. There are different ways of measuring the foreign exposure, including the net asset (net liability) measurement. Different strategies are open to businesses to counter the exposure to this risk, including the money-market hedge, the forward-market hedge, futures contracts, and options. Each involves different costs.

OBJECTIVE 6

In discussing working-capital management in an international environment, we find leading and lagging techniques useful in minimizing exchange rate risk and increasing profitability. In addition, funds positioning is a useful tool for reducing exchange rate risk exposure. The MNC may have a lower cost of capital because it has access to a larger set of financial markets than a domestic company. In addition to the home, host, and third-country financial markets, the MNC can tap the rapidly growing external currency markets. In making capital structure decisions, the MNC must consider political and exchange rate risks and host and home country capital structure norms.

OBJECTIVE 7
OBJECTIVE 8

The complexities encountered in the direct foreign investment decision include the usual sources of risk—business and financial—and additional risks associated with fluctuating exchange rates and political factors. Political risk is due to differences in political climates, institutions, and processes between the home country and abroad. Under these conditions, the estimation of future cash flows and the choice of the proper discount rates are more complicated than for the domestic investment situation.

KEY TERMS

Arbitrageur, 512

Asked Rate, 512

Bid-rate, 513

Bid-asked Spread, 513

Buying Rate, 513

Covered-interest Arbitrage, 512

Cross Rate, 513

Direct Quote, 509

Exchange Rate, 508

Exchange Rate Risk, 513

Floating-rate International Currency System, 508

Forward Exchange Contract, 513

Forward-spot Differential, 514

Indirect Quote, 509

Interest Rate Parity Theory, 517

Law of One Price, 519

Multinational Corporation (MNC), 506

Purchasing Power Parity Theory, 518

Selling Rate, 513

Simple Arbitrage, 512

Spot Transactions, 509

Transaction Exposure, 521

Transfer Price, 524

Triangular Arbitrage, 512

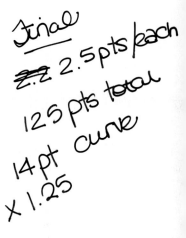

final
2.2 2.5 pts each
125 pts total
14 pt curve
x 1.25

STUDY QUESTIONS

16-1. What additional factors are encountered in international as compared with domestic financial management? Discuss each briefly.

16-2. What different types of businesses operate in the international environment? Why are the techniques and strategies available to these firms different?

16-3. What is meant by *arbitrage profits?*

16-4. What are the markets and mechanics involved in generating (a) simple arbitrage profits, (b) triangular arbitrage profits?

16-5. How do the purchasing power parity, interest rate parity, and the Fisher effect explain the relationships among the current spot rate, the future spot rate, and the forward rate?

16-6. What is meant by (a) exchange risk, (b) political risk?

16-7. How can exchange risk be measured?

16-8. What are the differences between transaction, translation, and economic exposures? Should all of them be ideally reduced to zero?

16-9. What steps can a firm take to reduce exchange risk? Indicate at least two different techniques.

16-10. How are the forward market and the money market hedges affected? What are the major differences between these two types of hedges?

16-11. In the New York exchange market, the forward rate for the Indian currency, the rupee, is not quoted. If you were exposed to exchange risk in rupees, how could you cover your position?

16-12. Compare and contrast the use of forward contracts, futures contracts, and options to reduce foreign exchange exposure. When is each instrument most appropriate?

16-13. Indicate two rocking-capital management techniques that are useful for international businesses to reduce exchange risk and potentially increase profits.

16-14. How do the financing sources available to an MNC differ from those available to a domestic firm? What do these differences mean for the company's cost of capital?

16-15. What risks are associated with direct foreign investment? How do these risks differ from those encountered in domestic investment?

16-16. How is the direct foreign investment decision made? What are the inputs to this decision process? Are the inputs more complicated than those to the domestic investment problem? If so, why?

16-17. A corporation desires to enter a particular foreign market. The DFI analysis indicates that a direct investment in the plant in the foreign country is not profitable. What other course of action can the company take to enter the foreign market? What are the important considerations?

16-18. What are the reasons for the acceptance of a sales office or licensing arrangement when the DFI itself is not profitable?

SELF-TEST PROBLEMS

The data for Self-Test Problem ST–1 are given in the following table:

SELLING QUOTES FOR THE GERMAN MARK IN NEW YORK		
COUNTRY	**CONTRACT**	**$/FOREIGN CURRENCY**
Germany—mark	Spot	.3893
	30-day	.3910
	90-day	.3958

ST–1. You own $10,000. The dollar rate on the German mark is $2.5823/DM. The German mark rate is given in the table above. Are arbitrage profits possible? Set up an arbitrage scheme with your capital. What is the gain (loss) in dollars?

STUDY PROBLEMS

The data for Study Problems 16-1 through 16-6 are given in the following table:

SELLING QUOTES FOR FOREIGN CURRENCIES IN NEW YORK		
COUNTRY	CONTRACT	$/FOREIGN CURRENCY
Canada—dollar	Spot	.8437
	30-day	.8417
	90-day	.8395
Japan—yen	Spot	.004684
	30-day	.004717
	90-day	.004781
Switzerland—franc	Spot	.5139
	30-day	.5169
	90-day	.5315

[handwritten: ¥/$ 130; P/$ 10; 154/P; $1,000 × 10P/$ = 10,000P; 10,000P × 15¥/P = 150,000¥; 150,000¥ × 1$ / 130¥ = $11.53 ; 8437 ; 9368]

16-1. An American business needs to pay (a) 10,000 Canadian dollars, (b) 2 million yen, and (c) 50,000 Swiss francs to businesses abroad. What are the dollar payments to the respective countries? *[handwritten: 25,695 ; 29,188.50]*

16-2. An American business pays $10,000, $15,000, and $20,000 to suppliers in, respectively, Japan, Switzerland, and Canada. How much, in local currencies, do the suppliers receive? *[handwritten: 2,134,920 ; 29,188.50 ; 23,705.88]*

16-3. Compute the indirect quote for the spot and forward Canadian dollar, yen, and Swiss franc contracts.

16-4. The spreads on the contracts as a percent of the asked rates are 2 percent for yen, 3 percent for Canadian dollars, and 5 percent for Swiss francs. Show, in a table similar to the one above, the bid rates for the different spot and forward rates.

16-5. You own $10,000. The dollar rate in Tokyo is 216.6743. The yen rate in New York is given in the previous table. Are arbitrage profits possible? Set up an arbitrage scheme with your capital. What is the gain (loss) in dollars?

16-6. Compute the Canadian dollar/yen and the yen/Swiss franc spot rate from the data in the table above. *[handwritten: C$/¥ = .00555 ; ¥/franc = 109.71839]*

COMPREHENSIVE PROBLEM

For your job as the business reporter for a local newspaper, you are given the assignment of putting together a series of articles on the multinational finance and the international currency markets for your readers. Much recent local press coverage has been given to losses in the foreign exchange markets by JGAR, a local firm that is the subsidiary of Daedlufetarg, a large German manufacturing firm. Your editor would like you to address several specific questions dealing with multinational finance. Prepare a response to the following memorandum from your editor:

TO: Business Reporter

FROM: Perry White, Editor, *Daily Planet*

RE: Upcoming Series on Multinational Finance

In your upcoming series on multinational finance, I would like to make sure you cover several specific points. In addition, before you begin this assignment, I want to make sure we are all reading from the same script, as accuracy has always been the cornerstone of the *Daily Planet*. I'd like a response to the following questions before we proceed:

a. What new problems and factors are encountered in international as opposed to domestic financial management?

b. What does the term *arbitrage* profits mean?

c. What can a firm do to reduce exchange risk?

d. What are the differences between a forward contract, a futures contract, and options?

Use the following data in your response to the remaining questions:

Selling Quotes for Foreign Currencies in New York

Country—Currency	Contract	$/Foreign
Canada—dollar	Spot	.8450
	30-day	.8415
	90-day	.8390
Japan—yen	Spot	.004700
	30-day	.004750
	90-day	.004820
Switzerland—franc	Spot	.5150
	30-day	.5182
	90-day	.5328

e. An American business needs to pay (a) 15,000 Canadian dollars, (b) 1.5 million yen, and (c) 55,000 Swiss francs to businesses abroad. What are the dollar payments to the respective countries?

f. An American business pays $20,000, $5,000, and $15,000 to suppliers in, respectively, Japan, Switzerland, and Canada. How much, in local currencies, do the suppliers receive?

g. Compute the indirect quote for the spot and forward Canadian dollar contract.

h. You own $10,000. The dollar rate in Tokyo is 216.6752. The yen rate in New York is given in the table above. Are arbitrage profits possible? Set up an arbitrage scheme with your capital. What is the gain (loss) in dollars?

i. Compute the Canadian dollar/yen spot rate from the data in the table above.

SELF–TEST SOLUTIONS

SS–1.

The German rate is 2.5823 marks/$1, while the (indirect) New York rate is 1/.3893 = 2.5687 marks/$.

Assuming no transaction costs, the rates between German and New York are out of line. Thus, arbitrage profits are possible.

Step 1: Because the mark is cheaper in Germany, buy $10,000 worth of marks in Germany. The number of marks purchased would be $10,000 × 2.5823 = 25,823 marks

Step 2: Simultaneously sell the marks in New York at the prevailing rate. The amount received upon the sale of the marks would be:

$$25,823 \text{ marks} \times \$.3893/\text{mark} = \$10,052.89$$

net gain is $10,052.89 − $10,000 = $52.89

Changes and Challenges in Finance

Recent Innovations in Risk Management • Finance in the '90s: The Consequences of Financial Innovation in Corporate Restructuring • Recent Innovations in Raising Capital: Hybrid Securities • The Agency Problem: Changes and Challenges • The CAPM and Market Efficiency: The Challenges from Academia

A s problems are uncovered, financial solutions appear. For example, as firms trade more and more internationally, the need to protect sales against undesirable currency fluctuations becomes increasingly important. To deal with this problem, currency options were developed. A currency option entitles its holder to buy or sell Japanese yen, British pounds, German marks, or some other currency at a set price over a specified period. For example, Cessna might use currency options to protect sales on its Citation V aircraft, which are sold in Europe to Swiss customers. Because the Citation V is built in the United States and sold abroad, its costs in labor and materials are based on the dollar. However, as the dollar fluctuates relative to the Swiss franc, so must the sales price in Swiss francs for Cessna to receive the same amount of dollars on each sale in Switzerland.

Problems surface when the value of the Swiss franc falls relative to that of the dollar. For each sale to bring the same amount of dollars back to Cessna, the selling price in Swiss francs would have to be increased. Unfortunately, increased prices may lead to lost sales. To guard against this situation, Cessna may purchase put options on the Swiss franc to cover the anticipated Swiss sales. These puts give Cessna the option to sell or convert Swiss francs into dollars at a present price. If after the put options are purchased, the Swiss franc falls, Cessna could keep its selling prices constant in terms of the Swiss franc and make up for the loss in the currency exchange with the profits on the puts. Conversely, if the value of the Swiss franc rises relative to the value of the dollar, Cessna could lower its Swiss price, sell more aircraft, and still bring home the same dollars per sale—all that would be lost is the price paid for the put options.

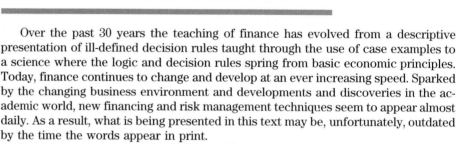

This chapter begins with a look at the dynamic nature of finance: how the financial world views problems as opportunities for innovation. Specifically, we focus on the development of the futures and options markets and their use by financial managers to manage risk, and the increased use of hybrid securities by smaller firms to reduce borrowing costs. The changes and challenges brought about by the wave of restructuring that swept corporate America in the 1980s is also examined. We then turn to the myriad of agency problems encountered in the financial world and the changes taking place right now to address them. Specifically, we will look at changes in executive compensation. Many of these changes are being motivated by academic research and the emergence of active institutional investors. Finally, we will examine some unsettling findings from academic circles dealing with market efficiency and the CAPM.

Over the past 30 years the teaching of finance has evolved from a descriptive presentation of ill-defined decision rules taught through the use of case examples to a science where the logic and decision rules spring from basic economic principles. Today, finance continues to change and develop at an ever increasing speed. Sparked by the changing business environment and developments and discoveries in the academic world, new financing and risk management techniques seem to appear almost daily. As a result, what is being presented in this text may be, unfortunately, outdated by the time the words appear in print.

How do you prepare for a field as dynamic as finance? The answer is to go beyond the answers and understand the logic that drives those answers. This is why the presentation in this text has been crafted around 10 underlying axioms. In this chapter we will examine how the practice of finance is evolving and pay special attention to recent developments in the theory of finance, and in particular to challenges to the use of the CAPM, spawned by discoveries in the academic world. In so doing, you will be provided with a sense of the future along with an appreciation of the assumptions and limitations of the theory of finance as we know it today.

OBJECTIVE 1 — RECENT INNOVATIONS IN RISK MANAGEMENT

In response to the volatile interest rates, commodity prices, and exchange rates of the late 1970s and early 1980s financial managers turned to the futures and options markets for relief. During this period the pace of innovation in these markets was staggering. These new financial instruments provided corporations with a low-cost means of hedging away many types of risk associated with possible price fluctuations. For example, futures and options can be used to eliminate risks associated with price fluctuations on raw materials in addition to risks associated with foreign exchange exposure that might be experienced by a corporation exporting goods to another country.

The development of new tools and techniques we see in the field of risk management is just one example of how dynamic and adaptive the field of finance is. The problems facing financial managers, in effect, become the seeds for innovation. The two areas that have seen the most dramatic change over the past 10 years and will continue to foster innovation are futures and options. For this reason we will now present a brief introduction to each of these areas.

A **futures contract** is a *contract to buy or sell a stated commodity (such as soybeans or corn) or financial claim (such as U.S. Treasury bonds) at a specified price at a specified future time*. It is important to note here that this is a contract that *requires* its holder to buy or sell the asset, regardless of what happens to its value during the interim. The importance of a futures contract is that it can be used by financial managers to lock in the price of a commodity or an interest rate and thereby eliminate one source of risk. For example, if a corporation is planning on issuing debt in the near future and is concerned about a possible rise in interest rates between now and when the debt would be issued, it might sell a U.S. Treasury bond futures contract with the same face value as the proposed debt offering and a delivery date the same as when the debt offering is to occur. Alternatively, with the use of a futures contract, Ralston-Purina or Quaker Oats can lock in the future price of corn or oats whenever they wish. Because a futures contract locks in interest rates or commodity prices, the costs associated with any possible rise in interest rates or commodity prices are completely offset by the profits made by writing the futures interest rate contract. In effect, futures contracts allow the financial manager to lock in future interest and exchange rate or prices for a number of agricultural commodities like corn and oats.

An **option contract** gives its owner the *right to buy or sell a fixed number of shares at a specified price over a limited time*. Although the market for options seems to have a language of its own, there are only two basic types of options: puts and calls. Everything else involves some variation. A **call option** gives its owner the *right to purchase a given number of shares of stock or some other asset at a specified price over a given period*. Thus, if the price of the underlying common stock or asset goes up, a call purchaser makes money. This is essentially the same as a "rain check" or guaranteed price. You have the option to buy something—in this case, common stock—at a set price. In effect, a call option gives you the right to buy, but it is not a promise to buy. A **put option,** on the other hand, gives its owner the *right to sell a given number of shares of common stock or some other asset at a specified price over a given period*. A put purchaser is betting that the price of the underlying common stock or asset will drop. Just as with the call, a put option gives its holder the right to sell the common stock at a set price, but it is not a promise to sell. Because these are just options to buy or sell stock or some other asset, they do not represent an ownership position in the underlying corporation, as does common stock. In fact, there is no direct relationship between the underlying corporation and the option. An option is merely a contract between two investors.

futures contract

option contract

call option

put option

Recent Innovations in the Futures and Options Markets

Recently, four additional variations of the traditional option have appeared: the stock index option, the interest rate option, the foreign currency option, and the Treasury bond futures option. In addition, there has been an explosion in the number and types of new futures contracts that are offered. Although there will undoubtedly be numerous other innovations in this market before you graduate, these additions to the options markets provide insights to the broad range of problems facing the financial manager that can be addressed with options.

Stock Index Options

The options on stock indexes were first introduced on the Chicago Board Options Exchange (CBOE) in 1983 and have since proved extremely popular. Although there are a variety of different index options, based on several different broad stock market indexes and also industry indexes such as a computer industry index, the broader stock market indexes have carried the bulk of the popularity of index options. Whereas the industry-based index options have received a somewhat mixed reception, stock index options, in particular the S&P 100 Index on the CBOE, have proved to be extremely popular. In fact, more than 80 percent of all stock index options trading involve the S&P 100 Index. Currently it accounts for over half of the volume of all option trading and has made the CBOE the second-largest U.S. securities market, with daily trading occasionally reaching nearly 700,000 contracts. (Remember, each contract involves an option on 100 "shares" of the index.)

The reason for this popularity is simple. These options allow portfolio managers and other investors holding broad portfolios to cheaply and effectively eliminate or adjust the market risk of their portfolio. When we talked about systematic and unsystematic risk, we noted that in a large and well-diversified portfolio, unsystematic risk was effectively diversified away, leaving only systematic risk. Thus, the return on a large and well-diversified portfolio was a result of the portfolio's beta and the movement of the market. As a result, because the movements of the market cannot be controlled, portfolio managers periodically attempt to adjust the beta of the portfolio when they think a change in the market's direction is at hand. Index options allow them to make this change without the massive transaction costs that would otherwise be incurred.

Interest Rate Options

Options on 30-year Treasury bonds are also traded on the CBOE. Although the trading appeal of interest rate options is somewhat limited, they do open some very interesting doors to the financial manager. In terms of the insurance and leverage traits, they allow the financial manager to ensure against the effects of future changes in interest rates. We know that as interest rates rise, the market value of outstanding bonds falls; thus, through the purchase of an interest rate put, the market value of a portfolio manager's bonds can be protected. Alternatively, a financial manager who is about to raise new capital through a debt offering and who is worried about a possible rise in interest rates before the offering occurs may purchase an interest rate put. This would have the effect of locking in current interest rates at the maximum level that the firm would have to pay.

Foreign Currency Options

Foreign currency options are the same as the other options we have examined, except the underlying asset is the British pound, the Japanese yen, or some other foreign currency. Although foreign currency options are limited to the Philadelphia Exchange, there is a considerable amount of interest in them largely because of the wide fluctuations foreign currency has had in recent years relative to the dollar. In terms of the insurance traits, these options allow multinational firms to guard against fluctuations in foreign currencies that might adversely affect their operations.

PAUSE AND REFLECT

An option on a Treasury bond future really holds little advantage over an option on a Treasury bond in terms of ability to reduce interest rate risk. Its advantages stem mainly from the great depth of the Treasury bond futures market.

Options on Treasury Bond Futures

Options on Treasury bond futures work the same way as any other option. The only difference between them and other bond options is that they involve the acquisition of a futures position rather than the delivery of actual bonds. To the creative financial manager, they provide a flexible tool to ensure against adverse changes in interest rates while retaining the opportunity to benefit from any favorable interest rate movement that might occur. Although a futures contract establishes an obligation for both parties to buy and sell at a specified price, an option only establishes a right. It is therefore exercised only when it is to the option holder's advantage to do so. A call option on a futures contract does not establish a price obligation, but rather a maximum purchase price. Conversely, a put option on a futures contract is used to establish a minimum selling price. Thus, the buyer of an option on a futures contract can achieve immunization against any unfavorable price movements, whereas the buyer of a futures contract can achieve immunization against any price movements regardless of whether they are favorable or unfavorable.

Introduction of New Futures Contracts

Between January 1991 and December 1995 the Chicago Board of Trade alone approved 85 new futures contracts. These included futures contracts on products like black-tiger shrimp, Brazilian bonds, recycled plastic, electricity, and milk. However, of those 85 new contracts, the success rate was only 20 percent. This flurry of new contracts continued into 1996, where in the first three months of the year 42 new contracts were approved by the Commodities Futures Trading Commission (CFTC), the industry's regulator, compared with 59 for all of the year 1995. As a result of all this activity, Aetna can use the Chicago Board of Trade's catastrophe insurance futures to guard against hurricane losses in Florida, and Hershey's can lock in the prices of both cocoa and milk supplies on the New York Coffee, Sugar, and Cocoa Exchange.

Future Changes and Challenges in the Futures and Options Markets

The growth of the futures and options markets clearly demonstrates that the markets view crises in financial management as opportunities to innovate. The rapid growth of these markets also demonstrates how quickly the tools of the financial manager change. No doubt we will see the same fast-paced innovation in the future; indeed, many of the tools available to you when you enter the workforce have yet to be developed. The financial markets are truly dynamic.

FINANCE IN THE '90S: THE CONSEQUENCES OF FINANCIAL INNOVATION IN CORPORATE RESTRUCTURING

OBJECTIVE 2

Corporate restructuring in the past decade has dramatically affected the perceptions most of us have about business and finance—not to mention the significant change in the number and structure of firms that existed only a few years ago. In the United States alone, the total value of assets changing hands in the past decade was $1.3

trillion. Of the 500 largest industrial corporations in the United States in 1980, 28 percent had been acquired by other firms by 1989. The decade was well-known even to the most casual observer as the period of the **hostile takeover,** meaning that *managers of the acquired firm resisted being taken over by investors who might be less than friendly to the current management.* These years were also characterized by the *use of large amounts of leverage in acquiring other companies;* this process came to be known as a **leveraged buyout (LBO).** In addition, management buyouts (MBOs), in which managers used large amounts of borrowed funds to buy the firms they managed, occurred with increasing frequency. In short, the business world has taken on a new look as a result of the innovation in financial restructuring of the '80s.

In the 1980s, several large investors, such as T. Boone Pickens and Carl Icahn, who came to be known as "corporate raiders," and several of the major investment banking houses became the brokers of the merger and acquisition activities. The pattern became that of acquiring a conglomerate, breaking it up into its individual business units, and selling off the units to large corporations in the same businesses. Several firms created in this process were temporary organizations intended to last only as long as was required to divest the pieces of the acquired firm to other corporations. Any remaining businesses were then offered to the public, especially when the business unit's value had been enhanced by improvements in the firm's operations.

The "decade of the deal" came to an end in the late 1980s, largely because the huge amounts of debt financing used to fund many of the acquisitions dried up. Also, a recession developed, which resulted in some major firms not being able to meet their debt obligations.

What may we conclude about this era of takeovers, a time when Michael Milken and Carl Icahn became household names? Some believe that it was a time of excesses and greed. Hostile takeovers and management buyouts, particularly, have been blamed for a multitude of problems, including massive layoffs. The fear of being taken over by the likes of T. Boone Pickens is thought to have caused managers to reduce significantly their planning horizons. The large debt loads of many of the acquiring and acquired firms have, according to some, increased the instability of the economy and resulted in the general decline of U.S. competitiveness. For these reasons, many states have all but banned hostile takeovers.

Whatever we believe about takeovers during the 1980s, they undoubtedly did include some excesses and greed. After all was said and done, however, the evidence suggests that takeovers during the 1980s represented a return to more specialized and focused firms after years of diversification. Most acquisitions during the latter years involved companies buying other firms in their own lines of business. Most often, firms were taken over, and their various business lines were sold off to different buyers in the same line of business. To a significant extent, hostile takeovers and leveraged buyouts that attracted so much public attention facilitated this process of deconglomeration. Some of the most common objections to takeovers, such as a reduction of competition and cutbacks in employment, investment, and R&D, are not supported by the data.[1]

Although the jury is still out as to the long-term consequences of the 1980s era of acquisitions, the mere fact that the conglomerates failed to deliver as they promised could mean that the performance of many firms as they gain increased focus will improve. We shall see in time.

---

[1]See, for example, Amar Bhide, "The Causes and Consequences of Hostile Takeovers," *Journal of Applied Corporate Finance* (Summer 1989): 36–59.

Mergers and acquisitions are usually justified by management on the grounds that merging diversifies the firm, thus reducing risk. However, it may be that the stockholder can diversify personally with more ease and less expense by buying stock in the two companies. There must be other reasons for the merger.

Why Mergers Might Create Wealth

Clearly, for a merger to create wealth it would have to provide shareholders with something they could not get by merely holding the individual shares of the two firms. Such a requirement is the key to the creation of wealth under the capital asset pricing model (CAPM). Restating the question: What benefits are there to shareholders from holding the stock of a new, single firm that has been created through a merger as opposed to holding stock in the two individual firms prior to their merger? Let's consider some of these benefits.

Tax Benefits

If a merger were to result in a reduction of taxes that is not otherwise possible, then wealth is created by the merger. This can be the case with a firm that has lost money and thus generated tax credits but does not currently have a level of earnings sufficient to use those tax credits. You will recall that losses can be carried back 3 years and forward a total of 15 years. As a result, tax credits that cannot be used and have no value to one firm can take on value when that firm is acquired by another firm that has earnings sufficient enough to employ the tax credits. In addition, a merger allows for previously depreciated assets to be revalued; thus, wealth is created from the tax benefits arising from the increased depreciation associated with this revaluation of assets.

Reduction of Agency Costs

As we know, the agency problem can occur when the management and ownership of the firm are separate. To compensate for the agency problem, stockholders and bondholders impose a premium on funds supplied to the firm to compensate them for any inefficiency in management. A merger, particularly when it results in a holding company or conglomerate organizational form, may reduce the significance of this problem, because top management is created to monitor the management of the individual companies making up the conglomerate. As a result, management of the individual companies can be effectively monitored without any forced public announcement of proprietary information, such as new product information that might aid competitors. If investors recognize this reduction in the agency problem as material, they may provide funds to the firm at a reduced cost, no longer charging as large an "agency problem premium."

Alternatively, it can be argued that the creation of a conglomerate might result in increased agency costs. Shareholders in conglomerates may think they have less control over the firm's managers as a result of the additional layers of management between them and the decision makers. Moreover, the resultant expenditures necessary to monitor conglomerates, because of their multi-industry nature, may give further rise to agency costs.

Free Cash Flow Problem: A Specific Case of the Agency Problem

free cash flow

The "free cash flow" problem was first identified by Michael Jensen in 1986. **Free cash flow** refers to *the operating cash flow in excess of what is necessary to fund all profitable investments available to the firm*—that is, to fund all projects with a positive net present value. As we know from our discussion of shareholder wealth maximization, this free cash flow should be paid out to shareholders; otherwise it would be invested in projects returning less than the required rate of return—in effect, less than shareholders could earn elsewhere.

Unfortunately, managers may not wish to pass these funds to the shareholders because they may think that their power would be reduced. Moreover, if they return these surplus funds, they may be forced to go outside for financing if more profitable investment opportunities are identified at a later date. Certainly, what we are describing here is a form of the agency problem; still, we need to see these actions in the context of the corporate management culture rather than as an attempt by the managers to maintain their own position. That is to say, as economic conditions change, managers who have successfully managed firms over the years of growing markets may have difficulty in adjusting their financial strategies to conditions in which not all cash flows can be invested at the required rate of return. Jensen argues that this was the case in the oil and gas industry in the late 1970s and resulted in much of the merger activity that took place in those markets during that period.[2] A merger can create wealth through allowing the new management to correct this problem by paying this free cash flow to the shareholders in increased dividends or stock repurchases, thus reducing free cash flow and allowing the shareholders to earn a higher return on this excess than would have been earned by the firm.

Economies of Scale

Wealth can also be created in a merger through economies of scale. For example, administrative expenses, including accounting, data processing, or simply top-management costs, may fall as a percentage of total sales as a result of sharing these resources.

The sharing of resources can also lead to an increase in the firm's productivity. For example, if two firms sharing the same distribution channels merge, distributors carrying one product may now be willing to carry the other, thereby increasing the sales outlets for the products. In effect, wealth would be created by the merger of the two firms and shareholders should benefit.

Unused Debt Potential

Some firms simply do not exhaust their debt capacity. If a firm with unused debt potential is acquired, the new management can then increase debt financing and reap the tax benefits associated with the increased debt.

Complementarity in Financial Slack

When cash-rich bidders and cash-poor targets are combined, wealth may be created as a result of the positive NPV projects taken by the merged firm that the cash-poor firm would have passed up. Thus, although these cash-poor firms are selling at a fair

---

[2]Michael C. Jensen, "The Takeover Controversy: Analysis and Evidence," *Midland Corporate Finance Journal* 4, no. 2 (Summer 1986): 6–32.

price, the discounted value of their future cash flow is below their potential price. In effect, a merger allows positive NPV projects to be accepted that would have been rejected if the merger had not occurred.

Removal of Ineffective Management

Any time a merger can result in the replacement of inefficient operations, whether in production or management, wealth should be created. If a firm with ineffective management can be acquired, it may be possible to replace the current management with a more efficient management team, and thereby create wealth. This may be the case with firms that have grown from solely production into production and distribution companies, or R&D firms that have expanded into production and distribution; the managers simply may not know enough about the new aspects of the firm to manage it effectively.

Increased Market Power

The merger of two firms can result in an increase in the market or monopoly power of the two firms. Although this can result in increased wealth, it may also be illegal. The Clayton Act, as amended by the Celler-Kefauver Amendment of 1950, makes any merger illegal that results in a monopoly or substantially reduces competition. The Justice Department and the Federal Trade Commission monitor all mergers to ensure that they do not result in a reduction of competition.

Reduction in Bankruptcy Costs

There is no question that firm diversification, when the earnings from the two firms are less than perfectly positively correlated, can reduce the chance of bankruptcy. The question is whether or not there is any wealth created by such an activity. Quite obviously, in the real world there is a cost associated with bankruptcy. First, if a firm fails, its assets in general cannot be sold for their true economic value. Moreover, the amount of money actually available for distribution to stockholders is further reduced by selling costs and legal fees that must be paid. Finally, the opportunity cost associated with the delays related to the legal process further reduces the funds available to the shareholders. Therefore, because costs are associated with bankruptcy, reduction of the chance of bankruptcy has a very real value to it.

The risk of bankruptcy also entails indirect costs associated with changes in the firm's debt capacity and the cost of debt. As the firm's cash flow patterns stabilize, the risk of default will decline, giving the firm an increased debt capacity and possibly reducing the cost of the debt. Because interest payments are tax deductible, whereas dividends are not, debt financing is less expensive than equity financing. Thus, monetary benefits are associated with an increased debt capacity. These indirect costs of bankruptcy also spread out into other areas of the firm, affecting things like production and the quality and efficiency of management. Firms with higher probabilities of bankruptcy may have a more difficult time recruiting and retaining quality managers and employees because jobs with that firm are viewed as less secure. This in turn may result in less productivity for these firms. In addition, firms with higher probabilities of bankruptcy may have a more difficult time marketing their product because of customer concern over future availability of the product. In short, there are real costs to bankruptcy. If a merger reduces this possibility of bankruptcy, it creates some wealth.

Financial Innovation with Efficiency in Mind: Divestitures or "Reverse Mergers"

Although the mergers and acquisition phenomenon has been a major influence in restructuring the corporate sector, divestitures, or what we might call "reverse mergers," may have become an equally important factor. In fact, preliminary research to date would suggest that we may be witnessing a "new era" in the making—one where the public corporation has become a more efficient vehicle for increasing and maintaining stockholder wealth.[3] Stern Chew calls it the "new math," when he writes that

> a new kind of arithmetic has come into play. Whereas corporate management once seemed to behave as if $2 + 2$ were equal to 5, especially during the conglomerate heyday of the 60's, the wave of reverse mergers seems based on the counter proposition that $5 - 1$ is 5. And the market's consistently positive response to such deals seems to be providing broad confirmation of the "new math."[4]

A successful divestiture allows the firm's assets to be used more efficiently and therefore to be assigned a higher value by the market forces. It essentially eliminates a division or subsidiary that does not fit strategically with the rest of the company; that is, it removes an operation that does not contribute to the company's basic purposes.

The different types of divestitures may be summarized as follows:

1. **Sell-off.** A sell-off is the *sale of a subsidiary, division, or product line by one company to another.* For example, Radio Corporation of America (RCA) sold its finance company and General Electric sold its metallurgical coal business.

   sell-off

2. **Spin-off.** A spin-off involves the *separation of a subsidiary from its parent, with no change in the equity ownership.* The management of the parent company gives up operating control of the subsidiary, but the shareholders retain the same percentage ownership in both firms. New shares representing ownership in the diverted assets are issued to the original shareholders on a pro rata basis.

   spin-off

3. **Liquidation.** A liquidation in this context is not a decision to shut down or abandon an asset. Rather, *the assets are sold to another company, and the proceeds are distributed to the stockholders.*

   liquidation

4. **Going private.** A *company goes private when its stock that has traded publicly is purchased by a small group of investors, and the stock is no longer bought and sold on a public exchange.* The ownership of the company is transferred from a diverse group of outside stockholders to a small group of private investors, usually including the firm's management. The leveraged buyout is a special case of going private. As noted earlier in the chapter, the existing shareholders sell their shares to a small group of investors. The purchasers of the stock use the firm's unused debt capacity to borrow the funds to pay for the stock. Thus, the new investors acquire the firm with little, if any, personal investment. However, the firm's debt ratio may increase by as much as tenfold.

   going private

---

[3]See G. Alexander, P. Benson, and J. Kampmeyer, "Investigating the Valuation Effects of Voluntary Corporate Sell-offs," *Journal of Finance* 39 (1984): 503–17; and D. Hearth, "Voluntary Divestitures and Value," *Financial Management* 14 (1984): 46–62.

[4]Joel M. Stern, and Donald H. Chew, Jr., eds., *The Revolution in Corporate Finance* (New York: Basis Blackwell, 1986), p. 416.

In summary, corporate restructuring does not always mean combining firms. It means structuring the firm in the way that makes the most economic sense. As we have seen here, it can mean either putting firms together or taking them apart.

| RECENT INNOVATIONS IN RAISING CAPITAL: HYBRID SECURITIES | OBJECTIVE 3 |

In the late 1980s, partly in response to several large corporate bankruptcies, the spread between interest rates charged to blue chip and non–blue chip borrowers became quite large. The financial markets attacked the problem through innovation. As a result, in the late 1980s and early 1990s there again was a flurry of innovation in the hybrid debt markets, where conventional debt issues were combined with futures or options. These innovations provided the issuing corporation and the investors purchasing these securities a low-cost method of hedging away interest rate volatility.

To understand many of these innovations it is necessary to understand first what a convertible bond is, as many of these new hybrids are simply variations of the convertible. A brief introduction to convertibles follows. **Convertible debt** is simply a *hybrid security that combines debt or preferred stock with an option on the firm's common stock.* Today, some of the hybrid securities combine debt with options on interest rates, stock indexes, foreign exchange rates, and commodities like silver, oil, and natural gas.

convertible debt

A **convertible security** is a *preferred stock or debt issue that can be exchanged for a specified number of shares of common stock at the will of the owner.* It provides the stable income associated with preferred stock or bonds in addition to the possibility of capital gains associated with common stock. This combination of features has led convertibles to be called "hybrid securities."

convertible security

When the convertible is initially issued, the firm receives the proceeds from the sale, less flotation costs. This is the only time the firm receives any proceeds from issuing convertibles. The firm then treats this convertible as if it were normal preferred stock or debenture, paying dividends or interest regularly. If the security owner wishes to exchange the convertible for common stock, he or she may do so at any time according to the terms specified at the time of issue. The desire to convert generally follows a rise in the price of the common stock. Once the convertible owner trades the convertibles in for common stock, the owner can never trade the stock back for convertibles. From then on the owner is treated as any other common stockholder and receives only common stock dividends.

Innovative Variations on the Convertible: The New Hybrids

Since 1980 the pace of innovative change through the use of hybrid financing has steadily quickened. While convertibles continue to be popular alternatives for raising funds, the new hybrids of today go well beyond traditional convertibles in terms of creativity. For example, in 1986 Pegasus Gold Corporation, a Canadian gold-mining firm, issued Eurobonds with detachable gold options. For the bondholder this issue provided both a traditional straight bond and gold options. If the price of gold rises, the bondholders benefit along with the firm, and, if not, the bondholders still have a straight bond. Structuring the hybrid in this way significantly reduces the interest rate on the bonds. Other hybrid variations include tying the interest payments to a commodity like copper or silver, or having interest payments vary as the creditworthiness of the issuing firm changes. For example, Magma Copper issued bonds in which the interest payment varied with the prevailing price of copper. Presidio Oil linked the interest payment to the price of natural gas, whereas Manufacturer's Hanover Bank issued bonds that provided for increased interest payments to bondholders if their creditworthiness declined. Again, each of these innovations allowed for funds to be raised at a lower cost than would otherwise have been available.

What has caused this burst of innovation in the debt market? It has been brought about by the competitive nature of the financial markets, where the problems businesses face are viewed by the financial markets as opportunities for innovation. In this case it was the increased spread between the interest rates paid by blue chip and less creditworthy corporations that inspired investment bankers to devise the recent wave of hybrids. In short, the less creditworthy firms were looking for a way to make their debt more attractive and therefore reduce its cost, and they found this through the creation of hybrids. In addition, the use of hybrids opened access to the long-term debt markets for some smaller firms that otherwise would not have had access to those markets.

What financial innovations will aid financial managers in raising capital in the future? The answer is that the problems financial managers face, both in an economic and a regulatory sense, will dictate what future financial innovations look like. However, one thing is clear: Very little remains the same in finance for long. Understanding the underlying principles—our 10 axioms—and the factors motivating these financial innovations makes the changes much easier to understand. We will now turn to the agency problem and the changes and challenges brewing in that area.

<table>
<tr><td>OBJECTIVE 4</td><td>THE AGENCY PROBLEM: CHANGES AND CHALLENGES</td></tr>
</table>

If the corporation is to truly maximize shareholder wealth, the interests of the managers and the shareholders must be aligned. In recent years much of the debate on how to resolve the agency problem has centered on how best to structure executive compensation so that managers act in the best interests of shareholders. More recently this debate has erupted into public outrage over large executive salaries. No doubt the controversy over how best to compensate managers and whether managers are overpaid will continue—in fact, it appears the debate is just heating up. After examining this question we will look at a phenomenon generating fewer headlines, but also addressing the agency problem—the emergence of relationship investing and the active investor.

BACK TO THE FOUNDATIONS

In this section we examine two topics related to the agency problem, which is presented in **Axiom 7: The Agency Problem—Managers Won't Work for the Owners Unless It's in Their Best Interest.** First, we examine the executive compensation package that should be used to align the managers' and owners' interests. Second, we look at the emergence of relationship investing, which also serves to control the agency problem by making managers more accountable to owners and allowing managers to take a long-term perspective with respect to investments.

Executive Compensation: The Debate and the Challenge

The recent outcry over the astronomical level of executive salaries has shifted the debate over executive compensation from the academic to the public arena. Much of the public debate was ignited by the disclosure of astronomical salaries of CEOs. For example, in 1995 John F. Welch, Jr. of General Electric had total direct compensation of nearly $22 million. This included restricted stock valued at $11.4 million at the time it was granted, in addition to a $5.3 million gain from exercising stock options. In fact, it was reported by the *Wall Street Journal* that the heads of about 30 major companies received compensation 212 times higher than the pay of the average American worker. This ratio of executive pay to worker pay is up nearly fivefold since 1965, when this ratio was 44 times.

All of this has sharpened the focus on excessive executive pay and has prompted proposals designed to cap CEO salaries. In fact, the Revenue Reconciliation Act of 1993 denies the deduction for certain compensation in excess of $1 million per year paid by a publicly traded corporation to the CEO and the four other most highly compensated officers beginning in 1994. Interestingly, compensation linked to productivity, as well as tax-qualified retirement plan contributions and certain fringe benefits, are excluded from the limit. To fully understand this debate and the changes it will bring in the 1990s, we must first understand how an executive compensation package should ideally be designed.

The purpose of an executive compensation plan is to align managerial behavior with shareholder objectives. Without such a plan the managers, regardless of how skilled they are, may simply seek to maximize their own personal wealth and perk consumption. The key to aligning managerial behavior and shareholders' objectives is to tie managerial compensation to changes in shareholder wealth within a plan that is easy to monitor. The plan should curb managers' accumulation of excessive and unnecessary perquisites and incorporate a long-term time horizon that matches that of the shareholders while maintaining shareholders' and managers' risk.

Perhaps the most common method of linking pay to performance is through stock option plans. With stock option plans the managers are given long-term call options on the company's common stock. As a result, the managers' compensation is tied directly to the returns received by common shareholders. In addition, the incentives provided by options are long-term. One criticism of such a plan is that stock price movements are not all caused by the managers' decisions, but instead may be caused by some underlying market movement. This has led some executive compensation packages to be based on relative stock performance. Another criticism of using stock options to compensate managers comes from the popular press and is that such packages lead to executive salaries that simply are too high. While citing individuals like Walt Disney's Michael Eisner, who in 1997 signed a 10-year contract estimated to be worth between $195 million and $771 million[5], the press many times overlooks the enormous gains in shareholder wealth that these managers oversaw for their shareholders.

Interestingly, although there are abuses in executive compensation, on average executive compensation increases only about $3 for every 1,000 increase in shareholder wealth.[6] Moreover, as the case of Eisner clearly demonstrates, pay for performance does work, and when the executive does an exceptional job, the pay will

---

[5]For further analysis of the relationship between executive compensation and performance, see Michael C. Jensen, "Performance Pay and Top-Management Incentives," *Journal of Political Economy* 98, no. 2 (1990): 225–64.

[6]Paul Farhi, "Disney Chief May Reap $771 Million From Stock Options," *Washington Post*, February 22, 1997, page D1.

be very high. A high level of compensation can result from a pay-for-performance system in which the executive has performed extremely well, or it can be the result of the agency problem, where the executive is taking advantage of the system. Keep in mind that an executive compensation committee, appointed by the firm's board of directors, generally recommends the CEO's compensation package. Also keep in mind the board of directors, although elected by the shareholders, is generally nominated for election by the CEO and thus may be more sympathetic to the CEO's desires than to the shareholders' best interests. This opens the door for "good old boy" networks to take care of their own and set up a compensation package that rewards, regardless of performance, without attempting to align managers' and shareholders' interests. It is this lack of control and monitoring of the CEO that leads to the agency problem. Still, the debate continues over how best to structure executive compensation packages to eliminate the agency problem. It is important to you as a student of finance to realize the significance of this debate and that it focuses on the elimination of the agency problem. It takes on importance because our goal of maximization of shareholder wealth cannot be realized if managerial behavior is not aligned with shareholder objectives.

Relationship Investing: The Emergence of the Active Investor

Another way in which the agency problem is being addressed is through relationship investing or the emergence of the active investor. Since the 1930s, managerial holding of common stock has declined dramatically, falling from roughly 3 percent to less than .03 percent today. Finally, the pendulum appears to be swinging the other way. Not only have management buyouts (MBOs) led to increased managerial ownership, but pensions, mutual funds, and large investors have increased their monitoring of corporate dealings. Some investors are taking large long-term positions in companies and, in return, are gaining a greater say in what management does and how it operates.

To those staking out large long-term positions in corporations, the advantages are twofold. First, it allows the firm to take on a long-term perspective with regard to investments. For a number of years CEOs have complained about the short-term outlook of investors. However, if the shareholders take on a long-term perspective and a patient attitude with respect to expectations, management may be able to focus on the long term, with the result being an increase in profits, productivity, and competitiveness.

The second advantage gained from relationship investing is increased manager accountability. This results from increased monitoring by large investors who have taken long-term ownership positions in the firm. Unfortunately, the board of directors does not do a good job of monitoring the behavior of the managers. Although shareholders vote for the corporate board of directors (generally through proxy voting), who in turn hire and fire management, as mentioned earlier, the system really works the other way around. In reality, management selects both the issues and the board of director nominees. Then management distributes the proxy ballots to the shareholders. Thus, the shareholders are, in effect, offered a slate of nominees selected by management from which to choose. The result is that management effectively selects the directors, who then may have more allegiance to the managers than to the shareholders. This sets up the potential for agency problems in which a divergence of interests between managers and shareholders is allowed to exist, with the board of directors not monitoring the managers on behalf of the shareholders as they should. During the 1992 presidential campaign Ross Perot highlighted this problem in describing his dealings with the General Motors board of directors, which he referred to as the CEO's "pet rocks."

Is relationship investing working? It appears that the regular, ongoing monitoring it affords, along with the long-term perspective it allows, does, in fact, work. Examples of relationship investing at work and succeeding include Avon, Sears, and Eastman Kodak. Where will all this lead? In the next decade we will no doubt see an increase in relationship investing. After all, it is a logical way to improve internal corporate control and make the boards more responsive to shareholder objectives rather than managerial objectives, thereby allowing managers to take a long-term perspective on investments. There is no question that the benefits from controlling the agency problem are enormous. Therefore, large shareholders will surely continue their efforts to ensure their voices are heard.

THE CAPM AND MARKET EFFICIENCY: THE CHALLENGES FROM ACADEMIA

OBJECTIVE 5

During the 1970s and 1980s the capital asset pricing model (CAPM) and the concept of market efficiency gained increased acceptance in the corporate world as a result of being relentlessly pushed in college classrooms across America. However, since the stock market crash of 1987, the CAPM has come under increasing attack from many of those who had championed its use just a few years earlier. Given the widespread use of the CAPM, we should become familiar with these criticisms; moreover, we should understand the assumptions and limitations surrounding its use. It does not appear that this problem, and the passionate debate it engenders, will go away soon. It is just one more example of the dynamic nature of financial theory and how important it is to understand its underlying principles.

BACK TO THE FOUNDATIONS

Much of the debate over the CAPM centers on how best to measure risk in the risk-return trade-off presented in **Axiom 1: The Risk-Return Trade-off—We Won't Take On Additional Risk Unless We Expect to Be Compensated with Additional Return.** The debate over the validity of the CAPM has taken on the trappings of an academic holy war. Although it may take some time for the field of finance to arrive at a consensus, you should be familiar with the limitations and uncertainties surrounding the CAPM.

The CAPM Debate: Beta Is Dead—No It's Not—Is Too!

In Chapter 8 we introduced the CAPM controversy that erupted in 1992 when Eugene Fama and Kenneth French of the University of Chicago published the findings of an exhaustive study. The study concluded over the past 50 years that beta, which is the CAPM's measure of systematic risk, has not been related to returns. In effect, the risk-return relationship predicted by the CAPM has not held for the past 50 years. To say the least, this is a disturbing finding, in particular to individuals who have for years been supporting the CAPM. It came on the heels of findings that investors may overreact to some announcements, and other studies that indicate the markets may be much more complex than presented by the CAPM. In fact, markets and prices may move based on nonlinear relationships, with bubbles building and eventually bursting. The bottom line is that the process of stock valuation may be much more complex than the CAPM states—in fact, so complex that valuation may be incomprehensible to all but a few. Given the importance of this debate, we will take a closer look at it and its implications.

Where does this leave us? First, the basic risk-return trade-off presented in **Axiom 1** still holds; we just can't be sure that beta is a reasonable way to measure risk. We know that according to the CAPM, systematic risk is the only relevant type of risk. However, as we saw earlier, lifting the assumption of no bankruptcy costs makes unsystematic risk relevant. Thus, although it is important to have a conceptual understanding of the CAPM, this understanding is virtually worthless without an understanding of the assumptions and limitations of the model. Whether the criticisms of the CAPM hold up and whether the CAPM continues to be used or is replaced by a newer alternative only time will tell. In response to the Fama and French allegations, two lines of attack have sprung up. The first involves refinements to the empirical research methods used by Fama and French.[7] Using different empirical techniques and looking at different time periods, these responses find evidence of a risk-return relationship that Fama and French found absent. The second line of attack against the Fama and French allegations involves a theoretical argument offered by Richard Roll and Stephen Ross. They contend that the findings by Fama and French indicate that either the market portfolio used by Fama and French in their testing may not have been efficient, or that a relationship between betas and returns were absent.[8] Unfortunately, we cannot tell which.

So what are we to conclude? Is beta dead? At the very least the latest salvo of criticism has forced the academic community to come to grips with the fundamental shortcomings of the CAPM. The model, like all models that attempt to explain complex real-world phenomena using simplifying assumptions, is an abstraction and does not "fit the facts" as to the way the world works. Does this mean the model lacks usefulness? We think not. The model points to the need to diversify and identifies the source of the market risk premium as being tied to the risk of the security that cannot be diversified away. Is the model a complete guide to the underlying determinants of the risk-return trade-off? Probably not. We know that bankruptcy risk is ignored by the CAPM, and this risk is a significant fact of life in the way investors evaluate and value securities. Then, just how useful is the model? We are reminded by the results of Fama and French that the CAPM is, at best, only a crude approximation of the relationship between risk and return. Thus, users are reminded to treat their beta estimates and the corresponding market-risk premium estimates with great care. Perhaps we should use only one decimal place rather than six for our CAPM-based cost-of-capital estimates. In summary, because the CAPM provides quantifiable insights into the risk-return trade-off, it will continue to be used in the absence of a workable alternative understandable to managers, but should only be used mindful of its limitations and underlying assumptions. In the next several years you will see the debate over the CAPM continue to rage—again, an example of the dynamic nature of the discipline of finance.

---

[7]See Yakov Amihud, Bent Christensen, and Haim Mendelson, "Further Evidence on the Risk-Return Relationship," working paper, New York University, 1992; Louis Chan and Josef Lakonishok, "Are the Reports of Beta's Death Premature?" working paper, University of Illinois, Champaign-Urbana, 1992; and S. P. Kothari J. Shankin, and R. Sloan, "Another Look at the Cross-Section of Expected Stock Returns," working paper, University of Rochester, 1992.

[8]See Richard Roll and Stephen A. Ross, "On the Cross-Sectional Relationship Between Expected Returns and Betas, Working Paper (University of California at Los Angeles, July 8, 1992).

This section relates to **Axiom 6: Efficient Capital Markets—The Markets Are Quick and the Prices Are Right** and presents a challenge to that axiom. It issues a warning that there may be much more going on in the capital markets than we understand now. Because there is no final answer at this time, we should be aware of the complexities and uncertainties involved in valuing assets in the capital markets.

Market Efficiency and the Crash of 1987

Market efficiency implies that stock price movements respond instantaneously and in an unbiased manner to new information, and that as a result stock prices "fully reflect" all relevant information. However, if stock prices truly reflect the value of the common stock, how could the stock market drop by 23 percent in one day, with a 16.5 percent decline taking place in 2 hours and 45 minutes? Certainly the crash of 1987 caused concern to those financial economists who like to view the stock market as a place of orderly and efficient pricing. Exactly why the market dropped as quickly and dramatically as it did may never be known with certainty. But one theory that has gained considerable backing is that stock prices had deviated from their true value and the crash was a permanent correction, returning prices to their true economic value. This theory asserts that market bubbles exist. That is, prices continue to climb past their economic value—the present value of the future cash flows—with overvaluation supported by the continued rise in prices and the expectation that more price rises will follow. Thus, investors invest in stocks not because of their underlying value but because "stocks are a good investment and they're going to go up in price." As a result, price increases become self-fulfilling. Investors think prices will rise further, so they buy stock, which pushes the stock price even higher. Eventually the market can no longer support these explosive and unjustified stock price increases, and the stock price increases slow down. This, in turn, causes investors to question whether future stock price increases will continue, thus making the future of the bubble more uncertain. Finally, when a news event causes the bubble to burst, prices drop to their economically justified level, or even lower initially, as investors overreact to the drop. Although this scenario seems to describe what happened during October 1987, it is hard to prove scientifically whether a bubble actually existed. Still, early evidence supports the bubble hypothesis.[9] No doubt in the next several years there will be more explanations offered as to what took place and why, but given that there is still no consensus about what caused the crash of 1929, it is not surprising that an explanation has not been found for the crash of 1987.

Other signals indicate there are perhaps pockets of pricing inefficiency in the stock market. For example, researchers have found that small firms, firms with low price-earnings ratios, and firms that attract less analyst attention tend to outperform the market. In addition, researchers have found there are a number of calendar effects. That is, higher returns can be generated by purchasing stocks at particular

---

[9]See Richard Roll, "The International Crash of 1987," in Rishard J. Barro et al. (eds.), *Black Monday and the Future of Financial Markets* (Homewood, IL: Dow Jones–Irwin, 1989).

times. Unfortunately, these pricing inefficiencies are quite interrelated and the problem of disentangling them continues.

In the next decade there will be continued attacks on the concept of market efficiency, with many of these attacks centering on the existence of pricing bubbles, questioning the rationality of investors. What is becoming evident is that there is a lot going on in the stock market. Although we can feel comfortable that security pricing is guided by the present value principles presented in this text, the process of security pricing is far from being completely understood. This makes it even more important that you have an understanding of the principles that guide us and the limitations of what we know about the pricing of assets. Here again is an area of finance where our understanding continues to evolve.

SUMMARY

OBJECTIVE 1

This chapter examines the dynamic nature of finance: how the financial world views problems as opportunities for innovation. We first examine the development of the futures and options markets and their use by financial managers to manage risk. A futures contract is a contract to buy or sell a stated commodity (such as soybeans or corn) or financial claim (such as U.S. Treasury bonds) at a specified price at some future specified time. A future contract *requires* its holder to buy or sell the asset, regardless of what happens to its value during the interim, and can be used to lock in the price of a commodity or an interest rate and thereby eliminate one source of risk.

A call option gives its owner the right to purchase a given number of shares of stock or some other asset at a specified price over a given period. A put, on the other hand, gives its owner the right to sell a given number of shares of common stock or some other asset at a specified price over a given period.

OBJECTIVE 2

The assertion that merger activity creates wealth for the shareholder cannot be maintained with certainty. Only if the merger provides something that the investor cannot do on his or her own can a merger or acquisition be of financial benefit.

A divestiture represents a variety of ways to let go of a portion of the firm's assets. It has become an important vehicle in restructuring the corporation into a more efficient operation.

OBJECTIVE 3

There have been dramatic innovations in methods of raising capital in recent years, particularly through the use of hybrid securities. To understand many of these innovations it is necessary to understand what a convertible bond is, because many of these new hybrids are variations of the convertible. Convertible debt is a hybrid security that combines debt or preferred stock with an option on the firm's common stock. Today, some hybrid securities combine debt with options on interest rates, stock indexes, foreign exchange rates, and commodities like silver, oil, and natural gas. This surge of innovation in the debt market has been caused by the competitive nature of the financial markets, where the problems businesses face are seen as opportunities for innovation by the financial markets.

OBJECTIVE 4

In recent years the debate on how to resolve the agency problem has centered on the question of how best to structure executive compensation so that managers act in the best interests of shareholders. The purpose of an executive compensation plan is to align managerial behavior with shareholder objectives. Without such a plan the managers, regardless of how skilled they are, may simply seek to maximize their own personal wealth. A common method of linking pay to performance is through stock option plans. Relationship investing is another way of addressing the agency problem. With relationship investing, investors take large long-term positions in companies and gain a greater say in what management does and how it operates. To those staking out large long-term positions in corporations, the advantages are two-fold: It allows the firm to take on a long-term perspective with respect to investments, and it increases manager accountability by allowing close and constant monitoring of them.

During the 1970s and 1980s the capital asset pricing model and the concept of market efficiency gained increased acceptance in the corporate world. However, since the stock market crash of 1987, the capital asset pricing model, with its beta as its measure of systematic risk, has come under attack from many who had earlier championed its use. These attacks have focused on the CAPM and the concept of market efficiency. Whether the criticisms of the CAPM hold up and whether the CAPM continues to be used or is replaced by a newer alternative remains to be seen. There does not seem to be a workable alternative today that is understandable to managers. Thus, in that the CAPM provides quantifiable insights into the risk-return trade-off, it will continue to be used, but with awareness of its limitations and assumptions.

Certainly the crash of 1987 has upset those financial economists who see the stock market as orderly and price efficient. Why the market dropped so quickly and dramatically may never be known with certainty. One theory with considerable backing is that stock prices had deviated from their true value and the crash was a permanent correction, returning prices to their true economic value. This theory says market bubbles exist. Moreover, other signals suggest there are pockets of pricing inefficiency in the stock market. Although we can confidently maintain that security pricing is guided by the present value principles presented in this text, the process of security pricing is far from being clearly understood. All this makes it important that you understand the principles and limitations of pricing assets and be prepared for change.

KEY TERMS

Call Option, 535

Convertible Debt, 543

Convertible Security, 543

Free Cash Flow, 540

Futures Contract, 535

Going Private, 542

Hostile Takeover, 538

Leveraged Buyout (LBO), 538

Liquidation, 542

Option Contract, 535

Put Option, 535

Sell-off, 542

Spin-off, 542

STUDY QUESTIONS

17-1. What is the difference between a futures contract and an option contract?

17-2. Describe a situation in which a financial manager might use commodity futures. Assume that during the period following the transaction the price of that commodity went up. Describe what happened. Then assume that the price of that commodity went down. Now what happened?

17-3. Describe a situation in which a financial manager might use interest rate futures. Assume that during the period following the transaction the interest rates went up. Describe what happened. Then assume that interest rates went down following the transaction. Now what happened?

17-4. Define *call option.*

17-5. Define *put option.*

17-6. Why might merger activity create wealth?

17-7. Explain the different types of divestitures.

17-8. Convertible bonds generally carry lower coupon interest rates than do nonconvertible bonds. If this is so, does it mean that the cost of capital on convertible bonds is lower than on nonconvertible bonds? Why or why not?

17-9. What caused the recent flurry of innovation in the debt market?

17-10. Why is it important to pay attention to the way executives are compensated?

17-11. What advantage can be gained from relationship investing?

17-12. What does the existence of market bubbles mean for the concept of market efficiency?

COMPREHENSIVE PROBLEM

For your job as the business reporter for a local newspaper, you are given the task of putting together a series of articles on the changing financial markets for your readers. Much recent local press coverage has been given to the dangers and losses that some firms have experienced recently in those markets. Your editor would like you to address several specific questions in addition to demonstrating the use of futures contracts and options and applying them to several problems.

Please prepare your response to the following memorandum from your editor:

TO: Business Reporter

FROM: Perry White, Editor, *Daily Planet*

RE: Upcoming Series on the Changes in Finance

In your upcoming series on the Changes in Finance, I would like to make sure you cover several specific points. In addition, before you begin this assignment I want to make sure we are all reading from the same script, as accuracy has always been the cornerstone of the *Daily Planet*. As such I'd like a response to the following questions before we proceed:

a. What opportunities do the derivative securities markets (i.e., the futures and options markets) provide to the financial manager?

b. When might a firm become interested in purchasing interest rate futures? Foreign exchange futures? Stock index futures?

c. What can a *firm* do to reduce exchange rate risk?

d. How would Treasury bond futures and options on Treasury bond futures differ?

e. What is an option on a futures contract? Give an example of one and explain why it exists.

f. Why might merger activities create wealth?

g. What is a convertible security?

h. Why has the agency problem been in the news lately?

i. What are market bubbles and how do they relate to the concept of market efficiency?

APPENDIX A

Using a Calculator

As you prepare for a career in business, the ability to use a financial calculator is essential, whether you are in the finance division or the marketing department. For most positions, it will be assumed that you can use a calculator in making computations that at one time were simply not possible without extensive time and effort. The following examples let us see what is possible, but they represent only the beginning of using the calculator in finance.

With just a little time and effort, you will be surprised at how much you can do with the calculator, such as calculating a stock's beta, or determining the value of a bond on a specific day given the exact date of maturity, or finding net present values and internal rates of return, or calculating the standard deviation. The list is almost endless.

In demonstrating how calculators may make our work easier, we must first decide which calculator to use. The options are numerous and largely depend on personal preference. We have chosen the Texas Instruments BAII Plus.

We will limit our discussion to the following issues:

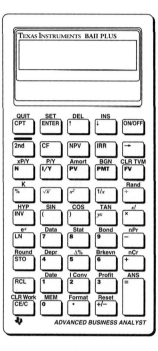

I. Introductory Comments
II. An Important Starting Point
III. Calculating Table Values for:
    A. Appendix B (Compound sum of $1)
    B. Appendix C (Present value of $1)
    C. Appendix D (Sum of an annuity of $1 for n periods)
    D. Appendix E (Present value of an annuity of $1 for n periods)
IV. Calculating Present Values
V. Calculating Future Values (Compound sum)
VI. Calculating the Number of Payments or Receipts
VII. Calculating the Payment Amount
VIII. Calculating the Interest Rate
IX. Bond Valuation
    A. Computing the value of a bond
    B. Calculating the yield to maturity of a bond
X. Computing the Net Present Value and Internal Rate of Return
    A. Where future cash flows are equal amounts in each period (annuity)
    B. Where future cash flows are unequal amounts in each period

I. Introductory Comments

In the examples that follow, you are told (1) which keystrokes to use, (2) the resulting appearance of the calculator display, and (3) a supporting explanation.

The keystrokes column tells you which keys to press. The keystrokes shown in a white box tell you to use one of the calculator's dedicated or "hard" keys. For example, if $+/-$ is shown in the keystrokes instruction column, press that key on the keyboard of the calculator. To use a function printed in a shaded box above a dedicated key, always press the shaded key 2nd first, then the function key.

II. An Important Starting Point

Example: You want to display four numbers to the right of the decimal.

KEYSTROKES	DISPLAY	EXPLANATION
2nd		
FORMAT	DEC =	
4 ENTER	DEC = 4.0000	Sets display to show four numbers to the right of the decimal
CE/C CE/C	0.0000	Clears display

Example: You want to display two payments per year to be paid at the end of each period.

KEYSTROKES	DISPLAY	EXPLANATION
2nd		
P/Y	P/Y =	
2 ENTER	P/Y = 2.0000	Sets number of payments per year at 2
2nd		
BGN	END	Sets timing of payment at the end of each period
CE/C CE/C	0.0000	Clears display

III. Calculating Table Values

A. The compound sum of $1 (Appendix B)

Example: What is the table value for the compound sum of $1 for 5 years at a 12 percent annual interest rate?

KEYSTROKES	DISPLAY	EXPLANATION
2nd		
P/Y	P/Y =	
1 ENTER	P/Y = 1.0000	Sets number of payments per year at 1
2nd		
BGN	END	Sets timing of payment at the end of each period
CE/C CE/C	0.0000	Clears display
2nd		
CLR TVM	0.0000	Clears TVM variables
1 +/− PV	PV = −1.0000	Stores initial $1 as a negative present value. Otherwise the answer will appear as negative.
5 N	N = 5.0000	Stores number of periods
12 I/Y	I/Y = 12.0000	Stores interest rate
CPT FV	FV = 1.7623	Table value

III. Calculating Table Values (continued)

B. The present value of $1 (Appendix C)

Example: What is the table value for the present value of $1 for 8 years at a 10 percent annual interest rate?

KEYSTROKES	DISPLAY	EXPLANATION
2nd		
P/Y	P/Y =	
1 ENTER	P/Y = 1.0000	Sets number of payments per year at 1
2nd		
BGN	END	Sets timing of payment at the end of each period
CE/C CE/C	0.0000	Clears display
2nd		
CLR TVM	0.0000	Clears TVM variables
1 +/− FV	FV = −1.0000	Stores future amount as negative value
8 N	N = 8.0000	Stores number of periods
10 I/Y	I/Y = 10.0000	Stores interest rate
CPT PV	PV = 0.4665	Table value

C. The sum of an annuity of $1 for *n* periods (Appendix D)

Example: What is the table value for the compound sum of an annuity of $1 for 6 years at a 14 percent annual interest rate?

KEYSTROKES	DISPLAY	EXPLANATION
2nd		
P/Y	P/Y =	
1 ENTER	P/Y = 1.0000	Sets number of payments per year at 1
2nd		
BGN	END	Sets timing of payment at the end of each period
CE/C CE/C	0.0000	Clears display
2nd		
CLR TVM	0.0000	Clears TVM variables
1 +/− PMT	PMT = −1.0000	Stores annual payment (annuity) as a negative number. Otherwise the answer will appear as a negative.
6 N	N = 6.0000	Stores number of periods
14 I/Y	I/Y = 14.0000	Stores interest rate
CPT FV	FV = 8.5355	Table value

III. Calculating Table Values (continued)

D. The present value of an annuity of $1 for *n* periods (Appendix E)

Example: What is the table value for the present value of an annuity of $1 for 12 years at 9 percent annual interest rate?

KEYSTROKES	DISPLAY	EXPLANATION
2nd		
P/Y	P/Y =	
1 ENTER	P/Y = 1.0000	Sets number of payments per year at 1
2nd		
BGN	END	Sets timing of payment at the end of each period
CE/C CE/C	0.0000	Clears display
2nd		
CLR TVM	0.0000	Clears TVM variables
1 +/− PMT	PMT = −1.0000	Stores annual payment (annuity) as a negative number. Otherwise the answer will appear as a negative.
12 N	N = 12.0000	Stores number of periods
9 I/Y	I/Y = 9.0000	Stores interest rate
CPT PV	PV = 7.1607	Table value

IV. Calculating Present Values

Example: You are considering the purchase of a franchise of quick oil-change locations, which you believe will provide an annual cash flow of $50,000. At the end of 10 years, you believe that you will be able to sell the franchise for an estimated $900,000. Calculate the maximum amount you should pay for the franchise (present value) in order to realize at least an 18 percent annual yield.

KEYSTROKES	DISPLAY	EXPLANATION
2nd		
BGN	END	Sets timing of payment at the end of each period
CE/C CE/C	0.0000	Clears display
2nd		
CLR TVM	0.0000	Clears TVM variables
10 N	N = 10.0000	Stores *n*, the holding period
18 I/Y	I/Y = 18.0000	Stores *i*, the required rate of return
50,000 PMT	PMT = 50,000.0000	Stores PMT, the annual cash flow to be received
900,000 FV	FV = 900,000.0000	Stores FV, the cash flow to be received at the end of the project
CPT PV	PV = −396,662.3350	The present value, given a required rate of return of 18 percent. (Note: The present value is displayed with a minus sign since it represents cash paid out.)

V. Calculating Future Values (Compound Sum)

Example: If you deposit $300 a month (at the beginning of each month) into a new account that pays 6.25 percent annual interest compounded monthly, how much will you have in the account after 5 years?

KEYSTROKES	DISPLAY	EXPLANATION
2nd BGN	END	Sets timing of payment at the end of each period
2nd SET	BGN	Sets timing of payments to beginning of each period
2nd P/Y	P/Y =	
12 ENTER	P/Y = 12.0000	Sets 12 payments per year
CE/C CE/C	0.0000	Clears display
2nd CLR TVM	0.0000	Clears TVM variables
60 N	N = 60.0000	Stores n, the number of months for the investment
6.25 I/Y	I/Y = 6.2500	Stores i, the annual rate
300 +/− PMT	PMT = −300.0000	Stores PMT, the monthly amount invested (with a minus sign for cash paid out)
CPT FV	FV = 21,175.7613	The future value after 5 years

VI. Calculating the Number of Payments or Receipts

Example: If you wish to retire with $500,000 saved, and can only afford payments of $500 each month, how long will you have to contribute toward your retirement if you can earn a 10 percent return on your contributions?

KEYSTROKES	DISPLAY	EXPLANATION
2nd BGN	BGN	Verifies timing of payment at the beginning of each period
2nd P/Y	P/Y = 12.0000	
12 ENTER	P/Y = 12.0000	Sets 12 payments per year
CE/C CE/C	0.0000	Clears display
2nd CLR TVM	0.0000	Clears TVM variables
10 I/Y	I/Y = 10.0000	Stores i, the interest rate
500 +/− PMT	PMT = −500.0000	Stores PMT, the monthly amount invested (with a minus sign for cash paid out)

VI. Calculating the Number of Payments or Receipts (continued)

500,000 FV	FV = 500,000.0000	The value we want to achieve
CPT N	N = 268.2539	Number of months (since we considered monthly payments) required to achieve our goal

VII. Calculating the Payment Amount

Example: Suppose your retirement needs were $750,000. If you are currently 25 years old and plan to retire at age 65, how much will you have to contribute each month for retirement if you can earn 12.5 percent on your savings?

KEYSTROKES	DISPLAY	EXPLANATION
2nd BGN	BGN	Verifies timing of payment at the beginning of each period
2nd P/Y	P/Y = 12.0000	
12 ENTER	P/Y = 12.0000	Sets 12 payments per year
CE/C CE/C	0.0000	Clears display
2nd CLR TVM	0.0000	Clears TVM variables
12.5 I/Y	I/Y = 12.5000	Stores i, the interest rate
480 N	N = 480.0000	Stores n, the number of periods until we stop contributing (40 years × 12 months/year = 480 months)
750,000 FV	FV = 750,000.0000	The value we want to achieve
CPT PMT	PMT = −53.8347	Monthly contribution required to achieve our ultimate goal (shown as negative since it represents cash paid out)

VIII. Calculating the Interest Rate

Example: If you invest $300 at the end of each month for 6 years (72 months) for a promised $30,000 return at the end, what interest rate are you earning on your investment?

KEYSTROKES	DISPLAY	EXPLANATION
2nd BGN	BGN	Sets timing of payments to beginning of each period
2nd SET	END	Sets timing of payments to end of each period
2nd P/Y	P/Y = 12.0000	
12 ENTER	P/Y = 12.0000	Sets 12 payments per year

VIII. Calculating the Interest Rate (continued)

Keystrokes	Display	Explanation
CE/C CE/C	0.0000	Clears display
2nd CLR TVM	0.0000	Clears TVM variables
72 N	N = 72.0000	Stores *n*, the number of deposits (investments)
300 +/− PMT	PMT = −300.0000	Stores PMT, the monthly amount invested (with a minus sign for cash paid out)
30,000 FV	FV = 30,000.0000	Stores the future value to be received in 6 years
CPT I/Y	I/Y = 10.5892	The annual interest rate earned on the investment

IX. Bond Valuation

A. Computing the value of a bond

Example: Assume the current date is January 1, 1993, and that you want to know the value of a bond that matures in 10 years and has a coupon rate of 9 percent (4.5 percent semiannually). Your required rate of return is 12 percent.

Keystrokes	Display	Explanation
2nd BGN	END	Verifies timing of payments to end of each period
2nd P/Y	P/Y = 12.0000	
2 ENTER	P/Y = 2.0000	Sets 2 payments per year; end mode (END) assumes cash flows are at the end of each 6-month period
CE/C CE/C	0.0000	Clears display
2nd CLR TVM	0.0000	Clears TVM variables
20 N	N = 20.0000	Stores the number of semiannual periods (10 years × 2)
12 I/Y	I/Y = 12.0000	Stores annual rate of return
45 PMT	PMT = 45.0000	Stores the semiannual interest payment
1,000 FV	FV = 1,000.0000	Stores the bond's maturity or par value
CPT PV	PV = −827.9512	Value of the bond, expressed as a negative number

Solution using the bond feature:

Keystrokes	Display	Explanation
CE/C CE/C	0.0000	Clears display
2nd BOND	STD = 1-01-1970	(This will be the last date entered)
2nd CLR WORK	STD = 1-01-1970	Clears BOND variables

Solution using the bond feature: (continued)

Keystrokes	Display	Explanation
1.01.93 ENTER	STD = 1-01-1993	Stores the current date (month, date, year)
↓	CPN = 0.0000	
9 ENTER	CPN = 9.0000	Stores the coupon interest rate
↓	RDT = 12-31-1990	(This will be the last date entered)
1.01.03 ENTER	RDT = 1-01-2003	Stores the maturity date in 10 years
↓	RV = 100.0000	Verifies bond maturity or par value
↓	ACT	
2nd		
SET	360	Sets calculations to be based on 360-day year
↓	2/Y	Verifies semiannual compounding rate
↓	YLD = 0.0000	
12 ENTER	YLD = 12.0000	Stores the investor's required rate of return
↓	PRI = 0.0000	
CPT	PRI = 82.7951	Value of bond as a percent of par value; i.e., value of bond is $827.95

IX. Bond Valuation

B. Computing the yield to maturity of a bond

Example: Assume the current date is January 1, 1994, and that you want to know your yield to maturity on a bond that matures in 8 years and has a coupon rate of 12 percent (6 percent semiannually). The bond is selling for $1,100.

Keystrokes	Display	Explanation
2nd		
BGN	END	Verifies timing of payments to end of each period
2nd		
P/Y	P/Y = 12.0000	
2 ENTER	P/Y = 2.0000	Sets 2 payments per year; end mode (END) assumes cash flows are at the end of each 6-month period
CE/C CE/C	0.0000	Clears display
2nd		
CLR TVM	0.0000	Clears TVM variables
16 N	N = 16.0000	Stores the number of semiannual periods (8 years × 2)
1100 +/− PV	PV = −1,100.0000	Value of the bond, expressed as a negative number
60 PMT	PMT = 60.0000	Stores the semiannual interest payments
1,000 FV	FV = 1,000.0000	Stores the bond's maturity or par value
CPT I/Y	I/Y = 10.1451	The yield to maturity, expressed on an annual basis

Solution using the bond feature:

CE/C CE/C 2nd	0.0000	Clears display	
Bond 2nd	STD = 1-01-1993	(This will be the last date entered)	
CLR WORK	STD = 1-01-1993	Clears BOND variables	
1.03.94 ENTER	STD = 1-03-1994	Stores the current date (month, date, year)	
↓	CPN = 0.0000		
12 ENTER	CPN = 12.0000	Stores the coupon interest rate	
↓	RDT = 1-01-2003	(This will be the last date entered)	
1.03.02 ENTER	RDT = 1-03-2002	Stores the maturity date in 8 years	
↓	RV = 100.0000	Verifies bonds maturity or par value	
↓	ACT		
2nd			
SET	360	Sets calculations to be based on 360-day year	
↓	2/Y	Verifies semiannual compounding rate	
↓	YLD = 0.0000		
↓	PRI = 0.0000		
110 ENTER	PRI = 110.0000	Stores the bond value as a percentage of par value	
↑	YLD = 0.0000		
CPT	YLD = 10.1451	Bond's yield to maturity	

X. Computing the Net Present Value and Internal Rate of Return

A. Where future cash flows are equal amounts in each period (annuity)

Example: The firm is considering a capital project that would cost $80,000. The firm's cost of capital is 12 percent. The project life is 10 years, during which time the firm expects to receive $15,000 per year. Calculate the NPV and the IRR.

KEYSTROKES	DISPLAY	EXPLANATION
2nd		
BGN	END	Verifies timing of payments to end of each period
2nd		
P/Y	P/Y = 12.0000	
1 ENTER	P/Y = 1.0000	Sets 1 payment per year; end mode (END) assumes cash flows are at the end of each year
CE/C CE/C	0.0000	Clears display
2nd		
CLR TVM	0.0000	Clears TVM variables
15,000 PMT	PMT = 15.0000	Stores the annual cash flows of $15,000

X. Computing the Net Present Value and Internal Rate of Return (continued)

KEYSTROKES	DISPLAY	EXPLANATION
10 N	N = 10.0000	Stores the life of the project
12 I/Y	I/Y = 12.0000	Stores the cost of capital
CPT PV +/−	PV = −84,753.3454 PV = 84,753.3454	Calculates present value Changes PV to positive
−80,000 =	4,753.3454	Calculates net present value by subtracting the cost of the project
80,000 +/−	−80,000.0000	
PV	PV = −80,000.0000	
CPT I/Y	I/Y = 13.4344	Calculates the IRR

B. Where future cash flows are unequal amounts in each period

Example: The firm is considering a capital project that would cost $110,000. The firm's cost of capital is 15 percent. The project life is 5 years, with the following expected cash flows: $−25,000, $50,000, $60,000, $60,000 and $70,000. In addition, you expect to receive $30,000 in the last year from the salvage value of the equipment. Calculate the NPV and IRR.

KEYSTROKES	DISPLAY	EXPLANATION
CE/C CE/C	0.0000	Clears display
CF	CF_0 = 0.0000	
2nd		
CLR WORK	CF_0 = 0.0000	Clears cash flow variables
110,000 +/− ENTER	CF_0 = −10,000.0000	Stores CF_0, the initial investment (with a minus sign for a negative cash flow)
↓ 25,000 +/− ENTER	CO1 = 0.0000 CO1 = 25,000.0000	Stores CF_1, the first year's cash flow (with a minus sign for a negative cash flow)
↓ ENTER	FO1 = 1.0000	Stores the number of years CF_1 is repeated (in this case, 1 year only)
↓ 50,000 ENTER	CO2 = 0.0000 CO2 = 50,000.0000	Stores CF_2
↓ ENTER	FO2 = 1.0000 FO2 = 1.0000	Stores the number of years CF_2 is repeated
↓ 60,000 ENTER	CO3 = 0.0000 CO3 = 60,000.0000	Stores CF_3
↓ 2 ENTER	FO3 = 2.0000	Stores the number of years CF_3 is repeated (here, 2 years, so our response is 2 to the FO_3 prompt)

X. Computing the Net Present Value and Internal Rate of Return (continued)

↓	CO4 = 0.0000	
100,000	CO4 = 100,000.0000	Stores CF$_4$, $70,000 plus expected $30,000
ENTER		
↓	FO4 = 1.0000	Stores the number CF$_4$
ENTER		
2nd		
QUIT	0.0000	Ends storage of individual cash flows
NPV	I = 0.0000	
15 ENTER	I = 15.0000	Stores interest rate
↓	NPV = 0.0000	
CPT	NPV = 29,541.8951	Calculates the project's NPV at the stated interest rate
IRR	IRR = 0.0000	
CPT	IRR = 22.0633	Calculates the project's IRR

APPENDIX B

Compound Sum of $1

n	1%	2%	3%	4%	5%	6%	7%	8%	9%	10%
1	1.010	1.020	1.030	1.040	1.050	1.060	1.070	1.080	1.090	1.100
2	1.020	1.040	1.061	1.082	1.102	1.124	1.145	1.166	1.188	1.210
3	1.030	1.061	1.093	1.125	1.158	1.191	1.225	1.260	1.295	1.331
4	1.041	1.082	1.126	1.170	1.216	1.262	1.311	1.360	1.412	1.464
5	1.051	1.104	1.159	1.217	1.276	1.338	1.403	1.469	1.539	1.611
6	1.062	1.126	1.194	1.265	1.340	1.419	1.501	1.587	1.677	1.772
7	1.072	1.149	1.230	1.316	1.407	1.504	1.606	1.714	1.828	1.949
8	1.083	1.172	1.267	1.369	1.477	1.594	1.718	1.851	1.993	2.144
9	1.094	1.195	1.305	1.423	1.551	1.689	1.838	1.999	2.172	2.358
10	1.105	1.219	1.344	1.480	1.629	1.791	1.967	2.159	2.367	2.594
11	1.116	1.243	1.384	1.539	1.710	1.898	2.105	2.332	2.580	2.853
12	1.127	1.268	1.426	1.601	1.796	2.012	2.252	2.518	2.813	3.138
13	1.138	1.294	1.469	1.665	1.886	2.133	2.410	2.720	3.066	3.452
14	1.149	1.319	1.513	1.732	1.980	2.261	2.579	2.937	3.342	3.797
15	1.161	1.346	1.558	1.801	2.079	2.397	2.759	3.172	3.642	4.177
16	1.173	1.373	1.605	1.873	2.183	2.540	2.952	3.426	3.970	4.595
17	1.184	1.400	1.653	1.948	2.292	2.693	3.159	3.700	4.328	5.054
18	1.196	1.428	1.702	2.026	2.407	2.854	3.380	3.996	4.717	5.560
19	1.208	1.457	1.753	2.107	2.527	3.026	3.616	4.316	5.142	6.116
20	1.220	1.486	1.806	2.191	2.653	3.207	3.870	4.661	5.604	6.727
21	1.232	1.516	1.860	2.279	2.786	3.399	4.140	5.034	6.109	7.400
22	1.245	1.546	1.916	2.370	2.925	3.603	4.430	5.436	6.658	8.140
23	1.257	1.577	1.974	2.465	3.071	3.820	4.740	5.871	7.258	8.954
24	1.270	1.608	2.033	2.563	3.225	4.049	5.072	6.341	7.911	9.850
25	1.282	1.641	2.094	2.666	3.386	4.292	5.427	6.848	8.623	10.834
30	1.348	1.811	2.427	3.243	4.322	5.743	7.612	10.062	13.267	17.449
40	1.489	2.208	3.262	4.801	7.040	10.285	14.974	21.724	31.408	45.258
50	1.645	2.691	4.384	7.106	11.467	18.419	29.456	46.900	74.354	117.386

n	11%	12%	13%	14%	15%	16%	17%	18%	19%	20%
1	1.110	1.120	1.130	1.140	1.150	1.160	1.170	1.180	1.190	1.200
2	1.232	1.254	1.277	1.300	1.322	1.346	1.369	1.392	1.416	1.440
3	1.368	1.405	1.443	1.482	1.521	1.561	1.602	1.643	1.685	1.728
4	1.518	1.574	1.630	1.689	1.749	1.811	1.874	1.939	2.005	2.074
5	1.685	1.762	1.842	1.925	2.011	2.100	2.192	2.288	2.386	2.488
6	1.870	1.974	2.082	2.195	2.313	2.436	2.565	2.700	2.840	2.986
7	2.076	2.211	2.353	2.502	2.660	2.826	3.001	3.185	3.379	3.583
8	2.305	2.476	2.658	2.853	3.059	3.278	3.511	3.759	4.021	4.300
9	2.558	2.773	3.004	3.252	3.518	3.803	4.108	4.435	4.785	5.160
10	2.839	3.106	3.395	3.707	4.046	4.411	4.807	5.234	5.695	6.192
11	3.152	3.479	3.836	4.226	4.652	5.117	5.624	6.176	6.777	7.430
12	3.498	3.896	4.334	4.818	5.350	5.936	6.580	7.288	8.064	8.916
13	3.883	4.363	4.898	5.492	6.153	6.886	7.699	8.599	9.596	10.699
14	4.310	4.887	5.535	6.261	7.076	7.987	9.007	10.147	11.420	12.839
15	4.785	5.474	6.254	7.138	8.137	9.265	10.539	11.974	13.589	15.407
16	5.311	6.130	7.067	8.137	9.358	10.748	12.330	14.129	16.171	18.488
17	5.895	6.866	7.986	9.276	10.761	12.468	14.426	16.672	19.244	22.186
18	6.543	7.690	9.024	10.575	12.375	14.462	16.879	19.673	22.900	26.623

Compound Sum of $1 (continued)

n	11%	12%	13%	14%	15%	16%	17%	18%	19%	20%
19	7.263	8.613	10.197	12.055	14.232	16.776	19.748	23.214	27.251	31.948
20	8.062	9.646	11.523	13.743	16.366	19.461	23.105	27.393	32.429	38.337
21	8.949	10.804	13.021	15.667	18.821	22.574	27.033	32.323	38.591	46.005
22	9.933	12.100	14.713	17.861	21.644	26.186	31.629	38.141	45.923	55.205
23	11.026	13.552	16.626	20.361	24.891	30.376	37.005	45.007	54.648	66.247
24	12.239	15.178	18.788	23.212	28.625	35.236	43.296	53.108	65.031	79.496
25	13.585	17.000	21.230	26.461	32.918	40.874	50.656	62.667	77.387	95.395
30	22.892	29.960	39.115	50.949	66.210	85.849	111.061	143.367	184.672	237.373
40	64.999	93.049	132.776	188.876	267.856	378.715	533.846	750.353	1051.642	1469.740
50	184.559	288.996	450.711	700.197	1083.619	1670.669	2566.080	3927.189	5988.730	9100.191

n	21%	22%	23%	24%	25%	26%	27%	28%	29%	30%
1	1.210	1.220	1.230	1.240	1.250	1.260	1.270	1.280	1.290	1.300
2	1.464	1.488	1.513	1.538	1.562	1.588	1.613	1.638	1.664	1.690
3	1.772	1.816	1.861	1.907	1.953	2.000	2.048	2.097	2.147	2.197
4	2.144	2.215	2.289	2.364	2.441	2.520	2.601	2.684	2.769	2.856
5	2.594	2.703	2.815	2.932	3.052	3.176	3.304	3.436	3.572	3.713
6	3.138	3.297	3.463	3.635	3.815	4.001	4.196	4.398	4.608	4.827
7	3.797	4.023	4.259	4.508	4.768	5.042	5.329	5.629	5.945	6.275
8	4.595	4.908	5.239	5.589	5.960	6.353	6.767	7.206	7.669	8.157
9	5.560	5.987	6.444	6.931	7.451	8.004	8.595	9.223	9.893	10.604
10	6.727	7.305	7.926	8.594	9.313	10.086	10.915	11.806	12.761	13.786
11	8.140	8.912	9.749	10.657	11.642	12.708	13.862	15.112	16.462	17.921
12	9.850	10.872	11.991	13.215	14.552	16.012	17.605	19.343	21.236	23.298
13	11.918	13.264	14.749	16.386	18.190	20.175	22.359	24.759	27.395	30.287
14	14.421	16.182	18.141	20.319	22.737	25.420	28.395	31.691	35.339	39.373
15	17.449	19.742	22.314	25.195	28.422	32.030	36.062	40.565	45.587	51.185
16	21.113	24.085	27.446	31.242	35.527	40.357	45.799	51.923	58.808	66.541
17	25.547	29.384	33.758	38.740	44.409	50.850	58.165	66.461	75.862	86.503
18	30.912	35.848	41.523	48.038	55.511	64.071	73.869	85.070	97.862	112.454
19	37.404	43.735	51.073	59.567	69.389	80.730	93.813	108.890	126.242	146.190
20	45.258	53.357	62.820	73.863	86.736	101.720	119.143	139.379	162.852	190.047
21	54.762	65.095	77.268	91.591	108.420	128.167	151.312	178.405	210.079	247.061
22	66.262	79.416	95.040	113.572	135.525	161.490	192.165	228.358	271.002	321.178
23	80.178	96.887	116.899	140.829	169.407	203.477	244.050	292.298	349.592	417.531
24	97.015	118.203	143.786	174.628	211.758	256.381	309.943	374.141	450.974	542.791
25	117.388	144.207	176.857	216.539	264.698	323.040	393.628	478.901	581.756	705.627
30	304.471	389.748	497.904	634.810	807.793	1025.904	1300.477	1645.488	2078.208	2619.936
40	2048.309	2846.941	3946.340	5455.797	7523.156	10346.879	14195.051	19426.418	26520.723	36117.754
50	13779.844	20795.680	31278.301	46889.207	70064.812	104354.562	154942.687	229345.875	338440.000	497910.125

n	31%	32%	33%	34%	35%	36%	37%	38%	39%	40%
1	1.310	1.320	1.330	1.340	1.350	1.360	1.370	1.380	1.390	1.400
2	1.716	1.742	1.769	1.796	1.822	1.850	1.877	1.904	1.932	1.960
3	2.248	2.300	2.353	2.406	2.460	2.515	2.571	2.628	2.686	2.744
4	2.945	3.036	3.129	3.224	3.321	3.421	3.523	3.627	3.733	3.842
5	3.858	4.007	4.162	4.320	4.484	4.653	4.826	5.005	5.189	5.378
6	5.054	5.290	5.535	5.789	6.053	6.328	6.612	6.907	7.213	7.530
7	6.621	6.983	7.361	7.758	8.172	8.605	9.058	9.531	10.025	10.541
8	8.673	9.217	9.791	10.395	11.032	11.703	12.410	13.153	13.935	14.758
9	11.362	12.166	13.022	13.930	14.894	15.917	17.001	18.151	19.370	20.661
10	14.884	16.060	17.319	18.666	20.106	21.646	23.292	25.049	26.924	28.925
11	19.498	21.199	23.034	25.012	27.144	29.439	31.910	34.567	37.425	40.495
12	25.542	27.982	30.635	33.516	36.644	40.037	43.716	47.703	52.020	56.694
13	33.460	36.937	40.745	44.912	49.469	54.451	59.892	65.830	72.308	79.371
14	43.832	49.756	54.190	60.181	66.784	74.053	82.051	90.845	100.509	111.190
15	57.420	64.358	72.073	80.643	90.158	100.712	112.410	125.366	139.707	155.567
16	75.220	84.953	95.857	108.061	121.713	136.968	154.002	173.005	194.192	217.793
17	98.539	112.138	127.490	144.802	164.312	186.277	210.983	238.747	269.927	304.911
18	129.086	148.022	169.561	194.035	221.822	253.337	289.046	329.471	375.198	426.875
19	169.102	195.389	225.517	260.006	299.459	344.537	395.993	454.669	521.525	597.625

Compound Sum of $1 (continued)

n	31%	32%	33%	34%	35%	36%	37%	38%	39%	40%
20	221.523	257.913	299.937	348.408	404.270	468.571	542.511	627.443	724.919	836.674
21	290.196	340.446	398.916	466.867	545.764	637.256	743.240	865.871	1007.637	1171.343
22	380.156	449.388	530.558	625.601	736.781	865.668	1018.238	1194.900	1400.615	1639.878
23	498.004	593.192	705.642	838.305	994.653	1178.668	1394.986	1648.961	1946.854	2295.829
24	652.385	783.013	938.504	1123.328	1342.781	1602.988	1911.129	2275.564	2706.125	3214.158
25	854.623	1033.577	1248.210	1505.258	1812.754	2180.063	2618.245	3140.275	3761.511	4499.816
30	3297.081	4142.008	5194.516	6503.285	8128.426	10142.914	12636.086	15716.703	19517.969	24201.043
40	49072.621	66519.313	89962.188	121388.437	163433.875	219558.625	294317.937	393684.687	525508.312	700022.688

APPENDIX C

Present Value of $1

n	1%	2%	3%	4%	5%	6%	7%	8%	9%	10%
1	.990	.980	.971	.962	.952	.943	.935	.926	.917	.909
2	.980	.961	.943	.925	.907	.890	.873	.857	.842	.826
3	.971	.942	.915	.889	.864	.840	.816	.794	.772	.751
4	.961	.924	.888	.855	.823	.792	.763	.735	.708	.683
5	.951	.906	.863	.822	.784	.747	.713	.681	.650	.621
6	.942	.888	.837	.790	.746	.705	.666	.630	.596	.564
7	.933	.871	.813	.760	.711	.665	.623	.583	.547	.513
8	.923	.853	.789	.731	.677	.627	.582	.540	.502	.467
9	.914	.837	.766	.703	.645	.592	.544	.500	.460	.424
10	.905	.820	.744	.676	.614	.558	.508	.463	.422	.386
11	.896	.804	.722	.650	.585	.527	.475	.429	.388	.350
12	.887	.789	.701	.625	.557	.497	.444	.397	.356	.319
13	.879	.773	.681	.601	.530	.469	.415	.368	.326	.290
14	.870	.758	.661	.577	.505	.442	.388	.340	.299	.263
15	.861	.743	.642	.555	.481	.417	.362	.315	.275	.239
16	.853	.728	.623	.534	.458	.394	.339	.292	.252	.218
17	.844	.714	.605	.513	.436	.371	.317	.270	.231	.198
18	.836	.700	.587	.494	.416	.350	.296	.250	.212	.180
19	.828	.686	.570	.475	.396	.331	.277	.232	.194	.164
20	.820	.673	.554	.456	.377	.312	.258	.215	.178	.149
21	.811	.660	.538	.439	.359	.294	.242	.199	.164	.135
22	.803	.647	.522	.422	.342	.278	.226	.184	.150	.123
23	.795	.634	.507	.406	.326	.262	.211	.170	.138	.112
24	.788	.622	.492	.390	.310	.247	.197	.158	.126	.102
25	.780	.610	.478	.375	.295	.233	.184	.146	.116	.092
30	.742	.552	.412	.308	.231	.174	.131	.099	.075	.057
40	.672	.453	.307	.208	.142	.097	.067	.046	.032	.022
50	.608	.372	.228	.141	.087	.054	.034	.021	.013	.009

n	11%	12%	13%	14%	15%	16%	17%	18%	19%	20%
1	.901	.893	.885	.877	.870	.862	.855	.847	.840	.833
2	.812	.797	.783	.769	.756	.743	.731	.718	.706	.694
3	.731	.712	.693	.675	.658	.641	.624	.609	.593	.579
4	.659	.636	.613	.592	.572	.552	.534	.516	.499	.482
5	.593	.567	.543	.519	.497	.476	.456	.437	.419	.402
6	.535	.507	.480	.456	.432	.410	.390	.370	.352	.335
7	.482	.452	.425	.400	.376	.354	.333	.314	.296	.279
8	.434	.404	.376	.351	.327	.305	.285	.266	.249	.233
9	.391	.361	.333	.308	.284	.263	.243	.225	.209	.194
10	.352	.322	.295	.270	.247	.227	.208	.191	.176	.162
11	.317	.287	.261	.237	.215	.195	.178	.162	.148	.135
12	.286	.257	.231	.208	.187	.168	.152	.137	.124	.112
13	.258	.229	.204	.182	.163	.145	.130	.116	.104	.093
14	.232	.205	.181	.160	.141	.125	.111	.099	.088	.078
15	.209	.183	.160	.140	.123	.108	.095	.084	.074	.065
16	.188	.163	.141	.123	.107	.093	.081	.071	.062	.054
17	.170	.146	.125	.108	.093	.080	.069	.060	.052	.045
18	.153	.130	.111	.095	.081	.069	.059	.051	.044	.038
19	.138	.116	.098	.083	.070	.060	.051	.043	.037	.031

Present Value of $1 (continued)

n	11%	12%	13%	14%	15%	16%	17%	18%	19%	20%
20	.124	.104	.087	.073	.061	.051	.043	.037	.031	.026
21	.112	.093	.077	.064	.053	.044	.037	.031	.026	.022
22	.101	.083	.068	.056	.046	.038	.032	.026	.022	.018
23	.091	.074	.060	.049	.040	.033	.027	.022	.018	.015
24	.082	.066	.053	.043	.035	.028	.023	.019	.015	.013
25	.074	.059	.047	.038	.030	.024	.020	.016	.013	.010
30	.044	.033	.026	.020	.015	.012	.009	.007	.005	.004
40	.015	.011	.008	.005	.004	.003	.002	.001	.001	.001
50	.005	.003	.002	.001	.001	.001	.000	.000	.000	.000

n	21%	22%	23%	24%	25%	26%	27%	28%	29%	30%
1	.826	.820	.813	.806	.800	.794	.787	.781	.775	.769
2	.683	.672	.661	.650	.640	.630	.620	.610	.601	.592
3	.564	.551	.537	.524	.512	.500	.488	.477	.466	.455
4	.467	.451	.437	.423	.410	.397	.384	.373	.361	.350
5	.386	.370	.355	.341	.328	.315	.303	.291	.280	.269
6	.319	.303	.289	.275	.262	.250	.238	.227	.217	.207
7	.263	.249	.235	.222	.210	.198	.188	.178	.168	.159
8	.218	.204	.191	.179	.168	.157	.148	.139	.130	.123
9	.180	.167	.155	.144	.134	.125	.116	.108	.101	.094
10	.149	.137	.126	.116	.107	.099	.092	.085	.078	.073
11	.123	.112	.103	.094	.086	.079	.072	.066	.061	.056
12	.102	.092	.083	.076	.069	.062	.057	.052	.047	.043
13	.084	.075	.068	.061	.055	.050	.045	.040	.037	.033
14	.069	.062	.055	.049	.044	.039	.035	.032	.028	.025
15	.057	.051	.045	.040	.035	.031	.028	.025	.022	.020
16	.047	.042	.036	.032	.028	.025	.022	.019	.017	.015
17	.039	.034	.030	.026	.023	.020	.017	.015	.013	.012
18	.032	.028	.024	.021	.018	.016	.014	.012	010	.009
19	.027	.023	.020	.017	.014	.012	.011	.009	.008	.007
20	.022	.019	.016	.014	.012	.010	.008	.007	.006	.005
21	.018	.015	.013	.011	.009	.008	.007	.006	.005	.004
22	.015	.013	.011	.009	.007	.006	.005	.004	.004	.003
23	.012	.010	.009	.007	.006	.005	.004	.003	.003	.002
24	.010	.008	.007	.006	.005	.004	.003	.003	.002	.002
25	.009	.007	.006	.005	.004	.003	.003	.002	.002	.001
30	.003	.003	.002	.002	.001	.001	.001	.001	.000	.000
40	.000	.000	.000	.000	.000	.000	.000	.000	.000	.000
50	.000	.000	.000	.000	.000	.000	.000	.000	.000	.000

n	31%	32%	33%	34%	35%	36%	37%	38%	39%	40%
1	.763	.758	.752	.746	.741	.735	.730	.725	.719	.714
2	.583	.574	.565	.557	.549	.541	.533	.525	.518	.510
3	.445	.435	.425	.416	.406	.398	.389	.381	.372	.364
4	.340	.329	.320	.310	.301	.292	.284	.276	.268	.260
5	.259	.250	.240	.231	.223	.215	.207	.200	.193	.186
6	.198	.189	.181	.173	.165	.158	.151	.145	.139	.133
7	.151	.143	.136	.129	.122	.116	.110	.105	.100	.095
8	.115	.108	.102	.096	.091	.085	.081	.076	.072	.068
9	.088	.082	.077	.072	.067	.063	.059	.055	.052	.048
10	.067	.062	.058	.054	.050	.046	.043	.040	.037	.035
11	.051	.047	.043	.040	.037	.034	.031	.029	.027	.025
12	.039	.036	.033	.030	.027	.025	.023	.021	.019	.018
13	.030	.027	.025	.022	.020	.018	.017	.015	.014	.013
14	.023	.021	.018	.017	.015	.014	.012	.011	.010	.009
15	.017	.016	.014	.012	.011	.010	.009	.008	.007	.006
16	.013	.012	.010	.009	.008	.007	.006	.006	.005	.005
17	.010	.009	.008	.007	.006	.005	.005	.004	.004	.003
18	.008	.007	.006	.005	.005	.004	.003	.003	.003	.002
19	.006	.005	.004	.004	.003	.003	.003	.002	.002	.002
20	.005	.004	.003	.003	.002	.002	.002	.002	.001	.001

Present Value of $1 (continued)

n	31%	32%	33%	34%	35%	36%	37%	38%	39%	40%
21	.003	.003	.003	.002	.002	.002	.001	.001	.001	.001
22	.003	.002	.002	.002	.001	.001	.001	.001	.001	.001
23	.002	.002	.001	.001	.001	.001	.001	.001	.001	.000
24	.002	.001	.001	.001	.001	.001	.001	.000	.000	.000
25	.001	.001	.001	.001	.001	.000	.000	.000	.000	.000
30	.000	.000	.000	.000	.000	.000	.000	.000	.000	.000
40	.000	.000	.000	.000	.000	.000	.000	.000	.000	.000

APPENDIX D

Sum of an Annuity of $1 for *n* Periods

n	1%	2%	3%	4%	5%	6%	7%	8%	9%	10%
1	1.000	1.000	1.000	1.000	1.000	1.000	1.000	1.000	1.000	1.000
2	2.010	2.020	2.030	2.040	2.050	2.060	2.070	2.080	2.090	2.100
3	3.030	3.060	3.091	3.122	3.152	3.184	3.215	3.246	3.278	3.310
4	4.060	4.122	4.184	4.246	4.310	4.375	4.440	4.506	4.573	4.641
5	5.101	5.204	5.309	5.416	5.526	5.637	5.751	5.867	5.985	6.105
6	6.152	6.308	6.468	6.633	6.802	6.975	7.153	7.336	7.523	7.716
7	7.214	7.434	7.662	7.898	8.142	8.394	8.654	8.923	9.200	9.487
8	8.286	8.583	8.892	9.214	9.549	9.897	10.260	10.637	11.028	11.436
9	9.368	9.755	10.159	10.583	11.027	11.491	11.978	12.488	13.021	13.579
10	10.462	10.950	11.464	12.006	12.578	13.181	13.816	14.487	15.193	15.937
11	11.567	12.169	12.808	13.486	14.207	14.972	15.784	16.645	17.560	18.531
12	12.682	13.412	14.192	15.026	15.917	16.870	17.888	18.977	20.141	21.384
13	13.809	14.680	15.618	16.627	17.713	18.882	20.141	21.495	22.953	24.523
14	14.947	15.974	17.086	18.292	19.598	21.015	22.550	24.215	26.019	27.975
15	16.097	17.293	18.599	20.023	21.578	23.276	25.129	27.152	29.361	31.772
16	17.258	18.639	20.157	21.824	23.657	25.672	27.888	30.324	33.003	35.949
17	18.430	20.012	21.761	23.697	25.840	28.213	30.840	33.750	36.973	40.544
18	19.614	21.412	23.414	25.645	28.132	30.905	33.999	37.450	41.301	45.599
19	20.811	22.840	25.117	27.671	30.539	33.760	37.379	41.446	46.018	51.158
20	22.019	24.297	26.870	29.778	33.066	36.785	40.995	45.762	51.159	57.274
21	23.239	25.783	28.676	31.969	35.719	39.992	44.865	50.422	56.764	64.002
22	24.471	27.299	30.536	34.248	38.505	43.392	49.005	55.456	62.872	71.402
23	25.716	28.845	32.452	36.618	41.430	46.995	53.435	60.893	69.531	79.542
24	26.973	30.421	34.426	39.082	44.501	50.815	58.176	66.764	76.789	88.496
25	28.243	32.030	36.459	41.645	47.726	54.864	63.248	73.105	84.699	98.346
30	34.784	40.567	47.575	56.084	66.438	79.057	94.459	113.282	136.305	164.491
40	48.885	60.401	75.400	95.024	120.797	154.758	199.630	295.052	337.872	442.580
50	64.461	84.577	112.794	152.664	209.341	290.325	406.516	573.756	815.051	1163.865

n	11%	12%	13%	14%	15%	16%	17%	18%	19%	20%
1	1.000	1.000	1.000	1.000	1.000	1.000	1.000	1.000	1.000	1.000
2	2.110	2.120	2.130	2.140	2.150	2.160	2.170	2.180	2.190	2.200
3	3.342	3.374	3.407	3.440	3.472	3.506	3.539	3.572	3.606	3.640
4	4.710	4.779	4.850	4.921	4.993	5.066	5.141	5.215	5.291	5.368
5	6.228	6.353	6.480	6.610	6.742	6.877	7.014	7.154	7.297	7.442
6	7.913	8.115	8.323	8.535	8.754	8.977	9.207	9.442	9.683	9.930
7	9.783	10.089	10.405	10.730	11.067	11.414	11.772	12.141	12.523	12.916
8	11.859	12.300	12.757	13.233	13.727	14.240	14.773	15.327	15.902	16.499
9	14.164	14.776	15.416	16.085	16.786	17.518	18.285	19.086	19.923	20.799
10	16.722	17.549	18.420	19.337	20.304	21.321	22.393	23.521	24.709	25.959
11	19.561	20.655	21.814	23.044	24.349	25.733	27.200	28.755	30.403	32.150
12	22.713	24.133	25.650	27.271	29.001	30.850	32.824	34.931	37.180	39.580
13	26.211	28.029	29.984	32.088	34.352	36.786	39.404	42.218	45.244	48.496
14	30.095	32.392	34.882	37.581	40.504	43.672	47.102	50.818	54.841	59.196
15	34.405	37.280	40.417	43.842	47.580	51.659	56.109	60.965	66.260	72.035
16	39.190	42.753	46.671	50.980	55.717	60.925	66.648	72.938	79.850	87.442
17	44.500	48.883	53.738	59.117	65.075	71.673	78.978	87.067	96.021	105.930
18	50.396	55.749	61.724	68.393	75.836	84.140	93.404	103.739	115.265	128.116

Sum of an Annuity of $1 for *n* Periods (continued)

n	11%	12%	13%	14%	15%	16%	17%	18%	19%	20%
19	56.939	63.439	70.748	78.968	88.211	98.603	110.283	123.412	138.165	154.739
20	64.202	72.052	80.946	91.024	102.443	115.379	130.031	146.626	165.417	186.687
21	72.264	81.698	92.468	104.767	118.809	134.840	153.136	174.019	197.846	225.024
22	81.213	92.502	105.489	120.434	137.630	157.414	180.169	206.342	236.436	271.028
23	91.147	104.602	120.203	138.295	159.274	183.600	211.798	244.483	282.359	326.234
24	102.173	118.154	136.829	158.656	184.166	213.976	248.803	289.490	337.007	392.480
25	114.412	133.333	155.616	181.867	212.790	249.212	292.099	342.598	402.038	471.976
30	199.018	241.330	293.192	356.778	434.738	530.306	647.423	790.932	966.698	1181.865
40	581.812	767.080	1013.667	1341.979	1779.048	2360.724	3134.412	4163.094	5529.711	7343.715
50	1668.723	2399.975	3459.344	4994.301	7217.488	10435.449	15088.805	21812.273	31514.492	45496.094

n	21%	22%	23%	24%	25%	26%	27%	28%	29%	30%
1	1.000	1.000	1.000	1.000	1.000	1.000	1.000	1.000	1.000	1.000
2	2.210	2.220	2.230	2.240	2.250	2.260	2.270	2.280	2.290	2.300
3	3.674	3.708	3.743	3.778	3.813	3.848	3.883	3.918	3.954	3.990
4	5.446	5.524	5.604	5.684	5.766	5.848	5.931	6.016	6.101	6.187
5	7.589	7.740	7.893	8.048	8.207	8.368	8.533	8.700	8.870	9.043
6	10.183	10.442	10.708	10.980	11.259	11.544	11.837	12.136	12.442	12.756
7	13.321	13.740	14.171	14.615	15.073	15.546	16.032	16.534	17.051	17.583
8	17.119	17.762	18.430	19.123	19.842	20.588	21.361	22.163	22.995	23.858
9	21.714	22.670	23.669	24.712	25.802	26.940	28.129	29.369	30.664	32.015
10	27.274	28.657	30.113	31.643	33.253	34.945	36.723	38.592	40.556	42.619
11	34.001	35.962	38.039	40.238	42.566	45.030	47.639	50.398	53.318	56.405
12	42.141	44.873	47.787	50.895	54.208	57.738	61.501	65.510	69.780	74.326
13	51.991	55.745	59.778	64.109	68.760	73.750	79.106	84.853	91.016	97.624
14	63.909	69.009	74.528	80.496	86.949	93.925	101.465	109.611	118.411	127.912
15	78.330	85.191	92.669	100.815	109.687	119.346	129.860	141.302	153.750	167.285
16	95.779	104.933	114.983	126.010	138.109	151.375	165.922	181.867	199.337	218.470
17	116.892	129.019	142.428	157.252	173.636	191.733	211.721	233.790	258.145	285.011
18	142.439	158.403	176.187	195.993	218.045	242.583	269.885	300.250	334.006	371.514
19	173.351	194.251	217.710	244.031	273.556	306.654	343.754	385.321	431.868	483.968
20	210.755	237.986	268.783	303.598	342.945	387.384	437.568	494.210	558.110	630.157
21	256.013	291.343	331.603	377.461	429.681	489.104	556.710	633.589	720.962	820.204
22	310.775	356.438	408.871	469.052	538.101	617.270	708.022	811.993	931.040	1067.265
23	377.038	435.854	503.911	582.624	673.626	778.760	990.187	1040.351	1202.042	1388.443
24	457.215	532.741	620.810	723.453	843.032	982.237	1144.237	1332.649	1551.634	1805.975
25	554.230	650.944	764.596	898.082	1054.791	1238.617	1454.180	1706.790	2002.608	2348.765
30	1445.111	1767.044	2160.459	2640.881	3227.172	3941.953	4812.891	5873.172	7162.785	8729.805
40	9749.141	12936.141	17153.691	22728.367	30088.621	39791.957	52570.707	69376.562	91447.375	120389.375

n	31%	32%	33%	34%	35%	36%	37%	38%	39%	40%
1	1.000	1.000	1.000	1.000	1.000	1.000	1.000	1.000	1.000	1.000
2	2.310	2.320	2.330	2.340	2.350	2.360	2.370	2.380	2.390	2.400
3	4.026	4.062	4.099	4.136	4.172	4.210	4.247	4.284	4.322	4.360
4	6.274	6.362	6.452	6.542	6.633	6.725	6.818	6.912	7.008	7.104
5	9.219	9.398	9.581	9.766	9.954	10.146	10.341	10.539	10.741	10.946
6	13.077	13.406	13.742	14.086	14.438	14.799	15.167	15.544	15.930	16.324
7	18.131	18.696	19.277	19.876	20.492	21.126	21.779	22.451	23.142	23.853
8	24.752	25.678	26.638	27.633	28.664	29.732	30.837	31.982	33.167	34.395
9	33.425	34.895	36.429	38.028	39.696	41.435	43.247	45.135	47.103	49.152
10	44.786	47.062	49.451	51.958	54.590	57.351	60.248	63.287	66.473	69.813
11	59.670	63.121	66.769	70.624	74.696	78.998	83.540	88.335	93.397	98.739
12	79.167	84.320	89.803	95.636	101.840	108.437	115.450	122.903	130.822	139.234
13	104.709	112.302	120.438	129.152	138.484	148.474	159.166	170.606	182.842	195.928
14	138.169	149.239	161.183	174.063	187.953	202.925	219.058	236.435	255.151	275.299
15	182.001	197.996	215.373	234.245	254.737	276.978	301.109	327.281	355.659	386.418
16	239.421	262.354	287.446	314.888	344.895	377.690	413.520	452.647	495.366	541.985
17	314.642	347.307	383.303	422.949	466.608	514.658	567.521	625.652	689.558	759.778
18	413.180	459.445	510.792	567.751	630.920	700.935	778.504	864.399	959.485	1064.689
19	542.266	607.467	680.354	761.786	852.741	954.271	1067.551	1193.870	1334.683	1491.563
20	711.368	802.856	905.870	1021.792	1152.200	1298.809	1463.544	1648.539	1856.208	2089.188

Sum of an Annuity of $1 for *n* Periods (continued)

n	31%	32%	33%	34%	35%	36%	37%	38%	39%	40%
21	932.891	1060.769	1205.807	1370.201	1556.470	1767.380	2006.055	2275.982	2581.128	2925.862
22	1223.087	1401.215	1604.724	1837.068	2102.234	2404.636	2749.294	3141.852	3588.765	4097.203
23	1603.243	1850.603	2135.282	2462.669	2839.014	3271.304	3767.532	4336.750	4989.379	5737.078
24	2101.247	2443.795	2840.924	3300.974	3833.667	4449.969	5162.516	5985.711	6936.230	8032.906
25	2753.631	3226.808	3779.428	4424.301	5176.445	6052.957	7073.645	8261.273	9642.352	11247.062
30	10632.543	12940.672	15737.945	19124.434	23221.258	28172.016	34148.906	41357.227	50043.625	60500.207

APPENDIX E

Present Value of an Annuity of $1 for *n* Periods

n	1%	2%	3%	4%	5%	6%	7%	8%	9%	10%
1	.990	.980	.971	.962	.952	.943	.935	.926	.917	.909
2	1.970	1.942	1.913	1.886	1.859	1.833	1.808	1.3783	1.759	1.736
3	2.941	2.884	2.829	2.775	2.723	2.673	2.624	2.577	2.531	2.487
4	3.902	3.808	3.717	3.630	3.546	3.465	3.387	3.312	3.240	3.170
5	4.853	4.713	4.580	4.452	4.329	4.212	4.100	3.993	3.890	3.791
6	5.795	5.601	5.417	5.242	5.076	4.917	4.767	5.623	4.486	4.355
7	6.728	6.472	6.230	6.002	5.786	5.582	5.389	5.206	5.033	4.868
8	7.652	7.326	7.020	6.733	6.463	6.210	5.971	5.747	5.535	5.335
9	8.566	8.162	7.786	7.435	7.108	6.802	6.515	6.247	5.995	5.759
10	9.471	8.983	8.530	8.111	7.722	7.360	7.024	6.710	6.418	6.145
11	10.368	9.787	9.253	8.760	8.306	7.887	7.499	7.139	6.805	6.495
12	11.255	10.575	9.954	9.385	8.863	8.384	7.943	7.536	7.161	6.814
13	12.134	11.348	10.635	9.986	9.394	8.853	8.358	7.904	7.487	7.103
14	13.004	12.106	11.296	10.563	9.899	9.295	8.746	8.244	7.786	7.367
15	13.865	12.849	11.938	11.118	10.380	9.712	9.108	8.560	8.061	7.606
16	14.718	13.578	12.561	11.652	10.838	10.106	9.447	8.851	8.313	7.824
17	15.562	14.292	13.166	12.166	11.274	10.477	9.763	9.122	8.544	8.022
18	16.398	14.992	13.754	12.659	11.690	10.828	10.059	9.372	8.756	8.201
19	17.226	15.679	14.324	13.134	12.085	11.158	10.336	9.604	8.950	8.365
20	18.046	16.352	14.878	13.590	12.462	11.470	10.594	9.818	9.129	8.514
21	18.857	17.011	15.415	14.029	12.821	11.764	10.836	10.017	9.292	8.649
22	19.661	17.658	15.937	14.451	13.163	12.042	11.061	10.201	9.442	8.772
23	20.456	18.292	16.444	14.857	13.489	12.303	11.272	10.371	9.580	8.883
24	21.244	18.914	16.936	15.247	13.799	12.550	11.469	10.529	9.707	8.985
25	22.023	19.524	17.413	15.622	14.094	12.783	11.654	10.675	9.823	9.077
30	25.808	22.397	19.601	17.292	15.373	13.765	12.409	11.258	10.274	9.427
40	32.835	27.356	23.115	19.793	17.159	15.046	13.332	11.925	10.757	9.779
50	39.197	31.424	25.730	21.482	18.256	15.762	13.801	12.234	10.962	9.915

n	11%	12%	13%	14%	15%	16%	17%	18%	19%	20%
1	.901	.893	.885	.877	.870	.862	.855	.847	.840	.833
2	1.713	1.690	1.668	1.647	1.626	1.605	1.585	1.566	1.547	1.528
3	2.444	2.402	2.361	2.322	2.283	2.246	2.210	2.174	2.140	2.106
4	3.102	3.037	2.974	2.914	2.855	2.798	2.743	2.690	2.639	2.589
5	3.696	3.605	3.517	3.433	3.352	3.274	3.199	3.127	3.058	2.991
6	4.231	4.111	3.998	3.889	3.784	3.685	3.589	3.498	3.410	3.326
7	4.712	4.564	4.423	4.288	4.160	4.039	3.922	3.812	3.706	3.605
8	5.146	4.968	4.799	4.639	4.487	4.344	4.207	4.078	3.954	3.837
9	5.537	5.328	5.132	4.946	4.772	4.607	4.451	4.303	4.163	4.031
10	5.889	5.650	5.246	5.216	5.019	4.833	4.659	4.494	4.339	4.192
11	6.207	5.938	5.687	5.453	5.234	5.029	4.836	4.656	4.487	4.327
12	6.492	6.194	5.918	5.660	5.421	5.197	4.988	4.793	4.611	4.439
13	6.750	6.424	6.122	5.842	5.583	5.342	5.118	4.910	4.715	4.533
14	6.982	6.628	6.303	6.002	5.724	5.468	5.229	5.008	4.802	4.611
15	7.191	6.811	6.462	6.142	5.847	5.575	5.324	5.092	4.876	4.675
16	7.379	6.974	6.604	6.265	5.954	5.669	5.405	5.162	4.938	4.730
17	7.549	7.120	6.729	6.373	6.047	5.749	5.475	5.222	4.990	4.775
18	7.702	7.250	6.840	6.467	6.128	5.818	5.534	5.273	5.033	4.812

Present Value of an Annuity of $1 for *n* Periods
(continued)

n	11%	12%	13%	14%	15%	16%	17%	18%	19%	20%
19	7.839	7.366	6.938	6.550	6.198	5.877	5.585	5.316	5.070	4.843
20	7.963	7.469	7.025	6.623	6.259	5.929	5.628	5.353	5.101	4.870
21	8.075	7.562	7.102	6.687	6.312	5.973	5.665	5.384	5.127	4.891
22	8.176	7.645	7.170	6.743	6.359	6.011	5.696	5.410	5.149	4.909
23	8.266	7.718	7.230	6.792	6.399	6.044	5.723	5.432	5.167	4.925
24	8.348	7.784	7.283	6.835	6.434	6.073	5.747	5.451	5.182	4.937
25	8.422	7.843	7.330	6.873	6.464	6.097	5.766	5.467	5.195	4.948
30	8.694	8.055	7.496	7.003	6.566	6.177	5.829	5.517	5.235	4.979
40	8.951	8.244	7.634	7.105	6.642	6.233	5.871	5.548	5.258	4.997
50	9.042	8.305	7.675	7.133	6.661	6.246	5.880	5.554	5.262	4.999

n	21%	22%	23%	24%	25%	26%	27%	28%	29%	30%
1	.826	.820	.813	.806	.800	.794	.787	.781	.775	.769
2	1.509	1.492	1.474	1.457	1.440	1.424	1.407	1.392	1.376	1.361
3	2.074	2.042	2.011	1.981	1.952	1.923	1.896	1.868	1.842	1.816
4	2.540	2.494	2.448	2.404	2.362	2.320	2.280	2.241	2.203	2.166
5	2.926	2.864	2.803	2.745	2.689	2.635	2.583	2.532	2.483	2.436
6	3.245	3.167	3.092	3.020	2.951	2.885	2.821	2.759	2.700	2.643
7	3.508	3.416	3.327	3.242	3.161	3.083	3.009	2.937	2.868	2.802
8	3.726	3.619	3.518	3.421	3.329	3.241	3.156	3.076	2.999	2.925
9	3.905	3.786	3.673	3.566	3.463	3.366	3.273	3.184	3.100	3.019
10	4.054	3.923	3.799	3.682	3.570	3.465	3.364	3.269	3.178	3.092
11	4.177	4.035	3.902	3.776	3.656	3.544	3.437	3.335	3.329	3.147
12	4.278	4.127	3.985	3.851	3.725	3.606	3.493	3.387	3.286	3.190
13	4.362	4.203	4.053	3.912	3.780	3.656	3.538	3.427	3.322	3.223
14	4.432	4.265	4.108	3.962	3.824	3.695	3.573	3.459	3.351	3.249
15	4.489	4.315	4.153	4.001	3.859	3.726	3.601	3.483	3.373	3.268
16	4.536	4.357	4.189	4.003	3.887	3.751	3.623	3.503	3.390	3.283
17	4.576	4.391	4.219	4.059	3.910	3.771	3.640	3.518	3.403	3.295
18	4.608	4.419	4.243	4.080	3.928	3.786	3.654	3.529	3.413	3.304
19	4.635	4.442	4.263	4.097	3.942	3.799	3.664	3.539	3.421	3.311
20	4.657	4.460	4.279	4.110	3.954	3.808	3.673	3.546	3.427	3.316
21	4.675	4.476	4.292	4.121	3.963	3.816	3.679	3.551	3.432	3.320
22	4.690	4.488	4.302	4.130	3.970	3.822	3.684	3.556	3.436	3.323
23	4.703	4.499	4.311	4.137	3.976	3.827	3.689	3.559	3.438	3.325
24	4.713	4.507	4.318	4.143	3.981	3.831	3.692	3.562	3.441	3.327
25	4.721	4.514	4.323	4.147	3.985	3.834	3.694	3.564	3.442	3.329
30	4.746	4.534	4.339	4.160	3.995	3.842	3.701	3.569	3.447	3.332
40	4.760	4.544	4.347	4.166	3.999	3.846	3.703	3.571	3.448	3.333
50	4.762	4.545	4.348	4.167	4.000	3.846	3.704	3.571	3.448	3.333

n	31%	32%	33%	34%	35%	36%	37%	38%	39%	40%
1	.763	.758	.752	.746	.741	.735	.730	.725	.719	.714
2	1.346	1.331	1.317	1.303	1.289	1.276	1.263	1.250	1.237	1.224
3	1.791	1.766	1.742	1.719	1.696	1.673	1.652	1.630	1.609	1.589
4	2.130	2.096	2.062	2.029	1.997	1.966	1.935	1.906	1.877	1.849
5	2.390	2.345	2.302	2.260	2.220	2.181	2.143	2.106	2.070	2.035
6	2.588	2.534	2.483	2.433	2.385	2.339	2.294	2.251	2.209	2.168
7	2.739	2.677	2.619	2.562	2.508	2.455	2.404	2.355	2.308	2.263
8	2.854	2.786	2.721	2.658	2.598	2.540	2.485	2.432	2.380	2.331
9	2.942	2.868	2.798	2.730	2.665	2.603	2.544	2.487	2.432	2.379
10	3.009	2.930	2.855	2.784	2.715	2.649	2.587	2.527	2.469	2.414
11	3.060	2.978	2.899	2.824	2.752	2.683	2.618	2.555	2.496	2.438
12	3.100	3.013	2.931	2.853	2.779	2.708	2.641	2.576	2.515	2.456
13	3.129	3.040	2.956	2.876	2.799	2.727	2.658	2.592	2.529	2.469
14	3.152	3.061	2.974	2.892	2.814	2.740	2.670	2.603	2.539	2.477
15	3.170	3.076	2.988	2.905	2.825	2.750	2.679	2.611	2.546	2.484
16	3.183	3.088	2.999	2.914	2.834	2.757	2.685	2.616	2.551	2.489
17	3.193	3.097	3.007	2.921	2.840	2.763	2.690	2.621	2.555	2.492

Present Value of an Annuity of $1 for *n* Periods
(continued)

n	31%	32%	33%	34%	35%	36%	37%	38%	39%	40%
18	3.201	3.104	3.012	2.926	2.844	2.767	2.693	2.624	2.557	2.494
19	3.207	3.109	3.017	2.930	2.848	2.770	2.696	2.626	2.559	2.496
20	3.211	3.113	3.020	2.933	2.850	2.772	2.698	2.627	2.561	2.497
21	3.215	3.116	3.023	2.935	2.852	2.773	2.699	2.629	2.562	2.498
22	3.217	3.118	3.025	2.936	2.853	2.775	2.700	2.629	2.562	2.498
23	3.219	3.120	3.026	2.938	2.854	2.775	2.701	2.630	2.563	2.499
24	3.221	3.121	3.027	2.939	2.855	2.776	2.701	2.630	2.563	2.499
25	3.222	3.122	3.028	2.939	2.856	2.776	2.702	2.631	2.563	2.499
30	3.225	2.124	3.030	2.941	2.857	2.777	2.702	2.631	2.564	2.500
40	3.226	2.125	3.030	2.941	2.857	2.778	2.703	2.632	2.564	2.500
50	3.226	2.125	3.030	2.941	2.857	2.778	2.703	2.632	2.564	2.500

APPENDIX F

Check Figures for Selected End-of-Chapter Study Problems

CHAPTER 1

1–1. Taxable income = $526,800
Tax liability = $179,112
1–3. Taxable income = $365,000
Tax liability = $124,100
1–5. Taxable income = ($38,000)
Tax liability = $0
1–7. Taxable income = $153,600
Tax liability = $43,154
1–9. Taxable income = $370,000
Tax liability = $125,800
1–11. Taxable income = $1,813,000
Tax liability = $616,420

CHAPTER 2

2–1. Inferred real rate on Treasury bills: 1.56%
Inferred real rate on Treasury bonds: 4.55%
2–2. 11.28%
2–4. 12.35%
2–5. a. The logic here is based on the expectations theory of the term structure of interest rates.

CHAPTER 3

3–1. $500,000
3–3. a. Total assets turnover = 2
   b. Sales = $17.5m
      Percentage increase = 75%
   c. For last year, OIROI = 20%
      Projected OIROI = 35%
3–5.

RATIO	1997
Current ratio	4.0x
Acid-test (quick) ratio	1.92x
Average collection period	107 days
Inventory turnover	1.36x
Operating income Return on investment	13.8%
Operating profit margin	24.8%
Total asset turnover	.56x
Inventory turnover	1.36x

Fixed asset turnover	1.04x
Debt ratio	34.6%
Times interest earned	5.63x
Return on common equity	10.5%

3–7. a.

Cash inflows from customers	$199,500
Cash paid to suppliers	$85,500
Other operating cash outflows and interest payments	$24,500
Cash tax payments	$2,500
Total cash flow from operations	$87,000
Purchase of fixed assets	($142,500)
Issue of preferred stock	$231,000
Mortgages payable reduced	($150,000)
Payment of dividend	($18,000)
Net change in cash	$7,500

Adjustments to Reconcile Net Income

Depreciation	$34,500
Amortization of patents	$9,000
Decrease in accounts receivable	$12,000
Decrease in inventory	$3,000
Increase in prepaid expenses	($1,500)
Decrease in accounts payable	($12,000)
Increase in taxes payable	$7,500

3–9. a. Total asset turnover = 2.25
   Operating profit margin = 11.11%
   Operating income return on investment = 25%
   b. Operating income return on investment = 19.5%
   c. Return on common equity
      Post-renovation analysis = 14.5%
      Pre-renovation analysis = 20%
3–11. a. Current ratio = 1.84
      Acid-test ratio = .72
      Debt ratio = .55
      Times interest earned = 8
      Inventory turnover = 5.48
      Fixed asset turnover = 2.22
      Return on equity = 23.4%

CHAPTER 10

10–1. a. $6,800
    b. $3,400
    c. No taxes
    d. $1,020
10–3. a. 2.75 years
    b. $10,628.16
10–5. a. $560,000
    b. Cash flow after tax: $116,170
10–7. $NPV_A = \$8,025$
    $NPV_B = \$10,112$

CHAPTER 11

11–1. a. $k_d (1 - t) = 6.53\%$
    b. $k_{nc} = 14.37\%$
    c. $k_c = 15.14\%$
    d. $k_p = 8.77\%$
    e. $k_d (1 - t) = 7.92\%$
11–5. $k_p = 7.69\%$
11–7. $k_p = 14.29\%$
11–9. a. $k_c = 17.59\%$
    b. $k_{nc} = 18.25\%$
11–11. $P_0 = \$1,063.80$
    $NP_0 = \$952.10$
    Number of bonds = 525
    $k_d (1 - t) = 7.14\%$

CHAPTER 12

12–1. a. 1.67 times
    b. 1.11 times
    c. 1.85 times
12–3. a. 1.67 times
    b. 1.11 times
    c. 1.85 times
    d. $18,326,693.23
    e. (25%) (1.85) = 46.25%
12–5. a. $F = \$780,000$
    b. $S_B = \$1,560,000$
12–7. a. $P = \$6.875$ (selling price per unit)
12–8. a. 1,200 units
    b. $600,000
    c. 1.316 times
    d. 26.32%
12–11. a. EBIT = $2,000,000
    b. EPS will be $1.00 for each plan
    d. Plan B

CHAPTER 13

13–1. 95,238 shares; $11,428,560
13–3. Value before and after dividend: $275

13–5. a.

Year	Dividend
1	$0.70
3	$0.93

    b. Target dividend: $0.90
13–7. 163,743 shares; $15,555,556

CHAPTER 14

14–1. Rate = 13.79%
14–3. a. Rate = 36.73%
    b. Rate = 74.23%
14–7. a. Rate = 16.27%
14–11. a. APR = 10%
    b. APR = 11.76%

CHAPTER 15

15–1. Yes; the company will save $250,000 annually by switching to the new concentration-banking system.
15–4. a. Need to speed up collections by more than 0.5214 day.
    b. Cash collections would have to be accelerated by more than 0.8110 day.
15–6. a. $4 million
    b. $240,000
    c. $48,600
    d. Yes; net annual gain = $191,400
15–8. a. $5,333
15–10. a. $912.44
    b. The loss will be $87.56.
    c. The capital loss here would be only $17.59.
    d. Interest rate risk. This leads to the maturity premium discussed in Chapter 2.
15–12. a. 36.36%
    b. 36.73%
    c. 55.67%
15–14. a. Average inventory = $90,000
    b. $53,333
15–16. a. EOQ = 7,071 units, or rounded to 7,100
    b. 35.2 orders per year

CHAPTER 16

16–1. a. $8,437
    b. $9,368
    c. $25,695
16–3. Canada: 1.1853; 1.1881; 1.1912
    Japan: 213.4927; 211.9992; 209.1613
    Switzerland: 1.9459; 1.9346; 1.8815
16–5. Net gain = $149.02

GLOSSARY

Accelerated Depreciation Techniques. Techniques that allow the owner of the asset to take greater amounts of depreciation during the early years of its life, thereby deferring some of the taxes until later years.

Accounts-Receivable Turnover Ratio. A ratio, credit sales divided by accounts receivable, that expresses how often accounts receivable are "rolled over" during a year.

Accrual Method. A method of accounting whereby income is recorded when earned, whether or not the money has been received at that time, and expenses are recorded when incurred, whether or not any money has actually been paid out.

Acid-Test Ratio. (Current assets − inventories) ÷ current liabilities. This ratio is a more stringent measure of liquidity than the current ratio in that it subtracts inventories (the least liquid current asset) from current assets.

Acquisition. A combination of two or more businesses into a single operational entity.

Agency Costs. The costs, such as a reduced stock price, associated with potential conflict between managers and investors when these two groups are not the same.

Agency Problem. Problems and conflicts resulting from the separation of the management and ownership of the firm.

Amortized Loans. Loans that are paid off in equal periodic payments.

Analytical Income Statement. A financial statement used by internal analysts that differs in composition from audited or published financial statements.

Annuity. A series of equal dollar payments for a specified number of years.

Annuity Due. An annuity in which the payments occur at the beginning of each period.

Anticipatory Buying. Buying in anticipation of a price increase to secure goods at a lower cost.

Arbitrage-Pricing Model. A theory that relates stock returns and risk. The theory maintains that security returns vary from their expected amounts when there are unanticipated changes in basic economic forces. Such forces would include unexpected changes in industrial production, inflation rates, term structure of interest rates, and the difference between interest rates of high- and low-risk bonds.

Arbitrageur. A person involved in the process of buying and selling in more than one market to make riskless profits.

Arrearage. An overdue payment, generally referring to omitted preferred stock dividends.

Asked Rate. The rate a bank or foreign exchange trader "asks" the customer to pay in home currency for foreign currency when the bank is selling and the customer is buying.

Asset Allocation. Identifying and selecting the asset classes appropriate for a specific investment portfolio and determining the proportions of those assets within the portfolio.

Automated Depository Transfer Check (DTC) System. A cash management tool that moves funds from local bank accounts to concentration bank accounts electronically. This eliminates the mail float from the local bank to the concentration bank.

Average Collection Period. Accounts receivable divided by (annual credit sales divided by 365). A ratio that expresses how rapidly the firm is collecting its credit accounts.

Balance Sheet. A basic accounting statement that represents the financial position of a firm on a given date.

Balance-Sheet Leverage Ratios. Financial ratios used to measure the extent of a firm's use of borrowed funds, calculated using information found in the firm's balance sheet.

Bankers' Acceptances. A draft (order to pay) drawn on a specific bank by a seller of goods in order to obtain payment for goods that have been shipped (sold) to a customer. The customer maintains an account with that specific bank.

Bank Wire. A private wire service used and supported by approximately 250 banks in the United States for transferring funds, exchanging credit information, or effecting securities transactions.

Benefit-Cost Ratio. See **Profitability Index.**

Beta. The relationship between an investment's returns and the market returns. This is a measure of the investment's non-diversifiable risk.

Bid-Ask Spread. The difference between the bid quote and ask quote.

Bird-in-the-Hand Dividend Theory. The view that dividends are more certain than capital gains.

Bond. A long-term (10-year or more) promissory note issued by the borrower, promising to pay the owner of the security a predetermined and fixed amount of interest each year.

Bond Par Value. The face value appearing on the bond, which is to be returned to the bondholder at maturity.

Book Value. (1) The value of an asset as shown on the firm's balance sheet. It represents the historical cost of the asset rather than its current market value or replacement cost. (2) The depreciated value of a company's assets (original cost less accumulated depreciation) less the outstanding liabilities.

Book-Value Weights. The percentage of financing provided by different capital sources as measured by their book values from the company's balance sheet.

Breakeven Analysis. An analytical technique used to determine the quantity of output or sales that results in a zero level of earnings before interest and taxes (EBIT). Relationships among the firm's cost structure, volume of output, and EBIT are studied.

Business Risk. The relative dispersion or variability in the firm's expected earnings before interest and taxes (EBIT). The nature of the firm's operations causes its business risk. This type of risk is affected by the firm's cost structure, product demand characteristics, and intra-industry competitive position. In capital structure theory, business risk is distinguished from financial risk. Compare **Financial Risk.**

Buying Rate.   The bid rate in a currency transaction.

Call Option.   The right to purchase a given number of shares of stock or some other asset at a specified price over a given time period.

Call Premium.   The difference between the call price and the security's par value.

Call Provision.   A provision that entitles the corporation to repurchase its preferred stock from their investors at stated prices over specified periods.

Capital Asset.   All property used in conducting a business other than assets held primarily for sale in the ordinary course of business or depreciable and real property used in conducting a business.

Capital Asset Pricing Model (CAPM).   An equation stating that the expected rate of return on a project is a function of (1) the risk-free rate, (2) the investment's systematic risk, and (3) the expected risk premium for the market portfolio of all risky securities.

Capital Budgeting.   The decision-making process with respect to investment in fixed assets. Specifically, it involves measuring the incremental cash flows associated with investment proposals and evaluating those proposed investments.

Capital Gain or Loss.   As defined by the revenue code, a gain or loss resulting from the sale or exchange of a capital asset.

Capital Market.   All institutions and procedures that facilitate transactions in long-term financial instruments.

Capital Rationing.   The placing of a limit by the firm on the dollar size of the capital budget.

Capital Structure.   The mix of long-term sources of funds used by the firm. This is also called the firm's capitalization. The relative total (percentage) of each type of fund is emphasized.

Cash.   Currency and coins plus demand deposit accounts.

Cash Breakeven Analysis.   Another version of breakeven analysis that includes only the cash costs of production within the cost components. This means noncash expenses, like depreciation, are omitted in the analysis.

Cash Budget.   A detailed plan of future cash flows. This budget is composed of four elements: cash receipts, cash disbursements, net change in cash for the period, and new financing needed.

Cash Flow Process.   The process of cash generation and disposition in a typical business setting.

Cash Flow Statement.   An accounting statement that computes the firm's cash inflows and outflows for a given time period.

Cash Flows from Investment Activities.   Cash flows that include the purchase of fixed assets and other assets.

Cash Flows from Financing Activities.   Cash flows that include proceeds from long-term debt or issuing common stock, and payments made for stock dividends.

Cash Flows from Operations.   Cash flows that consist of (1) collections from customers; (2) payments to suppliers for the purchase of materials; (3) other operating cash flows such as marketing and administrative expenses and interest payments; (4) and cash tax payments.

Certainty Equivalents.   The amount of cash a person would require with certainty to make him or her indifferent between this certain sum and a particular risky or uncertain sum.

Characteristic Line.   The line of "best fit" through a series of returns for a firm's stock relative to the market returns. The slope of the line, frequently called beta, represents the average movement of the firm's stock returns in response to a movement in the market's returns.

Chattel Mortgage Agreement.   A loan agreement in which the lender can increase his or her security interest by having specific items of inventory identified in the loan agreement. The borrower retains title to the inventory but cannot sell the items without the lender's consent.

Clientele Effect.   The belief that individuals and institutions that need current income will invest in companies that have high dividend payouts. Other investors prefer to avoid taxes by holding securities that offer only small dividend income but large capital gains. Thus, we have a "clientele" of investors.

Commercial Paper.   Short-term unsecured promissory notes sold by large businesses in order to raise cash. Unlike most other money-market instruments, commercial paper has no developed secondary market.

Common Stock.   Shares that represent the ownership in a corporation.

Company-Unique Risk.   See **Unsystematic Risk.**

Compensating Balance.   A balance of a given amount that the firm maintains in its demand deposit account. It may be required by either a formal or informal agreement with the firm's commercial bank. Such balances are usually required by the bank (1) on the unused portion of a loan commitment, (2) on the unpaid portion of an outstanding loan, or (3) in exchange for certain services provided by the bank, such as check-clearing or credit information. These balances raise the effective rate of interest paid on borrowed funds.

Compound Annuity.   Depositing an equal sum of money at the end of each year for a certain number of years and allowing it to grow.

Compound Interest.   The situation in which interest paid on the investment during the first period is added to the principal and, during the second period, interest is earned on the original principal plus the interest earned during the first period.

Compounding.   The process of determining the future value of a payment or series of payments when applying the concept of compound interest.

Concentration Bank.   A bank where a firm maintains a major disbursing account.

Concentration Banking.   The selection of a few major banks where the firm maintains significant disbursing accounts.

Constant Dividend Payout Ratio.   A dividend payment policy in which the percentage of earnings paid out in dividends is held constant. The dollar amount fluctuates from year to year as profits vary.

Contractual Interest Rate.   The interest rate to be paid on a bond expressed as a percent of par value.

Contribution Margin.   The difference between a product's selling price and its unit variable costs. It is usually measured on a per unit basis.

Contribution-to-Firm Risk.   The amount of risk that a project contributes to the firm as a whole. This measure considers the fact that some of the project's risk will be diversified away as the project is combined with the firm's other projects and assets, but ignores the effects of diversification of the firm's shareholders.

Convertible Debt. A hybrid security that combines debt or preferred stock with an option on the firm's common stock.

Convertible Preferred Stock. Stock that allows the stockholder to convert the preferred stock into a predetermined number of shares of common stock, if he or she so chooses.

Convertible Security. Preferred stock or debentures that can be exchanged for a specified number of shares of common stock at the will of the owner.

Corporate Bylaws. Regulations that govern the internal affairs of the corporation, designating such items as the time and place of the shareholders' meetings, voting rights, the election process for selecting members of the board of directors, the procedures for issuing and transferring stock certificates, and the policies relating to the corporate records.

Corporation. An entity that *legally* functions separate and apart from its owners.

Cost of Capital. See **Weighted Cost of Capital.**

Cost of Common Stock. The rate of return a firm must earn in order for the common stockholders to receive their required rate of return. The rate is based on the opportunity cost of funds for the common stockholders in the capital markets.

Cost of Debt. The rate that has to be received from an investment in order to achieve the required rate of return for the creditors. The cost is based on the debtholders' opportunity cost of debt in the capital markets.

Cost of Preferred Stock. The rate of return that must be earned on the preferred stockholders' investment to satisfy their required rate of return. The cost is based on the preferred stockholders' opportunity cost of preferred stock in the capital markets.

Cost-Volume-Profit Analysis. Another way of referring to ordinary breakeven analysis.

Coupon Interest Rate. The interest to be paid annually on a bond as a percent of par value, which is specified in the contractual agreement.

Coverage Ratios. A group of ratios that measure a firm's ability to meet its recurring fixed-charge obligations, such as interest on long-term debt, lease payments, and/or preferred stock dividends.

Covered Interest Arbitrage. Arbitrage designed to eliminate differentials across currency and interest rate markets.

Credit Scoring. The numerical evaluation of credit applicants where the score is evaluated relative to a predetermined standard.

Cross Rate. The computation of an exchange rate for a currency from the exchange rates of two other currencies.

Cumulative Feature. A requirement that all past unpaid preferred stock dividends be paid before any common stock dividends are declared.

Cumulative Voting. Voting in which each share of stock allows the shareholder a number of votes equal to the number of directors being elected. The shareholder can then cast all of his or her votes for a single candidate or split them among the various candidates.

Current Assets. Assets consisting primarily of cash, marketable securities, accounts receivable, inventories, and prepaid expenses.

Current Ratio. Current assets divided by current liabilities. A ratio that indicates a firm's degree of liquidity by comparing its current assets to its current liabilities.

Current Yield. The ratio of the annual interest payment to the bond's market price.

Date of Record. Date at which the stock transfer books are to be closed for determining the investor to receive the next dividend payment. See **Ex-Dividend Date.**

Debenture. Any unsecured long-term debt.

Debt. Liabilities consisting of such sources as credit extended by suppliers or a loan from a bank.

Debt Capacity. The maximum proportion of debt that the firm can include in its capital structure and still maintain its lowest composite cost of capital.

Debt Ratio. Total liabilities divided by total assets. A ratio that measures the extent to which a firm has been financed with debt.

Declaration Date. The date upon which a dividend is formally declared by the board of directors.

Default Risk. The uncertainty of expected returns from a security attributable to possible changes in the financial capacity of the security issuer to make future payments to the security owner. Treasury securities are considered default-free. Default risk is also referred to as "financial risk" in the context of marketable-securities management.

Degree of Combined Leverage. The percentage change in earnings per share caused by a percentage change in sales. It is the product of the degree of operating leverage and the degree of financial leverage.

Delivery-Time Stock. The inventory needed between the order date and the receipt of the inventory ordered.

Depository Transfer Checks (DTCs). A means for moving funds from local bank accounts to concentration bank accounts. The depository transfer check itself is an unsigned, nonnegotiable instrument. It is payable only to the bank deposit for credit to the firm's specific account.

Depreciation. The means by which an asset's value is expensed over its useful life for federal income tax purposes.

Direct Costs. See **Variable Costs.**

Direct Method. A format used to measure cash flow from operations, by which the different cash outflows occurring in regular operations of a business are subtracted from the cash flow collected from customers.

Direct Placement. See **Private Placement.**

Direct Quote. The exchange rate that indicates the number of units of the home currency required to buy one unit of foreign currency.

Direct Sale. The sale of securities by the corporation to the investing public without the services of an investment-banking firm.

Direct Securities. The pure financial claims issued by economic units to savers. These can later be transformed into indirect securities.

Disbursing Float. Funds available in the company's bank account until its payment check has cleared through the banking system.

Discount Bond. A bond that sells at a discount below par value.

Discounting. The inverse of compounding. This process is used to determine the present value of a cash flow.

Discount Rate. The interest rate used in the discounting process.

Discretionary Financing. Sources of financing that require an explicit decision on the part of the firm's management every time funds are raised. An example is a bank note which requires that negotiations be undertaken and an agreement signed setting forth the terms and conditions of the financing.

Diversifiable Risk. See **Unsystematic Risk.**

Dividend Payout Ratio. The amount of dividends relative to the company's net income or earnings per share.

Dividend Yield. The dividend per share divided by the price of the security.

Dunning Letters. Past-due letters sent out to delinquent accounts.

Du Pont Analysis. A method used to evaluate a firm's profitability and return on equity.

Earnings Before Interest and Taxes (EBIT). Profits from sales minus total operating expenses. Also called **Operating Income.**

Earnings Before Taxes (EBT). Operating income minus interest expense.

EBIT-EPS Indifference Point. The level of earnings before interest and taxes (EBIT) that will equate earnings per share (EPS) between two different financing plans.

Economic Failure. Situation in which a company's costs exceed its revenues. Stated differently, the internal rates of return on investments are less than the firm's cost of capital.

Efficient Market. A market in which the values of securities at any instant in time fully reflect all available information, which results in the market value and the intrinsic value being the same.

EPS. Typical financial notation for earnings per (common) share.

Equity. Stockholders' investment in the firm and the cumulative profits retained in the business up to the date of the balance sheet.

Equivalent Annual Annuity (EAA). An annuity cash flow that yields the same present value as the project's NPV. It is calculated by dividing the projects' NPV by the appropriate $PVIFA_{i,n}$.

Eurobond. A bond issued in a country different from the one in whose currency the bond is denominated; for example, a bond issued in Europe or Asia by an American company that pays interest and principal to the lender in U.S. dollars.

Eurodollar Market. This is a banking market in U.S. dollars outside the United States. Large sums of U.S. dollars can be borrowed or invested in this unregulated financial market. Similar external markets exist in Europe and Asia and for other major currencies.

Exchange Rate. The price of a foreign currency stated in terms of the domestic or home currency.

Exchange Rate Risk. The risk that tomorrow's exchange rate will differ from today's rate.

Ex-Dividend Date. The date upon which stock brokerage companies have uniformly decided to terminate the right of ownership to the dividend, which is two days prior to the date of record.

Expectations Theory. The concept that, no matter what the decision area, how the market price responds to management's actions is not determined entirely by the action itself; it is also affected by investors' expectations about the ultimate decision to be made by management.

Expected Rate of Return. (1) The discount rate that equates the present value of the future cash flows (interest and maturity value) with the current market price of a bond. It is the rate of return an investor will earn if the bond is held to maturity. (2) The rate of return the investor expects to receive on an investment by paying the existing market price of the security. (3) The arithmetic mean or average of all possible outcomes where those outcomes are weighted by the probability that each will occur.

Ex-Rights Date. The date on or after which the stock sells without rights.

External Common Equity. A new issue of common stock.

Factor. A firm that, in acquiring the receivables of other firms, bears the risk of collection and, for a fee, services the accounts.

Factoring Accounts Receivable. The outright sale of a firm's accounts receivable to another party (the factor) without recourse. The factor, in turn, bears the risk of collection.

Fair Value. The present value of an asset's expected future cash flows.

Federal Agency Securities. Debt obligations of corporations and agencies created to carry out the lending programs of the U.S. government.

Federal Reserve System. The U.S. central banking system.

Field Warehouse–Financing Agreement. A security agreement in which inventories pledged as collateral are physically separated from the firm's other inventories and placed under the control of a third-party field-warehousing firm.

Financial Analysis. The assessment of a firm's financial condition or well-being. Its objectives are to determine the firm's financial strengths and to identify its weaknesses. The primary tool of financial analysis is the financial ratio.

Financial Assets. Claims for future payment by one economic unit upon another.

Financial Intermediaries. Major financial institutions, such as commercial banks, savings and loan associations, credit unions, life insurance companies, and mutual funds, that assist the transfer of savings from economic units with excess savings to those with a shortage of savings.

Financial Leverage. The use of securities bearing a fixed (limited) rate of return to finance a portion of a firm's assets. Financial leverage can arise from the use of either debt or preferred stock financing. The use of financial leverage exposes the firm to financial risk.

Financial Markets. Institutions and procedures that facilitate transactions in all types of financial claims (securities).

Financial Policy. The firm's policies regarding the sources of financing it plans to use and the particular mix (proportions) in which they will be used.

Financial Ratios. Accounting data restated in relative terms to identify some of the financial strengths and weaknesses of a company.

Financial Risk. The added variability in earnings available to a firm's common shareholders, and the added chance of insolvency caused by the use of securities bearing a limited rate of return in the firm's financial structure. The use of financial leverage gives rise to financial risk.

Financial Structure. The mix of all funds sources that appear on the right-hand side of the balance sheet.

Financial Structure Design. The activity of seeking the proper mixture of a firm's short-term, long-term, and permanent financing components to minimize the cost of raising a given amount of funds.

Financing Costs. Cost incurred by a company that often include interest expenses and preferred dividends.

Finished-Goods Inventory. Goods on which the production has been completed but that are not yet sold.

Fixed-Asset Turnover. Sales divided by fixed assets. A ratio indicating how effectively a firm is using its fixed assets to generate sales.

Fixed Costs. Costs that do not vary in total dollar amount as sales volume or quantity of output changes. Also called **Indirect Costs.**

Fixed or Long-Term Assets. Assets comprising equipment, buildings, and land.

Float. The length of time from when a check is written until the actual recipient can draw upon or use the "good funds."

Floating Lien Agreement. An agreement, generally associated with a loan, whereby the borrower gives the lender a lien against all its inventory.

Floating Rate International Currency System. An international currency system in which exchange rates between different national currencies are allowed to fluctuate with supply and demand conditions. This contrasts with a fixed rate system in which exchange rates are pegged for extended periods of time and adjusted infrequently.

Flotation Costs. The transaction cost incurred when a firm raises funds by issuing a particular type of security.

Foreign Direct Investment. Physical assets, such as plant and equipment, acquired outside a corporation's home country but operated and controlled by that corporation.

Formal Control. Control vested in the stockholders having the majority of the voting common shares.

Forward Exchange Contract. A contract that requires delivery on a specified future date of one currency in return for a specified amount of another currency.

Forward-Spot Differential. The premium or discount between forward and spot currency exchange rates.

Future-Value Interest Factor ($FVIF_{i,n}$). The value $(1 + i)^n$ used as a multiplier to calculate an amount's future value.

Future-Value Interest Factor for an Annuity ($FVIFA_{i,n}$). The value $\left[\sum_{t=0}^{n-1} (1 + i)^t \right]$ used as a multiplier to calculate the future value of an annuity.

Futures Contract. A contract to buy or sell a stated commodity (such as soybeans or corn) or financial claim (such as U.S. Treasury bonds) at a specified price at a specified future time.

General Partnership. A partnership in which all partners are fully liable for the indebtedness incurred by the partnership.

Gross Income. A firm's dollar sales from its product or services less the cost of producing or acquiring the product or service.

Gross Profit Margin. Gross profit divided by net sales. A ratio denoting the gross profit of the firm as a percentage of net sales.

Hedge. A means to neutralize exchange rate risk on an exposed asset position, whereby a liability of the same amount and maturity is created in a foreign currency.

Hedging Principle. A working-capital management policy which states that the cash flow–generating characteristics of a firm's investments should be matched with the cash flow requirements of the firm's sources of financing. Very simply, short-lived assets should be financed with short-term sources of financing while long-lived assets should be financed with long-term sources of financing.

High-Yield Bond. See **Junk Bond.**

Holding-Period Return. The return an investor would receive from holding a security for a designated period of time. For example, a monthly holding-period return would be the return for holding a security for a month.

Hostile Takeover. A merger or acquisition in which management resists the group initiating the transaction.

Hurdle Rate. The required rate of return used in capital budgeting.

Income Statement. A basic accounting statement that measures the results of a firm's operations over a specified period, commonly one year. Also known as the profit and loss statement. The bottom line of the income statement shows the firm's profit or loss for the period.

Increasing-Stream Hypothesis of Dividend Policy. The hypothesis that dividend stability is essentially a smoothing of the dividend stream to minimize the effect of other types of company reversals. Thus, corporate managers make every effort to avoid a dividend cut, attempting instead to develop a gradually increasing dividend series over the long-term future.

Incremental Cash Flows. The cash flows that result from the acceptance of a capital-budgeting project.

Indenture. The legal agreement between a firm issuing bonds and the bond trustee who represents the bondholders, providing the specific terms of the loan agreement.

Indirect Costs. See **Fixed Costs.**

Indirect Method. An approach used to measure cash flows from operations, by which all operating expenses that did not result in a cash outflow for the period are added to net income.

Indirect Quote. The exchange rate that expresses the number of units of foreign currency that can be bought for one unit of home currency.

Indirect Securities. The unique financial claims issued by financial intermediaries. Mutual fund shares are an example.

Information Asymmetry. The difference in accessibility to information between managers and investors, which may result in a lower stock price than would be true in conditions of certainty.

Initial Outlay. The immediate cash outflow necessary to purchase an asset and put it in operating order.

Insolvency. The inability to meet interest payments or to repay debt at maturity.

Interest-Rate Parity Theory. The forward premium or discount should be equal and opposite in size to the differences in the national interest rates for the same maturity.

Interest Rate Risk. (1) The variability in a bond's value (risk) caused by changing interest. (2) The uncertainty that envelops the expected returns from a security caused by changes in interest rates. Price changes induced by interest rate changes are greater for long-term than for short-term financial instruments.

Internal Common Equity.   Profits retained within the business for investment purposes.

Internal Growth.   A firm's growth rate in earnings resulting from reinvesting company profits rather than distributing the earnings in the form of dividends. The growth rate is a function of the amount retained and the return earned on the retained funds.

Internal Rate of Return (IRR).   A capital-budgeting technique that reflects the rate of return a project earns. Mathematically, it is the discount rate that equates the present value of the inflows with the present value of the outflows.

Intrinsic or Economic Value.   The present value of an asset's expected future cash flows. This value is the amount the investor considers to be fair value, given the amount, timing, and riskiness of future cash flows.

Inventory Loans.   Loans secured by inventories. Examples include floating or blanket lien agreements, chattel mortgage agreements, field-warehouse receipt loans, and terminal-warehouse receipt loans.

Inventory Management.   The control of assets used in the production process or produced to be sold in the normal course of the firm's operations.

Inventory Turnover Ratio.   Cost of goods sold divided by inventory. A ratio that measures the number of times a firm's inventories are sold and replaced during the year. This ratio reflects the relative liquidity of inventories.

Investment Banker.   A financial specialist who underwrites and distributes new securities and advises corporate clients about raising new funds.

Investor's Required Rate of Return.   The minimum rate of return necessary to attract an investor to purchase or hold a security. It is also the discount rate that equates the present value of the cash flows with the value of the security.

Junk Bond.   Any bond rated BB or below.

Just-in-Time Inventory Control System.   A production and management system in which inventory is cut down to a minimum through adjustments to the time and physical distance between the various production operations. Under this system the firm keeps a minimum level of inventory on hand, relying upon suppliers to furnish parts "just in time" for them to be assembled.

Law of One Price.   The proposition that in competitive markets the same goods should sell for the same price where prices are stated in terms of a single currency.

Lead and Lag Strategies.   Techniques used to reduce exchange rate risk where the firm maximizes its asset position in the stronger currency and its liability position in the weaker currency.

Least-Square Regression.   A procedure for "fitting" a line through a scatter of observed data points in a way that minimizes the sum of the squared deviations of the points from the fitted line.

Leveraged Buyout (LBO).   A corporate restructuring where the existing shareholders sell their shares to a small group of investors. The purchasers of the stock use the firm's unused debt capacity to borrow the funds to pay for the stock.

Limited Liability.   A protective provision whereby the investor is not liable for more than the amount invested in the firm.

Limited Partnership.   A partnership in which one or more of the partners has limited liability, restricted to the amount of capital he or she invests in the partnership.

Line of Credit.   Generally an informal agreement or understanding between a borrower and a bank as to the maximum amount of credit the bank will provide the borrower at any one time. Under this type of agreement there is no "legal" commitment on the part of the bank to provide the stated credit. Compare **Revolving Credit Agreement.**

Liquidation Value.   The dollar sum that could be realized if an asset were sold independently of the going concern.

Liquidity.   A firm's ability to pay its bills on time. Liquidity is related to the ease and quickness with which a firm can convert its noncash assets into cash, as well as the size of the firm's investment in noncash assets vis-à-vis its short-term liabilities.

Liquidity Preference Theory.   The shape of the term structure of interest rates is determined by an investor's additional required interest rate in compensation of additional risks.

Liquidity Ratios.   Financial ratios used to assess the ability of a firm to pay its bills on time. Examples of liquidity ratios include the current ratio and the acid-test ratio.

Loan Amortization Schedule.   A breakdown of the interest and principle payments on an amortized loan.

Long-Term Residual Dividend Policy.   A dividend plan by which the residual capital is distributed smoothly to the investors over the planning period.

Mail Float.   Funds tied up during the time that elapses from the moment a customer mails his or her remittance check until the firm begins to process it.

Majority Voting.   Voting in which each share of stock allows the shareholder one vote, and each position on the board of directors is voted on separately. As a result, a majority of shares has the power to elect the entire board of directors.

Marginal Cost of Capital.   The cost of capital that represents the weighted cost of each additional dollar of financing from all sources, debt, preferred stock, and common stock.

Marginal Tax Rate.   The tax rate that would be applied to the next dollar of income.

Market Equilibrium.   The situation in which expected returns equal required returns.

Market Risk.   See **Systematic Risk.**

Market Segmentation Theory.   The shape of the term structure of interest rates implies that the rate of interest for a particular maturity is determined solely by demand and supply for a given maturity. This rate is independent of the demand and supply for securities having different maturities.

Market Value.   The value observed in the marketplace, where buyers and sellers negotiate a mutually acceptable price for the asset.

Market-Value Weights.   The percentage of financing provided by different capital sources, measured by the current market prices of the firm's bonds and preferred and common stock.

Marketable Securities.   Security investments (financial assets) the firm can quickly convert to cash balances. Also known as near cash or near-cash assets.

Maturity.   The length of time until the bond issuer returns the par value to the bondholder and terminates the bond.

Maturity Date.   The date upon which a borrower is to repay a loan.

Merger. A combination of two or more businesses into a single operational entity.

Money Market. All institutions and procedures that facilitate transactions in short-term instruments issued by borrowers with very high credit ratings.

Money-Market Mutual Funds. Investment companies that purchase a diversified array of short-term, high-grade (money-market) debt instruments.

Monitoring Costs. A form of agency costs. Typically these costs arise when bond investors take steps to ensure that protective covenants in the bond indenture are adhered to by management.

Mortgage Bond. A bond secured by a lien on real property.

Multinational Corporation (MNC). A corporation with holdings and/or operations in more than one country.

Mutually Exclusive Projects. A set of projects that perform essentially the same task, so that acceptance of one will necessarily mean rejection of the others.

Negotiable Certificates of Deposit. Marketable receipts for funds deposited in a bank for a fixed period. The deposited funds earn a fixed rate of interest. More commonly, these are called CDs.

Net Income. A figure representing a firm's profit or loss for the period. It also represents the earnings available to the firm's common *and* preferred stockholders.

Net Income Available to Common Equity (also **Net Common Stock Earnings**). Net income after interest, taxes, and preferred dividends.

Net Income Available to Common Stockholders (Net Income). A figure representing a firm's profit or loss for a period. It also represents the earnings available to the firm's common and preferred stockholders.

Net Operating Loss Carryback and Carryforward. A tax provision that permits the taxpayer first to apply the loss against the profits in the three prior years (carryback). If the loss has not been completely absorbed by the profits in these three years, it may be applied to taxable profits in each of the 15 following years (carryforward).

Net Present Value (NPV). A capital-budgeting concept defined as the present value of the project's annual net cash flows after tax less the project's initial outlay.

Net Profit Margin. Net income divided by sales. A ratio that measures the net income of the firm as a percent of sales.

Net Working Capital. The difference between the firm's current assets and its current liabilities.

Nondiversifiable Risk. See **Systematic Risk.**

Nominal Interest Rate. The interest rate paid on debt securities without an adjustment for any loss in purchasing power.

Normal Probability Distribution. A special class of bell-shaped distributions with symmetrically decreasing density, where the curve approaches but never reaches the X axis.

Offer Rate. Same as asked rate.

Operating Income. See **Earnings Before Interest and Taxes (EBIT).**

Operating Income Return on Investment. The ratio of net operating income divided by total assets.

Operating Leverage. The incurring of fixed operating costs in a firm's income stream.

Operating Profit Margin. Net operating income divided by sales. A firm's earnings before interest and taxes. This ratio serves as an overall measure of operating effectiveness.

Opportunity Cost of Funds. The next-best rate of return available to the investor for a given level of risk.

Optimal Capital Structure. The capital structure that minimizes the firm's composite cost of capital (maximizes the common stock price) for raising a given amount of funds.

Optimal Range of Financial Leverage. The range of various capital structure combinations that yield the lowest overall cost of capital for the firm.

Option Contract. The right to buy or sell a fixed number of shares at a specified price over a limited time period.

Order Point Problem. Determining how low inventory should be depleted before it is reordered.

Order Quantity Problem. Determining the optimal order size for an inventory item given its usage, carrying costs, and ordering costs.

Organized Security Exchanges. Formal organizations involved in the trading of securities. Such exchanges are tangible entities that conduct auction markets in listed securities.

Other Assets. Assets not otherwise included in current assets or fixed assets.

Over-the-Counter Markets. All security markets except the organized exchanges. The money market is an over-the-counter market. Most corporate bonds also are traded in this market.

Partnership. An association of two or more individuals joining together as co-owners to operate a business for profit.

Par Value. On the face of a bond, the stated amount that the firm is to repay upon the maturity date.

Payable-Through Draft (PTD). A legal instrument that has the physical appearance of an ordinary check but is not drawn on a bank. A payable-through draft is drawn on and paid by the issuing firm. The bank serves as a collection point and passes the draft on to the firm.

Payback Period. A capital-budgeting criterion defined as the number of years required to recover the initial cash investment.

Payment Date. The date on which the company mails a dividend check to each investor of record.

Percent of Sales Method. A method of financial forecasting that involves estimating the level of an expense, asset, or liability for a future period as a percent of the sales forecast.

Perfect Capital Market. An assumption that allows one to study the effect of dividend decisions in isolation. It assumes that (1) investors can buy and sell stocks without incurring any transaction costs, such as brokerage commissions; (2) companies can issue stocks without any cost of doing so; (3) there are no corporate or personal taxes; (4) complete information about the firm is readily available; (5) there are no conflicts of interest between management and stockholders; and (6) financial distress and bankruptcy costs are nonexistent.

Permanent Investment. An investment that the firm expects to hold longer than one year. The firm makes permanent investments in fixed and current assets. Compare **Temporary Investments.**

Perpetuity. An annuity with an infinite life.

Pledging Accounts Receivable. A loan the firm obtains from a commercial bank or a finance company using its accounts receivable as collateral.

Plowback Ratio.   The fraction of earnings that are reinvested, or plowed back, into the firm.

Portfolio Beta.   The relationship between a portfolio's returns and the market returns. It is a measure of the portfolio's non-diversifiable risk.

Portfolio Diversification Effect.   The fact that variations of the returns from a portfolio or combination of assets may be less than the sum of the variation of the individual assets making up the portfolio.

Preauthorized Check (PAC).   A check that resembles an ordinary check but does not contain or require the signature of the person on whose account it is being drawn. A PAC is created only with the individual's legal authorization. The PAC system is advantageous when the firm regularly receives a large volume of payments of a fixed amount from the same customer over a long period.

Preemptive Right.   The right entitling the common shareholder to maintain his or her proportionate share of ownership in the firm.

Preferred Stock.   A hybrid security with characteristics of both common stock and bonds. It is similar to common stock in that it has no fixed maturity date, the nonpayment of dividends does not bring on bankruptcy, and dividends are not deductible for tax purposes. It is similar to bonds in that dividends are limited in amount.

Premium Bond.   A bond that is selling above its par value.

Present Value.   The value in today's dollars of a future payment discounted back to present at the required rate of return.

Present-Value Interest Factor ($PVIF_{i,n}$).   The value $[1/(1 + i)^n]$ used as a multiplier to calculate an amount's present value.

Present-Value Interest Factor for an Annuity ($PVIFA_{i,n}$).   The value $\left[\sum_{t=1}^{n}\dfrac{1}{(1 + i)^t}\right]$ used as a multiplier to calculate the present value of an annuity.

Price-Earnings (P/E) Ratio.   The price the market places on $1 of a firm's earnings. For example, if a firm has an earnings per share of $2, and a stock price of $30, its price-earnings ratio is 15 ($30 ÷ $2).

Primary Markets.   Transactions in securities offered for the first time to potential investors.

Principle of Self-Liquidating Debt.   See **Hedging Principle.**

Private Placement.   A security offering limited to a small number of potential investors.

Privileged Subscription.   The process of marketing a new security issue to a select group of investors.

Processing Float.   Funds tied up during the time required for the firm to process remittance checks before they can be deposited in the bank.

Profit Budget.   A budget of forecasted profits based on information gleaned from the cost and sales budgets.

Profit Margins.   Financial ratios (sometimes simply referred to as margins) that reflect the level of firm profits relative to sales. Examples include the gross profit margin (gross profit divided by sales), operating profit margin (operating earnings divided by sales), and the net profit margin (net profit divided by sales).

Profitability Index (PI).   A capital-budgeting criterion defined as the ratio of the present value of the future net cash flows to the initial outlay. Also called **Benefit-Cost Ratio.**

Pro Forma Income Statement.   A statement of planned profit or loss for a future period.

Prospectus.   A condensed version of the full registration statement filed with the Securities and Exchange Commission that describes a new security issue.

Protective Provisions.   Provisions for preferred stock included in terms of the issue to protect the investor's interest. For instance, provisions generally allow for voting in the event of nonpayment of dividends, or they restrict the payment of common stock dividends if sinking-fund payments are not met or if the firm is in financial difficulty.

Proxy.   A means of voting in which a designated party is provided with the temporary power of attorney to vote for the signee at the corporation's annual meeting.

Proxy Fight.   A battle between rival groups for proxy votes in order to control the decisions made in a stockholders' meeting.

Public Offering.   A security offering where all investors have the opportunity to acquire a portion of the financial claims being sold.

Purchasing Power Parity Theory.   In the long run, exchange rates adjust so that the purchasing power of each currency tends to be the same.

Pure Play Method.   A method of estimating a project's beta that involves looking for a publicly traded firm on the outside that looks like the project and using that outside firm's required rate of return to judge the project.

Put Option.   The right to sell a given number of shares of common stock or some other asset at a specified price over a given time period.

Quick Ratio.   See **Acid-Test Ratio.**

Raw-Materials Inventory.   The basic materials purchased from other firms to be used in the firm's production operations.

Real Assets.   Tangible assets like houses, equipment, and inventories; real assets are distinguished from financial assets.

Real Interest Rate.   The nominal rate of interest less any loss in purchasing power of the dollar during the time of the investment.

Remote Disbursing.   A cash management service specifically designed to extend disbursing float.

Repurchase Agreements.   Legal contracts that involve the sale of short-term securities by a borrower to a lender of funds. The borrower commits to repurchase the securities at a later date at the contract price plus a stated interest charge.

Required Rate of Return.   See **Investor's Required Rate of Return.**

Residual Dividend Theory.   A theory that a company's dividend payment should equal the cash left after financial all the investments that have positive net present values.

Restrictive Covenants.   Provisions in the loan agreement that place restrictions on the borrower and make the loan immediately payable and due when violated. These restrictive covenants are designed to maintain the borrower's financial condition on a par with that which existed at the time the loan was made.

Retained Earnings.   Cumulative profits retained in a business up to the date of the balance sheet.

Return on Common Equity.   Net income available to the common stockholders divided by common equity. A ratio relating earned income to the common stockholder's investment.

Return on Total Assets. Net income divided by total assets. This ratio determines the yield on the firm's assets by relating net income to total assets.

Return-Risk Line. A specification of the appropriate required rates of return for investments having different amounts of risk.

Revolving Credit Agreement. An understanding between the borrower and the bank as to the amount of credit the bank will be legally obligated to provide the borrower. Compare **Line of Credit.**

Right. A certificate issued to common stockholders giving them an option to purchase a stated number of new shares at a specified price during a 2- to 10-week period.

Risk. Potential variability in future cash flows. The likely variability associated with revenue or income streams. This concept has been measured operationally as the standard deviation or beta.

Risk-Adjusted Discount Rate. A method for incorporating a project's level of risk into the capital-budgeting process, in which the discount rate is adjusted upward to compensate for higher-than-normal risk or downward to compensate for lower-than-normal risk.

Risk-Free Rate of Return. The rate of return on risk-free investments. The interest rates on short-term U.S. government securities are commonly used to measure this rate.

Risk Premium. The additional return expected for assuming risk.

Safety Stock. Inventory held to accommodate any unusually large and unexpected usage during delivery time.

Sales Forecast. Projection of future sales.

Salvage Value. The value of an asset or investment project at the end of its usable life.

Scenario Analysis. Simulation analysis that focuses on an examination of the range of possible outcomes.

Secondary Market. Transactions in currently outstanding securities. This is distinguished from the new issues or primary market.

Secured Loans. Sources of credit that require security in the form of pledged assets. In the event the borrower defaults in payment of principal or interest, the lender can seize the pledged assets and sell them to settle the debt.

Securities and Exchange Commission (SEC). The federal agency created by the Securities Exchange Act of 1934 to enforce federal securities laws.

Securities Exchange Act of 1933. A regulation that requires registration of certain new issues of public securities with the Securities and Exchange Commission (SEC). The registration statement should disclose all facts relevant to the new issue that will permit an investor to make an informed decision.

Securities Exchange Act of 1934. This act enables the SEC to enforce federal securities laws. The major aspects of the 1934 act include (1) major securities exchanges are required to register with the SEC; (2) insider-trading is regulated; (3) stock price manipulation by investors is prohibited; (4) the SEC has control over proxy procedures; and (5) the Board of Governors of the Federal Reserve System is given the responsibility of setting margin requirements.

Security Market Line. The return line that reflects the attitudes of investors regarding the minimum acceptable return for a given level of systematic risk.

Selling Group. A collection of securities dealers that participates in the distribution of new issues to final investors. A selling-group agreement links these dealers to the underwriting syndicate.

Selling Rate. Same as the asked rate.

Sell-off. The sale of a subsidiary, division, or product line by one firm to another.

Semifixed Costs. See **Semivariable Costs.**

Semivariable Costs. Costs that exhibit the joint characteristics of both fixed and variable costs over different ranges of output. Also called **Semifixed Costs.**

Sensitivity Analysis. The process of determining how the distribution of possible net present values or internal rates of return for a particular project is affected by a change in one particular input variable.

Shelf Offering. See **Shelf Registration.**

Shelf Registration. A procedure for issuing new securities where the firm obtains a master registration statement approved by the SEC.

Simple Arbitrage. Trading to eliminate exchange rate differentials across the markets for a single currency, e.g. for the New York and London markets.

Simulation. The process of imitating the performance of an investment project through repeated evaluations, usually using a computer. In the general case, experimentation upon a mathematical model that has been designed to capture the critical realities of the decision-making situation.

Sinking-Fund Provision. A protective provision that requires the firm periodically to set aside an amount of money for the retirement of its preferred stock. This money is then used to purchase the preferred stock in the open market or through the use of the call provision, whichever method is cheaper.

Small, Regular Dividend Plus a Year-End Extra. A corporate policy of paying a small regular dollar dividend plus a year-end extra dividend in prosperous years to avoid the connotation of a permanent dividend.

Sole Proprietorship. A business owned by a single individual.

Spin-off. The separation of a subsidiary from its parent, with no change in the equity ownership. The management of the parent company gives up operating control over the subsidiary, but the shareholders maintain their same percentage ownership in both firms. New shares representing ownership in the averted company are issued to the original shareholders on a pro rata basis.

Spontaneous Financing. The trade credit and other accounts payable that arise "spontaneously" in the firm's day-to-day operations.

Spot Transaction. A transaction made immediately in the marketplace at the market price.

Stable Dollar Dividend per Share. A dividend policy that maintains a relatively stable dollar dividend per share over time.

Standard Deviation. A statistical measure of the spread of a probability distribution calculated by squaring the difference between each outcome and its expected value, weighting each value by its probability, summing over all possible outcomes, and taking the square root of this sum.

Stock Buyback. See **Stock Repurchase.**

Stock Dividend. A distribution of shares of up to 25 percent of the number of shares currently outstanding, issued on a pro rata basis to the current stockholders.

Stock Market Value. (See **Market Value.**)

Stock Repurchase. The repurchase of common stock by the issuing firm for any of a variety of reasons, resulting in a reduction of shares outstanding. Also called **Stock Buyback.**

Stock Split. A stock dividend exceeding 25 percent of the number of shares currently outstanding.

Straight-Line Depreciation. A method for computing depreciation expenses in which the cost of the asset is divided by the asset's useful life.

Stretching on Trade Credit. Failing to pay within the prescribed credit period. For example, under credit terms of 2/10, net 30, a firm would be stretching its trade credit if it failed to pay by the thirtieth day and paid on the sixtieth day.

Subchapter S Corporation. A corporation that, because of specific qualifications, is taxed as though it were a partnership.

Subordinated Debenture. A debenture that is subordinated to other debentures in being paid in case of insolvency.

Subscription Price. The price for which the security may be purchased in a rights offering.

Sustainable Rate of Growth. The rate at which a firm's sales can grow if it wants to maintain its present financial ratios and does not want to resort to the sale of new equity shares.

Syndicate. A group of investment bankers who contractually assist in the buying and selling of a new security issue.

Systematic Risk. (1) The portion of variations in investment returns that cannot be eliminated through investor diversification. This variation results from factors that affect all stocks. Also called **Market Risk** or **Nondiversifiable Risk.** (2) The risk of a project from the viewpoint of a well-diversified shareholder. This measure takes into account that some of the project's risk will be diversified away as the project is combined with the firm's other projects, and, in addition, some of the remaining risk will be diversified away by shareholders as they combine this stock with other stocks in their portfolios.

Target Capital Structure Mix. The mix of financing sources that a firm plans to maintain through time.

Target Debt Ratio. A desired proportion of long-term debt in a firm's capital structure. Alternatively, it may be the desired proportion of total debt in the firm's financial structure.

Taxable Income. Gross income from all sources, except for allowable exclusions, less any tax-deductible expenses.

Tax Expenses. Tax liability determined by earnings before taxes.

Tax Liability. The amount owed the federal, state, or local taxing authorities.

Tax Shield. The element from the federal tax code that permits interest costs to be deductible when computing a firm's tax bill. The dollar difference (the shield) flows to the firm's security holders.

Temporary Financing. Financing (other than spontaneous sources) that will be repaid within a period of one year or less. Included among these sources of short-term debt are secured and unsecured bank loans, commercial paper, loans secured by accounts receivable, and loans secured by inventories.

Temporary Investments. A firm's investments in current assets that will be liquidated and not replaced within a period of one year or less. Examples include seasonal expansions in inventories and accounts receivable. Compare **Permanent Investments.**

Tender Offer. A formal offer by the company to buy a specified number of shares at a predetermined and stated price. The tender price is set above the current market price in order to attract sellers.

Terminal Warehouse Agreement. A security agreement in which the inventories pledged as collateral are transported to a public warehouse that is physically removed from the borrower's premises. This is the safest (though costly) form of financing secured by inventory.

Term Loans. Loans that have maturities of 1 to 10 years and are repaid in periodic installments over the life of the loan. Term loans are usually secured by a chattel mortgage on equipment or a mortgage on real property.

Terms of Sale. The credit terms identifying the possible discount for early payment.

Term Structure of Interest Rates. The relationship between interest rates and the term to maturity, where the risk of default is held constant.

Times Interest Earned Ratio. Earnings before interest and taxes (EBIT) divided by interest expense. A ratio that measures a firm's ability to meet its interest payments from its annual operating earnings.

Total Asset Turnover. Sales divided by total tangible assets. An overall measure of the relation between a firm's tangible assets and the sales they generate.

Total Project Risk. A project's risk ignoring the fact that much of the risk will be diversified away as the project is combined with the firm's other projects and assets.

Total Revenue. Total sales dollars.

Trade Credit. Credit made available by a firm's suppliers in conjunction with the acquisition of materials. Trade credit appears on the balance sheet as accounts payable.

Transaction Loan. A loan where the proceeds are designated for a specific purpose—for example, a bank loan used to finance the acquisition of a piece of equipment.

Transfer Price. The price a subsidiary or a parent company charges other companies that are part of the same MNC for its goods or services.

Transit Float. Funds tied up during the time necessary for a deposited check to clear through the commercial banking system and become usable funds to the company.

Treasury Bills. Direct debt obligations of the U.S. government sold on a regular basis by the U.S. Treasury.

Trend Analysis. An analysis of a firm's financial ratios over time.

Triangular Arbitrage. Arbitrage across the markets for all currencies.

Unbiased Expectations Theory. The shape of the term structure of interest rates is determined by an investor's expectations about future interest rates.

Underwriting. The purchase and subsequent resale of a new security issue. The risk of selling the new issue at a satisfactory (profitable) price is assumed (underwritten) by the investment banker.

Underwriting Syndicate. A temporary association of investment bankers formed to purchase a new security issue and quickly resell it at a profit. Formation of the syndicate spreads the risk of loss among several investment bankers, thereby minimizing the risk exposure of any single underwriter.

Undiversifiable Risk. The portion of the variation in investment returns that cannot be eliminated through investor diversification.

Unique Risk. See **Unsystematic Risk.**

Unsecured Loans. All sources of credit that have as their security only the lender's faith in the borrower's ability to repay the funds when due.

Unsystematic Risk. The portion of the variation in investment returns that can be eliminated through investor diversification. This diversifiable risk is the result of factors that are unique to the particular firm. Also called **Company-Unique Risk** or **Diversifiable Risk.**

Value of a Bond. The present value of the interest payments, I_1 in period t, plus the present value of the redemption or par value of the indebtedness, M, at the maturity date.

Value of a Security. The present value of all future cash inflows expected to be received by the investor owning the security.

Variable Costs. Costs that are fixed per unit of output but vary in total as output changes. Also called **Direct Costs.**

Volume of Output. A firm's level of operations expressed either in sales dollars or as units of output.

Weighted Cost of Capital. A composite of the individual costs of financing incurred by each capital source. A firm's weighted cost of capital is a function of (1) the individual costs of capital, (2) the capital structure mix, and (3) the level of financing necessary to make the investment.

Weighted Marginal Cost of Capital. The composite cost for each additional dollar of financing. The marginal cost of capital represents the appropriate criterion for making investment decisions.

Wire Transfers. A method of moving funds electronically between bank accounts in order to eliminate transit float. The wired funds are immediately usable at the receiving bank.

Working Capital. A concept traditionally defined as a firm's investment in current assets. Compare **Net Working Capital.**

Work-in-Process Inventory. Partially finished goods requiring additional work before they become finished goods.

Yield to Maturity. (1) See **Term Structure of Interest Rates.** (2) The rate of return a bondholder will receive if the bond is held to maturity. (Equivalent to the expected rate of return.)

Zero and Very Low Coupon Bond. A bond issued at a substantial discount from its $1,000 face value and that pays little or no interest.

Zero Balance Accounts (ZBA). A cash management tool that permits centralized control over cash outflow while maintaining divisional disbursing authority. Objectives are (1) to achieve better control over cash payments; (2) to reduce excess cash balances held in regional banks for disbursing purposes; and (3) to increase disbursing float.

INDEX

Subject

A

Accelerated cost recovery system (ACRS), 303
  modified, 9
Accountability, 337, 546–47
Accounting profits, 13, 296
Accounts receivable loans, 448–50
Accounts receivable management, 483, 485–88
  aging of accounts receivable, 83n
  collection efforts and, 485, 486, 487–88
  size of investment, 485–88
  terms of sale and, 486
  type of customer and, 486–87
Accounts receivable turnover ratio, 83, 87
Accrued taxes, 443
Accrued wages, 443
Acid-test (quick) ratio, 82
Active investor, emergence of, 546–47
Adams, F. Gerard, 115n
Added value, 215
Adkins, Arthur W.H., 224n
Advising function of investment banker, 43
Agency problem, 15–16, 379, 544–47
  agency costs
    dividend policy and, 411–12
    firm value and, 380–84
    mergers and reduction of, 539–40
  executive compensation, 545–46
  free cash flow theory, 381–83, 540
  relationship investing, 546–47
Aging of accounts receivable, 83n, 489
Alexander, G., 542n
Allen, Robert E., 1
Altman, Edward I., 380n
American Stock Exchange (AMEX), 40
Amihud, Yakov, 548n
Amortized loans, 157–58
Analytical income statement, 361
Annual percentage rate (APR)
  on accounts receivable loan, 448–49
  on commercial paper, 447–48
  on factored accounts receivable, 449–50
Annual percentage yield formula, 442
Annuities, 151–56

compound, 151–53
defined, 151
due, 156–57
equivalent annual (EAA), 279–80
future-value interest factor for, 152
present-value interest factor for, 154, 270–72
present value of, 154–56
Anticipatory buying, 495
Arbitrage, 512
Arbitrage pricing model (APM), 245
Arbitrageur, 512
Arendt, H., 337n
Argentina, inflation rate in, 162
Aronson, J. Richard, 389n
Asked rate, 512–13
Asset allocation, 239–40
  investor and, 241
Assets. *See also* Valuation
  balance sheet, 71–72
  current, 71, 118, 436–37. *See also*
    Working-capital management
  financial, 34
  fixed (long-term), 72
  long-term, 72
  as percentage of sales, 118
  permanent, 440
  real, 34
  return on, 85n, 92
  temporary, 440
  total asset turnover, 86
Asset-selection. *See* Capital budgeting
Asymmetry, information, 411
Automated depository transfer check system, 469
Average collection period, 83

B

Bakar, Todd, 208
Baker, H. Kent, 413–14
Balance sheet, 71–74, 373
Balance-sheet leverage ratios, 365–66
Bank credit, 444–46

Bankers' acceptances, 480, 484
Banking Act of 1933, 43
Bankruptcy
  cost of debt and, 378
  costs associated with, 311
    mergers and reduction in, 541
  financial risk and threat of, 438n
Banks for Cooperatives, 480
Bank Wire, 470
Barclay, Michael J., 404n
Barriers to entry, 14–15
Barro, Richard J., 549n
Barwise, Patrick, 301n
Base case, using the right, 301
Beebower, Gilbert L., 239–40
Benefit-cost ratio, 265–66
Benson, P., 542n
Berle, A.A. Jr., 380n
Bernstein, Peter, 405
Best-efforts basis of selling security issues, 44
Beta, 234–38
  controversy over, 243–45, 547–48
  defined, 234
  estimating, 314–16
    pure play method of, 316
    using accounting data, 314–16
  portfolio, 237–38
Bhide, Amar, 538n
Bid-asked spread, 513
Bid rate, 513
Bierman, Harold Jr., 281n
Biotechnology industry, 505
"Bird in the hand" theory, 406–7
Black, Fischer, 404–5, 408–9, 413n
Black, Pam, 228
Blue sky laws, 48
Blume, Marshall E., 339–40
Board of directors, 204, 546
Board of Governors of Federal Reserve System, 49
Board of Trade of the City of Chicago, 40n
Boesky, Ivan F., 18, 47–48, 49
Bond rating agencies, 177, 178
Bond ratings, 177–79

Corporate

Table B. Compound Sum of $1: $(1 + I)^n$

Period	1%	2%	3%	4%	5%	6%	7%	8%	9%	10%	12%	14%	15%	16%	18%	20%	24%	28%	32%	36%
1	1.0100	1.0200	1.0300	1.0400	1.0500	1.0600	1.0700	1.0800	1.0900	1.1000	1.1200	1.1400	1.1500	1.1600	1.1800	1.2000	1.2400	1.2800	1.3200	1.3600
2	1.0201	1.0404	1.0609	1.0816	1.1025	1.1236	1.1449	1.1664	1.1881	1.2100	1.2544	1.2996	1.3225	1.3456	1.3924	1.4400	1.5376	1.6384	1.7424	1.8496
3	1.0303	1.0612	1.0927	1.1249	1.1576	1.1910	1.2250	1.2597	1.2950	1.3310	1.4049	1.4815	1.5209	1.5609	1.6430	1.7280	1.9066	2.0972	2.3000	2.5155
4	1.0406	1.0824	1.1255	1.1699	1.2155	1.2625	1.3108	1.3605	1.4116	1.4641	1.5735	1.6890	1.7490	1.8106	1.9388	2.0736	2.3642	2.6844	3.0380	3.4210
5	1.0510	1.1041	1.1593	1.2167	1.2763	1.3382	1.4026	1.4693	1.5386	1.6105	1.7623	1.9254	2.0114	2.1003	2.2878	2.4883	2.9316	3.4360	4.0075	4.6526
6	1.0615	1.1262	1.1941	1.2653	1.3401	1.4185	1.5007	1.5869	1.6771	1.7716	1.9738	2.1950	2.3131	2.4364	2.6996	2.9860	3.6352	4.3980	5.2899	6.3275
7	1.0721	1.1487	1.2299	1.3159	1.4071	1.5036	1.6058	1.7138	1.8280	1.9487	2.2107	2.5023	2.6600	2.8262	3.1855	3.5832	4.5077	5.6295	6.9826	8.6054
8	1.0829	1.1717	1.2668	1.3686	1.4775	1.5938	1.7182	1.8509	1.9926	2.1436	2.4760	2.8526	3.0590	3.2784	3.7589	4.2998	5.5895	7.2058	9.2170	11.703
9	1.0937	1.1951	1.3048	1.4233	1.5513	1.6895	1.8385	1.9990	2.1719	2.3579	2.7731	3.2519	3.5179	3.8030	4.4355	5.1598	6.9310	9.2234	12.166	15.916
10	1.1046	1.2190	1.3439	1.4802	1.6289	1.7908	1.9672	2.1589	2.3674	2.5937	3.1058	3.7072	4.0456	4.4114	5.2338	6.1917	8.5944	11.805	16.059	21.646
11	1.1157	1.2434	1.3842	1.5395	1.7103	1.8983	2.1049	2.3316	2.5804	2.8531	3.4785	4.2262	4.6524	5.1173	6.1759	7.4301	10.657	15.111	21.198	29.439
12	1.1268	1.2682	1.4258	1.6010	1.7959	2.0122	2.2522	2.5182	2.8127	3.1384	3.8960	4.8179	5.3502	5.9360	7.2876	8.9161	13.214	19.342	27.982	40.037
13	1.1381	1.2936	1.4685	1.6651	1.8856	2.1329	2.4098	2.7196	3.0658	3.4523	4.3635	5.4924	6.1528	6.8858	8.5994	10.699	16.386	24.758	36.937	54.451
14	1.1495	1.3195	1.5126	1.7317	1.9799	2.2609	2.5785	2.9372	3.3417	3.7975	4.8871	6.2613	7.0757	7.9875	10.147	12.839	20.319	31.691	48.756	74.053
15	1.1610	1.3459	1.5580	1.8009	2.0789	2.3966	2.7590	3.1722	3.6425	4.1772	5.4736	7.1379	8.1371	9.2655	11.973	15.407	25.195	40.564	64.358	100.71
16	1.1726	1.3728	1.6047	1.8730	2.1829	2.5404	2.9522	3.4259	3.9703	4.5950	6.1304	8.1372	9.3576	10.748	14.129	18.488	31.242	51.923	84.953	136.96
17	1.1843	1.4002	1.6528	1.9479	2.2920	2.6928	3.1588	3.7000	4.3276	5.0545	6.8660	9.2765	10.761	12.467	16.672	22.186	38.740	66.461	112.13	186.27
18	1.1961	1.4282	1.7024	2.0258	2.4066	2.8543	3.3799	3.9960	4.7171	5.5599	7.6900	10.575	12.375	14.462	19.673	26.623	48.038	85.070	148.02	253.33
19	1.2081	1.4568	1.7535	2.1068	2.5270	3.0256	3.6165	4.3157	5.1417	6.1159	8.6128	12.055	14.231	16.776	23.214	31.948	59.567	108.89	195.39	344.53
20	1.2202	1.4859	1.8061	2.1911	2.6533	3.2071	3.8697	4.6610	5.6044	6.7275	9.6463	13.743	16.366	19.460	27.393	38.337	73.864	139.37	257.91	468.57
21	1.2324	1.5157	1.8603	2.2788	2.7860	3.3996	4.1406	5.0338	6.1088	7.4002	10.803	15.667	18.821	22.574	32.323	46.005	91.591	178.40	340.44	637.26
22	1.2447	1.5460	1.9161	2.3699	2.9253	3.6035	4.4304	5.4365	6.6586	8.1403	12.100	17.861	21.644	26.186	38.142	55.206	113.57	228.35	449.39	866.67
23	1.2572	1.5769	1.9736	2.4647	3.0715	3.8197	4.7405	5.8715	7.2579	8.9543	13.552	20.361	24.891	30.376	45.007	66.247	140.83	292.30	593.19	1178.6
24	1.2697	1.6084	2.0328	2.5633	3.2251	4.0489	5.0724	6.3412	7.9111	9.8497	15.178	23.212	28.625	35.236	53.108	79.496	174.63	374.14	783.02	1602.9
25	1.2824	1.6406	2.0938	2.6658	3.3864	4.2919	5.4274	6.8485	8.6231	10.834	17.000	26.461	32.918	40.874	62.668	95.396	216.54	478.90	1033.5	2180.0
26	1.2953	1.6734	2.1566	2.7725	3.5557	4.5494	5.8074	7.3964	9.3992	11.918	19.040	30.166	37.856	47.414	73.948	114.47	268.51	612.99	1364.3	2964.9
27	1.3082	1.7069	2.2213	2.8834	3.7335	4.8223	6.2139	7.9881	10.245	13.110	21.324	34.389	43.535	55.000	87.259	137.37	332.95	784.63	1800.9	4032.2
28	1.3213	1.7410	2.2879	2.9987	3.9201	5.1117	6.6488	8.6271	11.167	14.421	23.883	39.204	50.065	63.800	102.96	164.84	412.86	1004.3	2377.2	5483.8
29	1.3345	1.7758	2.3566	3.1187	4.1161	5.4184	7.1143	9.3173	12.172	15.863	26.749	44.693	57.575	74.008	121.50	197.81	511.95	1285.5	3137.9	7458.0
30	1.3478	1.8114	2.4273	3.2434	4.3219	5.7435	7.6123	10.062	13.267	17.449	29.959	50.950	66.211	85.849	143.37	237.37	634.81	1645.5	4142.0	10143.
40	1.4889	2.2080	3.2620	4.8010	7.0400	10.285	14.974	21.724	31.409	45.259	93.050	188.88	267.86	378.72	750.37	1469.7	5455.9	19426.	66520.	*
50	1.6446	2.6916	4.3839	7.1067	11.467	18.420	29.457	46.901	74.357	117.39	289.00	700.23	1083.6	1670.7	3927.3	9100.4	46890.	*	*	*
60	1.8167	3.2810	5.8916	10.519	18.679	32.987	57.946	101.25	176.03	304.48	897.59	2595.9	4383.9	7370.1	20555.	56347.	*	*	*	*

*FVIF > 99,999.

Table C. Present Value of $1: $\dfrac{\$1}{(1 + I)_n}$

Period	1%	3%	5%	6%	7%	8%	9%	10%	11%	12%	13%	14%	15%	16%	17%	18%	19%	20%	24%	28%
1	.9901	.9709	.9524	.9434	.9346	.9259	.9174	.9091	.9009	.8929	.8850	.8772	.8696	.8621	.8547	.8475	.8403	.8333	.8065	.7813
2	.9803	.9426	.9070	.8900	.8734	.8573	.8417	.8264	.8116	.7972	.7831	.7695	.7561	.7432	.7305	.7182	.7062	.6944	.6504	.6104
3	.9706	.9151	.8638	.8396	.8163	.7938	.7722	.7513	.7312	.7118	.6930	.6750	.6575	.6407	.6244	.6086	.5934	.5787	.5245	.4768
4	.9610	.8885	.8227	.7921	.7629	.7350	.7084	.6830	.6587	.6355	.6133	.5921	.5718	.5523	.5336	.5158	.4987	.4823	.4230	.3725
5	.9515	.8626	.7835	.7473	.7130	.6806	.6499	.6209	.5934	.5674	.5428	.5194	.4972	.4761	.4561	.4371	.4190	.4019	.3411	.2910
6	.9420	.8375	.7462	.7050	.6663	.6302	.5963	.5645	.5346	.5066	.4803	.4556	.4323	.4104	.3898	.3704	.3521	.3349	.2751	.2274
7	.9327	.8131	.7107	.6651	.6627	.5835	.5470	.5132	.4817	.4523	.4251	.3996	.3759	.3538	.3332	.3139	.2959	.2791	.2218	.1776
8	.9235	.7894	.6768	.6274	.5820	.5403	.5019	.4665	.4339	.4039	.3762	.3506	.3269	.3050	.2848	.2660	.2487	.2326	.1789	.1388
9	.9143	.7664	.6446	.5919	.5439	.5002	.4604	.4241	.3909	.3606	.3329	.3075	.2843	.2630	.2434	.2255	.2090	.1938	.1443	.1084
10	.9053	.7441	.6139	.5584	.5083	.4632	.4224	.3855	.3522	.3220	.2946	.2697	.2472	.2267	.2080	.1911	.1756	.1615	.1164	.0847
11	.8963	.7224	.5847	.5268	.4751	.4289	.3875	.3505	.3173	.2875	.2607	.2366	.2149	.1954	.1778	.1619	.1476	.1346	.0938	.0662
12	.8874	.7014	.5568	.4970	.4440	.3971	.3555	.3186	.2858	.2567	.2307	.2076	.1869	.1685	.1520	.1372	.1240	.1122	.0757	.0517
13	.8787	.6810	.5303	.4688	.4150	.3677	.3262	.2897	.2575	.2292	.2042	.1821	.1625	.1452	.1299	.1163	.1042	.0935	.0610	.0404
14	.8700	.6611	.5051	.4423	.3878	.3405	.2992	.2633	.2320	.2046	.1807	.1597	.1413	.1252	.1110	.0985	.0876	.0779	.0492	.0316
15	.8613	.6419	.4810	.4173	.3624	.3152	.2745	.2394	.2090	.1827	.1599	.1401	.1229	.1079	.0949	.0835	.0736	.0649	.0397	.0247
16	.8528	.6232	.4581	.3936	.3387	.2919	.2519	.2176	.1883	.1631	.1415	.1229	.1069	.0930	.0811	.0708	.0618	.0541	.0320	.0193
17	.8444	.6050	.4363	.3714	.3166	.2703	.2311	.1978	.1696	.1456	.1252	.1078	.0929	.0802	.0693	.0600	.0520	.0451	.0258	.0150
18	.8360	.5874	.4155	.3503	.2959	.2502	.2120	.1799	.1528	.1300	.1108	.0946	.0808	.0691	.0592	.0508	.0437	.0376	.0208	.0118
19	.8277	.5703	.3957	.3305	.2765	.2317	.1945	.1635	.1377	.1161	.0981	.0829	.0703	.0596	.0506	.0431	.0367	.0313	.0168	.0092
20	.8195	.5537	.3769	.3118	.2584	.2145	.1784	.1486	.1240	.1037	.0868	.0728	.0611	.0514	.0433	.0365	.0308	.0261	.0135	.0072
25	.7798	.4776	.2953	.2330	.1842	.1460	.1160	.0923	.0736	.0588	.0471	.0378	.0304	.0245	.0197	.0160	.0129	.0105	.0046	.0021
30	.7419	.4120	.2314	.1741	.1314	.0994	.0754	.0573	.0437	.0334	.0256	.0196	.0151	.0116	.0090	.0070	.0054	.0042	.0016	.0006
40	.6717	.3066	.1420	.0972	.0668	.0460	.0318	.0221	.0154	.0107	.0075	.0053	.0037	.0026	.0019	.0013	.0010	.0007	.0002	.0001
50	.6080	.2281	.0872	.0543	.0339	.0213	.0134	.0085	.0054	.0035	.0022	.0014	.0009	.0006	.0004	.0003	.0002	.0001	*	*
60	.5504	.1697	.0535	.0303	.0173	.0099	.0057	.0033	.0019	.0011	.0007	.0004	.0002	.0001	.0001	*	.0000	*	*	*

*The factor is zero to four decimal places.